FRONTIER RETREAT ON THE UPPER OHIO 1779-1781

EDITED WITH INTRODUCTION AND NOTES BY
LOUISE PHELPS KELLOGG

HERITAGE BOOKS
2008

HERITAGE BOOKS
AN IMPRINT OF HERITAGE BOOKS, INC.

Books, CDs, and more—Worldwide

For our listing of thousands of titles see our website at
www.HeritageBooks.com

Published 2008 by
HERITAGE BOOKS, INC.
Publishing Division
100 Railroad Ave. #104
Westminster, Maryland 21157

Copyright © 1917 Louise Phelps Kellogg

All rights reserved. No part of this book may be reproduced or transmitted in any form or by any means, electronic or mechanical, including photocopying, recording or by any information storage and retrieval system without written permission from the author, except for the inclusion of brief quotations in a review.

International Standard Book Numbers
Paperbound: 978-1-55613-942-0
Clothbound: 978-0-7884-7003-5

DANIEL BRODHEAD
From a Daguerreotype Presented to Dr. Draper by a member of Brodhead's Family

CONTENTS

	Page
Preface	9
Historical Introduction	13
Documents	39
Appendix	425
Index	499

ILLUSTRATIONS

	Page
Portrait of Daniel Brodhead	*Frontispiece*
Map of Western Pennsylvania	55
Portrait of Capt. Abraham Chapline	87
Contract for rescuing Indian captives	199
Portrait of Samuel Murphy	206
Portrait of Joseph Brant	287
Henry Baubee's drawing of Fort Lernoult at Detroit	303
Portrait of Samuel Huntington	333
Map of Southwest Virginia	402

PREFACE

To those who are familiar with the publications of the State Historical Society of Wisconsin no announcement need be made at this late date of its publications of source material in the field of the Revolution in the West under the general caption of the Draper Series. Four volumes have been issued thus far, the first three under the editorship of Reuben Gold Thwaites and Louise Phelps Kellogg, the fourth under that of Miss Kellogg alone. They cover, in general, the story of the Revolution in the West from the outbreak of Lord Dunmore's War to July, 1779. Drawn chiefly from the Society's rich store of material comprised in the Draper Collection of manuscripts, the contents of the volumes have been further enriched with the pertinent gleanings from other collections, notably from the manuscript treasures belonging to the Library of Congress. The volume now offered to the scholarly world covers the two year period from July, 1779 to July, 1781. Its title, *Frontier Retreat On the Upper Ohio*, aptly suggests the contrast between the conditions prevalent during these two years of revolution in the West and those dealt with in the volume issued last year, *Frontier Advance on the Upper Ohio*.

The privilege of indicating the character and historical significance of the documents presented in this volume is reserved to its editor in her historical introduction. Here it may properly be observed that only those who are possessed of a considerable degree of familiarity with the subject are likely properly to appreciate the painstaking labor which Miss Kellogg has undergone in order that a pathway might be blazed for students through this comparatively obscure portion of our Revolutionary struggle.

Readers of the present volume who are unfamiliar with the pressmark and editorial abbreviations are referred to the preface of the preceding volume (*Frontier Advance on the Upper Ohio*) for a convenient explanation.

PREFACE

As with volume four of the Draper Series, the labor of preparing the copy of the present volume for the printer and seeing it through the press has been chiefly borne by Lydia M. Brauer, editorial assistant, and Annie A. Nunns, assistant superintendent, of the Society's staff.

Madison, May 1, 1917

M. M. QUAIFE

HISTORICAL INTRODUCTION

HISTORICAL INTRODUCTION

The documents presented in this volume cover the two years from July, 1779 to July, 1781. Both in the East and in the West these were the most critical years of the American Revolution. After the flush of early victories and the hope of speedy independence had died away, the long strain of the struggle taxed the economic resources of the American people, and the uncertainty of the result wrought a change in their temper. Only the noblest and truest maintained their early ideals, while discontent, disaffection, and dishonesty on the part of many undermined the efforts of the colonial leaders. These tendencies, marked in the eastern army, intensified upon approaching the border. There were gathered the poorer sort of inhabitants upon whom the economic pressure bore most severely. Thither many of the disaffected fled from their Whig neighbors in the older settlements, hoping to find an asylum or means to escape to the western British posts. There dishonesty and peculation, freed from constant supervision and the danger of detection, flourished. There an inflated military authority exercised a petty tyranny over civilians who, having revolted from one government for the sake of liberty, complained of oppression from their whilom deliverers. There jealousy and selfish arrogance made patriotism a cloak for base actions, and the highest in rank connived with the meanest of the people to exploit the situation for personal advantage. In such an atmosphere, love of country and sacrifice for the people's welfare languished and died, and the problem of protecting and preserving the frontier grew ever more doubtful and difficult.

At the beginning of the period we are considering, the Revolution in the West seemed on the flood tide of success. The territory of the enemy had been repeatedly invaded, and posts were maintained in the heart of the Indian country. The British governor of Detroit had been captured, and both French inhabitants and Indian tribesmen rallied to the American standard. The British officials were seriously alarmed. In January, 1780 Gen. Frederick Haldimand wrote from Quebec to Sir Henry Clinton:

> I am sorry to acquaint your Excellency that very little is to be expected * * * from the Western Nations who resort to Detroit and that neighborhood. Indefatigable pains have been taken, and immense sums lavished to secure their affections, yet they are every day declining, particularly since the American alliance with the French to whom they have an old and a very firm attachment: Add to this, the misfortune of Mr Hamilton, the disappointment of reinforcements promised to them from year to year; the unwearied pains of the Spanish from the Mississippi to debauch them; and the advances of the enemy on all sides into their country; which with all the pains that were taken last year, they never could be brought vigorously to oppose, & it is plain that nothing but the example and continual remonstrances of the Five Nations prevent their abandoning us entirely.[1]

Col. Daniel Brodhead, commandant at Fort Pitt, who during the summer of 1779 had scored a success in his dealings with the western Indians, determined to invade the country of the Five Nations, hoping by laying waste the homes of these British allies to break their influence over the western tribesmen, and to take revenge for their raids into Westmoreland County, upon the borders of which Pittsburgh was situated. He secured the services of a number of friendly Indians from the Delaware tribe, who throughout the previous years of the Revolution had remained true to the American alliance. Their coöperation as spies and guides made possible an expedition to the upper waters of the Allegheny where were gathered a large number of the Seneca or Mingo, as the westernmost Iroquois tribe was frequently called.

The plan had originally been for this expedition to support an invasion of the Iroquois territory under the command of Gen. John Sullivan, which was to proceed by way of the Susquehanna River. The commander in chief was much interested in the success of this latter movement and thought a simultaneous advance along the Allegheny would take the Iroquois on the flank and prevent their escape from merited chastisement. On further consideration, however, Washington decided that the risk of joint action over so widely separated a field was too great; he thereupon revoked his orders to Brodhead, at the same time giving him permission to advance in whatever direc-

[1] See *post*, 122.

tion he thought best. When these messages reached Fort Pitt, preparations for the Allegheny expedition were in such a state of forwardness that Brodhead decided to carry out the original plan, and sent messengers to Sullivan to notify him of his intention. Then, without awaiting their return, he concentrated his regulars at Fort Pitt, called out volunteers from the neighboring militia, and on August 11 set forth on his march to the headwaters of the Allegheny River.

The little army thus collected, numbered about 600 men, most of whom were inured to rough traveling over wilderness trails. Provisions were transported by water to the head of navigation, then transferred to pack horses for the remainder of the way. The country through which they had to pass was wild and forbidding, "almost impassible by reason of the stupendous heights and frightful declivities, with a continued range of craggy hills, overspread with fallen timber, thorns and underwood, here and there an intervening valley, whose dark impenetrable gloom has always been impervious to the piercing rays of the warmest sun."[1] The advance was slow through this rough country where in the gloom of the frequent valleys and ravines might lurk a treacherous ambush. Only once, however, was an enemy encountered when, near the present site of Irvine, Pennsylvania, the advance guard descried an unsuspecting party of Indians dropping down stream in their canoes, and after a brief engagement scattered them in all directions. These fugitives warned the Indians on the upper river of the army's approach, so that upon reaching the towns Brodhead's men found that all the inhabitants had fled. They thereupon burned the villages, put the torch to immense fields of standing corn, and rendered the whole region uninhabitable to the tribesmen who had been collecting there in force in order to raid the frontier. It had been Brodhead's plan to press on and if possible secure a junction with General Sullivan. But upon reaching the upper towns, near the present boundary of New York, he could find no one to guide his army through the farther wilderness. The rough march had cut their shoes so that most of his men were barefoot. Thereupon he reluctantly ordered a retreat.

The effect of this invasion upon the Iroquois was very great. A horde of starving fugitives sought the British post of Niagara and communicated their alarm to its British officers, who reported

---

[1] See *post*, 56–57.

a possible attack upon that post.[1] Dread of American prowess was enhanced, and the baleful influence of the Five Nations upon the western tribesmen was severed. Upon his return to Pittsburgh, Brodhead reported that he had marched 400 miles in thirty-three days, and brought back his troops without the loss of a single man. This achievement marks the high tide of success upon the Fort Pitt frontier; thereafter, the fortunes of the American cause in that region began to ebb.

Upon his arrival Brodhead found a delegation of the most powerful and influential tribe of the western Indians awaiting his return. The Wyandot chiefs, having decided that the Americans were in the ascendency, asked for their alliance and for immunity during the anticipated advance from Fort Pitt to Detroit, promising on their part neutrality and friendship. With them came the Mequochoke branch of the Shawnee, who had withdrawn from their own tribe and were living with the Delawares. Brodhead gave reassuring answers to these prospective allies, and formed with them provisional treaties. These, together with the pacification of the Wabash tribes by Col. George Rogers Clark, quieted the trans-Ohio Indians and afforded an opportunity for an American advance against Detroit.

Throughout the summer and autumn of 1779 Detroit was in momentary expectation of an attack either from Vincennes or Fort Pitt. Its new fort was rendered more secure, and reënforcements were hurried on from Niagara and the East. In October, Major DePeyster, who had had much success in dealing with the Indians at the post of Mackinac, was transferred to the command of Detroit. He at once occupied a large island at the mouth of the river for a provision magazine. This, with the fleet commanding the surrounding waterways, rendered him capable of withstanding a considerable siege.[2] Although thus anticipated by the British officers, at no time during the latter part of 1779 was an attack by American forces upon Detroit really imminent. "Why do you conceive," wrote Brodhead to Morgan in the latter part of September, "that 500 men are now equal to the task of carrying that place which is rendered much stronger by men and works than it was two years ago, when 1800 men were thought necessary?"[3] Clark at the Falls of the

[1] See *post*, 78; also *Michigan Pioneer & Historical Collections*, XIX, 478.
[2] *Id.*, IX, 398; *id.*, X, 370; *id.*, XIX, 479; *Pennsylvania Archives*, XII, 198.
[3] *Ibid*, 160.

HISTORICAL INTRODUCTION

Ohio was chafing at his enforced inaction and at the nonarrival of reënforcements. His council of officers called to discuss the practicability of an immediate advance against Detroit reported that "not less than 1,000 troops would be requisite" for such an expedition.[1] It being impossible to procure such numbers the autumn months wore away with the British in apprehension of the attack that never seriously threatened.

In October, however, an episode occurred which, slight in itself, encouraged the British and affected the decision of hundreds of wavering tribesmen. Simon Girty had been sent to Sandusky to attempt to arouse the frightened savages to deliver another stroke against the American frontier.[2] Aided by his brother George, Girty assembled about a hundred hostiles — Seneca, Wyandot, Delaware, and Shawnee warriors — and set forth upon an intended raid into Kentucky. Advancing leisurely down the valley of the Little Miami, this party of warriors had arrived on October 4 where Cincinnati now stands, and was preparing to cross the river, when to their surprise they discovered a flotilla of boats ascending the Ohio, laden with a rich store of supplies and ammunition. This was the expedition of Col. David Rogers returning from New Orleans with a large store of goods and specie which he had obtained through the good offices of the Spanish officers at that place.

From the beginning of the Revolution the Spanish in the New World had connived at the transport of supplies for the revolutionists, and these had been of especial value to the defenders of the frontier. In 1777 Col. William Linn had brought from New Orleans a cargo of gunpowder which had been used to defend the border posts until the coming of Continental troops.[3] The success of this importation and the implication that more supplies would be forthcoming induced Virginia in 1778 to send David Rogers upon a similar mission to the Southwest. He had been eminently successful in his undertaking, and his arrival at the Falls of the Ohio in August, 1779 was greeted with much satisfaction. For his further progress Clark detailed an escort under the command of Lieut. Abraham Chapline, and the opportunity for an ascent of the dangerous Ohio under cover of such

---

[1] *Illinois Historical Collections*, VIII, 376.
[2] C. W. Butterfield, *History of the Girtys* (Cincinnati, 1893), 113.
[3] R. G. Thwaites and Louise P. Kellogg, *Revolution on the Upper Ohio* (Madison, 1908), 252–53.

a guard was embraced by several civilians and retired officers who wished to make their way from Louisville to Pittsburgh.

Upon this unsuspecting party Girty's warriors fell. When the Americans, surprised at the attack, attempted to land, the enemy boarded their boats and massacred their passengers indiscriminately. One of the five boats escaped down the river, the others were taken; most of their crews and escort, including Colonel Rogers himself, were murdered. Chapline and Col. John Campbell of Pittsburgh were made prisoners and reserved for savage tortures. An immense amount of booty fell into the victor's hands, including provisions and specie, and a number of letters which revealed Clark's conditions at the Falls, his lack of men and resources. The British at Detroit were not slow to take advantage of this information. "During the succeeding autumn and winter," writes Clark in his *Memoir*, "Detroit had pretty well recovered itself the Shawanees, Delawares and other prominent Indian tribes were so exceedingly Troublesome that our hunters Had no suckcess numbers being cut off and small skirmishes in Cuntrey so common that but little notice was taken of them." [1]

The news of Rogers' defeat reached Fort Pitt through the medium of the Moravian missionaries and was at first received with incredulity. When confirmed, it revealed the hopelessness of a march through the Indian country without a formidable body of troops. Washington warned Brodhead not to undertake another expedition unless he was certain of success. He suggested, however, the possibility of a winter campaign, when the Indian warriors would be hunting and the enemy's fleet useless. He thought swift transport might be possible along frozen ways, and advised Brodhead to make careful but veiled inquiry concerning the various possible routes.[2]

Pending the execution of a campaign against Detroit, by the close of 1779 the American frontier was withdrawn to the Ohio, where a series of posts was planned to make that stream an effective protection for the western settlements. In this process of withdrawal the most advanced post was abandoned first. In August, Fort Laurens, which had been built in 1778 about midway between Pittsburgh and Detroit, was divested of its garrison in preparation for Brodhead's Allegheny expedition. Upon the return from that incursion the regulars were posted at

[1] Draper Mss., 47J122, printed in *Ill. Hist. Colls.*, VIII, 302.
[2] See *post*, 101.

HISTORICAL INTRODUCTION 19

Fort Pitt and Fort McIntosh, while the subsidiary forts from Kittanning on the Allegheny to Wheeling on the Ohio were maintained by militia and rangers enlisted in their immediate vicinity. In the department of the Far West, during the latter half of 1779 the troops were gradually withdrawn from the Illinois and concentrated at the Falls of the Ohio. Vincennes remained the only trans-Ohio village protected by any considerable force of Americans. Preparations were also made for a strong fort at the mouth of the Ohio, which should cover the Kentucky settlements from the west, and control the entire system of western transportation. In addition to Fort Jefferson, as the new station was called, Virginia planned to fill the gap between the fort at the Falls and Fort Henry at Wheeling with posts at the mouths of the Kanawha, Little Kanawha, Guyandotte, Big Sandy, and Licking, with one in Powell's Valley commanding the eastern end of the Wilderness Road.[1]

This system of protective posts was never completed. While its details were being considered, the British were planning for the first time during the Revolution in the West a sweeping offensive. Large detachments were to advance both from Mackinac and Florida, and after capturing the Spanish and the American posts on the Mississippi, were to drive along the Ohio River with such force as would crush the puny American posts, and sweep the frontier across the Appalachian Mountains.[2] The commandants at Pensacola and Mackinac were ordered to arrange for this movement. But the Spanish upon the lower river were beforehand with their preparations. Word no sooner reached New Orleans, in July, 1779, of Spain's declaration of war against England than the energetic young governor, Bernardo de Galvez, gathered his forces and quickly possessed himself of all the British posts above him on the Mississippi. By the spring of 1780, he had organized for a descent upon Mobile, and the British at Pensacola were effectively hindered from performing their part in the Mississippi-Ohio drive.

At Mackinac, however, arrangements were carried on unhindered for an attack on the upper Mississippi posts. A large concourse of Indians and fur traders gathered in the spring of 1780 for a descent upon St. Louis, while to "amuse Clark" at the Falls of the Ohio, Capt. Henry Bird was ordered from Detroit with a force of regulars, a contingent of artillery, and a thousand

[1] See *post*, 51.
[2] See *post*, 230; *Ill. Hist. Colls.*, VIII, pp. cxxiv–cxxvi.

Indian warriors to divert attention from the Mississippi expedition. St. Louis, the one Spanish post on the upper Mississippi, was warned of the British approach in good season, and hastily erected a series of barricades, so that when, on the morning of May 26, 1780, the Mackinac forces arrived before that place they met with a stout resistance, and retired after merely raiding the outlying fields and gardens. It was said that the presence of Clark, who had been hastily summoned to its defense, was sufficient to turn aside the contemplated attack by the same Indian contingent on Cahokia and the other posts in Illinois.

At the Falls of the Ohio news of Bird's approach was brought by Lieut. Abraham Chapline, who in May made good his escape from the Indians, and warned Kentucky of its danger. The settlements were greatly alarmed. The protecting posts along the Ohio had not yet been built. Messengers were dispatched to summon Clark from Fort Jefferson, and to implore help from Brodhead at Fort Pitt and from the militia officers of southwest Virginia.[1] Again the terror of Clark's presence turned aside the Indian horde. News of his arrival at the Falls having reached Bird's Indian warriors, they refused to be led thither. Thereupon the formidable British contingent moved up the Licking and after besieging and capturing two small stations retired to the Indian country with its captives and booty. With this slight success the British were content to rest their attempt to conquer the entire West.

During the spring of 1780 the neighborhood of Fort Pitt suffered severely from Indian hostilities. All the treaties and promises of the preceding year were deliberately broken, and the British emissaries stirred up their now repentant allies to new border raids. The winter of 1779–80 was the most severe ever known to western annals, but before its protective immunity had disappeared the severity and frequency of the attacking parties caused cries of distress and appeals for help to pour into Pittsburgh from many localities. As early as March a party of Wyandot, led by the sons of the chief, Half King, who had made the treaty at Fort Pitt the previous autumn, attacked a sugar camp on Raccoon Creek, not more than thirty miles below Fort Pitt, killed several young men, and carried six children into captivity.[2] On April 17 Col. Archibald Lochry

[1] See *post*, 184–87, 192–95.
[2] See *post*, 150–54.

HISTORICAL INTRODUCTION

wrote that the savages had struck Westmoreland County in four places. "Our country is worse depopulated than ever it has been, * * * if the savages were acquainted with our weekness they might very easily drive the people over the Youghogania."[1] In May, Brodhead wrote urgently to the Pennsylvania authorities: "For heavens sake hurry up the Companies voted by the Honble Assembly or Westmoreland county will soon be a wilderness."[2] By the first of June all the people north and west of the Youghiogheny River had been driven into forts, the county records had been removed, and petition after petition was being hurried across the mountains for help.[3]

In spite of these disconcerting conditions in the spring of 1780, immigrants, lured by the favorable reports of Indian neutrality the previous autumn, began to pour into the West in numbers described as "incredible." In May, Brodhead wrote to a correspondent in the Indian country: "The settlements at Kentucky by next Fall will be able to turn out 15,000 men, and the villainous Shawanese and their allies will soon find very troublesome neighbours from that quarter as well as from this."[4] Another estimate of the migrating populace states that no less than 20,000 people removed to Kentucky in the latter part of 1779 and the year 1780.[5] The western counties of Pennsylvania shared in this increase of population. By 1781 there were 2,500 effective men in the recently erected county of Washington alone.[6] Westmoreland County and the northwestern Virginia counties filled up with newly arrived and eager immigrants. From the standpoint of frontier defense, however, these new settlers were a source of weakness rather than of strength. They knew little of Indian warfare, and they were frequently the first to fall victims to the scalping knife and tomahawk. Their helpless families added to the fear and confusion of the situation. In 1781 John Floyd wrote from Kentucky: "Indigent Widows and Orphans make up a great part of the Inhabitants of this County who are bereaved of their Husbands and Fathers by Savages and lef among strangers without the common necessaries of life."[7]

[1] See *post*, 171.
[2] *Pa. Archives*, VIII, 246.
[3] *Ibid.*, 283–84.
[4] *Id.*, XII, 227.
[5] Draper Mss., 4CC25.
[6] See *post*, 410.
[7] *Ill. Hist. Colls.*, VIII, 541–42.

Unlike the earlier pioneers few of these recent immigrants were Indian fighters. When Clark, in the summer of 1780, wanted recruits for his Shawnee expedition he appealed in vain for volunteers sufficient for the enterprise, and it was only upon his summary closing of the land office and ordering a draft of the militia that the newcomers could be brought out for a raid on the Indian towns.

It was strongly suspected, moreover, that many of the immigrants were Tories driven from the older settlements and seeking an asylum upon the frontier.[1] This was so well understood among the borderers that a visitor to Kentucky writes to Col. George Morgan: "Should the English go there and offer them Protection from the Indians the greatest part will join."[2] It was even strongly asserted that no effort was made to defend the Licking stations against Bird's expedition, because their commanders and the greater part of the inhabitants desired to remove to British protection. Brodhead, for his part, complained that the more loyal portion of the population about Fort Pitt was fast removing farther West which "has given opportunity to disaffected people from the interior part of the Country to purchase and settle these lands."[3] The presence of these Loyalists was a constant source of danger to the patriot defenders of the frontier; they refused to volunteer for expeditions either toward Detroit or the Indian villages, and strongly resisted any attempts at a draft. "I am sensible," wrote Brodhead in the latter part of 1780, "that there are a great number of disaffected inhabitants on this side the mountain, that wish for nothing more than a fair opportunity to submit to the British Government, and, therefore, would be glad to have the regular troops withdrawn."[4]

The disputed jurisdiction of Pennsylvania and Virginia gave to many of the disaffected a chance to shirk payment of taxes as well as military service. Moreover, they paid slight heed to the American attempt to maintain a boundary on the Ohio River. Numbers of squatters insisted upon trespassing upon the Indian side of the stream, and from the mouth of Beaver Creek as far down as that of the Muskingum the ax of the settler was heard in the timber, and improvement rights were made in

[1] Draper Mss., 26J30.
[2] *Ibid.*, 46J09.
[3] *Pa. Archives*, XII, 274.
[4] See Draper Mss., 3H26.

HISTORICAL INTRODUCTION

defiance of American treaties with the allied Indians. Twice during the troubled autumn of 1779 Brodhead was compelled to detach a party of troops from Fort McIntosh to clear away the squatters' cabins, and forcibly eject their dwellers from the land guaranteed to the Indians. "It is hard to determine," wrote Brodhead to the president of Congress, "what effect this imprudent conduct may have on the minds of the Delaware Chiefs and Warriors, but I hope for a favorable answer to the speech I sent them."[1] The Delawares accepted Brodhead's apologies in the given instance,[2] but no doubt the distrust implanted by this breaking of sacred treaties gave point to the reiterated claim of the British that the American object was to dispossess the aborigines, and drive them from their ancestral homes.

Late in 1780 the Loyalists around Fort Pitt attempted to establish communication with Detroit and induce another desertion similar to that of 1778.[3] Brodhead, however, more wary than General Hand, arrested the British agents, retook the few who succeeded in deserting, and put down what might have led to a formidable Loyalist uprising.

Such a movement, during the period we are considering took place upon the headwaters of the Kanawha in the border counties of southwest Virginia. There the Loyalists had for their objective the capture of the lead mines of Montgomery County, which were of great importance to the patriot cause. As early as April, 1779, information reached the officers of Montgomery and Washington counties that a number of nonjurors existed in the several militia companies of the neighborhood of New River, Walker's and Reed creeks. Two of these turned informers, and reported that meetings had been held at the house of Michael Price, and that a certain John Griffith from the south fork of the Holston was administering an oath of allegiance for the benefit of George III. "The people on all Quarters Round him and from Carolina Says that the County is Sold to the French, and that they may as well fight under the King of Great Britain, as to be Subjects to France."[4]

[1] *Pa. Archives*, XII, 176.
[2] See *post*, 96–97, 106–7, 114–15.
[3] R. G. Thwaites and L. P. Kellogg, *Frontier Defense on the Upper Ohio* (Madison, 1912), 249–56.
[4] Draper Mss., 5QQ2; *The John P. Branch Historical Papers of Randolph-Macon College*, IV, 302–7.

Upon receipt of this information Colonel Preston, lieutenant of Montgomery County, secured the persons of the ringleaders and tried them at the May session of the county court. The informants' characters appeared so untrustworthy that Griffith was released upon bail, while certain of the other nonjurors were sent to Staunton jail.[1] During the summer of the same year, the disaffection broke forth afresh. The malcontents attempted to burn houses, kill domestic animals, and even to murder the most active of their prosecutors. The officers of Montgomery County were terrorized and appealed to the neighboring counties for assistance. Whereupon Col. William Campbell, a bold Scotch-Irishman of Washington County, marched towards the lead mines, and, being joined by Maj. Walter Crockett, their combined force of 130 men broke up the nest of Loyalists, "Shot one, Hanged one, and whipt several," and ended with a sale of their estates.[2] The State approved of these high-handed measures and on Oct. 22, 1779 the House of Delegates "Resolved That William Campbell, Walter Crockett, and others, concerned in supressing a late conspiracy and insurrection on the frontiers of this State, ought to be indemnified for any proceeding therein not warranted by law."[3]

The Loyalist conspiracy of 1780 was more extensive and threatening than were these earlier sporadic outbursts of discontent. It was a part of the concerted movement to capture all the southern states for the royal cause, and was sanctioned and incited by the highest British officers. One of the organizers of the conspiracy in western Virginia was said to have visited British headquarters near Charleston, and to have been commissioned by Sir Henry Clinton in person. The danger for the frontier was enhanced by the inclusion of Indian forces in the plan of operation. Agents sent out from Florida stirred up the Cherokee, and reports were rife that 1,500 warriors with twenty horseloads of ammunition were preparing to time an attack with the uprising of the Loyalists.[4]

Among the British agents in western Virginia were many who had been concerned in the plots of the year before. John Griffith enrolled many of his Welsh neighbors. Michael Price, William Ingles, and other prominent frontiersmen were suspected of com-

[1] *Ibid.*, 306-7.
[2] *Wisconsin Historical Collections*, XXIII, 405.
[3] *Journal Virginia House of Delegates* (Richmond, 1827), 21.
[4] *John P. Branch Historical Papers*, IV, 310-11.

plicity. The common sort of citizens was attracted by large promises of reward. Those who joined the associations were to receive during active service two shillings sixpence per day, and upon its successful conclusion 450 acres of land free from quit rents for twenty-one years. A roll of their names was to be sent to England and laid before the King and Parliament.[1] The temptation these proposals offered to the poor and ignorant among the border settlers was great. They were told that the British army had overrun both North and South Carolina, and would soon be in their midst. Then their loyalty would be recognized and their future fortunes secured. The purpose of the conspirators was to seize the lead mines and "burn and cut their way" to the British army in the Carolinas, by whose officers they expected to be received with acclaim.

The details of the plot were known to the patriot officers as early as March, 1780. At the risk of their lives two of the borderers turned informers, and brought to Colonel Preston news of the dangerous character of the plans of the local malcontents. At the same time he received warnings from the Whigs of North Carolina showing the extent of the conspiracy and its connection with similar operations along the entire range of the up-country settlements from Virginia to Georgia. Preston acted promptly. He seized three of the disaffected ringleaders, disarmed the militia companies in which they were numerous, strengthened the guard at the lead mines, and sent out spies toward the Cherokee country. The discovery of their plans, and the arrest of their leaders disconcerted the plotters, and reports of Whig successes in the upper portions of the Carolinas dampened their ardor. The Cherokee, probably at the prompting of the Raven chief who had been at Fort Pitt in 1779, refused to rise. For the time being the danger was averted. Preston reported to Governor Jefferson the suppression of "this daring and treasonable Conspiracy" and received the latter's approval of the measures he had taken. Jefferson considered that the discontent arose from "no grievance but what we all feel in common, as being forced on us by those to whom they would now join themselves." In case, however, of further danger from invasion or insurrection, he authorized Preston to summon Clark from Kentucky to his aid.[2]

[1] See *post*, 145.
[2] *Ill. Hist. Colls.*, VIII, 402–4.

Clark was, as we have seen himself sorely in need of assistance. The danger call from Kentucky in anticipation of Bird's approach, reached the borders of Virginia about the middle of June. Preparations were at once made to send several companies of militia to assist in repelling the expected foe. Maj. Thomas Quirk was ordered to march to Kentucky from Fort Chiswell at the lead mines. All unwittingly the patriots were exposing their most vulnerable point. The secret agents of the Loyalists seized the opportunity. Concerting with the King's men in North Carolina they gave orders for their henchmen to embody in force. On June 24, the Whigs were surprised by the news that more than 200 disaffected men had secured arms, and were stationed in the Glades at the head of the Holston River not five miles from the site of the lead mines. On their way thither they had already slain nine patriots who had resisted their march.[1]

Fortunately the company stationed at the mines had not yet started for Kentucky. The whole neighborhood was aroused and offers of aid poured in from every side. The killing of their countrymen and the threatened massacre of the most respected men upon the frontier, for whose lives large rewards were offered in the Tory camp, struck a thrill of horror to the heart of every patriot. Among the conspirators were many of the lawless class, horse thieves, petty thieves, and the suspected criminals of the border. The better element of the entire countryside flocked to the support of the county officers. The neighboring counties also hastened to support Montgomery at this time of trial. Col. Arthur Campbell, lieutenant of Washington County, with part of the militia already embodied for the Kentucky expedition marched to Fort Chiswell. Thence he pursued the Loyalist force to the North Carolina border, where the insurgents heard of the defeat of their confederates at Ramsour's Mills in North Carolina. Fugitives from that battle having crossed the mountains reported keen pursuit by the Whig forces. The Virginia Loyalists scattered to the mountains and wooded ravines. Colonel Preston sent out disarming parties upon whom he impressed his desire for lenity and mercy. By July 12 he wrote that the "late insurrection" was in a large measure suppressed.

[1] See *post*, 195–98; *John P. Branch Historical Papers*, IV, 314–16.

HISTORICAL INTRODUCTION 27

But the pacification was more apparent than real. Encouraged by British success in overrunning all of South Carolina, and in driving the revolutionists of North Carolina into the foothills of the mountains, a new and even more serious attempt to seize the mines and the government was timed for the latter days of July. An officer at Fort Chiswell, hearing a hint of danger, persuaded a Whig refugee from Charleston to take a friend and go among the malcontents in the disguise of British officers. In this way all the plans of the conspirators were learned, and their success was thus "providentially" forestalled. Col. William Campbell, who had been excused from his seat in the Virginia House of Delegates, and sent by the governor and council to aid in protecting the frontier, arrived at this opportune moment. To his command was entrusted a body of mounted riflemen who rode at once for the lead mines. Reënforced at this strategic point, Campbell turned south along New River to its head streams. The approach of this noted border warrior alarmed the insurgents, who scattered before him in every direction. At the North Carolina line, Col. Benjamin Cleveland, hard in pursuit of Tories fleeing from his own state, was met. Together Campbell and he scoured the neighborhood for lurking fugitives, hung one, whipped several, and deprived large numbers of their horses and cattle lest they be tempted "to join in the like designs again."

A reign of terror now ensued in the back counties of Virginia. Everyone suspected his neighbor. Col. Charles Lynch, purveyor of ammunition for the state, came over from Bedford County, where he had just stamped out an incipient insurrection. Proceeding to the lead mines, his force arrested all stragglers and suspected persons encountered en route and brought them to that place for summary trial. Some were whipped, the ringleaders were shot or hung. Col. William Preston and other officers of moderation insisted upon more orderly proceedings. They summoned courts-martial which occupied the greater part of August. Most of the younger offenders were pardoned on condition of enlisting in the Continental service. Some men of property concerned in the plot were held under heavy bonds. By September the insurrection had been put down, but with such a heavy hand that the Virginia Assembly found it necessary in October, 1782 to pass an immunity act for the benefit of Preston, Lynch, and others who had participated in the trials and executions.[1] A smouldering spirit of revenge lurked among the backwoods people. The life of Col. William Campbell was threatened more than once, but far from avoiding danger, this intrepid officer sought new opportunities for service and enlisted in the expedition which he led to victory at the battle of King's Mountain.

While the officers of southwest Virginia were thus contending against the Loyalists and those of Kentucky were fending off the western Indians, Brodhead at Pittsburgh was planning means to repeat his invasion of the Indian country, and chafing because he had "the mortification to remain on the defensive." His first proposal in 1780 was for an expedition against the Scioto towns of the hostile Shawnee. Early in April orders were sent to draft 800 militia, and invitations were issued to the Delaware Indians to participate in this campaign. To the latter Brodhead wrote, "I am only waiting to receive a letter from our great Warrior, but I am weary of sitting here & am now standing with my Tomhawk in my hand."[2] Washington had sent to the Western Department a detachment of artillery, which was detained so long by the deep snows in the mountains that it did not arrive at Fort Pitt until June. For lack of this artillery force, and because the constant distress of the frontier made the militia loath to leave their homes, the expedition was postponed from week to week, until finally on May 20 Brodhead with great reluctance abandoned the campaign.[3]

Meanwhile diplomacy was tried to accomplish what could not be undertaken by an armed force. The devotion of the Indian tribesmen to the French was utilized to minimize their hostility to the allies of France. This loyalty to their former friends was well expressed by the Delaware chiefs when in the spring of 1779 they said to the French envoy at Philadelphia:

Father: it is now twenty Years since we saw your Face or heard your Voice. When you left us you told us we should see you again, before we left our Town we were informed that we should see you here, this made our Hearts glad, for we longed to see our true father & to hear his Voice * * * We love our Father—We love our Father and we desire to hear him speak from his Heart.[4]

[1] William Walter Hening (ed), *Statutes at Large; Being a Collection of all the Laws of Virginia* * * * (Richmond, 1823), XI, 134–35.
[2] See *post*, 166.
[3] See *post*, 182.
[4] *Wis. Hist. Colls.*, XXIII, 337–38.

HISTORICAL INTRODUCTION   29

Brodhead on Nov. 10, 1779 wrote to Washington that "a couple of French gentlemen of good address would be very serviceable in this district," to which the commander in chief replied that he would send "any Frenchman that answers your description, as soon as one might be met willing to be so employed."[1] Just as Brodhead's hopes of a Shawnee expedition began to wane a French-Canadian officer who had had much experience in dealing with the Indians arrived at Fort Pitt, and was immediately requested to undertake a mission to the western tribes. Daniel Maurice Godefroy de Linctot had been Clark's agent for the Mississippi tribesmen during the summer of 1779, when he had shown much address in winning the red men to the American cause. During the winter of 1779–80 he had visited Williamsburg, and upon his return by way of Fort Pitt was glad to accept the offer Brodhead made him. He set forth early in May for the Delaware villages, whence he was to send formal messages to the western tribes, inviting them in the name of their French father to join the American alliance. By July, Linctot with about thirty Indian chiefs returned to Fort Pitt, where another French officer had lately arrived on his way to the farther west.

Col. Augustin Mottin de la Balme was a comrade of Lafayette, and had seen service as a cavalry officer in the Continental army. The circumstances of his death, and the loss of all his papers have obscured the purpose of his western mission, and the value of his services in the preservation of the frontier. It is now generally accepted that his object was to arouse the French inhabitants of the West to coöperate in a movement to recover Canada, a project Lafayette had much at heart.[2] Meanwhile his advent at Pittsburgh was most opportune. Together with Linctot he held a council with the friendly chiefs, assuring them of French support and urging them to obey the behests of the American commandant. La Balme was much incensed at the conduct of the inhabitants of the frontier. "Aside from the commandant of Fort Pitt," he wrote "all have a revolting behaviour towards the Indians. While the question of peace was being treated at the fort, a band of eight men went to the nations in order to massacre a few Indians; others went to steal four

[1] See *post*, 124.
[2] *Ill. Hist. Colls.*, II, p. lxxxiv.

horses near their camp."[1] Thus the frontiersmen were themselves to blame for the increasing Indian animosity, and the French officers rendered a commendable service to the American cause by postponing for several months the general Indian war.

La Balme with a few companions and a "Shawnee princess some-what old," left Fort Pitt for the West in mid-July, while Linctot went overland through the Indian villages, bringing everywhere the influence of French attachment to bear upon the councils of the tribesmen. La Balme at the Illinois was "received by the Inhabitants as the Hebrews would receive the Messiah," and by his influence pacified the Indians of the Far West.[2] But his disastrous expedition in October overthrew the French influence with the tribesmen, and restored to the British the prestige they had lost upon the capture of Governor Hamilton.

At Fort Pitt during all the summer of 1780, Brodhead continued to hope for the opportunity for another advance movement. By June the long-awaited artillery had arrived and prospects of an abundant harvest encouraged the expectation of plentiful provisions. Brodhead thereupon planned an expedition against the Wyandot towns to coöperate with Clark's campaign against those of the Shawnee.[3] To the latter officer Brodhead wrote: "I think it probable that before next Winter I shall have the pleasure of taking you by the Hand somewhere upon the Waters of Lake Erie."[4] In furtherance of this project he summoned a contingent of mounted militia to rendezvous at Fort Pitt in August, and taking fifteen days' provisions, to make a cavalry dash for the Wyandot towns upon the Sandusky. In order to secure information of their situation, Capt. Samuel Brady was sent early in July on a scout towards these towns with instructions to bring back a prisoner to be interrogated. Brady and his men succeeded in their reconnoiter, and captured two Wyandot squaws, but on the homeward route, both of these prisoners made their escape—the second in the confusion incident to Brady's rescue from a marauding party of a prisoner, Mrs. Jane Stoops. The chief killed upon this occasion was a noted Wyandot brave, and another Wyandot defeat about this time increased the prestige of the American soldiers with this

[1] *Id.*, V, 163-67.
[2] *Ibid.*, 196.
[3] Jared Sparks, *Correspondence of the American Revolution* * * * (Boston, 1853), III, 33.
[4] *Ill. Hist. Colls.*, VIII, 408.

HISTORICAL INTRODUCTION 31

perfidious tribe. Warnings were received in July from the Moravian Indians that a large band of Wyandot warriors was advancing towards Wheeling. A party of regulars dispatched from Fort McIntosh discovered the canoes hidden by this party when they crossed the Ohio. The soldiers prepared a skillful ambush, and as the warriors returned after killing some harvesters and capturing a prisoner they were met by a volley of musketry; most of their number were killed, and the prisoner was rescued. The Wyandot towns were deeply stricken by these disasters, and for the time being the tribe was effectively chastened.

This unexpected turn of affairs gave the militia excuse for not volunteering for Brodhead's August expedition, and he therefore had again the mortification of countermanding his orders for a campaign into the Indian territory.[1] In the meantime conditions at Fort Pitt were growing ominous. Notwithstanding a plentiful harvest, provisions for the daily needs of the troops were obtained with more and more difficulty. The inhabitants of the neighboring country refused to accept the depreciated Continental paper currency, and the commissaries went out and returned without success. At Pittsburgh the troops marched in a body to the commandant's house and made a respectful protest against their lack of rations. The Pennsylvania authorities, feeling the necessity of sustaining Fort Pitt, acquiesced in the use of force to secure the needed supplies. Thereupon several detachments of soldiers under competent officers were sent from headquarters to impress provisions. Recourse was also had to hunting parties who brought in wild meat, and the Moravian Indians were importuned to come to the garrison's aid with the products of their chase. Even in the midst of such destitution Brodhead's hopes did not desert him. Late in the autumn of 1780 he made a third attempt to rendezvous for an expedition, but this effort like the previous ones was destined to prove abortive.

Had the commandant's prudence and integrity been commensurate with his ambition the story of his régime at Fort Pitt might have ended in a different manner. It is impossible to ignore the fact that Brodhead was guilty of gross impropriety in his conduct of the affairs of the Western Department. Whether or not he was guilty of all the crimes with which he was charged by his numerous enemies, the conclusion is irresis-

[1] See *post*, 234.

tible that he took advantage of his official position to further his private interests. Moreover he was surrounded by a circle of favorites whom he allowed to imitate his example, and the destitution of the troops and the distress of the frontier were in a large measure due to their petty peculations. Brodhead was a man of no mean military attainments, but his ideas of subordination, and martinet discipline alienated his own officers; his pride and overbearing manner caused the militia officers to rebel at his demands; and his oppression of the civil inhabitants of Pittsburgh led to the proferring of charges against his methods, which in the end caused his downfall and recall.

Brodhead's disposition was such that he could brook no rival, nor could he maintain any effective coöperation with his equals or his superiors in rank. His relations with Clark afford evidence of this unfortunate habit of mind. Although both in 1779 and in 1780 Brodhead had made overtures to the latter for a simultaneous advance against the foe, it is clear that he anticipated claiming the greater share of the credit of a success, since as a Continental officer he would outrank Clark, who only held a state commission. So well was this understood by the Virginia authorities that early in 1780 Jefferson, writing to Washington of Clark's proposed movement against Detroit, thought it incumbent upon him to say, "It may be necessary, perhaps, to inform you, that these two officers [Brodhead and Clark] cannot act together, which excludes the hope of ensuring success by a joint expedition."[1] It was thus with some misgivings that Washington gave his consent and approval to the Virginia plan, formulated in the last months of 1780, for an expedition against Detroit wholly under the management of Clark, who had been raised to a brigadier-generalship in the State's forces. The plan contemplated only such coöperation from Brodhead as the lending of a large share of his infantry and his one artillery company to unite with Clark's forces. It remanded the commandant of Fort Pitt to the inglorious role of acting on the defensive, and protecting a wide frontier with a greatly depleted force. Washington sent orders for these arrangements for Clark to deliver in person, and upon their receipt Brodhead wrote to the Pennsylvania authorities: "I shall not be surprised to see his Expedition fall through for it is clear to me, that wise men at a great distance, view things in the western Country very differently from

[1] See *post*, 134.

HISTORICAL INTRODUCTION   33

those, who are more immediately acquainted with Circumstances & situations."[1] That Brodhead's opposition, covert though it was, had much to do with ruining Clark's project is clear from the documents in the latter portion of this volume. Quibbling about the wording of the peremptory commands, Brodhead forced Clark to send messengers to Philadelphia in order to secure the regulars which had been assigned to him, and to obtain permission from the authorities of Pennsylvania to raise volunteers within their territory. The dispute over the Pennsylvania-Virginia jurisdiction, which had lain dormant after the compromise agreed upon by commissioners from both commonwealths, was revived and utilized against Clark's recruiting officers and commissary. It was charged by contemporaries that Brodhead timed his Coshocton expedition to interfere with Clark's securing men for his Detroit enterprise. Col. John Gibson, who had been detailed with his Virginia regiment to accompany Clark, was detained at Fort Pitt by Brodhead's departure for Philadelphia to combat the charges that his arbitrary conduct had brought upon him. Before this, however, he had secured one slight advantage and had made his final incursion into the Indian territory.

The catastrophe which all the commandants of Fort Pitt had struggled to avert had fallen upon the frontier by the spring of 1781. The Delawares of Coshocton after the departure of Linctot yielded to the pressure they could no longer resist and abandoned the American alliance. Early in April they sent a delegation of chiefs to make their peace at Detroit, and beg its commandant to take them into his favor and under his protection. The condition on which they were received was to bring in "live meat" from among the Virginians. This defection of the Delawares was especially serious to the American frontier because of their proximity to, and their familiarity with its inhabitants and garrisons. When the certainty of their hostility was made known to Brodhead by the ever-loyal Moravians, he determined to be the first to strike. With remarkable celerity he gathered his militia auxiliaries, and dropping down with his regulars to Wheeling, marched thence overland to the Delaware towns on the Muskingum. A few of the tribe, who had been with Brodhead at Fort Pitt, persisted in their former allegiance, and guided the little army to their ancient homes, where the inhabi-

[1] *Pa. Archives*, VIII, 767.

tants were completely surprised, many taken prisoners, and the remainder dispersed. The Moravian converts were profuse in their hospitality to the invading army, and after but nineteen days absence Brodhead returned to Wheeling laden with booty and prisoners.

A characteristic episode of the expedition reveals the vindictive temper of the frontier militia. During the stay near the Moravian villages a chief of the hostiles was invited into camp under the strictest promises of safe-conduct from the commandant. As they were conferring together a noted hater of Indians among the soldiers crept silently forward, and without excuse or warning buried his tomahawk in the envoy's forehead. By such savage deeds as this must the frontier spirit be judged. The continuance of the conflict increased the vindictiveness of both the white and the red races. La Balme, the French visitor in 1780, had prophesied truly when he said: "From all these dishonesties and perfidies there must result a great fund of hatred which of necessity engenders war of which many families are victims."[1]

After Brodhead's departure for the East the frontier looked to General Clark as its only savior. Many were of opinion that an offensive campaign was what "alone under Providence can give us Ease in this Quarter,"[2] and the one proposed by Clark had the sanction of the chiefs of the army, the heads of the states, and the prestige that his former successes had given the western hero. Most of the prominent officers and magistrates upon the frontier gave the expedition their support, and notwithstanding the factious opposition of a few newcomers many volunteers from both Virginia and Pennsylvania offered themselves for this service. But the demoralizing tendencies had gone too far to save the frontier from its fate. With all the Indian nations arrayed in complete hostility, with the army of defense honeycombed with dishonesty and intrigue, with discord and discontent rife among the inhabitants, even the Herculean efforts of Clark were insufficient to restore the morale of the frontier. After the departure of his troops, the forces of disintegration reigned supreme and the defeat which the British could not accomplish was nearly achieved by the lack of integrity and virtue on the part of the officers stationed on the frontier.

[1] *Ill. Hist. Colls.*, V, 166.
[2] *Pa. Archives*, IX, 241.

HISTORICAL INTRODUCTION 35

The history of the recovery and support of the demoralized border during the closing years of the Revolution will be that of the succeeding volume of this series. After Brodhead was displaced a new confidence sprang up, and although the seeds he had sown continued to bring misfortunes to harvest, the disintegration and confusion never again reached the point which marks the close of the present volume of documents.

The sources for these are similar to those of the preceding volumes of the series. The Draper Manuscripts in the Wisconsin Historical Library supplemented by the Washington Papers in the Library of Congress have supplied the body of the text. Some of the Brodhead and Clark papers from the former collection having been printed hitherto, summaries of such as are essential to the history of the Upper Ohio frontier during the critical years of 1779, 1780, and 1781 have been presented at their appropriate place in the unfolding of the story contained in the present volume.

DOCUMENTS

July, 1779—July, 1780

FRONTIER RETREAT

PREPARATIONS FOR ALLEGHENY EXPEDITION

[Summary of a letter of Col. Daniel Brodhead, Pittsburgh, July 29, 1779, to Col. Archibald Lochry.[1] Printed in *Pennsylvania Archives*, XII, 139–40.]

Regrets to hear that more mischief has been done in Lochry's region by the savages; proposes to strike at the root of the evil by an expedition to raid their villages. Lieut. Gabriel Peterson,[2] following the trail of the Indian war party that lately visited the settlements, found only three canoes. If the Indians escape Captain Jack's[3] pursuing party, they may find Captain Brady[4] in their rear. The Westmoreland people must be convinced of the necessity of destroying the towns upon the upper Allegheny River.

[Summary of a letter of Col. Daniel Brodhead, Pittsburgh, July 30, 1779, to Col. Richard Campbell.[5] Printed in *ibid.*, 141.]

Has received Campbell's extraordinary letter, dated yesterday, which must have come with unusual expedition unless there was a mistake in the date. An experienced officer should not misconceive the language of orders. "Sir, I mean as I said

---

[1] For Col. Archibald Lochry, who was county lieutenant for Westmoreland County, Pennsylvania, see *Frontier Defense*, 39, note 79.
[2] For a sketch of Lieut. Gabriel Peterson see *Wis. Hist. Colls.*, XXIII, 327, note 2.
[3] For Capt. Matthew Jack see *ibid.*, 299, note 1.
[4] For a sketch of Capt. Samuel Brady, the noted border partisan, see *ibid.*, 158, note 4.
[5] Lieut. Col. Richard Campbell, the second officer of the Virginia regiment on the western frontier, was commandant at Fort Laurens. For a sketch of his career, see *ibid.*, 59, note 2.

before, that Fort Laurens must be evacuated,[1] and as Captain Harrison[2] told you, he was sent to bring off the stores on the Pack Horses, under his escort, and they are not to be slaughtered." Grants Campbell's request for an investigation.

[Summary of a letter of Col. Daniel Brodhead, Headquarters, Pittsburgh, July 31, 1779, to Ensign Jacob Coleman.[3] Printed in *ibid.*, 141.]

Upon receipt of letter, Coleman is ordered to evacuate his post[4] immediately and bring off the stores.

[Summary of a letter of Col. Daniel Brodhead, Fort Pitt, July 31, 1779, to Gen. George Washington. Printed in *ibid.*, 146–48.]

Has been honored with Washington's instructions of June 23 and July 13.[5] Fort Armstrong has been built at Kittanning; Fort Laurens is to be evacuated. Hopes to march for Seneca country early in August, before the men's terms of service expire, and before the Indian corn is ripe. Men will turn out between seeding and harvest. Scouting parties have brought in one scalp and some booty. Western Indians—Wyandot, Chippewa, Ottawa, and Potawatomi—have not come as they promised to make a lasting peace; suspects they and the Shawnee are trying to deceive him. Encloses articles of treaty with Cherokee chiefs.[6] If Seneca expedition is successful, requests permission to reduce Detroit. Needs more artillery and an artillery officer. Terms of most of the men of Rawlings' regi-

---

[1] The British and their Indian allies rejoiced when the Americans evacuated Fort Laurens. See *Mich. Pion. & Hist. Colls.*, XIX, 468.
[2] This was probably Capt. Benjamin Harrison of the Thirteenth Virginia, for a sketch of whom see *Wis. Hist. Colls.*, XXIII, 386, note 3.
[3] Jacob Coleman was commissioned ensign in the Ninth Virginia Regiment (formerly the Thirteenth), April 5, 1779. On December 20 of the same year he was promoted to a lieutenancy. In 1781 he was transferred to the Seventh Virginia, and retired April 2, 1782.
[4] Coleman was in command of Fort Crawford, for which see *Wis. Hist. Colls.*, XXIII, 164, note 1.
[5] See *ibid.*, 371, 388.
[6] Given in *ibid.*, 392–400.

ment[1] have expired. Troops suffering for lack of shoes, some of their clothing given to Indians. Captain Killbuck[2] is there; has sent for Delaware warriors to join the expedition. Desires to coöperate with General Sullivan,[3] but will be in Seneca towns before a messenger can reach him. Has sixty boats ready for the stores.

P. S. August 4. Has just heard that two soldiers have been killed at Fort Laurens, two boys on Wheeling Creek, two captured on Raccoon Creek, a soldier killed and one wounded at Fort McIntosh. Inhabitants are so intent on removing to Kentucky, that there will be few volunteers.

INDIAN RAIDS NEAR FORT PITT

[Summary of a letter of Col. Daniel Brodhead, Headquarters, Pittsburgh, Aug. 1, 1779, to Ensign John Beck.[4] Printed in *ibid.*, 142.]

Has received Beck's letter of July 30, telling of capture of two boys near Wheeling. Has also heard of wounding of Anderson near "Dillars Fort" and capture of his two sons.[5] Delawares sent word that two war parties of twenty each were on their way to the Tuscarawas; it is they, doubtless, who did the mischief. Hopes the troops coming in from Fort Laurens will meet and punish them. The inhabitants must be on their

[1] This was a Maryland regiment ordered to Fort Pitt in 1779. See *ibid.*, 229, 350.

[2] For this Indian chief see *Rev. Upper Ohio*, 38, note 64.

[3] Gen. John Sullivan was in command of an expedition preparing for an invasion of the Iroquois country by way of the Susquehanna River.

[4] John Beck entered the service Feb. 4, 1777 as sergeant of the Thirteenth Virginia Regiment. He received an ensign's commission Oct. 31, 1778, and was promoted to a lieutenancy Dec. 15, 1779. He continued in active service until retired, on Jan. 1, 1783.

[5] William Anderson, a settler on the upper waters of Raccoon Creek, was surprised and wounded by Indians while at work in his field. His wife and one child hid in the bushes and were not discovered by the assailants. An older son and a stepson named Logan, four and seven years old respectively, were captured and carried off. Anderson succeeded in reaching the house of a neighbor, who carried him almost two miles to the protection of the blockhouse of Matthew Dillon, in Hanover Township, Washington County, Pa. The older boy was returned from captivity after the Treaty of Fort McIntosh (1785). The younger child grew up among the Indians, married a half-breed, and had sons, named Anderson, who became noted Indian warriors.

guard, and the garrison at Beck's post[1] in constant readiness; advises that a spy be kept out if possible. Speedy retaliation will be made on the villains who did this mischief.

CONGRATULATIONS FOR CLARK

[Summary of a letter of Col. Daniel Brodhead, Headquarters, Pittsburgh, Aug. 2, 1779, to Col. George Rogers Clark. 49J63. A. L. S. Printed in *Illinois Historical Collections*, VIII, 352–53.]

Although he has not the honor of a personal acquaintance, extends his congratulations on Clark's success. Hears that a Shawnee expedition is contemplated; hopes to coöperate with him in future military movements. Writer is now at liberty to make an advance into the Seneca country. Orders Capt. Robert George lately of Captain Willing's company to apprehend deserters and return to Fort Pitt.[2]

PREPARATIONS FOR ALLEGHENY EXPEDITION

[Summary of a letter of Col. Daniel Brodhead, Headquarters, Pittsburgh, Aug. 2, 1779, to Gen. Nathaniel Greene. Printed in *Pennsylvania Archives*, XII, 146.]

Under McIntosh's command there was great waste of public stores, for which Colonels Morgan and Steel[3] are responsible. The "Hobby Horse he [McIntosh] built at Beaver Creek occasioned a delay of military operations and consequently an useless consumption of Stores." Has sixty boats finished and in a few days will march toward Seneca towns.

[1] Beck was stationed at Holliday's Cove Fort. See *Frontier Defense*, 45, note 89.
[2] For a sketch of Captain George see *Wis. Hist. Colls.*, XXIII, 259, note 2. Brodhead's letter to this officer is in *Pa. Archives*, XII, 143.
[3] For Col. George Morgan, who was commissary for General McIntosh's army, see *Rev. Upper Ohio*, 31, note 59. Col. Archibald Steel, who was deputy quartermaster-general at Fort Pitt, is sketched in *Frontier Defense*, 139, note 7.

[Summary of a letter of Col. Daniel Brodhead, Headquarters, Pittsburgh, Aug. 2, 1779, to Capt. Samuel Dawson.¹ Printed in *ibid.*, 145.]

Volunteers may not join the expedition in sufficient number, therefore all the garrison of Fort McIntosh, except forty, must come in. Bring all the boats except the flatboats, which are to be secured and sunk.

[Summary of a letter of Col. Daniel Brodhead, Headquarters, Pittsburgh, Aug. 3, 1779, to Pres. Joseph Reed.² Printed in *ibid.*, 150–51.]

The Ottawa, Chippewa, Wyandot, Potawatomi, and Shawnee tribes are apparently acting deceitfully; the Allegheny expedition may cause them to change their policy. As the terms of 200 of the men of his regiment soon expire, asks permission to call out militia. Requests that Capt. John Finley³ may remain. Officers and men are ragged and without blankets or stockings.

[Summary of a letter of Col. Daniel Brodhead, Fort Pitt, Aug. 3, 1779, to Timothy Pickering. Printed in *ibid.*, 149–50.]

The light swivels and Indian goods asked for are not yet forwarded. The regiment needs clothing. Encloses a copy of the Cherokee treaty. Hopes to set out on the Seneca expedition on August 7.

[Summary of letter of Col. Daniel Brodhead, Headquarters, Pittsburgh, Aug. 6, 1779, to Gen. John Sullivan. Printed in *ibid.*, 154–55.]⁴

Has directions from the commander in chief to correspond on subject of a Seneca expedition. Ready to start, waiting only for garrison to come from Fort Laurens, when he will march for

¹ For Capt. Samuel Dawson see *Wis. Hist. Colls.*, XXIII, 286, note 1.
² Reed was the presiding executive of the state of Pennsylvania. See sketch in *ibid.*, 261, note 1.
³ For a sketch of this officer see *ibid.*, 73, note 1.
⁴ This letter is also printed in *Magazine of American History*, III, 655–57, together with a good secondary account of Brodhead's Allegheny expedition.

Conewago,[1] expects to be there about August 20, and to advance from there. Has with him twelve Delaware warriors and the promise of more. Scouting parties have scattered two Munsee war parties.[2] The Munsee are now willing to make peace, but it will not be granted them until they have been punished.

[Summary of a letter of Col. Daniel Brodhead, Headquarters, Pittsburgh, Aug. 7, 1779, to Col. Richard Campbell. Printed in *ibid.*, 154.]

Provision return of commissary shows twelve days' flour. "Your obstinacy has already delayed the expedition I informed you of, & I expect, unless this meets you near at hand, to march without your Garrison."

WYANDOT INDIAN WAR PARTIES

[Captain Johnny[3] to Col. Daniel Brodhead and Captain Killbuck. 3H159–61. Transcript.]

COOSHOCKUNG,[4] Augt ye 9th 1779.

Mr Gerard to Maghingwe Geeschuch[5] and Galalemend (Captn John Killbock)

BROTHERS:

The reason why I am so late in meeting you is, because I have had some troublesome matters to consider. But now you may depend on seeing me with you in 5 days. You have mentioned 3 in particular whom you had desired to come, but as one of these three (Mamawókunund) cannot come, there being nobody

---

[1] For the location of this Indian town see *Wis. Hist. Colls.*, XXIII, 273, note 1.

[2] For a sketch of the Munsee Indians see *Frontier Defense*, 147, note 11.

[3] The Delaware chief known to the whites as Captain Johnny was one of the delegation that in 1779 visited Congress and had interviews with Washington and the French envoy, Monsieur Gérard. Captain Johnny assumed the name of the latter as a title of distinction. He was the same chief whom the Moravians called Israel. See sketch in *Wis. Hist. Colls.*, XXIII, 225, note 2.

[4] For a sketch of this town see *Rev. Upper Ohio*, 46, note 73.

[5] For this title conferred upon Colonel Brodhead see *Wis. Hist. Colls.*, XXIII, 282.

besides him to speak to the Cherokees; we send another (Cold) in his place.

Brothers: I can now inform you that our friends that left us last fall, are daily coming in; many are round about us already, the rest close by.

Brothers: A few days ago I had an opportunity of speaking to 14 warriors of the Wyondott Nation. I explained to them the good friendship between us & the United States, & by much trouble turned them back from going against you. A few days after there came six of the same nation to our town from war against you. They say they had one prisoner, who after two days journey made his escape. Those latter upon meeting some of our hunters, made ready to fire upon them, but finding the company to be too many for them, altered their design. These two parties were both headed by the Half King's sons.[1]

MORAVIAN INFORMATION

[Rev. John Heckewelder[2] to Col. Daniel Brodhead. 3H161–62. Transcript.]

COOSHOCKING, Augst 9th 1779.

DEAR SIR:

As I have understood by some of the Dellaware who came from Phillad^a that I had been represented as one who listens to any story he may hear, & for that reason has sent such fearful letters to several officers in the service of the United States. I therefore think best to leave the communication of all news to the Delawares themselves, & no further trouble myself about such matters, as they are indeed not properly my business. I thought to do some service to my country to which I am close attached; and always have made it a rule to write nothing but what I had from a trusty body; likewise to distinguish my news by the words—*facts* & *reports*. And I think the most of what I wrote has appeared to be true already, & the other part may appear true yet.[3]

[1] For this chief see *Rev. Upper Ohio,* 91, note 14. See also his visit to Fort Pitt, *post,* 66.

[2] For a sketch of this Moravian missionary see *Rev. Upper Ohio,* 202, note 43.

[3] Heckewelder had previously furnished information that had been extremely serviceable to the officers of the American posts. See *Frontier Defense,* and *Wis. Hist. Colls.,* XXIII, *passim.*

I am, dear Sir, with every mark of esteem, Your most humble Servant,

JOHN HACKENWELDER.

Brothers: By a Dellaware who comes from over the Lake we hear that the Wyondotts have made out at Detroit to keep constantly a good watch-out between two forts. We judge it must be between Fort M°Intosh & Fort Pitt. These men will be about 50.

Brothers: When I shall come to you myself, I shall acquaint you of many matters. I only mean now to inform you that you may depend on my being with you in the time I mentioned.

GERARD.

To BROTHER MAGHINGWEE GESHUCH, Col° Coman^{dt} West^n Dep^t, Fort Pitt. By a messenger from Cooshocking

---

THE WYANDOT EMBASSY

[The Delaware chiefs at Coshocton to Col. Daniel Brodhead and Captain Killbuck. 1H115–16. In handwriting of John Heckewelder.]

COOSHOCKUNG Augst ye 11th 1779

Israel & the Councill of Cooschockung to Brother Maghingwe Geeshuch, and Gelelemend[1]

BROTHERS:

Hear what I have to say to You! My Oncles, who are Your Brothers[2] are now come to Cooshachking.

Brothers: I am at a loss what to do. I had sent to the Wyondotts desiring them only to go as far as Fort McIntosh.

Brothers: I now desire You will take a Coal from Our Councill fire at Fort Pitt, and kindle a Fire at Fort M°Intosh, and there I will meet You with my Oncle; Your Brother and consult with one another about Our good Friendship.

[1] This is the Indian title of the Delaware chief, Capt. John Killbuck, who at the date of this letter was with Colonel Brodhead at Fort Pitt.

[2] "Oncle" is the French word for uncle. The Delawares applied this term of relationship to the Wyandot. The expression, "who are your Brothers," signified that the Wyandot had come seeking the American alliance.

Brothers: The reason I desire this is because I heard You speak of it first. I believe it will suit Us both best.

Brothers: In 5 Days from this I shall get up and go with my Oncles the Wyondotts to You, and mean to be with You in 9 Days.

Brothers: My Oncle who is now come to my Town, is the Man (Captn Bawbee) who sent You a Letter some time ago.[1]

Brothers: Captn Pipe and Wingenund[2] will be here tomorrow, to whom I intend to communicate all the good Words spoke to me by Genr^l Washington & Congress, which is the reason that I cannot meet You sooner.

Brothers: I now desire You to send imediately for our Brother Taimenend (Geo: Morgan) as he desired me to inform him when Our Oncles came, and he would come himself, and speak with them.

Brothers: The same Day that those Men who are to join You, were to set off from here the Wyondotts came, and now we intend to go all together.

ISRAEL

[*Endorsed:*] Indian Israel Augt 11th 1779

THE SIX NATIONS ALARMED

[Col. Mason Bolton[3] to Gen. Frederick Haldimand. 58J58–59. Transcript.]

I enclose you copies of letters received from Major Butler,[4] which will inform your Excellency of the enemy's arrival at Tioga,

[1] For the message of this Wyandot chief in 1778 see *Wis. Hist. Colls.*, XXIII, 128–29; a sketch of his life is in *ibid.*, 128, note 2.

[2] These were two Delaware chiefs who are sketched in *Rev. Upper Ohio*, 46, note 75, and 80, note 6.

[3] For this British officer in command at Fort Niagara see *Frontier Defense*, 285, note 46.

[4] Maj. Walter Butler was the son of Col. John Butler, a Tryon County Loyalist, who commanded a regiment of Canadian rangers. Walter Butler, before the Revolution, was a law student at Albany, where he was known as a clever and aristocratic youth. On the outbreak of the Revolution he went to Canada, where he was commissioned ensign in the Eighth Canadian Infantry. In 1776 he was sent to Niagara, and the succeeding year took part in St. Leger's campaign in the Mohawk Valley. There he was captured and would have been executed as a spy but for the intercession of some American officers who had known him at Albany. He was kept in close confinement at that place until the spring of

and the disagreeable situation the Six Nations are in. That the Rebels are determined to oblige them to observe neutrality, I have scarce a doubt of, and they appear to me in general extremely dissatisfied that the troops y^r ex^y promised them had not taken post at Oswego. Several Chiefs came in lately, and in Council requested to know the reason why the Great King their Father did not assist them in the time of their distress, after the many promises made by the General and the commanding officer here; that they could not resist the force the Rebels were now bringing against them, and were even at a loss which way to go, as the enemy were advancing from all quarters. They desired I would send part of the Garrison to their relief, otherwise their villages would be cut off, and they could no longer fight the King's battles. They even in Council said I had not kept my word, and that I talked of nothing but provisions, while they were well convinced there was a great quantity at Quebec, therefore I could have no excuse for not assisting them. I informed them of what Major Butler had wrote and notwithstanding I attended their Councils three days, and gave them every thing they wanted in clothing, provisions, &c., I could only prevail on 44 to set off out of 200 warriors. Kiasheeta desired an hundred soldiers might be sent with him in order to attack 600 Rebels and 100 Delawares, who have taken post in his neighbourhood,[1] 15 miles this side of Venango.[2] In short, to answer all their demands, I must have given them every soldier in this garrison. Their behaviour altogether was very different from what I had ever seen before, and if Major Butler should be defeated, I am convinced they will follow the example of their brethren at Detroit. * * *

1778, when he succeeded in escaping, and in retaliation for his imprisonment planned and carried out the raid against Cherry Valley. In 1779 he vainly attempted to oppose Sullivan's invasion of New York, and was defeated in the battle of Newtown. Thereafter he was in the border service until October, 1781, when he was killed while retreating from an unsuccessful raid.

[1] Guyashusta (Kiasheeta) was a Seneca chief who lived upon the Allegheny. See sketch in *Rev. Upper Ohio*, 38, note 65. The "rebels" here mentioned were the men of Brodhead's expedition.

[2] For this site see *ibid.*, 162, note 88.

TROOPS RETURN FROM KENTUCKY

[Capt. Robert Beall's[1] passport for Capt. William Harrod.[2] 4NN76. A. D. S.]

FORT M^c INTOSH 23^d August 1779

Then Arived Captain Willm Harrod on his way from the falls of Ohio to Muddy Creek.[3] and Producing proper Athority from the County Lieutanent of that place. is Noted for his Carceter in Distinguishing himself in his Conterys service And has promition to pass with his Craft & Reepass

ROBERT BEALL Capt Comd^t

To ALL CONCEARNED

[*Endorsed by Draper:*] Capt. Wm Harrod reaches F^t M°Intosh 23^d Aug. 1779—from the Falls of Ohio. Passport

---

BRODHEAD'S MESSENGERS TO SULLIVAN

[Extract from the journal of Major James Norris.[4] 19 U141.—Transcript.]

[Aug.] 25th We find great difficulty in getting ready to march for want of a sufficiently [*sic*] number of horses to carry our provisions, ammunition, &c. However, we are to move tomorrow without fail, with twenty-seven days flour and live beef. Our whole force that will march from here is about five thousand men, officers included, with nine pieces of artillery. And three of the Oneida warriors arrived here this afternoon who are agoing on with us as guides. Two runners arrived from Colonel Brodhead at Fort Pitt, informing that Col. Brodhead is on his way with about eight hundred men against the western Indians.

[1] For a sketch of Capt. Robert Beall see *Wis. Hist. Colls.*, XXIII, 326, note 1.

[2] Capt. William Harrod is sketched in R. G. Thwaites and Louise P. Kellogg, *Documentary History of Dunmore's War*, 1774 (Madison, 1904), 68, note 14. At the time this present document was written Harrod was returning from service under Col. George Rogers Clark.

[3] For this locality see *ibid.*, 36, note 63.

[4] Maj. James Norris was a New Hampshire officer who accompanied Sullivan's expedition. His manuscript journal of this campaign is owned by the Buffalo Historical Society, whence Dr. Draper secured a transcript in 1879.

UPPER BRITISH POSTS

[Extract from a letter of Gen. Frederick Haldimand to Gen. Henry Clinton. 58J38–39. Transcript.]

QUEBEC 29th Aug. 1779:
* * * The demands from all the Posts in the Upper Country are enormous, owing to the necessity of feeding not only the Indians collected in different places, but the old men, women & children, of the Mohawks, Onondaga & Cayuga Nations (whose villages have been destroyed) at Niagara; and those of the Shawanese & Delaware Nations in the same predicament at Detroit.
* * * I have as much as possible, reinforced Detroit, and the forwardness of a work now constructing there, will, I hope, ensure the safety of that place, unless the Rebels should be able to make their way to it in great force, which the growing slackness of the western nations (from the impossibility of marching into the field with them) may perhaps enable them to effect. Every means in my power to encourage the Five Nations to defend their country, and annoy the enemy, have been employed, and I hope your Excellency's operations have been, in some measure, facilitated by their vigilance and activity. They likewise heavily complain that the burthen of the war in that country is left upon their shoulders, without provisions and men, particularly the former; it is impossible to assist them materially.

WESTERN GARRISONS FOR VIRGINIA

[Gen. Andrew Lewis and Col. William Fleming[1] to Gov. Thomas Jefferson. 2ZZ82. A. L. S. of Fleming.]

BOTETOURT Augt 31. 1779
SIR:
In compliance with the order of Councel[2] of July the 23d directing Genl Lewis William Fleming & Willm Christian[3] to meet for the purpose of fixing the Stations proper for the Troops designed for

---

[1] For these officers see *ibid.*, 426–29.
[2] For these orders see *Wis. Hist. Colls.*, XXIII, 401–4.
[3] For a sketch of this officer see *Dunmore's War*, 429–30.

the Defence of the S⁰ western Frontiers—Andrew Lewis & Wm Fleming accordingly met; and on Maturely considering the order of Councel, to Comply therewith, in forming as compleat a Chain of defence as the number of men allotted for that service will admit of It is our oppinion that at, or as near the following places mentioned as a proper situation will suit—Fifty Men with the usual Officers be stationed at or near the Mouth of Guayandot and Fifty Rank & File with the proper Officers at or near the Mouth of Big Sandy River, One hundred Rank & File at or near the Junction of Licking Creek with the Ohio. And Fifty at or near Martins Cabbin in Powels Vally[1]—We imajine these posts occupied on the Ohio, will be of more service for the protection of the Frontier than stationing the Battaleon[2] nearer the Inhabitants. The Station at Licking is not a great distance from some Shawnese Towns and near the place they generally cross the Ohio from these Towns, when they make inroads on our Southern Frontiers. it may be a proper Station for the Command^t of the S⁰ department, as he may at short notice command any detachment from Sandy, or Guandot Stations and Joind with the Inhabitants of Kentucky conveniently carry on any Offensive Opperations against the Enimy on Meamee [Miami] or elsewhere to the westw^d of Licking. The Station we mention to Your Honbl^e Board in Powels Vally, will not only keep the communication open with Kentucky County but be a defence to the Western Frontier of Washington,[3] by being near the path of the Northern Tribes in their way either to the Cherokees or Chuchamoga [Chickamauga] Indians[4]—We think it would forward the Service for the Men raised in or near the Frontier Counties to be immediatly employed in the defence thereof and might save unnecessary marching. We therefor recommend it that the 50 Men we mention to be Station'd at Guyandot & the 50 at Big Sandy River be raised from Montgomery, Botetourt & Rockbridge Counties. The 100 at Licking from Kentucky, Pitsilvania & Henry Counties & the 50 in Powels Vally from Washington & Bedford. And should the Districts of the above mentioned Counties be insufficient for

---

[1] For this locality see *ibid.*, 4, note 6.

[2] The battalion referred to was that under the command of Col. Joseph Crockett, raised by the Virginia authorities for western defense. See *Wis. Hist. Colls.*, XXIII, 401–2.

[3] Washington County in Southwest Virginia was then the state's frontier county in that direction. See sketch, *ibid.*, 120, note 1.

[4] For the location of this tribe see *ibid.*, 37.

the Men requir[ed] the Honb^le Board may please to make up the deficiencies from Bu[ck]ingham, Amherst or other convenient Counties.—We beg leave to mention we think 5 Doz falling Axes. Eight broad Axes 1½ Doz Mattocks or Grubinghoes. 1½ Doz Agurs of different sizes. 1 D[oz] drawing knives Eight Tro's & Four Cross cut saws with some Spikes Nails tenpenny D° & Gimblets will be sufficient for the South^n Troops with one Camp kettle that hold two Gallons, these articles can not be procured here & ought to be provided below   Riffles are the properest fire Arms for Our Service we wish the board to give an encouragement to the Volunteers to furnish themselves with Guns, Shot pouches & Powder horns. You will perceive Sir we have only turnd our Attention to the Southw^d of the Kanhaway, and make no doubt the Commiss^rs for the Northern District will establish a post of Communication between Fort Randolph[1] & Green Brier County.

We are Sir Your most Ob^t Humb[le] Servants

And^w Lewis
Willm Fleming

[*Endorsed by Draper:*] Col. Wm Fleming Commissioners—Aug '79

BRODHEAD ALARMS BRITISH INDIANS

[John Docksteder[2] to Col. Mason Bolton. 58J61. Transcript.]

Cataragaras, Septr 1st 1779.

Sir:

A runner is just arrived at this place from the Ohio, who informs me that thirty of our Indians were attacked by a large body of the Rebels about four miles below Canawago. From what I can

---

[1] For a sketch of this post, see *Rev. Upper Ohio*, 185, note 7.

[2] John Docksteder, who was an officer in the British Indian service, belonged to a family of New York Loyalists. In the spring of the year in which this letter was written he was wounded while leading an Indian raid. In 1781 Col. Marinus Willett defeated Docksteder and his Loyalist party at Sharon Center, N. Y. After the Revolution, Docksteder settled in Ontario where he received a military grant on Grand River in the township of Canborough. There he died in the latter part of 1804, his estate being entered for administration on December 1 of that year. His wife was a Mohawk Indian, and their children lived among the Indians. The modern spelling of the name is Doxtater; several persons of that name now live among the Oneida Indians in Wisconsin.

learn we have had three Senecas killed, but the number of Delawares are not known. It is expected that the Rebels have destroyed ere this time the Delaware Town and Oanackadago.

I am now going, with about forty warriors, to meet the enemy, but the Chiefs beg that you would send them some assistance, and that soon, as their distressed condition requires it.

I am, Sir, Your most obed^t servant,

JOHN DOCKSTEDER.

LIEUT. COL. BOLTON.

[Col. John Butler[1] to Col. Mason Bolton. 58J62–63. Transcript.]

CANAWAGARAS,[2] 8th September, 1779.

I endeavoured, but to no purpose, to prevail upon the Indians to make a stand at Canadasego;[3] the Rebels took possession of that Village the 7th instant in the evening. Joseph Brant[4] who stayed to reconnoitre them, and was near the place when they entered it says that to all appearance they cannot be less than 3000. The chiefs have now determined to collect all the force they can and meet them before they reach this, and I send in Captain Power[5] to bring off with him such Indians as may be about Niagara, in which I must beg you to give him all the assistance you can, and also to send out with him every body you can spare.

The 7th Instant in the evening a runner came in from the Ohio, informing that the Rebels were come up the Alleghany, and had penetrated as far as Canawaga, the village at which Mr Dock-

[1] For a sketch of this Loyalist see *ibid.*, 152, note 67.

[2] Canawaugus was the Indian town to which Butler and his troops withdrew after their defeat at Newtown, Aug. 29, 1779, by the troops of Gen. John Sullivan. Canawaugus was near the site of the present town of Avon in Livingston County, N. Y.

[3] The site of this important Seneca town was a mile and a half northwest of Geneva, N. Y., where Butler had a trading house. Canadasega was composed of sixty large, well-built houses, and a stockade fort built during the French and Indian War. Its inhabitants fled upon Sullivan's approach, and the town was completely destroyed by his troops, who found there no human being but a captive white child about three years of age.

[4] For a sketch of this Indian chief see *Wis. Hist. Colls.*, XXIII, 269, note 2.

[5] Capt. Thomas Power was a New York Loyalist who after the Revolution became a Spanish subject and engaged in attempts to separate the western states from the Union.

stead was stationed last winter; and another runner who came in this morning says they have destroyed a village called Naradago,[1] a day's journey on this side Canawaga, but says they returned from thence, and were building a Fort at a place which the Indians called Ningaracharie, and I believe the same as Le Beuff.[2] The Indians seem in better spirits and more determined than I have seen them since they left Chucknut,[3] and if they get any succours from Niagara, I am in hopes I shall be able to persuade them to attack the Rebels on their march; at any rate I shall do my endeavour to get them to make a stand.

Joseph and the Chiefs think that a few troops from Niagara would be of the greatest service at this juncture, as they would encourage and give them spirits, and they imagine this cannot be of any bad consequences to your part, as you can always be reinforced from Caleton [Carleton] Island.[4]

I am, &c.

JOHN BUTLER.

LIEUT. COL. BOLTON.

[1] This is the same Indian town that John Montour named to Colonel Brodhead as Yoghroonwago. See *post* 55. Its site was near the New York border on the Allegheny River in Warren County, Pa.

[2] French Creek was formerly known as Le Bœuf River. Brodhead's troops camped at its mouth, where the town of Franklin, Pa., now stands.

[3] Choconut (Chucknut, Chugnutt) was an Iroquois town situated on the southern bank of the Susquehanna, where Vestal, Broome County, now stands. Sullivan's forces destroyed this Indian village on Aug. 19, 1779.

[4] Carleton Island lies at the foot of Lake Ontario. It was called by the French *Isle aux Chevreuils*, variously translated Deer or Buck Island. In the month of August, 1778, three companies of the Forty-seventh British Infantry built a post on this island, and renamed it for their popular general. Carleton Island was a naval and military supply station for the posts of the upper country. After the close of the Revolution a fort was erected at Kingston, Ontario, when the garrison from Carleton Island was transferred thither. A small guard was thereafter maintained at the island post, which in July, 1812 was captured by a patriot party from New York. Carleton Island is now part of Jefferson County in that state. Until recent years ruins of the old British post might be seen upon this site.

THE ALLEGHENY EXPEDITION

[Summary of a letter of Col. Daniel Brodhead, Pittsburgh, Sept. 16, 1779, to Gen. George Washington. Printed in *Pa. Archives*, XII, 155-56.][1]

Returned on September 14 from the expedition herewith reported. Left there the eleventh of last month with 605 rank and file, including militia and volunteers. One month's provision sent by water (except the cattle) to Mahoning,[2] there loaded on pack horses. Ten miles this side of Conewago, Lieut. John Hardin[3] and advance guard discovered thirty or forty of the enemy descending the river in canoes. Immediate preparation made for action in which five of the Indians were killed and several wounded. Their party suffered only slight wounds. Next morning Brodhead's army advanced to Buckaloons,[4] threw up a breastwork, and after finding they were not attacked marched to Conewago. This town appeared to have been deserted for eighteen months. As no guide could be found, they followed a trail for twenty miles to some towns that were evacuated as the army approached. These villages were seven in number and contained 130 houses. Montour[5] called the uppermost town Yoghroonwago.[6] Three days were occupied in destroying standing corn and burning houses. Booty to the value of $30,000 was taken. On the return, Conewago, Buckloons and Mahusquechikoken[7] were burned. The army returned via the old Venango

[1] This letter, in a somewhat abbreviated form, is also printed in *Mag. of Amer. Hist.*, III, 672-73; and John Almon, *Remembrancer*, IX, 673-75.

[2] Mahoning Creek is an eastern affluent of the Allegheny, in Armstrong County. Its mouth is about fifteen miles above the site of Fort Armstrong, and in Brodhead's time was the limit of navigation on the main stream.

[3] For Lieut. John Hardin see *Wis. Hist. Colls.*, XXIII, 326, note 2.

[4] This was an ancient Seneca town near the mouth of Broken Straw Creek. In 1749 a French officer noted a recently built town just below this creek, wherein he held a council. Apparently it was continuously occupied until its destruction by Brodhead, after which it was not rebuilt. Traces of the breastworks thrown up during Brodhead's advance were said to be visible as late as 1887.

[5] For John Montour see *Rev. Upper Ohio*, 28, note 57.

[6] This appears to have been a Seneca town, but the other seven villages were those of the Munsee, and were never rebuilt. The whole region was part of the reserve granted in 1785 to the Seneca chief, Cornplanter.

[7] This town was on French Creek. See Jack's account, *post*, 61.

road.[1] It was the apparent intention of all the Seneca and Munsee to congregate on the upper Allegheny. This object now defeated. Men and officers worthy of all praise, made no complaint although their clothing was in tatters. Delawares, Wyandot, and Mequo-choke-Shawnee were at Fort Pitt when he returned. The former desire a fort among them. So many regulars had to be discharged that he has no adequate force for a Detroit expedition. Indian negotiations of Col. George Rogers Clark.

[Extract from an anonymous letter. Printed in *Maryland Journal*, Oct. 26, 1779. 2E109–13. Transcript.]

PITTSBURGH, September 16th, 1779:
"The many savage barbarities and horrid depredations committed by the Seneca and Muncy Nations upon the Western frontiers, had determined Col° Brodhead, as the most effectual way to prevent such hostilities in future, and revenge the past, to carry the war into their own country, and strike a decisive blow at their towns.

"On the 11th of August, our little army, consisting of 605, rank & file, marched from Pittsburgh with one month's provision; at Mahoning, 15 miles above the old Kittanning, we were detained four days by the excessive rains, from whence (leaving the river which rolls in a thousand meanders) we proceeded by a blind path leading to Cuscushing,[2] thro' a country almost impassible, by reason of the stupendous heights and frightful declivities, with a continued range of craggy hills, overspread with fallen timber, thorns and underwood, here and there an intervening valley,

---

[1] The old Venango trail ran from the mouth of French Creek to Pittsburgh. Its course was some distance east of the river, through Salem Township, Clarion County, across Clarion River at Bullock's Ford near the present Callensburg. Thence it ran southeast to Red Bank Creek at the mouth of Town Run, and from there turned south, heading the branches of the Allegheny.

[2] This was an important Munsee town built about 1765 near the present Tionesta, Forest County, Pa. Thomas Hutchins calls it Kushkushing, and on his map of 1778 locates it on the northwest side of the river. See *Wis. Hist. Colls.*, XXIII, 321. John Heckewelder writes the name Goschgoschuenk, and states that in English it means "place of hogs." *Narrative of the Mission of the United Brethren* (Philadelphia, 1820), 106. The Moravians attempted to establish a mission at this place in 1768–69, but were forced to abandon it in the latter year. At the time of Brodhead's march this village was unoccupied.

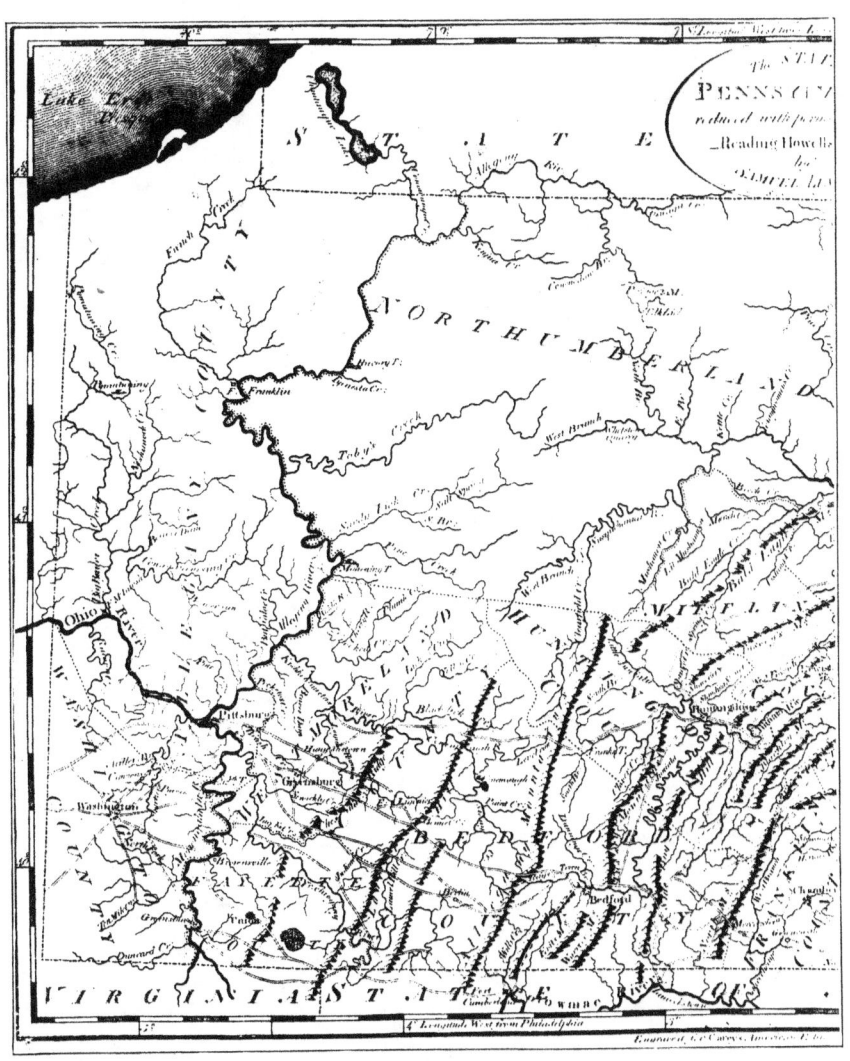

WESTERN PENNSYLVANIA
Reproduced from a Map of Samuel Lewis in 1880

whose deep impenetrable gloom has always been impervious to the piercing rays of the warmest sun. At Cuscushing (which is 15 miles above Venango), we crossed the Alleghany, and continued our route upon its banks. But here our march was rendered still more difficult by the mountains which jutted close upon the river, forming a continued narrow defile, allowing up [us] only the breadth of an Indian path to march upon. In the midst of one of these defiles, our advanced party, consisting of 15 white men & 8 Delawares, discovered between 30 & 40 warriors landing from their canoes, who having also seen part of our troops, immediately stripped themselves and prepared for action. Lieutenant Harding, who commanded our advance, disposed his men in a semi-circular form, and began the attack with such irresistable fury, tomahawk in hand, that the savages could not long sustain the charge, but fled with the utmost horror and precipitation, some plunging themselves into the river, and others, favoured by the thickness of the bushes, made their escape on the main, leaving five dead on the field, without any loss on our side, except three men slightly wounded. Upon the first alarm, supposing it to be more serious, the army was arranged for fight, both officers and men, enraged at their former cruelties, and animated by the calmness, resolution and intrepidity of the commandant, showed the utmost ardor to engage; and had the action been general, we had every prospect of the most ample success from a brave commander, at the head of brave men."

[The article] Then goes on to say, that they burned eight Indian towns, and cut down & piled into heaps near 600 acres of corn: Says they arrived at Buckloons the same day as the skirmish with Hardin's advance.

"After burning the old towns of Conauwago and Mahusguachiakocken, we arrived at Pittsburg the 14th instant with the scalps we had taken, and 30,000 dollars worth of plunder, having in the course of 33 days completed a march of near 400 miles, through a country the Indians had hitherto thought impenetrable by us, and considered as a sufficient barrier for the security of their towns, and indeed nothing but the absolute necessity of such a measure, and a noble spirit of enterprise, could be a sufficient inducement to undertake so arduous a task, and encounter those difficulties and obstacles which require the most consummate fortitude to surmount."

58 WISCONSIN HISTORICAL COLLECTIONS

[Recollections of Capt. Jesse Ellis.[1] 2S319–22.]

Brodhead's campaign of '79. My informant was in the militia—commanded by Col. John Gibson, Lt. Col. George Verlandigham,[2] & Maj. Samuel McCulloch.[3] The whole army numbered 600 privates, beside the requisite officers—Thos Nicholson interpreter,[4] & John Montour pilot—the former c^d speak 7 Indian languages; the latter was a half breed. The army rendezvoused at Pittsburg the 1st of Aug.—marched up the Allegheny by land; the baggage in canoes. Nicholson was ahead with 30 men—about a mile ahead of the main army; & espied 3 canoe loads of Indians descending the river, 10 Indians in each: (Don't recollect about Brady[5] being with the advance) The men Squatted in weeds &c. in a gut putting into the river; & Nicholson (not the one out with Crawford) hallowed to the Indians & they came ashore & landed taking their guns; & while Nicholson, at some distance off was talking with them, some of the men peeping up were discovered by the Indians who quickly fired at Nicholson & then treed—[Nicholson] dodged behind a tree and was slightly wounded across the top of the thigh—the fight lasted hotly & severely about ten minutes (about 10 o'clock in the forenoon—&

[1] For a sketch of Jesse Ellis see *Wis. Hist. Colls.*, XXIII, 161, note 2.

[2] George Vallandigham was born about 1738 near Alexandria in Fairfax County, Va., of Huguenot parents, who had emigrated to America at the close of the seventeenth century. After a liberal education young Vallandigham became a teacher and surveyor, and about 1772 visited the neighborhood of Fort Pitt. There he and his brother-in-law, Henry Noble of Maryland, located lands on Robinson's Run, twelve miles southwest of Pittsburgh, and there in 1775 they made their permanent homes. In the meantime Vallandigham served as a lieutenant in Dunmore's army of 1774. After settling in the West, he was chosen justice of the peace, and on Mar. 25, 1778, lieutenant-colonel of Yohogania County militia. In that capacity he served with Brodhead on his expeditions of 1779 and 1781. During the Whisky Rebellion Vallandigham supported the government, and was recognized as a valuable and able citizen. His death, which occurred Oct. 4, 1810, was widely deplored. His grandson, Clement L. Vallandigham, afterwards notorious for his opposition to the government of Lincoln, in 1848 sent Dr. Draper the account herein abridged. Draper Mss., 11E151–56.

[3] For Maj. Samuel McColloch see *Rev. Upper Ohio*, 234, note 77.

[4] Joseph, not Thomas, Nicholson, was Brodhead's pilot. See *Pennsylvania Colonial Records*, XVI, 504–6. For a sketch of the two Nicholsons see *Dunmore's War*, 13, note 26.

[5] Tradition in Pittsburgh claimed that Capt Samuel Brady commanded the advance party that had the skirmish with the Indians; it was in fact, Lieut. John Hardin. See *ante*, 55.

about the 20th Aug.)—during which the Indians lost 15 killed, & 14 wounded, & only one got off uninjured—the whites lost none killed,—& besides Nicholson, Sargent Askens was wounded, & a pet Indian—the latter about 16 years—all slightly wounded: The Indian was shot across the back of his hand, & Askens was shot in the left thumb (ball of) while scalping an Indian. The Indians scattered off, leaving trails of blood—& leaving their dead (the wounded got off) their canoes, provisions, 7 war-clubs in canoes, &c.—The Indian who got off unharmed, forded to an island in the river, & thence through it unseen & reached the opposite shore; where he gave three yells, as if to notify some other Indian party if within hearing. This fight was over before the main army got up—who hearing the firing hurried on—Brodhead in the bottom, & the militia along the adjacent hills. Went to the Muncy Towns—which they reached the 3^d day after the fight—a town on either side of the Allegheny, near its head, & within some 8 or 10 ^{ms} of what is now the N. York line. Reach^d the towns near midday—it was deserted, apparently that very morning; set about destroying all the cabins, some 500 acres of corn in roasting ears, cattle were taken for beef; captured upwards of 30 horses—30 brass kettles were found sunk in the river. This was Simon Girty's town[1]—the Indians at this time were mostly absent opposing Gen. Sullivan: Some of Girty's papers were found in the town. Then returned to Pittsburg. The Muncies never re-settled their town; the place was given [in 1785] by Gov^t to Cornplanter[2] & his party, who were friendly—Provisions plenty.

[Recollections of Daniel Higgins.[3] 3S128–29.]

Was on Brodhead's campaign up the Allegheny against the Muncy Towns, in Capt. John Clark's company—[Frederick]

[1] For Girty see *Dunmore's War*, 152, note 4. Ellis intends to say that this was the town where Simon Girty lived when as a boy he was a captive among the Seneca.

[2] For this chief see *Rev. Upper Ohio*, 160, note 84; his portrait appears opposite 162.

[3] Daniel Higgins was an Irishman who emigrated to Pittsburgh about the year 1778 and performed his first military service on the expedition of 1779. He was out in 1782 under Crawford. After the war he removed to Ohio, and in 1846, then in his eighty-eighth year, he was living near Warren, where Dr. Draper visited him and secured this interview.

Vernon,[1] maj^r of the reg^t. A major McCulloch was out on the campaign.

Capt. Brady commanded the spies,—was in advance—with some friendly Indians under com^d of Capt. Wilson, a small man, a Delaware.[2] The next day after passing Kittanning, Brady in the advance met a party of Indians—about 60—said to be Muncys, & under Simon Girty, a little below the mouth of Sugar Creek, & on the west side of the Allegheny: The Indians had several canoes—going on an expedition against the settlements—& had landed & just finished their repast when Brady came upon them—a Skirmish ensued—both parties treed. Capt. Wilson, the Delaware, got wounded across the back of the hand—none others of Brady's party hurt: Soon drove the Indians into the river, which they swam, leaving their canoes, some of their accoutrements, & provisions. One fellow, a large, fat man, was left dead. * * * One of the Indians in swimming the river dropped his rifle; & one of Brady's Indians dove & brought it up. * * *

Burned two towns—& cut up a large quantity of corn both sides of the river: Got a good deal of plunder, traps, furs & skins, &c. The Indians had deserted the towns: The war party that Brady defeated, went to the first town, & doubtless gave notice of Brodhead's approach—& this body posted themselves on a high hill a little distance above the town, & watched Brodhead's movements—so Cornplanter subsequently told my informant—but said he was not there, nor was he then in that part of the country.

Jonathan [Joseph] Nicholson, who spoke several Indian languages, was pilot—& with Brady's attacking party. The army lay only one night at the Indian town—then marched for Pittsburgh—after crossing French Creek at its mouth, took over the hills direct to Pittsburgh. Took out beeves for use on out-march —none on return, but some beef, & flour.

---

[1] For these officers see *Wis. Hist. Colls.*, XXIII, 205, note 1, and 139, note 4.

[2] George Wilson, whose Indian name was Nanowland, was a friend of Samuel Brady, and accompanied him on many scouts. In 1776 he brought messages to Pittsburgh from the Delaware chiefs, and was frequently employed as a messenger during the Revolution. See *ibid., passim*. In 1781 Wilson accompanied Brodhead's Coshocton expedition and returned with the troops to the neighborhood of Pittsburgh. There, while encamped with others, on an island in the Ohio, these friendly Indians were attacked by frontiersmen, and Wilson was among those who were murdered.

[Recollections of Capt. Matthew Jack. 6NN188.]

I again in the Spring of 1779 by order of Genl McIntosh I raised a Company of Six months men to Join Genl Brodhead in a Campaign against the Indians at the Monsey Towns high up on the Allegheny river & I raised the Company and Joined Genl Brodhead in the Said expedition the[y] were about 1700 men in all when we marched Composed of Pennsylvanians & Virginians and on our march up the Allegheny river about 16 miles below the Muncy Towns we met a body of Indians Supposed to be about 100 on their way to war—The Indians attacked our advance guard & after returning their fire fell back and the Indians followed them up and we met them, and they Stood but one or two fires; we killed 12 of them and the rest ran; 4 or 5 of our men was killed & wounded; we went on to the Muncy Towns but the Indians of Course knew of our Coming as those we met I expect returned back there again—we found none at their Town—all big & little had fled—we destroyed three Towns & Cornfields and left.

We then on our return back down the river as far as the mouth of French Creek where Franklin now Stands & remained there a day or two and while there Genl Brodhead ordered two Companies to be Selected out of his Brigade under the Command of Capt Samuel Brady & myself to march up French Creek to the Indian Towns where Meadville[1] now Stands, we went there and when we arrived the Indians old and young had all fled I expect the[y] had heard of us Coming we burnt their Town and distroyed their Cornfields

We got a quantity of Fur and Traps and returned with them to the mouth of French Creek—and from there we returned with Genl Brodhead to Pittsburgh where I was discharged and went home.

[1] This was the town called "Mahusquechikoken," or "Mahusguachiakocken." See *ante*, 55, 57. Dr. Draper thought (Draper Mss., 6NN209-10) that this was the village usually termed "Kiskakoquille," and that it was not as far up French Creek as the present Meadville, but seven miles lower down that stream in Wayne Township, Crawford County.

[Recollections of Ezekiel Caldwell. 3S143-44.]

Brodhead's campaign, 1779. [John] Caldwell[1] was on this campaign up the Allegheny: Several head of cattle had been taken along for supplies for the troops—these ran off from the trail to the water's edge of the Allegheny to slake their thirst—at this moment two canoes filled with Indians descending the river, discovered the cattle, & evidently curious to know the meaning of this unusual sight in that region, landed cautiously some little distance above, when they were attacked by a party in ambush, & routed & some killed.—In the Indian town were found poles erected with scalps on them, as if left to taunt the whites. Cut up a large quantity of corn—that convenient to the river was thrown into the stream—the other was thrown in heaps to heat & destroy.

[Recollections of Charles O'Bail.[2] 4S122-24.]

Brodhead's Expedition, 1779. Na-tah-go-ah, or Capt. Crow was the leader of the party who were defeated by Brodhead's advance. Crow, Red-Eye & 4 others went down the river in a canoe to hunt: They first went to an island 2 miles below Warren; some were posted on the island at a crossing place, while the others went upon the main Western Shore, & running yelping, dog-like, through the woods, start the deer & drive them for the crossing place, & as they would take the river for the island, those on the island would shoot them.

Brodhead's friendly Indian spies heard the shooting, & reported. Crow's party now moved to the island below Broken Straw 3 miles, for another similar hunt. There they discovered the Americans approaching pretty near. Crow's small party disagreed as

---

[1] For John Caldwell see *Frontier Defense*, 61, note 18. His son, Ezekiel, narrated to Dr. Draper in 1846 his father's adventures.

[2] Charles O'Bail, son of the famous chief, Cornplanter, was born in 1778 at the Seneca town of Conesus. He remembered that his mother and her children were driven from their home by Sullivan's invasion in 1779 and spent the following winter at Fort Niagara. They then lived for five years at Tonawanda, removing in 1785 to Cornplanter's reserve on the Allegheny. There on Feb. 21, 1850 Dr. Draper interviewed O'Bail, who gave him the Indian traditions of Brodhead's expedition. The old chief died on Dec. 31, 1868 near the present town of Cornplanter, Pa.

to the best mode of escape—all of them then being on the western shore. Crow & two of the others took to the woods, who escaped: Red-Eye & his two companions pushed off in the canoe, aiming to reach the eastern bank of the river, thinking they would be safest when there. Brodhead's succeeded in getting fair shots at them, & killed two of them. Red-Eye jumped out of the canoe, finding himself too much exposed to the fire of the Americans, & swam over just around the foot of the island—diving & swimming till he got over—a great many balls striking near & around him. And after he got over, & was climbing up the bank or hill, a ball came so near him as to knock him down, yet without actually touching him.

O'Bail thinks Brodhead did not go above Broken Straw—that the Cornplanter town[1] had Indian sentinels out, & were momentarily expecting the Americans: Hearing loud singing in the woods—or a rude attempt to sing—below the town, they thought surely the Americans were close upon them,—finally a few bolder spirits than the rest, ventured carefully to reconnoitre & discovered a lone white man, without a gun or any weapon of defence, evidently deranged, who had probably wandered off from Brodhead's army. He was kindly taken care of—not harmed—thinks he was sent to the British at Fort Niagara. Indians never harm an idiot or insane person.

Thus O'Bail heard Capt. Crow relate this affair. * * * Capt. Crow died on the Alleghany Reservation, at Cold Spring,[2] about 20 years ago: Red-Eye died at Cold Spring about the same time,—he was only a common warrior when opposing Brodhead, but an extra or unusually good one.

[Recollections of Blacksnake.[3] 16F150-53]

Capt. Redeyes Escape from fifty 50 men By Crossing the Allegany River

While we are gon to Wyoming and others places to war with our own america whites Brotherns Captain Redeyes and another

[1] The narrator refers to the Munsee town on the site of the village later built by Cornplanter.
[2] Cold Spring is on the upper Allegheny in Cattaraugus County, N. Y.
[3] For a sketch of the Seneca chief, Blacksnake, and for other excerpts from his manuscript see *Rev. Upper Ohio*, 159, notes 82 and 83.

Indians was with Redeye about ten of them together following Down Stream on the Allegeny River with Bark canoes and hunting furs. Redeyes and his comrates was Down about five miles below Brokenstraw now called warrent county Pennsylvania they had been camp out on the Bank of the River, Captain Redeye took his Rifle and walk it Down on the Bank the River, about quarter of a mile from his camp there he Saw a company of men of war, and count them, how many it was the company they was about 500 men in the company and they Saw him and he Run Back to his camp, they fire it at him But not toucth him the Ball, But he Run as fast as he could, then they put after him about 50 of them, But he Rather out Run them as soon as he got into their camp he told his comrate that the whites company are coming close to hand that they had Better Run soon as possible, So they start it and Run for their lives, some Run up the River, and Redeye and 3 others went with him and got into their Bark canoe and put cross the River But before Reaching crossing, the company come upon them and fire it and this 3 Indians was kill in the River while crossing and Redeye jump it out the canoe into water and Dove in the water as far as he could go under water But the company kept fire gun at him as far as they see him. But he made out cross the River life [alive] as soon as he got out the water and Run to the first tree and got behind that—till water Drin from him and made out Escape from them But the whites company kept pursued him up the River, Captain Redeye Kept it going Day and Nights untill he came up to now called Cornplanter Reservation at that time and at that place was no Regular settlement only a few Indians family Stop it there for to Rase some corn that year 1769[1] the Indians and women and children made them prepared themselves for to get out, away from Danger of their anemy that are coming up the River, that Redeye aurge [urged] his people to get Ready as soon as posible and also made all the Indians to march up the River, and they took Backages with some provisions and vinisions, and the young one and get them a way as soon as posible, for the Danger near at hand, of the 500 men are coming to Destroyed them So they got away, and left all those unmoveable Such [as] crops on the ground and come into state new york, and made a stop at now Cold Spring and made retirement for a few days, and send messnger over to Genesee River immidiatly

[1] All of the dates in Blacksnake's narrative are incorrect.

and to the head quarter, to let them know the disturbantes and the persons that who was Kill at the time Redeye was first drove from hunting &c &c. when Redeye first got up at Cold Spring and his company Buried their corn and vensions under the ground you have seen the hold frequently a long side the River like potatoe holds when the Indians has been Buried up their provisions and cooking utenstial those Indians wandering about in the woods or in when is having forest &c till uncle Cornplanter and Red Jacket[1] and myself come over to protect them, when we got down to Cornplanter now Reserved in P^a where the Redeye had it corn that season, the whites has been there, and cut all the corn and throw [in] the River, so that we could not have any if Redeye should come back and the whites were gone down again and we persued them as far as warren Pennsylvania and see nothing of them so we returnit again and called upon all the Indians and we went long up stream and over to Genesee River and down home at avon[2] about winter sit in.

[Recollections of Capt. John Decker.[3] 4S99–100.]

1779—Brodhead's Expedition. A party of between 30 & 40 warriors, mostly Senecas, some Delawares, were descending the Alleghany in canoes, going on an expedition against the American settlements. Deh-gus-way-gah-ent, or the Fallen-Board, a Seneca; & Day-oos-ta, or It-is-light-to-be-lifted, a Delaware, were the war-leaders of the party.

The friendly Delawares with Brodhead discovered the Seneca war-party, & reported to Brodhead, who ordered some of his

[1] For a sketch of Red Jacket see *Rev. Upper Ohio*, 160, note 84; his portrait appears opposite p. 164.
[2] For this town see *ibid.*, 161, note 85. It is the same town as that noted *ante*, 53. Blacksnake was mistaken about spending the winter of 1779–80 at this place, since Sullivan's troops completely destroyed the village, and all its inhabitants retired to Niagara.
[3] Capt. John Decker was a Seneca Indian whose tribal name was Dah-gan-non-do, or "He who patches." He claimed to be over one hundred years of age when Dr. Draper interviewed him in February 1850. Decker was born on the site of the modern Franklin, Pa. He remembered the events of Braddock's Defeat in 1755, of the siege of Niagara in 1759, and the capture of Fort Venango in 1763. He said he had visited Fort Duquesne while the French were in possession, that is before 1758. The only campaign in which he took part was that against Hannastown in 1782. He died in April, 1851.

men to the East side of the river up the hills, while the main body kept on up the road on the West side. As the Senecas got into the Channel on the West side of the island, about 3 miles below Da-gah-she-no-de-a-go or Broken Straw Creek—with a high hill skirting the river on the western [as well as eastern] bank— finding themselves between two fires, fled to the island: The Seneca & Delaware leaders, & a Seneca warrior named Gen-ne-hoon, or Double-Door, were killed; & a Delaware warrior was wounded in his arm. The others escaped. Cornplanter was not there.

Brodhead's men camped at Broken Straw, & there left several bloody bandages—hence the Indians thought he had a good many wounded. The Indian town known as the Burnt-Houses, where Cornplanter afterwards settled, was burned by Brodhead. The Delaware town or settlement destroyed was on Kenjua Flats,[1] on the South side of the river—extending from Kenjua Creek 5 or 6 miles above—the extent of the flats.

THE WYANDOT EMBASSY

[Col. Daniel Brodhead's speech to the Wyandot chiefs. 1H117–18. In handwriting of Brodhead.]

HEAD QUARTERS PITSBURGH Sepr 17th 1779
Maghingwe Keeshuch to Doonyontat[2] principal Chief of the Hurons[3]

BROTHER:

I rejoice to find that you are at last come to this great Council fire and that I have the pleasure of seeing you here & to hear from your own mouth that the heavy Clouds which have so long hung over us are almost dispersed and that the Sun will soon shine clear upon us

Brother: It is likewise very pleasing to me that your Heart is inclined as your Nephews for good Works and that you have laid hold of the same chain of Friendship with your Brothers of the United States to secure your Women & Children & that you are

[1] This place is now known as Kinzua, in Warren County, Pa.
[2] This is the Indian title of the Wyandot chief known as Half King.
[3] For a brief sketch of the Huron (Wyandot) Indians see *Rev. Upper Ohio*, 36, note 62.

fully convinced that so long as they the English kept you in darkness they told you many lies to deceive you and engage you to murder your best Friends

Brother: I have told you before that I can freely take you by the Hand but the wicked every where must be punished. Your Nephews have told you that the flesh & blood of the Americans are on your Hands and that you must take care to cleanse them by delivering up

Brother: I have much more to say to you   Listen to me

The English & the Mingoes have by the Assistance of the bad Spirit who put flattery & lies in to their Mouths excited you to do much Mischief against your Brothers of this Island[1] and for this they must die because the great Spirit will not take into his Arms bad Men And you ought to assist your Brothers of the United States to destroy them so that each of our Children & Grand Children may live under the tree of peace which God has planted for his Children on this Island

Brother: When I have heard your answer I shall again speak to you so that every [thing] may be fully settled for your Nation before you return home and then I shall wish you a Good Journey

Brother: The Belts & Strings with the Scalp you delivered to Capt Heth[2] I do not well understand the meaning and shall be glad you would explain it to me

[*Endorsed:*] Mahingweegeesuch to Noonyoondat, Sepr 17th —79

[The Wyandots' speech to Col. Daniel Brodhead. Reprinted from *The Olden Time* (Pittsburgh, 1848), II, 311–14.]

September 17th, 1779.

The Speech of Doonyontat, the Wyandot Chief, to Maghingive Keeshuch,

Brother, listen to me.

Brother, It grieves me to see you with the tears in your eyes. I know it is the fault of the English.

---

[1] "Island" was the term used in Indian councils for the continent of North America.

[2] For Capt. Henry Heath see *Wis. Hist. Colls.*, XXIII, 164, note 2. He was left in command at Fort Pitt during Brodhead's absence on the Allegheny expedition.

Brother, I wipe away all those tears, and smooth down your hair, which the English and the folly of my young men has ruffled.

Now *my Brother*, I have wiped away all the stains from your clothes, and smoothed them where my young men had ruffled them, so that you may now put on your hat, and sit with that ease and composure which you would desire.

(Four strings of white wampum.)

Brother, Listen to the Huron Chiefs.

Brother, I see you all bloody by the English and my young men. I now wipe away all those stains and make you clean.

Brother, I see your heart twisted, and neck and throat turned to the one side, with the grief and vexation which my young men have caused, all which disagreeable sensations I now remove, and restore you to your former tranquility, so that now you may breathe with ease, and enjoy the benefit of your food and nourishment.

Brother, your ears appear to be stopped, so that you cannot listen to your brothers when they talk of friendship. That deafness I now remove, and all stoppage from your ears, that you may listen to the friendly speeches of your brothers, and that they may sink deep into your heart.

(Seven strings of white wampum.)

Brother, Listen to me.

When I look around me, I see the bones of our nephews lie scattered and unburied.

Brother, I gather up the bones of all our young men on both sides, in this dispute, without any distinction of party.

Brother, I have now gathered up all the bones of our relations on both sides, and will bury them in a large deep grave, and smooth it over so, that there shall not be the least sign of bones, or any thing to raise any grief or anger in our minds hereafter.

Brother, I have now buried the bones of all our and your relations very deep. You very well know that there are some of your flesh and blood in our hands prisoners: I assure you that you shall see them all safe and well.

(Eight strings of white wampum.)

Brother, I now look up to where our Maker is, and think there is still some darkness over our heads, so that God can hardly see us, on account of the evil doings of the King over the great waters. All these thick clouds, which have [been] raised on account of that bad King, I now entirely remove, that God may look and see in our treaty of friendship, and be a witness to the truth and sincerity of our intentions.

(Four strings of white wampum.)

Brother, As God puts all our hearts right, I now give thanks to God Almighty, to the chief men of the Americans, to my old father the King of France, and to you, Brother, that we can now talk together on friendly terms, and speak our sentiments without interruption.

(Four strings of black and white wampum.)

Brother, You knew me before you saw me and that I had not drawn away my hand from yours, as I sent word last year by Captain White Eyes.

Brother, I look up to Heaven, and call God Almighty witness to the truth of what I say, and that it really comes from my heart.

Brother, I now tell you that I have for ever thrown off my Father the English, and will never give him any assistance; and there are some amongst all the nations that think the same things that I do, and I wish they would all think so.

Brother, I cannot answer for all the nations, as I don't know all their thoughts, and will speak only what I am sure of.

Brother, Listen to me. I love all the nations, and hate none, and when I return home they shall all hear what you say, and what is done between us.

Brother, I have just now told you, that I loved all the nations, and I see you raising up the hatchet against my younger brothers the Shawanese. I beg of you to stop a little while, as he has never yet heard me; and when he has heard me, if he does not choose to think as we do, I will tell you of it immediately.

Brother, I intend to speak roughly to my younger brother, and tell him not to listen to the English, but throw them off, and listen to me and then he may live as I do.

Brother, I thank you for leaving the fortress at Tuscarawas, and am convinced by that you have taken pity on us, and want to make us your friends.

Brother, I now take a firmer hold of your hand than before, and beg that you will take pity upon other nations who are my friends, and if any of them should incline to take hold of your hand, I request that you would comply and receive them into friendship.

(A black belt of eleven rows.)

Brother, Listen. I tell you to be cautious, as I think you intend to strike the man near to where I sit,[1] not to go the nighest way to where he is, lest you frighten the owners of the lands who are living through the country between this and that place.

Brother, You now listen to me, and one favour I beg of you is, that when you drive away your enemies you will allow me to continue in possession of my property, which if you grant will rejoice me.

Brother, I would advise you, when you strike the man near where I sit, to go by water, as it will be the easiest and best way.

Brother, If you intend to strike, one way is to go up the Allegheny and by Prisquille;[2] another way is to go down this river and up the Wabash.

Brother, The reason why I mentioned the road up the river is, that there will be no danger of your being discovered until you are close upon them, but on the road down the river you will be spied.

Brother, Now I have told you the way by Prisquille, and that it is the boundary between us and your enemies; if you go by Wabash your friends will not be surprised.

Brother, You must not think that what I have said is only my own thoughts, but the opinion of all the Huron Chiefs, and I speak in behalf of them all. If you grant what favours I have asked of you, all our friends and relations will be thankful and glad as far as they can hear all round.

Brother, The reason why I have pointed out these two roads is, that when we hear you are in one of them we will know your intentions without further notice, and the Huron Chiefs desired me particularly to mention it that they may meet you in your walk, and tell you what they have done, who are your enemies and who are your friends, and I in their name request a pair of colors to shew we have joined in friendship.

(*Fourteen strings of black wampum.*)

Brother, The chiefs desired me to tell you that they had sent Montour before to tell you their intentions, and they leave him to go with you, that when you meet your brothers, you may consult together, and understand one another by his means.

---

[1] The chief refers to an anticipated attack upon Detroit by the American forces.

[2] For this site see *Wis. Hist. Colls.*, XXIII, 207, note 1.

FRONTIER RETREAT 71

[Col. Daniel Brodhead's speech to the Wyandot chiefs. 3H162-65. Letter Book.]

HEAD QUARTERS, PITTSBURGH, Sepr 18th 1779.
Maghingwe Keeshuch to Dooyontat, principal chief of the Wyondats,

BROTHER:
Yesterday I had the pleasure to hear you speak. But when I had heard all, & you had taken no notice of what I mentioned to you before, against the English, I could not tell what to think.

Brother: The Chiefs of the Wyondats have lived too long with the English to see things as they ought to do. They must have expected when they were councilling, that the Chief they sent to this Council fire would find the Americans asleep. But the sun which the Great Spirit has set to light this island, discovers to me that they are much mistaken.

(*Four strings of white & black wampum.*)

Brother: I will tell you why they are mistaken; they must have thought that it was an easy matter to satisfy us, after doing all the mischief they could. They must have heard that the English were getting weaker & the Americans stronger, & that a few flattering words would, with giving up our prisoners, secure to them their lives, the lives of their women & children, & their lands; and the wicked Shawnese who have so often embrued their hands in the blood of the Americans And that in my military operations they had a right to mark out the road I should march on.

(*Six strings white and black wampum.*)

Brother: I, however, thank you for wiping away the blood & burying the bones of our young men, & for casting off that bad father the King of Britain over the great Lake.

(*Three strings of white wampum.*)

Brother: I left the fort at Tuscarawas because it gave uneasiness to several of the Indian Nations which I pitied & promised to save, if they would do what was right before God, & I still intend to do it. But I have said, they must do what is right, & they must send some of their great men to me to remain as hostages until they have complied with the terms. If this is not done, all words will be considered as wind & no regard will be paid to them: And though I love peace, & could wish to save the lives of my countrymen of this Island, I am not afraid of war.

(*Four strings of black wampum.*)

Brother: I will now tell you what I conceive to be right, & I will leave it to all the world to judge it. I think the Nations you mention & wish me to receive into friendship, ought to send hostages to me. As I said before, until they have killed & taken as many from the English & their allies as they have killed & taken from the Americans, & return whatever they have stolen from their brothers, together with their flesh & blood, & on every occasion join us against our enemies—upon these terms, which are just, they & their posterity may live in peace & enjoy their property without disturbance from their brethren of this Island, so long as the Sun shines or the waters run.

(*A black belt—Rows.*)

Brother: I have now spoke from my heart. I am a warrior as well as a Councillor; my words are few, but what I say I will perform. And I must tell you that if the Nations will not do justice, they will not be able, after the English are driven from this Island, to enjoy peace or property.

(*Four strings black wampum.*)

Brother: When I go to war, I will take my choice of roads; if I meet my friends I shall be glad to see them, & if I meet my enemies I shall be ready to fight them.

Brother: You told you had not yet spoken to the Shawnese: You likewise say that you had not yet let slip my hand; if so, why did you not speak to them? They have heard their Grand Fathers the Delawares, & they have heard me. I sent them a good talk, but they threw it into the fire.

Now, *brother*, I must tell you that I cannot now prevent the Shawnese being struck: Col° Clark, I hear, is gone against them & will strike them before I can send to him to call him back; but if the Shawnese do what is right, as I have told you, they shall enjoy peace & property. This belt confirms my words.

(*A white & black belt—Rows.*)

Col° Brodhead to Noonyoondat.—

MEQUOCHOKE-SHAWNEE SEEK AMERICAN ALLIANCE

[Captain Killbuck's speech to Col. Daniel Brodhead. Reprinted from *The Olden Time*, II, 316–17.]

Kelleleman to Maghingive Keeshuch.[1]
September 21, 1779.

BROTHER:
I told my grand-children, the Shawanese, when they came to me yesterday, to remain with their grandfathers, until they had spoken to their brothers, the Americans. They answered, they would comply with the request of their grand-fathers. This our grand-children spoke to us, and said, grand-fathers, we are humble, and are now come unto you—now I am come to you, I take my hands and wipe your eyes, that you may clearly see the light, and that these are your grand-children who now appear before you, and likewise remove every obstruction from your ears, that you may hear and understand me. I also compose your heart, that you may be disposed to pity your poor grand-children, as your ancient Chiefs used to pity their grand-children, the Macquichees,[2] when they were poor or humble before them. Now my grand-fathers, I tell you to pity your grand-children, the Macquichees, and whatever you direct them to do, will be done. Now you have heard your grand-children speak, and you will judge what to say to your brother Maghingive Keeshuch.
(*Two strings of white wampum.*)
Now *grand-fathers*, here is a little tobacco to fill your pipes, that you may consider and pity your grand-children Macquichees.
Keeshmattsee, to his grand-fathers, the Delawares.
Grand-fathers, I now take my Chief and Councellor Nimwha,[3] and set him down on the ground before you that he may assist you in considering the distressed situation of your grand-children.

Killbuck to Colonel Brodhead.
Brother Maginghive Keeshuch, listen to me.
You always told me, that when any nations came to treat of peace, I should first speak to them, and tell you my sentiments of

[1] These are the Indian titles of Captain Killbuck and Colonel Brodhead.
[2] For this branch of the Shawnee see *ibid.*, 280, note 1.
[3] For this chief see *Rev. Upper Ohio*, 41, note 67.

them, which I am now come to do, in regard to my grand-children, the Macquichees.

I told them I was much obliged to them, for clearing my eyes, my ears, and composing my heart, and that it was time, that many bad things enter my ears.

I remember you told me to pity you, and it is true, I have pitied you, my grand-children, the Shawanese.

Now, I tell you, my grand-children, it is very well you put me in mind of my wise ancestors, who, out of pity to you, took you up, and placed you before them.

My grand-children, the Maquichees, it is true, you have done no harm, but I see some stains of blood upon you, which the mischief and folly of your young men have occasioned. Now, my grand-children, I will advise you how to be cleansed from your bloody stains, deliver to our brother Maghingive Keeshuch, all his flesh and blood which are prisoners in your hands, and the horses you have stolen from the Americans. My grand-children, when you have done this, you will then be clean, your flesh and heart will be the same as mine, and I can again take you up, and set you down before me, as our wise Chiefs formerly did.

Now, my grand-children, I tell you, for several years past you have been fraught with lies, which I am tired of hearing, and in future you must tell me nothing but truth.

Now listen to me, my grand-children, you see how dreadful the day looks, and how thick the clouds appear; don't imagine this day to be like that on which you first came to your grand-fathers. I tell you that I have finished the chain of friendship. The thirteen United States and I are one. I have already assisted my brother, in taking the flesh of the English and Mingoes. You told me just now, that whatever I told you, you would do; now I offer you the flesh of the English and Mingoes to eat, and that is the only method I know of, by which your lives may be preserved, and you allowed to live in peace, (delivering them a string of wampum and two scalps.) They received the string and scalps, and said they were glad to know this, and as they had before said, whatever their grand-fathers told them, they would do, so they told them again on receiving the scalps. They said, now grandfather, I am very glad to hear what you have said; I have got in my hand what you say will save my life, and immediately sung his war-song. The speaker, having danced, delivered the scalps to the King, who likewise rose and sung his war-song, and said,

Now grand-fathers, although you have often sent good speeches to the other tribes of the Shawanese nation, yet they would not receive them, but still took up the tomahawk to strike your brothers, I will now go and deliver them what I have in my hands, which I suppose they will receive.

Delaware Chief to Maghingive Keeshuch.

Brother, We are come to let you know the result of our Council, respecting the Maquichees.

Brother, Listen, This is the way I have considered the matter, and if I am mistaken, I am very sorry for it. Brother, let us both consider of it. I thought, when I looked in his eyes, that he was sincere.

Brother, I think the Maquichees are honest. In former times they were the best of the Shawanese nations. I think we may take them by the hand; and you know, you told me, that any nation I took by the hand, you would also receive.

DELAWARE NEGOTIATIONS

[The Delawares' speeches to Col. Daniel Brodhead. 1H119-20. Contemporary Transcript.]

Delaware Chiefs Speech Sepr 23^d 79

Listen to your BROTHERS:

The have all consulted upon what they before said & think it right

Brother: you Remember what passed between us last fall & it is true—Brother you told me that if I wanted a Fort you would build it for me to keep my Women & Children safe when I should be absent from them—you also told me that you would perform whatever you promised. At Tuscarawas you repeated the same promise which I told you to defer it But now I have occasion for it[1] Brother when that is done my Warriors can go where they please—Remember exactly w^t we have said to one another.

[1] Note on original manuscript: "In reference to the above request see P. S. to Col. Brodhead's official Report of his expedition against the Senecas & Monseys, Sept. 1779—L. C. D."

BROTHER: PITTSBURGH 24th Sep' 1779.

listen to the chiefs of the Delawares Formerly when our Ancestors when they first kindled the Council fire at Philad^a

After that we took a few coals & fire and kindled one at this place

Brother: now with this string of wampum I now take a few Coals of fire and kindle one at Beaver Creek Where we or any that are desirous of treating of peace may meet, & consult together as we are one & the same people let us join and both put our Hands together to remove it to that place When this is agreed on I shall inform all my People that the Council fire is removed to Beaver Creek.

[Endorsed:] Removal of the Council fire to Beaver Creek Sep' 24th 79

THE ALLEGHENY EXPEDITION

[Summary of a letter of Col. Daniel Brodhead, Pittsburgh, Sept. 23, 1779, to Pres. Joseph Reed. Printed in *Pa. Archives*, VII, 710–11.]

Incloses the account of his successful expedition against the Seneca and Munsee. The Delawares, Wyandot, and Mequochoke-Shawnee seem disposed for peace, a few goods and trinkets would engage them against the enemy. The Delawares seem ready to follow him anywhere. The troops are ragged and there is great need of clothing and of money. Lieut. John Hardin's services; he is recommended for promotion. Unless Pennsylvania allows a larger bounty for recruits, most of the men in his regiment whose terms have expired will enlist in the Virginia corps.

[Summary of a letter of Col. Daniel Brodhead, Pittsburgh, Sept. 23, 1779, to Timothy Pickering. Printed in *id.*, XII, 158–59.][1]

Thanks Pickering for having placed his letters before Congress. Awaits its decision. Is equipping Captain McIntire's[2] company as light dragoons. Incloses copy of letter to General Washington on Allegheny expedition and the talks of Delawares, Wyan-

[1] This letter is also printed in Almon, *Remembrancer*, IX, 152.
[2] For Capt. Thomas McIntyre see *Wis. Hist. Colls.*, XXIII, 400, note 2.

dot, and Mequochoke-Shawnee. "Since my last, this Frontier has enjoyed perfect tranquility, but the new settlement on the Kentucke has suffered greatly." Boat builders are returning to the East, therefore there is need for more.

DETROIT REËNFORCED

[Summary of a letter of Col. Daniel Brodhead, Pittsburgh, Sept. 24, 1779, to Col. George Morgan. Printed in *ibid.*, 159–60.]

Desires Morgan's presence at Pittsburgh. Has applied for permission to undertake an expedition against Detroit. For lack of men and provisions, it must be postponed. How can 500 men take a place stronger by men and works than two years ago when 1,800 were then thought necessary? Secrecy impossible because of Indian interests.

CLARK REPLIES TO BRODHEAD

[Summary of a letter of Col. George Rogers Clark, Headquarters, Falls of Ohio, Sept. 24, 1779, to Col. Daniel Brodhead. Printed in *Ill. Hist. Colls.*, VIII, 366–67.]

Hopes for Brodhead's success against the savages. Captain George has taken a commission under Virginia, which it appears he was at liberty to do. Will endeavor to send back all troops belonging to Continental regiments, but many deserters have gone to Florida. Plans to prevent this evil. Desires to maintain a correspondence.

[Summary of a letter of Capt. Robert George, Falls of Ohio, Sept. 25, 1779, to Col. Daniel Brodhead. Printed in *ibid.*, 367–68.]

Has received his favor of August 2. When he joined Captain Willing he was in the marine service; had orders to return to Colonel Clark in the Illinois, under whose orders he now considers himself. Has taken a few deserters, but Spanish territory is a convenient refuge, and deserters cannot be taken there without the consent of the Spanish.[1]

NIAGARA ENDANGERED

[Gen. Frederick Haldimand to Gen. Henry Clinton. 58J59–60. Summary and transcript.]

QUEBEC, 28th Sept. 1779—
From the force of the enemy, & the great caution they observe in advancing, and from their penetrating at the same time to Venango and Le Bœuf, it would appear that they have more in view than merely to awe the Six Nations. Niagara seems now to be their object by a junction of those two bodies, which they certainly may effect unless the appearance of the reënforcement should reunite the Indians and determine them to fall vigorously upon the enemy. I cannot say I apprehend much from any attempt they can make upon that place, provided that no accident should happen to Sir John Johnson[2] in the field that may prevent his throwing himself into it.
* * * [Then speaks of "the usual supplies cannot be had from Detroit, the crop there having so entirely failed that applications have been made to me for passes to carry grain & flour from hence to that place."]

[1] The letters of both Clark and George were sent by Col. David Rogers' expedition, and were captured by the British. See *post*, 79–94.
[2] Sir John Johnson, born in 1742, was the eldest son of Sir William Johnson, to whose title and estate he succeeded in 1774. A prominent Loyalist, Sir John commanded a body of rangers in St. Leger's expedition of 1777, and in the succeeding years of the Revolution frequently raided the Mohawk Valley. After the war he resided at Montreal, where he was superintendent of Indian affairs for British North America until his death in 1837.

ALLEGHENY POSTS REGARRISONED

[Summary of a letter of Col. Daniel Brodhead, Headquarters, Pittsburgh, Oct. 2, 1779, to Capt. Thomas Campbell.[1] Printed in *Pa. Archives*, XII, 160–61.]

Orders Campbell to Fort Crawford. Captain Irwin[2] is to garrison Fort Armstrong. Scouts to go out daily between that post and Kiskiminitas Creek, and from there to Fort Pitt. Hopes he will find new post more agreeable than Fort Hand.[3]

[Summary of a letter of Col. Daniel Brodhead, Headquarters, Pittsburgh, Oct. 2, 1779, to Francis McIlwaine. Printed in *ibid.*, 161.]

Has ordered Captain Irwin to relieve McIlwaine at Fort Armstrong, the latter to come in to Fort Pitt.

ROGERS' DEFEAT

[Narrative by Dr. Lyman C. Draper. 5D21–30, and 11E225. A. D.]

Rogers' Defeat, Remarkable Adventure of Basil Brown and Robert Benham

When the mighty struggle for independence was forced upon the American people in 1775, they were illy prepared for it. They were poor; they had no accumulated wealth—no supply of arms and munitions of war—no manufactories. It was the policy of the mother country to blockade the ports of the rebellious Colonies, and cut off all supplies from abroad.

Not unfrequently the patriot army was scantily provided with arms and ammunition. At the battle of Han[g]ing Rock, Sumter's men went into the fight with scarcely two rounds of powder per

---

[1] Thomas Campbell was an officer in the Pennsylvania Battalion, and was captured Nov. 16, 1776 at Fort Washington on the Hudson. He suffered two years' imprisonment before his exchange. Upon his release he returned to his home in Westmoreland County, where in 1779 he was chosen captain of a ranging company.

[2] For a sketch of Capt. Joseph Irwin see *Wis. Hist. Colls.*, XXIII, 391, note 1.

[3] For a sketch of this post see *Frontier Defense*, 41, note 83.

man, re-supplying themselves from their vanquished foes. During the terrible winter of 1777-78 at Valley Forge—a winter of great severity—Washington's army suffered greatly from hunger and nakedness, and could be tracked by their bleeding feet. No less than two thousand, eight hundred and ninety-eight men were in camp unfit for duty, because they were barefoot or otherwise naked; and, for want of blankets, many were obliged to sit up all night by fires to keep themselves comfortable. For three days successively, the troops were without bread, and two without meat; and these were no uncommon occurrences. Washington declared, that he could not enough admire the incomparable patience and fidelity of his army.[1]

Nor did the troops encamped on the Highlands of the Hudson that winter suffer less terrible privations. "There is not one blanket," wrote General Putnam, "in Colonel Dubois' regiment; very few have either a shoe or a shirt; and most of them have neither stockings, breeches, or overalls."[2] At a later period of the war, it is related of Greene's Southern army, that all were in clothes nearly worn out, many in tatters, many with but a remnant of some garment pinned around their waists with the thorn of the locust tree. The heavy musket bruised sorely the naked shoulder. The cartouch-box pressed roughly upon the unprotected loin. More than a thousand were so naked that they could not be put on duty of any kind; three hundred were without arms.[3]

The people throughout the country resorted to every make-shift to supply their own and the pressing wants of the army. Some fabrics were woven in the rude looms of their own construction; even the wild nettle, in some instances, was brought into requisition as a substitute for flax. But while these proved essential aids, they did not lessen the necessity for resorting to additional sources of supply, and especially for the more important munitions of war. Ambassadors were dispatched to foreign countries, to enlist their sympathies, and invoke their assistance. A million of francs were given from the French treasury in 1776; while cannon and military stores, to the value of a million of dollars, were placed at our disposal. Spain, the same year, sent the

[1] Note on original manuscript: "Sparks' *Washington*, V, 193, 199, 239.—L. C. D."

[2] Note on original manuscript: "Lossing's *Field Book of the Revolution*, I, 705—L. C. D."

[3] Note on original manuscript: "Greene's *Greene*, III, 448, 449—L. C. D."

revolted Colonies a free gift of a million of francs; and cargoes of military stores from the port of Bilboa.[1]

Important supplies came from an unexpected quarter. Oliver Pollock migrated from his native Ireland several years before the Revolutionary war, and settled in Carlisle, Pennsylvania, in the humble capacity of bar-keeper to his brother James, who kept a tavern there.[2] In 1769, he arrived in New Orleans, in a brig from Baltimore, with a cargo of flour, at a time of great scarcity when the price had risen to twenty dollars a barrel. He sold the cargo to Governor O'Reilly, for military supplies, at fifteen dollars a barrel, which so much pleased the Governor that he promised the enterprising adventurer free trade to Louisiana as long as he lived, and a favorable report to the King.[3]

Establishing himself as a merchant in New Orleans, and marrying a Spanish lady, a friend of the subsequent Governor Galvez, he acquired wealth and influence. The Spanish Government had not only sent to the American Colonies a present of money, and military stores from Bilboa, but tendered a gentle hint that there were three thousand barrels of powder stored at New Orleans which should be at their service; and, as early as August, 1776, on application of Patrick Henry, Governor of Virginia, through the friendly intercessions of Mr Pollock, a cargo of this precious article, consisting of ninety-eight barrels, aggregating about ten thousand pounds, was despatched by Governor Unzaga, passing up the Mississippi and Ohio, under the charge of Lieutenant William Linn, in safety, and proving of essential service to the country.[4]

[1] Note on original manuscript: "George Sumner's Boston Oration, 1859 p. 16, note—L. C. D."
[2] Note on original manuscript: "Ms. notes of conversations with the late John B. Gibson, long Chief Justice of Pennsylvania—L. C. D."
[3] Note on original manuscript: "Martin's *History of Louisiana*, II, 12—L. C. D."
[4] Note on original manuscript: "Lieut. William Linn's letter to Oliver Pollock, in Ms. Archives of Virginia, dated Arkansas, Nov. 30, 1776, gives the number of barrels; a statement in Butler's *Kentucky*, on authority of one of Linn's party, specifies one hundred and fifty-six kegs of powder as the number carried around the Falls of Ohio—indicating that, for convenience of handling, the powder, after reaching the Arkansas Post had been transferred from barrels to kegs. Col. David Shepherd's Ms. letter, June 8, 1789, shows that the total weight of powder delivered at Wheeling by Lieut. Linn was 'ten thousand pounds, or thereabouts,' and Shepherd's certificate of Jan. 31, 1791, shows that nine thousand pounds were sent forward to Col. Crawford, at Fort Pitt. Capt. George Gibson, who headed this expedition to New Orleans, returned himself by sea to Philadelphia, as Pollock's Memorial, of September, 1782, to Congress, states —L. C. D."

The sufferings of the troops at Valley Forge, and the extreme difficulty of procuring military supplies, induced Governor Henry again to look to New Orleans for succor in this time of sore distress. Colonel David Rogers was selected as a proper person for this delicate and important mission. A native of Ireland, he had migrated to this country when quite young, settling himself as a merchant at Old Town, Maryland; and subsequently, in 1775, making a settlement five miles above Wheeling on the Ohio.[1] In the fall of this year, he marched a company to Pittsburg; and, in 1776, was chosen to represent the district of West Augusta in the Senate of Virginia.[2] In December, 1776, while a Major of militia, he was appointed a Captain in one of the six Virginia regiments on Continental establishment, but did not qualify.[3] Retaining his position in the militia service, he was ordered, in February, 1777, to station fifty men at the mouth of Wheeling, and as many more at the mouth of the Little Kenawha, properly officered, for the defence of those posts, and the protection of the neighboring settlements.[4] When Ohio County, Virginia, was organized, he was appointed its County Lieutenant, March 4, 1777; and, the next month, was re-elected to the State Senate. But shortly after, the incursions of the Indians broke up the settlement where he resided.[5]

Colonel Rogers sojourned awhile at Mount Braddock, half a dozen miles north-east of Union Town, Fayette County, Pennsylvania; but returning to the Potomac region, he married the widow of Captain Michael Cresap, and located on the Potomac, in Hampshire County, Virginia, opposite to Old Town. Changing his residence from Ohio County, he resigned his commission as County Lieutenant; and was succeeded, in June, 1777, by Colonel David Shepherd.[6]

[1] Note on original manuscript: "Ms. notes of conversations with Michael Cresap, 1845; and with Mrs. Lydia Cruger, 1846—L. C. D."
[2] Note on original manuscript: "Virginia Ms. Archives—L. C. D."
[3] Note on original manuscript: "*American Pioneer*, II, 397—L. C. D."
[4] Note on original manuscript: "Ms. letter of Patrick Henry to Major Rogers, Feb. 13, 1777—L. C. D." Printed in *Rev. Upper Ohio*, 232–33.
[5] Note on original manuscript: "Virginia Ms. Archives. Ms. petition of Samuel McColloch, John Canon and J. P. Duval, Dec. 7, 1778, to the Virginia Senate, submitting whether Rogers had not vacated his seat in that body —L. C. D."
[6] Note on original manuscript: "Col. James Paul's Ms. statement. Recollections of Michael Cresap. McColloch, Canon and Duval's petition. Virginia Ms. Archives—L. C. D."

FRONTIER RETREAT 83

Proving himself active and energetic in the public service, Col. Rogers was prevailed on by Governor Henry to convey, by the way of the Ohio and Mississippi, a letter to Bernardo de Galvez, the Spanish Governor of Louisiana. He was authorized to engage a Lieutenant, Ensign, and twenty-eight men, with directions for General Hand, at Pittsburgh, to assist in supplying boats for the expedition. In addition to conveying despatches to Governor Galvez, he was to act in the capacity of private ambassador in behalf of Virginia, consulting with the Governor as to the most suitable point on the Mississippi for the establishment of an American garrison; making to him a full representation of the resources, strength and condition of Virginia, the progress of the war, together with any additional information he might desire. Colonel Rogers was, on his return, to take into his care such supplies as Governor Galvez, or Mr Pollock, the American commercial agent, might have to transmit for the use of the State. He was, furthermore, to be the bearer of despatches to Colonel G. R. Clark, connected with his expedition against the Illinois country; who, when Rogers should ascend the Ohio, was directed to furnish him a proper escort for the safety of his vessels and cargo. These instructions, which met the approval of the Council, were given January fourteenth, 1778; and, six days thereafter, the sum of six hundred and twenty-five pounds, Virginia currency, was advanced to Colonel Rogers to defray the expenses of the Expedition.[1]

He raised his little company of thirty men[2] in the Red Stone region. Isaac Collyer was appointed Lieutenant, Patrick McElroy Ensign, and Robert Benham Commissary.[3] Two keel-boats

---

[1] Note on original manuscript: "Virginia Ms. Archives. Ms. copy of Henry's letter to Galvez, Jan. 14, 1778—L. C. D." See also letter of Governor Henry to Gen. Edward Hand, in *Frontier Defense*, 199.

[2] When Clark raided the Shawnee towns in 1786, a roll of Col. David Rogers' company was found among the Indians' effects. See Draper Mss., 5D211.

[3] Robert Benham was born at Monmouth, N. J., and there brought up by his maternal grandfather, Robert James. In 1772 Benham emigrated to Westmoreland County and after marrying Elizabeth Miller, settled upon Ten Mile Creek. Thence he volunteered on Rogers' expedition and thither he returned after his escape. In 1789 he removed to Cincinnati, and is said to have owned the land on which Rogers' defeat occurred. Benham later lived at Newport, Ky., in 1791 he went out with St. Clair, and was severely wounded. In the succeeding years he served under Harmar and Wayne. After the Indian wars he settled at Lebanon, Ohio, whence he was sent to represent his county in the first state assembly. He died in the month of February, 1809.

were built at Pittsburgh, one of which was taken to Red Stone Old Fort for the baggage and supplies of the party; and, in June, 1778, Colonel Rogers set out on his voyage down the Ohio and Mississippi, encountering many hardships in descending those rivers. With a plentiful stock of flour, the commissary had to rely for wild meat upon the success of squads of hunters, who took their turns, in following along the margin of the streams, while the boats were being carried down by the current, aided by the oarsmen of the party.

Arriving, at length, at the Arkansas Post,[1] fifty miles up the Arkansas River, where a Spanish garrison was established, Rogers and his party were kindly received by the commandant, and informed that the goods he sought had been sent up to St. Louis; but that it would be necessary for him to go to New Orleans to get the proper order for them. Selecting half a dozen of his men, among whom were Robert Benham and Basil Brown,[2] Colonel Rogers descended the Arkansas and Mississippi in a canoe, and narrowly escaped capture in passing the British post of Manchac in the night.[3]

He at length reached New Orleans, about the twentieth of September, where he met a very cordial reception by Mr Pollock and Governor Galvez. Rogers had confirmed to him what he had learned at Arkansas Post, that a very considerable quantity of goods had been sent up the river by Pollock, for the use of Congress or Virginia—having, apparently, like the Governor, no very clear distinction between the States in their separate and federal relations. As Governor Henry had been the medium of former negotiations for supplies, and renewed despatches now coming from him, there was no difficulty in securing an order for the goods. As for the loan Governor Henry solicited in behalf of Virginia, Galvez had to defer that matter to his superiors at

---

[1] For this post see *Frontier Defense*, 199, note 71.

[2] Two of the earliest settlers in the Redstone region of the Monongahela were Thomas and Basil Brown, who claimed settlement rights as early as 1768. Basil Brown Jr., who went with Rogers, was but sixteen years old when he volunteered. After this adventure he returned to his home in Luzerne Township, Fayette County, and after 1786 drew a yearly pension of £12 for the disabilities caused by his wounds received at Rogers' defeat. His later life was spent at Brownsville, where he lived with an invalid sister. His death occurred in 1837.

[3] Note on original manuscript: "Ms. copy of letter of Col. Rogers to Patrick Henry, New Orleans, Oct. 4, 1778. Basil Brown's deposition, Sept. 12, 1834, in Virginia Archives. Butler's *Kentucky*, 103—L. C. D."

Madrid—a request which, he was quite confident, would be granted.[1]

There was a British sloop of war in port, the Captain of which, suspicious of the presence of Colonel Rogers and his American party, watched their movements closely, ready to take any advantage if any infringements were made on the treaty relations existing between the courts of London and Madrid. While this state of affairs was perhaps somewhat perplexing, yet the fact that the goods and military supplies for which Rogers was in quest, were out of the reach of British interference on the Mississippi, rendered this espionage less harmful than it otherwise might have been. As the Spanish Government, from motives of public policy, was privately disposed to promote the interests of the new Republic, Colonel Rogers found no difficulty in holding such interviews with Governor Galvez as he saw fit to solicit. Benham was sent with despatches, it is conjectured, to Governor Henry, and probably to Colonel Clark and General Hand, through the long intervening wilderness; and, with the hardihood characteristic of the times, subsisted principally on Indian corn boiled in lye, to preserve it from the weevil. He went first to Kaskaskia, and proceeded thence to the Falls of the Ohio.[2]

It was near the close of the year before Colonel Rogers took his departure from New Orleans, going about ninety miles by water, to the point where Plaquemine village is now situated, a little distance below Manchac; thence by land, to avoid the English garrisons at Manchac and Natchez, where all passing boats were rigidly overhauled; and the bare suspicion that any party was friendly to the American cause, was very certain to subject them to seizure and imprisonment, with the confiscation of all their property. After leaving the river, their course lead them about sixty miles to Opelousas, and thence about one hundred and twenty miles to Natchitoches on Red River, where [they] arrived on the first of February, 1779. Their journey had been much impeded by almost continual rain, and consequent high waters, which compelled them to tarry a couple of weeks at Natchitoches. Resuming their toilsome travels they passed through the wilderness—partly by canoe, and partly by land—in a north-eastern direction, over two hundred miles, and, at length, after great hazard and fatigue reached their point of des-

---

[1] Note on original manuscript: "Rogers to Henry, Oct. 4, 1778—L. C. D."
[2] Note on original manuscript: "Butler's *Kentucky*, 103—L. C. D."

tination. Over this route some goods were conveyed, which seem to have been brought from New Orleans.[1]

From Arkansas Post, Rogers and party descended the Arkansas River to the Mississippi, and thence, in the slow and tedious manner of that day, they proceeded up the latter stream to St. Louis, where the goods, for which they had orders, were obtained from Mons. Eugene Pouree, alias Beausoliel, who had conveyed them from New Orleans, under cover, doubtless, of his being a well-known enterprising French trader of Upper Louisiana.[2] Here Joseph Francis Perrault,[3] a merchant of St. Louis, who had furnished Colonel Clark, for the supply of his troops in the Illinois country, goods to the amount of $11,814, for which he had received drafts on the State of Virginia, now took passage with Colonel Rogers, in order to collect these drafts, in tobacco

[1] Note on original manuscript: "Rogers to Henry, Oct. 4, 1778. Rogers to Oliver Pollock, 'Natchitash' Feb. 15, 1779. Brown's deposition already cited—L. C. D."

[2] Note on original manuscript: "Ms. letters and statements of Oliver Pollock —L. C. D." For a sketch of Eugène Pourée dit Beausoleil see Wis. Hist. Colls., XVIII, 431, note 41.

[3] Joseph François Perrault was born in 1753 in Canada, son of Louis François Perrault and Marie-Josephe Baby. About the year 1769 his father emigrated to New Orleans and soon thereafter established himself as a merchant at St. Louis. In 1772 the children went from Canada to join their father, taking the route via the Atlantic and the West Indies. They were twice shipwrecked, and nearly a year elapsed before they joined their father at St. Louis. Joseph soon became a fur trader, and made several voyages to New Orleans and return. On one of these in 1778 he accepted in payment for his peltry drafts on the Virginia government, which he was on his way to collect when captured by the Indians with Rogers' unfortunate men. At the first Indian town Perrault was compelled to run the gauntlet, and suffered many indignities, which he vividly narrates in his autobiography. Upon reaching Detroit he was rescued from captivity by his uncle, Jacques Duperon Baby of that place. Nevertheless, he was sent as a prisoner to Canada in 1780, where he was pardoned by Haldimand, and permitted to return to Detroit. There he spent the winter of 1780–81 in the vain endeavor to return to St. Louis. In the following spring he went back to Montreal, where he soon became a prosperous merchant. After having studied law, he was chosen prothonotary of Quebec in 1795. Removing thither, he became an honored and valued citizen. His efforts in founding schools gave him the name of "Father of Canadian Education." In 1834 he presented his autobiography to the governor of Canada. It has been published several times, first in 1834. More recently it appeared as part of P. B. Casgrain, La Vie de Joseph-François Perrault (Quebec, 1898). See also P. Bender, Old and New Canada * * * or the life of Joseph François Perrault (Montreal, 1882). Perrault died at Quebec in 1844, ninety-one years of age.

CAPT. ABRAHAM CHAPLINE

From an Etching Made by James R. Stuart from a miniature Owned by one of the Chapline Family

or flour, and ship them by sea to New Orleans.[1] Perrault's papers show that Rogers was in St. Louis on the fifth of August; and probably, not long thereafter, descended the river to the mouth of the Ohio, and up that stream to the Falls—now Louisville.

Benham was found at the Falls, and there rejoined the expedition.[2] Colonel Clark, then making his head-quarters at that place, assigned Lieutenant Abraham Chapline,[3] and some twenty three men of the Illinois regiment, together with an additional boat, to escort Colonel Rogers, with his two boats laden with supplies, to Pittsburgh. Colonel John Campbell, of Yohogania County, Virginia,[4] and perhaps others, there took passage with Rogers, as affording a supposed safe opportunity of returning to the Pittsburgh country. There were also half a dozen British prisoners, who had, in some way, come into Clark's possession, and were now ordered up the river, where they could be used in effecting exchanges. A negro woman, and two negro boys, probably employed as cooks, were attached to the expedition. Thus, including all classes, Rogers' party must have numbered about sixty-five persons.

With nothing unusual to interfere with the monotony of a voyage up the Ohio at that early day, enjoying the romantic

[1] Note on original manuscript: "Ms. memorial of J. F. Perrault to the Virginia legislature, May 17, 1784—L. C. D." Transcribed in Draper Mss., 11S150–53. Perrault says in his autobiography that his claim on the state of Virginia was never settled.

[2] Note on original manuscript: "Butler's *Kentucky*, 103—L. C. D."

[3] Abraham Chapline was born Dec. 17, 1754 in Frederick County, Va. Having been orphaned while young, he began to care for himself at the age of fifteen, and in 1773 went west and raised a crop of corn on Chartier's Creek in Washington County, Pa. In 1774 he joined James Harrod's party on a prospecting tour to Kentucky, where Harrodsburg was laid out. In the autumn of that year Chapline participated in the battle of Point Pleasant. The next year he returned to Kentucky, and in 1778 was a member of Clark's Kaskaskia expedition, first as ensign, later as lieutenant. In 1779 Clark detailed him to escort Rogers' party to Fort Pitt. During the captivity that followed, Chapline was taken to the headwaters of Great Miami River, forced to run the gauntlet, and then adopted into an Indian family. For his escape in 1780 see *post*, 185. Chapline served throughout the Revolution; in 1783 he was a captain at Fort Nelson. After the war he settled in Mercer County, Ky. He commanded a company on Clark's Wabash expedition of 1786. Later he was a member of the Kentucky legislature and a practising physician. He died on his farm near Harrodsburg, Jan. 19, 1824.

[4] For Col. John Campbell, see *Rev. Upper Ohio*, 231, note 74.

scenery presented on either side of that noble river, Colonel Rogers, on the morning of the fourth of October, reached the mouth of the Licking, one hundred and thirty miles above the Falls.[1]

[Basil Brown's deposition. 60J429–43. Transcript.]

State of Pennsylvania,
Fayette County, S. S.

Bet [sic] it remembered that on the day & date hereof, Basil Brown of the said County of Fayette personally appeared before the subscriber, a Justice of the Peace in & for the county aforesaid, & being duly sworn deposes & says, that from the best information he has been able to obtain on the subject, he the said affiant is now between seventy one & seventy two years of age: That during the Revolutionary war he resided for the most part at or near what was then called Red Stone Old Fort on the Mon[on]gahela River in what was then claimed as Yohogania County, Virginia. That whilst living at his father's near that place in the year 1778, David Rogers, who was an officer in the Virginia State line, was ordered by the executive of that State to bring up the Mississippi & Ohio Rivers to Fort Pitt from New Orleans, certain military stores, munitions of war, &c. which had been previously purchased by that State from the Spanish Government or people at that place—said Rogers, as well as affiant recollects, had been a captain in the Virginia State Line previous to undertaking the said expedition, but was promoted at that time, as affiant always understood, & now believes, to the office of Colonel in consequence of the great hazard that was supposed would, & that did, attend the said expedition. The said David Rogers was always after the undertaking of said expedition called & recognized as a Colonel in the Virginia State Line. Affiant further States, that the said Colonel Rogers built or procured to be built two boats for said expedition, at what was then Fort Pitt, now the city of Pittsburgh, Penn. That after their completion he brought one of said boats to Red Stone Old Fort on the Monongahela, for the purpose of receiving at that point the stores &c. necessary for the expedition, & the men who were to compose & who did compose the party under his command;

[1] At this point Dr. Draper's narrative ends.

after which he returned with it to Fort Pitt & was there joined by the other boat. The whole party consisted, as well as affiant now recollects, of about forty men, & accompanied by one or perhaps more family boats, embarked from Fort Pitt sometime in the month of June, 1778. The party descended the Ohio & Mississippi Rivers without meeting with any material obstruction, & at length landed at the mouth of what was then called the *Ozark*, now the *Arkansas*, River, and ascended it a short distance to a small fort or military post built & then occupied by the Spaniards. Here Col. Rogers was informed, that the stores, munitions, &c. for which he had been despatched had been forwarded by the Spanish authorities at New Orleans to a post then held by them at the point now occupied by the city of St. Louis on the Mississippi, several hundred miles above the Ozark or Arkansas. It here, however, became necessary to go on to New Orleans in order to obtain from the authorities there some order or direction to the persons having said stores, munitions &c. in charge, to deliver to Col. Rogers & his party. For this purpose Col. Rogers having left his boats at the post on Ozark procured a large *perogue*, & with some six or seven of his men, amongst whom was affiant himself, he descended the Ozark & Mississippi rivers to New Orleans. At this period the British occupied the post of Natchez on the Mississippi, between Ozark or Arkansas & New Orleans, which rendered a voyage from one of those places to the other very dangerous. Having arrived at the place of their destination & procured the necessary order to the proper officer or authorities for said stores, munitions of war, &c. Col. Rogers & his party, owing to the danger of navigating the Mississippi in consequence of the British post at Natchez, were compelled to return to the Post on Ozark by an inland trip, which was accomplished with great hazard & fatigue, the entire country being a wilderness, & the journey several hundred miles in length. Having reached Ozark they re-entered their boats & ascended the Mississippi & procured said stores, &c. Col. Rogers & his party returned to the mouth of the Ohio & ascended that river a considerable distance above the Falls where Louisville now stands, nearly to the mouth of Licking river, when a small party of Indians were seen crossing the river a short distance above them. By order of Col. Rogers the boats were landed in the mouth of Licking river, & the most of his party, a few being left in charge of the boats, ascended the bank of the river, when an engagement immediately ensued. Instead of the small party before mentioned it was now discovered there was a very large party of the Indians. Col. Rogers & his party were surrounded almost immediately, & overpowered by numbers. Of the whole party but thirteen, as well as affiant now recollects, escaped, & two of those were severely wounded. Col. Rogers himself was mortally wounded shortly after the commencement of the engagement, but escaped at that time as affiant was afterwards frequently informed by one John Knotts who belonged to the party & who escaped at the same time. Knotts also informed affiant that Col. Rogers & himself remained together in the woods during the night after the battle—& described his wound as being in the abdomen & mortal. That during the night & the succeeding morning when he left him he was in extreme pain & utterly passed recovery as [he] thought, particularly in a wilderness where no aid could be rendered. Left in this situation, Col. Rogers was never afterwards seen or heard of by the survivors of the party. Affiant was himself severely wounded in the right arm & in the left shoulder in said engagement, by means whereof he has always since been disabled, & from the nature of his wounds must so continue through life. Affiant & another of the party whose name was Robert Benham, & who acted as commissary to the party, & who was also wounded, remained for some time after the close of the battle & until the Indians had withdrawn. They afterwards subsisted for nineteen days on the game that chanced to pass by there [erased, but legible—"Benham, from his wound, being unable to walk, but having the use of his hands could shoot whatever came in reach, & affiant whose hands were disabled, but who could walk & bring to"—] when with much difficulty they succeeded in getting on board of a boat which had descended the Great Kenhawa & Ohio, & we were carried to the post at the Falls.

Affiant further States that he then & always since that time considered Colonel Rogers as acting throughout said expedition in a military capacity. That affiant & the other men under his command were soldiers, except so far as he now recollects, two other officers in the party, to wit, Isaac Collier & Patrick M°Elroy —the former a Lieutenant & the latter an Ensign to the company. Col. Rogers & the said last mentioned officers were always respected & obeyed by affiant & the other soldiers composing the party according to their said ranks respectively.

Affiant further states, that the wife & family of Col. Rogers at the time he came to Red Stone Old Fort, resided on the Potomac river near Old Town, Maryland.

Affiant always esteemed Col. Rogers, as all others who knew him, & that he has heard speak on the subject declare they esteemed him, a worthy man & brave officer. Affiant further states that the battle in which Col. Rogers was killed occurred, as well as he now recollects, in the month of October, 1779. And further affiant saith not.

BASIL BROWN.

Sworn & subscribed before Nath¹ Islor, J. P. Sept. 12, 1834.

[Recollections of Basil Brown.[1] 10ZZ66–69.]

On the fourth of October in 1779 the boats reached the mouth of Licking opposite the site [of] Cincinnati. A little befor the landing of the boats some indians were discovered crossing the river from the indian to the Kentucky shore As soon as the boats were landed about forty men asenended the bank and went up the bottom to try to kill them The indian canoe the only one seen by our men contained only Seven Indians. As soon as they landed on the beach of the river they were fired on but at too great a distance for doing much excution The party were instantly attacked by about one hundred and Seventy Indians who in less than two minutes almost surrounded them Only thirteen escaped two of whom were left wounded in the woods Those who escaped unhurt made [the] best of way to the settlements in Kentucky One of boats was taken by the Indians The other having three or four men on board was rowed off during the battle Two men were killed in the captured boat in attempting to push her off

My informant Basil Brown was one of the two wounded men left in the woods He was wounded severely in the right arm and left shoulder Robert Benham the other was wounded in the hip These unfortunate men remained nineteen days in the wood without the aid or even the sight of any human being. * * * The captured boat furnished a rich booty to the half

---

[1] The following account was obtained from Basil Brown by the Rev. Joseph Doddridge, whose daughter sent the manuscript to Dr. Draper.

naked Indian conquerers   The other boat returned to Louisville and furnished a seasonable supply of clothing and ammunition to the destitute troops of Gen¹ Clark

The narrative of the sufferings of my informant Basil Brown and his companion Benham was very affecting to me and perhaps may be so to the reader.

Brown was wounded on his retreat   He had pursued a buffaloe path some distance and had descended a steep bank of a little branch and thought himself pretty well out of danger when two indians at the distance of about thirty yards sprang up and shot at him nearly at the same time   He attempted to return the fire but both his arms refused to obey the command of his will   The indian[s] instead of dispatching him with their tomahocks as he expected both ran off   After running some distance he fell and fainted from the loss of blood.   After he came to himself he heard the report of a gun on the opposite side of the river Licking   He hallooed and after some time was answered by Benham but before he could reach his companion in misfortune he had to travel three miles up the Licking before he could cross it   When they got together they were illy able to assist each other   Benham could not use his feet   Brown was equally helpless as to his hands but between [them] they made shift to live   Benham had killed a racoon before Brown reached him.   The river bottom was full of wild turkies of these Benham killed as many as they needed   Brown made shift to drag them to him and he having the use of his hand[s] picked and dressed them after some fashion   They dressed their wounds with slippery elm bark

On the nineteenth day after the battle they heard the whooping cough of some persons in a family boat   Brown went to the shore hailed the boat and was answered but the people in the boat afraid of an ambuscade by the Indians declined coming to shore

A project was hit upon for the safety of both parties.   Some distance below them a bar¹ put out a long distance into the river   The river being then quite low   It was proposed to Brown that he should go to the point of the bar and if they found things as he said they would take him in but if they discovered any signs of a decoy they would shoot him and make their escape   After they had taken Brown into the boat it was with considerable hesitation they sent out two men to bring his companion Benham

---

¹ This sand bar ran out into the river opposite the present town of Dayton, Ky., about two miles above the mouth of Licking River.   Draper Mss., 5D220.

FRONTIER RETREAT 93

They were taken to Louisville and there for the first time received surgical aid for the care of their wounds.

[Recollections of Joseph Jackson.¹ 11C62, p. 27.]

Campbell's boats taken, 1779. In the month of October, 1779, a party of Shawanoes captured two boats, called Campbell's boats, loaded with Spanish goods, destined for Fort Pitt. Among the articles on board were a large number of barrels of flour. There were four boats in company—seeing Indians, all on board went on shore at the mouth of Pond Creek, now Mill Creek,² but finding the Indians too strong, they retreated to their boats— two of the boats got off; while the other two being unable to get off, were taken—a good many whites were killed, & Campbell himself was taken prisoner. Girty was with this Indian party, & he favoured Campbell by taking him *around* Chillicothe so as to avoid his running the gauntlet. The flour was in tight barrels —the boats were scuttled & sunk in the mouth of Mill Creek— flour sunk with the boats, the Indians not liking it as well as their pounded corn. Two years after, when their corn was destroyed, they used to go & raise the sunken flour; it was wet only an inch or two in from the staves, & was as good as ever. Jackson ate of it.—Girty so told it.

[Extract of a letter of Col. George Rogers Clark, printed in Lloyd's *London Evening Post*, Feb. 18, 1780, from a letter dated Williamsburg, Virginia, Nov. 27, 1779. 23J29. Transcript.]

FALLS OF OHIO, October 9, 1779.

By one of Col. David Rogers' boats just returned to this place, I have the mortifying account, that, on the 4th inst., near the

¹ Joseph Jackson was born in the year 1755, in Bedford County, Va. In July, 1777 he enlisted in a militia company which was sent to the relief of Boonesborough. There he remained during the succeeding winter, and in February he was captured by Indians while boiling salt at Blue Licks under the direction of Col. Daniel Boone. Jackson was adopted into a Shawnee family at New Chillicothe on Little Miami. He voluntarily remained with the Indians until 1799, then returned to Kentucky and settled in Bourbon County. There Dr. Draper interviewed him in 1844. His memory was good, and he related the events of the war as known in the Indian towns.

² On the site of the city of Cincinnati.

mouth of the Miami, a party of Indians was discovered ahead crossing the Ohio. A proposal was made to land and attack them, which was generally agreed to, and Col. Rogers with fifty men landed, and began the attack. The first parties of the enemy they met with retreated before them; but the Indians being strongly re-inforced, our people were obliged to give way. The Indians pressed hard on our men in their retreat, and boarded two of their batteaus; the third, having about a dozen soldiers on board as a guard, a brave fellow among them refused to surrender her, and assuming the command, brought her off through a heavy fire from the shore.[1] Our loss is Col. John Campbell,[2] of Yohiogany, Col. Rogers and supposed between 30 and 40 of his best officers and men, beside a considerable amount of public and private property.

WESTERN EXPEDITION PROPOSED

[Summary of a letter of Col. Daniel Brodhead, Pittsburgh, Oct. 9, 1779, to Gen. George Washington. Printed in *Pa. Archives*, XII, 164–65.]

Has now enough provisions for 1,000 men for three months. Recent Indian raids on Cheat River and in Kentucky. Would have been glad to have destroyed western Mingo, Wyandot, and Shawnee settlements had not his orders been to act on the defensive. If an expedition against Detroit is not permitted, any number of volunteers, especially from Virginia, will turn out against the Indian towns. Encloses court-martial proceedings. The independent companies: Heath's, useless and expensive; O'Hara's,[3] annexed to Ninth Virginia; Moorhead's,[4] to Eighth Pennsylvania.

[1] Note on original manuscript: "Andrew Linn and nephew Dr. Andrew Johnson Linn said their uncle William Linn commanded this boat which escaped to the Falls, and Abraham Chapline's son said the same—L. C. D." For a sketch of William Linn see *Rev. Upper Ohio*, 144, note 51.

[2] See letter from Col. John Campbell, dated "Shawney Town," Oct. 23, 1779, to Captain Lernoult, commandant at Detroit, in *Mich. Pion. & Hist. Colls.*, IX, 368.

[3] For Capt. James O'Hara see *Rev. Upper Ohio*, 253, note 1. The muster roll of his independent company is in *Frontier Defense*, 302–3.

[4] For Capt. Samuel Moorhead and his company see *ibid.*, 3, note 6.

FRONTIER RETREAT 95

[Summary of a letter of Col. Daniel Brodhead, Pittsburgh, Oct. 9, 1779, to John Jay. Printed in *ibid.*, 163.]

Asks confirmation of the appointment of Capt. Thomas Ferroll[1] as deputy commissary of military stores. September 21, a ten-year-old child was killed, and a girl of seventeen captured near the forks of Cheat River.[2] Western Indians are hostile to Kentucky settlements. Would have marched against their towns had he been at liberty to do so.

[Summary of a letter of Col. Daniel Brodhead, Pittsburgh, Oct. 9, 1779, to Pres. Joseph Reed. Printed in *ibid.*, 163–64.]

Desires to know if ranging companies of Westmoreland County commanded by Capt. Joseph Irwin and Capt. Thomas Campbell are under his command or that of Colonel Lochry; they are subsisted from public stores, and are in need of blankets. Mingo and Munsee routed; excursion proposed against Western Indians or Detroit, when frontier will enjoy tranquillity. Recent raids have been destructive. Bounty money for recruits.

[Summary of a letter of Col. Daniel Brodhead, Headquarters, Pittsburgh, Oct. 10, 1779, to Gen. John Sullivan. Printed in *ibid.*, 165–66.]

Sullivan's letter sent express from Catherine town[3] received soon after returning from Seneca expedition. Had 600 rank and

[1] For a sketch of Capt. Thomas Ferroll see *Wis. Hist. Colls.*, XXIII, 197, note 2.
[2] This raid occurred on Cheat River, near Granville, Monongalia County, W. Va. The two victims were Phebe and Fanny, daughters of David Scott. One was killed outright, the other taken prisoner. Their father came to Fort Pitt to attempt the rescue of the latter, but on his return home learned that she also had been killed by her captors, and her body found by the wayside. See R. G. Thwaites (ed.), *Withers' Chronicles of Border Warfare* (Cincinnati, 1895), 283.
[3] The native name of Catherine's Town was Sheoquaga. It was situated in Schuyler County, N. Y., on high ground just south of the head of Seneca Lake. It was composed of about thirty houses under the Chieftess, Catherine Montour, kinswoman of Andrew and John Montour. Her husband was the well-known Seneca, Thomas Hudson or Telenenut, and her mother was a half-breed, known

file, marched to upper town called Yahrungwago, said to be about forty miles this side of Genesee, would have gone thence, but for lack of shoes for the men. Met no opposition, except one party of forty defeated by advance guard without loss to his men. Destroyed 130 cabins, each large enough for three or four families. Appearances indicated intention of Indians to collect in great force. Congratulations on Sullivan's success. "Something still remains to be done to the westward, which I expect leave to execute, & then I conceive the wolves of the forest will have sufficient cause to howl as they will be quite destitute of food."

TRESPASSERS ON INDIAN LANDS

[Col. Daniel Brodhead to Col. David Shepherd. 1SS173. A. L. S.]

HEAD QUARTERS PITSBURGH Octr 10th 1779

DEAR SIR:

I have received your oblidging favor of yesterdays Date.

The Contents give me the utmost pain because I fear the imprudence or design of the Trespassers will involve the innocent in new Calamities.

I shall take the most prudent steps to prevent any ill consequence arising from such folly or villainy and in the mean time will endeavour to make an example of some to terrify the rest.

It would give me an additional uneasiness should the inhabitants of your County forfeit my esteem by so rash an undertaking as you represent against the laws of the State of which they profess themselves Members and the repeated Genl Orders issued at Fort M°Intosh for its prevention.

I hope however that every good Member of Soci[ety] will discountenance a practice so base & impoli[tic] and the incorrigible may depend on meeting the severest Military Punishment where the civil magistrate fails to execute the Laws he is sworn to administer. I shall rely on your exertions to prevent a trespass so big with Danger to the peaceable Inhabitants and request you will call on the Magistrates of your County to put an immediate Stop to the Evil by bringing to Justice the violators of the Laws

as French Margaret. Sullivan's army reached Catherine's Town on Sept. 1, 1779, and destroyed it the next day. The Indians fled to Niagara, and in that vicinity Catharine spent the rest of her life. She was still living as late as 1791.

FRONTIER RETREAT 97

of your Country and the Laws of Nations And am with great regard your most obed^t Servt
DANIEL BRODHEAD, Col° command^g W. D.
COL° DAVID SHEPHERD

[Col. Daniel Brodhead to Capt. John Clark. 1NN68. Transcript.]

Oct. 11th 1779

Col. Brodhead orders Capt. John Clark to proceed to the Wheeling region, & dispossess all settlers on the Indian lands on the Western side of the Ohio, & make prisoners of the violators of the law, & send them to Head Quarters—Capt. Clark to return to F^t McIntosh.

[Col. Daniel Brodhead to the Delaware chiefs. 2H45. Contemporary transcript.]

HEAD QUARTERS PITTSBURGH Octr 11th 1779.

Mahingweegeesuch to the Delaware Council at Coochocking

BROTHERS:
I informed you by Caleylemont that I did not know whether you had not changed your minds about the strong houses you wanted me to build at your Towns because your young men who were to have gone with mine went home—I am still ready to do what you requested but want to hear from you again & to see the Men that were to go with mine, & then perhaps I will go & see my friends at Coochocking & have the work well done for them.

Brothers: I have heard that some foolish white men have gone over the River near wheeling & cut trees & built little Cabbins on your lands   I dont know whether it is true but I send one hundred men this day to see & if it is true they will pull down those Cabbins & bring the offenders to me & you may depend I will punish them so severely that they will never venture to behave so again

Brothers: You may depend on my taking care that no injustice shall happen to you & I desire you will not be uneasy on account of what I have heard.

Brothers: I am sorry to [hear] that Pipe & Wingemund['s] people are not yet come in to live at your towns & I desire you will advise them to make haste so that my friends may live together & be strong against the bad nations

7

Brothers: I will be glad to hear from you soon & know the news that is brought from our enemies.
I am your friend & Brother

MAHINGWEEGEESUCH

WESTERN EXPEDITION PLANNED

[Col. Daniel Brodhead to Col. David Shepherd.[1] 1SS175. L. S.]

HEAD QUARTERS PITTSBURGH Octr 12th 1779

DEAR SIR:

As I expect to be at liberty to make at least one more excursion against the Savages before the close of the Champaign, And the Terms of a great number of my non Commissioned Officers & Privates being expired, the Regula[rs] alone may not compose a Body sufficient for the undertaking. It may therefore be necessary to draw forth a Body of Militia to aid them, should it be approven by His Excellency the Commander in Chief agreeable to my wish—

You are therefore on receipt hereof to order Sixty Men of the Militia of your County and a proportion of Commissioned & non Commissioned Officers to hold themselves in perfect readiness to march at an hours warning

I have the honor to be with greatest regard yo[ur] most Obe^{dt} Servt

DANIEL BRODHEAD, Col^o command^g W. D.

COL^o DAVID SHEPHERD

BRODHEAD AND HIS OFFICERS

[Summary of a letter of Col. Daniel Brodhead, Headquarters, Pittsburgh, Oct. 13, 1779, to Capt. Joseph Irwin. Printed in *Pa. Archives*, XII, 169–70.]

Rebukes Irwin for recent letter; has disobeyed positive orders. This conduct will be reported to authorities. Improper to send an officer to Philadelphia without Brodhead's consent. Irwin's company to be marched to Fort Armstrong and a detachment to relieve McIlwaine. "How you can take upon yourself to continue with your company at Hannah's town, wasting their time at the public expense" is unaccountable.

[1] A similar letter was addressed to all the county lieutenants near Fort Pitt. For that to Colonel Lochry of Westmoreland County see *Pa. Archives*, XII, 169.

FRONTIER RETREAT

[Summary of a letter of Col. Daniel Brodhead, Headquarters, Pittsburgh, Oct. 13, 1779, to Francis McIlwaine. Printed in *ibid.*, 170.]

Captain Irwin's company will soon be at Fort Armstrong. Cannot send regulars there; new Pennsylvania levies best for that service. Firing heard near that fort was probably by hunters, not Indians.

[Summary of a letter of Col. Daniel Brodhead, Headquarters, Pittsburgh, Oct. 13, 1779, to Col. John Gibson. Printed in *ibid.*, 171.]

The will to comply with orders appears wanting; always disposed to oblige, but not to dispense with authority. "It always creates in my breast a great share of uneasiness when I find a gentleman with whom I have contracted an intimacy under pretensions of friendship, aiming to destroy my peace of mind. But more particularly where an officer travails so far out of the line of his duty as to disobey my orders."

GARRISONS FOR ALLEGHENY POSTS

[Summary of a letter of Col. Daniel Brodhead, Headquarters, Pittsburgh, Oct. 16, 1779, to Capt. Thomas Campbell. Printed in *ibid.*, 171–72.]

Colonel Lochry reported that Campbell was at Fort Hand, supposed whole company there also. Supplies forwarded were taken to Fort Armstrong. If both garrisons are maintained, cattle will be sent. Shoes and blankets not yet available. Campbell summoned to headquarters where project for building barracks for company will be discussed.

[Summary of a letter of Col. Daniel Brodhead, Headquarters, Pittsburgh, Oct. 18, 1779, to Lieutenant Glass or commanding officer of Capt. Thomas Irwin's company. Printed in *ibid.*, 171–72.]

Orders Lieutenant Glass to Fort Armstrong to relieve McIlwaine. Douglass,[1] is assistant commissary of issues. Scouts to

Ephriam Douglass entered the army in 1776 as quartermaster for the Eighth Pennsylvania Regiment. The following year, while serving as aid-de-camp for

be sent to Kiskiminitas and spies up the Allegheny. Orders for conduct of garrison.

PLANS FOR DETROIT EXPEDITION

[Gen. George Washington to Col. Daniel Brodhead. Washington Papers. Draft.]

D^R SIR: HEAD Q^{RS} WEST POINT October the 18 1779

I have on the 15 the pleasure by Captn McIntire to receive your Letter of the 16th ult^o continued to the 24th. I am exceedingly happy in your success in the expedition up the Alleghany against the Senecca & Muncy nations—and transmit you the inclosed Extract from General Orders which will convey to you the sentiments I entertain of your conduct and of that of the Officers and Men employed in the expedition. This you will be pleased to communicate to the Troops thro the Channel of your orders. I trust from this stroke and the operations of Genl Sullivan, who I am happy to inform you is now on his return to join the Army, after having laid waste the whole of the Senecca Towns their Crops & their Country except in the Quarter where you were and a Town or two higher up on the Alleghany and compelling the whole of the Nation to flee to Niagara for refuge—the eyes of the savages will be opened—and that they will be convinced, that it will be their true interest & policy at least to hold themselves in a state of neutrality. I approve the sale you directed of the plunder & of the distribution of the profits among the Troops.

I have transmitted that part of your letter which relates to the want of Cloathing—to James Wilkinson Esquire Cloath^r General at Philadelphia and directed him to take measures for supplying it. I wish however that you had ascertained the number of those to be supplied and their Regiments & Corps—as this is essential to govern the Cloathier in his conduct.

Gen. Benjamin Lincoln, he was captured at Bound Brook, N. J. Released upon parole he was made ensign in 1778 and lieutenant in 1779. While awaiting an exchange, which did not occur until 1780, he served as commissary in the Western Department. At the close of the war Douglass was sent to Niagara on a mission connected with the terms of peace. His journal of this mission is published in Buffalo Historical Society *Publications*, XIV. His later home was in Fayette County, Pa., of which he was prothonotary, 1783–1808, and where he died in 1833.

I have also written to Colo Palfrey Pay master General who is also at Philadelphia & inclosed the paragraph which respects the pay of the Troops—and requested him to pursue measures for having them paid.

With respect to an Expedition against Detroit—I can not at this time direct it to be made, as the state of the force at present with you is not sufficient to authorise the clearest hopes of success and indeed to ensure it and because it is not in my power circumstanced as things are at this critical moment to say how far it may be practicable to afford sufficient aid from hence. In any other view than that of a certainty of success I would not undertake the reduction of the post—as a miscarriage would be attended with many disagreable consequences. However, as it is of great importance to reduce it—and I shall willingly attempt it, whenever circumstances will justify it, you will turn your close[s]t attention to the subject and make such preparations & obtain such necessary information as may be in your power without exciti^g much alarm—as may facilitate the work whenever it is undertaken either this winter when the lake is frozen which appears to me to be the only season when an effectual blow can be struck or next Campaign.—In the meanwhile the nature & strength of the works should be ascertained—whether any & what kind of Bomb proofs.—what aid can be drawn from the Country of men, provisions Horses &c—what opposition, or assistance is to be expected from the Indians &c^a &c^a &c^a—& prospect of supplies.

I shall have no objection to your making occasional excursions against any of the Indian Nations that may prove inimical & hostile, when circumstances will permit you to do it with safety.

The powers of making peace or War are in general cases, which affect the common interest, entirely with Congress as they ought of right to be. And therefore—if overtures of peace are made by the Seneccas & Muncies—You will communicate the same to them who will act in consequence. either by appointing Commissioners or otherwise as to them shall seem most proper.

Col^o Clark is not an Officer in the Continental line—nor does he act under my instructions. He is in the service of the State of Virginia. I make no doubt however that the Instructions he has received are calculated to promote the general good—and from the character he seems justly to have acquired I should suppose he will act with the caution and prudence—and do nothing that will not be promotive of it.

With respect to supplies & trinkets for the Indians—you must try to keep them in the best humour you can—and I dare say on your application to the Honble the Board of War—they will direct such to be furnished as may be in their power to procure.

We are anxiously waiting for advices from the Southward. His Excellency Count D'Estaing arrived at Savannah in Septr with His fleet & a considerable land force—with a design of striking a blow against the Enemy in that Quarter—which from his vast superiority he was able easily to do, if they have not found means of escaping. His arrival there of itself was very interesting —and if it has been attended with all the expected success—He will have crushed the Enemy and relieved Georgia & South Carolina from the dangers which had already in great part overwhelm^d the one—and from which the Other was not entirely free.

I am &c

G W

Col^o Brodhead

P. S. I duly rec^d your letter of the 31st of July.

P. S. You will let me know by the first opportunity what Military Stores & Artillery will be necessary, in case an expedition should be undertaken against Detroit—and whether they could be supplied at Fort Pitt or what part of them. If from the information you gain in the points I have mentioned above, as necessary to be inquired into, and your accounts of our Affairs in this quarter—you should have reason to conclude the expedition will be undertaken, and the Military Stores essential for it cannot be furnished at Pittsburg—You will apply to the Board of War in the first instance to prevent delay, to whom I have written & requested that they may be supplied. You will however take the earliest opportunity to furnish me with an Estimate as above required, both of the Cannon &c & Stores—and of any deficiency—And indeed I wish to have a Return of the military stores of the Garrison & Cannon, particularly distinguishing whether any of the latter & of what size are on travelling Carriages.

[*Endorsed:*] transmitted to Colo Mitchell—to be forwarded by Express—19 Oct 1779

GARRISON AT FORT McINTOSH

[Summary of a letter of Col. Daniel Brodhead, Headquarters, Pittsburgh, Oct. 22, 1779, to Capt. Simon Morgan.[1] Printed in *Pa. Archives*, XII, 173.]

Beef and salt pork for garrison. Regulations for armorers; Koonty's work in repairing and cleaning arms.

[Summary of a letter of Col. Daniel Brodhead, Headquarters, Pittsburgh, Oct. 22, 1779, to Capt. John Clark. Printed in *ibid.*, 174.]

Warnings to trespassers on Indian lands. Supplies for Fort McIntosh. Clark with all of Eighth Pennsylvania except the armorer, Koonty, ordered to headquarters. Capt. Simon Morgan and Ninth Virginia to remain at garrison. Craft to be brought up; cautions for the march.

ROGERS' DEFEAT

[Col. George Rogers Clark to Col. William Fleming. 23J93. A. L. S.]

LOUISVILLE Octob[r] 22[d] 1779

D[r] Gen[l]

I Received your Let[r] by the Express and Congratulate you on your safe arrival in this part of the world[2] I dont suppose that you Injoy much satisfaction In a Country so much Harassed by Savages as this is without being able to repell them which has already occationed so much reflection in me that I was fixed in

[1] Before the Revolution Simon Morgan resided in the West, serving in 1775 as a justice of the West Augusta District, Va. In December, 1775 he enlisted as an ensign in the Eighth Virginia Regiment. He was promoted in the latter part of 1776 to a lieutenancy in the Thirteenth Virginia, and on Mar. 15, 1778 he was commissioned captain. In 1781 Morgan was serving with the Seventh Virginia in the southern states. In April he led a division at Hobkirk's Hill, and in September was wounded at the battle of Eutaw Springs.

[2] Col. William Fleming was one of the commissioners sent to Kentucky by the governor and council of Virginia to settle public accounts and investigate the titles to land.

my Resolutions Respecting the Shawoneese my greatest ambition has been to once get a body of Troops suffitient to Reverse our General conduct in the Indian Department: untill some person does it we shall have no peace from them. had it not been for that little flight from their Towns last Spring,[1] we now should be able to march against them but that has occationed all the mischief that has been done Since and put them on their Guard, Expecting a greater force against them. if they have not left their Towns they are prepared for our Reception and less than Six or Seven Hundred men would not be safe to march against them which number we cannot possibly Raise at present but by puting a stop to the people leaving the Countrey. I think we might in a few weaks Raise a Body suffitient to put the matter out of Doubt, the greatest sirvice we Could expect to Render would be in the numbers that we might destroy in a pitched Battle nothing else we may expect without they are so Foolish as many Imagine them to be in fortifying their Towns which I think Fallatious but in Case we attemp an Enterprise we ought to prepare for that as well as a Suffitient body to defeat them in the Field, which I think their is a probability of geting by the Middle of next month except the Ohio is Intirely Block up in some part or other, in mean time we ougt if possible to have spies in their Cuntrey that might give valuable Inteligence. It is what I have wished for and nothing shall be wanting in me to Facilitate it whether we shall be able to execute it or not I think we ought to make every preparatory stroke possible for the Expedition as their is a probability of its being put in execution if to the Contrary the loss cant be great. if we meet with second defeat at them Towns this County is lost a few Days ago several Gentlemen arrive from the Illinois St Vincent, & a Considerable number of Sav [ages] have lately Concluded peace with us Espetialey the Delaware, in that Cuntrey thought proper to Sue for peace which was granted them a few weaks past by our Ageants my Mineuevers this Summer has occation the English to Evacuate Michilimackinic St Josephs and to abandon their Interest in that Quarter by which the Savages in that Cuntrey have declared for us the Capture of Co^l Rogerses Boats is a very great loss, and will Incourage the Savages much. the Savages on the Ouabash and Wesward would to a man take up the Tomahawk against the

[1] Clark refers to the Shawnee expedition of Col. John Bowman which took place in May, 1779. See *Wis. Hist. Colls.*, XXIII, 365, note 1.

Showanees if we had a few goods only to present them with. three French men and several Indians is gone from St Vincents have gone to the Shawne Nation with Speaches if they Return atall, they will be at this place in fourteen Days by which we may expect to Receive some Inteligence of Importance.

I shall be happy to see you at this place and Remain with Respect Genl your Very H Servant

G R CLARK

MESS^{RS} FLEMING, BARBER & LIN[1] Harrodsburgh
[*Addressed:*]General Clark To Col William Flemming St Asaph Kentucky p^r Express

---

[Captain Killbuck and Rev. John Heckewelder to Col. Daniel Brodhead. 1H121. A. L. S. In handwriting of Heckewelder.]

COOSCHOCKUNG Oct^{br} ye 23^d 1779.

BROTHER MACHINGWE GEESCHUCH:

I will inform You in the first place that in 2 Days I shall set off from here for Pittsburg. Captn Pipe and others will be in company with me.

We had a report some Days ago of a Battle somewhere on the big River, of which I thought at first but little, but as a Man came here last Night who had been himself in the engagement, I am persuaded to believe it, and herewith imediately aquaint You likewise of it. There had been 135 Indians, Shawnese, Mingoes, Wyondotts and Dellawares at the big River in order to cross and go to War; part of which had cross'd already, in order to recogniter the banks if clear of White People. In the mean time those on this side making ready to cross likewise, were fired upon out of the thickets, when 2 Men of the Ind^s fell on the spot, upon which the White People run off, but were followed by the Enemy and many of them killed, likewise 14 taken Prissoners, namely: 3 Americans, 7 Englishmen, 1 French-man, 1 Negro Wench and 2 Negro boys. It is said that Mr John Campbell is among the Prissoners. That the whole company was with him, and on his own private buissness, they going with Boats up to Fort-Pitt. What Number of Boats they had I cannot tell, but the Man says

---

[1] James Barbour and Edmund Lyne were the other members of the Virginia commission in Kentucky. They held their first meeting at Harrodsburg, Oct. 13, 1779.

they got 2 of them with all what was in them. The Man says that by the Prissoners they learn that the White People were 80 in Number, 30 of which only had Arms, and which were near all killed or taken Prissoners.

When I shall come to you I hope I shall be able to inform You more about this matter.

I am Your friend and Brother.

JOHN KILLBOCK

DEAR SIR:

This is indeed an unhappy affair, I am exceeding sorry for the whole of it, but in particular for the unfortunate Mr John Campbell. I could not believe it to be him at first, but the Man says most of the Indians know him, and call him by that Name. What his fate further may be God knows alone, but I wish they might spare him.

I am Your sincere friend and very hum^{bl} Servt

JOHN HACKENWELDER.

MR DANIEL BRODHEAD Col^o Command^r ect.

TRESPASSERS ON INDIAN LANDS

[Summary of a letter of Col. Daniel Brodhead, Pittsburgh, Oct. 26, 1779, to Gen. George Washington. Printed in *Pa. Archives*, XXII, 176–77.]

After sending letter of 9th instant, heard from Colonel Shepherd of Ohio County about trespassers on Indian lands. Ordered Capt. John Clark and sixty men to cross the river, apprehend trespassers, and destroy their huts. Extent of trespassers' settlements. Delawares to be propitiated. Blockhouse not built at their towns. Influence of Wyandot uncertain. Colonel Clark's success. Brodhead desires to visit East.

[Summary of a letter of Col. Daniel Brodhead, Pittsburgh, Oct. 26, 1779, to Gen. Nathaniel Greene. Printed in *ibid.*, 174-75.]

Quartermaster's department; purchase of horses, lack of forage. No tents have arrived. Colonel Steel appears to be honest but has poor judgment. Preparations for a winter expedition.

[Summary of a letter of Col. Daniel Brodhead, Pittsburgh, Oct. 26, 1779, to John Jay. Printed in *ibid.*, 176.]

Trespassers on Indian lands extend from Muskingum River to Fort McIntosh, and thirty miles up the branches of the Ohio. Captain Clark found that the trespassers had returned. Excuses offered to Delawares; uncertain of their attitude. Governor and council of Virginia should be informed.

BRODHEAD AND HIS OFFICERS

[Summary of a letter of Col. Daniel Brodhead, Headquarters, Pittsburgh, Oct. 27, 1779, to Lieut. John Jameson.[1] Printed in *ibid.*, 177.]

Jameson's arrival at Fort Armstrong. Supplies for garrison; whiskey expensive; to be issued only in rainy weather. Sentry boxes for protection against weather. Forty-five in garrison.

[Summary of a letter of Col. Daniel Brodhead, Headquarters, Pittsburgh, Oct. 29, 1779, to Col. Thomas Gaddis.[2] Printed in *ibid.*, 178.]

Virginians cannot avail themselves of boundary dispute to escape militia duty; both legislatures have passed laws establishing jurisdiction.[3] Deplores depredations in Monongalia County;

[1] Jameson was an officer in the Westmoreland County rangers.
[2] For Col. Thomas Gaddis see *Rev. Upper Ohio*, 234, note 78.
[3] May 21, 1779 the Virginia Assembly passed a resolution appointing a commission of three (Rev. James Madison, Rev. Robert Andrews, and Thomas Lewis) to meet and confer with the Pennsylvania commissioners (George Bryan, John Ewing, and David Rittenhouse) on the adjustment of the boundary dispute between the two states. The joint board met on Aug. 27, 1779 at

108   WISCONSIN HISTORICAL COLLECTIONS

scouting between Wheeling and Fish Creek;[1] rangers will be sent out. Defensive versus offensive operations and advantages of latter. Militia aid needed.

[Summary of a letter of Pres. Joseph Reed, In Council, Oct. 30, 1779, to Col. Archibald Lochry. Printed in *id.*, VII, 770–71.]

Officers of ranging companies are under control of county lieutenant unless offensive operations are to be undertaken. This arrangement, in the opinion of Council, affords best protection. Good understanding with Colonel Brodhead will promote the public service. Favorable reports from operations in the East and South.

[Summary of a letter of Pres. Joseph Reed, In Council, Oct. 30, 1779, to Col. Daniel Brodhead. Prin ted in *ibid.*, 771–73.]

Differences concerning command of ranging companies, not on continental establishment. They should be under the county lieutenant. Colonel Lochry justified. Clothing and supplies forwarded by Captain McIntyre for twenty-four officers and 250 privates of Eighth Regiment. Difficulty of procuring these. Bounty for recruits. War news from the South.

Baltimore, all being present except Thomas Lewis. On August 31 an agreement was reached, compromising the claims of both parties to the dispute and arranging for a boundary line substantially as it now runs. This agreement was ratified by Pennsylvania on November 19, but not until July 1, 1780 by Virginia, which in the meantime had granted land certificates within the territory in dispute. Pennsylvania vigorously protested, but later, to close the difficulty, accepted the conditions Virginia imposed and ratified her titles. On Sept. 23, 1780 this final adjustment was reached. The boundary line, however, was not run until 1784.

[1] Fish Creek is about twenty-four miles below Wheeling, in Marshall County, W. Va. A famous Indian war road ran along this stream.

CONDITIONS AT FORT PITT

[Summary of a letter of Col. Daniel Brodhead, Pittsburgh, Nov. 3, 1779, to Timothy Pickering. Printed in *id.*, XII, 179-80.]

Return of Continental troops; necessary winter clothing. Wyandot of Sandusky, Mingo of Tankhonnetick,[1] Piqua and Chillicothe tribes of Shawnee[2] continue hostilities; they have lately killed and taken some inhabitants. Other tribes are friendly. Troops' pleasure in paymaster's arrival.

[Summary of a letter of Col. Daniel Brodhead, Pittsburgh, Nov. 4, 1779, to Pres. Joseph Reed. Printed in *ibid.*, 180-82.]

Complains of lack of information in this distant and separate command. Has orders to act entirely on defensive. Proportion of officers to men. Recommendation for Capt. John Finley and for Capt. Joseph Finley.[3] Indian news. Boundary line needed as Virginia laws are disregarded.

[Summary of a letter of Col. Daniel Brodhead, Headquarters, Pittsburgh, Nov. 4, 1779, to Capt. Thomas Campbell. Printed in *ibid.*, 179.]

Approves of scouting parties up and down the river. Barracks not to be built at present. Blankets and supplies for garrison.

[1] For the site of this village, known to the whites as Pluggy's Town, see *Wis. Hist. Colls.*, XXIII, 266, note 1.
[2] For these Shawnee tribes see *Frontier Defense*, 20, note 45.
[3] Joseph Lewis Finley was born in 1748 in Lancaster County, Pa. He studied at Princeton College, and was preparing for the ministry when the Revolution began. He immediately enlisted in the Pennsylvania Rifle Regiment, of which he was commissioned lieutenant. In 1777 he became a captain, and on July 1, 1778 was transferred to the Eighth Regiment, in which he served to the end of the war. At its close he was appointed United States surveyor for Westmoreland County, whither he removed and where he resided for many years. In 1808 he was chosen president of a college in Kentucky, where he served for four years. His final home was in West Union, Ohio, where he died May 9, 1839. The letters of his son to Dr. Draper are found in Draper Mss., 5E20-21.

VIRGINIA MILITIA DRAFTED

[Order for returns. 5SS94. D. S.]

In pursuance of an Act of the General Assembly of this Commonwealth intitled An Act for Raising a Body of Troops for the Defence of the Commonwealth Passed May Session 1779[1] We the Subscribers Having Met agreeable to appointment The Captains failing to appear with Proper Muster Rolls of their Campanies Rendered it out of our Power to proceed Agreeable to the Tenor of the above Receited Act—

Order'd that the Said Captains be and They are hereby desired to meet at the House of Robert Taylor[2] on Monday the 27th of December with a Just Return of all the Effective men in their Companies or Districts

Given Under our hands in Ohio County this 8th day of November 1779.

JAMES CALDWELL[3]   DAVID SHEPHERD
E. W. ROBINSON[4]   SILAS HEDGES[6]
GEORGE McCULLOCH[5]   DAVID McCLURE[7]

[1] This law required each county of the state to send out one twenty-fifth of their militia, after the county lieutenant with a board of senior justices, and the field officers of the county had laid off the militia into divisions, each of which was required to furnish one able-bodied man. See Hening, *Statutes of Virginia*, X, 32–34.

[2] Robert Taylor's residence was on the site of the present Taylorstown, in Buffalo Township, Washington County, Pa. This part of Washington County was, at the period of this document, a portion of Ohio County, Va.

[3] James Caldwell was commissioned a justice of the peace for Ohio County in 1777; his residence was in the region of Grave Creek. He was probably a brother of John, for whom see *ante*, 62.

[4] E. W. Robinson probably resided on Robinson's Run in the present Washington and Allegheny counties, Pa.

[5] George McColloch was either uncle or older brother of Maj. Samuel McColloch. The McColloch family emigrated in 1770 from the south branch of the Potomac to the waters of Short Creek, not far above Wheeling. In 1787 George McColloch was a trustee of the town of West Liberty.

[6] A sketch of Silas Hedges is given in *Wis. Hist. Colls.*, XXIII, 303, note 1.

[7] For David McClure see *Rev. Upper Ohio*, 234, note 77.

FRONTIER RETREAT

[Militia draft. 1SS178. D. S.]

We do hereby Certify that we have Carefully Classed and proceeded agreeable to an Act of the General Assembly of this Commonwealth passed May Session 1779 To draught one 25th man of the Militia within Mentioned they having failed To produce the Said man in the limited Time
Given under our Hands this 8th day of Novr 1779

Field officers { DAVID SHEPHERD / SILAS HEDGES / DAVID M^{C}CLURE

Magistrates { JAMES CALDWELL JUS^T / E. W. ROBINSON JUS^T / GEORGE M^{C}COLLOCH

PLANS FOR DETROIT EXPEDITION

[Summary of a letter of Col. Daniel Brodhead, Pittsburgh, Nov. 10, 1779, to Gen. George Washington. Printed in Jared Sparks, *Correspondence of the American Revolution* (Boston, 1853), II, 349–52.][1]

Honored with Washington's letter of October 18, and grateful for his approval of the Allegheny expedition. Clothing and pay for the troops; artillery estimates. An expedition against Detroit would give command of Lake Erie. Winter campaigns usually result in great loss of horses and cattle, but compensation would be found if the garrison of Detroit was taken. Will endeavor to have everything in perfect readiness for the advance; many Indians will join him. Has heard that the enemy has built a strong work, that his garrison is about 300 regulars and the same number of militia.[2] Some of the latter will join the Americans. Unless expedition is undertaken before February it will be too late, because of floods. If Detroit expedition proves impracticable, troops with volunteers might be employed against the Shawnee and thence to Natchez, and return early enough in the spring to march against Detroit. French gentlemen would be serviceable

[1] This letter is likewise printed in *Pa. Archives*, XII, 184–85, but with several omissions and errors.
[2] On Nov. 15, 1779 the British reported that the Detroit garrison comprised 393 regulars. See *Mich. Pion. & Hist. Colls.*, XIX, 479.

112   WISCONSIN HISTORICAL COLLECTIONS

in case of an expedition. Has news from Sandusky that 2,000 Indians are in great distress at Niagara; are afraid to hunt, and therefore live on the pittance afforded by the British.

[Summary of a letter of Col. Daniel Brodhead, Pittsburgh, Nov. 11, 1779, to Timothy Pickering. Printed in *Pa. Archives*, XII, 183.]

Commander in chief directs application for Indian goods and trinkets; probability of a winter expedition against either Detroit or Natchez.

GARRISON AT FORT McINTOSH

[Summary of a letter of Col. Daniel Brodhead, Headquarters, Pittsburgh, Nov. 11, 1779, to Maj. Richard Taylor.[1] Printed in *ibid.*, 182–83.]

Matters of public concern delayed reply to letter of November 7. Armorer and masons for Fort McIntosh; discomforts of post. Mr. Eels, an Indian warrior, hunting for Brodhead. Delaware delegates expected; expedite their journey here. Indians not on public business must pay for provisions. Supplies, except forage, considerable. Reënforcements expected. Remainder of Ninth Virginia Regiment will be sent to Taylor soon. Captain Vance's[2] detail against trespassers.

RETURNS AND SUPPLIES

[Summary of a letter of Col. Daniel Brodhead, Pittsburgh, Nov. 11, 1779, to Col. Alexander Scammell.[3] Printed in *ibid.*, 185.]

Returns were enclosed to commander in chief; copy now sent. Difficulty of transporting returns; express charges high.

[1] For Maj. Richard Taylor see sketch in *Wis. Hist. Colls.*, XXIII, 205, note 2.
[2] Robert Vance received a commission as lieutenant in the Thirteenth Virginia Regiment in December, 1776; on Aug. 19, 1778 he was promoted to a captaincy; he resigned Dec. 31, 1780.
[3] Col. Alexander Scammell was adjutant-general of the Continental army from 1778 to 1781.

FRONTIER RETREAT

[Summary of a letter of Col. Daniel Brodhead, Pittsburgh, Nov. 12, 1779, to Pres. Joseph Reed. Printed in *ibid.*, 186.]

Capt. John Finley is sent for regimental clothing; an excellent officer. "This frontier is in perfect tranquility at present." Indian refugees at Niagara. Detroit inhabitants wish to see an American army. "I hope to gratify them this next winter."

WESTERN BATTALION OF VIRGINIA

[Gov. Thomas Jefferson to county lieutenant of Ohio County. 1SS174. L. S.]

W<small>MSBURG</small> Novr 13th 1779.

S<small>IR</small>:

I am to ask the favour of you to give notice to the Officer recommended by you for the Western Battalions that as soon as one half his quota of men is raised and delivered by you, he shall be entitled to his commission and must march the men on to Fort Pitt, the remaining half you must send on under a Serjeant to the same rendezvous. Lieutenant Colo. Knox[1] is appointed to take command of the Battalion of which your men will be. But your distance renders it impracticable to join them to their battalion till the Spring. They will do duty under Colonel Gibson this winter. The subsistence Account previous to their Delivery to the Officer you will settle with the Auditors here.

I am sir Your very humble Servt

T<small>H</small>: J<small>EFFERSON</small>

"T<small>HE</small> C<small>OUNTY</small> L<small>IEUTENANT OF</small> O<small>HIO</small>."

RANGERS REËNLISTED

[Summary of a letter of Capt. Joseph Finley, Headquarters, Pittsburgh, Nov. 16, 1779, to Lieut. John Jameson, Fort Armstrong. Printed in *Pa. Archives*, XII, 186–87.]

Sergeant John Parker, William Blake, John McCinney, and John Miller of Capt. Joseph Irwin's ranging company under

[1] For a sketch of this officer see *ibid.*, 402, note 2.

8

Jameson's command were enlisted by Captain Brady in the Eighth Pennsylvania. Ordered to headquarters for suitable clothing.

[Summary of a letter of Col. Daniel Brodhead, Headquarters, Pittsburgh, Nov. 20, 1779, to Capt. Thomas Campbell. Printed in *ibid.*, 187.]

Pack horses unnecessary at this season; river transportation may be relied upon. Sends cattle, flour, and liquor. Subaltern, sergeant, and fifteen rank and file, among whom any butchers, coopers, or masons in company are to be included, ordered to Pittsburgh to assist in laying in provisions. Any who have enlisted in the Eighth Pennsylvania to be also included.

TRESPASSERS ON INDIAN LANDS

[Summary of a letter of Col. Daniel Brodhead, Headquarters, Pittsburgh, Nov. 21, 1779, to Maj. Richard Taylor. Printed in *ibid.*, 188.[

Captain Vance should have apprehended trespassers who seem determined to provoke new calamities by encroachment on Indians' hunting grounds. Order out another party for that purpose. Colonel Gibson has leave to go to Carlisle. Flour sent.

PLANS FOR WESTERN EXPEDITION

[Gen. George Washington to Col. Daniel Brodhead. Washington Papers. Draft.]

Hd. Qrs. West Point 21st Novr 1779

Dr Sir:

I have been favored with your letters of the 9th and 26th of October with their enclosures.

You will find by my letter of the 10th [18] (a copy of which I transmit) that you are at full liberty to act against the hostile Indians, in such excursions as your circumstances will admit. I make no doubt of your particular attention to the several objects regarding Detroit; and that you will spare no pains to collect such information as may enable us to judge precisely of its state and force, that we may know how to regulate our measures.

With respect to Heaths and Ohara's companies, I find they were raised by the State of Virginia for the particular purpose of garrisoning some of the frontier posts. They were to be enlisted for the war, and to be entitled to Continential commissions, but whether this deprived the State of interfering with their subsequent arrangements I will not undertake to say.—If the incorporation proposed by the Lt Governor will be for the good of the service I think it had better be adopted. And I dare say the State will have no objection to the company's being annexed to one of its own regiments while it remains on the frontiers.

I herewith return you the proceedings of the court-martial on Adjutant Gordon.[1] The sentence of the Court on the second charge is founded on a right which the States exercise of filling up vacancies in their regiments.

The steps you have taken to obviate any impressions which the trespass on the Indian lands may produce in their minds, are judicious and I hope will answer a good purpose. While we blame these people for cruelties, we should avoid giving them cause of complaint.

I wish to oblige you with leave of absence from your command, but as our eyes are turned towards Detroit, and in procuring information from that quarter you will see the necessity of waiting a more favorable opportunity.

I am &c
COL. BRODHEAD
G W

CONDITIONS AT FORT PITT

[Summary of a letter of Col. Daniel Brodhead, Pittsburgh, Nov. 22, 1779, to Gen. George Washington. Printed in *Pa. Archives*, XII, 188–89.]

Visit from Delaware chiefs, who report that the new fort at Detroit is very strong; garrison about 300. British have refused supplies to Wyandot, because of treaty made at Pittsburgh. Wyandot chiefs en route here; must be supplied by us or will be obliged to submit to British. Wyandot can give better informa-

---

[1] Arthur Gordon was commissioned first lieutenant of the Thirteenth Virginia Regiment on Dec. 19, 1776. For his court-martial, which occurred Feb. 9, 1780, see Appendix, *post*, 433.

tion about Detroit than Delawares. Inquiries are veiled, apparently directed toward Niagara. Delawares came to Fort Pitt intending to visit Congress, prefer to join an expedition. Need of money for commissaries. Report of defeat of supply boats under a Virginia commander [Colonel Rogers] near the Little Miami. Artillery estimates.

[Summary of a letter of Col. Daniel Brodhead, Pittsburgh, Nov. 22, 1779, to Timothy Pickering. Printed in *ibid.*, 190.]

Delaware chiefs dissuaded from visiting Congress; must be supplied by us. Encroachment by Pittsburgh inhabitants on garrison's quarters.

[Summary of a letter of Col. Daniel Brodhead, Pittsburgh, Nov. 22, 1779, to Col. Archibald Steel. Printed in *id.*, VIII, 21.]

House occupied by Edward Ward and Thomas Smallman[1] needed for defense in case of attack; Maryland corps to be quartered therein. Offers his own rooms to present occupants.

GARRISONS FOR OHIO POSTS

[Summary of a letter of Capt. Joseph Finley, Headquarters, Nov. 24, 1779, to Maj. Richard Taylor. Printed in *id.*, XII, 192.]

Commissioned officers and prisoners ordered to headquarters for a general court-martial. All of Maryland corps at Fort McIntosh, Wheeling, or Holliday's Cove to be relieved; there are ten at one of the two latter stations.

[1] For a sketch of Edward Ward see *Rev. Upper Ohio*, 171, note 97. For Thomas Smallman see *Frontier Defense*, 73, note 39.

FRONTIER RETREAT 117

DELAWARE SPIES

[Summary of a letter of Col. Daniel Brodhead, Headquarters, Pittsburgh, Nov. 26, 1779, to Rev. David Zeisberger.[1] Printed in *ibid.*, 192–93.]

Supplies for Indians—powder, lead, coffee, sugar, salt, and clothing—at hand; blankets en route. Information wanted about Detroit: the strength of the garrison and fort, the number and size of cannon, the sympathies of the inhabitants. Will pay an Indian spy eighty to one hundred bucks. Is sending a spy to Niagara.

ALLEGHENY POSTS EVACUATED

[Summary of a letter of Capt. Joseph Finley, Headquarters, Pittsburgh, Nov. 27, 1779, to Lieut. John Jameson. Printed in *ibid.*, 193.]

Brodhead orders immediate evacuation of Fort Armstrong, with all stores; transport either by water or by pack horses. The latter may be secured from Captain Carnahan[1] at Bull Town at mouth of Kiskiminitas.

[Summary of a letter of Col. Daniel Brodhead, Headquarters, Pittsburgh, Nov. 27, 1779, to Capt. James Carnahan.[2] Printed in *ibid.*, 193–94.]

Pack horses used improperly for hunting purposes; punishment for those guilty of this practice. Lieutenant Jameson must be granted use of pack horses to bring stores from Fort Armstrong. Report requested.

[1] Rev. David Zeisberger was a Moravian missionary at the Delaware towns. See sketch in *Rev. Upper Ohio*, 45, 71.
[2] For Capt. James Carnahan see *Wis. Hist. Colls.*, XXIII, 286, note 2.

[Summary of a letter of Col. Daniel Brodhead, Headquarters, Nov. 27, 1779, to Capt. Thomas Campbell. Printed in ibid., 194.]

Terms of men nearly expired. No danger threatens frontier, therefore Fort Crawford ordered to be evacuated and all stores brought off.

[Summary of a letter of Capt. Joseph Finley, Headquarters, Pittsburgh, Nov. 28, 1779, to Maj. Richard Taylor. Printed in ibid., 194–95.]

Brodhead orders the six-pound cannon from Fort McIntosh, with all its cartridges, to be sent to Fort Pitt. Detachment of Maryland troops at Wheeling to be relieved.

CHARGES AGAINST BRODHEAD

[Maj. Frederick Vernon's charges. 2E106. Transcript.]

PITTSBURG, Decr 1779

. States that he would not associate or dine with him.
1—For preventing the artificers from making necessary furniture for the officers rooms, while he suffers Nancy McCauley (his girl) to sell furniture made by the public officers.
2. For "sporting away" public money designed for recruiting his regiment.
3. That Nancy McCauley has taken unbecoming liberties, in the presence of Col. Brodhead, with some of his officers.

COMMANDANTS AT OHIO POSTS

[Summary of a letter of Col. Daniel Brodhead, Headquarters, Pittsburgh, Dec. 3, 1779, to Capt. Benjamin Biggs.[1] 4JJ54. Printed in Pa. Archives, XII, 195.]

Biggs granted leave of fourteen days to appear before the Virginia land commissioners[2] to settle title to a tract of land disputed by McCullough.

[1] For a sketch of Capt. Benjamin Biggs, who was at this time in command of Fort Henry at Wheeling, see ibid., 256, note 1.
[2] According to the act of the May session of the legislature Francis Peyton, Philip Pendleton, Joseph Holmes, and George Meriwether were appointed com-

[Summary of a letter of Col. Daniel Brodhead, Headquarters, Pittsburgh, Dec. 5, 1779, to Ensign Jacob Springer.[1] Printed in ibid., 195–96.]

Sends one month's allowance of flour for garrison. Apply for Indian meal for winter's supply. Maryland troops at Springer's post called in.

INFORMATION CONCERNING DETROIT

[Summary of a letter of Col. Daniel Brodhead, Headquarters, Pittsburgh, Dec. 12, 1779, to Rev. David Zeisberger. Printed in ibid., 196.]

Light dragoons arrived yesterday, bringing enclosures. Joshua[2] appears willing to go as spy to Detroit; his fitness referred to missionary; spy will be suitably rewarded.

missioners to settle disputed land titles in the Northwest Virginia counties. Meriwether did not serve. The other three commissioners held their first session at Redstone in December, 1779, with James Chew as clerk of the board. A number of the certificates granted by this commission are in Draper Mss., 1SS6–11.

[1] Jacob Springer was commandant of the garrison of Holliday's Cove. He was a descendant of the Springer family which emigrated from Sweden to Delaware early in the seventeenth century. One branch of this family removed to the Monongahela region, and there Jacob enlisted, and on Oct. 31, 1778 was commissioned ensign of the Ninth Virginia. Later he became a lieutenant and served throughout the war. He died June 16, 1823.

[2] A Mahican Indian from the Connecticut River visited the Moravians at Bethlehem, and in 1742 was baptized by Count Zinzendorf, under the name of Joshua. Joshua was a faithful member of the Moravian church and emigrated with Zeisberger to the villages on the Tuscarawas. The elder Joshua died in 1773. His son, also named Joshua, was born in Connecticut in 1741, brought as a babe to live with the Moravians, and was one of their most valued members. He was a remarkable linguist and for many years employed as chapel interpreter. Two of his daughters perished in the Gnadenhütten massacre of 1782. In 1801 Joshua went on a mission to the White River Delawares, and remained among them as their preacher. In 1805 he was accused, by the Prophet, Tecumseh's brother, of witchcraft and burned at the stake. See Heckewelder, Narrative, 408; Benjamin Drake, Life of Tecumseh (Cincinnati, 1841), 88–89.

[Summary of a letter of Col. Daniel Brodhead, Pittsburgh, Dec. 13, 1779, to Gen. George Washington. Printed in ibid., 197–99.]

Washington's letter of November 21 received. Reliance for Detroit information on Moravian missionaries and intelligent Indians of their congregation. Enemy at Detroit expected our troops last fall; their provision magazine is on an island. O'Hara's company is merged in Ninth Virginia. Clothing for troops. Ordnance and military stores; need of a competent engineer. Tranquillity of frontier. Terms of Gibson's men expire in February; few new levies. Indian goods needed and also a superintendent of trade.

CLOTHING FOR TROOPS

[Summary of a letter of Col. Daniel Brodhead, Pittsburgh, Dec. 13, 1779, to Gen. James Wilkinson. Printed in ibid., 199.]

Glad to learn ample supply of clothing for troops has been forwarded. Need of hats and shoes. Three hundred cocked hats wanted before spring.

WESTMORELAND RANGERS

[Summary of a letter of Col. Archibald Lochry, Hannastown, Dec. 13, 1779, to Col. Daniel Brodhead. 1NN48. Printed in id., VIII, 42.]

Command of Irwin's and Campbell's ranging companies vested by state authorities in Lochry; will station them for protection of frontier; requests their return from Fort Pitt, and also a supply of provisions. Will support any offensive measures against the savages.

[Summary of a letter of Col. Daniel Brodhead, Pittsburgh, Dec. 13, 1779, to Pres. Joseph Reed. 1NN49. Printed in *ibid.*, 38–40.]

Extraordinary that ranging companies should be subsisted from public stores, while under command of county lieutenant. These companies, stationed at Forts Armstrong and Crawford, were ordered to Pittsburgh when closing of river with ice seemed likely. No danger from Indians. Writer hopes to be either in Detroit or Natchez before spring.

[Summary of a letter of Col. Daniel Brodhead, Headquarters, Pittsburgh. Dec. 18, 1779, to Col. Archibald Lochry. Printed in *ibid.*, 50–51.]

Has received Lochry's letter of the 13th instant. Ranging companies will not be prevented from marching for Hannastown. County authorities must supply provisions. Troops destitute of clothing.

CONDITIONS AT OHIO POSTS

[Summary of a letter of Col. Daniel Brodhead, Headquarters, Pittsburgh, Dec. 19, 1779, to Maj. Richard Taylor. Printed in *id.*, XII, 200.]

Loss of boat containing flour is irreparable; negligence of garrison, who deserve to suffer hunger. Searching party to be sent out on each side of river if weather is favorable. Because of illness of Col. Richard Campbell Taylor cannot be relieved. Fresh supplies of provisions and forage being sent.

[Maj. Richard Taylor to Capt. Benjamin Biggs. 5NN6. Transcript.]

FORT M^{c}INTOSH, 26th Decr 1779.

DEAR SIR:

I rec^d y^r favor by the express, & am sorry to hear your men are so sickly, as it is out of my power to send the Doctor down, for a horse cannot cross the river, & there is no such thing as travelling by water. As for sending men to supply the places of those discharged, I must wait for instructions from Head Quarters for that purpose. I have wrote the Comd[t] for instructions how to act in that matter. As the men's time expire, you will send them to Pittsburgh for their discharges, as both Col° Gibson & Col° Campbell are there, tho' they had best call here. You will be so good as to take the names of all such men at your post as have not received the six months gift, & send it to me by some of the men who are coming up. &c.

R[D] TAYLOR

To CAPT. BEN. BIGGS, at Fort Henry.

[Summary of a letter of Col. Daniel Brodhead, Headquarters, Pittsburgh, Dec. 30, 1779, to Maj. Richard Taylor. Printed in *Pa. Archives*, XII, 201.]

Supplies of beef and cattle in store. The sick at Wheeling need a physician; surgeon's mate at Fort McIntosh hospital. Soldiers' discharges; Sullivan[1] reports men of Ninth Virginia Regiment for the most part enlisted for war. Fresh supplies of flour and forage. Leave of absence is inadvisable.

BRITISH LOSE INDIAN SUPPORT

[Extract of a letter of Gen. Frederick Haldimand to Gen. Henry Clinton. 58J113–114. Transcript.]

*　*　*　*　*　*　*　*

QUEBEC, January, 1780.

I am sorry to acquaint your Excellency that very little is to be expected, in co-operation, from the Indians upon the frontiers of Virginia, at least from those with whom we have any intercourse—I mean the Western Nations who resort to Detroit and that neighbourhood. Indefatigable pains have been taken, and immense sums lavished to secure their affections, yet they are every day declining, particularly since the American alliance with the French, to whom they have an old and a very firm attachment: Add to this, the misfortune of M[r] Hamilton, the disappointment of reinforcements promised to them from year to year; the unwearied pains of the Spanish from the Mississippi to debauch them; and the advances of the enemy on all sides into their

[1] For Capt. James Sullivan see *Frontier Defense*, 174, note 40.

country; which with all the pains that were taken last year, they never could be brought vigorously to oppose, & it is too plain that nothing but the example and continual remonstrances of the Five Nations prevent their abandoning us entirely.

I have however, the pleasure to acquaint your Excellency, that since my last letter, I have had accounts from thence, informing me that a scout, conducted by white men, fell in with, and totally defeated a party of the enemy on their way to Fort Pitt from New Orleans, where they had been sent to treat with, and to solicit supplies from the Spanish Governor. They succeeded, & were returning with three loaded batteaux up the Ohio, when they were attacked. The party consisted of about 60 men, commanded by Colonel David Rogers, who, with about 40 men, were killed upon the spot, and a Colonel Campbell, with 5 more, were taken prisoners: Some letters & papers were found upon them; I transmit for your information copies of the most interesting.

DETROIT EXPEDITION INEXPEDIENT

[Gen. George Washington to Col. Daniel Brodhead. 1H122. Transcript.][1]

HEAD QUARTERS MORRIS TOWN Jany 4th 1780

SIR:

I have successively received your letters of the 10th 22^{d} of November & 13th of Decem^{r}.

Persuaded that a winter expedition against Detroit would have great advantages over a summer one, and be much more certain of success, I regret that the situation of affairs does not permit us to undertake it. We cannot at present furnish either the men or supplies necessary for it. From the estimate you make of the enemy's force there, your Garrison with all the aid you could derive from the militia would not be equal to the attempt, especially as it must soon suffer so large a diminution, by the departure of the men whose terms of service are expiring and (even were it not too late in the season to march men such a distance in time) the same circumstance and the detachment, we are making to South Carolina, put it out of our power to supply

[1] The original of this letter was in the possession of Brodhead's descendants, who made this transcript for Dr. Draper in 1846.

the defect of your numbers from this quarter. We must therefore of necessity defer the prosecution of the enterprise to a more favorable opportunity, but I would not wish you to discontinue your inquiries and preparations as far as convenient, for it is an object of too much importance to be lost sight of.

I fear also that you will not have force for the expedition you propose to the Notches [Natchez], though this is much more within the compass of our abilities. It would scarcely be prudent to leave Fort Pitt without a proportion of Continental Troops for its defence. Sufficient dependence cannot be placed in the militia, and it is too valuable a Post to be exposed to an accident.

If you should leave only an hundred men here besides those at the dependent posts you would not have above one hundred and fifty for the expedition. Unless the num^s of the Volunteers you expect exceed what I should imagine, there would be great danger to the party. We are too little acquainted with the situation of the Notches to count with assurance, upon success, and if we should fail the party returning against stream so great a distance after a disappointment might run no small risque of being intercepted by the unfriendly Indians through whom it would have to pass. I do not however mean to discourage the undertaking altogether but to suggest the difficulties that occur to me, that every circumstance may be well weighed previous to entering upon it. As the business will be attended with little additional expence, I should be glad you would make every necessary preparation and let me know when you will be completely ready giving me an exact state of the force you will be able to employ on the expedition and to leave at the Garrison under your command. Whatever you do should be under the veil of the greatest secrecy, as on this your success will depend. I shall be glad also after closely examining your means you will give me your sentiments on the practicability of the enterprise.

If I can meet with any Frenchman that answers your description willing to be so employed, I will send him to you, and you shall have an Engineer if you go upon anything that requires one.

I shall write to the Board of War recommending you may be supplied with a few pieces of Artillery & a proportion of stores to be ready against there may be a call for them—

I am with great regard Dr Sir Your most obet Servt

G^o Washington

Col Brodhead

[*Endorsed:*] His Excelly G^l Washington   Rec^d 18th April 1780.

WESTMORELAND RANGERS

[Summary of a letter of Col. Daniel Brodhead, Headquarters, Pittsburgh, Jan. 2, 1780, to Capt. John Clark. Printed in *Pa. Archives*, VIII, 68.]

Lochry ordered to arrest Capt. Thomas Campbell for an insolent letter, and Capt. Joseph Irwin for disobedience of orders. As Irwin is Lochry's father-in-law, the duty will devolve upon Clark. Recruiting service; rangers to be enlisted. Numbers of Irwin's company.

[Summary of a letter of Col. Daniel Brodhead, Headquarters, Pittsburgh, Jan. 2, 1780, to Capt. Joseph Irwin. Printed in *ibid.*, 68–69.]

Men of Irwin's ranging company enlisted in Eighth Pennsylvania ordered to join the regiment.

[Summary of a letter of Col. Daniel Brodhead, Headquarters, Pittsburgh, Jan. 2, 1780, to Col. Archibald Lochry. Printed in *ibid.*, 69–70.]

President of state wrote that rangers were raised by order of Congress; should be reënlisted in Continental troops. Supplies at Hannastown. Support given to Westmoreland. Irwin's men enlisted for war to be sent to Fort Pitt; if he refuses orders him placed under arrest. Also order for arrest of Capt. Thomas Campbell for an insolent letter. Brodhead does not consider it his duty to supply troops not under his command.

[Summary of a letter of Col. Archibald Lochry, Hannastown, Jan. 9, 1780, to Pres. Joseph Reed. Printed in *ibid.*, 77–79.][1]

Details of difference with Brodhead about command of ranging companies; arbitrary removal from Allegheny River posts. West-

[1] For the reply to this letter see *Pa. Archives*, VIII, 405.

moreland people uneasy at exposed condition of frontier; anticipate early Indian attacks. Lochry cannot call out militia for lack of provisions; Brodhead refuses a supply; rangers billeted by fours and fives on inhabitants. Ranging companies should be enlisted for another year. Brodhead's recruiting officers have enlisted rangers before their time expired and he has ordered these to Fort Pitt. Lochry has refused to send them or to arrest officers as required. Moorhead's independent company removed to Fort Pitt and annexed to Eighth Pennsylvania. If that company and the rangers were in the field better support could be given to offensive measures of Continental troops.

[Summary of a letter of Col. Daniel Brodhead, Headquarters, Pittsburgh, Jan. 20, 1780, to Col. Archibald Lochry. Printed in *id.*, XII, 202–3.]

Powers of president of state with regard to rangers. "Who has been the best Guardian to the frontiers will hereafter be discovered." Lochry's confessed inability. Has no concern for supplies for troops not under his own command. Capt. Thomas Campbell sent to Philadelphia to avoid trial for insolence; he shall not be excused. Lochry's military knowledge and the propriety of his conduct sarcastically treated.

TROOPS EN ROUTE TO ILLINOIS

[Summary of a letter of Col. Daniel Brodhead, Headquarters, Pittsburgh, Jan. 20, 1780, to Col. Francis Peyton[1] and Col. Philip Pendleton.[2] Printed in *ibid.*, 201–2.]

The bearer, Capt. John Rogers, brought to Fort Pitt some Virginia troops who were on their way to Illinois; no provision for

[1] Francis, son of Valentine Peyton, was born in Prince William County, Va. Sometime before the Revolution the younger Peyton removed to Loudoun County, which he represented in the Virginia Constitutional Convention of 1776. He was also county lieutenant for several years, a member of the House of Burgesses from 1777 to 1785, and state senator from 1798 to 1803.

[2] Philip Pendleton, son of Nathaniel Pendleton of Culpeper County, Va., removed to Berkeley County near Martinsburgh, where he was admitted to the bar in 1772. From 1777 to 1781 he was an officer of the county militia, and its representative in the State Assembly of 1779.

[3] John Rogers, a cousin of George Rogers Clark, was born in 1757. At the age of nineteen he was commissioned lieutenant in the Fourth Virginia Regiment

their subsistence; have been subsisted on march from Winchester from Continental magazines. Improper to open United States magazine to troops of one state without authorization from Congress or commander in chief. Advises employment of a commissary on credit of state. Will afford a temporary supply.

THE BOUNDARY DISPUTE

[Gov. Thomas Jefferson to Col. David Shepherd. 1SS189. L. S.]

W<small>MSBURG</small> Jany 30th 1780

S<small>IR</small>:
I find that the execution of the Commission for determining disputed titles to land, so far as the same has taken place in the controverted territory, has given great alarm & uneasiness to the State of Pennsylvania, who have applied to Congress on the occasion, and produced their interference.[1] I hope no other Act has taken place subversive of the quiet of the Settlement. I must entreat you to exert the whole of your influence & to call in that of the Captains & subordinate officers under you, to keep the inhabitants on both sides in good temper with each other, and to induce ours rather to neglect little circumstances of irritation, should any such happen, than by embroiling their two Countries

and during the early years of the Revolution embarked on a privateering venture. In 1778 he became second lieutenant in Capt. Leonard Helm's company on Clark's Kaskaskia expedition. In 1779 Rogers was given command of the war galley against Vincennes, and after the capture of that place was sent to convey the British prisoners to Williamsburg. In Virginia he received thanks and honors from the Assembly and was commissioned captain of a troop of horse, raised for the western service. With this reënforcement he arrived at Fort Pitt in January, 1780. Upon reaching the Illinois, Rogers took part in Montgomery's Rock River expedition and in the autumn of that year was appointed commandant at Kaskaskia by Montgomery. Being young and inexperienced, he became involved with the adventurers, John Dodge and Thomas Bentley, and by harsh and arbitrary measures alienated the French-Canadian habitants. See his letter of defense in *Ill. Hist. Colls.*, VIII, 545–46. In August, 1781 Rogers returned to Virginia, and resigned from the service in February, 1782. Thereafter he resided at Richmond, where he died in 1794 from the effects of a fall. See Dr. Draper's correspondence with Rogers' brother, Thomas, in Draper Mss., 10J113.

[1] See resolution alluded to in *Journal of Continental Congress* (Washington, 1909), XV, 1411.

to Shipwreck the general cause & bring on events which will destroy all our Rights. I put great confidence in your discretion on the present occasion & the effect of your recommendations to the people to be temperate in word & deed with their brethren of Pennsylvania.

I am with great respect Sir Your most humble serv^t

TH: JEFFERSON

SPANISH SUCCESS ON THE MISSISSIPPI

[Col. William Christian to Col. William Fleming. 2U73. A. L. S.]

DEAR SIR: MAHANAIM February the 5th 1780.

A man who at present has his Family at the Lick on Roan Oak has called, and tells me he is now on his Way to Kentuckey to claim Land he has a Right to, which gives me an opportunity of writing to you. I suppose my Sister has written you of Family Affairs, so that I will not touch upon them. Our Assembly broke up at Christmas, after passing 52 Acts, but I have seen none of them but one, for laying some further Taxes. Three pounds per Tithable and four pounds per poll is to be paid immediately, the first upon white & the latter on black People. And next summer 30^{lb} Tob° p^r Tithable is to be collected for raising money to pay to Congress. The sum designed to be paid is ten million of Pounds, one half there of to be borrowed in Philadelphia the other to be paid out of this Extra Tax. The Tob° was rated at £30 per hundred, the present Current Price. The Assembly &c except the Navy Board are to remove to Richmond, notwithstanding repeated Efforts last session to prevent it. I dont know any other Laws that immediately concerns the Frontiers. Money is very scarce all over the back Country, although nothing falls in the Price; Credit being introduced every where. Corn hereabouts is £6. and in Botetourt £10, but I expect it will be ten everywhere on this Side of the Mountains. If there is no Indian War, nor no purchases made, next Summer on the Frontiers there will be no Money amongst us, as we have no Commodities to bring any. A good crop of Grain this Year will raise our Currency four fold but a bad one will make it worse. Whiskey is four Dollars the half pint at Sam Thompsons, and Rum eight

Dollars the half Pint at Col Ingles's. If the War slackens Money will get better, or Traffic must End here. At the first sales of British Property Negroes sold generally from 1700 to 3000 Pounds. The farmers had no money, but the Traders attended the Sales with enough & furnished every Tobacco maker with what he wanted. One Mitchell an Irishman at Richmond alone attended with £80,000. A Gentleman who purchased Stoners Land in Cumberland had hundreds of thousands; and Ross had Agents with a great deal In short all the money in the State Centers with the Traders. Salt a month ago in Botetourt was at £65, but now there is none to be had on this side of Bedford. There seems to be no Traffic among us now but for Grain, or Liquor. The Assembly had no Intelligence from England but Reports that America gains Ground in Europe. Nothing of Note has happened between England & France. I have heard nothing from Savannah since our Repulse there. Nor has any Thing happened to the Northward this Winter. Genl Sullivan destroyed some Indian Towns, and drove Butler from some Breast works; and returned. The Virg & Carolina Continental Troops are on their Way for Charles Town, where the People dread an Attack. About 6,000 of Clintons Army embarked for the Southward, but for what spot is unknown. We have had a Report that the Spaniards have taken all West Florida; I have conjectured that the English were going to the aid of that Colony. A Man on Foot, came here this morning & says he left Pensacola the 6th of December, & that it was certain that the Natches & Mushack [Manchac] was taken,[1] with one Col Dickson

[1] The Spanish capture of the British forts on the Mississippi in September, 1779 was one of the most brilliant operations of the Revolution in the West. Bernardo de Galvez, governor of Louisiana (for a sketch of whom see *Frontier Defense*, 289, note 53) received word late in August of Spain's declaration of war against England. He immediately had the recognition of American independence proclaimed at New Orleans, and made preparations for a movement against Fort Bute at Manchac, on the Mississippi, 115 miles above New Orleans. A terrific hurricane, that occasioned great loss of water craft, delayed his advance for a few days, but on September 7, his forces, consisting of about 500 regular troops and nearly 1,000 auxiliaries of militia, Indians, and negroes, stormed the British fort and took it at the first assault. The garrison was small; the British commandant having withdrawn to Baton Rouge, determined to make his stand there. Galvez at once advanced upon that post, which surrendered on September 21, after a four days' siege in which the Spanish cannon played havoc with the British entrenchments. The capitulation included all the British posts on the Mississippi; thus Natchez, under the command of Capt. Anthony Forster with a garrison of nearly a hundred, fell to the Spanish

& 700 men.[1] That one of the Places defended itself four Days and then surrendered. And he says Gen[l] Campbell[2] was preparing to defend Pensacola where he looked for the Spaniards before Christmas. This poor man says he was taken near New England two Years ago & was carried to Pensacola from whence he now run away. He says 500 of the Choctaws joined the Spaniards; and that there were no Goods for the Indians at Pensacola.

Webb, resigned his Treasurers Place & one Moore was app[d] Jamey Madison, Jn° Walker Cyrus Griffen, Joseph Jones, and some other Person goes to Congress. And Col Fleming of Botet[t] is app[d] of the council. I suppose you cant be in before some Time without a blow. In a report written before Baton Rouge three days before its capitulation Galvez claimed that the British forces were equal or superior to his own. (*Archives of Cuba*, transcripts in Wisconsin Historical Library.) Within fifteen days he took three forts one by assault, one by capitulation, one by evacuation; captured 550 British regulars including 28 officers, making with voyageurs and camp followers 667 prisoners; secured more than fifty vessels ranging in size from large transports to launches and canoes; and retired to New Orleans with the loss of only one man. Oliver Pollock and eight other American residents of New Orleans accompanied the expedition as volunteers. For a recent account see Wilbur H. Siebert, "The Loyalists in West Florida and the Natchez District" in Mississippi Valley Historical Association *Proceedings*, 1914–15, 108–22.

[1] Lieut-Col. Alexander Dickson was a veteran British officer, having been commissioned captain of the Sixteenth Infantry June 17, 1761. He served in America during the French and Indian War, and as early as 1767 was stationed at Pensacola, Fla. On May 20, 1771 Dickson became major, and on Jan. 11, 1776, lieutenant-colonel of his regiment. In 1776 the regiment was summoned to New York, but because of its familiarity with Florida, it was the next year recalled to that colony. In 1778, Colonel Dickson commanded the garrison at Mobile; early in 1779 he was sent to the Mississippi. After his capture by Galvez he was detained at New Orleans until exchanged. On Nov. 20, 1782 he was promoted to a colonelcy. Apparently he died soon afterwards, as by 1783 his name disappears from the *Army List*. The garrison at Baton Rouge was composed of large detachments from the sixteenth and sixtieth regiments and a number of Waldeckers, who in the summer of 1779 had been sent to reënforce the Mississippi posts.

[2] Gen. John Campbell was a veteran officer, having been in the army before 1763. In 1773 he was major of the Sixtieth or American Regiment, and in 1777, its colonel. On Feb. 19, 1779 he was commissioned major-general, and honorary colonel of the Fifty-seventh Foot. He was sent to Pensacola early in 1779, and entrusted with the defense of both the Floridas. While personally brave, Campbell was careless and dilatory, failing to relieve Mobile in 1780, when it was besieged by Galvez. In 1781 General Campbell surrendered Pensacola to the Spanish, and was made prisoner of war, but was released the succeeding year. In 1787 he became lieutenant-general, in 1797, general, and died in 1809.

in May. I shant write Stephen [Trigg] now,[1] but all is well with him. If he can see opp^y he had better try to come in to represent Kentuckey. That country ought to be divided in three or four Counties, & it will be done, if the People ask it. The two Batt. are not going to Ohio this Winter Col Crocket is ordered to command at Albamarle & Col Knox is Assembling the Recruits at Lynch's Ferry.—

Perhaps one Batt. may be sent to Ohio; perhaps not. Every Thing will be discharged next Spring that can be spared in order to retrench our Expences, and make the Currency more precious. Every Engine will be set to work for that End. People are forbid settling over Ohio, or on the Land reserved for the Army on Cumberland &c in the strongest Stile. I have procured Patents for the great bone & the Lick on Salt river, and shall endeavour to do something at the latter next Summer; if public affairs dont wheel about the wrong way before then. But the war gives no concern, now. It is expected that the Spaniards are to have both the Florida's as soon as they can take them, for themselves. Tell Stephen not to depend on my selling any of his mares before he comes in: although every Thing is held as high as ever, and rather more so, there is no one has ready money to give for any Thing that can be done without hereabouts. The Rule with Tradesmen is now 30 for one, but many talk of forty. Pork is held at £50. per hundred, & scarce at that. This River has afforded a Bridge of Ice Six Weeks; we have hardly seen the Earth for two months. Food for Cattle is nearly exhausted every where, and many Families will soon have no Bread to eat. People talk less of Kentuckey lately than hitherto. For my Part I intend to begin to move next Fall and finish the next one. The first will be to make a crop. I shall lay off a Town at the Salt lick, and give Lotts to those who choose to settle there. As the Falls are sickly this must be the next suitable Place on Acc° of its interior Navigation I believe Land warrants sells but slowly The sales are yet under a million of Acres, perhaps a good deal under.

Mason[2] Damns the back country Speculators for frightning People from purchasing.

The comm^s. have never met in this District as yet, nor do I hear of them. They met lately at Greenbrier, but did nothing

[1] For a sketch of this pioneer see *Dunmore's War*, 44, note 79. He was secretary of the commission to settle Kentucky land titles.

[2] George Mason, the prominent Virginia statesman.

perhaps owing to the weather. I hear they meet next Week at Jamey Barnets,[1] I suppose it must be to do the Botet[ourt] Business.

I believe I may as well conclude now, that I am Your affectionate Brother

COL FLEMING

W^M CHRISTIAN

CAPTAIN PIPE'S MESSAGE

[Captain Pipe to Col. Daniel Brodhead. 1H124. L. S.]

Whinguakeshoo[2]   FORT M^cINTOSH 6th Feby 1780

BROTHER: I am Very Glad your Message Overtook me it gives me pleasure almost Eaqual to that of Seeing & Speaking with you Brother: myself Capt Pekelen & all my men Sends our Sincer Love & friendship to you in this my words, to you and are all very Glad your Love has overtaken us.

Brother Whinguakeshoo: I am glad I have So Great, So Good, & Strong a Man to make a Lasting peace with one that I Hope will not forget me: for my part I Shall Ever hold fast the Chain, & Should Be very Sory there Should be any Holes Broke therein any thing that may Happen for my Part I Can wipe away & think no more thereon.

Brother Whingua Keshoo: the words you told me in your Letter I find to be very true, I am very Sorry any of my men belonging to the Woolf Tribe Should behave in So Rediculous a maner as to bring Scandle on the Whole Tribe, Capt Pekelen is also very Sorry & hopes you will not think worse of him for the Ill behaviour of a bad man.

Brother Whingua Keshoo: I now Send you the watch I hope you will Look at it & See that I never tell you any Lies, according to your Desire I have made him give the watch up: & now Brother I hope you will Consider Captⁿ Pekelens Case in Reguard to the Horses he Lost at Fort Pitt Last Sumer by some of your People & try to make them give them up by Spring, & now Brother as

---

[1] For a sketch of James Barnett see *Wis. Hist. Colls.*, XXIII, 52, note 6.
[2] This is a variant of Brodhead's Indian name, usually written "Mahingwe Keesuch."

you may See I never intend to Deceive you I hope you will not forget him
Brother Whingua Keshoo: I hope you will think no more of this matter but Let it go with the wind, and wipe it all away & not think that my Self or Captn Pekelen Encourages any of our People in Such Measures—the young man was foolish & thought he [would] get his Horses sooner by takeing the watch as he thought it would Hurry them to find the Horses, and as we have not Deceiv'd you Brother we hope you will not Deceive us but Endevour to get our Horses by Spring if there is any thing more Lost Perhaps you Can Let me Know by the first that Comes to the Meravion Town, I Shall allways be Glad to hear of your wellfair, I Can any time get your Letter from there—
from Your friend & Brother
CAPT^N PIPE

VIRGINIA PLANS DETROIT EXPEDITION

[Gov. Thomas Jefferson to Gen. George Washington. 27S58–59. Transcript.]

WILLIAMSBURG, February 10, 1780.

SIR:
It is possible you may have heard, that in the course of last summer an expedition was meditated, by our Colonel Clarke, against Detroit: that he had proceeded so far as to rendezvous a considerable body of Indians, I believe four or five thousand, at St. Vincennes; but, being disappointed in the number of whites he expected, and not choosing to rely principally on the Indians, he was obliged to decline it. We have a tolerable prospect of reinforcing him this Spring, to the number which he thinks sufficient for the enterprise. We have informed him of this, and left him to decide between this object, and that of giving vigorous chastisement to those tribes of Indians, whose eternal hostilities have proved them incapable of living on friendly terms with us. It is our opinion, his inclination will lead him to determine on the former. The reason of my laying before your Excellency this matter, is, that it has been intimated to me that Colonel Broadhead is meditating a similar expedition. I wished, therefore, to make you acquainted with what we had in contemplation. The enterprising and energetic genius of Clarke is not altogether

unknown to you. You also know (what I am a stranger to) the abilities of Broadhead, and the particular force with which you will be able to arm him for such an expedition. We wish the most hopeful means should be used for removing so uneasy a thorn from our side. As yourself, alone, are acquainted with all the circumstances necessary for well-informed decision, I am to ask the favor of your Excellency, if you should think Broadhead's undertaking it most likely to produce success, that you will [be] so kind as to intimate to us to divert Clarke to the other object, which is also important to this State. It will, of course, have weight with you in forming your determination, that our prospect of strengthening Clarke's hands, sufficiently, is not absolutely certain. It may be necessary, perhaps, to inform you, that these two officers cannot act together, which excludes the hopes of ensuring success by a joint expedition.

I have the honor to be, with the most sincere esteem, Your Excellency's most obedient and most humble servant,

TH: JEFFERSON

MESSAGES FOR DELAWARES

[Summary of a letter of Col. Daniel Brodhead, Headquarters, Pittsburgh, Feb. 10, 1780, to Rev. David Zeisberger. Printed in *Pa. Archives*, XII, 203-4.]

Proposal to remove Delawares to Big Beaver River; Moravians invited to remove their congregation likewise; dangers and difficulties of their present location; supplies could be more easily furnished in new location. Requests information of decision. Desires aid in procuring intelligence. Reports of general American success.

[Col. Daniel Brodhead to Captain Pipe. 2H48-50. Letter Book.]

HEAD QUARTERS PITTSBURGH Feb[y] 11th 1780
BROTHER CAPTAIN PIPE:

I am very glad to hear from you & that you have sent back the watch I can freely forgive the man who took it, and I am very sorry on my good friend Pekeeland's account that the watch was taken

Brother: It would give me great pleasure to recover Pakeeland's horses for him but I fear it will be out of my power; However I will do all I can to get them & I hope you will likewise endeavour to make your people return all the Horses they have stolen from their Brethren the Americans, & if my people have stolen more than yours I will give you as many horses as will pay for what you may be looser & I hope you will do the same with me.

Brother: Many Horses have been stolen on both sides & perhaps we shall do wisely not to say much about them but leave the matter as it is & do all we can to hold fast of our good Chain of Friendship; if I hear of any more goods that may have been stolen I will inform you of it.

Brother: I likewise esteem you as a great good man & I hope that so long as God lets us live we will do all the good we can

I am your Friend & Brother

MAHINGWEEGEESHUCH

To Capt Pipe

HARD WINTER AT FORT PITT

[Summary of a letter of Col. Daniel Brodhead, Fort Pitt, Feb. 11, 1780, to Gen. George Washington. Printed in Sparks, *Corr. Amer. Rev.*, II, 399–400.]

Has received no reply to letters of November 10 and 22 and December 13; encloses report of court-martial of Lieut. Arthur Gordon. Has not seen Col. George Morgan since coming to this department. Need of provisions. Public craft carried away by ice; such deep snow and such ice never known there before. Prisoner, escaped from Wyandot towns, brings word of strength of new fort at Detroit; garrison, 450 regulars; 1800 at Niagara and many Indians. Danger of invasion; requests reënforcement. Need of boat builders and armorers. Plans to drive off the Shawnee.

[Summary of a letter of Col. Daniel Brodhead, Pittsburgh, Feb. 11, 1780, to Pres. Joseph Reed. Printed in *Pa. Archives*, VIII, 106–7.]

Defends action with regard to Westmoreland ranging companies; poor opinion of Capt. Joseph Irwin. Severity of winter. Danger of invasion from Niagara. Escaped prisoner's report of strong defenses at Detroit. If reënforcements arrive will chastise hostile Indians and probably take Detroit. Delawares talk of nearer settlement. Will regarrison Forts Armstrong and Crawford when weather permits.

SUPPLIES FOR FORT PITT

[Summary of a letter of Col. Daniel Brodhead, Pittsburgh, Feb. 11, 1780, to Gen. Nathaniel Greene. Printed in *id.*, XII, 204–5.]

Col. Archibald Steel's inattention to duties; not dishonest, but weak in detecting frauds. Lack of tents, 200 needed; marquee for holding Indian councils desireable. Davis as quartermaster. Condition of the public horses. Danger of invasion from Niagara.

[Summary of a letter of Col. Daniel Brodhead, Fort Pitt, Feb. 12, 1780, to Richard Peters.[1] Printed in *ibid.*, 207–8.]

Estimate of cannon and military stores needed. Reports from Western Indians favorable. Large garrisons at Detroit and Niagara; danger of invasion; need of cannon and artillerymen in early spring. Boat builders and armorers wanted. Provisions supplied to Virginia state troops.

BRODHEAD REBUKED

[Summary of a letter of Pres. Joseph Reed, In Council, Philadelphia, Feb. 14, 1780, to Col. Daniel Brodhead. Printed in *id.*, VIII, 109–10.]

Representations of Capt. Thomas Campbell and Col. Archibald Lochry concerning dispute with Brodhead. State authorities had hoped much from his appointment; regrets the breach with

[1] Richard Peters was elected, June 13, 1776, secretary of the Continental Board of War, an office which he retained until December, 1781. Upon his resignation he received the thanks of Congress "for his long and faithful services."

Westmoreland County. Impropriety of enlisting men from ranging companies before their time had expired. Powers of state president called in question; regard for Brodhead's previous services lessens rebuke administered.

HARD WINTER IN SOUTHWEST VIRGINIA

[Rev. Caleb Wallace[1] to Col. William Fleming. 2U74. A. L. S.]

15th Feby 1780

D^r SIR:

The Opportunity forbids me being so particular as I wish. We have rec^d your Letters inclosing Two Certificates for Milatary Warrants and one for a preemption, which we have sent to W^{ms}burg agreeable to your Directions, and now expect a return every Hour. When the Warrants come to hand they shall be forwarded to you by the first safe opportunity. Mrs Fleming and all your Family are in good health. I removed my effects from Charlotte about the begining of the long spell of very hard Weather which we have had. And Capt Christian's sudden and unexpected removal, the Humphries keeping possession of your places this Winter with some other Circumstances, laid me under the necessity of removing immediately to Green Spring.—The Inclemency of the Weather, Getting the old Houses in a condition so that we could subsist in them, and riding almost continually on the hunt of Corn for my Family, made it impossible for

[1] Caleb Wallace was born in 1742 in Charlotte County, Va. He was educated at Princeton, graduating with the class of 1770. Two years later he was licensed to preach and was given charge of the Presbyterian church of Cub Creek in his native county. In 1779 he removed to Botetourt County, where he married Rosanna, sister of Col. William Christian, and of Mrs. William Fleming. In 1782 Wallace was one of the commissioners to settle land titles in Kentucky, when he was elected to represent Lincoln County in the Virginia Assembly. The next spring he removed his family to Kentucky, and settled on Elkhorn Creek in what was then Fayette, later Woodford County. He gave up the ministry and entered the legal profession, and was one of the first judges of the Kentucky District Court. He was a member of all the Kentucky conventions, presidential elector in 1797, and in 1799 declined the honor of drafting the Kentucky Resolutions. On the erection of the state he was chosen judge of the Court of Appeals, a position which he retained until 1813. He died at his Woodford County home in 1814. See William H. Whitsitt, "Caleb Wallace" in *Filson Club Publications* (Louisville, 1888), No. 4.

me to do all the Services for your Family which I anxiously desired. Nothing however shall be neglected that is in my power. Your Fodder and Straw is nearly gone. But Dr Smith & myself have lately bought you 20 or 30 Bushels of Corn, and as the most of your Stock are yet in pretty good Case and Mrs Fleming has a good Supply of Salt, I hope your loss will not be great if the Winter should end favourably. The Condition of this Country is truely distressing. Corn has risen to 10, 12 & 15 pounds the Bushel, and it is to be feared that Multitudes will not get it at any Price.

My Affairs have taken a different turn from what I expected, I need only mention my being disappointed of the Grain which I was encouraged to expect from the congregation, and which I had made the Condition of my settlement with them, I do not therefore think of spen[d]ing another Winter in this Quarter. I have therefore wrote to our friend Mr Trigg to seek a settlement for me at Kentucky, if he can make a valuable purchase and obtain Credit until I can raise it and Transmit it to him. I have directed him to advise with you, and as the Bearer is gone on his Way and I must follow him quickly with my letters, I beg leave to refer you to his Letter. If you find it in your power to serve me in the Case, I shall thankfully acknowledge the favour, and shall give you my thoughts more fully by the next medium of Conveyance that offers. I expect land will rise in value very fast as a great many are going out as soon as the winter Breaks to purchase. If I could get a Convenient Tract of Land in a Good Neighbourhood, I would not pay much regard to the Prospect of a Congregation. Should however desire to officiate as a Clergyman among them, upon proper encouragement, But more of this when I write again. If I do not remove to Kentucky next Fall, I purpose to go as far as Houlston, for here I cannot,—I may say, I will not stay. The truth in a Word is, I shall sink in one year the Earnings of my Life among an ungrateful People, and the greatest part through their Default.

I am Dr Sir, Your's most Affectionately

CALEB WALLACE

To COL. W^M FLEMING, Kentucky.

INDIAN ALLIES NEED GOODS

[Delawares and Mequochoke-Shawnee to Col. Daniel Brodhead, with his reply. 1H126. Contemporary document.]

PITTSBURGH Feby 17th 1780

Speech delivered by Capt Killbuck sent to him from Cooshocking

BROTHER:

All your Brothers at Coocking greet you by this speech & request that after you hear it you will assist them in the execution of their designs

Brother: Listen: I formerly desired you at the Grand Council fire at Philad^a to send some traders amongst us with goods as our women & Children are poor & naked & in danger of perishing by the severity of the winter, if you have got up any goods we wish you would send them to us two horse loads of powder & lead with eight horse load of other goods would help us very much

Maguchee–Shawanese to the Delawares

Grandfathers listen: My chief Nimwha is dead whom I used to listen to & whom Kishinotsey set before you the king of the Maguichees has sent for me & I am going to him as soon as I see him I will know better where I shall live

Grandfather: Here is a pipe full of tobacco which when you smoke you will see us rising up & going away but do not be uneasy at it

Mahingweegeeshuch'^{s} Answer

Brothers: I am sorry to hear that you are in a bad situation for want of Clothing. Your Brethren of this Isle in this contest have suffered much for sake of their freedom but the worst is now over—the deep snow has prevented our getting supplies over the mountains for the Delawares. Some goods we have & such as we have you shall have in welcome & perhaps it may be sufficient as the warm weather will soon come But the people who have the Goods are unwilling to send them to Coochocking as your people are not all of one mind about building some strong place to secure the Goods which may be sent for your use. You desired me last fall to build a Fort for you but afterwards you said you did not want it this is the reason why Goods cannot be sent to your Towns & you must blame yourselves for being under the necessity of coming here to buy them. When you are all collected to one place Goods shall be sent you according to promise.

MESSAGE FROM NIAGARA

[Col. Guy Johnson[1] to Alexander McKee. Printed in J. Watts De Peyster (ed.), *Miscellanies by an Officer* (New York, 1888), app., p. xliv.[2]]

SIR: NIAGARA, 18th Feby., 1780.

I arrived at this Place the 4th Octr. last after a variety of Disappointments and Difficulties which I must defer entering upon until we meet. A few days after I went to Oswego with a body of Indians, on an Affair which was rendered impracticable from the late arrival of the Troops, and the hasty Retreat of the Rebels,[3] and on my Return, the 18th Novr. I wrote you a few Lines to notify my arrival and to acquaint you that the General had sent your Letter to me, and that I should take the first Opportunity to arrange all matters, since which I heard that you went to the Southward, and the other Day I read your Letter from the Shawanese Town of Novem'r last to the Commanding Officer of Detroit, by which I perceive you had no intelligence respecting me. I hope this letter will come safe to your hands and I wish it may do so at the Shawanese Village, as I would have you acquaint them People that after my having been sent by the King's Orders to attend a proposed Movement from New York which at length was laid aside, I obtained Permission to come this way, but was near lost in a Storm at Sea, and obliged to winter in Nova Scotia, from which I set out as early as I could procure conveyance, and have been here these Six Months, furnished with His Majesty's Royal Commission and Authority as Superintendent of the Six Nations and all Allies, &c., and as their Colonel. That I am particularly pleased to hear of the Fidelity of many among them, which I mean to reward, and that they will always find me their True Friend, and a follower of Sir William Johnson's Footsteps, and that I think it necessary

---

[1] For a sketch of Col. Guy Johnson see *Rev. Upper Ohio*, 65, note 95.

[2] *Miscellanies by an Officer* was the work of Col. Arent Schuyler De Peyster, commandant at Mackinac, 1774–79, who replaced Hamilton at Detroit in 1779. The first edition of his *Miscellanies* was published at Dumfries, Scotland, in 1813. In 1888 J. Watts De Peyster of New York issued a new edition to which he added an *Appendix, Explanatory Notes*, etc., under a separate cover. In this latter is contained a number of hitherto unpublished letters obtained from the Johnson and the De Peyster family papers.

[3] This refers to Gen. John Sullivan's expedition in the autumn of 1779.

in the present state of affairs to see some of their Chiefs, as early as possible in the Season to Concert Matters for their Honor and advantage. If you have left the Place you can forward this with any Additions necessary accompanied with a Belt to them. But as I have some Cash for you, and many important Points to settle, I think it will be best that you accompany them, or if they are tardy that you come yourself as soon as it is practicable. Possibly I may be to the Westward of this; but as this must depend upon the Posture of Affairs, I think it the best to direct you to this Place, from whence you can proceed as the service may require, so as to render the Indians of your District as useful as I know they are capable of being. The General wrote to me that you had been recommended as of much Use in Detroit, which gave me much Pleasure, as I am always, with much Esteem, Sir, Your Friend & Well-Wisher

G. JOHNSON

I have near 3000 Indians at this Place, all hearty in the cause, and about 300 are Just gone out against the Enemy.
ALEXR. McKEE, Esqr.

HARD WINTER IN KENTUCKY

[Col. John Floyd to Col. William Preston.[1] 33S317–18. Transcript.]

HARRODSBURG, 20th Feb. 1780.

D^R SIR:
I came up here a few days ago to adjust a little business. * * * Notwithstanding the severest winter that ever was known, I have only lost one cow, & she died since the warm weather: I lost two horses, but they strayed away last December; but poor Bob [whose foot was badly hurt by the first tree he cut on the place, lodging & sliding off the stump.] died about three weeks ago, after all I could do. He got frost bitten in camp before I could get him a cabin, & was reduced to a mere skeleton.

I have no bread yet, but expect a small supply from my friend Col. Henderson at Boonesborough, who has greatly befriended

[For a sketch of John Floyd see *Dunmore's War*, 9, note 15. For Col. William Preston see *ibid.*, 430–31.

me by sparing that which he may want himself, & only waits for high water to send it down with his own, on the way to the mouth of Green river where he is about to form a settlement.[1]

I shall not be able to do much surveying this spring, as the hard winter & the loss of my negro have prevented my getting one acre cleared on my place. We have but ten families with us yet, but I expect about fifteen in the whole, which I think will make us tolerably safe. * * *

J[N] FLOYD.

HARD WINTER AT FORT PITT

[Summary of a letter of Col. Daniel Brodhead, Headquarters, Pittsburgh, Feb. 22, 1780, to Capt. Simon Morgan. Printed in *Pa. Archives*, XII, 208.]

Forage and provision sent by boat; safeguarding the craft. Packhorses carried last supplies. Provisioning the Indians; hopes for the breaking of winter, that they may go beaver hunting.

[Summary of a letter of Col. Daniel Brodhead, Headquarters, Fort Pitt, Feb. 27, 1780, to James Wilkinson. Printed in *ibid.*, 209.]

Great depth of snow prevented the transportation of clothing; suffering of troops. Woolen garments to be kept for next winter; supplies of linen requested. Ninth Virginia better supplied than Eighth Pennsylvania. Requests scarlet cloth for himself.

[Summary of a letter of Col. Daniel Brodhead, Headquarters, Pittsburgh, Feb. 28, 1780, to Capt. Thomas McIntyre. Printed in *ibid.*, 209–10.]

Will send horses and kegs as soon as weather permits; conveyance too uncertain to send money. Need of full complement of shoes for ensuing campaign.

[1] Col. Richard Henderson, for whom see *Rev. Upper Ohio*, 1, note 3, had come from a survey of the North Carolina-Virginia boundary line, which he abandoned in November, 1779. Henderson remained at Boonesborough until March, 1780, when he set out for the tract between the Green and Ohio rivers, which had been granted by the Virginia Assembly on Oct. 5, 1778, to the Transylvania Company as a recompense for its efforts in founding Kentucky. The town of Henderson was later built within this land grant.

LOYALISTS IN SOUTHWEST VIRGINIA

[Col. William Preston to Gov. Thomas Jefferson. 5QQ28. Autograph draft signed.]

[March, 1780]

SIR:

I am sorry to acquaint your Excellency that three Days ago an Information was made to a Magistrate in the County That a Number of Men Dissafected to the present Government had combined to disturb the Peace of this unhappy Frontier as soon as the Season would Permit and the british Troops could gain any Footing in S° Carolina & were making the Necessary Preparations for that Purpose. That 75 or thereabouts had taken the Oath of Allegiance to the King of Great Britain in one Neighbourhood & carried on a constant Correspondence with all the other Disaffected People not only in this & Washington County but on the Frontiers of N° Carolina but that they had Persons employ'd to carry Intelligence to & from our Enemies in Georgia & Elsewhere on the Continent. That there is now fifteen British Commissions in this County and Washington, & that these People intended to perpetrate the most horrid murders [on all] Individuals in Authority on this Quarter, with many other Things of the like Nature that would be too tedious to Relate. The Information being made at the Risque of the Informers Life & the Lives of his Family he would not suffer his Name to be made known.

Another Information of the same kind had been made on a Number of Inhabitants on another Frontier Settlement, where a few had actually got under Arms & Were dispersed had been made a Day or two before, tho' not so Circumstantial.

Upon hearing the first I gave Orders to four Captains to Disarm all suspected Persons in their respective Companies; and on the second Information ordered a trusty officer with a Party of Men immediately to Sieze three of the Ringleaders & bring them well tied before Justice to be dealt with as the Law directs; and as soon as that can be done two Captains with 25 Men each are to march privately into that settlement by different Routes & at the same Instant to begin and Disarm the whole & the Arms when taken I have ordered to be deposited at the Lead Mines[1] where a Guard of Men ought to be kept, & as I have not a doubt

---

[1] For this location and the fort located there see *Dunmore's War*, 52, note 90.

but the destruction of that Place will be attempted on the first breaking out of the Tories. But as [we] have no Prison in this County & but an Indifferent one in Botetourt nor have we any Sherif here at present, our Sherif being deprived of his Office the other Day for not giving security for the Collection I am really at a loss to know what to do with any of these Ringleaders or others that may be taken in the Course of this Conspiracy; and the rather as our Informer will not for the above reasons suffer his name to be used nor can he appear against the Prisoners. So that I am doubtful the Magistrates will be obliged to send some of those well known Villians to the Prison in Augusta without further Evidence or Form, of Trial untill the impending storm blows over or untill some other Evidence may providentially be discovered which I hope may be the Case as I have ordered the strictest search to be made for Papers & the attack to be made with the greatest secrecy that they may be surprized be[fore] the[y] Suspect any Danger or Discovery being made of their infernal Schemes.

I thought is [sic] my Duty to give your Excellency this early Information by Express to beg that you will be pleased to give me such Instructions and Advice herein [as] may most effectually bend to the suppression of this daring & treasonable Conspiracy; as also what steps are to be taken for the Defence of the Frontiers against the Savages should they Disturb us this spring & whether it would not be necessary to order out some good Woodsmen in the mean Time as Scouts.

I am your Excellency's most Obed[t] & very hble serv[t]

W. P.

[Endorsed:] L[r] to the Gov[r]   Mar 1780

[Col. William Preston's account of Loyalist plot. 5QQ27. Autograph draft.]

The Reports against the Nonjurors or those who have not taken the Oath of Allegience to the State in this County, and some others, are, That a Plot or Conspiracy has been forming for near a twelve month Past, in which John Griffith has been very active, to disarm the Friends to the Country & kill some. To destroy the Lead Mines.—To Join the Indians & with them to burn Destroy & cut their Way to the English Army and assist them in reducing the Country.—That s[d] Griffith has administered the Oath of allegience to King George, to a Number of People, who also took an Oath of Secrecy not to discover the Plot.—That it is beleived from many Circumstances and Information that many People in this Neighbourhood, Sinking Creek[1] & other Places are Joined herein.—That said Griffith was in the Neighbourhood, about the 21st or twenty eighth of Feby to administer an Oath to those People, several of whom met him; & knowing the Man & not finding him properly authorized for that Purpose declined taking it at that Time, That Griffith assured them he would return to them by the 28th or 29th of March with one Col Robinson[2] from the British Army properly Authorized to Administer the Oath, to enroll their Names, to promise each man 2/6 sterling a Day from that Time and 450 acres of Land to clear of Quit Rents 21 years & that the Roll of their Names should be sent to the King and Parliament of England that it might be known what Friends they had here.—That the People on Sinking Creek and down the River had due notice hereof, many of whom came, on various pretences & that some took the Oath, others refused as Robison did not come in according to promise, and only Griffith appeared; who being alarmed by a Report that men were raising to take him made off & the People who had attended dispersed for that Time. That frequent meetings and Consultations are held privately on this Subject.

These are the principal Reports or Informations that I have had. I might mention names who were active herein; but as I hope every one will endeavour to disprove the same generally: and as I am desirous to have the Matter amicably Settled and full assurance given of the Peacable intentions of the People I do not incline to descend to further particulars. Should I do so, many things might be added.

[*Endorsed:*] Charge vs. Nonjurors

[1] For the location of this stream see *Wis. Hist. Colls.*, XXIII, 75, note 1.
[2] This officer may have been the South Carolina Loyalist, Joseph Robinson, who in 1775 was repulsed when attacking the Whig forces at Fort Ninety-six. After the fall of Charleston in May, 1780 Robinson received a British commission and served during the succeeding summer in Ferguson's brigade.

ARTILLERY ORDERED TO FORT PITT

[Richard Peters to Gen. George Washington. Washington Papers. A. L. S.]

SIR: WAR OFFICE March 4, 1780

We beg to apologize for omitting the Acknowledgment of your Excellency's Favour of the 8th of Feby relative to the Ordnance & Stores to be lodged at Fort Pitt. Immediately on receipt of that Letter Orders were given for the provision of the Articles which are now ready to proceed when the roads will admit

If any offensive Operations are intended in that Quarter we wish to be favoured with the earliest Intelligence of them. We have directed a retrenchment in the Quarter Master's Department of a vast Number of hired Horses which have been kept at a most enormous Expence in Berkley Virginia. It will therefore be necessary to have the Information requested that if any Enterprize is intended Orders may be given for providing Horses as well as other necessary Matters in due Season. From the Intelligence received from Genl Schuyler relative to Indian Affairs it should seem that the Savages are disposed for Peace. But it may notwithstanding be proper to prepare for War as they are artful & perfidious.

We have the Honour to be with the greatest Esteem & Respect Your very obedt Servant

RICHARD PETERS By Order

HIS EXCELLENCY GENL WASHINGTON

MONONGALIA MILITIA

[Summary of a letter of Col. Daniel Brodhead, Headquarters, Pittsburgh, Mar. 11, 1780, to Col. John Evans.[1] Printed in *Pa. Archives*, XII, 210.]

Men raised without Brodhead's consent must be paid and subsisted by local authorities. Petty posts useless. No apparent danger.

[1] For Col. John Evans of Monongalia County see *Rev. Upper Ohio*, 234, note 78.

PERMISSION FOR OFFENSIVE OPERATIONS

[Gen. George Washington to Col. Daniel Brodhead. 3H166–69. Transcript.]

HEAD QUARTERS, MORRIS TOWN, 14th March, 1780.

DEAR SIR:
I have rec^d your favor of the 11th ult^o. You will, I imagine, long before this time, have received mine of the 4th January, which acknowledges yours of the 10th & 22^d Novem^r & 13th December. What I hinted in that letter, respecting an expedition against the Natchez & the English settlements upon the Mississippi, is now at an end, the Spaniards having already possessed those posts.

From the accounts which you have received of the enemy's force at Detroit, and my ideas of yours (having rec^d no late returns) it is evident that you can make no attempt at that place: But if you think yourself competent to an excursion against any of the hostile tribes of Indians, you are at liberty, as I have mentioned in some of my former letters, to undertake it.

In your next return be pleased to let me know the different terms of service of your own Regiment, & of the 9th Virginia—& let the returns of the late Rawlin's & the independent companies, not only specify the terms of service, but to what States the men, who compose them, belong. This is necessary to enable me to give the States credit for their men serving in detached corps.

I had, upon the 8th February, desired the Board of War to prepare a certain quantity of ordinance & stores for Fort Pitt, & recommended to them, to endeavor to send them up while the snow was on the ground, if they should be of opinion that it would be possible to pass the mountains at that season. I imagine it was deemed impracticable, as they wrote me on the 4th instant, that the stores were ready, & would go off as soon as the roads would permit. I have directed General Knox to detach an officer of artillery with a proper number of men for the duty of the Garrison of Fort Pitt.

I am under the necessity of disapproving the sentence against Lt. Gordon on account of the irregular constitution of the Court. A general Court Martial can only be held by order of the Commander-in-Chief- or, of a General Officer commanding a separate department, or in any one of the States. But that justice may be duly administered, I enclose a power, by which Mr Gordon may be brought to a new trial, as may any other prisoners, whose cases may require a General Court. I return the former proceedings.

My apprehensions that the boats would be lost, if they were suffered to be taken into employ, for common purposes, was the reason of my directing them to be carefully laid up, until wanted. And I perceive by your letter, that my fears were not groundless. The expense of the materials for boat-building, & the wages of proper workmen are at this time so enormous, that, as there is little or no prospect of any offensive operations, I shall not give orders for the number of carpenters you mention. The boats that have been saved, are, I imagine, more than sufficient for the purposes of transporting stores, &c. from post to post. I have desired the Board of War to direct a few armourers to be sent up.

In one of your former letters you expressed a wish of coming down the country to visit your family. Upon the prospect of matters at that time, I did not think it expedient for you to leave the post: But I think in the present situation of affairs to the westward, you may take an opportunity of doing it. You will be the best judge of the matter when this gets to your hands, & will determine upon the propriety of the measure from circumstances. I take it for granted that Col° Gibson will remain at the post should you come down, as I would not chuse that a place of such consequence should be entrusted to an officer of inferior rank. I am with great regard, dear Sir, your most humb^le Servt,

G° WASHINGTON.

A general Court Martial whereof Colonel John Gibson is President to sit at Fort Pitt on Monday the 5th day of June for the trial of all persons who may be brought before them.

Given at Head Quarters at Morristown, this 17th day of March, 1780.

G° WASHINGTON.

[Endorsed:] (Rec^d 22^d Ap^r 1780.)

OFFICER REQUESTS TRANSFER

[Col. Richard Campbell to Gen. George Washington. Washington Papers. A. L. S.]

PITTSBURGH March the 16th 1780

MAY PLEASE YOUR EXCELLENCY:

I take the Liberty to Inform you the Strength & Circumstance Of the 9th Virg^a Reig^t in the Western Department as I now Command in the absence of Co^l John Gibson.

The Strength of the Reigement at this Time is not more than Two Hundred men for within this Fifteen days I have discharged a Hundred men that was Entitled to their Discharges & Only Enlisted for three years & their Times being Exp[i]red that they Engaged for.

But the Remainder of the Reig^t is for During the War, but I Can assure your Excellency from the Depre[cia]ation Of the money & the Encouriagement of Settling the Kentucky Lands that it is impossible to Recruit our Reigement In this Cuntery, Therefore i Should wish to have the Reigem^t from this quarter if your Excellency Thought Proper, for Reasons if We are Continued in this Department it will not be in Our Powers to Recruit any Part of our Reig^t & there are Several Gentlemen in The Reig^t that would wish to have it in their Powers to make Themselves Acquainted with Millitary Decepline, & the Rules of the Armey which is not in their Powers when they are Kept in The Woods & Stationed at Diff[er]a[n]t Posts.

I Can Assure your Excellency that I think it would Be for the Good of the Reig^t & the Service to have them Removed from here, for the Reig^t have been Raised in this Countery & thus have So many Acquaintances & the Opening for Setteling the New Cuntery that they are Constantly Deserting.

But as Colon^l John Gibson Command^s the Reig^t and his Connections in this Country i make no doubt but he would wish the Reig^t Continnued in this Department, But I Can assure your Excellency it is the wish of the Officers to be Releave'd if it would meet with Your Approbation.

If your Excellency thinks Proper to Con[t]inue the Reig^t in this Department, I will thank your Excellency for leave to Join Some Other Coare for the Ensuing Campeign Or Some Other Command as The Reig^t is but Small & a Sufficient Number of

Officers To the Reigiment & Two Field Officers Besides myself, when I Stept forth in the Armey it was my determination to Render my Cuntry Ever[y] Service, In my Power & wish to be allways where i Could take an Active Part, & as there has Been Officers Ordered from Differant Reig^{ts} To Command Troops to the Southward I Should be Glad to meet with the Same Indulgance if Your Excellency Thought Proper I am Sensible your Excellency is not Unacquainted with my Charrictor While with the Meine Armey therefore I Will not Trouble you Any Further & hope to Receive Your Excellencyes Answer.

I Have the Hon^r to be Your Most Obedient & Hble Servant
RICHARD CAMPBELL Lt Colo^l 9th Virg^a Reigem^t
On Publick Service His EXCELLENCY GENERAL WASHINGTON Commander in Chief Of the Amarican Armey.

INDIAN RAIDS BEGIN

[Summary of a letter of Col. Daniel Brodhead, Fort Pitt, Mar. 18, 1780, to Gen. George Washington. Printed in Sparks, *Corr. of Amer. Rev.*, II, 416–17.]

Savages have begun hostilities. Last Sunday killed five men at a sugar camp on Raccoon Creek; three girls and three lads taken prisoners.[1] Delawares thought to have done this; their hostility would greatly distress the settlements. Return of troops. Col. George Rogers Clark writes from the Illinois proposing to coöperate in an expedition. More regulars needed.

[Summary of a letter of Col. Daniel Brodhead, Headquarters, Mar. 18, 1780, to Capt. Samuel Brady. Printed in *Pa. Archives*, XII, 213.]

Directs pack-horse train to bring stores; to return via the Glade road as the old road may be dangerous.[2] Attack on Raccoon Creek, two men[3] of his regiment killed.

[1] The captives were George and Elizabeth Foulks, Lewis and Mary Tucker, and James and Elizabeth Turner. See the reminiscences, *post*, 151–54. The captors were not Delawares, but Wyandot from Sandusky.

[2] The "old road" was the regular Pennsylvania thoroughfare through Ligonier and Hannastown direct to Fort Pitt. It was built by Gen. John Forbes on his expedition in 1758 to capture Fort Duquesne. The Glade road was the one from the Turkey Foot, or three forks of Youghiogheny River, northwest to Fort Pitt. See map in *Frontier Defense*, frontispiece.

[3] The two men of the Eighth Pennsylvania Regiment who were killed were named Deaver. See Draper Mss., 19S278.

FRONTIER RETREAT

[Summary of a letter of Col. Daniel Brodhead, Fort Pitt, Mar. 18, 1780, to Richard Peters. Printed in *ibid.*, 211-12.][1]

Raiders on Raccoon Creek supposed to be Delawares. Need of cannon and military stores; no tents at hand; if not of good material militia will cut them up for hunting shirts. Convoy of cloth. Commissary of forage. Wishes Congress would send commissions for some of the Delaware chiefs.

THE CAPTURED CHILDREN

[Reminiscences of Mrs. Cline, daughter of George Foulks.[2] 16S289-90.]

George Foulk's father, John Foulks, dropped dead while plowing in the fall of 1779, & then his widow shortly after married one Tucker, father of Lewis Tucker.[3]

At the sugar camp (perhaps some 5 miles off from their home, & on Raccoon waters) Indians came in a moonlight night: Elizabeth Foulks asked her brother George to go & get some sugar water to make some sassafras tea for supper—he went & said he could fine [sic] none at the first tree—she wished him to go to another, pointing to one, but he got some at a nearer tree, & the Indians afterwards said if he had gone to the tree his sister had directed him to go, some of the Indians were behind it, & would have had to [have] tomahawked him. During the evening the

[1] See also similar letters of the same date from Brodhead to Pres. Joseph Reed and to Capt. Thomas McIntyre, in *Pa. Archives*, VIII, 140; *id.*, XII, 212-13.

[2] George Foulks was born in 1769 at Leesburgh, Va. His family removed to the neighborhood of Pittsburgh two or three years before he was captured. After being taken to the Indian towns George remained among them for about twelve years. He escaped in the summer of 1791 or 1792, and reached the Ohio alone, where he was ferried across by two young girls, one of whom, Catherine Ullery, afterwards became his wife. Foulks joined the spy service and was often out under Brady, his knowledge of Indian languages and customs making him especially useful. After Wayne's treaty in 1795, Foulks revisited his Indian captors upon the Sandusky. He was married Nov. 21, 1796, and settled the next spring on Little Beaver Creek in Beaver County, Pa. There he died July 10, 1840.

[3] Lewis Tucker returned from captivity in the same year as George Foulks. About the year 1793 he married Mary Turner and began farming in Washington County, Pa., but soon thereafter died, leaving no children.

dogs barked & made much fuss: John Foulks laid down in a large sugar trough with his gun, & had a dog with him; & when the Indians attacked, & rushed up, they tomahawked George on the top of his head but did not enter the skull, & made him senseless, & when he recovered his senses, he found himself before the fire with a hoppus string around his neck. Indians chased John Foulks, & he made off towards the Run, & his alarmed dog ran before & tripped him & threw him, so the Indians overtook & tomahawked him. It was about eleven o'clock at night—four were killed. There were seven Indians of the party; they had brought some horses, & left them over the Ohio: when they reached there, the girls had their gowns cut off, so as to travel better, & their shoes were thrown into the Ohio, & moccasins were given them, which the Indians had brought along. There were horses enough for each of the girls to ride, & Elizabeth Foulks would sometimes put her little wounded brother on in her place, but the Indians would soon drag him off, & make him walk—weak & feeble from the loss of blood. It was the second or third day after being taken before his wound was dressed. On the return trip to their towns, the Indians had but little to eat—a very scanty supply of dried venison; but when they reached the nearest Indian settlement at Old Town, & Snip's Town,[1] just south of Rome, Richland County, they there got plenty of homony, venison, & wild turkey's boiled in sugar water. Here his wound was dressed with slippery elm bark and bear's oil. As they were children, they did not have to run the gauntlet.

[Reminiscences of George F. Whitaker, son of Elizabeth Foulks.[2] 22S95-97.]

Miss Foulks was captured within a few miles of Pittsburg, with several other young people, in March [1780] while making

[1] This village belonged to a Shawnee chief whom the whites called Captain Snip.

[2] Elizabeth Foulks was eleven years old the Christmas before her capture. She never returned from among the Indians but married James Whitaker, a fellow captive for whom see *Frontier Defense*, 254, note 9. After the death of her husband in 1806, Elizabeth Foulks Whitaker lived on the west bank of Sandusky River, below Fremont, Ohio. In the Indian treaty of 1817 she was granted a reserve of 1,280 acres at this place, and there she died in May, 1831. These facts were obtained from her son, George Foulks Whitaker, who in 1868 resided at Hannibal, Mo. See Draper Mss., 22S95.

maple sugar. She had a brother killed at the time—& another, George, taken. Several families would join in sugar making, & the young men would go of nights to guard them.

Among the other captives were Polly,[1] John & Lewis Tucker—the latter perhaps a dozen or fourteen years old. When they reached the Tuscarawas it was high, & the Indians feared they would not be able to get the children over safely, as they had no canoe. So they obtained a dry sapling, & fastened the children, boys & girls to it, & placed it in the stream to float over, with their heads above the water's surface, & the Indians swimming & pushing it over.

Lewis Tucker was bold & saucy to the Indians—so much so, that the other prisoners were afraid the Indians would kill him. But they seemed to admire his spirit & fearlessness. Don't know when or how he got away—nor what became of him.

*　　*　　*　　*　　*　　*　　*　　*

There were nineteen of the party of Wyandotts who captured the sugar makers—& Half King was the leader; & it was in Half King's family that Elizabeth Foulks lived, as her son believes.

[Reminiscences of John McCormick, son of Elizabeth Turner.[2]　17S201-2.]

[His mother] was Elizabeth Turner, daughter of Wm Turner, with Elizabeth Foulks & Nancy McKeever[3] (don't know what

---

[1] Mary (Polly) Tucker married during her captivity an elderly Frenchman named Wine. After Wayne's treaty in 1795 she and her husband returned to her father's home in Pennsylvania. There her husband died in 1798. She survived him several years. See *ibid.*, 16S277.

[2] Elizabeth Turner was kept as a prisoner in Half King's family and in 1782 was obliged to witness the torture and death of Col. William Crawford. About the year 1785 she married Alexander McCormick, for whom see *Wis. Hist. Colls.*, XXIII, 246, note 2. Soon after her marriage she visited her family in Pennsylvania, where she found that her father had died, while her mother's death occurred during her visit. Mrs. McCormick then returned to her home on the Maumee Rapids where in 1790 her son, John, was born. After Wayne's victory in 1794 the McCormick family withdrew from the Maumee and in 1796 settled at Colchester, Essex County, Ontario. There Mrs. McCormick died on June 6, 1838. John served with the British in the War of 1812. He personally knew Tecumseh and the famous chiefs of his day. In 1863 Dr. Draper visited him at Colchester and secured this interview.

[3] McCormick's memory is at fault in this instance, for the third of three captured girls was Polly Tucker.

became of her)—a young youth Foulks, & perhaps a young M⁰-Keever also taken. George Turner, a young man grown, was killed in camp, & his younger brother William also—perhaps five killed altogether.

There were nine Indians of the party, who took them—had been watching all the previous Saturday afternoon. When the whites first went there to make sugar, took out Kettles &^{c} with teams, & some of the young colts strayed away from their dams, & remained at camp, when the teams returned—colts were caught & tied up; & the young men returned on Saturday for the colts, intending to return home the next day—were playing, jumping, & shooting at a mark, during Saturday afternoon, which rather intimidated the Indians. The Indians took the colts & horses. Three of the Old [Half] King's sons were along.

COUNTY OFFICERS CALLED TO COUNCIL

[Col. Daniel Brodhead to Col. David Shepherd. 1SS197. A. L. S.]

HEAD QUARTERS FORT PITT March 21st 1780

DEAR SIR:

The savages having begun their Depredations earlier than (considering the season) could reasonably have been expected, & before a reinforcement of Regulars could possibly arrive from the main Army. I find it indispensably necessary to take the advice of the Lieutenants of Counties in this part of the Department in order to establish either some general defensive plan, or to consult & fix upon some well calculated offensive operations against one or more of the hostile Tribes, which latter will in my opinion prove the most eligible, and therefore I request you will meet the Lieutenants of the other Counties at my quarters on the first day of next month without fail, as nothing but a hearty concurrence of the Counties can at present enable me to give any considerable protection to the Frontier.

I have the honor to be Dear sir with due respect your most obed^t serv^t

DANIEL BRODHEAD Col⁰ command^g W. D.

COL⁰ DAVID SHEPHARD

LOYALISTS AND RAIDS IN VIRGINIA

[Summary of a letter of Gov. Thomas Jefferson, Williamsburg, Mar. 21, 1780, to Col. William Preston. 5QQ24. Printed in *Ill. Hist. Colls.*, VIII, 402-4.]

Disaffected persons have no more grievances than all feel in common; are subject to pains of law, and should be brought to trial; may be removed from county if absolutely necessary; prefer militia guards to keep them safe. If evidence insufficient to convict of treason, a capital crime, try for misprision of treason punishable by a fine and imprisonment. Lead mines must be protected at all hazards. No probability of Indian disturbance. Coöperate with Colonel Clark in keeping peace with them.

[Maj. John Taylor[1] to Col. William Preston. 5QQ26. A. L. S.]

SIR:
 The 18th Instant the Indians was In this Neighbourhood and Fell in at James Roark's[2] where they Scalped seven of his Children And his wife They are all Dead only one Girl They took Seven Head of Horses Five of which was the property of Wm Patterson. This part of y^r County is In a scene of Confusion And I make no doubt but the Country will Break up without they Can Get Some Assistance, I am as yet Living at home but Capt Maxwell's[3] Comp^y are Chiefly Gathered together in Small Parties, Corn is very Scarce Here but if a few men Could be raised I think they Could be found. Sir if you have Resigned y^r Commission Pray let the County Lieu^t Have this Letter or a few lines from y^r Self which I think will Answer a better End.

[1] For a sketch of this officer see *Dunmore's War*, 45, note 80.
[2] Roark's house was probably at or near Roark's Gap in Tazewell County, Va., near what is now known as Gap Store. An Indian trail led across Indian Ridge, up the Dry Fork of Big Sandy, and approached Clinch River at this gap. The course of this trail indicates that the raiders were northern Indians.
[3] Capt. James Maxwell lived near the modern Maxwell in Tazewell County. In 1782 two of his daughters were killed and scalped. Within a month afterwards Captain Maxwell, following another band of marauding Indians, was shot and instantly killed at what is now known as Maxwell's Gap in Tug Ridge.

I expected a few lines from you By Capt Moor[1] but Dont hear of any   My family is In Health As I hope yours are and I am Sir, y^r Most Hum^{le} Srt.

JN° TAYLOR

HEAD CLINCH 23 March 1780
C B the Murder was Commited In seven miles of here

DELAWARES SUSPECTED

[Summary of a letter of Col. Daniel Brodhead, Headquarters, Pittsburgh, Mar. 22, 1780, to Rev. David Zeisberger. Printed in *Pa. Archives*, XII, 214–15.]

Delawares strongly suspected of murder of five men, and capture of six children upon Raccoon Creek; no news from missionaries is ominous; has almost resolved on offensive operations. Requests that he send word whether the tribe is hostile or not merely by "yes" or "no."

RECRUIT FOR CLARK

[Col. Richard Campbell to Col. George Rogers Clark. 50J22. A. L. S.]

PITTSBURGH March ye 29th 1780

DEAR SIR:

This will be Handed you By Captn Harrison who was Formerly a Captain in my Reig^t & For Reasons he has Resigned. But I Can assure you he is a Gentleman of Charactor & has Allways Supported The Charrector of a Good & Brave Officer & Wishes to join you and any thing you Can Serve him in   I would thank

---

[1] This officer was probably Capt. James Moore. His father, James, was a Scotch-Irish emigrant, who settled in Rockbridge County not far from Staunton. There the younger James grew up, married Martha Poage, and in 1772 removed to Abb's Valley in the present Tazewell County, Va. The neighborhood forted at Captain Moore's during Dunmore's War, when Daniel Boone was militia officer in charge. During the early years of the Revolution Moore was a captain of militia. In 1781 he joined General Greene's army and took part in the battle of Guilford Court House. In 1784 the valley in which he lived was raided, and one of his sons was captured. In 1786, during another raid, the Shawnee Indians killed Captain Moore and took his wife and children prisoners.

you to Give him your Interest I am Sensible you Will find him Worthy of your notice—
The News of this Place I Refer you to the Bearer—I Should be happy to hear from you please to Except of my wishes for your well fare—

RICH^D CAMPBELL Lieu^t Col^o 9 Virg^a Reig^t

COLONEL GEORGE ROGERS CLARK in the Elyonie Country p^r Favour of Capt Benjamin Harrison.

DELAWARES LOYAL

[Delawares to Col. Daniel Brodhead. 1H128. In handwriting of Heckewelder.]

COOSHOCKUNG March ye 30th 1780.

Walawpachtschischen Mr Gerrard and the Council of Cooshockung to Co^l Brodhead and Col. John Henry[1] as follows.

BROTHERS:
Listen now to what I shall say unto [you]. I can now inform You as a fact who it was that Murdered Your Chilldren, (our Brothren) at Raccoon Creeck. Some time ago I had heard that bad People were gone past towards you, but knew not the truth. Now I assure You that it was done by a party of Mingoes and Monsys together, who first took a great numner of Skins scaffled in the Woods belonging to Pakeelend and others of our People, these Skins they first destroyed and took some of the best along. I can assure You that neither Capt Pipe nor any of his Men has had a hand in this Murder.

Brothers: While I am sitting in my House in peace, I am at once surprised to see three Warriors at the head of a large party carrying Your Flesh and Blood by here. It makes me indeed sorry to see it for I always remember that I and You are one. I and You have agreed together that We always will aquaint one another of any such thing we hear, this I also am determined to do at all times. These three Warriors were first the Mingo Hawtatscheek. Neeshawsh a Mohican. Washenaws. a Monsy. These three carryed 20 Chilldren and 3 grown People Prissonners past here Yesterday.

[1] This was the adopted name of Capt. John Killbuck, taken to honor a prominent Pennsylvanian. See Pennsylvania Historical Society, *Bulletin*, I, No. 12, 151.

Brother: I desire You to let me only know when You are ready to march that I may send a few Men to You in time, who shall go with You wherever you go. I also desire You to march as quick as possible, let nothing hinder You from doing this.

2 branches of Wampum.

Brother: You told me to call my friends from Wabash here, I accordingly have sent to them, and only wait to see them back again, and this shall be the last time I speak to any of the bad People. I lay this down and will have no more to say unto any of those foolish Nations, or People, to whom I have spoke so often in vain.

Brother: Again my Messengers are gone off to Gehnhenshecan where Wingenund is to hurry those to Cooshachking as quick as possible. This is all that I am waiting for yet.

Brother: Now I only wait for those I have sent for, and for nobody else for then when they are here all which are Your friends I shall let You know that You may not be at a loss when you march for knowing Your friends from You Enemies

Brother: What You have always told me namely to gather all our friends together here at Cooshacking, that now will soon be done, We shall be together, and then You may look on all those whom You see back towards the lake of this place as Your Enemies be they who they will, and even if You meet with some of my Nation You may remember that they belong no more to me.

Brother: I hear that Pemowagen the half King head of the Wyondotts on this Side of the Lake, is gone himself out to War against You.

Brother: I have before informed You how the back Nations were, and that they were good inclined. I have not at present heard any thing to the contrary, but such as is good.

Brother: This is all what I can tell You, I know of nobody that is striking You but those who live on Unamy Sepu,[1] and from that towards the Lakes, all those that live beyond Us here to that River on this Side of the Lake or those who are striking You.

6 branches of Wampum.

Brother: This what I have told You now is indeed the truth. I had indeed heard a good while ago that the bad People intended to strike You as soon as the ground would be bare. I also told Geshahsee to inform You of it, but it seems he never told You of it.

---

[1] This is the Indian name for the river now known as the Maumee.

FRONTIER RETREAT 159

WELAWPACHTSCHIECHEN

Monsi Gerrard desires his Brother Col. Brodhead and Gelelemend also to look on all the above as the real truth, as he knows it to be as it is mentioned herein.

I am Your friend and Brother

GERRARD

Addressed: To Col Daniel Brodhead Comandt W. Departm^t at Pittsburgh by Express from Cooshokung.

[Extract of a letter of Rev. John Heckewelder to Col. Daniel Brodhead. Washington Papers. Contemporary transcript.]

COOCHOCKING March 30th 1780

We have heard nothing at all this whole winter what the Enemy are about: The Snow being so deep & the weather so continually cold has I suppose prevented this, but this day I am informed that three young fellows, two Delawares & one Wyandott have turned back from a body of warriors consisting of Twenty six men. They inform that five or six Companies of warriors are gone out, two parties of Wyandotts towards Beaver Creek & the others down this River—The Half King it appears is at the head of one of the parties & Neeshawsh (a Mohicon) heads a party of Muncies & Delawares

It is also reported here this day that the Shawanese & others are gone to fight with the Army at the *Big Bone Lick*, likewise that the Wabash Indians are all gone to war.

We here intend to leave this place entirely in about two weeks & move nearer to Gnadenhutten.[1]

I am with sincere regard your most Obed^t Hbl^e Servt

JOHN HACKENWELDER

An Extract[2]

[1] For this locality see *Rev. Upper Ohio*, 45, note 71.
[2] The correct date of this letter is Mar. 30 (not Mar. 20), 1780. See *Calendar of Correspondence of George Washington with his Officers* (Washington, 1915), 1280. Brodhead enclosed this letter in his to Washington of April 24.

EMIGRANTS ATTACKED

[Capt. William Harrod to Mrs. Amelia Harrod.[1] 4NN79. A. L. S.]

LOVING WIFE:
                              FORT HENRY March ye 30th [1780][2]

I have the Disagreable News to Inform you off that on Monday Morning th 27th I went a shore at Fishing Creek with Adam Rowe[3] and Isaac Perry in a Canoe for some Iron ware of Rows the Boats Not stopping which was to overtake but after we had Got Near Rows house Rowe & Perry was Fired upon By Five or Six Indians and perry was killed as I was Some Distance from them when they was fired on I made toward the the Firing and met Rowe after he had made his Escape the Indians being between us and our Canoe so that we Could [not] Get [to] the Boats again we were Obliged to Retreat up to this place being from Monday morning Till Tuesday in the after Noon before we got here I Intend yet to pursue my Jorney as there has a Number of Boats Arived here on their way to the Falls in which I shal go so no more at present by my kind Love to you and Remains Loving Husband Till Death

                                                  WIM HERROD
[To MRS. AMELIA HARROD, Muddy Creek]

---

[1] Amelia Stephens married William Harrod, Oct. 1, 1765, in Cumberland County, Pa. She died in April, 1793 at her home in Washington County, Pa.

[2] Note on original manuscript: "This was in Spring of 1780 as W^m. Harrod Jr. thinks. See his manuscript statement. Mem^o—By reference to Col. W^m. Fleming's journal for 1779 & '80, it appears that the 27th of March '80, came on Monday—hence that must have been the year—L. C. D."

[3] For the location of Fishing Creek see *Rev. Upper Ohio*, 207, note 51. Adam Rowe was in garrison at Grave Creek Fort in 1776, and that year lost two sons by an Indian raid. *Ibid.*, 220, 225. The son of Capt. William Harrod told Dr. Draper many additional details of the skirmish herein narrated. See Draper Mss., 37J170–71.

DELAWARES LOYAL

[Rev. David Zeisberger to Col. Daniel Brodhead. Washington Papers. Contemporary transcript.]

TUPAKING[1] April 2nd 1780

DEAR SIR:
I have been very much disappointed in sending an answer to your several letters you wrote me. This place is quite out of the way, no Indians which are going to the Fort pass by here & though I wrote to Mr Edwards[2] at Gnadenhutten several times to let me know of an opportunity but all in vain. In Feby some of our people was on the way with them, I had also wrote, but after travelling a day & half they turned back because of the deep snow they met with.

In your letter of the 26th Novr last you desired me to procure you some intelligence from over the Lake, but was not in my power to do & much less now as I live such a distance from Coochocking where I might perhaps bring it about one way or other. Joshua intended to go but hard winter & deep snow

---

[1] Tupaking was the Indian name for the Moravian village of Schönbrunn, for whose location and history see *Rev. Upper Ohio*, 45, note 71. Zeisberger, in 1779, removed his mission from Lichtenau, two miles below Coshocton, to Schönbrunn, which was forty miles farther up the Tuscarawas. Later in the same year he built New Schönbrunn on the west bank of the stream, which was finished and occupied in December, 1779. This latter village was abandoned in 1781.

[2] William Edwards, a Moravian missionary, was sent in the fall of 1776, from Bethlehem, Pa., to reënforce the mission on the Muskingum. G. H. Loskiel, *History of the Mission of the United Brethren* (London, 1794), III, 115. Stationed first at Lichtenau, in the summer of 1779 Edwards was placed in charge of Gnadenhütten, where he remained until 1781, when the Moravians were carried captive to Sandusky. With the other missionaries he visited Detroit early in 1782, and in July of that year settled the mission of New Gnadenhütten in St. Clair County, Mich. In 1785 Edwards visited Pittsburgh to arrange for a removal of the mission to American territory. Having received assurances of protection, the Moravians, in the summer of 1786, made a settlement on the Cuyahoga River; later, because of Indian hostilities, they crossed to Canada and settled at Fairfield on the Thames. Thence in 1798, Heckewelder and Edwards brought their flock to their first location on the Tuscarawas, and built the mission village of Goshen. At this time Edwards was seventy-four years old, and soon afterwards he died, worn with years of faithful service for his Indian neophytes. His grave is still to be seen in the Indian cemetery at Goshen, Ohio. *Ohio Archæological and Historical Publications*, 1909, 159.

coming on he dropped it—But hearing that a white man who was a prisoner among the Wyandotts, & who was well acquainted as I was told with all the particulars at Detroit went by Gnadenhutten for the Fort last winter I thought he could & would give you more sufficient intelligence than any Indian could procure because Indians have no knowledge about such matters; and I think it would be of very little service to send an Indian on such an errand who is a stranger to the place. In your 2nd letter of Feby 10th you proposed that our Indians might move nearer to the Fort; Sir, this indeed would not only be very hard & difficult, but also impossible for us to undertake now except our people would leave behind all what they have, for they are not like the rest of the Indians who can take their whole estate on their backs & go where they please & tho' they might go round by water we would not be able to procure such a number of Canoes as it would require—Our people have been travelling & moving from one place to another till we at last came to this place where we hoped to remain in possession of our settlements & enjoy the fruit of our labour at least for a good many years. I dare not think about moving nor even propose it to our people for it would quite discourage them unless there was great necessity—therefore pray Sir, let us remain in possession of our settlements; Have we held it out so long? I hope with the help of God we shall get over until peace is restored again. Neither warriors nor other Indians come to our towns now because it is out of their way & we live very quiet.

Of the murder committed on Racoon Creek I heard nothing before I received your letter About eight days before we heard of a company of warriors having been tracked who came from towards the Wyandott towns, but did not learn what Indians they were, they must either be Mingoes, Muncies or of Wyandaughland's Gang.[1] I have not heard of any hostile thoughts from the Coochocking Indians yet, & if I should perceive anything of that kind I would give you intelligence by express.

But yesterday we heard that a party of warriors amongst which was the well known Muncy Washnaws have attacked a boat in the River, killed three men & have taken twenty one men, women & children prisoners & likewise the whole Boat.[2] No

[1] For a sketch of this hostile chief, usually known as Wyondochella, see *Wis. Hist. Colls.*, XXIII, 214, note 1.

[2] This was the boat in which the Malott family was emigrating. See succeeding document.

doubt this action will encourage them to do more mischief. I am much oblidged for sending me the three packets of letters, & likewise for communicating the agreeable news contained in your letter. Those of our people which lived yet nigh Coochocking are all moving up this way & in a few days more they will be all gone from thence

I am with great esteem Dr Sir your most Hbl^e Servt
DAVID ZEISBERGER

P. S. After I wrote the above I had more full intelligence— the murder on Racoon Creek was committed by the Wyandotts & the other on the Big River by the Muncies, which is a true account.

MALOTT FAMILY CAPTURED

[Reminiscences of Mrs. Predeaux Girty.[1] 17S193–94.]

Mr Joseph Malott[2] (father of Mrs Girty) had started from Maryland with his family to migrate to Kentucky. On the Monongahela united with a Mr Reynolds & got two boats— Mr Malott (of French descent) had the cattle & horses placed in one, & the families in the other, Reynolds having charge of this boat— & Mr Malott of the stock boat. They descended the river & somewhere on the Ohio in March (ab^t 1778 [1780]) while near shore in a bend or elbow of the river, concealed Indians fired, killed Reynolds, a small child, & captured the family boat & about twenty prisoners altogether. There were Ralph Nailor & one Dowler, young men, & a Mr Hardin[3] & wife whose child

[1] Predeaux, son of Simon Girty and his wife, Catherine Malott, was born Oct. 20, 1797. He lived most of his life in Canada, where he was esteemed as a man of probity and honor. He died at Dayton, Ohio, in January, 1853. His wife, who was born in St. Louis, Jan 3, 1799, was residing in 1863 with her son, Thomas Girty, at Gosfield, Can. There Dr. Draper visited her and secured these reminiscences.

[2] Joseph (other members of the Malott family speak of him as Peter or Theodore) Malott escaped to Louisville in his boat. Supposing his family to be dead, he returned to Maryland and there married again. His son, Peter, some time afterwards visited his father. None of the other captive Malotts ever returned to their former home. Draper Mss., 20S204–7.

[3] John Hardin (not the same person as Lieut. John Hardin) was in the rear boat and was not captured. His cousins, Thomas and William Hardin, were in the leading boat, and also escaped. They afterwards settled in Kentucky. See *ibid.*, 13CC9–10; also *post*, 199–200.

was killed. Nailor said before giving up, he would have one shot, & shot & killed an Indian.¹ Mr Malott had his cue shot off, & an eye of one of his horses shot out; but finally escaped with his boat and stock. He & his wife had besides Catherine (afterwards Mrs Simon Girty) Theodore, Keziah, & Peter.—Keziah married Robert Forsyth, who died at St. Louis in Indian trade & agency.² Peter & Theodore settled in Canada, & left many descendants.

Mrs Reynolds had a black woman, & the Indians, by some freak, constrained the negro woman to put on the best of Mrs Reynolds' clothing, & made Mrs Reynolds act as her waiter.

Catherine Malott when taken was fourteen years old, & was four years & four months in captivity.

ALLEGHENY POSTS REGARRISONED

[Summary of a letter of Col. Daniel Brodhead, Headquarters, Pittsburgh, April 2, 1780, to Col. Archibald Lochry. Printed in *Pa. Archives*, XII, 215.]

Draft sixty militia for two months, one third to be posted at Fort Crawford, one third at Fort Armstrong, the remainder at forks of Blacklegs Creek.³ Regulars also ordered to Fort Armstrong; these arrangements should provide a sufficient protection; advise people to be on their guard.

¹ Nailor was at first condemned to death for having shot an Indian; his sentence was finally remitted in order to secure the large reward offered by the British for prisoners. Draper Mss., 20S205.

² Thomas, son of William Forsyth (for whom see *Wis. Hist. Colls.*, XXIII, 346, note 2), was born Dec. 5, 1771 at Detroit. While still young he entered the Indian trade, wintering several years on Saginaw Bay, and in 1798 on an island in the Mississippi near Quincy, Ill. In 1802 he formed a partnership with his half-brother, John Kinzie, for trade at Chicago and Peoria, and was occupied therewith until the War of 1812. In 1804 Forsyth married Keziah Malott. In April, 1812 he was appointed subagent of Indian affairs, and throughout the war rendered valuable services to the borderers of Illinois. In 1819 he was appointed agent for the Sauk and Fox Indians at Rock Island, where he remained until 1830. His wife died the preceding year, and after retiring from office Forsyth removed to St. Louis, where he died Oct. 29, 1833. See Dr. Draper's interview in 1868 with his son, Robert, in Draper Mss., 22S99–111.

³ For this location see *Wis. Hist. Colls.*, XXIII, 210, note 1. The occupation of this site was only temporary.

COÖPERATION WITH CLARK

[Summary of a letter of Col. Daniel Brodhead, Fort Pitt, April 4, 1780, to Col. George Rogers Clark. 50J24. A. L. S. Printed in *Ill. Hist. Colls.*, VIII, 408–9.]

Reply to Clark's of December 22 last. Proposals with regard to Detroit pleasing; has written the commander in chief. "I think it is probable that before next Winter I shall have the pleasure of taking you by the Hand somewhere upon the Waters of Lake Erie." Delawares still profess friendship, many villains among them; expedition against the Shawnee desirable. Spanish have taken Natches and Manchac. Capt John Rogers accompanied by Thomas Bentley[1] who lately escaped from Canada, takes this letter. Captain George's Returns. Deserters on lower river.

[Summary of a letter of Col. Daniel Brodhead, Headquarters, Pittsburgh, April 4, 1780, to Capt. John Rogers. Printed in *Pa. Archives*, XII, 217.]

Orders all public craft in private hands on Ohio and Mississippi to be seized. Deserters to be arrested; those who are penitent may receive pardon on return.

[1] Thomas Bentley, a merchant at Kaskaskia for some years before the Revolution, is thought to have suggested to Clark the invasion of Illinois. See *Ill. Hist. Colls.*, V, pp. xvi–xxv. Before Clark reached Kaskaskia, however, Bentley had been suspected of sympathy with the Americans, and had been sent under arrest to Canada. Thence he escaped during the winter of 1779–80. At the time this letter was written Bentley was on his return to the West. At Vincennes in July, 1780, he was attempting to safeguard his own position by giving surreptitious information both to Clark and to the commandant of Detroit. *Ibid.*, 168–73; Illinois Historical Society, *Transactions*, 1909, 112, note 1. In the summer of 1781 Bentley visited Virginia in order to collect money for the script he had purchased from the Illinois inhabitants. Sometime about July, 1783 he died, probably at Richmond.

DELAWARE COÖPERATION

[Col. Daniel Brodhead to the Delawares. 2H51. Letter Book.]

HEAD QR^s PITTSBURGH April 6th 1780
Mahingweegeesuch to the Delaware Council at Coochocking
BROTHERS:
I have received your favor of the 30th of last month & I thank you for the news contained in it—Your determination to send some of your warriors to join me is a fresh proof of the sincerity of your regard for you[r] american Brethren & it must convince the whole world of the wisdom of your Council. I hear with great pleasure that our friends will be collected together & that I shall know them Because I wish to shew every mark of regard to them & at the same time to destroy my Enemies—I cannot inform you certainly in how many nights I shall set out to Destroy the Enemy But you may rely upon my word that the time is near at hand & I desire you will immediately send as many of your young men to join mine as you intend shall go along with me. I have plenty of provisions & I want them to get well acquainted with my people by seeing them every day.

Brothers: I am only waiting to receive a letter from our great Warrior, but I am weary of sitting here & am now standing with my Tomhawk in my hand wherefore I request you will send me another letter immediately & inform me of the number of warriors you can furnish for an expedition.

Brothers: I have ordered some goods to be given to the messengers for their trouble
I remain your friend & Brother
MAHINGWEEGEESUCH

DANGER ON THE OHIO

[Gabriel Madison to William Madison.[1] 5ZZ73. A. L. S.]

MONONGALIA April 10th 1780

DEAR W^m:

I have Started John[2] of[f] to W^{ms} Burg for the Surveyors Comⁿ which I Could not get for him without his appearing there in person (how ye lad will make out I Cannot tell for he Drives on partly in ye Old Way). But let that be as it will it has taken all the money I Could spare to fitt him out for the trip Besides Given Richard[3] Orders to Draw on you for £300 to help out with his exspences which Ric^d is to Borrow from some One and you must by no means Refuse the Order in Case he should Draw one on you—I shall leave this place in a day or two for the falls—there is Certain Accounts Brought to pitt of the Indians taken 2 Boats and that they are very thick on the River the passage without great Care will be Daingerous.

the people is in great Confusion heare on Account the of [sic] Dissputed line and is Determined to Declare them Selves a Seperate State which will be Done before the Last of this Month[4] George Roohs is at the head of it

I am y^r Aff^t B^r

GAB^L MADISON

I shall rite to you by the first op^y from the falls if I g^t th^e

[Addressed:] To Mr William Madison, Botetourt

[1] For William Madison see *Wis. Hist. Colls.*, XXIII., 89, note 2. His brother Gabriel, born in Augusta County, served during the early years of the Revolution as captain of militia. About 1782 he emigrated to Kentucky and in the autumn of that year volunteered for Clark's expedition. In 1783 Gabriel Madison was magistrate of Lincoln County; in 1786 he held a similar office in Mercer County. In 1785 he married Miriam Lewis, and settled on a plantation in Jessamine County, where he died in 1804. His wife survived until 1845. They had seven children.

[2] For John Madison Jr. see *Frontier Defense*, 296, note 61.

[3] Richard Madison was commissioned lieutenant in the Augusta County militia on May 19, 1778. In 1781, as ensign of cavalry he aided in the defense of the state. When John Madison Sr. (for whom see *Dunmore's War*, 280, note 98) resigned his office as county clerk on Nov. 21, 1778, Richard was appointed in his father's stead, and he held the office until his death in February, 1781.

[4] This was the new state movement described by F. J. Turner in "Western State Making during the Revolutionary Era," in *American Historical Review*, I,

PREPARATIONS FOR AN EXPEDITION

[Summary of a letter of Col. Daniel Brodhead, Fort Pitt, April 10, 1780, to Gen. Horatio Gates. Printed in *Pa. Archives*, XII, 218.]

Encloses letters from Delawares and Moravian missionaries. Indians will harass frontier unless offensive operations are undertaken. These will require some provisions from below the mountains. Further purchases for this department forbidden. Last campaign Brodhead avoided calling out militia and encouraged industry; by August supplies can be drawn from this side of the mountains; expense of transportation saved. "The prisoners mentioned in the Indian's letter were taken out of some Craft going to the new settlements upon Kentuck a few miles below Capteening Creek."[1]

[Receipt of Capt. Benjamin Biggs. 1SS196. A. D. S.]

FORT HENRY April 11th 1780

Receivd of Coll David Shepherd sixteen pair of Shoes for the use of this Garrison Giving under my hand this Day

BENJ^N BIGGS Capt 9 V Reg^t

To COLL° DAVID SHEPERD.

[Col. Daniel Brodhead to Col. David Shepherd.[2] 1SS199. A. L. S.]

HEAD QUARTERS PITTSBURGH April 13th 1780.

DEAR SIR:

Inclosed I send you the Copy of a Letter just received from the Delaware Council of Coochocking and Extracts of Letters from

85–86. See also James Veech, *Monongahela of Old* (Pittsburgh, 1858–92), 257; Boyd Crumrine, *History of Washington County, Pennsylvania* (Philadelphia, 1882), 232; and document in the present volume, *post*, 410.

[1] For this location see *Frontier Defense*, 106, note 66.

[2] This was a circular letter to the neighboring county lieutenants. Those to Colonels Evans and Lochry are printed in *Pa. Archives*, XII, 219–20. That to Lochry includes a rebuke for the Westmoreland inhabitants who were trespassing on Indian lands.

the Reverend Missionaries Messrs Zeisberger & Hackenwelder, who live in the Delaware Towns and by whom I have hitherto been furnished with authentic Intelligence.

It remains to strike a home stroke against one of the hostile Nations and I conceive that a lasting tranquility will ensue to the Inhabitants of this Frontier. This I have in contemplation and expect the hearty concurrence & aid of the Country. Let industry be encouraged, let your Farmers have their spring Crops in the ground by the tenth of next Month and do you have seventy five Men with a proportionate number of officers rendevouzed at Fort Henry by the twenty second. Those with the number I expect from the other Counties will enable us to strike terror into the Hostile Western Nations. And as the Expedition will be rapid & of short duration it will be attended with very small inconvenience to the planters.—Encourage such as can afford it to take eight or ten days Provisions with them, for which they shall be paid out of the public funds.

Please to write me your opinion of this measure by the bearer.

I have the Honor to be very respectfully your most obed^t Servt

DANIEL BRODHEAD Colo. commandg WD.

COLO. DAVID SHEPERD

[Summary of a letter of Col. Daniel Brodhead, Headquarters, Pittsburgh, April 14, 1780, to Rev. John Heckewelder. Printed in *Pa. Archives*, XII, 221.]

Thanks Heckewelder for intelligence; indifferent who are enemies, if they can be distinguished from friends. Stroke up Allegheny last fall successful; Six Nations have applied to Congress for peace. Expedition soon to be undertaken against Western tribes; one by sea and land against Quebec and Montreal will end British influence with Indians. Moravian Indians will be safer if gathered closer together.

[Summary of a letter of Col. Daniel Brodhead, Headquarters, April 15, 1780, to Rev. David Zeisberger. Printed in *ibid.*, 221–22.]

Honored by his letter of April 2. Sorry Joshua was prevented by cold weather from visiting Detroit; his reliability due to

Christian education and good natural ability. Moravian Indians would do well to assemble; should watch the other Delawares and send information. Plans for a western expedition.

LOYALIST PLOT IN THE SOUTHWEST

[Summary of a letter of Col. Walter Crockett,[1] April 15, 1780, to Col. William Preston. Printed in *John P. Branch Historical Papers of Randolph-Macon College*, IV, 310–11.]

Encloses letter of Col. Martin Armstrong[2] of North Carolina, dated Surry County, North Carolina, April 10, 1780, which gives alarming intelligence concerning a proposed Tory insurrection. Has been requested to disarm three militia companies on New River, but people so busy putting in crops it is impossible to get men.

An insurrection threatened on the frontiers from Georgia to Virginia; twenty horseloads of ammunition are to come from the Cherokee who are to send 1,500 warriors. The date for embodying is April 25. Similar reports come from H. Benjamin Johnston[3] of Virginia. Time is short; must suppress this attempt at once; it is a deeply laid scheme. One Dolly on New River is one of the chiefs of the conspiracy, and has lately visited General Clinton.

WESTMORELAND RAIDED

[Extract of a letter of Col. Archibald Lochry to Pres. Joseph Reed. 1NN50. Transcript.]

WESTMORELAND Co Ap^l 17th 1780

The savages have begun their hostilities—have struck us in four different places—taken & killed 13 persons, with a number

[1] For Col. Walter Crockett, who at the date of this letter was lieutenant-colonel of Montgomery County militia see *Dunmore's War*, 44, note 79.
[2] For Col. Martin Armstrong, county lieutenant for Surry County, N. Car., see *ibid.*, 221, note 53.
[3] Possibly this is the Benjamin Johnston who succeeded Col. William Crawford as surveyor of Yohogania County, and involved Virginia in difficulties with Pennsylvania concerning the boundary line. Johnston, the surveyor, lived after 1782 in North Strabane Township, Washington County, Pa.

of horses & other effects of the inhabitants: Two of the unhappy people were killed one mile from Hannastown. Our country is worse depopulated than ever it has been. I have got a few militia to support the frontiers, but am doubtful I cannot keep them long on duty for want of provisions. Our situation at present seems very deplorable, & if the savages were acquainted with our weekness they might very easily drive the people over the Youghogania. There is no amunition in the country but what is public property.

BRODHEAD UPHELD

[Summary of a resolution of Congress, April 18, 1780. Printed in *Journal of Continental Congress* (Washington, 1908), XVI, 372–73.]

Brodhead's letter of February 27 received. Resolved that Colonel Brodhead be supported in acts which the service at Fort Pitt makes necessary for the commandant.

[Summary of a letter of Col. Daniel Brodhead, Headquarters, Pittsburgh, April 19, 1780, to Col. Archibald Steel. Printed in *Pa. Archives*, XII, 222.]

Instructions must be carried out; if offensive operations occur, number of public horses is inadequate. Has requested information of inspection committee.

[Summary of a letter of Col. Daniel Brodhead, Headquarters, Pittsburgh, April 20, 1780, to Pres. Joseph Reed. Printed in *id.*, VIII, 197–99.]

Keenly sensitive to rebuke in letter of February 14 last. Instructions from commander in chief permitted reënlistment of rangers when terms had nearly expired; question of subsisting ranging companies discussed. Personal regard for Colonel Lochry, who is unduly influenced by Captains Irwin and Campbell. Protection will be assured to the inhabitants of Westmoreland.

DELAWARES LOYAL

[The Delaware chiefs to Col. Daniel Brodhead and Captain Killbuck. 1H131. In handwriting of Heckewelder.]

NEW TOWN, Apr 23^d 1780.

Walawpachtschiechen and the Councellors to Machingwe Geeshuch and Gelelemend as follows:

BROTHER:

You desired me to send some of my Young Men to You to join Your Army. I therefore now send Six to join You there, but when You once will be on Your March then two of my Capt^{ns} shall join You with more Men.

Brother: I assure You all what I have promised You that I would do, I also will do, but I see no ocasion of sending so many Men to Pittsburgh, as the Enemy we are about to destroy live quite an other Way, therefore I, when I shall know that You certainly March, will soon send Men to meet and join You.

Brother: I do at present not know which way You intend to March, wheither below Coschocking, thro it, or by Tuscorawas, but if You only give me timely Notice, I shall in no way be backward, to meet You at an appointed place.

Brother: I desire You to send two of these my Young Men to me again as soon as You begin to March With these two Young Men You will inform me of the place You may apoint for me to meet You.

Brother: I am so much mocked at by the Enemy Ind^s for speaking so long to them for You. Now they laugh at me, and ask me where that great Army of my Brothers, that was to come out against them so long ago, and so often, stays so long. They say to me, did We not tell that they had no Army and that we were nearly done killing them all, and yet You would believe them? They further desire me to tell You now to make haste and come soon, the sooner, and the greater Your Number the better.

Brother: I desire You to comply with their wish, and make up as great an Army against them as You possibly can. If you are strong all will end well.

Brother: I desire Captn Killbock to be with You when You March, do not let him go to Phillad^a till this buissness is over, for then I and many more intend to go with him.

Brother: I must yet mention to You that the Enemy is continually threatening Me, calling me big Knife and saying they will serve me the same. therefore Brother I long to see You come, and with as many Men as You possibly can get.

Brother: I desire You to send me with Nechnawalend 10 large Caggs of Powder, with Lead in proportion and flints. He is to fetsch it by Water to me. I am in want of these articles.

I am Your friend and Brother

WALAPACHTSCHIECHEN

Mr Gerrard remembers his Compliments to Col^1 Brodhead and Gelelemend, and desires them to comply with what is required above.

COL^o BRODHEAD. Comd^r W. Depart^t

[*Addressed:*] To Col^o Brodhead Comand^r West^n Departm^t at Pittsburgh.

PREPARATIONS FOR AN EXPEDITION

[Summary of a letter of Col. Daniel Brodhead, Fort Pitt, April 24, 1780, to Gen. George Washington. Printed in Sparks, *Corr. Amer. Rev.*, II, 437–39.]

Acknowledges receipt of his letters of January 4 and March 14, the former not received until April 18. Since reënforcements are not possible, an expedition against Detroit must be laid aside, unless Colonel Clark's troops join Brodhead's. Has called out 825 militia from neighboring counties for a Shawnee expedition; disputed jurisdiction will probably interfere with their coming. As Shawnee have been joined by many Indian renegades, a defeat by them would be fatal. Artillery and an artillery officer promised by Board of War. Water carriage and public boats. Thanks Washington for leave of absence, but as Colonel Gibson is absent and Indians remarkably hostile must remain at post. Encloses letters from Delaware council and from Heckewelder. Provisions and rations. "Since the 1st of March, the Indians have killed and taken forty-three men, women, and children, in the counties of Youghiogany, Monongalia, and Ohio, including those killed and taken upon the river; and they have destroyed a number of horses and cattle in Tiger Valley."[1]

[1] For this locality see *Frontier Defense*, 279, note 37.

PROTECTION FOR WESTMORELAND

[Orders for Capt. Thomas Beall.[1] 1NN68. Summary and transcript.]

Ap[l] 23[d] 1780, Capt. Tho[s] Beall is ordered with the party assigned him to take post at Fort Armstrong, & there receive under his command the militia ordered there by the Lieut. of Westmoreland: To keep out spies "towards Mahoning up the river" and "down to Kiskemonitas Creek."

[Summary of a letter of Col. Daniel Brodhead, Headquarters, Pittsburgh, April 25, 1780, to Col. Archibald Lochry. Printed in *Pa. Archives*, XII, 225-26.]

Lack of clothing has delayed detachment for Fort Armstrong. Capt. Thomas Beall sets out tomorrow with party and provisions for Forts Crawford and Armstrong; militia to be supplied thence. Desires Lochry's opinion on proposed expedition and whether he can furnish quota of militia; encouraging reports from Colonels Shepherd and Evans.

NEEDS AT FORT PITT

[Summary of a letter of Col. Daniel Brodhead, Fort Pitt, April 25, 1780, to Richard Peters. Printed in *ibid.*, 224-25.]

Employment of express for letters; hopes "to do something clever in the course of this Campaign," so desires early advices. Capt. A. Tannehill[2] goes to procure clothing allowed officers by act of Congress.[3] Bad condition of finances. Artillery reënforcement. Many raids since March 1.

[1] For a sketch of Capt. Thomas Beall see *Wis. Hist. Colls.*, XXIII, 350, note 3.

[2] Adamson Tannehill was a Marylander, who enlisted on July 1, 1776 as second lieutenant in Stephenson's rifle corps. In 1777 Tannehill became first lieutenant of Col. Moses Rawlings' Continental Regiment, and was employed during 1779 in the recruiting service. His captaincy was secured July 20, 1779, and thenceforward he served on the Pittsburgh frontier, until retired, Jan. 1, 1781. In 1812 he was brigadier-general of Pennsylvania volunteers. He died July 7, 1817.

[3] Congress passed a resolution, Nov. 25, 1779, denoting the amount and price of the clothing to which officers of Continental rank were entitled. *Jour. of Cont. Cong.*, XV, 1304-1306.

[Summary of a letter of Col. Daniel Brodhead, Headquarters, Pittsburgh, April 27, 1780, to Gen. James Wilkinson. Printed in *ibid.*, 226.]

Captain Tannehill's mission for officers' clothing; pay will not support them; need for summer clothing. Clothing for troops.

[Summary of a letter of Col. Daniel Brodhead, Pittsburgh, April 27, 1780, to Pres. Joseph Reed. Printed in *id.*, VIII, 210–11.]

Acknowledges receipt of letters of March 30 and April 22. Glad four companies are to be raised for frontier defense; need great. Between forty and fifty people taken in Ohio counties, no damage in Westmoreland yet. Recommendation of officers; those from neighboring families use soldiers as servants on their farms. Difficulties with Ward and Smallman. Drafting militia for a Shawnee expedition; hopes to do something important at Shawnee towns in course of six weeks.

ARTILLERY REËNFORCEMENT

[Summary of a letter of Pres. Joseph Reed, Philadelphia, April 29, 1780, to Col. Daniel Brodhead. Printed in *ibid.*, 218.]

Has received letter of March 18; sorry Delawares are so ungrateful and perfidious. Reënforcements cannot be sent, except Captain Craig's artillery,[1] which started two weeks ago. Penn-

[1] Isaac Craig was born in 1742 in the north of Ireland; in 1767 he emigrated to Philadelphia and was employed there as a master carpenter until the beginning of the Revolution. His first commission was as lieutenant of marines, and he served in 1775–76 in Hopkins' expedition to the West Indies in the ship Doria, Capt. Nicholas Biddle commanding. In 1776 Craig entered the infantry. The next year he was commissioned captain in Col. Thomas Proctor's artillery regiment and was wounded at the battle of Brandywine. In April, 1779 Craig received the thanks of the commander in chief for his gallant defense of Billingsport on the Delaware. In the summer of the same year he was detached for Sullivan's expedition, and the next spring to Fort Pitt. In 1781 Craig and his artillery company went with Clark to the Falls on the Ohio, returning Dec. 20, 1781. Upon his arrival at Pittsburgh, Craig heard of his promotion to a majority. The next year he volunteered for a reconnoitering expedition to Cuyahoga River. After the war Major Craig settled at Pittsburgh, and in

176 WISCONSIN HISTORICAL COLLECTIONS

sylvania Assembly voted four companies for frontier defense; depleted treasury may prevent execution. Protection of Westmoreland entrusted to Brodhead. Reward for scalps offered. Congress has justified Brodhead against improper action of Virginia courts.

FRENCH AGENT SENT TO DELAWARES

[Summary of a letter of Col. Daniel Brodhead, Fort Pitt, May 4, 1780, to Rev. John Heckewelder. Printed in *id.*, XII, 227–28.]

Thanks Heckewelder for letter of April 22. Indian reports discredited. Shawnee falsely report Americans defeated and fleeing. Kentucky will soon have 15,000 men; Shawnee will find them troublesome neighbors. Promising aspect of American affairs in general. Should Mingo attack Fort Pitt, will repent it. Delawares' desire for an expedition will soon be granted; awaiting only artillery. Delawares must no longer act double part. Major Linctot's[1] mission to their council.

1785 married the only daughter of Col. John Neville. In partnership with James O'Hara, he began the Pittsburgh glassworks. Craig also served as quartermaster-general during the Indian wars. He died in 1826 at his home on Montour's Island.

[1] Daniel Maurice Godefroy de Linctot (Lanctot) was one of two sons of a French officer who in colonial times commanded posts on Lake Superior and the Mississippi. Before the fall of New France, Daniel had attained the rank of ensign in the French colonial troops. In 1761 he and his brother went to France, but petitioned in 1762 to be allowed to return to the New World, and in the beginning of the Revolution they were fur traders on the Mississippi. The elder brother died in 1778 at Cahokia. *Ill. Hist. Colls.*, II, 8. Daniel entered the American service in May, 1779 and raised at Cahokia a troop of horse for an expedition against Detroit. With his new levies he crossed to Peoria and Ouiatanon, causing great alarm among the British. Having been commissioned by Clark captain in the Indian service Linctot exerted much influence for the Americans over the Mississippi tribes as far north as Prairie du Chien. Later in 1779 he went with a party of Indians to visit the governor of Virginia. During that visit he met several French officers and had a conference with the Marquis de Vaudreuil. *Id.*, V, 177. The Virginia authorities commissioned Linctot major of Indian affairs, and he set out for Fort Pitt, whence he went as agent to the Ohio tribesmen.

He reached Vincennes in December, 1780, and in the spring of 1781 organized relief for Fort Jefferson. In July of that year he was at St. Louis, and about a year later removed to Natchez, where he died sometime before 1797. His son, Bernard Lintot (so spelled), was on the Natchez Committee of Safety in the latter year. One of his sisters married Estevan Minor, last Spanish governor of

FRONTIER RETREAT 177

[Summary of a letter of Col. Daniel Brodhead, Headquarters, Fort Pitt, May 4, 1780, to Council at Coochocking. Printed in *ibid.*, 228-29.]

Acknowledges receipt of letter of April 23. Delaware young men are scouting with whites. Awaiting cannon before marching into enemies' country; route unknown, may be devious. Orders best warriors to be sent to accompany army. Enemies, who wish to see Brodhead, shall soon be gratified. French flag being sent to Delawares. Present of ammunition.

[Summary of a letter of Col. Daniel Brodhead, Fort Pitt, May 8, 1780, to Rev. David Zeisberger. Printed in *ibid.*, 231.]

Colonel Gibson brings letters that are forwarded by a French officer who goes with messages to Delaware council; requests honorable treatment for him. Will be glad of information when he returns.

SUPPLIES FOR EXPEDITION

[Summary of a letter of Col. Daniel Brodhead, Fort Pitt, May 5, 1780, to Gen. Horatio Gates. Printed in *ibid.*, 229.]

Expedition against hostile Indians is absolutely necessary. Application for large supply of salt provisions; may be brought up by horses in one trip. Propriety of application.

[Summary of a letter of Col. Daniel Brodhead, Headquarters, Fort Pitt, May 6, 1780, to Col. Archibald Steel. Printed in *ibid.*, 230.]

Orders for forwarding salt beef belonging to this district. Is to wait on General Gates with reference to purchase of bacon.

Natchez, and the other married the well-known adventurer, Philip Nolan. Linctot's descendants in the Minor family live in Terre Bonne Parish, La.

ALARM IN WESTMORELAND

[Summary of a letter of Col. Daniel Brodhead, Headquarters, Fort Pitt, May 6, 1780, to Capt. Thomas Beall. Printed in *ibid.*, 230.]

Sergeant Clark arrived express, brings news of a party of Indians discovered opposite Fort Crawford; singular that they should steer that way; has sent Bill Brady[1] for information. Beall has sent Guthrie[2] for militia; hopes he will not cause great alarm. Orders for Beall's movements.

EXPEDITION POSTPONED

[Col. Daniel Brodhead to Col. David Shepherd. 1SS201. L. S.][3]

HEAD QUARTERS FORT PITT May 9th 1780

DEAR SIR:

I find it will not be in my power to provide for the number of men I have ordered to be called into service so soon as I expected; Besides I have heard that a number of Artillery & stores and two Regiments of Infantry are now on their March to reinforce my Command. The account of Artillery & Stores I have received officially, & I believe the other may be credited.

It will be essentially necessary for the leading officers of your County to excite the greatest Industry in planting & sowing the Summer Crop & to have your Troops at Fort Henry by the fourth day of next Month—The Militia should be drafted for two Months, altho' the Expedition will probably end in one, and let them be as well armed & accoutred as Circumstances will admit —Encourage them to bring two weeks allowance of provisions lest there should be a deficiency.

I have no doubt but you & all the good people of your County are convinced of the necessity there is for prosecuting some offen-

---

[1] See mention of William Brady in *Frontier Defense*, 217.
[2] For references to Ensign John Guthrie see *Wis. Hist. Colls.*, XXIII, *passim*.
[3] For similar letters to Col. John Evans of Monongalia County, and Col. Joseph Beeler of Yohogania County see *Pa. Archives*, XII, 231-32.

sive operations against the Savages, and I trust that by a well timed movement from the new Settlements down the River to favor Our expedition we shall be enabled to strike a general panic among the hostile Tribes—I am averse to putting too much to hazard as a defeat would prove fatal to the Settlements & therefore I expect the full quota of men will be furnished which with the blessing of Divine Providence will ensure Success. Indeed I expe[ct] besides the Militia many will turn out volun[teers] to secure to themselves the Blessings of peace

I have the honor to be with great respect Your most Obed^t serv^t

DAN^L BRODHEAD Col^o Command^g W. D.

COL^o SHEPHERD.

[Summary of a letter of Col. Daniel Brodhead, Fort Pitt, May 10, 1780, to Col. Archibald Lochry. Printed in Mary C. Darlington, *Fort Pitt* (Pittsburgh, 1892), 235–36.]

Expedition postponed for a short time. Stroke on Brush Run[1] unexpected; had hoped country east of here would enjoy quiet. Militia should be drafted for two months. Must not run too great a risk.

WESTMORELAND RAIDED

[Summary of a letter of Col. Daniel Brodhead, Headquarters, Fort Pitt, May 11, 1780, to Maj. George Slaughter.[2] Printed in *Pa. Archives*, XII, 232.]

"The County of Westmoreland is again infested with the cursed Mingoes. The Inhabitants are flying from every quarter and it

[1] For this location, just east of Pittsburgh, see *Wis. Hist. Colls.*, XXIII, 292, note 4.

[2] George Slaughter, youngest son of Robert Slaughter, was born in 1739 in Culpeper County, Va. George, with his elder brother, Thomas, visited Kentucky in 1775. The next two years he was captain in the Continental service, and in Oct. 4, 1777 was commissioned major of the Twelfth Virginia Regiment, resigning two months later because of ill health. In the summer of 1779 he paid a second visit to Kentucky, and on returning to Virginia raised reënforcements for Clark's army. His troop, being detained by deep snows, wintered in the mountains, and arrived in April, 1780 at Fort Pitt, en route for Louisville.

will be necessary for you to keep a lookout where you are." Asks for detachment of fifteen or twenty soldiers to pursue raiders. Lieut. Col. Richard Campbell not yet returned from down the Ohio.

[Summary of a letter of Col. Daniel Brodhead, Fort Pitt, May 13, 1780, to Gen. George Washington. Printed in ibid., 233–34, and in Sparks, *Corr. Amer. Rev.*, II., 448–50.]

Assembling of militia postponed until June 4, hoping to secure provisions. General Gates has ordered commissaries to stop purchases. Mingo raids in Westmoreland, several killed and wounded; will probably prevent aid from their militia; they have stationed sixty men on their frontier. A Delaware brings news of two Indian parties crossing at Logstown and Chartier's Creek.

Artillery officer delayed en route. Enemy intend to attack some post; garrisons at Fort McIntosh, Holliday's Cove, Fort Henry, and Fort Armstrong. Delaware professions of friendship mistrusted.

[Summary of a letter of Col. Daniel Brodhead, Fort Pitt, May 13, 1780, to Pres. Joseph Reed. Printed in *Pa. Archives*, VIII, 246–47.]

Mingo, having received English goods, are again induced to attack Westmoreland, tracks of four parties seen in last four days; two more Indian parties crossed Ohio today. Have only cullings of last years' men to prevent incursions. Delaware friendship dubious because of lack of goods. "For heavens sake hurry up the Companies voted by the Honble Assembly or Westmoreland county will soon be a wilderness." Prevail on commander in chief to send 500 good regulars.

From the latter place they went out on the Shawnee expedition, and when Clark returned soon afterwards to Virginia he left Major Slaughter in command of the Kentucky regulars. During Clark's absence Slaughter built Fort Nelson. Soon thereafter he became lieutenant-colonel of all the Virginia forces in Kentucky. In 1784 he was a member of the Virginia Assembly from Jefferson County, Ky., whence he removed to Charleston, Ind., where on June 17, 1818 he died. His nephews, Lawrence, Joseph, James and John Slaughter, were all in Clark's Illinois battalion.

[Summary of a letter of Col. Daniel Brodhead, Fort Pitt, May 14, 1780, to Richard Peters. Printed in *id.*, XII, 234-35.]

Indian raiding parties; has provisioned the few men Westmoreland has raised for protection. Alarm at orders to commissaries to stop purchase of provisions. Poverty of Delawares may endanger their loyalty; chiefs intend to visit Congress again and take more children to be educated at college. A few goods would work wonders. Captain McIntyre's allowance while on command.

ARTILLERY REËNFORCEMENT

[Summary of a letter of Col. Daniel Brodhead, Headquarters, Fort Pitt, May 13, 1780, to Capt. Isaac Craig. Printed in *ibid.*, 233.]

Some weeks since news was received that Craig was ordered here with cannon and stores. Realizes difficulties of transportation, but considering great need of counteracting enemy's designs by offensive operations, urges him to try and arrive by first of June. Pennsylvania road very hazardous; advises coming by Virginia road. Requests a return of ordnance and stores.

SCOUT DOWN OHIO

[Summary of a letter of Col. Daniel Brodhead, Fort Pitt, May 18, 1780, to Timothy Pickering. Printed in *ibid.*, 237.]

Thanks for the favor of Congress. Estimate of Indian stores. Militia called out for an expedition; need of stores. Seventy-eight tents unfit for service. Colonel Campbell returned from a scout to mouth of Muskingum; made no discoveries. Good behavior of Delawares who accompanied him.

EXPEDITION ABANDONED

[Col. Daniel Brodhead to Col. David Shepherd. 1SS203. A. L. S.][1]

DEAR SIR:
HEAD QU^{rs} FORT PITT May 20th 1780.

I find it impossible to procure a sufficient quantity of Provisions to subsist the Troops which were intended to be employed on an Expedition against the Indians in alliance with Great Britain; Wherefore you will be pleased to give immediate notice to such as have been warned not to March untill you receive further Notice from me. In the mean time I shall endeavour to give every possible protection to the Settlements and amuse the Indians with Speeches. I am sorry for having given you the trouble of Drafting the Militia. But the disappointment with regard to the means of obtaining supplies are very embarassing, and must apologize for the alteration in our Measures. I have the Honor to be with great respect Your most Obed^t Servt

DANIEL BRODHEAD Col^o command^g W D.

COL^o DAVID SHEPHERD

[Summary of a letter of Col. Daniel Brodhead, Headquarters, Fort Pitt, May 20, 1780, to Col. George Rogers Clark. 50J39. A. L. S. Printed in *Ill. Hist. Colls.*, VIII, 419–20.]

Had planned an expedition, abandoned for lack of resources; no reënforcement expected. Urges Clark to attack Shawnee who are the most hostile of the tribes, and whose chastisement would end the war. Major Slaughter with 100 men on his way to Kentucky will join in expedition. Proposed junction of forces.

[1] For similar letters to Colonels Evans, Beeler, and Lochry see *Pa. Archives*, XII, 238.

BOUNTY FOR SCALPS

[Summary of a letter of Col. Daniel Brodhead, Fort Pitt, May 18, 1780, to Pres. Joseph Reed. Printed in *Pa. Archives*, VIII, 249-50.]

Received letter of April 29. Glad to assure Reed that Delawares were not concerned in murders as at first suspected; they acted with the scouts; will join an expedition. Depletion of treasury. Subsistence of troops. Fears bounty for scalps will be used against friendly Delawares and occasion a general Indian war. Delawares have been steady and serviceable; goods would be useful; cannot be taught to consider paper money as a proper reward. Congress' justification of Brodhead's actions.

[Summary of a letter of Col. Daniel Brodhead, Headquarters, Fort Pitt, May 20, 1780, to Col. Archibald Lochry. Printed in *id.*, XII, 239.]

Sends proclamation of Pennsylvania executive offering high premium for scalps of Indians and Tories found in arms against them, and for Indian prisoners. Danger of abuse; some are malicious enough to employ it against friendly Delawares. Their influence is considerable with twenty different tribes; due to them that so few are against them. Notice wanted of designs against friendly Indians.

[Col. Daniel Brodhead to the Delawares. 2H54. Letter Book.]

FORT PITT. May 27th 1780

Mahingweegeesuch to the Delaware Council at Coochocking

BROTHERS:

I sent you word by our friend Mon^{sr} Gerard that, The wise American Congress had sent up six Blank Commissions for me to fill up with the names of such trusty men of the Delaware nation as I thought best, But I am desirous first desirous [sic] to take the opinion & recommendation of your Council, because you know which of your own Captains can raise men to go with him against the Enemy & I desire you will immediately send me their names, I expect Captn Wilson will be one

Brothers: The Gov[r] & Council of Pen[a] have offered a high reward for Prisoners & Indian scalps They have carefully avoided offering a reward for white men[s] scalps but a bad use might be made of it by some & our Friends the French & Americans at Detroit suffer by it.

Brothers: The reward offered for scalps & Prisoners will encourage many of your Brethren of this Island to form themselves into parties to pursue or waylay the Enemy Indians, & as many of them are unexperienced & may not know our Friends I must advise you not to suffer your people to walk upon the warrior paths nor any of the paths leading to the Ohio River all the way from the mouth of Muskingum River to Fort M[c]Intosh, but let such of them as want to transact Business here, travel the old Cuscusky path[1] & proceed with great caution

Brothers: you have seen how careful I have always been to advise you for the best, & you may rely on my friendship still, But as I have said you must shew your friendship by your actions & now you have an excellent opportunity. every thing turns in our favor. The English must soon leave this Island & you will be well rewarded for prisoners & scalps

Brothers: Be wise & strong for the good of your posterity & believe me to be your Friend & Brother

MAKINGWEGEESUCH

P. S. When my Cannon & Soldiers arrive you will hear from me again.

KENTUCKY ENDANGERED.

[Col. John Bowman[2] to Col. Daniel Brodhead. 16S5–8. Transcript.]

KENTUCKY COUNTY May 27th 1780.

COL. BRODHEAD, SIR:

At this most alarming period, I think it necessary to inform you of the designs of our cruel enemy, the British and Indians, against this part of the western frontiers of Virginia.

[1] This was the trail taken by McIntosh's army when Fort Laurens was built. See description of the route in *Wis. Hist. Colls.*, XXIII, 183, note 1. For the Indian town of Kuskuskies see *Frontier Defense*, 178, note 46.

[2] For a sketch of Col. John Bowman, who at the time this letter was written was county lieutenant of Kentucky, see *Rev. Upper Ohio*, 170, note 94.

Lieutenant Abraham Chaplin, who was taken last November at the time Col. Rogers was defeated by the Indians on the Ohio, and George Hendricks who was likewise taken at the Salt Springs on Licking in the year 1777 with Major Boone,[1] made their escape from the Wyondott Nation of Indians, living on the waters of Sandusky,[2] the 27th or 28th ultimo, who bring intelligence that a larger number of the different tribes of Indians in conjunction with some of the troops belonging to the King of Great Britian, to the Amount of two thousand in the whole, six hundred of whom are green coat rangers from Canada, were preparing to attack the garrison at the Falls of Ohio with cannon,[3] &c. And after reducing the same, their next destination is to Illinois, in order to take that post. Likewise that Capt[n] Matthew Elliott[4] gave them information that the different tribes of Indians were gathering their horses in order to assist the enemy on their expedition over the carrying place from Omey to Large Miami,[5] and that they expect that the enemy will be at the Falls of Ohio in about four weeks from this time.

Though I have not had the honor of being personally acquainted with you, but from character am well assured of your great zeal for the welfare of the United States in general, and that you have been always ready to render them your services on all occasions—therefore I am induced to request of you all your assistance of men, amunition, and provisions, together with artillery, in order to relieve us from the approaching danger which seems to threaten this part of the world, as far as is in

[1] For the capture of the salt makers under Daniel Boone see *Frontier Defense*, 252, note 7. For a sketch of George Hendricks see *Wis. Hist. Colls.*, XXIII, 244, note 1.

[2] See a British account of the escape of these men in *Mich. Pion. & Hist. Colls.*, XIX, 528.

[3] The company known as the "green coat Rangers" was a detachment from the Loyalist regiment called the King's Royal Regiment of New York. This was enlisted in 1776 by Sir John Johnson, and served in St. Leger's campaign of 1777 and in later border raids. The "Royal Greens" was disbanded in 1783, and its members settled on the Ottawa and St. Lawrence rivers. The leader of the expedition threatening Kentucky, was Capt. Henry Bird. See *id.*, IX, 528, 584; *id.*, X, 501-2; *id.*, XIX, 519, 528, 533.

[4] For a sketch of Elliott see *Frontier Defense*, 249, note 5.

[5] The portage from the Maumee (Omey) to the Great Miami might be made either by ascending the Auglaize River to its source and portaging to Lorimier's trading post on Laramie Creek; or by ascending the St. Mary's branch of the Maumee and portaging to the same place. Bird's expedition took the former route.

your power, consistent with the line of your duty, which I am in hopes you will not deny. I am certain you are sensible, that should this country give way, the Illinois will fall of course, which will enable our enemy the Britons, to call all the Indians at the westward into their service, which would I am persuaded, be of very bad consequence to the United States in general. Pray pardon the freedom I have taken, as I assure you it is from no other motive but the public good.

I am with esteem your Most Ob^t & very humble Servt
 JOHN BOWMAN, County Lieutenant of Kentucky County
To COLONEL BRODHEAD.

[Col. John Floyd to Col. William Preston.[1] 33S318–19. Transcript.]

The savages have done no damage on this [Beargrass] Creek for some weeks past, but have frequently visited other parts of the county. Col° Slaughter has demanded 1400 militia from this county to go against the Towns, & to rendezvous at the Big Bone by the middle of July; but I doubt the men cannot be raised by Col° Bowman, as such numbers are daily flocking to the interior parts of the country.

The expedition of the enemy against the Falls, I hear nothing more about, tho' this is about the time they were to have been here. Dr Walker has not returned from the Mississippi;[2] & I believe Col. Clark has gone with his troops to a village about 60 miles above Illinois called Coho, where was said a large number of Indians were about to make an attack.[3] We are in a very defenceless situation in this country, & I hear of reinforcements from you, but I fear if they come they can do us but little service. They will be obliged to return for want of provisions as we have none but bread.

People [in] this [country] seem generally to have lost their health, but perhaps it is owing to the disagreeable way in which

[1] This letter is undated. On the manuscript Dr. Draper wrote: "Without date—but doubtless written in June, 1780."

[2] For Dr. Thomas Walker, who was one of the commissioners for running the Virginia-North Carolina boundary to the Mississippi, see *Dunmore's War*, 242, note 70.

[3] Floyd alludes to the joint attack on St. Louis and Cahokia (Coho) by a large body of British and Indians sent out by the commandant at Mackinac. See *ante*, 19–20.

we are obliged to live crowded in forts, where the air seems to have lost all its purity & sweetness. Our poor little Billy[1] has been exceedingly ill for several weeks & is reduced to a mere skeleton by a kind of flux which is common here & of which numbers die: His mother is almost disconsolate, & I myself am much afraid we shall lose the child; & if we do, I shall impute it to nothing but living in dirt & filth. My uncle Davis & his son, I am told, were both killed near Cumberland Mountain about five weeks ago as they were going to the settlement. There were four brothers of them who have been all murdered in the course of 7 or 8 years. * * *

J^N FLOYD

[Capt. William Harrod to Mrs. Amelia Harrod. 4NN80. A. L. S.]

HERRODS FARM May the 30 1780.

LOVING WIFE:

I Take this opertunity To Let you no that I am well at present Hoping you are all in the same state Luttⁿ Chaplain has just made his Escape from the indians and informs that thare is a Large party of english and indians and Canaidins on thier March Toward this Contry

I Entend [going] home as soon as poseble I can Setle my Consarns here you Will have opertunity of hering the situation of this Cuntry By the people that is gon home

From your Loving Husband
WIM HERROD

[To AMELIA HARROD, Ten Mile.]

BRADY'S SANDUSKY EXPEDITION

[Summary of a letter of Col. Daniel Brodhead, Fort Pitt, May 30, 1780, to Gen. George Washington. Printed in Sparks, *Corr. Amer. Rev.*, II, 458–60.]

Since last letter ten have been killed, wounded, or captured in Westmoreland County. Widely differing accounts of Detroit

[1] William Preston Floyd, eldest son of Col. John Floyd and Jane Buchanan, died of smallpox shortly after his father's death in 1783.

garrison. Is sending Captain Brady with five white men and two Delawares to Sandusky to try to take a prisoner; has offered Delawares $50 hard money for a British soldier. Expedition against Indian towns abandoned. Deserters and provisions.

[Summary of a letter of Col. Daniel Brodhead, n. d., to Pres. Joseph Reed. Printed in *Pa. Archives*, VIII, 300–301.]

No mischief done since last letter. Expecting salt provisions from below mountains. French envoy in service of Virginia sent to Indians; while means to chastise them, are lacking, it is well to amuse them. Reward for scalps less useful than a few goods would be. Captain Brady has been gone ten days to Sandusky; expects his return in as many more days; he deserves promotion.

WESTMORELAND RAIDED

[Summary of a letter of Col. Archibald Lochry, Twelve Mile Run, June 1, 1780, to Pres. Joseph Reed. Printed in *ibid.*, 282–84.]

Great distress in county; three parties of Indians have visited them; killed five near Ligonier, two on Braddock's Road near Brush Creek; two killed and one wounded near Brushy Run; Laughlin's mill burned. All forted north of Youghiogheny. Brodhead able to afford little assistance; Lochry is raising a volunteer ranging company. Requests ammunition; large amounts issued to militia at forts. Reward for Indian scalps. Permission for an expedition into enemies' country. Public records removed from Hannastown to Lochry's home. Hannastown petition against Lochry.

[Summary of a letter of Pres. Joseph Reed, June 2, 1780, to Col. Archibald Lochry. Printed in *ibid.*, 290.]

Sum of £10,000 forwarded for recruiting or other exigencies. Blank commissions for officers. Commissary Amberson[1] must subsist rangers.

[1] For a sketch of Maj. William Amberson, see *Wis. Hist. Colls.*, XXIII, 140, note 5.

INDIAN INFORMATION

[Rev. David Zeisberger to Col. Daniel Brodhead. Washington Papers. Contemporary transcript.]

SCHOENBRUN June the 1st 1780.

DEAR SIR:

I am much obliged for your favour of the 8th last month & also the Inclosed letters from Lancaster, by these last I learned that we have to expect some of our Brethern from Bethlehim very soon—when they arive at Pittsburgh I desire the favour to send an Messenger immediately here & give us notice of their Arrival and I will send a party of our Indians to conduct them hither.

Of Major Lanctots affair and what sucksess he had at Coochocking I can mention nothing as I only had a little Intelligence from here say, but I believe Mr Heckewelder who undoubtedly knows more of it has wrote to you—Your last message to the Chiefs at Coochocking I hear has given them much uneasiness & they are comeing to speak with you concerning that matter. A muncy Indian who was in the Company you had a skirmish with at or near Conawaen [Conewago] last year came here some days ago from Niagara, he says he tells no lie that all the Mingoe & muncy towns were destroyed & not one left—That those Munceys are on their way to come this way again & would be here this Summer, that at Niagara three hundred Indians Men, Women & Children Dyed of a distemper last year & at Conawaen Eighty by the small Pox. Cayashooto [Guyashusta] with a party of Mingoes is gone to the Wyandotts so as we hear to treat of good matters We are and have been very quiet all this spring but it seems by your last message [to] the Councill of Coochocking as if the road betwen here and the Fort would be unsafe to Travel, if it should be so you will be pleased to let me hear more of it, for our people will be most in danger because we are on the Frontiers & if our Indians go out hunting they might easily meet with some of your parties.

I am dear sir your most obedient & humble servant

D. ZEISBERGER

To DANEL BRODHEAD Co^l

[Rev. David Zeisberger to Col. Daniel Brodhead. Washington Papers. Contemporary transcript.]

TUPAKING June 7th 1780.

DEAR SIR:

I wrote to you some days ago when Major Lanctot came here from Cooshocking on his return to the Fort, but was afterwards detained by Cap't Killbuck and the Councillors who turned back again from this place to Cooshocking.

By these two Mesengers you will receive all the News from M'r Heckewelder in Writing which Cap't Killbuck brought to him from Cooshocking, but Major Lanctot will not give Credit to it, that Three Hundred English are marched, but perhaps only some few along with the Shawneese. He is very much for going with these Messengers, to the Fort but Cap't Killbuck sent Word to him to wait yet four days when he and others would go with him in a few days hence. He has sent Messages to the Wyandats and Shawneese but the latter was gone to War before this Message arrived there, and they are waiting yet for an Answer from the Wyandats.

I am Dear Sir your most Humble Servant—

D. ZEISBERGER.

TO COL. BRODHEAD

[Captain Killbuck to Col. Daniel Brodhead. 1H134. In handwriting of Heckewelder.]

SALEM[1] June y'e 7th 1780

Cap't'n John Killbuck, and the Councill of Cooshockung to Mahingwee Geeshuch as follows:

BROTHER:

You told me when I came away from You, to let You know what I might see or hear when at home. A few Days ago I was on my Horse already to come to You, and would have told You all I seen or heard, but again I was stop'd by Your Speech with the French Man, in which I was desired to listen to what he had to say.

[1] Salem was a village for the Moravian Indians, established in the spring of 1780 by Heckewelder, who removed thither those of his mission who had not gone to Gnadenhütten and Schönbrunn with Edwards and Zeisberger. Salem was situated on the Tuscarawas River, five miles below Gnadenhütten, a little southeast of the modern Port Washington, in Tuscarawas County, Ohio.

Brother: Some of the News which we had hear'd before was not so as reported, but now depend on what I tell You that it is truth. Eight Nights ago 300 English (some French along with them) with 4 pieces of Cannon; 500 Indians of diferent Nations, Wyondoughella with 50 Dellawares, 19 Dellawares from Keenhanshicanink went off to War against the Settlements at Kentuckee. furthur Geijashuta (the Mingoe Chieff) is arived at Sandusky with a great many Belts, from whence he sent for the half King, Wyondoughella, Captn Pipe and Wingeenund, and now it is 2 Nights past since they set off for Detroit, there to hear the Speeches and have a Councill.[1] I hear Geijashuta is on a good arrant, but cannot know yet the truth. No Wyondotts are gone with those Warriors, they spoke strong to all of their Nation and told them that is was true they formerly were the greatest Warriors of all Nations, but that now the Shawnese were eager to gain that Name, that *they* were become the greatest Wariors of all Nations, they therefore (the Wyondotts) would leave all over unto them, and they might now try and do their best.

Brother now listen to me further: You told me that You had received Orders to give Comisions to 6 of my Men, namely such as could be recomended as true and faithfull. I have Considered about this matter, and shall give You my Oppinion of it when we will come together again. I am glad to hear You and shall come soon to You, and when we shall see one another in the Face we will know more about our good and great Friendship.

Brother: I desire You will open me imediately my old Road by Beaver Creeck to Pittsburgh again for I do not like to take such a round about way, when I come to see an speak with You. This Brother I desire You to do and let me know imediately by one of these my Young Men what you have determined on. In 4 Nights more I shall set off for Pittsburg, I now am only waiting to hear the News the Big Cat[2] will bring from the Wyondotts and then will go, and wish to meet my Messenger half ways between this and Beaver Creeck that I may hear there from him Your determination.

[1] For this embassy see *Mich. Pion. & Hist. Colls.*, X, 404. Because of the absence of the chiefs upon Capt. Henry Bird's expedition no formal council could be held by Guyashusta. The messages, which were sent by the Six Nations urging the western warriors to maintain the British alliance, he left with the Wyandot. In August, 1780 the chiefs assembled at Detroit to consider this matter. *Id.*, XIX, 555.

[2] For this chief see *Wis. Hist. Colls.*, XXIII, *passim*.

Brother: I must yet inform You that 3 Men from Wyondoughellas gang went by here towards You, it is likely they will do some mischieff.

Brother: Some Days ago one Man and an old Woman came from Niagara, who aquaint me that last Winter 3 Hundred Ind^s died at that place on the Flux. You shall hear furthur when I come to You.

I am Your friend and Brother

JOHN KILLBUCK.

BROTHER MAGHINGWE GEESHUCH at Pittsburgh

[*Addressed:*] To Mr Daniel Brodhead Col° Comand^t W^n Dep^t at Pittsburgh by 2 Dellaw^s from Cooshokung.

[*Endorsed:*] Col° Henry alias Jn° Killbuck

WESTERN GARRISONS FOR VIRGINIA

[Summary of proposals of Virginia Council, June 8, 1780. 50J42. Printed in *Ill. Hist. Colls.*, VIII, 423–24.]

Posts to be garrisoned at mouth of Little and Great Kanawha, Sandy, and Licking rivers, one at Kelly's on the Great Kanawha, and one at Martin's cabin in Powell's Valley. Proportion of militia to be raised by each of the several western counties.

KENTUCKY ENDANGERED

[Summary of a letter of Col. Arthur Campbell,[1] Goodwood, June 7, 1780, to Col. William Preston. Printed in *John P. Branch Historical Papers*, IV, 311.]

An express from Col. John Bowman brings word that Lieut. Abraham Chapline, taken prisoner at Rogers' defeat, escaped from Sandusky, April 28, and reached the Falls of Ohio, May 19. He reports also that Col. John Butler with 600 regulars and 1,000 Indians is on his way from the lakes to attack the post at the Falls and other forts. They have cannon and are coming up the Maumee and down the Great Miami. Colonel Bowman sends for aid. Plans for furnishing relief. The fate of Charleston, S. C., will encourage the Tories.

[1] For a sketch of Col. Arthur Campbell see *Dunmore's War*, 39, note 70.

[Rev. David Zeisberger to Col. Daniel Brodhead. Washington Papers. Contemporary transcript.]

TUPAKING June 12th 1780.

DEAR SIR:
This is the third time I write to you sin[c]e the French Officer is here in our Town waiting for the Chiefs to go with him to the Fort. He has sent speeches to the Wyandats, and Shawnesse, but it seems they are not attentive, for they are already at War. He sees very well there is nothing to be done now. Fifty English and Fifty French, with some Hundreds of Indians are Marched to Kentucke, but most part of the French are Deserted. they have with them some Canon,—At Detroit there Cayashoota party of Mingoes is gone, and where a great Council is to be held undoubtedly a new Indian War is preparing for—for that is I think, not the place to treat for peace. We have no peace to expect so long as that place remaineth in that situation, by the Gentleman who was a prisoner among the Wyandats, you will [receive] a good deal of Inteligence, concerning that place, Sixteen Wyandats, in one, and Six Delawares from thence in another Company, are gone by Tuscarawas towards Pittsburgh to War, it is likely we shall have troublesome times this Summer.

I am Dear Sir Your most Obedient & Humble Servant

D. ZEISBERGER

[Col. Arthur Campbell to Maj. William Edmiston.[1] 9DD20. A. L. S.]

June 12th 1780.

SIR:
The requisition of the Commanding Officer of Kentuckey County for Aid from this to enable him to oppose the Enemy that are about to invade that Country, has made it my Duty to Order, Three Companys of the Militia of this County which you are to take Command of and to March with all possible dispatch to Louisville (ye Falls of the Ohio), or such other Post in that County, that from, the events of the Invasion, you may judge most advisable for the public Good.

Your Corps are to be furnished with Provision for the Journey by Mr Baker[2] Colo Clarks Commissary, and they are to escort

[1] For a sketch of William Edmiston see *ibid.*, 84, note 32.
[2] Evan Baker was a namesake of Col. Evan Shelby. He and his father, Isaac Baker, removed from Maryland with the Shelby family, where the Bakers settled

such supplys of provision &c. as may be judged necessary to send. Mr Robert Irvine is instructed to provide Pack Horses &c. for your use, to whom you are to apply from time to time, and give him such necessary advice and instructions as the promotion of the Service may require   I have it from good authority that the Assembly is about passing a Law to pay the Militia at old rates, (or in other Words at Tobacco rates) this will enable the frontier Counties more readily to send Men into the Service, without hurting their Families. For Provisions, Horse Hire &c. and the officers and Men in the Staff Department to be paid in the same manner. In short I hope as our Rulers seems to be departing from their late narrow System, we ought on our part to display, the greater readiness and activity in the defence of our Country, especially as our own security so immediately depends on it.

I am Sir Your very Humble Servant

ARTHUR CAMPBELL

MAJOR EDMISTON

[*Addressed:*] Major William Edmiston of Washington, Public Service.

[Summary of a letter of Col. Arthur Campbell, Goodwood, June 13, 1780, to Col. William Preston. 5QQ33. A. L. S. Printed in *Ill. Hist. Colls.*, VIII, 424–25.]

Indecision and consternation in Kentucky; Col. John Butler coming in great wrath, boasts he will give no quarter. Three companies of militia to go from this county; desires one or two companies from Montgomery County. Aid in furnishing ammunition requested.

[Summary of a letter of Col. Arthur Campbell, Goodwood, June 23, 1780, to Col. William Preston. Printed in *John P. Branch Historical Papers*, IV, 312–13.]

On receipt of Colonel Bowman's requisition, concluded to send supplies directly overland to Colonel Clark at the Falls.

on the Holston River near the Virginia-Tennessee border line, at the modern Goodson, Va. Evan Baker was commissary of Washington County, Va., during the later years of the Revolution.

FRONTIER RETREAT   195

Three companies are almost ready to march; cattle and pack horses to accompany them. Captain May[1] confirms the expectation of a heavy blow to the westward, which explains recent immunity. Beginning of the campaign is unfavorable; it would be an additional humiliation to have a British government established on the Ohio and Mississippi. The times call for the assistance of every wise man.

[Summary of a letter of Capt. Thomas Quirk,[2] June 23, 1780, to Col. William Preston. Printed in *ibid.*, 313.]

Acknowledges receipt of his letter of the 22nd, would be willing to march to the Ohio with his few men, were they in condition for that service. All of them at the lead mines amount to no more than two sergeants and twenty-nine privates and are without arms or clothing. As it is almost impossible for those men to march in time to the assistance of Kentucky would be glad to have the conditions reported to the governor.

LOYALIST PLOT IN SOUTHWEST

[Col. Arthur Campbell to Maj. William Edmiston. 9DD21. A. L. S.]

GOODWOOD June 24, 1780

DEAR SIR:

A Letter just received from the Commanding Officer at the Lead-Mines, I am informed that the Tories have embodied them-

[1] For Capt. John May see *Dunmore's War*, 21, note 34.
[2] Thomas Quirk, an Irish emigrant, came to America sometime before the Revolution and in 1775 prospected in Kentucky. The next year he was commissioned ensign in the Seventh Virginia Regiment, and on November 13 was promoted to a lieutenancy. On Sept. 14, 1778 Lieutenant Quirk was transferred to the Fifth Virginia. Having resigned, July 4, 1779, from the eastern army, Quirk recruited during the succeeding summer for Clark, and took reënforcements to the Illinois, where he was stationed at Cahokia. In 1780 Quirk was in Virginia, in charge of a company of militia posted at Fort Chiswell to protect the lead mines. It was from this place that this letter of June 23, 1780 was written. After a summer's campaign against the Virginia Loyalists Quirk went in 1781 to Kentucky, serving as major of the troops stationed at Louisville. He died at that place on Sept. 6, 1803. By his demise was lost "a brave man and an excellent officer." See his obituary in Draper Mss., 36J23, 28.

selves up New River, and intend to take that place also that they have killed nine Men, and are committing various outrages. I am also call'd upon in a most pressing manner to send assistance as the Mines is in great danger.

You are therefore desired to Order four full Divisions out of the Companies commanded by the Captains Montgomery,[1] Beattie,[2] Dysart,[3] Edmondson,[4] Lewis,[5] Neil,[6] and John Campbell R[oyal] Oak,[7] to go under the Command of the Captains Dysart,

[1] Capt. James Montgomery lived on the south fork of Holston River, eight miles from the present Abingdon, Va. For a sketch of his career see *Dunmore's War*, 65, note 9.

[2] David Beattie was born about the year 1752 on Carr's Creek, Rockbridge County, Va. About the year 1772 his father, John Beattie, removed with his family to Glade Spring in Washington County. There, on Feb. 26, 1777, David was commissioned lieutenant in the county militia, and in April, 1780 was promoted to a captaincy. After the summer's campaign of 1780 against the Loyalists, David Beattie and his younger brothers, William and John, volunteered for the campaign of King's Mountain, where on October 7, the latter of the three brothers was killed. David Beattie died in the spring of 1814 at his home in Washington County. See Draper Mss., 14DD72.

[3] James Dysart was born in 1744 in Ireland, and in 1761 emigrated to America. In 1770 he was one of the group known as the "Long Hunters," which explored Kentucky and Tennessee. Later Dysart settled on Little Holston, where in 1775 he married Agnes, sister of David Beattie. Dysart was for many years a magistrate and a militia officer of Washington County, serving also as its sheriff from its organization until June 5, 1784. He was captain of volunteers in the expedition to King's Mountain, and was wounded in the battle. The next year he was commissioned major of militia, and later represented his county in the Virginia Assembly. Late in life he removed to Rockcastle County, Ky., where he died May 26, 1818.

[4] Capt. William Edmiston (Edmondson) was either nephew or cousin of the officer to whom the above letter is addressed. After the campaign against the Loyalists, Captain Edmondson volunteered for the King's Mountain campaign and was killed in the battle that ensued.

[5] Aaron Lewis was from Albemarle County, and belonged to the same family as the explorer, Meriwether Lewis. Aaron, after removing to Washington County, was justice and coroner, major, and later lieutenant-colonel of militia. In 1783 he was assistant county surveyor, and soon thereafter removed to Kentucky. There in 1787 he was trustee of Boonesborough, and the next year member of the Kentucky convention. In 1794 Col. Aaron Lewis represented Madison County in the State Assembly. In 1804 he was official surveyor of Logan County, when he made his home at Russellville.

[6] William Neil (or Neal) was promoted in 1779 to a captaincy in the Washington County militia, wherein he had served as ensign since Feb. 26, 1777. Captain Neil with his company went on the King's Mountain campaign. See Lyman C. Draper, *King's Mountain and its Heroes* (Cincinnati, 1881), 405.

[7] For a sketch of Capt. John Campbell of Royal Oak see *Dunmore's War*, 47, note 83.

and Beattie, and such Subalterns as you may think proper, and the whole to be headed by yourself. Give caution to the Officers not to Order any of the Men or Officers, already ordered for the Kentucky Service, for altho. that trip is laid asside another is ordered, from which you may be excused, but it will be proper the others hold themselves in readiness. I think the Men ought at farthest to set out Tuesday Morning, taking with them provision to Serve them some days, as they cannot be supply'd until they get to the Mines. Such as chooses had better take Horses. The Governor has ordered no assistance from the Counties this way to Kentucky, but has ordered an Expedition against the Chuckamoggas. The French have Landed a fine Army in America. We have lately taken 700 of the Enemys Horse in one Body in the South. The Tories on the Frontiers are deceived once more, it may be for our good if they all thro' off the Mask, but can they claim the same lenity as have on former occasions been shown. Let both of the Companies rendezvous at Charles Bowens[1] one time where I will met them on giving me notice as it may be proper to take different routs from thence. I judge it improper to leave home, therefore cannot see you as I intended. Charlestown Surrendered the 11th of May after a close Seige of 30 days.—Capt May from Kentucky says that he thinks the Main Body of the Enemy are gone to the Illinois, however he says 200 Indians was seen crossing the Ohio near the Falls a few days before he left Kentucky.

I am Sir Your most Obedient Servant

ARTHUR CAMPBELL

MAJOR EDMONDSON

P. S. I have just heard that one of the heads of the Tories from Carolina was on Reed Creek[2] yesterday,—It may be proper to caution the Companies your way to have their Arms all in order and to be on their guard, indeed it may be dangerous for so many Men to be assembled tomorrow unarmed, now seems to be the time to try the sincerity of those who have professed themselves Citizens of America.

A. C.

[*Addressed:*] To Major William Edmondson, Public Service.

[1] Charles Bowen lived at Crab Orchard at the head of Holston River, probably in the modern Bland County, Va. Bowen, who was born in 1747, was in Capt. William Edmiston's company on the King's Mountain campaign. In 1832 he was living in Blount County, Tenn. See Draper Mss., 2DD228.

[2] For this location see *Dunmore's War*, 63, note 4.

[Col. Arthur Campbell to Maj. William Edmiston. 9DD22. A. L. S.]

June 25 [1780] 3 OClock Afternoon
DEAR SIR:
I have just received another Express from Col⁰ Crockett and Capt Quirk the Tories are actually embodied in the Glades,[1] to the Amount of Two Hundred, and some have certainly kill'd nine Men.—Send Expresses to the different Captains to hurry them along, let no time be lost either night or day, the Men had better come this way to be supply'd with powder. Public Lead I have none, but there is some of my own here, that such as chooses may be supply'd with you had better desire, that every one that can—should come along. the matter will be decided in a few days.
I am Sir Your Obedient Ser^{vt}

ARTHUR CAMPBELL

[Addressed:] To Major William Edmiston, Public Service

[Summary of a letter of John Breckinridge,[2] Fort Chiswell, June 25, 1780, to Col. William Preston. Printed in *John P. Branch Historical Papers*, IV, 314.]

News of the rising of the Tories on New River confirmed. Husk, supposed to be a spy, came to the mines, was detained by Captain Quirk. A gathering in the Glades, including nine light horsemen refugees from Carolina. A captain of militia named Swift brings the same accounts and adds that there were British officers among them. Preston's neighbors will no doubt be active on this occasion.

[1] The "Glades" lay at the head of the south fork of Holston River in Wythe County, Va., not far from the lead mines.
[2] For a sketch of John Breckinridge see *Wis. Hist. Colls.*, XXIII, 66, note 1.

CONTRACT FOR RESCUING INDIAN CAPTIVES

CONTRACTS FOR RESCUING CAPTIVES

[Agreements to recover captives.[1] 1H137–38. D. S.]

Articles of Agreement made by and bettween Lewis (an Indian) of the One Part and Henry Mc Bride[2] of the Other Part—Witnesseth

1st That the said Lewis doth hereby engage as far as lies in his power to release & bring in from the Indians, the Undernamed Persons now prisoners in their Custody, Viz^t Mary Tucker, Lewis Tucker, Elizabeth Turner, James Turner, Elizabeth Faulks & George Faulks, taken off the Waters of Racoon, from a sugar Camp.

2^d The said Henry Mc Bride doth hereby engage to deliver unto the afforsaid Lewis for his Services as afforementioned Two Milch Cows or Cows with calf, for each & every of the abovementioned prisoners when they are delivered up.

3dly And as each of the afforesaid prisoners will require a Horse to ride home the said Henry Mc Bride doth hereby engage to give a Horse or Mare in Good Order for each of said Horses that may be rendered Invalid by such services.

In Witness whereof the parties engaging have hereunto set their Hands & Seals this 27th Day of June 1780

HENRY M^{c}BRIDE

Witness Present
Wm BONIFACE

his
LEWIS + LAPANDIER
mark

[*Endorsed:*] Articles of Agreement between Indian Lewis & Mc Bride

---

Articles of Agreement made & concluded on between Lewis (an Indian) of the One Part and John Harden of the Other Part—Witnesseth——

1st That the Said Lewis hereby engageth to release & bring in from the Indians the Undernamed persons now in their Custody, Viz^t Mary Harden wife of John Hardin & her Two Children One

---

[1] This agreement and the succeeding one were made at Fort Pitt at the time of the council held by the French officers. See *Ill. Hist. Colls.*, V, 163–67.

[2] James McBride, who lived on Little Raccoon Creek, in Robinson Township, Washington County, Pa., was the father of ten sons, of whom Henry appears to have been one. The McBrides were neighbors of the Tuckers and Turners, whose children were in captivity.

a Boy of Five Years old and the Other Four Years Old, taken on the River Ohio about Forty Miles below Wheeling.

2^d The Afforesaid John Hardin doth hereby promise to pay unto the afforesaid Lewis for the abovementioned Services, two Milch Cows, or Cows with Calf, for each and every of the Above Mentioned prisoners at the time of Delivery.

3dly And As the s^d Lewis will require Horses to carry the said prisoners into the American Lines, or be thereby Invalided by such services, then the Afforesaid John Hardin doth hereby engage to make good the Damages that said Horses may receive on account of said Services.

In Witness Whereof the parties have hereunto set their Hands & Seals this 28th Day of June and in Year 1780
Witness Present
JACOB COLMAN[1]   JOHN HARDIN
JACOB SPRINGER
[*Endorsed:*] Articles of Agreement between Lewis (an Indian) and John Hardin

FRENCH AGENT AT FORT PITT

[Summary of a letter of Col. Mottin de la Balme,[2] Fort Pitt, June 27, 1780, to Chevalier de la Luzerne.[3] Printed in *Ill. Hist. Colls.*, V, 163–68.]

Found on arrival here that the United States was threatened with a general Indian war. Linctot, who had wandered some

[1] According to reminiscences in Draper Mss., 13CC9, "Coonrod Coleman and another man, went to Detroit to get these [the Hardin family] exchanged. Brought back Mrs. Hardin."

[2] Col. Augustin Mottin de la Balme came to the United States in 1778 and offered his services to Congress, by whom he was appointed inspector-general of cavalry, an office for which his previous military training had prepared him. Upon the appointment of Pulaski as head of the Continental cavalry La Balme resigned, and spent the winter of 1779–80 in Philadelphia. There he met the French minister, and, apparently authorized by him, came West in June, 1780, possibly in response to Brodhead's request for a French officer to treat with the Indians. La Balme arrived at Vincennes sometime before July 30, thence he proceeded to the Illinois, and raised a force of French-Canadians destined to attack and capture Detroit. Late in October the expedition arrived at the Miami village on the site of Fort Wayne. This they captured and plundered, but the Indians and traders, rallying a few days later, defeated La Balme's force at Aboite Creek, killed their leader, and entirely dispersed the expedition. See brief account in M. M. Quaife, *Chicago and the Old Northwest* (Chicago, 1913), 97–99. See also Ill. Hist. Soc., *Transactions*, 1909, 104–34.

[3] Anne César, Chevalier de la Luzerne, was born in Paris in 1741 of an illustrious family. His first career was that of arms, which he relinquished in 1776

years among Indians because he refused to serve under English flag, left here May 7, accompanied by thirty trusty Indians, to go and ward off threatened attacks on the frontiers. His messages received by several tribes; some chiefs came back here with him for a council. Writer as a French chief spoke to them. They promise entire obedience to the French, but ask for goods; say that last year a thousand promises were made them at Philadelphia; now they are neglected and abandoned, and threatened by the English. Writer told them the French king wished them to be quiet and listen to Spanish and Americans. Bad treatment by all whites here except commandant. While treating for peace, one band of men attempted to massacre them; another to steal their horses. Writer descends the river with three Frenchmen and an old Shawnee princess.[1] Linctot is to go overland and try and attach Indians to cause of United States. Value of Linctot's services. Relations between French and Indians advantageous. One Pierre Thibau of Captain Craig's artillery is a French deserter, desires reënstatement.

A LOYALIST LETTER

[Jacob Peteson to Michael Price.[2] 5QQ35. A. L. S.]

HOLESTON June the 29th 1780

RESPECTIVE FRIEND:

I beg Leave to congratulate You my Dear Friend on a Subject of no small importance concerning the Disturbances in your County which I have heard of Late which is that the county is like to be torn to pieces by the Whigs since they heard that Charlestown was taken by the British but Dear Sir I have a Lamentable Story to Inform you off and indeed I would be glad that you would keep it Secret which is that Charlestown is re-

for diplomacy. In that year he was French minister to the Court of Bavaria. In 1779 he was appointed minister to the United States arriving in September, but he was not formally presented to Congress until November. La Luzerne was a prudent and gracious diplomat, on confidential terms with Washington and Lafayette. He served throughout the Revolution, returning to France in 1783. In 1788 he was appointed ambassador to London where he died in 1791.

[1] Probably this was the Grenadier Squaw, for whom see *Frontier Defense*, 26, note 57.

[2] As early as 1777 Michael Price was suspected of Loyalist tendencies. See *ibid.*, 169.

taken by the French and likewise New York which is for certain tho I beg to be excused for my short Epistole tho if you will be pleased to meat me at Shells [Shulls] this 29th Day of June I would inform you in a more inteligible manner. I have no more to say at present but still remain your resp^t Friend

JACOB PETESON [?]

To Mr MICHAEL PRICE Montgomery County

BRADY RESCUES MRS. STOOPS

[Summary of a letter of Col. Daniel Brodhead, Fort Pitt, June 29, 1780, to Gen. George Washington. Printed in Sparks, *Corr. Amer. Rev.*, III, 9–11, and in *Pa. Archives*, XII, 243.]

Encloses letters from Colonel Bowman and Rev. David Zeisberger. Accounts alarming; Brodhead's messages to Indians may prevent British expedition. Capt. Samuel Brady has just returned from Sandusky; took two squaws, one escaped after six days; he brought the other to Kuskuskies where he met seven warriors with a woman and child captured on Chartier's Creek. Brady killed the Indian captain, brought in white woman, squaw escaped. Was without provisions six days, but brought in whole party safe. His zeal and good conduct commended.[1] Artillery safely arrived, with company of twenty-five men and three officers.

[Summary of a letter of Col. Daniel Brodhead, Fort Pitt, June 30, 1780, to Timothy Pickering. Printed in *ibid.*, 244.]

Alarming accounts of British activity. Brady's return from Sandusky; rescue of a white woman. Has provisions for only four weeks; alarming message from Colonel Steel; forced supplies will be necessary.

[1] Brady's Sandusky expedition and his rescue of Mrs. Stoops on the return trip are among the best-known events of his career, and many descriptions thereof are contained in the Draper Mss. We choose for publication, in addition to Brodhead's official reports, the account of Brady's brother, Hugh, who obtained his knowledge from Brady himself; the recollections of the captive boy, related to Dr. Draper by his widow; and those of one of Brady's scouts, related by his son.

[Reminiscences of Gen. Hugh Brady.¹ 7NN39, pp. 3-5, 8.]

Not long after this affair [rescue of the Henry children]² the captain at the solicitation of his colonel visited the upper Sandusky town³ with only eight men. on his near approach to the village he discovered men, women, and children amusing themselves in horse raceing. From the position which he had taken he witnessed the running of the Horses, which was continued throughout that day and until late in the afternoon of the next, when a gray horse which had proved the victor was beaten only by over-weighting him with two riders—after which, the men returned to the village, the women & children to picking berries. As no chance of taking a warrior prisoner presented, he caught two squaws and started for home. That night it commenced raining very hard and continued throughout all the next day, which destroyed their provisions and all the powder but a few charges which the captain had in a priming horn—The weather continued cloudy for several days after, and being without a compass to stear by, their progress was slow, and not very direct until the sun made its appearance, shortly after which they struck an old Indian path—which the captain knew led to the mouth of the Big Beaver. Having then been two days without provisions —he informed his men he would go in advance and try to kill something to eat—he had proceeded but a little way when he met on the path a party of Indians—the man in advance was riding, and accosted the Capt as a friend, who being disguised in Indian costume he mistook as such—and turning his head to announce him to his friends the Captain shot him, as he fell out of his saddle—the capt gave the war whoop which being answered by his friends in the rear (they supposing he had killed something for supper) induced the Indians to retreat—when the captain got to the dead Indian, he found a white boy fastened to his back, before he could extricate him he discovered the Indians returning, and seizing the mother of the child dragged her off much against her will, and escaped the Indians—His own men, on seeing the Indians supposing the captain was killed and having

¹ For a sketch of Gen. Hugh Brady see *Wis. Hist. Colls.*, XXIII, 375, note 2.
² General Brady's narrative of this incident is in *ibid.*, 375–76. It directly precedes the account we here publish.
³ The Indian village of Upper Sandusky was located on the eastern bank of Sandusky River three miles above the present town of that name in Wyandot County, Ohio.

no powder, let the squaws run and mad[e] their way to Fort McIntosh below the mouth of the Big Beaver—about 12 miles from the Fort the captain was met by a detachment sent out to bury him, his men having arrived and reported him killed—(Here I think it not out of place to say that the boy remained with the Indians until after Wayne's Treaty in 1795—when agreeably to its stipulations he was surrendered and brought to Pittsburgh. And when the Land West of the Ohio was brought into market, he purchased the sight on which the above affair took place, and built a cabin as near the spot the Indian was killed as could then be pointed out—and remained there till the fall of 1833 when he was killed by the fall of a tree—This I learnt from his son in 1837, his name was Stoopes.)

* * * * * * * *

Brady's Lake he named having discovered it as he went to Sanduskey, he never met an enemy there, as I have seen it stated, in some accounts of him. Brady's leap[1] is I apprehend a fiction, for I never heard him speak of it.

[Reminiscences of Mrs. Nancy Stoops.[2] 4S170–75.]

James Stoops & his wife Jane, probably came from Ireland with Gen[l] Hand:[3] They had 15 sons & one daughter—William

[1] One of the most persistent traditions with regard to Brady was that when pursued by Indians he leaped across Cuyahoga, just below Franklin Mills, where the breadth of the stream is over forty feet. It has been assumed that this event occurred on his first Sandusky expedition. His brother's refutation would seem sufficient to disprove the tradition.

[2] Mrs. Nancy Stoops, then nearly sixty-seven years of age, was interviewed Mar. 1, 1850 by Dr. Draper at Pittsburgh. She stated that she was married in 1808 to William Stoops, who was captured in childhood, and that he died July 24, 1835.

[3] James Stoops came to Fort Pitt before the Revolution as sergeant in the Irish regiment that formed its garrison. Securing his discharge from the army, he settled as a tenant on the land of Gen. Edward Hand, two miles above the mouth of Chartier's Creek. There the capture of his wife and child occurred. Mrs. Jane, or Jenny, Stoops became in after years a devoted champion of Captain Brady. When he was arrested and tried in 1792 for the murder of an Indian, she planned to rescue him from the officers of the law in case he should be convicted and sentenced for the crime. Mrs. Stoops died about the year 1793 and was buried in the graveyard of the First Presbyterian Church of Pittsburgh.

was the youngest,—the four youngest residing with their parents —the others in Ireland: William Stoops used pleasantly to say, that there were fifteen brothers of them, & each had a sister.

Three of the children were at Pittsburgh attending school. Mrs Stoops thought all day she had seen the shadows of Indians on the hill in the woods near the house, but her husband hooted at it. In the night they were awakened by Indians trying to break into the front door. Mr S. made several efforts to carry off the child, but every time he would cry out lustily—finally Mrs S. seeing the futility of an attempted escape with the little affrighted boy, & not willing to abandon him herself, she urged her husband to escape, that he might be a father to the children in town— & perhaps he might be able to get help in time to rescue her & the child. He went off through the back door, in his shirttail, taking his gun; he soon shot at the Indians, & made off, they following him some distance.

Mrs Stoops got into the potatoe-hole under the floor, leaving little William (between 3 & 4 years old) in bed. The Indians first set the house on fire, then broke in—going to the bed where the child was—a mother's affection prevailed, & she called out in agony, begging them to spare her child. One of the Indians replied by asking in broken English, where she was? She told, & directed which board to lift up, & let her out of her hiding place. Both mother & child were saved.

After robbing the house, particularly of victuals—as also milk from the milk-house—they departed with their prisoners, leaving the house in flames. Mrs Stoops would break twigs by the way, to enable her husband to pursue—& discovering this, the Indians beat her. They cut off her petticoats, squaw fashion, to enable her to travel better.

On the northern bank of Mahoning Creek, 33 miles from Beaver, & about a mile & a half below where the state line crosses the Mahoning—& two miles below Lowell.[1] (Mrs N. Stoops is certain as to the spot where the Indian's remains were found by Mr John McFarland, about 1796, who married a sister of hers—she has often been there)—was where Mrs Jane Stoops was rescued, & the Indian killed.[2]

[1] This place is now called Lowellville in Mahoning County, Ohio.

[2] "A brother-in-law of W$^{m.}$ Stoops, John McFarland, purchased the spot where M$^{rs.}$ Stoops was rescued—& there died, his descendants yet residing there. When McFarland cleared up the land, some years ago, he found the bones—& for several years after they were yet lying there." Draper Mss., 4S169.

Brady & 2 or 3 others were returning from Sandusky with one Squaw prisoner. Brady was in advance, with (as Mrs S. thinks) his last load of powder but one, in his rifle—met the seven Indians—only the head one on horseback, with little William tied behind him—Mrs Stoops near her son, & the other Indians following behind on foot. Brady shot the Indian dead, to whom the little boy was tied—he fell off his horse: The other Indians quickly treed. Don't recollect about Brady trying to get the powder-horn—nor of an Indian snapping his gun at him. Mrs Stoops seeing Brady in Indian dress, & painted, & not doubting but he was a real Indian, enquired—"What did you kill your brother for?"—"Brother, be d—d," replied Brady, "come with me!" Neither Brady nor Mrs Stoops though well acquainted, at first recognized each other—though soon discovered. They made off. Near by, Brady & his party crossed the Mahoning—& the squaw waded (or swam) over, carrying Mrs Stoops on her back—& once over, she exclaimed to Mrs Stoops "Puck-e-she! Puck-e-she!"—which meant[1]—"make your escape—clear yourself!"—& then the squaw re-crossed the stream & disappeared. Either Brady did not notice it, or if he did was indifferent about her under the new circumstances of the case.

When the squaw arrived where the Indians were, they were debating whether to kill the little white boy, since his mother had escaped & their leader had been killed—& one of the Indians had already struck him a tomahawk blow on the head, inflicting a wound an inch & a half long. The squaw now coming up, begged the boy's life—which was granted her, she becoming nurse. At Detroit he was sold to the British, & sent to school.[1]

That night Brady & his party lay under a shelving rock—& the Indians in pursuit came so close by, that the whites held their breath to avoid the least noise. Brady went to Fort McIntosh. Mrs Stoops was badly scratched & lacerated with thorns & bushes, & was lame a considerable time. After she reached home, she became so much effected with reflections upon her captivity, & the uncertain fate of her little boy, that her friends thought she would go crazy.

William Stoops was detained in captivity 3 years. Recollects something about an Indian giving information about the boy, & being offered a reward to return him to his parents—he prob-

---

[1] Samuel Murphy when prisoner at Detroit in 1781 saw William Stoops among the other prisoners. *Ibid.*, 3S61.

SAMUEL MURPHY
From a Daguerreotype Presented by him to Dr. Draper

ably failed in his efforts to do so. He was sent with other prisoners to the East & Sam¹ Stoops, his oldest brother, went & got him, aided by Gen¹ Hand, & brought him home to Pittsburgh on a salt pack-horse. His mother at the time of his arrival, was 3 miles distant attending a sick woman—& returned in haste, not putting on her clothes: She knew her boy by a mark on his body.

[Reminiscences of Samuel Sprott.[1] 19S274–75.]

Brady with a party—four or five altogether—went to Sandusky to catch a prisoner & learn information about the Indian towns and designs in that quarter. They were returning, had run out of provisions, & had only one load [of powder] left, & that was in Brady's gun—they came on the Mahoning, & Brady bleated up a doe, he snapped, but his gun missed fire. He picked out a few dry grains of powder from his horn & re-primed his gun, & started after the retreating deer to try to bleat her up again; and as he came round a large log, he discovered a party of Indians approaching—one Indian on horseback with a small boy fastened behind him—Mrs. Stoops, a prisoner, also mounted—the rest all on foot. Brady said he happened to discover a little hand around the Indian's breast—it instantly flashed upon his mind that it was a prisoner child, & he aimed a little higher & shot—the gun fired clear, and the Indian fell from his horse, with the lad fastened to him—Brady ran up, & tried to jerk loose the Indian's powder horn, as he had no powder to re-load with; one of the Indians flashed his gun at Brady, the Indians having treed—& Brady's men, having no loads nor amunition, could only halloo & thus help to scare the enemy. Brady driven by the enemy's fire and position from securing the coveted powder horn, now less

[1] Samuel Sprott was born in June, 1761 in County Down, Ireland. When he was two years of age his father and family emigrated to Pennsylvania, settling first at Cumberland, then in 1773 removing to Westmoreland, where they made their home on Montour's Run. Samuel was employed, in 1791, in the spy service and later carried dispatches for Wayne; he was one of Brady's scouts, and accompanied him on several expeditions. Sprott was in service for about four years, and at one time acted as paymaster of the militia. He died at his home on Little Beaver Creek, Jan. 23, 1832. Dr. Draper interviewed Sprott's son, John, in 1863, and obtained from him his recollections of what his father had heard Captain Brady relate.

exposed jerked Mrs Stoops from her horse, & ran taking her by the hand. Brady's party now scattered, & the Indians did not pursue.

LOYALIST PLOT IN SOUTHWEST

[Summary of a letter of James McGavock,[1] Fort Chiswell, June 30, 1780, to Col. William Preston. Printed in *John P. Branch Historical Papers*, IV, 315–16.]

Last night a man who was afraid to come in person lest it should be discovered, sent his wife to inform me that John Griffith has been rousing and encouraging the Tories on Walker's Creek and rewards of many guineas are offered for the capture of the principal men, particularly of Preston and McGavock. Griffith has now gone promising to return in two weeks with a large body of Tories. Colonel Campbell, who was here this morning, says that the Tories are not removing their property; this makes him fear they will soon be back in great force. His advice is to secure assistance from neighboring counties. He promises to raise a hundred men and keep them ready to march on the shortest notice.

NO REËNFORCEMENTS AVAILABLE

[Gen. George Washington to Col. Daniel Brodhead. 1H139. Transcript.]

HEAD QUARTERS BERGEN COUNTY JERSEY 4th July 1780.
DEAR SIR:
I have duly rec[d] your favors of the 18th March 24th April and 13th and 30th of May. It is much to be regretted that the state of our regular Troops will not admit of a detachment sufficient to reduce the posts of the enemy to the Westward, or even to undertake anything offensive against the hostile tribes of Indians. Militia, besides being very expensive, are so exceedingly capricious, that I should be loth to attempt anything with them which depended upon more than a very short time to accomplish the object.—

[1] For a sketch of James McGavock see *Wis. Hist. Colls.*, XXIII, 154, note 3.

We are in hourly expectation of a considerable French land and sea force, which is intended to cooperate with us against the common enemy. We are, for this purpose, endeavoring to draw out a competent reinforcement of Men and supplies to enable us, in conjunction with our allies, to strike decisively at the Enemy. I fear, we shall, notwithstanding the emergency of the occasion, fall very far short of the number of men required. I mention these matters to shew the impracticability of detaching any troops at present to the Westward, altho' I look upon the reduction of the post of Detroit as a measure most desirable; and without which I believe the savages upon that quarter will never be kept in proper order.

I do not conceive that I have a right to delegate a general power to hold Courts Martial. There must be an application for a Court whenever particular objects present themselves. This may, it is true in some measure delay the course of justice, but it cannot, from the necessity of the case, be avoided.

I am with great Regard Dear Sir Your most ob^t Servant

G° WASHINGTON

COL° BRODHEAD.

LOYALISTS DEFEATED IN SOUTHWEST

[Summary of a letter of Gov. Thomas Jefferson, Richmond, July 3, 1780, to Col. William Preston. 5QQ38. L. S. Printed in *Ill. Hist. Colls.*, VIII, 434.]

Protection of lead mines by militia of Washington, Botetourt, and Montgomery counties a wise measure. Col. Joseph Crockett's battalion must aid in garrisoning western posts and in strengthening Colonel Clark. Distress of western frontier is general. Five thousand militia have been sent to Carolina. Col. William Campbell[1] is to turn his force against internal enemies; offensive operations are most effective.

[1] For a sketch of Col. William Campbell see *Dunmore's War*, 43, note 58. In 1780 he was a member of the Virginia legislature, and in June was excused from attendance in order to protect the frontier.

[Summary of a letter of Col. Arthur Campbell, Camp in Baker Settlement, July 3, 1780, to Col. William Preston. Printed in *John P. Branch Historical Papers*, IV, 316–17.]

Have proceeded this far up New River in pursuit of insurgents under Roberts, who are several days' march in advance and it is hopeless to try to overtake them. Their total defeat at Ramsour's Mills June 22[1] has given General Rutherford's[2] militia leisure to intercept Roberts. Have apprehended some runaways from the battle. Have sent out several parties to disarm, distress, and terrify the disloyal settlements. A letter from Rutherford to Col. Benjamin Cleveland[3] reports that the English have retreated from Camden towards Charleston, which is besieged by a Spanish and French fleet. The prisoners taken here are to be sent to

[1] The battle of Ramsour's Mills between the Whigs and Loyalists of North Carolina occurred June 20 (not 22) near the site of the present Lincolnton in that state. The Loyalists were commanded by Col. John Moore and Nicholas Welch, and brought on the action contrary to orders from Cornwallis. See full account in Draper Mss., 22VV62.

[2] Griffith Rutherford was a Scotch-Irishman, born in 1721, whose parents died on the voyage when emigrating to America. Young Rutherford was brought up by a relative in New Jersey. He first came West as a surveyor, and in 1753 settled on the frontier of North Carolina near Salisbury. He was a militiaman in the French and Indian War, and later served against the Regulators. In 1775 Rutherford was chairman of the local Committee of Safety, and suppressed a Loyalist movement in his district. In 1776 he was chosen brigadier-general and commander of an expedition against the Cherokee. After the fall of Charleston in 1780 General Rutherford embodied the Whig militia, and after defeating the Loyalists at Ramsour's Mills, joined General Gates and was wounded and captured at Camden. While a prisoner he was confined on a ship off St. Augustine, Fla. Released in 1781, he was employed during the latter part of the year in another campaign against the Loyalists. After the Revolution General Rutherford served in the State Senate, and in the convention of 1788 for ratifying the Federal Constitution. In 1792 he removed to Sumner County, Tenn., where he was elected president of the territorial council. He died at his Tennessee home, Aug. 10, 1805.

[3] Benjamin Cleveland was born May 26, 1738 in Prince William County, Va. In early life he removed to the frontier, where he became famous as a hunter and woodsman. About the year 1769 he settled on the Yadkin River in North Carolina. Thence, incited by Daniel Boone, Cleveland explored Kentucky, and visited the Cherokee country. During the Revolution Cleveland was a militia colonel for Wilkes County, and led its forces in the battle of King's Mountain. Throughout the war he was active in the suppression of Loyalist uprisings. In 1784 he removed to South Carolina, where he died in 1806. For an extended sketch of his life see Lyman C. Draper, *King's Mountain and Its Heroes*, 425–54.

North Carolina, those in our state to be confined at the lead mines. Property of insurgents sold for benefit of troops, but if governor requires will refund money to state. At the battle of Ramsour's Mills Colonel McDonald[1] with 350 men totally defeated 1,500 Tories; they had 500 killed and taken on the spot, many drowned in the mill pond. General Rutherford's horsemen, 500 in number, came up towards the end of the action and pursued them several miles until they dispersed. This should put an end to Toryism in this country.

[Col. William Preston to Capt. James Byrn.[2] 5QQ37. A. L. S.]

July 5th 1780

Capt Byrn:

The Insolence of the Tories and the Disturbance given by them to the well affected Inhabitants of this and the Neighbouring Counties demands every Exertion in our Power to suppress them by every legal Means that God and the Government of the Commonwealth have put into our hands. And as many of our Friends & Neighbours are at present engaged in this necessary Service, to the great prejudice of their private Affairs, there is therefore the greatest Reason and Justice that we in this part of the Country should give them all the Assistance we can at this important Juncture; and the rather, as it may be a Means of reducing those unhappy People to reason and of bringing them to a Just Sense of the Duty they owe their Country, in which the[y] Live, and by which they have hitherto been protected in the peaceable Enjoyment of their Lives Liberties & Property.

You will therefore be pleased to collect and embody any Number of Men you can not exceeding fifty with the proper officers out of the Companies commanded by Capt Wm Robinson of

---

[1] Joseph McDowell, known as "Quaker Jo" from his home at Quaker Meadows was born near Winchester, Va., in 1756. Having removed to Burke County, N. C., he entered the service in 1776, and went out on Rutherford's Cherokee campaign. In 1780 McDowell was in the battle of Ramsour's Mills, as subordinate to Col. Francis Locke, the chief in command of the Whig forces. McDowell commanded a detachment at King's Mountain, and in 1781 at the Cowpens. Later he was prominent in social and political life, served in the state legislature, and represented North Carolina in the Third and Fifth Congresses. He died Aug. 11, 1801.

[2] For a sketch of James Byrn see Wis. Hist. Colls., XXIII, 75, note 3.

Botetourt[1] and Capt Trigg[2] and yourself in this County, and proceed without loss of Time up the great Road to near Peek Creek[3] under Colour of going to Garrison the Fort at the Mines a few Days. When you get to the fork of the proper place you are to turn off & without loosing time to proceed immediately to Walkers Creek[4] where a great many of those disafected People reside which you are to Disarm with all imaginable Secrecy and Dispatch beginning above Shannons[5] and thence up the several Branches of the creek where there are Settlements as well as on Wolf Creek[6] if you can spare a Party for that Purpose Those who make it appear to the Court or any two Magistrates that they are & have been friends to american Liberty are to have their Arms delivered back to them, but in the mean time I think there ought to be no distinction made except in the Case of Capt Thomas Ingles[7] whose Arms are not to be disturbed. You will also make a diligent Search at every Place for Papers, and if you find any of a treasonable tendency to Secure them & the Persons in whose Possession they are found & bring them to Justice. If Britain,[8] that Infamous Vilain and traitor to his Country, can be found be sure to bring him in well secured. The arms when taken are to be delivered to the Commandant at the Lead Mines taking his receipt for the same and distinguishing by proper marks who is the Owner of each Piece, You are also to secure all the Ammunition that you find in Possession of those People. Such as obstinately persist in concealing their Arms or refusing to deliver them are to be taken into Custody & brought off; but no Violence is to be offered to Women or Children, or the old & helpless, nor indeed to any either in their Persons

---

[1] For this officer see *ibid.*, 76, note 2.

[2] Daniel, brother of Col. Stephen Trigg, was an early settler on the western waters. In 1773 he was chosen sheriff of Fincastle County, and the succeeding year guarded the frontier during Col. William Christian's absence on the Point Pleasant campaign. In 1777 Daniel Trigg was a captain in the Montgomery County militia, and throughout the Revolution was active in protecting the border.

[3] For this stream see *ibid.*, 52, note 8.

[4] For Walker's Creek see *Dunmore's War*, 56, note 96.

[5] Shannon's was at the "big crossing" of New River near the mouth of Walker's Creek. See *Wis. Hist. Colls.*, XXIII, 274, 276.

[6] For Wolf Creek see *ibid.*, 52, note 2.

[7] For a sketch of Col. Thomas Ingles see *Dunmore's War*, 179, note 24.

[8] Nathaniel Brittain was apprehended, tried, and sentenced in August, 1780. See *post*, 263.

or Property who will give up their Arms and Ammunition peaceably

As many Circumstances may Occur which will make it necessary to vary from the above Instructions you are therefore in such Cases to use your own discretion & to treat those People with all the Lenity your Duty to your Country will admit & their Behaviour on the Occasion Merit. On your Return you may disarm such People beyond New River as you have Just cause to believe are dissaffected to the present Government and Aiding or Assisting by any Means, the Enemies thereof.

That the foregoing Instructions may be put into Execution with Propriety and Dispatch the officers and soldiers must go on horseback; & for such as have not Horses you are hereby Authorized to Impress Horses & Saddles from such as cannot go themselves, taking care to comply with the Law herein, as well as in Impressing Provisions should you find such a step Necessary. By this means you may perform this service and return to your house by next Tuesday or Wednesday at furthest when this Tour of Duty will be at an End and the Company are to be discharged. Indeed nothing but the Importance of this Undertaking could have induced me to call Men from home at this critical Season; but I have hopes that if the Plan is properly Executed it will be a means of humbling those People and of course removing the Cause of so much disturbance for the future. Should you meet the Botetourt Militia on their return, whether they have succeeded or not, you are to proceed to perform the above Service.

You will get Pilots Either in Capt McCorkles or Capt Pattons[1] Company but you must be catious in the Choice of them.

I wish you Success and am Sir your hble Servt

Wm Preston

To Capt. James Byrn

[1] For a sketch of James McCorkle see *Wis. Hist. Colls.*, XXIII, 135, note 8. For Capt. Henry Patton see *ibid.*, 51, note 5.

FRENCH AGENT SENT TO DELAWARES

[Summary of a letter of Col. Daniel Brodhead, Headquarters, Pittsburgh, July 7, 1780, to Maj. Daniel Maurice Godefroy de Linctot. Printed in *Pa. Archives*, XII, 246.]

Linctot requested to carry messages to Coshocton, to encourage the Delawares to maintain their allegiance and to bring in British prisoners, to inform them of the proposed punitive expedition, and persuade them to take the first steps toward peace. Ordered to find out the disposition of each tribe, and return to this place without loss of time.

PLANS FOR AN EXPEDITION

[Summary of a latter of Col. Daniel Brodhead, Headquarters, Fort Pitt, July 9, 1780, to Col. Archibald Lochry. Printed in Darlington, *Fort Pitt*, 236–37.]

Men should be protected during harvest. The sixty rangers proposed to be raised in Westmoreland County must be subsisted by state. Strict economy necessary to subsist Continental troops. "If I can possibly obtain supplies, I shall yet make an excursion into the Indian country in time to destroy the corn, etc. But I conceive the best method will be to march on horse if they can be furnished."

[Summary of a circular letter of Col. Daniel Brodhead, Headquarters, Fort Pitt, July 10, 1780, to the county lieutenants. Printed in *Pa. Archives*, XII, 246–47.]

Necessary to make a rapid excursion on horses to attack some hostile Indian town when corn is ripe. Secrecy a condition of success. Engage volunteers to furnish fifteen days' provisions for themselves. Rendezvous at Fort McIntosh August 12. Send in returns of those engaged by August 4. Each volunteer to furnish a cutlass. "A severe blow at the intended Season may send our Enemies to a greater distance and prevent a greater Effusion of blood in future."

LOYALISTS SUPPRESSED IN SOUTHWEST

[Col. William Preston to Capt. Isaac Taylor.[1] 5QQ40. Autograph draft signed.]

July 12th 1780

SIR:
The Insolence of the Tories, and the Disturbance given by them to the well affected Inhabitants of this County demands all the Exertions in our power to suppress them by every means that Providence and the Government of the commonwealth have put into our hands. And as the late Insurrection had been in a great measure suppressed by the activity of our Militia & the friendly & timely assistance of the Militia of the neighbouring Counties, whose conduct on these Occasion's deserves great applause, to prevent anything of the kind for the future it has been Indeed absolutely neccessary for the safety and protection of the well affected Inhabitants, as well as to overawe those that are yet dissafected, to raise two small Troops of light Horse to remain on Duty for two or three months should there be Occasion to continue them so long.—Capt Robert Sayers[2] is to command one of those Troops & You, Sir, are to take the Command of the other.

You will therefore be pleased, with the Assistance of Mr Wm Glaves the L^t & Mr John Ward the Cornet in s^d Troop immediately to engage Thirty Men, each to find a good Horse fit for the Service. When you[r] men are embodied You will proceed up New river and disarm all the Tories that reside in the four Companies of Militia there. And as I am informed that many of the Insurgents who Joined roberts their Commander have deserted from him and returned, you will endeavour to take all such and bring them to Justice. They may continue in Confinement at the Lead

[1] For Capt. Isaac Taylor see *ibid.*, 76, note 1.
[2] Robert, son of Alexander Sayers, was born in 1752, probably on the family estate of Beverly Manor, where his grandfather, Robert, died in 1746. Robert Sayers Jr. was educated in Bedford County, and was attending school when his father died in 1765. In 1767 Robert Breckinridge was appointed his guardian. Young Sayers entered the army in 1776 as first lieutenant of the Seventh Virginia Regiment; on April 4, 1777 he was promoted to a captaincy. He served in Morgan's brigade, his regiment becoming in 1778 the Fifth Virginia. In May, 1779 Sayers was honorably discharged and returned to Montgomery County, where his home was situated not far from that of Colonel Preston. In 1781 Sayers represented his county in the Virginia Assembly. He was still living in 1805.

mines untill the Court can meet to try them. You will also proceed to disarm all the Tories above the Court House, a List of whom you are to demand from each of the Cap^{ts} in that district. The Arms & Ammunition taken from these People are to be Deposited at the lead mines. Any further Instructions you may receive from Col Walter Crockett or myself from time to time you will please to observe.

In conducting this Business I beg that you will proceed in the most Orderly Manner & with the utmost Caution. That the friends to american Liberty may be distinguished from its Enemies; and even to the latter, I would hope that no cruelty or unnecessary outrage be committed upon them or their Property Especially on the Women & Children or the old & helpless. In taking any property from the Tories, I would have it secured but by no means Sold untill you have the Opinion of the Court thereon that they may have an Opportunity to be heard in their own Defence.—As true Bravery & humanity are inseparable; Your Company Exercising the latter on every Occasion will convince Mankind that they are possessed of the former. Mr Baker the Commissary & Quarter Master for the Western Department will Supply you with Provisions and Ammunition. You will please to make a report to me when Opportunity Offers of your Proceedings; and should any thing extraordinary happen you will inform me by Express.

Let me again entreat you to keep up good order and discipline amongst your men, & always to hold them in readiness to assist in repelling or pursuing any Parties of Savages that may appear in an hostile manner on our Frontiers.

W P

CAP^T ISAAC TAYLOR

Capt Sayers Instructions to be dated the 11th 1780
[*Endorsed:*] Instructions to the Cap^{ts} of Troops July 11th & 12th 1780 Ja^s Mores L^t R Simpson Cornet[1]

---

[1] These men were probably the subordinate officers in Capt. Robert Sayers' troop of horse.

FRONTIER RETREAT 217

[Col. Arthur Campbell to Col. William Campbell. 8DD3. Transcript.]

FORT CHISWELL, July 12th, sunrise [1780]
DEAR SIR:
I received intelligence last night that the enemy then embodied was about forty or fifty strong, the fort at the mines is prepared for defence. They may do mischief outside as robbers, but I hope strength enough will be collected today to chastise them. The men I mentioned last night to come from our county, may proceed without over-marching themselves, and act as future intelligence may make necessary. They have plundered two or three houses, and perhaps that is their real object.
I am Sir Your ob^d Servt
A. CAMPBELL
I think by the intelligence, the insurgents yesterday had not left the upper settlements of N. River, so I suppose can't be down before tomorrow.
To COL. WILLIAM CAMPBELL.

INDIAN COUNCIL AT DETROIT

[Captain Killbuck and the Delaware Council to Col. Daniel Brodhead. 1H140. In handwriting of Heckewelder.]

SALEM July ye 19th 1780.
Captn John Killbock & others the Councellors of Cooshocking to Col^o Brodhead as follows:
BROTHER MAHINGWE GEESHUCH:
I will aquaint You that Captn Pipe & Wingeenund are come back again from the Councill which was held at Detroit. Geyjachshuta was gone back already when they came there, but the Speeches was shown unto them, namely: a large Belt of 36 rows from the King of England with the Name of the Indian Agent marked therin. Again another Belt with 12 rows and a Tomhowk, likewise the Agents Name theron. Again another Belt of 12 rows with 8 spot's—Again another black Belt which is said to be a Speech from the Chibways—The contens of the large Belt was not fully understood, on account the chieff Interpreters not being present, but part of the Speech was thus: That the

King of England desires the 5 Nations to speak to all Nations, & desire them to be strong in being one People, so as had been concluded on from the beginning. That it was true, the 5 Nations had divided themselves, the one half having gone over to the Americans, but that no other Nation should follow their Example, for those who had done so should never again come in favour with him, he had thrown them away entirely.—With the 2^d Belt the English says to the Nations: That as the Tomhowk they had used hitherto, had been but a small one, they therefore supposed it was wore out by this time. Now they would give them a large Ax which was strong made, very Sharp and well hardened, so that it could not wear out so soon—The 3^d Belt with the 8 spott's is a Speech from the Mingoes, in which they tell all Nations that now they were 8 Nations who were one, and had joined themselves to strike the Americans with all their might, and not to give way to them on any Account. That as before they had been of different minds, they had been backward, but now the time was come, where they would do all that lay in their Power in fighting the Americans—After this Speech was delivered the Major [De Peyster] rose with the Belts in his hands making much noise and great talk, then handing the Belts, fi[r]st to the Chibways and from them to the Wyondott's the Ax was sharpened over and over again. After this all was over (Captn Pipe & Wingeenund present at the time) they was breaking up, when the half King's Brother rose, desired them to stay and hear a Speech he had brought from the French, (Major Lenkto's [Linctot's] Speech.) This Wyondott, delivered the Speech with great courage, then laid it down in the middle of them, opposite to the Wyondott Chieff, who taking it up very chearfully, put it under his Arm, then after smoking a Pipe laid it on the ground before him, but soon taking the Belt up again he put it in his Breeches till he had smoked an other Pipe being silent all the time but very glad, when at last he put it on the ground again, on which imediately the English Major arose took the Belt and threw it on the Ground tramping thereoon, saing: "I do not know from whence the Speech of such an ugly Bird comes." It is impossible that this Bird whom I destroyed but of late, and mashed him against the Ground, should have recovered again, and be so impudent as to sing again ect., The French present began to speak boldly theron, and a Quarrell between them and the English arose At last of all the Wyondott Chieff took the Belt up again, rose and made a long Speech, then threw the Belt to the English Major, who taking it spoke in the French Language to the French present, and then threw it out of Doors again an other House standing close by, where a Man seing it, took it away with him so that nobody knows what is become of the Belt.

This *Brother* is all I can tell You of this Matter from over the Lake. When Captn Pipe and Wingenund had returned to Sandusky the half King made a Speech to the former, desiring him not to force his People to go to live at Cooshocking, saing that they might go and see one another and return back here again. Then he (the half King) spoke to the People of Cooshocking in the following maner:

Cousin You that live at Cooshocking hearken unto me:
Cousin I tell You that as You told me what I desired of you, You would do; I therefore now desire of You not to listen any more to the Virginian Devils—The reson that I tell You this is because I find You are become to great with the Virginians, by which I lost 2 of my Woomen.[1] This Cousin what has been done unto me I dont mind yet, but I desire You now to leav off, and do so no more. I now furthur say unto You Cousin, that if You dont leave off soon to be so great with the Virg^s You will find yourselves in a miserable Condition. I will set up Bark between You and them. I also say unto You, make haste and fetch all Your People away from among the Virginians, free yourselves from them, be together at Cooshoking make great haste, for it will otherwise soon be to late for You, Cousin at Cooshacking. We are of Old Friends together, there is not a scar to be seen on You, caused by me, neither is there a Scars on me made by You. Cousin it is enough, I desire You now to leave off stealing my Horses, do it no more. Likewise Cousin I desire You to fetch me my Friends back again. Their Number is 4. two White Men, and to Woemen of my Collour. These my friend I love equal, the White as much as the others. Cousin I will tell You more: There came a party of Wyandotts (Warriors) over the Lake lately, among which was the Oncle of one of them Woemen which was taken away; the same was ready to go and watch the Road at Little Beaver Creek, there to kill any one of You my Cousins that he might meet with on the Way. I stop'd him for the present, thinking to speak once more to You my Cousin first—

Captn Pipe and Wingeenund saw when at Sandusky a party of 60 Warriors several others of 10 marching for to watch the Roads about little Beaver Creek in Order to kill every Dellaware they came across. The half King made a Speech to them to stay a little while yet, upon which they agreed to divide in smaller party's about little Beaver Creek and cross the big River for to do mischieff about Fort Pitt. We also hear by a relation of John Montures who went to War with the English & Shawnese

[1] This is a reference to the Indian women captured by Capt. Samuel Brady at the Upper Sandusky town. See *ante*, 202.

against the Settlements of Kentuck; that these have burnt 2 Forts. & taken 340 Prissoners, Men Woemen & Chilldren.[1]

Now *Brother Maghingwe Geeshuch:* This Is what I had to inform You. I have heard a great deal more than what is Wrote down here, but think part of it must be Lyes, yet my Boys will tell You all what I know.

Brother: Believe me, that I am very buisy a Working here at Cooshacking, but I begin now to be astonished.

Brother: I assure You that nobody shall break our Friendship We are one Man Brother. In a very short time Brother You shall hear me. As soon as these my 2 Boys return again 2 of my Captn^s shall go up to You, and then You will hear me—Take care of these my 2 Boys that they return safe, guard them to Fort McIntosh—Send me a Flag wherby You may know me when I come—My Boys are very Naked, I beg You may give them a Shirt a piece. All our Capt^{ns} remember their Compliments to You.

I am Your friend & Brother

JOHN KILLBUCK

COL^o BRODHEAD Comand^r W^n Departm^t

VIRGINIA LOYALISTS WARNED

[Col. William Preston to Loyalist leaders. 5QQ41. L. S.]

Thursday Morning July 20 1780

GENTLEMEN:

Since the Troubles which began in this County in June last, I am sorry to say that your Behaviour has been very distant. You cannot be insensible that the resentment of the well affected in this, and the Neighbouring Counties runs very high against you; & that you have enjoyed every Protection, that the best Citizens enjoyed notwithstanding your Conduct This resentment has been hitherto restrained, I may say without Vanity, by

---

[1] This is the Indian report of the capture of Ruddell's and Martin's Stations in Kentucky by Capt. Henry Bird's expedition. See a brief description in *Ill. Hist. Colls.*, VIII, p. cxxxvii; a more extended account is found in *Withers' Chronicles of Border Warfare*, 294–99. For Major De Peyster's letter on the arrival, Aug. 4, 1780, of a portion of the prisoners at Detroit, see *Mich. Pion. & Hist. Colls.*, XIX, 553.

myself, though not without diffaculty & Censure; which I have done, not from any love to your Political Sentiments but from a Regard for you as Neighbours.

I much expected that your own Peace and Safety would have induced you to fall on some publick method to secure both, by giving, or at least proposing some farther Security to the State of your peceable Intentions, in order to satisfy the Government as well as the Enraged Multitude How far you have complied with that formerly given you must be able to Judge & to which I am no Stranger — In short I must tell you plainly, That your Conduct on this Occasion has been Dark Sul[len] Disgusful Suspicious and Offensive to the Government of this state, & such a[s] will draw down its highest resentment—This I have long doubted & have laboured for Years past to convince you of your folly & Danger but to no purpose—I now find the Storm gathering against you from every Quarter which will surely burst upon you without prudent & Speedy Measures be fallen upon to prevent it. For which Reason I would request you all, and as many more as you Judge Proper, to come to my House next Saturday Morning, to consult in a Neighbourly way, the Proper steps for you to take for your own Peace, safety & security; & at the same time to to secure the Peace of the Community so far as relates to You & others in the same situation in this Company—I hereby Pawn my Veracity, that your Persons & Property shall be safe during this Interview That only two or three unarmed friends will attend to see & hear what passes & that I have no one thing in View but your Benifit & to secure the internal Peace of the State—Should you refuse to comply with this invitation to confer on such an important Subject, I shall then take it for Granted that you have farther Views which are distructive to the Peace of the country—I request of Mr Price to forward this to those to whom it is directed.

I am your hbl Servt

W^M PRESTON

To MR MICHAEL PRICE, MR JOHN & HOWARD HEAVIN MR JAMES BEANE MR JACOB SHULL, MR JOHN WALL & MR HARLESS & POOPICKHOOVER

The mutual Agreement[1] entered into last year, broke by M P in the first Instance by sending Expresses &^{ca} Trying Guns & preparations for War.

Our Property Divided by Garlick & Morgan & they Encouraged & Caressed.

Trees Blazed & Marked as Insults to the Country.

The Bond given, forfeited by the refusal of complying with the Law in giving in the Taxable Property as well as by Speeches. Correspondance carried on & Letters rec^d from hill & others,

The Express stop^d made Drunk, Exam'd & King George Huzzad for, on that, as well as at Walls & Banes Rollings & all public Occasions. & an agreement entered into to begin after harvest the work of murder. Did not Tom Hale threaten to kill my other Express? for what Reason?

A new Riffle and a large Sum of Money offered to an Asassin to Murder me in this Neighbourhood.—John McDonald threatens my life if the Sherif does his Duty in Collecting.—My Sons life threatened.

A Purse of Guineas offered for me on Walkers Creek & Elsewhere. H Ogle & four others to come to my house under the pretence of Buying a still & then to Murder me.—For what these Threatnings? what have I done?

Although the Troubles were Extensive, no One came to consult his own or his friends Safety, but listened to false reports kept a Suspicious Distance & made Preparations for extending the Trouble.

Col^o Campbells appointment & Instructions proceeding immediately from the Govr & Council, I cannot restrain him unless a proper Compliance now.—What can you promise y^{r}selves by standing out? [The Tories are used by the British as draught Horses or beasts of Burden] Can a few dispersed people without a Leader fly in the face of Continent?—it is true some secret Stabs may be given, & some murder committed, but will it not end in the Destruction of the Perpetrators & their Adherents? [*Endorsed:*] Copy of a Letter to the Nonjurors in Capt Byrn's Company July 20th 1780

[1] This that follows is a list of subjects which Colonel Preston intended to discuss with his Loyalist neighbors.

WYANDOT DEFEAT NEAR FORT McINTOSH

[Summary of a letter of Col. Daniel Brodhead, Fort Pitt, July 21, 1780, to Gen. George Washington. Printed in Sparks, *Corr. Amer. Rev.*, III, 32–34.]

Party of more than thirty Wyandot[1] crossed the Ohio five miles below Fort McIntosh, hid thirteen canoes, killed four reapers, and captured the fifth. Captain McIntyre ambushed Indians on their return, sunk two canoes, killed a number of Indians, took much plunder, and retook prisoner. Latter gave information of fifteen Wyandot who had marched toward Hannastown. Sent off another party to intercept them. Scarcity of provisions. Fall campaign planned against the Wyandot towns. Colonel Clark to visit Shawnee.

P. S. July 22. The fifteen Indians crossed the Ohio at Crow's Island, four miles above Fort McIntosh,[2] killed one man and returned; pursuing party sent out.

[Summary of a letter of Col. Daniel Brodhead, Fort Pitt, July 21, 1780, to Timothy Pickering. Printed in *Pa. Archives*, XII, 248–50.]

McIntyre's attack on Wyandot party. Return of provisions. David Duncan[3] employed to purchase supplies. If these can be obtained intend to penetrate Indian country on or near Lake Erie before corn is ripe. Col. George Morgan no longer acting; recommends new commissaries. Crops best ever known; a public mill would be a great advantage.

[1] See letter of Major De Peyster in *id.*, X, 404, stating that on account of the influence of Guyashusta over the Wyandot, their parties had gone toward Fort Pitt on war raids.
[2] This island, in Beaver County, Pa., is still known as Crow's Island.
[3] For a sketch of David Duncan see *Rev. Upper Ohio*, 61, note 89.

[Alexander Fowler[1] to Gen. Edward Hand. 3E1. A. L. S.]

PITTSBURGH 22^d July 1780.

DEAR HAND:

The last Letter I wrote you was dated the 27th of April wherein I related the transactions of this Quarter at that period. Since that time a Second Attempt has been made on Che^{t}ees [Chartiers] Settlement with the Indians, and Stoopes has suffered; having had his House Burnt and all that was in it. Seven Wyandots and Delawars attacked him in the dead of the Night—which you know is somewhat uncommon—he escaped, but his Wife and youngest Child were taken Prisoners. After taking what they could conveniently carry with them, they set fire to the poor fellows House, and left him without a Shirt but the one that covered him when he made his escape. Having traversed the Woods most part of the Night to Alarm his Neighbours, and seeing his House Consumed, and not knowing but his Wife and Child perished in the Flames, he made a melancholy and shocking appearance on his Arrival at Fort Pitt. I have rendered him every service in my power; but I beleive the Poor Man knows not well what to do, and he has entreated of me to inform you of his situation. His Wife however was restored to him in the folowing providential manner.

Captn Bradey a young Gent^n of the 8th Pen^l R^t with a party of Seven Men Attempted to surprise one of the Wyandot Towns, and succeeded so far as to bring off two Squaws Prisoners:—One of them made her escape Six days after she was taken, the other he brought with him to Beaver Creek, within about Thirty Miles of Fort McIntosh. By this time he had but three Men in his party besides himself; the other three being overcome w^t Fatigue, were obliged to Steer their Course by a different rout. Having got to the Waters of Beaver Creek, he espyed a Party of Warriours, on what I beleive they call the Warriours Path. He

[1] Alexander Fowler came to America in 1768 as lieutenant in the Eighteenth British Infantry. About the year 1769–70 the regiment was stationed at Fort Pitt, and in 1771–72 at Fort Chartres in Illinois. There Fowler was for a time commandant of the post at Kaskaskia. Sometime before the Revolution Lieutenant Fowler retired from the army and became a permanent resident of Pittsburgh. He embraced the patriot cause, acting as auditor of military accounts and deputy judge-advocate for the Western Department. Fowler died soon after the close of the war. One of his daughters became the wife of Samuel Sample, the well-known inn-keeper of Pittsburgh.

accordingly tree'd himself and party and Waited untill the Leader of the Indians, (who was Riding with Stoopes Son behind him) was withing ten paces of the muzzle of his Riffle, when he saluted him with a Brace of Balls which brought him from his Horse dead. The other Ind^s being ignorant of Bradeys party, Tree'd and soon Run, and left their Prisoner Mrs Stoopes, who informing Captn Bradey of the Strength of the Indians, he thought it unadviseable to Pursue, as he must have fought two to one;—besides his party was wore down with fatigue and want of Provisions, and had but one Load of Powder p Man, which had been carefully dryed the day before by the Sun. This was occas^d by the Crossing of Creeks and Rivers. Cap^{tn} Bradey brought Jenny Stoopes to Fort McIntosh with him; but in crossing Beaver Creek, soon after he had the Skirmish with the Indians; the other Squaw by some means or other left him and Joined the Indians. Bradey was then convinced he wold be pursued, which was the Case for Eight or Ten Miles, but without Success, for Cap^{tn} Bradey with his three Men got safe to McIntosh with the Prisoner he retook, when he immediately reinforcd his Party and pursued the Indians in turn; but notwithstanding his Vigilance they escaped: He took this opportunity of Scalping the Indian—which he had not time to do when he Shot him—and brought his Scalp and Mrs Stoopes to Fort Pitt in Triumph; and it appears from what Mrs Stoopes relates that he [the Indian] was undoubtedly the Leader of the Party.

This young officer Cap^{tn} Bradey, has great Merit as a Partisan in the Woods. He has had the Address to surprise and beat the Indians three different times since I came to this department. I have formed a great opinion of him. He has and I am sure may still be made more usefull; for he is *Brave, Vigilant,* and successfull.

A few days ago Thirty Wyandots made a Stroke, on the upper parts of Raccoon Settlement. They killed and Scalped four Men, and took one Prisoner. By great good Luck their Bark Canoes were discovered concealed on the Banks of the Ohio the very day they Crossed. An Ambuscade was Accordingly prepared for them, by a formidable Party on the opposite side of the River, and had it been well Conducted the whole of them must have fallen into our Hands. Some of the Soldiers, it seems, seeing such a large party of Indians recrossing the River with such a formidable Fleet of Canoes as Sixteen got timid and left their Concealment, by which means the Indians discovered the Party.

At this time the leading or Van Canoe of Kayashutas Fleet was about two thirds a Cross, and about 40, or 50, yards from the Party, when they immediately gave a Horrid yell, turned and paddled back, and at the same time were Saluted w^t a Volley, which as there were several good Marksmen, it's imagined four or five of them at least were killed and as many Wounded; However they immediately Sunk and no Scalps were got. They had taken four Scalps on the Waters of Racoon, and one Prisoner,[1] who was retaken and restored to his Family, so that they cannot boast of their Expedition; and 'tho the Stroke was not so effectuall as it might have been, yet I think it will prove serviceable. The Militia from Chertees were Vigilant on this Occassion, having got to the Ohio where the Indians Attempted to Cross about two Hours after they were dispersed.

We understand from the Prisoner that was retaken, who seems to be an intelligent Man that 15 of the same Gang had Crossed the Alleghaney to make a Stroke on some of the Westmoreland Settlements; but as yet we have heared of nothing they have done in that quarter, and I hope they may be disappointed and meet with a drubbing, as the Country is effectually Apprised of their intention and are on the look out for them.

The fall of Charles Town is much against us; yet I hope it will Rouse America from that Stupor and Lethargey, which she seems to have been in every since my Arrival on the Continent. I wished to have been employed in the Line of the Army, where I knew I could have been Serviceable, and I would have Accepted of such Rank, as I think could not have given offence to the officers of the American Army; But it was settled otherwise, and I know not for what reason. I am sure that neither my Conduct, Principles, nor experience, would have disgraced an Army contending for the Rights of Mankind. But you know my Ambition—'tho a Soldier—is not Great; for my Greatest Ambition is to be free, and my greatest happiness is to see America Independ^t

---

[1] Note on original manuscript: "Wm Bailey. See *Hazard's P^a . Reg^r . vol. Xth, p. 199.*" This reference gives an obituary of the rescued prisoner, William Bailey, who died Aug. 4, 1832 in Robinson Township, aged eighty-two. Bailey was a native of Ireland, who when young was brought to Adams County, Pa. He came to the West in the spring of 1780, and was captured on July 16 of that year. On crossing the Ohio, he was tied to the canoe, and was nearly drowned when the Indian who was propelling it was shot. One of McIntyre's men swam out with a knife between his teeth, cut Bailey's bonds, and rescued him from death.

Pray let me hear from you—favor me with the transactions below. Is our Money to be d—d, or is their any Chance of its appreciating?
I am with great Affection and regard Dear Hand, Your Sincere And obed^t Servant

A: FOWLER

BRIG^{DR} GENERAL EDWARD HAND.
[*Endorsed by Hand:*] Letter from Alex^r Fowler Esqr Dated Pittsburgh 22^d July 1780. Private.

LOYALISTS PUNISHED IN SOUTHWEST

[John Heavin to Col. William Preston. 5QQ42. A. L. S.]

July 22nd 1780

S^R:
Mr Price brought me the Letter Concerning the Distroying our Small Estates it is out of my power to tel for what I have not giveen any offence Neighther has my Children (Mr Shells tels me they are actually so—we have Concerned with Nothing of what I Suppose you Judg us for—I have seen several of the Neighbours that all say they are Clear and I Can say no farther than what they tel me) they all say they only want pease My Disappearing shall be no token of my Gilt and for to sattisfy the Internal peas of this State I know not How to doe that, I have no way to sattisfy you I Can find by your riteing unless it is to sweare and that I Cannot doe for my part for I Never meddleed with war from the first moment and Cant think of Intangleing my selfe with it now I hope that theire may be Cumpassion Useed with our wives and Innocent Children and as to the Distroying our Liveing that is in your own hands to my knowledg no man means to Rais arms Against you I nor mine Shall not I never useed any Dissate but am always for peas I hope this may sattisfy you and those that are Disturbed
I am your Humble serv^t

JOHN HEAVIN

To COL^o W^M PRESTON

[Joseph Grey's[1] warrant to Capt. James Barnett. 5QQ43. D. S.]

Montgomery Js

Complaint being this Day made to me that Jn° M°Donald of Said County (who having formerly taken the Oath of Allegiance to the State) hath behaved himself Indecently by declaring that he would pay no Taxes & that if they were Inforced Col° Preston might take care of himself & if any harm followed he might blame himself. That he would Support George Robison with his Life. That he would loose his Life before he would give up his Arms & that there would Soon he Supposed be a king in every County. That he thought We had been fighting for Liberty but Slavery was the Consequence, with many others Speeches of the like Nature contrary to the Peace of the Commonwealth.

These are there in the Name of the Commonwealth to Command you to bring the S^d John before me or some other Justice for S^d County to Answer to the above Complaint giving him Notice to bring with him two Sufficent Securities for his Appearance at next Court & his good Behaviour untill then. You are to Summon Such Witnesses as the Plantiff in Behalf of the Commonwealth may direct, as also such as the Defendant may require in order to Exculpate himself of the Charge. Given under my hand this 24th July 1780

Jos. Grey

To Cap^т Barnet to order to be Executed as the Man made his Escape from the Civil Officer

---

[Robert McGee's bond.[2] 5QQ45. D. S.]

Know all Men by these Presents that We Robert Magee James Magee & John Henderson are held and firmly Bound unto Thomas Jefferson Esqr Governor of Virginia or the Governor for the time Being in the Just and full sum of five Thousand Pounds Current Money of Virginia. To the Payment of which well and truly to be made We Bind ourselves Jointly and Severall our Joint an

[1] See sketch of Capt. Joseph Grey in *Wis. Hist. Colls.*, XXIII, 137, note 4.
[2] Bonds similar to the above, given by Jacob Seiler, James Bean (Bane) Jr., Thomas Burke, John McDonald, Samuel Robinson, and Walter Stewart, are preserved, and are in the Draper Mss., 5QQ44, 46–49, 51–52.

severall Heir's Executors & Adm^s firmly by these Presents. Sealed with our Seals and Dated this 26th Day of July 1780.

The Condition of the above Obligation is Such that whereas the above Bound Robert Magee formerly took the Oath of Allegience to the State of Virginia notwithstanding which he hath since repeatedly refused to comply with the Laws of the State by not giving in his Taxable Property on Oath when thereunto demanded & by Separating from the Friends & Citizens of S^d State in a great Measure & Associating with Nonjurors & other Suspected Persons & making Speeches on many Occasions which tended to subvert the present Government. Now if the Said Robert Magee for the future do behave himself in a Manner which becomes a good Citizen and Subject of S^d State, by paying a decent and due Obedience to the Laws thereof & not be Aiding, Abbeting, Consulting or Comforting the Enemies thereof or any of the Enemies of the United States of America by whatever Names they may be termed denominated or Distinguished; but on the Contrary that he will discover and make known all Treasons, Combinations or traitourous Conspiracies that may come within his knowledge entered into by the Enemies of S^d States; & that he will be ready and willing to defend the S^d State against the Enemies thereof when legally thereunto called, as other good subjects thereof ought to do then the Condition of the above Obligation to be void otherwise to be and remain in full Force & Virtue

Sealed & Delivered in presence of
W^M PRESTON
JOHN PRESTON

ROBERT M^{C}GEE
JAMES MCGEE
JOHN HENDERSON

[*Endorsed:*] Robert Magees Bond 1780

PROPOSED CONQUEST OF OHIO VALLEY

[Capt. John Rogers to Lieut. William Clark.[1] 1M1. A. L. S.]

SIR: CAHOES [CAHOKIA] July 28th 1780

I have Just received the Distressing News from your Village by fav^r of your & Mr Carnys[2] Letters for which I am Much obblidged to you both and In return send you what we have with us which you will make out by Compareing the two Letters which you will be so good as to Excuse as I have said more than my paper would hold in the manner I write   I shall ask no more Excuses from you but say on Begining where I Left off   the Man I Last Mentioned in Mr Carnys Letter Brings News in 21 Days from Michelemcanaugh[3] and says the Governor of that place was then setting of to Detroyt to fight A Great Man that Was Coming there as he tells the Indians and Informs them at the same time that he shall then Go to the falls of Ohio where he shall Fight a second time from thence to Fort Pitt but shall have a third fight on the way   his forth Battle to be at Pitt and his Fifth and Last Battle to be at Fort Cumberland & Garrison that and then return and Go home to his King for a reward   by this [time] they may have word of the Col. [Clark] Marching that way

[1] Lieut. William Clark, born in Virginia in 1760, was the son of Benjamin, and the cousin of George Rogers Clark. In 1780 the younger Clark was commissioned lieutenant and came to Kentucky, probably in the company of Capt. John Rogers. Lieutenant Clark served until Feb. 15, 1784, in the earlier years at Fort Jefferson, later at Louisville. In 1782 he took part in the Wabash campaign, and two years later was chosen a commissioner and the surveyor for the Indiana land grant to Clark's regiment. Thereafter Lieutenant Clark resided in Clarksville, Ind., where he was appointed a magistrate, and whence, in 1785, he carried an important message to the northern Indians. In 1790 he returned to Louisville where in November, 1791, he died. He was never married, and his will bequeathed his estate to his surviving brothers and sisters. His papers are in the Draper Mss., series M.

[2] Martin Carney of Botetourt County, Va., served as a private in the Point Pleasant expedition of 1774. During the Revolution he was first quartermaster of the Eighth Virginia Regiment, then ensign and lieutenant of the Fourth, resigning from the latter position Jan. 1, 1780. Before that date he had been with Clark in the Western Department; as early as 1779 he conveyed for him a message from Vincennes to Detroit. During 1780–81 Carney was quartermaster at Fort Jefferson. Upon its abandonment he returned to Louisville where he was living in 1785.

[3] The early name of Mackinac.

Maj^r Wiliams[1] who Comands here has sent for me to Go to his Logings Imediately I must go
I am Sir your Hum^l Servt

J^{no} ROGERS

My Com^s to Capt George & Miss Nancy
[*Addressed:*] Wm Clark Esqr F^t Jefferson P^r fav Lt Clark

DELAWARES LOYAL

[Rev. John Heckewelder to Col. Daniel Brodhead. Washington Papers. Contemporary transcript.]

SALEM July 26th 1780

DEAR SIR:

I wrote a long Letter for the Chiefs of Coochocking to You a few days ago, but understood since that the Messengers out of fear for a number of Warriors whom they tracked turned back again, but as now others are sent, I suppose the Letter will come safe to hand, At present I know of no other news concerning the Enemy, than what is mentioned in the Letter. It seems to me by conversation I and several of the head Men from Coochocking had the other day, that the Delewares would willingly join you in a Campaign against the Enemy for they think themselves in great danger of other Nations who begin to threaten them again, but I can hardly believe it to be so bad as they think. Out of a Letter from from Mr Zeizberger I see that some of his Men who had been out Hunting tracked a great number of Warriors who were turned back and gone by Tuscarawas to Sandusky again. Whether there be still any between this & Fort M^{c}intosh I cannot tell. Not one Warrior has passed through our Town here this Spring. The French Major, Captain & Company are gone to Coochocking their Business I cannot tell, It is indeed my Duty

---

[1] John Williams served in Dunmore's War with the troops from the Holston. In 1778 he was commissioned lieutenant in Clark's forces, and took part in the Kaskaskia and Vincennes campaigns. Having become major, Williams in 1779 commanded Fort Clark at Kaskaskia, and the following year the post of Cahokia. He married at the former town, and about the year 1783 removed to Natchez. In 1791 he received a military land grant, and about 1798 was living thirty miles below Natchez at Dead Man's Bend, where he died in 1808. His descendants secured from Congress the full amount of his claim for services. See *ibid.*, 36J37, 37J188–95.

Dr Sir to return you my most hearty thanks for your kind services to the Rever^d Mr Grube & Company[1] when at Fort Pitt, & I wish to have the pleasure of making a more fully acknowledgment to You for this and all your kind services to Us.

I am indeed Sir with great regard Your sincere friend & most Obed^t humble Servt

J^{no} HACKENWELDER

COL^o BRODHEAD Comm^g West^n Dep^t

[Col. Daniel Brodhead to Rev. John Heckewelder. 2H63. Letter Book.]

FORT PITT Jully 31^t 1780

DEAR SIR:

I have received your kind favour of the 26th Instant, togither with that from the Delaware Council & am sorry to find that the British have met such great sucess in the new settlement of Kentucke The Party of warriors tracked by the Messingers & Mr Zeisbergers Men Paid dearly for Coming this Way & were severely Chastised by a Party of white men which I sent to pursue them, of which you will Probably be informed and I beg you will write me a Particular account of their loss.

I am glad to hear of the good disposition of the Delaware Council and will shortly Put it in their Power to take satisfection of the scoundrels who threaten them

It is with Great satisfection I hear the Enemy have not Pass^d through your town this Campaign & I wish you to Discountenance their coming that way to Prevent Jealous apprehensions from these Inhabitants who allready Entertain an unfavourable oppinion of the Delawares in General.

---

[1] Rev. Bernard Adam Grube was born in 1715 near Erfurt, Germany. Educated at Jena, he became a missionary to America, arriving at Bethlehem, Pa., in the year 1746. Later he established the Moravian mission in North Carolina, and in 1755 barely escaped massacre at Gnadenhütten on the Susquehanna. Grube was finally made superintendent of the central missions and in that capacity visited in 1780 the Tuscarawas towns. He conveyed thither from Bethlehem the young woman to whom Heckewelder was married in July of that year. On their outward journey from Fort Pitt they were pursued by white ruffians, and narrowly escaped massacre. Heckewelder, *Narrative*, 211. Grube's last years were spent peacefully at Bethlehem, where he passed away on Mar. 20, 1808.

Please to Prevent [sic] My respectfull Compliments to your Revd Brethren & the Ladies & belive me to be with great respect & Esteen Dr Sir your most Obed^t Servt
       Danl Brodhead Co^l Comd^g W^t Dep^t
Rev^D MR Jno Hackenweller

[Col. Daniel Brodhead to the Delaware chiefs. 2H57. Letter Book.]

       Head Qr^s Fort Pitt July 31^t 80
Mahingwe Geeshuch to Capt John KillBuck and the council at Coochocking
I thank you for your Message by the two young men, but you forgot to inform me of the Purport of the Chipoways speech, wherefore I hope you will inform me in your next letter
Brothers:
the King of Britain and the five Nations, or a part of them, will Doutless Continu to deceive the Indians as long as they can by any means influence them, but I flatter myself there are Indians whose councils are too wise to be Deceived by them, We shall hear what will be done with this large Ax which has been given to the foolish Indians, likewise who is afriad of the loud talk of the British King against his masters
 Brothers: I intend to go to the Countrey of those fools who carry the big Ax, it will not be long before they will see me and then you will see what the big knife can do.
 Brothers: as to the speech of the half King it is a Great discharge of wind, he dare not hurt a hair of your head
 Brothers: if what you heard from Montours Relation is true, the British and their Indians have got many Prisoners, but Perhaps it is not all true as the Intilligence comes from a bad man I Desire you will find out the truth and write to me all about it. Because I am Determined to make them Pay Dearly for all the mischief they have Done
 Brothers: What you have requested, shall be Done for your boys, But they have nothing to fear, I have cleared the Road Give my Compliments to your Father, I hope he is doing Good for his Children likewise to all the Captains & all our friends
 I am your friend & Brother
         Mahingwe Geeshuch

[Col. Daniel Brodhead to Maj. Daniel Maurice Godefroy de Linctot. 2H61. Letter Book.]

HEAD QR^s FORT PITT Jully 31^t 1780

DR MAJOR:

I am honord with your favour of the 27th Instant If the account you have Rec^d from KaneTucke be true, the British savages have been too successfull

It is with Pleasure I hear of the good Disposition of the Delaware Council & I hope your speeches and adress will have weight with the other Nations, the Hurons have Lately been very Hostile but one of their Parties has been severly chastised, by a Party I Detachd to Pursue them

Every Posible Exertion is now making to Procure a suficient suply of Provisions for carying an enterprize into the enemys Country & I hope to be in Readiness in the month of september, wherefore I request you will endeavour to Return by the midle of that month if it should [not] be Convenient to return, sooner there is not a Person here who can Properly Translate your letters, wherefore I cannot be Particular in my answer, Yet I must request you will write me by every oppertunity and give me every Posible Intiligence Relative to the Disposition of the Indians, & the Intention of the British

I hope the Captain is agreeably entertained by the Ladies of the Wilderness

Please to Present my respectfull Compliments to him & belive that I am with much respect & Esteem Your Most Obed^t serv^t

DAN^L BRODHEAD Col Commd^g W D^t

MAJ^R G^Y LANCTOT

EXPEDITION POSTPONED

[Summary of a circular letter of Col. Daniel Brodhead, Headquarters, Fort Pitt, July 31, 1780, to Col. John Evans and other county lieutenants. Printed in *Pa. Archives*, XII, 253–54.]

Colonel Beeler[1] and his officers have decided that volunteers cannot furnish salt provisions for fifteen days and fresh ones cannot be preserved for that time. Public magazines are empty.

[1] For a notice of Col. Joseph Beeler see *Wis. Hist. Colls.*, XXIII, 162, note 1.

FRONTIER RETREAT 235

It is therefore necessary to postpone rendezvous of troops. Council called for sixteenth of next month.

ALLEGHENY POSTS EVACUATED

[Summary of a letter of Col. Daniel Brodhead, Headquarters, Aug. 3, 1780, to Capt. James Carnahan. Printed in *ibid.*, 254.]

No rations to send to his garrison, is impressing sheep etc.; no prospect of getting flour. Orders him to bring in garrison and public stores, to direct Captain Lochry[1] to do the same if he cannot secure stores from the state commissary.

[Summary of a letter of Col. Daniel Brodhead, Headquarters, Fort Pitt, Aug. 3, 1780, to Capt. Thomas Stokeley.[2] Printed in *ibid.*, 255.]

If Colonel Lochry cannot furnish stores through the state commissary Fort Crawford must be evacuated until foraging brings in sufficient supplies. Westmoreland is in no immediate danger. Proposed expedition delayed for lack of means.

COMMISSARY APPOINTED

[Summary of a letter of Pres. Joseph Reed, Philadelphia, Aug. 5, 1780, to Col. William Amberson. Printed in *id.*, VIII, 487–88.]

Early in the summer appointed Amberson commissary of purchases for Westmoreland and sent state money therefor. Alarming reports from Brodhead that he may be obliged to evacuate Fort Pitt for lack of provision: importance of post to frontier. Harvest plentiful, there should be no difficulty in securing supplies. Impress them if necessary. Virginia has ratified the boundary line.

[1] A sketch of Capt. William Lochry is given in *Frontier Defense*, 139, note 6.
[2] For Capt. Thomas Stokeley see *Wis. Hist. Colls.*, XXIII, 300, note 1.

WISCONSIN HISTORICAL COLLECTIONS

LOYALISTS REORGANIZE

[Col. Walter Crockett to Col. William Preston. 5QQ48. A. L. S.]

Dear Col°
          Fort Chiswill 9 Oclock Augt 6th 1780

I have Collected about Two hundred and fifty men and shall begin our March towards New River in about three hours and continue it untill I hear from you by this Express, I have been informed the Tories have murdered one Letcher in the Hollow the other day, the Murderours were, Meeks and Nicholas: Thursday last they Stole six horses from Col° Green,[1] within six Miles of Herberts ferry,[2] endeavourd to catch his Negro fellow in the Wood, and threatned to rob him that Night, but were prevented by a party from the Lead Mines. I should think, it very necessary to send a party to Greesey Creek, and Towards the flower Gap,[3] and the rather so as it is Generally believed a large body of those wretches are Collected in the Hollow, or the head of Fishers River.[4]

                        Yours &°
                    Walter Crockett.

[Col. William Campbell to Col. Arthur Campbell. 8DD4. Transcript.]

Sir:
                              [About July 25, 1780][5]

Upon receiving your letter which you wrote from Fort Chiswell, informing me that the insurgents were embodying up New

[1] Probably this person was John Green, who was one of the Kentucky surveyors of 1774. See *Dunmore's War*, 172; Draper Mss., 3B109, 131.

[2] Thomas Herbert operated a ferry above that of Ingles over New River, in Pulaski or Wythe County.

[3] Greasy Creek is an eastern affluent of Reed Island Creek, which empties into the New, not far below Reed Creek. Greasy Creek lies in Carroll and Floyd counties. Flower Gap is through the Blue Ridge on the boundary line of Virginia and North Carolina, between Carroll and Surry counties. In 1751 Christopher Gist returned from his western journey through this gap.

[4] Fisher Branch is a tributary of Cripple Creek, which flows into New River just below the site of Fort Chiswell.

[5] Dr. Draper assigned this undated manuscript to the year 1780 and considered that the letter of Col. Arthur Campbell (referred to at the beginning of this

River, and that their design was to destroy the works at the lead mines, I immediately wrote to Captains Edmiston, Lewis and Dysart, directing to order fifteen men out of each of their companies, to assemble at my house early next day, equipped to march with me to the lead mines. I also wrote to Captain Campbell of R[oyal] Oak to order ten men out of his company who were directed to join me on my way up. The men met as early as I could expect, and we left this place about twelve or one o'clock. That night we got about twelve miles from this place, the next day we got to Radcliffs marsh where we halted for a small party I had detached the day before to apprehend some persons that were much suspected, and it being late before they joined us, we were obliged to lie at that place all night. We got to the mines next day soon in evening. There I was informed two men had been sent up the river, to discover, if possible, the designs of the insurgents, and that it was expected they would return that night. About an hour and a half before day next morning they came to the mines and informed me that they had been as far as Captain Cox's,[1] where they counted one hundred and five men assembled and in arms, beside a considerable number without arms. They also reported that they had been detained as prisoners about twenty four hours, and that when they were suffered to come away, the people that had assembled were dispersing, apparently with a design to return home. They brought with them a piece of writing signed Cox's and Osbornes Companies, directed to Colonel Preston, of which the enclosed is a copy. I then determined to go up New River with the men who went with me from this county; but some of the Militia officers of Montgomery County being there, they proposed to collect as many men that day as they possibly could, and to be in readiness to march early next day, which we did with about one hundred and forty men.

document) is his of July 12, 1780, *ante*, 217. It seems to the present editor that there are good grounds for thinking that this manuscript may be one of 1779, and that it describes Col. William Campbell's operations in that year. There is, however, documentary proof that Campbell and Walter Crockett coöperated against the Loyalists both in 1779 and in 1780. See H. J. Eckenrode, *The Revolution in Virginia* (Boston, 1916), 237. It has thus seemed best to insert this description of Campbell's New River campaign among the documents of 1780, where Dr. Draper placed it.

[1] John Cox received in 1765 a grant from the Loyal Land Company of a tract known as "Peach Bottom" in southeastern Grayson County, Va., where he made his home. He served in 1774 as a captain of militia and was living on the farm as late as 1805.

That evening we got about sixteen miles above the lead mines without getting any certain intelligence of the designs of the insurgents. Next day we continued our route up the river, through the most populous part of the settlement, and found no people at home but the women and children, excepting a few very old men. Upon our arrival at Captain Cox's, in the evening, we were informed that about forty of the insurgents, about two hours before, had crossed the river, and taken Captain Cox's son a prisoner. They expected we would have gone up the south side of the river, in which they would have met us, and designed to give us battle. We then followed after them in the best order we could, lest they should attempt to surprise us, until it became so dark that we could no longer follow their track, and turned off the path, about a quarter of a mile, and tied up our horses in the most silent manner we could, conjecturing the enemy were not far before us. There was a house about a mile from where we lay, to which I sent a few men, to make what discovery they could, who soon after returned without making any that was satisfactory. I then concluded they were encamped in the woods, and determined if possible to surprise them, and for that purpose set out on foot about two or three hours before day, leaving all our horses tied, where we halted in the evening. In this order we marched about a mile, when we again made a halt, and sent off four or five very trusty men, to find if possible where the enemy lay. I also sent with them a man whom I the day before had caused to come with me. Being informed he had a brother among the insurgents, I imagined he knew something of their schemes and designs, and told him if he did not discover where the insurgents lay, I would put him to death. They returned in about an hour and informed me they had been within twenty yards of the enemy's camp, and was fired upon by one of their sentries; that their encampment was in piece of woods in a large glade and perfectly clear for at least a quarter of mile all around where they lay. At this place (I then understood) they were that day to be joined by a considerable number more, and concluded that these would in such a place so secure themselves that the lives of a great many good men must be lost in an attempt to dislodge them, which I was unwilling should be the case in subduing such worthless wretches. I then, with the advice of the officers, went back to where we left our horses, it being then about break of day.

As soon as it became so light that we could see a small distance around us, we set out a second time toward the enemy's camp on horseback. We got to the side of the glade just as the sun was rising. The morning was very foggy, which prevented our discovering the flight of the enemy, nor did we know they had fled until Captain Cox's son came to us, who in their hurry they had suffered to escape. Upon going to their camp, we found they had gone off with the greatest precipitation, having left everything behind them excepting their arms. Before we followed them we had to wait a few minutes to get a horse for Captain Cox's son, who said he could conduct us the way they purposed to go. As soon as he was ready we pursued with all the expedition we could upon the trace; but upon their discovering that we [were] pursuing them, they dispersed and hid themselves among the bushes and weeds. We had not the fortune to find any but one of them, who was immediately shot. The woods were searched upon the way they fled for three or four miles. Some of them ran into the mountains and laurel thickets where it was impossible to pursue them on horseback. You cannot conceive my chargrin when I saw the situation of the enemy's camp. I found that had I known it myself, it was in my power to have destroyed nearly the whole of them, though it may perhaps be better ordered, as I believe the most of them are now well convinced of their folly, and may yet become very good citizens.

After the pursuit was over we all assembled at the enemy's camp and breakfasted upon the provision they left behind them, having eaten very little from early in the morning the day before. That night we went again to Captain Cox's. I then considered that it was to no purpose to search for those people in that mountainous country, and that there was a probability of their embodying again, if they could not then be prevailed upon to surrender. These considerations induced me to disperse among them copies of the enclosed, signed by Major Crockett and myself. It has had the wished for effect, only a few of the principals having refused to come in.

That night we went again to Captain Cox's where we were next morning met by a party of 130 men under the command of Colonel Cleveland from Wilks County, North Carolina. They had the day before apprehended a certain Zechariah Goss, a fellow who belonged to a party under the command of Samuel Brown and [James] Coyle, two noted murderers, horse-thieves and robbers.[1] Goss was immediately hung, I believe with the joint consent of near three hundred men, and two other villains were very well whip'd. I then detached between sixty and seventy men under the command of Captain Francis,[2] with instructions to collect all the stocks of horses and cattle belonging to the insurgents they possibly could, only leaving to each family one horse creature and what milch cattle were necessary for its support, having previously sent out by some of the inhabitants of the place copies of the enclosed, signed by Major Crockett and myself. This step I was induced to take from the consideration that it was impossible to find those people in that mountainous country—that there was a probability of their being stimulated to join in the like designs again, and that if I could see them they might be reasoned out of those mad schemes. That evening I went up to Captain Osborne's, where I was informed above forty of the insurgents had been embodied in that neighborhood, and that they were dispersed by Colonel Cleveland's party who left Captain Cox's about two hours before me. There were very few of the insurgents came in next day, they being afraid to venture even to their own houses. Those that came in first I disarmed and sent out in search of the others. I lay there two days in which time the greatest[3]

[Col. William Campbell to Col. William Preston and officers. 8DD6. Transcript.]

GENTLEMEN:

You will please to accept of my most hearty thanks for the obliging and polite manner in which you have expressed your approbation of my conduct in the excursion against the insurgents upon New River. As I thought I had done nothing but my duty, I by no means expected such a reward for my services—a reward which must stimulate every generous breast to the noblest

[1] The bands of Brown and Coyle ravaged the upper Carolinas for several months. Their leaders were apprehended and hung in November, 1780.
[2] In 1779–80 Capt. Henry Francis was an officer in the Montgomery County militia.
[3] Note on manuscript: "The remainder of this document missing—It is in the handwriting of Col. Wm Campbell. L. C. D." The original manuscript was obtained from Campbell's grandson, Gen. John S. Preston of South Carolina. After transcribing it, Dr. Draper returned it, Sept. 24, 1880, to its owner.

FRONTIER RETREAT   241

exertions. I owe much to the salutary advice of the officers who were with me, nor can I avoid taking the opportunity of testifying the particular obligation I am under to the militia of Montgomery county who did me the honor of accompanying me in that service. The cheerfulness with which they submitted to my command gave me the greatest satisfaction (pleasure), and I shall always entertain the most lively sense of it.

May the Almighty Disposer of all events always provide ample means for the preservation of our liberty and lives; and may the breast of every American be inspired to render that tribute of gratitude and praise which is justly due to *Him* who is the source of all our blessings, and in whose hands we are but the instruments of his will.

I am, Gentlemen, Your much obliged, and very humble servant,
W^M CAMPBELL.

COLONEL WILLIAM PRESTON & others, the militia officers of Montgomery County.

[Col. William Preston to Gov. Thomas Jefferson. 5QQ50. Autograph draft.]

MONTGOMERY Augt 8th 1780

SIR:

A most horrid Conspiracy amongst the Tories in this Country being providentialy discovered about ten days ago obliged me not only to raise the militia of the County but to care for so a large Number from the Counties of Washington and Botetourt that there are upwards of four hundred men now on Duty exclusive of a Party which I hear Col Lynch marched from Bedford[1] towards the Mines yesterday. Col^o Hugh Crocket[2] had sent two young men amongst the Tories as tory officers, with whom they agreed to Embody to a very great Number near the the Lead Mines the 25th Instant, and after securing that Place to

[1] For Col. Charles Lynch see *Rev. Upper Ohio*, 174, note 4. The term "Lynch law" is supposed to have arisen from this officer's summary executions while suppressing the Tory revolt.

[2] Col. Hugh Crockett, a brother of Joseph and Walter Crockett, removed in 1749 to the Roanoke River. In 1767 Hugh was constable of Botetourt County, and later a militia officer in Montgomery County. In 1781 he joined Greene in the Carolinas and served until the close of the Revolution. Col. Hugh Crockett was living in Montgomery County as late as 1788.

over run the Country with the assistance of the british Troops, who they were made to believe would meet them, and to relieve the Convention Prisoners[1] These they were to Arm & then subdue the whole State. A List of a Number of Officers was given to our Spies.—This Deception gave our Militia an Opportunity of fixing on many of them who have been taken and I believe there are near sixty now in confinement.—A number of Magistrates were called together from this County and Botetourt to examine Witnesses and enquire fully into the Conduct of those deluded Wretches In which we have been Engaged three Days; & I am convinced the Enquiry will continue at least a fortnight, as there are Prisoners brought in every hour and new Discoveries making. One has been enlarged on giving Security in £100,000 to appear when called for, some have been whipped & others, against whom little can be made appear, have enlisted to serve in the Continental Army. There is yet another Class who comes fully within the Treason Law, that we cannot Punish otherwise than by sending to the best Prisons in the Neighbouring Counties, untill they can be legally tried according to an Act of the last Session of Assembly to which however we are strangers, as we have not been able to procure a Copy of the Act & have only heard of it.

Some of the Capital offenders have disappeared whose personal Property has been removed by the soldiers & which they insist on being sold & divided as Plunder to which the Officers have submitted otherwise it would be almost impossible to get men on those pressing Occasions. I would beg your Excellency's Opinion on this head; as also what steps you Judge necessary to be taken by the Officers & Magistrates with the Prisoners, other than what I have mentioned.

I am your Excellency's most obed^t Servt

---

[1] When Burgoyne surrendered in 1777 his soldiers were termed "Convention" prisoners. In 1779 they were brought to Virginia and stationed in barracks built for the purpose at Charlottesville. In May, 1780 there were about 1,500 "conventioners" in Virginia, most of whom were German mercenaries. They remained at Charlottesville until released at the close of the war.

WESTERN GARRISONS FOR VIRGINIA

[Gen. Andrew Lewis to Col. Joseph Crockett. 50J55. Contemporary transcript.]

RICHMOND Aug. 10. 1780

SIR:

As you will be soon in motion for your Station on the Ohio I have taken the liberty of hinting to you the method I think most adviseable for you to observe in making your Establishments You will find in your Instructions from His Excellency that a Fort is to be erected at Kelley's[1] on the great Kanhaway where you are to station 26. of your Command for the purpose of keeping open the communication to Fort Randolph this fort is to be a receptacle for your Provisions as they are carried over the Mountains from thence it is supposed you will take down all your stores (Powder excepted) by Water whilst you are erecting this Your first Fort you will find it necessary to not only order your Commissary to send back all your Horses for a further Supply of Provisions but to have some kind of Craft constructed as may best suit the navigation of the River—Give me leave to further recommend it to you when you march from Kelleys to take no more of your Beef Cattle with you than you may think necessary for your support until you have constructed a Fort of sufficient capacity where stood Fort Randolph, built your Barracks and store Houses and prepared for salting your Winter Beef.—Should you not use this precaution the Indians may have it much in their power to destroy or drive off your Cattle. You cannot be too much on your guard against surprize therefore you will no doubt employ as scouts some of your most expert Woodsmen well accustomed to the Indian method of making War.

It need not be recommended to you to give the Inhabitants the most speedy notice in case you discover any body of the Enemy directing their course against them As you are under the direction of Col° Clarke and he may find it necessary on many Occasions to form a Junction of the greatest number of the Troops under his Command & such Junction cannot be effected without a sufficient number of Boats you will no doubt have them constructed as soon as your time and Circumstances will permit.

[1] For this location see *Dunmore's War*, 112, note 62.

Your Posts too below Fort Randolph must be supplied from that Post & Fort Pitt by water
I am Y^r most obed^t Servt

ANDREW LEWIS

P. S. Should any thing I have hinted at prove in any way contradictory to your Instructions I beg you may disregard my Hints.

A. L.

LOYALISTS SUPPRESSED IN SOUTHWEST

[Capt. Patrick Lockhart[1] to Col. William Preston. 5QQ53. A. L. S.]

BOTETOURT August 12th 1780
SIR:

The Officers from this County forgot to Consult you Relative to giving Credit at the sale of the Tories Effects shall be Obliged for your Advice in the Matter for I think whatever Measures is Adopted in regard to the Effects sold in your County ought to be here. We brought all the prisoners &c. safe as I came home I took a Young Man Named Stewart on Suspicion of being Connected with those Disaffected on the North Fork but nothing more appeared against him than that Polson had been makeing some proposals to him & he had failed to inform upon him but gladly agreed to inlist. Capt May seems displeased because he was one of his Company & demands him as a Recruit for his Division I told him I would Submit it to the Officers &c appointed to lay off the County in Divisions to say who was entitled
I am Sir your M^o Ob^t H^{ble} Servt
COL. PRESTON

PAT. LOCKART

[Col. Arthur Campbell to Col. William Campbell. 8DD5. Transcript.]

August 13, 1780
SIR:

I am just now creditably informed that an express is come from Chota sent by the Raven[2] chief, that a body of 700 tories and

[1] For this officer see *Rev. Upper Ohio*, 155, note 75. Lockhart died about the year 1802 at Fincastle Court House, Draper Mss., 25S239.
[2] For the town of Chote see *Wis. Hist. Colls.*, XXIII, 105, note 2; for Raven the Cherokee, see *ibid.*, 365, note 1.

Indians had actually set out against the frontiers of this state and Carolina, and that the men from Sullivan and Wattago[1] were to march this day to meet them. Our frontier in Powell's Valley is much exposed, also Clinch and the North Fork [of Holston] may suffer. You will therefore see the necessity speedily to return with the men from this county.
Your humble servant,
ARTHUR CAMPBELL.

P. S. The Sullivan and Wattago men are returned, after being successful.

COLONEL Wm CAMPBELL, [on New River.]

WYANDOT DEFEAT NEAR FORT McINTOSH

[Rev. John Heckewelder to Col. Daniel Brodhead. Washington Papers. Contemporary transcript.][2]

SALEM Augst ye 14th 1780

DEAR SIR:

Your kind favor of July the 31st I received by the Indian Messenger, and wish it was in my power to give you a full account of the loss of the Enemy, when pursued by a party of your Men, but I aprehend they will take as much care as they can to keep it private. However, I was informed the day before yesterday by a Man who came from the Wyondott Towns, that somewhere about the mouth of Yellow Creek a party of Wyondotts Crossing the River on Rafts were attacked by a party of White men, when Eight of the Indians were killed on the Spot, and two besides them mortally Wounded, one of witch had Died since, the other being Carried over to Detroit. It has also been reported here yesterday that Eight Hundred White men where marching towards the Shawnee Towns, that the latter had fetched at two Different times Scalps from them and one Prissoner, to the num-

---

[1] The first settlement of western North Carolina (now a part of Tennessee) was made in 1769 on the Watauga, an affluent of the north fork of Holston River. For ten years this was thought to be included in Virginia. In 1779 the boundary line was run, and on Feb. 7, 1780 Sullivan County, N. C., was organized and named for Gen. John Sullivan. Isaac Shelby was appointed colonel of the county militia, and in this capacity commanded its forces at the battle of King's Mountain.

[2] This letter was enclosed in Brodhead's of Aug. 21, 1780, to Washington.

ber of ten, but how much this report may be Depended on I know not.[1]

As soon as I shall hear any particular News, you may Depend on my favoring you with it.

Should the Re^d Barnard Grube who is going on his Journey back again Stand in need of any thing, You will greatly Oblige Us all in lending him your assistance.

The Brethen and their Ladies return most humbly their thanks for your good Wishes and Compliments, and desire me to remember them in the same respect to you again

I am Dr Sir, your Sincere friend and obed^t humb^l Servt

JOHN HACKENVELDER[2]

COL^L BRODHEAD Comd^t Wes^{tr} Depart^m

VIRGINIA LOYALISTS OFFERED PARDON

[Col. William Preston's proposal to Thomas Heavin and other Loyalists. 5QQ55. Autograph draft.]

Thomas Heavin, having withdrawn his Fidelity and Allegiance from the Commonweath of Virginia, by accepting a Commission in the british Service, by enlisting a Number of Men to serve the King of great Britain and administering the Oath of Allegience to such Persons to the S^d King; by swearing others not to lift Arms in the defence of American Liberty; by Poisoning the Minds of Other good Subjects to this State; & by holding private and Treasonable meetings with the Enemies thereof, in order to Subvert the Government and disturb the Internal Tranquility of the same.

Being conscious to himself of these Facts and of his Treasonable Practices, he has withdrawn himself from a public Enquiry into his Conduct & from the Punishment which he might reasonably expect would follow such an Enquiry.—But the Govern-

---

[1] For Clark's official account of his campaign against the Shawnee see *Ill. Hist. Colls.*, VIII, 451–53. Several men of Capt. Hugh McGary's company, who were hunting on the north side of the Ohio as they made their way from Louisville to the rendezvous at the mouth of the Licking, were killed by the Indians, *ibid.*, 477–78. This was the incident noted in this document.

[2] Concerning the spelling of this name see *Wis. Hist. Colls.*, XXIII, 247, note 1.

ment of Virginia being full of Mercy & ever willing to forgive her rebel & Dissafected Sons would rather reclaim & Pardon a number of them than Punish one.—Therefore We the Subscribers do hereby Invite and Exhort the Said Thomas Heavin or any other in the same situation with him to return to his or their Allegience to the Commonwealth. And we do in the Name and Behalf of the Government promise him or them so returning & his & their Families and property future Protection. That the Punishment for their past Offences shall not extend to their Persons nor property on their future good Behaviour & that if he or they shall not agree to the Proposals that may be made to them when they surrender themselves, they will then be at full Liberty to withdraw themselves forty eight hours before any Search or Enquiry shall be made for him or them. And that he or they may have the utmost Confidence in these Proposals & Promises We and each of us for ourselve do hereby Engage our Veracity and Honour that every thing we have promised or proposed in the above Writing shall be Strictly and punctually [Ms. torn] Given u der our] hands this 14th Day of August 1780

REUBEN REMEMBER

PETER POOR & Son
JACOB WAGGONER & Sons
NATH^L MORGAN & Son
JOHN CROOM w^d not go on duty

lodged at S. Thompsons & have
Piloted him over the River

PETER KINDERS Confession from
Griffiths Report
JOSHUA JONES an Officer
LAURENCE KITTERING D^o
WILLIAM BLEVINS D^o
TH HEAVIN'S D^o
JN^o WILLEY D^o
L HUFF D^o
a meeting at Peppers, Gresham

MICH^L ROGER an Officer perhaps
Briton piloted him
BANE & M^{c}DONALD spoke of
RICH^D OWENY

CONDITIONS AT FORT PITT

[Gen. George Washington to Col. Daniel Brodhead. Washington Papers. Draft.]

HEAD QUARTERS ORANGE TOWN 14th Augt 1780.

DEAR SIR:

I have rec^d your favors of the 29th June and 21st July. Col^o Bowmans apprehensions of the force expected from Canada is certainly groundless, as what men can be spared from the Garrisons of the upper Country—St Johns Montreal and Quebec are now acting in conjunction with the Indians upon the Mohawk River, where they have lately done considerable mischief.[1]

The distress on the score of provision has not been confined to you alone, but has been severely e[x]perienced in every quarter, and I think you will be very happy if you can adopt any expedient to supply yourself without depending wholly upon the Commissary in a regular way.

I am pleased to hear of the success of the parties under Captains Brady and McIntire to whom you will be pleased to express my thanks for their conduct. These affairs tho' apparently small have considerable influence upon Indians.

The first division of the French Fleet and Army consisting of 8 ships of the line and 5000 men are yet at Rhode Island waiting the arrival of the 2^d division now hourly expected. We look for very important news from the West Indies, the whole combined force of France and Spain in those seas having gone down it is said against Jamaca.

I am Dear Sir Yr

COL.^{o} BRODHEAD.

[Summary of a letter of Col. Daniel Brodhead, Fort Pitt, Aug. 18, 1780, to Gen. George Washington. Printed in Sparks, *Corr. Amer. Rev.*, III, 62–63.]

Ten men have been killed on forks of Cheat River. Troops are suffering for lack of bread. Courts-martial and their findings.

[1] The Mohawk Valley during the summer of 1780 was the scene of several raids conducted by Sir John Johnson, Col. John Butler, and Joseph Brant. For a good summary of these movements see Francis W. Halsey, *The Old New York Frontier* (New York, 1901), 287–94.

Enclosed letters from Delaware towns. Delawares might be involved in war with Wyandot had we means to encourage them. Forts and prisoners taken in Kentucky will probably encourage similar raids in future.

[Summary of a letter of Col. Daniel Brodhead, Fort Pitt, Aug. 18, 1780, to Pres. Joseph Reed. Printed in *Pa. Archives*, VIII, 513–11.)

Ten men on Cheat River have been killed by a Wyandot party. Troops begin to murmur for lack of bread; waters are too low to manufacture meal or flour. Pack-horse men have deserted. Forts captured on Licking Creek; British may attempt similar attack on this part of country; notice would, however, be given by friendly Indians. Temporary evacuation of Forts Armstrong and Crawford.

[Summary of a letter of Col. Daniel Brodhead, Headquarters, Fort Pitt, Aug. 19, 1780, to Col. Archibald Lochry. Printed in *id.*, XII, 257.]

Mistake in dating circular letters August 1 instead of July 31 deprived him of pleasure of seeing Lochry on August 16. Hopes to see him soon. Monongahela River rising; garrisons may soon be returned to stations. No immediate apprehension of danger. Ranging companies supplied.

CLARK'S SHAWNEE EXPEDITION

[Summary of a letter of Col. Daniel Brodhead, Fort Pitt, Aug. 21, 1780, to Gen. George Washington. Printed in Sparks, *Corr. Amer. Rev.*, III, 63–64.]

Captain Duplantier,[1] just arrived from Delaware towns, brings word that Clark with about a thousand men has destroyed

---

[1] Captain Duplantier would appear to have been a Frenchman who had offered his services to the American cause. He had no commission in the Continental army, but may have been serving under Virginia. See reference to him in *Calendar of Correspondence of George Washington with the Officers* (Washington, 1915), 1247.

Shawnee town of Chillicothe. French at Detroit, badly treated by British, desire approach of our troops. Letters from Delawares inclosed. "Had I provisions, I should be happy to march against some of the hostile Indian towns."

[Captain Killbuck to Col. Daniel Brodhead. Washington Papers. Contemporary transcript.]

CASHAQUIN[1]

DEAR BROTHER:

the Occupation the Indiens gives me hinders me to Come to Fort Pitt to Bring you the news our french father, is Come to tell you, and in the Same time that what layes in our power we do to make peace he will tell you the hearts of all our Brothers. We desire that you will march with an Army as Sone as posible the Sircumstances is Very good the Shawnes is Defeated by an Army of our brothers, i Believe that you might go where you pleas. I Expect our French-father will have a Considerable party of our young Wariors to go with you. Send Sum Salt and flower and Soap for me and Nancy white Eyes.

Sir I am your friend and Brother

COL^L HENRY

DISAFFECTION SUPPRESSED IN SOUTHWEST

[Col. Charles Lynch to Col. William Preston. 5QQ57. A. L. S.]

M^R McGAVOCKS August ye 17th 1780

D^R S^R:

I was Honour'd with yours a few days past, in which you Desire Me to Desist in trying torys &c &c—What sort of tryals you have been inform'd I have given them I know not, but I can assure you I only Examine them strictly & such as I believe not Very criminal I set at Liberty. Others I have for a proper tryal, some I have kept for soldiers, some as witnesses, some perhaps Justice to this Country May require they shou'd be Made Exampels of.

[1] This undated letter was enclosed in that of Brodhead to Washington, Aug. 21, 1780. "Cashaquin" may be a copyist's error for Coshocton, but see *ibid.*, 1496.

it may also appear Very Od to you at first View that I shou'd be in your county apprehending some of those you have had Before you & nothing appear'd against them, all which Dificultys I hope to reconcile to you Esspetially and to Every good Man, When first I was inform'd about the Conspiracy, and March to the hed of Little river, & soon Discover'd the Conspiracy to be so great as well in Bedford as in your parts, I thought it best to have something Done in Bedford, without Delay, fully Determining to have inform'd you by Expres of all the information I had got, about the Matter in your Parts and at the same time offer'd you My Assistance with 100 good Men to have apprehended those traytors to their Country, if you Needed it, but 1st so it happen'd I was ten Days Latter than I Expect'd before I with Convenience cou'd get along; from the upper part of Bedford I had the Express all ready & in Less than one hour shou'd have sent it of. When I receiv'd Saertain information there was a body of Bottetourt Militia had March'd to your assistance and you were a Doing the Needfull. I then Determin'd to March by the head of Reed Iseland[1] Near the Mountains, where I was inform'd Several Principal Villians Harber'd & Expecting I might fall in with some from your parts Makeing their Escape, and so on to the Lead Mines where my information also reach'd. I apprehended the Welch Men, David Herbot, Roger Oats & John Jenkins Acknowledges agreable to the information I had to have Swore into the Secrets twelve Mo^s past, and have Given Me a good Deal of information on Others, some of Which I Shall have apprehended ready to Deliver before you I intended this Day to have Done My Self the Pleasure to have Waited on you, but last Evening I receiv'd information of some Men up the River Who were great Offenders, it was some Carolinians who fram'd themselves torys Comeing to the Mines to give up, brought me the intelligence. I have sent out a party of Men to bring them in which I Expect will be Done tomorrow, after which the whole will be ready to wait on you at any Place you Please—I found Such Poor fare at the Mines that I was Oblidg'd to Dismiss the Most of My small Detachment the Second Day, and therefore Cou'd by No Means advise you with the flying Camp that Way. Capt McCorcle Will inform you and as I said I will Wait on you I can get word from fort Chiswell as you Pass, Let these Broken hints apologise for My

---

[1] Reed Island Creek is an eastern tributary of New River in Carroll and Pulaski counties, Va.

Conduct untill I have the Pleasur of Seeing you I wou'd also request the favour of you to Let Me have a sight of Letters you receiv'd relative to my conduct &c &c
I am Sr With Esteem your Most Obedient Humble Servt &c
             CHA^s LYNCH
N. B. I sent your Express to Col° Armstrong   C L
[Addressed:] Col° William Preston Montgomery favour'd by Capt McCorcle

---

[Nancy Devereaux to Col. William Preston. 5QQ58. A. L. S.]

[August, 1780]
DEAR COL°:

Col° Lynch, with a party of Militia have come from Bedford, in quest of Tories, they are now at the Lead Mines, and have in Custoday Several and my Husband among the rest. I am very certain, nothing can be made appear against him, but as there is a missunderstanding between Col° Lynch and the Welsh in General, I am very uneasy at present least my Husband should not have the Strictest Justice, done him at the Trial, therefore request the favour of you to send for him, and the Witnesses against him and have him Try'd, at Prices or where yourself and the rest of the Gentlemen are conveined, and then if my Husband should be convicted of any misconduct against the State, I only wish he may get a punishment Suitable to his deserts.
I am Your Obedient Servant.
            NANCY DAVEREUX
COL° PRESTON
  [Lower line of manuscript missing]

[John Jenkins's confession. 5QQ54. Contemporary transcript.]

John Jenkins confession Before Chas Lynch & Alexander Cumings August ye 17th 1780 acknowledges to have been swore into the secret by David Harbert La[s]t Summer, and Before John Griffith Was Brought as a prisoner to the Mines—that Roger Oats in the hard Wether got some rum of Mr Sanders as he said to treat some of the Neigbours, Particularly some to be carried to John Griffith, that the s^d Oats & Herbert did go to Griffiths as he heard them say together that he ask'd Herbert Whether they carried any to Griffiths he said they Did—Herbert also inform'd him that Griffith was going about in Many Places to inlist and Warn all his Men to be ready at a short Notice &c. Roger Oats told Jinkins Griffith inform'd him he had been ask'd at the Brittish Camp^s Who Work'd the Lead Mines, & that he inform'd them it was carried on by Brittainers, they Answerd they were supris'd that they shou[l]d Do it—Roger Oats Also said he was Glad Jinkins had Quitted it for he woud surely been ruined if he had Not, When the English got the Day, but as it was they Might be Well of &c—

[David Herbert's confession. 5QQ54. Contemporary transcript.]

David Harbot confession, Says he was swore into the secret by Old Whover, and that Roger Oats is Listed & swore in by John Griffith and that about the time or soon after the Battle in Georegee on Sevanah Last Sumer Roger Oats inform'd him he had seen Griffith and he had inform'd him a great Deal that the Country surely wou'd be Conquer'd &c and that Roger Oats communicated it to John Jinkins, and that he the s^d Herbert then about Did Swore the s^d Jinkins to Keep the Matter a secrett and from time to time convers'd with Jinkins on the subject, and that Roger Oats Purchas'd a Cag of Rum from Mr Sanders in the Hard weather that he went with Oats to Griffiths Carrying some rum when they had a good Deal of conversation about the Griffith telling them he intended so[o]n to turn out & try to get as many as possible, And to be ready at a short Notice to turn Out, & Particularly said that he Was Ask'd at the Brittis Camp who workd at the Lead Mines & carried them On, griffith inform'd them it was carried on by Brittainers, & that they Anserd they were surpris'd Brittainers wou'd assist in Makeing Lead to fight against the King of Brittain &c

[Summary of Peter Kinder's confession, Aug. 17, 1780. Printed in *John P. Branch Historical Papers*, IV, 317–18.]

Enlisted under John Griffith twelve months ago; James Douglas on Cripple Creek,[1] Brittain, Cox, and Martin on Walker's Creek, Joseph McFarlan on Reedy [Reed] Creek likewise implicated. Kinder piloted Griffith through Brushy Mountain to Walker's Creek. Samuel Thompson, and young Greyson on New River, Leonard Huff, and Griffith Lewis on south fork of Holston concerned. Richard Oweny in Baptist Valley at head of Clinch[2] raised a company for the king. David Ross and John Hook messengers to British camp. Roger Oats told Kinder that George Forbush, George Caggley, and Charles Detrick were enlisted, and Tom Gillehan of Nolichucky.[3] Nicholas Darter was at Ramsour's Mills. Implicates Andrew Vault on Cripple Creek, Andrew Sidney on Wolf Creek, [Philip] Lambert, Richard Ward, Joshua Jones of Walker's Creek, and William Clevings on Holston River.

[Confession of James Douglas. 5QQ59. Contemporary transcript.]

James Duggless Confession August 18th 1780

That John Griffith listed him this last april was a twelve months At his own house the Said Griffith sent for me time after time before I would Go—also the said Griffith told me that the Leading men of our Cuntry was at the foundation of it—also Co^l Inglish was at the head of it and all the beafe Cattle he Drove to the northward went the write way And he ricevd hard money for them.—The said Griffith further told him that David Ross Employ'd one George Bell to take the Sheriff, Plase in this county for the good of all the inhabitants that will Come in to be Subjects to his magisty the Said Griffith further Saith that James McCorkle & James McGaffick Had a warm side for the Tory Party. the said Griffith further inform'd him one Capt William Austin had never taken the state Oath and fain would had

---

[1] For this locality see *Dunmore's War*, 163, note 13.
[2] The location of Baptist Valley is given in *Wis. Hist. Colls.*, XXIII, 120, note 2.
[3] The Nolichucky River was in eastern Tennessee. See *Dunmore's War*, 41, note 73.

persuaded all his men to not take the oth the said Griffith further Saith to Dugglis that Old Vault and all his sons, and John Newland & Andrew Bronstetter & Fredrick Slimp and likewise that Moses Wells is concernd and Richard Ward and likewise that James Romine had been at Nolechuckee and saw Griffith And that Griffith wrote Some letter or nother and made answer To Dugglis no matter what also the said Dugglis Saith His Brother Thos Dugglis had talked with him on the subject and he thought he was Gilty and said Dugglis Further Saith that George Vault told him David Bustard Told him that he new the Carreyngs on of the torys and Some men had revealed the whole secret to Him and thretneted him if he Devulged it he would kill Him and the next time he Met Bustard he told him that He had told it and Drew his knifes on him the said Dugglis further Saith that Griffith met his o[w]n son in the woods and wanted him to Join but there was no Book To Sweare him yet his son George Gave his Consent and likewise that Joshua Jones pass^d for Griffith & Enlisted men and Old Bronsteter likewise is Gilty Dugglis further Saith that Griffith told him that Sam. Thompson had conceald him at his House and told him that tompson was good and George Pemberton on elk Creek was hal[f] and half that is to signify every wind will turn him

---

[Confession of Thomas Douglas. 5QQ60. Contemporary transcript.]

Thos Dugglis Confession August 19th 1780

that James Dugglis told him he was not in the write way the said Duglis told the said Thos Duglis that ther was a man in the parts that knew More than either of them That if I wanted to see this man he could tell Me where to go and at the Same time that he would Leave it to my self to Do as I saw caus and not to blaim him if he ever come to Trouble hereafter the same Dugglis told The sa[i]d Thos Dugglis to Go to Philip Duttons the same Thos Dugglis went to Philip Duttons and saw John Griffith and had some conversation with him in a private room by themselves In the first place asked him if he ever took the State Oath I told him I had the Said Griffith replyd I am sorry for that the said Griffith said to me if you can cleare your Conchance of that Oath I will take me in: and he told me that He had been acting for the king ever since these times begun the said Griffith furthe[r] told him he should have six pence starling per day and a suit of Good Close and Should have land and should be cleare of taxes for one and twenty years and the said time I was to be ready at a moments Call and he then took the oath to keep secret the said word told the said Dugglis that he was for the british side.

[Capt. William Preston's safe conduct for Philip Lambert. 5QQ61. A. L. S.]

Augt 21st 1780

If Philip Lambert returns to his Allegience to the State and delivers himself up to a Magistrate or to the Court he will be treated with Lenity & his Person shall be protected from Injury; & if he don't like the Proposals to be made by the Court he will then be at Liberty to depart from the Place forty eight hours without search or Enquiry.

By order of Court

W^M PRESTON

[Confession of Robert King. 5QQ71. A. D. S.]

To the Worshipfull Court of Montgomery County Humbly Prayeth Jentlemen of the Court whereas I Understand that Information has been Laid Before your worships Court that I have been Guilty with many others of being a tory and as fare as I understand it has been proved against Me that I had a Capt Commission to List Men But Jentlemen the Case is Bad anough I confess and am hartly Sorry for Myself But Jentlemen I am Not in so High Commission as that for I Do not positivly [know] whither I am A Leu^t or Ensign But I must Confess that I Have Been Working in a Rong Cause and all through Bad Advice and A Rong Aperehension of the Matter and Jentlemen as it has been the first fault that Ever I have Commited in this Respect[or any Other since I have Come into the parts I Do Beg that your worships would Look over it as Easey as you posablely Can Not that I am any Better than another Man or that I would Vindicate My own Cause But there is several of Your worships Knows If you would pleas to speak what you know that

my Corrector has Ever been Good and Jentlemen I think it is Very Hard to Give my self up and to Have my Estate taken from me or my small and Helpless family to which it is well Known they would be so were You to pleas to Do it and there is nothing that I have But what I have worked hard for and got it all in a Honest way for which I Defy the world to Say any thing Els and I Likewise I Defy any Body iff the[y] would tell the truth that Ever I Intinded to hurt any Either in Body or Estate But only of my own Simple Notion and the Bad avice of Others that this was the Best Way But Now I see that I was Ronng in my opinion and am Now willing to Give up to your will and to Come under any obligations that your worhsips pleases to Lay on me in the Way of afine or giving Security for my Good behaver for the time to Come and Now Jentlemen I Beg that Your Worships would Look over my fault as Easy as you Posablely Can and I will for Ever be your Real friend
ROB^T KING

N B Dear Si^r I Beg you will send me aline By the Bearer to my wife that I may Know what You would avise Me to Do If it is not two much against the Intrest of the Contrys and I am si^r as before
To Co^L WILLIAM PRESTON
To Co^L WILLIAM PRESTON in Mountgomery County

[Proceedings of the courts of Montgomery and Botetourt counties at the trial of Loyalists. 5QQ73–79. A. D.]

At a meeting of the Justices of Montgomery County and Botetourt for the Examination of Col° Wm Ingles of Montgomery County,[1] who stands charged with being guilty of Treason against the Commonwealth.

Present

Col° Wm Preston   Capt John Taylor[2]   Patrick Lockart
Col° Wm Christian   Capt Ja^s Thompson   Andrew Boyd[3]

[1] For Col. William Ingles see *ibid.*, 101, note 46.
[2] For a sketch of Capt. John Taylor see *ibid.*, 45, note 80; for Capt. James Thompson see *ibid.*, 43, note 78.
[3] Andrew Boyd was an Augusta County pioneer who married Mary, daughter of Col. John Buchanan, about the year 1769. In 1776 Boyd successfully undertook a perilous mission to the hostile Cherokee. Soon thereafter he removed

258   WISCONSIN HISTORICAL COLLECTIONS

Col⁰ James   Capt Dan¹ Trigg   Robert Sayers
    Robertson¹   Capt James Barnett William Campbell
        &
George Rutlidge²   Capt Jo⁸ Grey   James Byrns
      William Neeley³

Whereupon the Witnesses were examined as well in Behalf of the Commonwealth as for the Prisoner &. The charge not being fully proven and information being made that further evidence may appear,

The Court are unanimously of Opinion that the final determination of the matter be defer'd & that in the mean time Col⁰ Ingles, do enter into Bond with—suffcitent security, to appear at any time when Call'd on, under the Penlʸ of £100,000

Robert Grayson,⁴ is allso charged for the same offense & Witness being sworn & examined, as well for the Commonwealth as the Prisoner The Court are of Opinion that the charge is not fully proven, & he offering to enlist into the Continental Army till the last of Decʳ 1781. He is received & he took the oath accordingly. & so long as he serves; his Familly & property is to be protected.

Joseph Mᶜ Donald allso stands charged with the same offense and Witnesses being examined, as well, in Behalf of the Commonwealth as for the prisoner. The Court are of Opinion that the charge is proven but he being 58 years of age, & a large Familly, & his Two Sons Joseph and Edward offering to enlist into the Continental Army untill the last day of Decʳ 1781. to have their

to Montgomery County, where he became a county magistrate. His home was in that portion of the county later laid off as Wythe County, and there he was living as late as 1807.

¹ For a sketch of James Robertson see *ibid.*, 44, note 79.

² George Rutledge, of the South Carolina family of that name, came to the frontier at the opening of the Revolution and served in 1776 on Christian's campaign against the Cherokee, and in 1779 on that of Shelby against the Chickamauga. In 1780 Rutledge was lieutenant in Capt. Gilbert Christian's company at King's Mountain, where, tradition holds, he fired the shot that proved fatal to Maj. Patrick Ferguson. Rutledge was later sheriff of Sullivan County, and a member of the constitutional convention for Tennessee. He was the first state senator for his district, and succeeded John Sevier as military commander of East Tennessee. Rutledge died in July, 1813 on his farm near Blountville.

³ William Neeley volunteered for the campaign of 1774, and on April 15, 1778 was commissioned ensign in the Botetourt militia. He was still living in Botetourt County in 1787.

⁴ Robert Grayson (Grissom) became a good citizen of the commonwealth, and died shortly before the year 1795.

Father excused. & of opinion that they be rec^d as soldiers & their Fathers Familly & Property protected during their Service— (Mr Lockhart disents)

John Mc Donald, is charged as above. & Witnesses being examined as well in Behalf of the Commonwealth as the prisoner, The Court is of Opinion that the charge is proven & that He be sent to Augusta Goal for a further Tryal

Joseph Poppecaughfer is charged as the rest & the Witnesses sworn & examined as before. & The Court are of Opinion that the charge is fully proven & that he be sent to Augusta Goal for further Tryall.

Jacob Shull Junr is allso charged as the rest. & the Witnesses sworn & exam^d as well in behalf of the Commonwealth as the prisoner, The Court are of Opinion that the Charge is proven, & that he be sent to Augusta Goal for further Tryal.

John Grayson, Gasper Reid & Jeremiah Patrick, stands charged with being Guilty of Treason against the Commonwealth. Witnesses being sworn & examined, The Court are of Opinion that the charge is only [blank in Ms.]

Gasper Garlick is charged as the above, & the Witnesses being sworn and examined, The Court are of opinion that the charge is supported & He appears to be a Simple Fellow do acquit him on his agreeing to take 39 Lashes

Henry Stafford being charged as the rest, & Witnesses being examined, The Court are of opinion that the charge is not supported, & that he be Acquited.

Abraham Morgan, stands charged as the rest, & the Witnesses being sworn & examined, The Court are of opinion that the charge is supported, but it appearing that he is an Ignorant Poor Man with a small Familly do order him to be acquited after getting 39 Lashes.

Swain Polson, stands charged as the rest, & Witnesses being sworn and examined, The Court are of Opinion that the charge is proven that he be sent to Augusta Goal for further Tryal

Robert McGee, stands as the rest, charged for Treason, & Witnesses being sworn & examined, The Court are of opinion that he be sent to Goal for further Tryal

Jeremiah Stover, stands charged as the rest, & the Witnesses being sworn & examined, the Court are of Opinion that the charge is so far proven, as finding him with his Gun Hid in a Barn with Several Tories, & has been known frequently and always since in this part of the Country to live among them, therefore do order him 39 Lashes.

Thomas Copeley is charged as the rest & witnesses being sworn & examd The Court are of Opinion that the Charge is [blank in Ms.]

Henry Lawer, stands charged as the rest, & being examined, Acknowledged He was an enlisted Soldier under Howard Haven, for the British Service. But it appearing to the Court that he was a Youth & advis'd to do so by, Haven, & on his agreeing now to enlist into the Continental Service, for 18 Months, after his arival in the G^d Camp The Court are of Opinion that he be admitted to do so—& he took the Oath

Andrew Lawer, stands charged as the rest & being examined, acknowledged himself as an enlisted Soldier under Howard Haven for the British Service, But it appearing to the Court that he was a Youth & might have been perswaded, to enlist into that service without properly understanding the matter & he now recanting & offering to enlist into the Continental Service & there to Serve for 18 Month after his Arival at the Grand Camp, they are of Opinion that he be admitted to do so—and he took the Oath.

George Walter, is charged with Treason as the rest, & Witnesses being sworn & examined, The Court are of Opinion that the Charge is fully proven He having been enlisted as a Soldier for the British Service But he appearing to be a poor & ignorant Man They agree to excuse him on his Volunt[arily] offering to enlist into the Continental Army for 18 Months from the time of his arival in Genl Washingt[ons] Camp. & he took the Oath accordingly

John Harrison is charged as the rest & Witnesses being sworn & Examined The Court are of Opinion that the charge is not proven & that he be acquited.

John Henderson is charged as the rest & Acknowledges himself sworn by Thos Heaven, not to lift arms against the British Army & to adhere to the King of England The Court are of Opinion that he [blank in Ms]

William Grant is charged as the rest. But he Voluntarily agreeing to enlist into the Continental Army, to serve for 18 Months from the time of his arival in the Grand Camp The Court did not go into the Examination of Witnesses, But admited him to the Oath of a Soldier.

Walter Stewart is charged as the rest, & Witnesses being sworn & exam^d The Court are of Opinion that the Charge is not fully supported & that he be acquited on entering into Bond with suffictient Security in the sum of £20000 for his Good Behaviour.

Samuel Robinson being charged as the rest, & Witnesses sworn & exam^d the court are of Opinion that the charge is not fully supported, & that he be Acquited on entering into Bond with Suffictient Sec^y in the sum of £20,000 for his Good Behaviour.

John Haven & his two Sons James & William being charged as the rest. but nothing appearing to fix the Charge fully on them; & William Voluntarily offering to enlist into the Continental Army, to serve as long as those troops order'd to be raised by the last Assembly (for that service) & the said John & his Other Son James offering to take the State Oath at the Table; The Court are unanimously of Opinion that the s^d William be received as a Soldier, upon which he took the Oath for that purpose, & that John & James be Acquited, & that they & their property be protected during the service of the said William & for ever after so long as they behave as becomes Good Citizens.

William Grant stands charged as the rest & Witnesses being sworn, & examined, The Court are of Opinion that the charge is [blank in Ms]

Adam Liveer being charged as the rest & he acknowledging himself Guilty of the Charge, & Offering to enlist himself in the Cotinental Army, to serve as long as the Troops ordered by the last Assembly. The Court are of Opinion, that as he is a Youth & it is probable he was inadvertedly drawn to the Wrong side of the Dispute. he be admitted as a Soldier, & thereupon he took the Oath of a Soldier

Jacob Francisco is charged as the rest & he Confesses that has been Sworn & enlisted With Howard Haven for the British service, [blank in Ms]

Hezekiah Phillips & Henry Laybrook being charged for assaulting & Beating Christian Snido, an Officer on duty, & Witnesses being sworn & exam^d The Court are of Opinion the charge is proven,

Jacob Shull, charged as the rest, and voluntarily enlists a Soldier in the Continental Army until the last Day of Decr 1781.— and also John Shull enlists on the same Terms. On which their & their Fathers property is to be protected, whilst the said Jacob & John & their said Father behaves well.

David Price, charged as the rest; and the Court are of Opinion that he be rec^d as a Soldier in the Continental Army he having voluntarily enlisted himself for that Purpose till last Decr 1781. Capt Lockart Dissents.

Jacob Francisco, charged as the rest, and enlists as a Soldier until the last Day of Decr 1781.

Robert Magee charged as the rest. He stands a prisoner upon Parole that he will appear at Decr Court next, then & there to answer to all Charges heretofore laid, & that may be laid against him in the mean Time under penalty of losing his Estate.

Samuel Ingram charged as the rest. And his Sons Jonathan & James voluntarily enlisting themselves as Soldiers in the Continental Army untill the 31 of Decr 1781. upon which the said Samuel Ingrams & his two Sons property is to be protected, whilst he & them behaves well

Wm Grayson charged as the rest. He voluntarily enlists himself as a Soldier in the Continental Army until the last Day of Decr 1781. upon which him & his property is to be protected, while he behaves well

Abraham Beaver, charged as the rest. He voluntarily enlists lists himself as a Soldier in the continental Army until the 31st of Decr 1781. upon which him & his property is to be protected, so long as he behaves well.

Henry Laybrook charged for misbehaviour. Voluntarily enlists himself as a Soldier in the continental army until the 31 Decr 1781.

Robert King charged for Treason. The Court waved giving Judgment upon it upon his enlisting as a Soldier in the Continental Army until the last Day of Decr 1781. and his pledging his own Estate real & personal; also his Father in law Joseph Reburn pledging his Estate, real & personal as Security that the s^d King will find another good and fit Soldier, for the Term as above when Col Preston calls for him.

Frederick Smith being charged with Treason against the State But the charge not being fully proven, & his Son offering to enlist into the Continental Army during the Term for which the Troops are to be raised, agreeable to an Act of Assembly, lately passed, for Filling up the Virginia Quoto. The Court are of Opinion that he be admited as a Soldier, & thereupon He took the Oath of a Soldier & the prisoner is Acquited during the Service of his Son.

Robert Henderson is charged as the rest, & Witnesses being sworn and examined, The [blank in Ms]

Thomas Downard being charged as the rest & the Witnesses being sworn & examined, The Court are of Opinion [blank in Ms]

Nathaniel Britton being charged as the rest, & the charge being examined into, The Court are of Opinion that he be sent to Augusta Goal & there to be confined for a further Tryal

James Kerr being charged as the rest & the charge being exam^d into, The Court are of opinion that he be sent to Augusta Goal & there to be Confined for a further Tryal

Jeremiah Patrick being charged, now singly, as the rest, & Witnesses sworn & examined, the charge not being fully supported & He offering to enlist himself a Soldier in the Continental Army untill the last day of December 1781. The Court are of Opinion that He be admitted as a Soldier, & that his Familly & property be protected so long as he remains in the Service, & thereafter so long as he behaves himself as becomes a Good Citizen (Mr Lockart desents to this order)

Gasper Reid being charged, now Singly, for Treason against the Commonwealth. & the charge being examined into; & proven, But he appearing to be Sixty Years old, & his son David appearing & offering to Enlist into the Continental Army untill the last day of December 1781. The Court are of Opinion He be rec^d as a soldier, & that during the Term of his Service. the old man & his Familly & property is to be protected provided he himself go to the Minds by the 25th of this month of August & there serve as a Soldier Two & a half months from that time.

Samuel Pepper is charged as the rest. & [blank in Ms]

Abraham Beaver stands charged as the rest & Witnesses being sworn & examined the Court are of Opinion [blank in Ms.]

James Bane Senr being charged as the rest, But his Son Edward comeing into Court & agreeing to enlist into the Continental Army untill the Last day of Decr 1781. Whereupon the Court received his Son as a Soldier, & let the old man go. & so long as his Son Serves in the Army his Familly & property is to be protected and afterwards so long as behaves as becomes a Good Citizen.

Samuel Sadler is charged as the rest, But he offering to enlist into the Continental Army to serve to the last day of Decr 1781. Whereupon the Court did not proceed to the full Hearing of the charge but received him as a Soldier & he took the Oath ac-

cordingly. & so long as he serves as a Soldier, his Familly & property is to is to be protected, & for ever after if he behaves well
James Bane Jun[r] stands charged as the rest, But he agreeing to enlist into the Continental Army to the last day of Dec[r] 1781. & his Father comeing into Court & Acknowledgeing that he will forfiet his Estate if his son deserts & the s[d] James Agreeing to forfiet his on the same Conditions The Court are of Opinion that he be received. & he took the Oath accordingly & during his Service his Familly & property is to be protected. & forever after so long as he behaves well.

[Patrick Henry to Capt. Thomas Madison.[1] 29J111. Transcript.]

LEATHERWOOD,[2] Aug. 23[d] 1780

DEAR SIR:

Yours with £800 I rec[d] by your messenger, and inclose your Bond as you desire, and shall write my brother & inform him of the contents of yours. We shall please ourselves with the expectation of seeing you and sister, with sister Christian, & I hope the Col° next month, & don't let any thing stop you. We shall set out down with our family in October, when the Assembly sets. The Torys have been plotting hereabouts as well as over the Mountains, but I hope they are pretty well suppressed. We have partys out in pursuit of them, and several have been detected, but as yet none are confined for Tryal in this county, but I guess some soon will. I hope the enemy you mention will be stopped before they penetrate any distance. Six ships of the Line, & 5000 men, land troops, composing the first division of the French, are arrived to the Northward. The enemy have retreated before Gen[l] Gates in Carolina.

With love to Sister & the children, I am, Dear Sir, Y[r] Aff[te],

P. HENRY.

CAPT THOMAS MADISON, Bottetourt Co. Virginia

[1] For Capt. Thomas Madison, whose wife was a sister of Patrick Henry, see ibid., 59, note 99.
[2] Patrick Henry in 1778 bought from Thomas Lomax the estate of "Leatherwood" for a consideration of £5,000. It comprised nearly 10,000 acres and was situated in Henry County, about eight miles from the courthouse, and 192 miles southwest of Richmond. This was then a pioneer region. Henry and his family lived at "Leatherwood" for about five years.

FRENCH AGENT IN INDIAN COUNTRY

[Summary of a letter of Col. Daniel Brodhead, Headquarters, Fort Pitt, Aug. 23, 1780, to Maj. Daniel Maurice Godefroy de Linctot. Printed in *Pa. Archives*, XII, 259.]

Supplies soon to be sent Linctot. Directed to inform Delaware council that their desire to march against the common enemy shall soon be gratified. Wyandot are determined for war. Shawnee have been rewarded by Colonel Clark. Linctot ordered to return unless he can influence some other hostile, or some neutral, tribe.

WESTMORELAND PROTECTED

[Summary of a letter of Col. Archibald Lochry, Twelve Mile Run, Aug. 24, 1780, to Pres. Joseph Reed. Printed in *id.*, VIII, 518–19.]

Supplies received; expedition against some hostile Indian town proposed, not yet accomplished for lack of provisions. Commissions for militia officers. Recruiting for ranging company. Pennsylvania volunteers supplied from Continental stores until 7th instant, now quartered on inhabitants, have had no pay since April 10. "We have had no dammage done by the savages since aprile which in a great meashure must be ascribed to the cair & Vigolence of our troops."

CONDITIONS IN KENTUCKY

[Col. John Floyd to Col. William Preston. 17CC130–31. Transcript.]

August 25th, 1780

DEAR SIR:

On my return home from our little Expedition about ten days ago, I received your kind letter of the 22nd. of June. I am sorry to hear of the losses we have met with at Charlestown, but I hope our Troops immediately under the direction of the great General have made retaliation by retaking N. York. The occurrencies in this Country in the course this Summer would far exceed the bounds of a Letter and as Mr Madison is going in it will be useless to enumerate them—The stroke the Enemy has made at Licking has raised many doubts and fears in the minds of the Inhabitants so that numbers are preparing to remove back to the interior parts of the country. I am sensible of the fears and anxieties you have had for the safety of this country, and the Friendly part you have acted by raising men for our relief, and indeed I am doubtful the storm is not over tho' perhaps it may[be] for this season. Col° Crockett's Batallion Stationed in the manner you mention will be of great service to this County, but we have very small expectations from Col° Slaughter's Regiment as it does not exceed forty effective men, who must suffer this winter for clothing. And if the 600 men from the three upper counties on the Ohio should come without any provisions as the others who came down have done, they cannot subsist without distressing the Inhabitants very much. From what I have seen of the situation of the Enemy's Country, they can at any time they please carry on a campaign against this part of the country with equal success to that above without some considerable alteration in our affairs for the better, or the immediate interposition of Providence. We have no spies out, nor had we one on duty when the attack was made on the Garrisons at Licking.[1] And although they were twelve days in going from the Ohio, and cleared a waggon road great part of the way they were never discovered till they marched in sight.

Poor Capt. Byrn[2] lies at Falls in a most deplorable situation with *his wounds*, and it is out of my power to do much for him. I attempted to have him removed out here with Billey M°Afee[3] who is also wounded; but Mr. Byrn could not bear to be removed off the Bed to lay him on the Bier; and Dr. Smith informs me he cannot live many days. Mʳ Byrn press'd to write to his Brother to come to him immediately, and it will be necessary for him to

[1] Note on original manuscript: "Ruddell & Martin's Stations. L. C. D."
[2] This wounded man, who soon afterwards died, was a brother of Capt. James Byrn of Montgomery County, Va. See Draper Mss., 17CC133.
[3] William was the youngest of the McAfee brothers, pioneer explorers of Kentucky. He was born about the year 1755 in Botetourt County, Va., and in 1779 removed and settled a station not far from Harrodsburg, Ky. He commanded a company in Col. Benjamin Logan's division of Clark's troops on the Shawnee expedition, and was severely wounded at the Indian town of Piqua. He died at Floyd's Station soon after this letter was written. *Ibid.*, 4CC26, 56–58.

FRONTIER RETREAT 267

come as his Brother has considerable property here, & he is appointed one of the Executors.

If an Expedition is gone out against Chuckamogo I think Charles[1] might come out with the greatest safety & I expect by this time he is surely on the way—You sent 1000 acre warrant for Capt. Smith. Pray how is he? No Surveying is to be done till October. The little mare I bought from Mr. Gardner was stolen from here last May and think she was taken back to the settlem^t. I wish he could find her out as I value her very much— Billey Breckenridge[2] is here and I believe would have gone in but his Horse is poor being just off the campaign and I have none left but Pompey and cannot supply him with a horse but his own will be in order by the middle of Sept. Jenny sends you her best wishes & very hearty thanks for your Fatherly care and supplications for the preservation of herself and little Will who is now a fine white Headed Chattering Boy—and please Dear Sir to accept of the sincere & grateful acknowledgments of your ever affectionate Friend & Servt

JNO FLOYD.

LOYALISTS REVENGEFUL

[Summary of a letter of Col. William Christian, Mahanaim, Aug. 30, 1780, to Col. William Preston. Printed in *John P. Branch Historical Papers*, IV, 318-19.]

A young negro lad belonging to Col. William Campbell was waylaid by four armed and one unarmed man at Sinking Spring, said they would hang him as soon as they reached Peak Creek, that his master had destroyed their property and they would destroy his, and that they were on their way to kill Colonel Campbell and wife. They opened the letters he carried, but finding

[1] Charles, younger brother of John Floyd, was born about the year 1752 in Amherst County, Va., and in 1773 married Mary Stewart of Hanover County. In 1778 he served in Clark's western army. In 1780 Floyd removed his family to his brother's station on Beargrass Creek, and was with the latter when he was killed. Thereafter he resided at Pond's Settlement, where his son, Charles Floyd Jr., enlisted for the Lewis and Clark expedition, whence he was never to return. Charles Floyd the elder died in 1828 while visiting a daughter in Todd County. His widow survived until 1850, when she passed away in Bond County, Ill.

[2] For a sketch of William Breckinridge see *Wis. Hist. Colls.*, XXIII, 275, note 2.

them of a private nature threw them down; were frightened off by the approach of some wagons. Requests a guard for Campbell's house. Letter forwarded to Fort Chiswell, where Preston is said to be. News of French armament. Colonel Crockett to march down this river soon with 400 or 500 men.

LOYALISTS ENLISTED

[Col. William Preston to Gen. John Peter Gabriel Muhlenberg.[1] 5QQ81. Autograph draft.]

SIR: [September, 1780]

Numbers of People in the County have been so stupid and lost to their own Interest as to be dissaffected to the present Governm^t of the Commonwealth ever since it took Place. Their Confederacy at length extended not only through this & some of the neighbouring Counties but into the neighbouring Frontiers of Carolina. Their Combinations were carried on with such amazing Secrecy that we were apprehensive they could not be fully discovered untill some desperate Blow would be struck. In order to Discover their designs we were obliged to employ two Men last July to go amongst them in the Character of british officers. One of these young men called John Wyatt[2] had been a Prisoner at Charles Town but made his Escape & had by some Means procured Protection from another Person & some of Clintons Proclamations which enabled him to pass amongst these people unsuspected & make many important Discoveries, & thereby opened a Door to an enquiry into their Conduct which Cost the Officers & magistrates of this County supported by the Militia near five Weeks. I believe they are now suppressed & I have enlisted near one hundred of them into the Continental Army as Security for their own & friends future good Behaviour. But Wyatt is called back to the Service, to which he is affraid to return lest some of these People might Secretly revenge the discovery

[1] For a sketch of this officer see *Frontier Defense*, 211, note 77.
[2] This was probably John Wyatt of North Carolina, who was born in 1759 of the Virginia family of that name. At the close of the Revolution he removed to Lincoln County, Ky., and thence in 1817 to Warren County, Mo. There he was living when in 1832 he made a declaration of his services in order to obtain a pension. His wife was Polly Pearl of Virginia.

he has made. Therefore the Officers & Magistrates of this County have desired me to make this Matter known to you, Sir, & to beg the Favour of you to give Wyatt a Discharge, for this Important Service; or if that cannot be granted to accept a Man in his room untill the last of December 1781 & that he may not be called on till then. His Behaviour here has gained him the Esteem of all good Men & it is hoped will [be] looked upon in a favourable light elsewhere A Line from you on this head will be deemed a particular favour.

A Youth called Ballard Smith[1] a Brother in law of mine has been in the Continental Army Some Years. I understand he is an old Lieutenant and expects to be promoted to the Command of a Company this Campaign. Should this be the Case I would take it as a singular Favour of You to give him the Command of the Company of Recruits that I have raised in this County, & who marches from hence for Richmond this Day. The Young man seems extremely fond to get the Company, as they are very likely & understands the use of Arms.—I beg Sir You will excuse this Request in favour of a Relation that I have esteemed from his Childhood, and who I have with pleasure heard is not destitute of Military Merit. Were it otherwise I should not have given you this Trouble.

I am with real Esteem, Sir Your most Obed^t Servt

A Copy of a Letter to Genl Mulenberg Sepr 1780

EMIGRATION CHECKED

[Extract of a letter from Pittsburgh, sent from Philadelphia, Oct. 10, 1780, published in *Maryland Journal*, Oct. 17, 1780. 29J20. Transcript.]

PITTSBURGH, Sept. 1 [1780]

Since my last, the savages have killed and scalped ten men, about 60 miles up the Monongahela;[2] and Cap^n Bird, with a

[1] Ballard Smith, born in Hanover County, Va., was the son of Francis Smith, whose daughter, Susannah, married Col. William Preston. Young Smith entered the army in October, 1776 as ensign in the First Virginia Regiment; on Aug. 9, 1777 he was promoted to a lieutenancy; and on May 12, 1779 became captain-lieutenant in his regiment. He served until the end of the war. In 1790 Smith was commissioned captain of the First United States Infantry; the next year he became major, and on Sept. 4, 1792 was assigned to the Fourth Sub-legion. Major Smith died Mar. 20, 1794.

[2] Probably this was the raid, narrated in *Withers' Chronicles of Border Warfare*, 282–83, that took place at Martin's Fort on Crooked Run, on the west side of the

few regulars and Canadians, and, they report, 700 savages, hath entirely broke up one of the Kentucky settlements, having made prisoners 400 men, women and children. But this stroke may prove serviceable to us, as it will, I hope, if not finally stopped, give a check to the emigrations to the Ohio, which is prodigious, and which must weaken the country below. The grasping hand of the covetous and avaricious monopolizer, not only of American money but of American lands, has in a manner put arms into the hands of our enemies. The former practice is now, I hope, effectually abolished, and I wish the latter was.

EXPEDITION PLANNED

[Col. Daniel Brodhead to Col. David Shepherd. 1SS209. A. L. S.][1]

HEAD QU^{rs} FORT PITT Sepr 4th 1780

DEAR SIR:

The Service requires that fifty Men well mounted on Horseback, besides proper officers, and fifty spare Horses, be furnished from your County and Rendevouz on the fifteenth Day of next Month at George Croghan's place, upon alleghany River;[2] to enable me to carry an Expedition into the Enemies Country & Cover the Settlements—

Such Horses as are lost in actual Service will be paid by the publick.

Encourage such as are of ability to bring with them Rations for fifteen Days, for which they shall likewise be paid the common price, if Demanded.

As the issue of the proposed Expedition will in all human probability be attended with salutary effects to the Settlements on

Monongahela River in what is now Monongalia County, W. Va. Withers assigns this event to 1779, but his dates are mostly given from reminiscences, not documents. The locality and the number of persons captured, as related by Withers, correspond with the account of the event described in this letter of 1780.

[1] This letter was a circular to the several county lieutenants. See a similar one to Col. Archibald Lochry, printed in *Pa. Archives*, XII, 260.

[2] For a sketch of Col. George Croghan see *Dunmore's War*, 7, note 12. His place, where Washington dined with him Oct. 19, 1770, was four miles above the confluence of the Allegheny with the Monongahela, on the eastern bank of the former stream in what was McCandlass Township. It is now within the city limits of Pittsburgh, near the United States arsenal.

this side the Hills, I doubt not but every Man who has the cause of his Country and Humanity at Heart, will readily contribute to carry it into the fullest execution

I have the Honor to be with great regard and Esteem Dear Sir your most obed^t Hble Servt

DANIEL BRODHEAD Col^o command^g W D.

COL^o DAVID SHEPHERD.

[Summary of a letter of Col. Daniel Brodhead, Fort Pitt, Sept. 5, 1780, to Gen. George Washington. Printed in Sparks, *Corr. Amer. Rev.*, III, 77.]

Yesterday two inhabitants killed by Indians on Robinson's Run[1] in this county; two soldiers taking some provisions in a canoe to Fort Henry were fired upon, one was wounded. No provisions, therefore cannot send out a pursuing party. Clark has destroyed two Shawnee towns, killed six men and one woman.[2] If provisions can be obtained, "I will yet visit the Wyandots by the 1st of November; and I believe the country will be unanimous in joining me upon an expedition."

[Summary o a letter of Col. Daniel Brodhead, Fort Pitt, Sept, 5, 1780, to Timothy Pickering. Printed in *Pa. Archives*, XII, 263–64.][3]

Orders misconstrued. Commissary Steel discharged a brigade of pack horses at Old Town with flour for Fort Pitt. Troops frequently without bread for two or three days at a time; meat sometimes lacking. Virginia has appointed no commisssary for West, and Westmoreland not purchasing beef for winter supplies. Recent Indian attacks. Encloses Major Linctot's letter with news of Clark's Shawnee success.

[1] Robinson's Run is a western affluent of Chartier's Creek in Allegheny and Washington Counties, Pa. See map, *Frontier Defense*, frontispiece.
[2] See the British account in *Mich. Pion. & Hist. Colls.*, X, 419.
[3] A similar letter to Pres. Joseph Reed is printed in *Pa. Archives*, VIII, 536–37.

[Summary of a letter of Col. Daniel Brodhead, Headquarters, Fort Pitt, Sept. 6, 1780, to Col. George Vallandigham. Printed in *ibid.*, 261-62.]

Distressed to hear his neighbors have again felt the cruel hand of the murdering savage. Moses Killbuck gave information of a party of forty Wyandot, and another of six Munsee coming against the settlements. As he is a notorious liar, did not alarm the people. Why were these men without a guard? Indians' leaving a Continental gun seems odd; directs that it be sent to him as some one may recognize it as the gun of a soldier killed by the savages. Pity and protection for the inhabitants. Vallandigham has his consent to raise thirty or forty scouts to range until fall crops are sown. Inhabitants must furnish provisions. If best men volunteer for proposed expedition there will be little to fear from the savages next year. British have evacuated New York.

ALLEGHENY POSTS REGARRISONED

[Summary of a letter of Col. Daniel Brodhead, Headquarters, Fort Pitt, Sept. 6, 1780, to Col. Archibald Lochry. Printed in *ibid.*, 261.]

Lochry's letter of September 3 brought pleasing news and a presage of final victory for America. Allegheny River raised by rains. Garrisons should be restored to Fort Armstrong and Fort Crawford to protect frontier against danger from Niagara. Two men killed on Robinson's Run on Monday.

HOSTILE INDIAN PARTIES

[Big Cat to Col. Daniel Brodhead. 1H144. In handwriting of Heckewelder.]

SALEM Sept^{br} ye 12th 1780.

M'hingwe Pushees (or the big Cat) to Col^o Brodhead as follows:

BROTHER M'HINGWE GWEESUCH:

I am very glad that we can inform one another all matters so freely. I now acquaint You that in 14 Days from to day I shall meet You at Pittsburgh where we will speak with one another. You must excuse my staying so long, as We had to consider Worshiping, and this great Work is not quite finished yet, but as soon as it is quite over, You may depend of seing all the Chieffs, Captains and their young Men with You.

Brother: All the Chieffs, Capt^{ns} & Young Men remember their Compliments to You.

Now *Brother:* I will inform You that Mechmewocunund whom We sent to Keenhanschican, heard that Alex^{dr} McKee was building a Fort on the Miami River, he had an 100 English there with him.

Brother: I was not able to stop a party of 20 Young Men which went by some Days ago to do Mischieff unto our American Brothers; They were headed by Captn Pipe Brothers & Relations. Again a Son of Wyondoghella threatens to kill the French Major & Captn

Brother: I met 3 Monsy's to Day who as I understand had been doing Mischief somewhere near Fort Pitt. They are Relations to the Monsy Chieff & one is lately come from the Miami River.

I am Your friend & Brother

M'HINGWEE PUSHEES.

[*Addressed:*] To Daniel Brodhead Col^o Comand^t West^n Departm^t at Pittsburgh. by 3 Messengers from Cooshocking

---

[Summary of a letter of Col. Daniel Brodhead, Fort Pitt, Sept. 14, 1780, to Gen. George Washington. Printed in Sparks, *Corr. Amer. Rev.*, III, 84–85, and in *Pa. Archives*, XII, 265–66.]

Your letter of July 4 received. Regret want of resources to enable you to act offensively against enemy. French at Detroit are in own interest; 1,200 men could carry that place. Fort Pitt garrison recently represented that they had had no bread for five days. Temporary supply obtained partly by compulsion. Recent letter from Heckewelder reports that a Wyandot party of thirty experienced warriors was almost entirely destroyed by a pursuing party from Fort McIntosh.

[Summary of a letter of Col. Daniel Brodhead, Fort Pitt, Sept. 16, 1780, to Pres. Joseph Reed. Printed in *id.*, V, 258–59.]

Garrison's request for bread; daily supplies procured with much difficulty. Intelligence just received of seven killed and captured on Ten Mile Creek;[1] no provisions for a pursuing party. Importance of Delaware friendship; must have goods to clothe them. Has just received letter from Major Linctot, written in French, translation enclosed. "Had I but Men & provisons,[2] I might do something to gain a Laurel, but in my present circumstances, it is probable I may loose my Reputation."

THREATENED INVASION FROM DETROIT

[Maj. Daniel Maurice Godefroy de Linctot to Col. Daniel Brodhead. Washington Papers. Contemporary translation.]

SIR:

I have Received the Letter that you did me the Honor to write by Mr Deplanteur, I am sorry to hear of the scarcity of provisions with you. I hope that my wishes may be accomplished, that at present you may have sufficient to cary on an Expedition which will be the only Method to stop the Nations, if they have not Faith, I loose intirely their confidence, I have already lost a party (here is something particular) they were twelve Days coming from Coochoquin, and the Meravians went to meet Mr Deplanteur that was sick, a party paid by the English have stop't me, and I dare not follow them, a great quantity of the party were in search of me, and would have taken me to Detroit, I hid myself till the party had seperated.

I understand the English is a going to send One Hundred men to the Shawnese to Build a Fort. They also say, that a party of a

[1] Ten Mile Creek is a western affluent of the Monongahela, dividing Greene County from Washington County. There seems to be no other record of the raid here mentioned, unless it was the one that occurred near Jackson's Fort on the south fork of the Ten Mile, in Franklin Township, Greene County, described by Samuel P. Bates, *History of Greene County, Pennsylvania* (Chicago, 1888), 500.

[2] See several letters on the subject of obtaining provisions, about this date, in Brodhead's Letter Book, in *Pa. Archives*, XII, 264–69.

Thousand men is a coming to Attack Fort Mᶜintosh, I imagine they will come with the Savages.

I have the Honor to be with the most Respectfull attachment Sir Your most Humble & Obedient Servᵗ

GODFREY LANCTOT.

I have sent some Belts to the Shawnese¹ & Mingoes & they would not make peace

---

[Col. Daniel Brodhead to Col. David Shepherd. 1SS211. A. L. S.]

HEAD QUᴿˢ FORT PITT Sepʳ 17ᵗʰ 1780

DEAR SIR:

Two Delaware Runners with Letters from Major Lanctot & Captⁿ LaᵥLuzerne,² arrived last Evening from Coochocking. As that from the Major is much the same in substance with the other I have got it translated into our language, and enclose you a copy for perusal. The Contents if true, in our present circumstances is alarming; and I must therefore request you will immediately upon receipt hereof, cause in the who[le] three-fourths of the Men in your county, to be equipped with Arms & accoutrements and as much provision as will last them fifteen Days and be in readiness to March at an hours warning but this additional number need not furnish Horses to ride as they are intended to act Defensively.

The messengers add that a party of twenty Muncies & Delawares, were discovered about six days ago, near the new Moravian Town, on their march towards our settlements, which it is expected will cross the River near to the old Mingoe Town.³ And that they have heard that the Seneca Indians intend to come in a large body down the Alleghany River to attack our Inhabitants. They likewise inform me that in the attack lately made by Captⁿ Mᶜlntyre's party, on the Wyondot warriors, eighteen or nineteen were killed, & some are still missing.

¹ For the message sent by Linctot to the Shawnee, and a description of the belt accompanying it see *Mich. Pion. & Hist. Colls.*, X, 427–29.

² In compliment to the Chevalier de la Luzerne, French minister to the United States, one of the Delaware chiefs assumed his name. This chief was steadfast in upholding the American alliance even after the defection of most of his tribe in 1781.

³ For this locality see *Frontier Defense*, 4, note 8.

Advise the Inhabitants to be unanimous and I will undertake to give a good account of the Enemy.

The former orders tending to offensive operations we are not to loose sight of, For should the Ene[my] fail of coming in force against us, I will if possible visit them.

I have the Honor to be with much respect Dear Sir your most obed^t Servt

DANIEL BRODHEAD Col° command^g W [D]

COL° DAVID SHEPHERD

[Summary of a letter of Col. Daniel Brodhead, Fort Pitt, Sept. 17, 1780, to Gen. George Washington. Printed in Sparks, *Corr. Amer. Rev.*, III, 90–91, and in *Pa. Archives*, XII, 269.][1]

News just received from Major Linctot of probable attack from Detroit. Delaware scouts report twenty warriors on the march, and a large party of Seneca soon to come down the Allegheny. Supplies for Delawares promised by treaty are lacking. With men and provisions would meet the enemy en route. Will do all possible to oppose their designs. Regulars few; inhabitants will doubtless think of flight rather than resistance.

IMPRESSING PROVISIONS

[Summary of a letter of Col. Daniel Brodhead, Headquarters, Fort Pitt, Sept. 21, 1780, to Capt. Samuel Brady. Printed in *id.*, VIII, 565–66.][2]

Money not yet sent to pay for provisions; permission from Pennsylvania to impress; Brady as assistant commissary is ordered to take such cattle and sheep as can be spared without injury to inhabitants or to further increase; on no pretense to take from the poorer people, or those who have suffered by the enemy. The levy to be confined to Pennsylvania.

[1] For a letter of the same date to Richard Peters, conveying substantially the same information, see *Pa. Archives*, XII, 274.

[2] Similar orders for the impressing of wheat, rye, and oats were issued about this same date to Capt. Uriah Springer. Draper Mss., 1NN69.

[Summary of a letter of Col. Daniel Brodhead, Fort Pitt, Sept. 23, 1780, to Col. Moses Rawlins. Printed in *id.*, XII, 272–73.]

Requests that flour Rawlins has offered be forwarded by pack horses. Drought continues to affect transportation.

DANGER FROM LOYALISTS NEAR FORT PITT

[Summary of a letter of Col. Daniel Brodhead, Fort Pitt, Sept. 23, 1780, to Gov. Thomas Jefferson. Printed in *ibid.*, 273.]

Board of War has instructed writer to make application for provisions to the state commissioners; Virginia has appointed none; impressment necessary to keep troops from starving. He has received notice of the approach of 1,000 British regulars and great numbers of Indians; officers of the Ninth Virginia Regiment think if inhabitants received promises of protection, they would join the invaders.

[Summary of a letter of Col. Daniel Brodhead, Fort Pitt, Sept. 23, 1780, to Richard Peters. Printed in *ibid.*, 274.]

Has heard nothing more of approaching enemy; has sent out spies to report. Officers of Ninth Virginia think if enemy approach and offer protection, half of inhabitants would join them. Emigration to Kentucky and the Falls incredible; disaffected from other parts come in and purchase lands of those leaving. Last meat in store issued; commissary impressing. Many deserters are harbored by inhabitants.

IMPRESSING PROVISIONS

[Summary of a letter of Col. Daniel Brodhead, Headquarters, Fort Pitt, Oct. 1, 1780, to Capt. Uriah Springer.[1] Printed in *ibid.*, 274–75.]

Glad to hear of his success; hopes good people will show zeal in present emergency. Troops have been three days without bread; nothing heard of pack-horses masters sent for flour. Rivers are raised; should endeavor to send flour and forage by boat.

EXPEDITION PLANNED

[Col. Daniel Brodhead to Col David Shepherd. 1SS213. L. S.][2]

HEAD QUARTERS FORT PITT Octr 7th 1780

DEAR SIR:

As it is yet uncertain whether an adequate supply of provisions can be obtained for the Regular Troops which it will be necessary to employ upon the intended Expedition. Likewise whether a sufficient number of Horses are engaged to carry them & their provisions. You will be pleased to direct the Militia Drafts & volunteers of your County not to march until you hear from me again. But they are to hold themselves in readiness to march at an hours warning; and in the mean time you will make me a return by the bearer of the number of men & Horses & of the spare

[1] Uriah Springer was born about the year 1755 in New Jersey, whence his family emigrated at an early day to the present North Union Township in Fayette County, Pa., then considered a part of Virginia. In 1774 Lord Dunmore commissioned young Springer ensign and placed him, during his campaign, in command of the fort at Redstone. In 1776 Springer enlisted in the Thirteenth Virginia, becoming lieutenant in that regiment Dec. 19, 1776 and captain Aug. 25, 1778. Almost all of his service was performed on the western frontier. After the Revolution he retired to his home near Connellsville, Pa., where he married Sarah, daughter of Col. William Crawford and widow of Capt. William Harrison. Captain Springer reëntered the regular army in 1791 as an officer in the Third Sub-legion, and served four years with distinction. During the War of 1812 he was appointed brigade inspector and took part in one winter campaign. He died early in the year 1826 at his Fayette County home.

[2] This was a circular letter; similar ones were sent to the other neighboring county lieutenants. See the replies of Colonel Beeler and Colonel McCleary, *post*, 279.

horses I may depend on from your County and as soon as I find it practicable to execute the proposed incursion, I will give you immediate notice to order them to march to a place of rendezvous that may then be most convenient for our Destination

I cannot but lament the repeated Disappointments we have met with for want of Resources to enable us to retailate upon the Hell-hounds of the Forest But I must console myself with a conscientiousness that the blame lies not at my Door

I have the honor to be with great Respect Dear Sir Your most obed^t Servt

DANIEL BRODHEAD Col° command^g W D

COL° DAVID SHEPHERD

[Summary of a letter of Col. Joseph Beeler, Oct. 10, 1780, to Col. Daniel Brodhead. Printed in *Pa. Archives*, VIII, 583–84.]

Your letter of October 7 received. Could not get volunteers; have impressed horses and draughted men. Embarrassed by lack of government and laws; those of Virginia not operative; not yet under protection of Pennsylvania. Have risked my private fortune for sake of an expedition.

[Summary of a letter of Col. William McCleary,[1] Monongalia County, Oct. 11, 1780, to Col. Daniel Brodhead. Printed in *ibid.*, 584–85.]

In Colonel Evans' absence, replies to Brodhead's recent letter. Officers at a general muster decided that since all hope of relief from a campaign this fall is abortive, and since frontiers for sixty to seventy miles are infested with savages, no men can be spared. Were ready for an expedition twice this summer. State of frontier deplorable; helpless women and children; "even while part of us is engaged in burying of our Neighbours that have been butchered by them, Others of us is falling a sacrifice to their Hellish inventions."

[1] This name is variously spelled McCleary, McCleery, and McClerry. For a sketch of this officer see *Rev. Upper Ohio*, 235, note 79.

IMPRESSING PROVISIONS

[Summary of a letter of Col. Daniel Brodhead, Headquarters, Fort Pitt, Oct. 11, 1780, to Capt. Samuel Brady. Printed in *id.*, XII, 276.]

Distressed at aversion of people to affording supplies; no alternative between using force and suffering. Colonel Lochry's share of provisions for regulars. If force must be used directs Brady to notify Captain Springer at Little Redstone to detach a party to assist. Thanks of commander in chief for Brady's services.

THE BOUNDARY AGREEMENT

[Summary of a letter of Gov. Thomas Jefferson, Richmond, Oct. 12, 1780, to Col. Daniel Brodhead. Printed in *id.*, VIII, 641–42.]

Supplies must be secured under laws of Pennsylvania since by boundary agreement the vicinity of Fort Pitt will be in that state; Mason and Dixon's line will be Pennsylvania's southern boundary; other line will run a little east of Ohio. Ohio posts are suffering for supplies. Our treasury is utterly empty.

[Summary of a letter of Col. Daniel Brodhead, Fort Pitt, Oct. 14, 1780, to Col. Ephraim Blaine.[1] Printed in *id.*, XII, 278.]

By late instructions of Pennsylvania Council, Blaine's deputy to receive supplies; he has no deputy here. Some supplies taken by force, inadequate for daily use. Hopes he is securing provision; troops cannot subsist on wind.

[1] Ephraim Blaine, of Scotch-Irish ancestry, was born near Carlisle, Pa., in 1741. His first military service was in Bouquet's expedition of 1764. Later he was appointed sheriff and lieutenant of Cumberland County. At the beginning of the Revolution he embraced the patriot cause, and on Jan. 1, 1780, at Washington's request, accepted the office of commissary-general of purchases, which he retained until July 24, 1782. By this service he seriously impaired his private fortune. After the war Colonel Blaine lived at Carlisle, where he died on Feb. 16, 1804. He was the great-grandfather of the statesman, James G. Blaine.

EXPEDITION POSTPONED

[Col. Daniel Brodhead to Col. David Shepherd. 1SS215. A. L. S.]

HEAD QU^{RS} FORT PITT October 13th 1780

DEAR SIR:
Finding that the fairest proposals to the people, and the faith of the publick, will not procure a sufficient quantity of provisions to enable me to secure the Inhabitants, by acting offensively against the Savages. I have determined to take provisions, agreeable to recent Instructions, And in order to facilitate the Business, have called for the Garrisons of Fort Henry and Hollidays Cove.

I do not mean to detain those Garrisons longer, than untill, they have executed the Business they are to be sent upon. And in the mean time You will be pleased to order a Captn & about twenty five Militia includ^g a Subaltern two Sergeants to take post at Fort Henry and a Subaltern two Sergeants & fifteen Rank and file to Hollidays. Let them be supplied as the Regulars were and they shall be paid by the publick.

I have received discouraging acc^{ts} from Col^{os} Beeler & McCleary, but all these will not deter me from doing every thing I can for the good Inhabitants.

I am very respectfully Your most obed^t Servt
DANIEL BRODHEAD

[Summary of a letter of Col. Daniel Brodhead, Headquarters, Pittsburgh, Oct. 13, 1780, to Capt. John Clark. Printed in *Pa. Archives*, XII, 277.]

Intended expedition postponed, provisions being taken by parties of troops. Evacuate Fort Henry and Holliday's Cove, and bring all stores to Fort McIntosh. There leave under Capt. Benjamin Biggs thirty-four of those least fit for active service and march the remainder to this place. Colonel Shepherd is to send militia to the posts. Assure inhabitants of protection; desire them to be on guard until expedition secures their safety.

SCARCITY OF PROVISIONS AT FORT PITT

[Gen. George Washington to Col. Daniel Brodhead. 1H146. Transcript.]

HEAD QUARTERS NEAR PASSAIC FALLS 13th October 1780.
DEAR SIR:

Your favors of the 18th and 21st of August reached my hands a few days before I sat out for Har[t]ford to meet the French admiral and General. This has occasioned their remaining unanswered to this time. I have approved the sentences of the Court Martial against Capt [Thomas] Beal, Peter Davis of the 9th Virginia and David Gamble of the 8th Penn^a Regiment—Gamble appearing to me the most proper object for an example, I have directed his execution. The time and place is left to your option. The adjutant General transmits you the extract from General Orders respecting the above.

I am sorry that I cannot, considering the former good conduct of Capt Beal, comply with the recommendation of the Court in his favor. The circumstance of his receiving the Grain and Rifle Gun for transferring McCloud to another Corps is so inconsistent with the character of an officer, that I cannot, with any degree of propriety, reinstate him.

I return you part of the proceedings of a court martial upon John Gosset of the 9th Virginia Reg^t: I imagine the remainder has been left out when your packet was made up.

The want of provisions is a clog to our operations in every quarter. We have several times, in the course of this campaign, been without either Bread or meat, and have never had more than four or five days beforehand. The smallness of your force will not admit of an expedition of any consequence, had you Magazines, You must therefore, of necessity, confine yourself to partizan strokes, which I wish to be encouraged.

The State of Virginia are very desirous of an expedition against Detroit, and would make great exertions to carry it into execution. But while the enemy are so formidable to the Southward, and are making such strides in that quarter, I fear it will require a greater force of men and supplies to check them than we since the defeat near Campden,[1] shall be able shortly to draw together.

I am Dear Sir Your most ob^t Servt

G^o WASHINGTON

[1] The battle of Camden, S. C., was fought Aug. 16, 1780 when Gen. Horatio Gates, in command of the Continental forces in the South, was defeated by Lord Cornwallis. It was in this battle that Baron De Kalb was slain.

COL^N BRODHEAD.
P. S. Since writing the foregoing, I have received your favors of the 5th 14th and 17th Septem^r. Your distress for provision, considering the distance you are from supplies and the approach of winter is very alarming, and I shall therefore take the earliest opportunity of laying before Congress the situation of the Garrison, and the necessity which there seems to be of furnishing the department with more certain means of procuring provisions, than a bare dependance upon the requisitions made from the States. Necessity must in the mean time justify the measure of taking by impress what the inhabitants can spare.

When the Court Martial have finished the business before them, it may be dissolved.

N. B. The foregoing letter is enclosed in an envelop and endorsed. "On public service To Colonel Brodhead Commanding at Fort Pitt. Recommended to the particular care of the Board of War by G° Washington See the P. S. of this respecting provisions"

[*Endorsed:*] His Excell^y General Washington Oct 13th 1780.

[Col. Daniel Brodhead to Gen. George Washington.[1] 3H1–3. Transcript of Letter Book.][2]

FORT PITT, October 17th 1780.

DEAR GENERAL:
Your favor of the 14th of Augt I had the honor to receive on the 7th instant, and am very thankful for the contents. You must be convinced ere now that Col° Bowman's apprehensions were founded on certain intelligence of an expedition intended against the forts on Kentucky.

[1] See a letter of the same date and of similar character to Pres. Joseph Reed, printed in *Pa. Archives*, VIII, 588.
[2] In 1846 a descendant of Colonel Brodhead, Col. Andrew J. Foulk of Kittanning, Pa., lent Dr. Draper a letter book of his ancestor, comprising his correspondence from October, 1780 to December, 1781. This letter book chronologically follows the one printed in *id.*, XII, 105–299, most of which has been summarized in the preceding pages. Dr. Draper made a careful transcript of the book sent him by Colonel Foulk and returned the original manuscript to its owner. It is not known whether or not it is still extant. Part of its contents was printed in Neville B. Craig, *Olden Time* (Pittsburgh, 1848), II. It is believed that many of these letters of Brodhead have not hitherto appeared in print.

I have sent out parties to take cattle and grain from the inhabitants, & expect to obtain a considerable supply of flour as the mills begin to have water sufficient to manufacture it; but the inhabitants, disappoint us of getting beef by driving their cattle into the mountains; and we have at present neither bread nor meat, but expect a small supply immediately.

Captn Brady is on command, & Captn McIntyre has leave of absence to Phil^{ada}; as soon as they return I will express your Excellency's thanks for their conduct.

In full confidence that a sufficient supply of provision would sooner or later be furnished for the troops in this district, as well as such number of militia as policy or the exigency of affairs might render it necessary to call into action; I with a view to cut off the Wyandotts & other Indian towns that were very troublesome to our Settlements called for a draught from the militia three different times, & was as often disappointed in obtaining provisions, which with the unsettled state of the boundary line between Pen^a & Virg^a, has greatly discouraged the inhabitants, & I apprehend had given a handle to the disaffected. I take the liberty to enclose copies lately received from Colonel Beelor & McClerry purporting some of the above facts.

The Delaware Chiefs with upwards of thirty warriors come to aid me upon an Expedition, but as I have neither bread nor meat to give them they will soon discover that it is not in my power to act offensively. They appear much dejected on account of the total want of goods which they were promised in exchange for their peltry.

Unless supplies of beef &c are procuring below the mountains which I know nothing of, the troops here will be reduced to great hardships before spring, and desertions will be very frequent.

I have frequently represented to the Honb^{le} Board of War the hardships of the troops, & am now informed by their Secretary that compulsion is tolerated by the Supreme Executive Council of Pen^a for a temporary supply.

I continue my inquiries respecting the strength of Detroit, & my intelligence is of a piece with that formerly communicated.

I have the honor to be, with the most exalted respect, &c

D. B.

His Excellency Gen^L Washington.

[Col. Daniel Brodhead to Col. John Davis.¹ 3H4. Transcript of Letter Book.]

FORT PITT, Octr 18th 1780.

SIR:
I am honored with your favor by Capt. Postlewait² & am glad to find this District is, by the new arrangement, under your direction, as I expect it will be well attended to.

Agreeable to your wish Mr D. Duncan has accepted the appointment of A. Q. Master. Capt. Postlewaite & he have settled the number of clerks & appointed a Forage Master, & I have reason to believe that with a competent sum of money business will be properly transacted.

Captn Postlewaite takes with him an estimate of stores indespensably necessary for the District, & I beg you will have them provided as soon as circumstances & situation will admit.

I have the honor to be, &c.

D. B.

COL° JN° DAVIS.—

[Summary of a letter of Col. Daniel Brodhead, Headquarters, Fort Pitt, Oct. 20, 1780, to Capt. Uriah Springer. Printed in *Pa. Archives*, XII, 278-79.]

Sorry to find people above Redstone intend to rise in arms against impressing party. Many doubtless are disaffected. Avoid harsh action if possible; if safety of party requires succor it shall be given by infantry and artillery.

¹ Col. John Davis lived neighbor to Col. Ephraim Blaine, in Middleton Township, Cumberland County, near Carlisle. In 1777 Davis was colonel of the Second Battalion of Cumberland County militia; after 1780 he was a deputy commissary under Blaine.
² Capt. Samuel Postlethwaite was deputy quartermaster from Oct. 6, 1777 to December, 1782. His home was at Carlisle, where he died, Aug. 24, 1810, in his seventy-second year.

[Gen. George Washington to President of Congress. Washington Papers. Draft.]

HEAD QUARTERS NEAR PASSAIC FALLS
21st Octob^r 1780

SIR:

I have been honored with your Excellency's favors of the 10th and 14th Instants. The advance of the British Army towards the borders of North Carolina is an alarming circumstance, more especially, as there is every reason to beleive that the force which lately sailed from New York is intended to cooperate with them. The enemy, by several accounts, received a reinforcement from Europe in the last Fleet, it is said by some to consist of two British Regiments—about 700 German Recruits and some from Scotland. If so, this new accession is nearly equal to their late detachment—but others again say the reinforcement consists wholly of Recruits. I have heard nothing directly from the Northward since my letter of the 16th. There are reports that the enemy retired after destroying Fort Ann Fort George and burning some Houses.[1] It is thought, and perhaps not without foundation, that this incursion was made upon a supposition that Arnolds treachery had succeeded.

Col^o Brodhead has in many of his late letters expressed his apprehension of the consequences which may result from the Want of provision should the enemy, agreeable to their threats, invest the post of Fort Pitt this Winter. But, by a letter from him of the 14th of September, matters had proceeded to such extremities, that the Garrison, headed by the non Commissioned officers, had waited upon him, and, he says, in a decent manner remonstrated upon the hardship at having been without Bread for five days. Upon being told that every thing would be done to releive them they retired in good order. Col^o Brodhead adds—the Country is not deficient of Resources, but that public credit is exhausted, and will no longer procure supplies. Congress will

[1] Washington here refers to the expedition of Maj. Guy Carleton, nephew of Lord Dorchester. In the autumn of 1780, with a force of a thousand Loyalists and Indians, Carleton advanced via Lakes Champlain and George into northern New York and laid siege to the protecting forts. On October 10 Fort Anne was surrendered, its garrison captured, and its buildings burned; the next day Fort George capitulated. Meanwhile Carleton had sent out a detachment as far as Ballston in Saratoga County, which captured Col. James Gordon and a number of Whig inhabitants. After these successful raids, a rapid retreat was made to Montreal.

SUPPLIES FOR FORT PITT

[Col. Daniel Brodhead to Col. John Perry. 3H4. Transcript of Book.]

HEAD QR^s FORT PITT, October 27th 1780.

SIR:

I am instructed by the Honb^{le} Board of War that our State of Pen^a is to furnish for the troops under my command a certain quantity of hay, grain, flour & rum. I, therefore, wish to see a copy of your latest instructions relative to supplies; and as the season is at hand for laying in winter stores, you'l please to inform me by Mr Duncan what part of the articles mentioned in your instructions are purchased bona fide, and what your future expectations are. You & Mr Duncan by conversing together may prevent any interference in purchasing.

Your deliveries in future must be to Mr Duncan, he being appointed a Deputy under Col^o Blaine. I am &c.

COL^o JN^o PERRY. 	D. B.

[Col. Daniel Brodhead to Maj. William Taylor.[1] 1NN70. Summary and transcript.]

Oct. 27, 1780

Maj. R. [William] Taylor ordered to Tyger's Valley to purchase cattle, & impress such as cannot be purchased &c—Capt. Springer near Red Stone to join him.

[Col. Daniel Brodhead to Maj. Frederick Vernon. 1NN70. Summary and transcript.]

Oct. 28, 1780.

Maj. Vernon was ordered to proceed immediately to Westmoreland county—relieve Capt. Brady, take his instructions relative

[1] William Taylor, a native of Orange County, Va., and a cousin of Col. Richard Taylor, enlisted in 1776 in the Second Virginia Regiment as lieutenant in the company of his brother Francis. By the close of the year William was himself a captain, and on Dec. 7, 1779 he was appointed major and transferred to the Ninth Virginia. On the same date his cousin, Richard, was transferred from the Ninth to the Second Virginia as its lieutenant-colonel. After the war Maj. William Taylor removed to Oldham County, Ky., where he resided upon Taylor's Creek and where he died April 14, 1830.

JOSEPH BRANT
Copied from a Painting belonging to H. B. Johnson, a descendent

herefore see the necessity of either furnishing the Commissary to the Westward with a competent sum of money, or of obtaining from the State of Pennsylvania an assurance that the part of the quota of supplies demanded of her by the requisition of Congress of February last and directed [to] be deposited in the Magazines to the Westward, which was intended for the support of Fort Pitt, shall be immediately laid in, if it has not been already done. The importance of that post to the whole Western Frontier is so great, as not to admit of its being left to any risque, if it can be avoided.

I take the liberty of inclosing your Excellency, for the determination of Congress, the Copy of a letter of the 18th [See Gen¹ Knox letter of that date respecting the dismission of Col° Mason] from Brig. Gen¹ Knox, representing the injury to the service, should the Resolve for the dismission of Lᵗ Col° [David] Mason, be immediately carried into execution. I am ignorant whether the Resolve proceeded from a motive of Oconomy or any thing improper in the conduct of Col° Mason. If only from the former, I should hope that General Knox's request would be complied with. If from the latter his services, however material, must be dispensed with.

Since I began this letter I have received advices from Gov. Clinton, at Albany who mentions that the party of the enemy which came from the Northward had retired by the way of Lake George, but that another party from the Westward had penetrated as far as Scoharie which valuable settlement they had destroyed.¹ The Governor himself was going to Schenectady to make a disposition of the force in that quarter. I have sent up two Continental Regiments to his assistance which I hope will be sufficient to repel the Enemy, as they are not represented as very numerous. Fort Schuyler² is well garrisoned and has forty days provision in it. I therefore hope no great danger is to be apprehended from the present incursion.

HIS EXCELLENCY PRESIDENT OF CONGRESS.

¹ The destruction of the Schoharie settlement was accomplished by Sir Joʰ Johnson and Joseph Brant with a force of Loyalists and Indians. Coming frᵒ Canada via Oswego and Lake Oneida, they rendezvoused at Unadilla and ᵖ taged to the Schoharie, where they attacked a fort on the site of Middleb There they were repulsed, but succeeded in devastating the valley and captᵘ about a hundred prisoners. On October 19 the New York forces under Robert Van Rensselaer defeated the invaders at Stone Arabia. See oᵗ documents in Draper Mss., 10F56.

² Fort Schuyler, originally Fort Stanwix, stood on the site of Rome, N

to taking cattle &c—Col. B. understands that there are cattle in the Forks of Yough which may be spared: "The season is so far advanced, & our necessities so great, that I must leave it to your discretion to get cattle & sheep where you find it most convenient until we are otherwise supplied." Capt. Robt Beal to go with Maj. Vernon.

COMMANDANT FOR FORT McINTOSH

[Col. John Gibson to Capt. Benjamin Biggs. 5NN7. Transcript.]

FORT PITT, Nov. 1st 1780.

SIR:

I rec^d your letter this morning by Express & immediately applied to Col. Brodhead to have you relieved; Captn Tannehill is ordered for that purpose, & will set out in a day or two. I am in some hopes that the whole of the officers and men will soon be relieved. No news from below. Please present my compliments to the gentlemen of your garrison, & believe me to be yours sincerely

J^{no} GIBSON, Col. 9th Vir. Reg^t

To CAPT. B. BIGGS Com^g at Fort McIntosh.

[Receipt of Capt. Adamson Tannehill to Capt. Benjamin Biggs. 5NN5. A. D. S.]

Rec^d of Captain Benjamin Biggs of the 9th. V. Reg^t one Brown Horse the property of the U. States,—Six falling axes and two Iron wedges for the use of the Garrison of Fort McIntosh Novr 6th 1780

TANNEHILL Captain Command^g F. McIntosh.

REDUCTION OF ARMY

[Summary of a letter of Gen. Anthony Wayne, Camp at Totowa,[1] Nov. 2, 1780, to Col. Daniel Brodhead. Printed in *Pa. Archives*, VIII, 595.]

New arrangement of the army. Pennsylvania line is reduced to six regiments; provision for supernumerary officers.[2] This arrangement to go into effect January 1, 1781. Return of Eighth Regiment desired, with dates of officers' commissions.

PLOT TO MURDER FRIENDLY INDIANS

[Summary of a letter of Col. Daniel Brodhead, Fort Pitt, Nov. 2, 1780, to Pres. Joseph Reed. 3H5–7. Printed in *ibid.*, 596.]

Disappointed not to conduct an expedition against hostile Indians; provisions scarcely sufficient for daily consumption. Nearly forty friendly Delawares came to his aid against hostile tribes; a band from Hannastown have attempted to destroy them, women and children as well as men; this massacre prevented by a guard of regulars posted for Indians' protection. Captains Irwin and Jack, Lieutenant Brownlee,[3] and Ensign Guthrie were concerned in this base attempt. Thomas Smallman's secret purchase from Delawares of McKee's Island[4] is illegal.

[1] Wayne's headquarters were not far from the present city of Paterson in Passaic County, N. J.

[2] Congress had at intervals during 1780 discussed the reduction of the army, until October 3 an act was agreed upon reducing the number of Continental regiments and assigning the quotas to the several states. The officers who were retired were well rewarded for their past services. See *Jour. of Cont. Cong.*, XVIII, 893–97, 958.

[3] Lieut. John Brownlee served in the early years of the war as a non-commissioned officer in the Eighth Pennsylvania Regiment. Having been honorably discharged he returned to his Westmoreland County home, and was successively lieutenant and captain of the militia and rangers. In 1782 during an attack by the Indians on Hannastown, Brownlee, who had a profound hatred of them, was captured and, his indentity having been learned, killed by a blow of his captor's tomahawk.

[4] The first island below Pittsburgh, a mile in length and 300 acres in area, was successively called McKee's, Hamilton's, and Brunot's, the latter name for Dr. Felix Brunot, a French physician who resided there early in the nineteenth century. See description in Fortescue Cuming, "Tour," in R. G. Thwaites (ed.), *Early Western Travels* (Cleveland, 1904), IV, 93–95.

SCARCITY OF PROVISIONS AT FORT PITT

[Col. Daniel Brodhead to Col. Ephraim Blaine. 3H8–9. Transcript of Letter Book.]

FORT PITT, Novr 3^d 1780.

DEAR SIR:
I have received your favor of the 22^d of Sept^r, & am sorry to hear of your inability to supply the troops under my command.
Hitherto by great exertions & the most plausible assurances of money to defray the debts we contract, we have barely subsisted, & it is clear to every body that a supply of meat cannot be had even for ready money equal to half the present consumption, to say nothing of what quantity ought to be laid in to enable me to act vigorously the ensuing campaign.
Flour, I conceive, may be furnished on this side the mountains, but too great a quantity of salt cannot be sent us as that article will procure meat when money cannot. Pack-horses can be furnished to transport it from Conogocheague. Mr Duncan does all in his power & is sure of every assistance in my power; but pork is out of the question—everywhere the kidney worm & vermin together having destroyed 9/10 [nine tenths] of the swine in this country, so that unless you can supply us with a quantity of meat from below the mountain, I shall have the mortification to remain on the defensive another campaign, which above all things I detest & abhor.
You must be convinced of the necessity of supporting this new country which is of great importance to the public, & that the only sure way to defend the settlements is to act offensively; to do which I expect to be reinforced next spring—& I trust your utmost exertions will not be wanting to afford us ample supplies.
I have the honor to be, &c.

D. B.

COL° EPHRAIM BLAINE.

[Col. Daniel Brodhead to Maj. Frederick Vernon. 3H9-11. Transcript of Letter Book.]

HEAD QR⁸, FORT PITT, Nov. 7ᵗʰ 1780

DEAR SIR:

I am favored with yours of the 5ᵗʰ instant, & am glad to find your prospect of further supply is enlarged. I am informed that several of the cattle you sent in, are unfit for consumption on account of their poverty; if this is their case, it is losing time & money to purchase or take such cattle—wherefore I have to request you may not suffer lean cattle to be purchased or taken whilst good cattle can be had for the troops. The commissaries are not to promise salt to any but the suffering frontier inhabitants who probably have no other method to obtain a supply. I suppose that purchasing commissaries advertisements have by this time been generally seen and understood, & as I am certain that Col. Blaine would not pledge his honor to the people without having a certainty of money to pay off the certificates in January next, apprehend such as have cattle, swine or sheep to spare will not now hesitate to sell them to his assistants. Be this as it may, we must at all events be supplied, & I hope & expect you will exert yourself to that end at this crisis, for a few weeks more will put it out of our power to procure supplies for the winter at any rate, & then the posts must inevitably be evacuated to the ruination of this country.

I am, &c.

D. B.

MAJOR F. VERNON.

CONDITIONS IN KENTUCKY

[Col. John Todd¹ to Col. William Fleming. 2U75. A. L. S.]

HARRODSBURG 14th Nov. 1780

HONBLE SIR:

I arrived safely here a few days ago. My friends here seem surprized that I venture to Lexington² a place of supposed Danger

¹ For a sketch of Col. John Todd see *Dunmore's War*, 343, note 64.
² A single log house, built in 1775 on the site of Lexington, Ky., gave a name to the place which was permanently settled in April, 1779. There Col. Robert Patterson went thither from Harrodsburg, and under the protection of the

but if I can be supplied with ammunition & a Good Magazine I shall stand to the post with Alacrity. I hope your honble Board will not neglect me in this Article I know not what Instructions Quirk may have for delivering the powder & Lead but Suspect that the necessary proportion will be denied me.

I expect a Warm attack next Spring from our Enemy Indians & I pray the attention of the Executive to our dangerous Situation The Ohio Adventurers chagrined with their disappointments in the Land Way & the Sickliness of the pond Stations have many of them deserted our Country & left us much weaker than we were last Spring. We have no important News from the West

I have the Honor to be with Respect Your mo. obed^t & hble Servant

J_N^o TODD jr

IMPRESSING PROVISIONS

[Col. Daniel Brodhead to Maj. William Taylor. 3H11–12. Transcript of Letter Book.]

HEAD QR^s, FORT PITT, Novr 15th 1780.

SIR:

I have duly rec^d your favor of the 12th instant, by Mr Bradford, and am really sorry to find that after so much time has been spent, you have not procured either by purchase or compulsion as much provisions as was necessary for the subsistence of your own party.

Immediately after Mr Carmichal's[1] acceptance he was under your command, & should not have delayed a moment. But perhaps Captn Berry [Perry] was not so expeditious as he might have been—he left this about the first instant. Please to enquire into the matter particularly & write me.

blockhouse that he built settlers came in rapidly. In the summer of 1780 John and Levi Todd made Lexington their home.

[1] John Carmichael was born in 1751 in Cumberland County, Pa. Before the year 1775 he removed to what is now Fayette County, Pa., and on the waters of Redstone Creek built a mill. In 1776 he was a member of the Pennsylvania Constitutional Convention and in 1777 of the assembly. He died in 1796, leaving two sons, James and Thomas.

I do not know whether it may answer the best purpose for you to go to the Glades, & then to Tygert's Valley, but expect you will go to the latter before you return.

Should Mr Carmichal refuse to attend you, any honest man who is a judge of the value of cattle &c may be appointed & disappointed by yourself.

When you wrote me before you could not have read your instructions with attention, otherwise you could not have been mistaken in so clear a point. The Q. Master has not a single horse at his command that I know of, but if upon enquiry one can be had, he shall be sent you. But if all fail, upon this particular command you shall be at liberty to hire one reasonably, & draw upon the Q.M. to pay the hire.

You will be pleased to make strict enquiry relative to swine, noting down what numbers & in whose possession they are, & give me the fullest information possible as to what number may be had for the troops.—I wish you success, & am

B. B.

Major Wm Taylor.

[Col. Daniel Brodhead to Maj. Frederick Vernon. 3H13. Transcript of Letter Book.]

Head Qr^s Fort Pitt, Novr 28th 1780.

Dear Sir:

I am favored with yours of the 18th inst. & should have answered it before now had not your messenger returned without giving me the pleasure of seeing him.

I conceive your success will [not] answer the fatigue & expense of collecting cattle in the present mode, & as ready money and Salt are scarce articles we must endeavor to get cattle on the advertisements of the Commissary, or learn to live without them.

The season is come for quartering the troops, & to that end it is necessary to collect the whole, lest there may be a lapse of duty for want of men. You will, therefore, on receipt hereof, march your party to this place, bringing all the cattle you may have collected.

I am, &c.

D. B.

P.S.—Please present my compl^{ts} to Captn Beall: I hope his horse will bring him in.

Major F. Vernom.

[Col. Daniel Brodhead to Maj. William Taylor. 3H14. Transcript of Letter Book.]

HEAD QR^s, FORT PITT, Nov. 28th 1780.

DEAR SIR:

The season being at hand that quarters must be assigned to the different corps, you will upon receipt hereof, march your party to this place, bringing with you all the cattle &c. you may have collected in pursuiance of your instructions.

Mr Duncan will deliver you this, & it is probable he will be able to inform you where you may take a few cattle on your return.

It appears to me, that we must depend much upon killing wild cattle for our subsistance, & therefore the sooner we set out parties for that purpose the better.

D. B.

MAJ. W^M TAYLOR.

A WYANDOT SPY

[Col. Daniel Brodhead to the Delaware chiefs. 2H66-69. Letter Book.]

FORT PITT Novr 19th—80

Mahingweegeesuch to Wm Pen & others the Council at Coochocking

BROTHERS:

Henry Bawbee[1] who lately came from Detroit says he belongs to the English & is paid by them to observe the conduct of you who live at Coochocking & to let the Commanding Officer know if any are friends to the Americans

Now *Brothers:* I believe that Bawbee intends to carry a bad report about you to the Enemy & excite them to strike you for he was very angry when he heard you had declared war against the Mingoes & he persuaded some of your warriors to turn back after they had marched, wherefore to prevent his doing harm to your people I have confined him

Now *Brothers* listen to me: You that are true Friends to America will rejoice on account of this bad man's Confinement & none but Tories will be sorry for it. His own bad Heart & words has

[1] This is probably the person referred to in *Rev. Upper Ohio*, 126, note 21.

brought this trouble upon him & I shall keep him confined for your sakes & not for my own until he can be tried agreeably to the Articles of our Confederation.

Brothers: I tell you that had Bawbee been a white American, a Frenchman, Spaniard or Englishman acting like a spy & carrying letters to the Enemy, he should be hanged before now. But because he is half an Indian and therefore to be tried as mentioned in the articles of Treaty—He will be kept alive until I hear from you & afterwards from Congress

Brothers: I hear great news but I will not tell you that all is true altho every body here believes it as well as myself. Our news is that Mons.ʳ Bouganville has certainly taken Quebec & all the English Troops therein, likewise that we have killed & taken Gen.ˡ Cornwallis & all his Army in South Carolina And that the French & Spaniards & Americans have taken near one hundred ships from the British in which were several thousand men

Brothers: All these accounts I believe to be true & I thank God that our troubles are near an end & that the Americans and their real Friends will be rich & happy whilst the British & their Children are poor & miserable

Brothers: Now from all I have spoke to you you will see who are the true Friends to the Indian Nations whether strangers or the people whom God hath raised up with you may be best trusted hereafter

I am your friend & Brother

[Delaware chiefs to Col. Daniel Brodhead. 1H149–50. In handwriting of Heckewelder.]

SALEM Nov.ᵇʳ 30ᵗʰ 1780.

Will.ᵐ Penn & others the Councill of Cooshockung to Col° Brodhead as follows:

BROTHER MAGHINGWE GEESHUCH: I am very glad, & thank You for the Intelligence You gave me. I rejoice that You remember me, & aquaint me of all circumstances

Brother: You told me You was desirous of hearing from me.

Brother: What shall I say unto You ? All I can say is to mention our great Friendship which we have made with one-another, this We will keep firm and fast, and not suffer it to be broke by one bad Man, nor even if there were ten of them or more, we could not be in the least inclined to speak for them, but to let them stand their chance for their bad Work, according to the Articles of our Confederation.

Brother: We love one another alike, I love You as much as You Love me, and I remember my Compliments to You.

WILL^m PENN

Now *Brother:* I will also inform You of the News I have heard. One of my Young Men, who just comes from Detroit, says, that while he was there the Comander sent for all the Wyondotts to come in, & when they were assembled together, he demanded all the Prissoners from them, saying it was his Flesh and Blood, and therefore they should fetch them all in quick. The Wyondotts upon hearing this, hung their heads a while, but afterwards agreed to what was demanded, & accordingly went home, and gathered them altogether, & fetched them over to him at Detroit, so that now the Wyondotts have not a single Prissoner among themselves no more.

Also my Young Man says, That while he was at Detroit, there came the Chieff of the Potowatamen with some of his Men, with the following News to the Comander viz. That an Army of French, Spaniards and Americans had come already as far as Chubhicking, and were marching on, in order to take Detroit, upon which the Comander ordered them some Liquor, and after they being Drunk, the Chibways fell upon them, and killed their Chieff one Captn and one comon Man. The Potawattamen are very Angry at this what has happened, and threaten to fall upon the former, and destroy them.

Now *Brother:* This is the News which my Young Man has brought, he saw both the former & the latter with his Eyes.

I am Your friend & Brother

WILL^m PENN.

Now *Kaylalemend:* You spoke to me by 4 strings of Wampum, desiring me to do my best for Your Cousin Henry Bawbee, that he might be set at Liberty again. What shall I do ? How shall I speak for him ? Listen to me! Remember on what Buissness we were last Year with Congress, consider the Articles of our

Confederation, and You will understand the Matter. This is all I have to say to You.

2 *Strings of Wampum*
Will[m] Penn

Col[L] Brodhead Comand[t] ect.

DELAWARES URGED TO WAR

[Col. Daniel Brodhead to Wingenund. 2H70–71. Letter Book.]

Fort Pitt Dec[r] 2nd 1780

Brother Wyngeenund:

Listen to me   It is not many nights since you came to see me & when you came I did not keep my words from you; No they entered your ears & you seemed to like them & then you told me that you laid fast hold of my words & that your heart was the same as mine

Now *Brother* listen to me: As you have been absent a long time from your Brothers here & it is necessary you should shew your friendship by your works—1 do not tell you to strike people of your own Colour that you are at peace with. But I tell you there are some Englishmen at Sandusky & other places thereabouts who are our Enemies & I desire you will get up & take them & their Goods & bring them here to me. This Brother will shew your friendship & serve your people

I am your Friend & Brother

Capt[N] Wyndgeenund

[Col. Daniel Brodhead to Indian Penn. 2H72-73. Letter Book.]

FORT PITT Decr 2nd 1780

Mahingweegeesuch to Mr Wm Penn

BROTHER:
When you look at your Grand Children the Shawanese you must remember they have done us much harm & that they must pay for all the mischief they have done before long

Now *Brother* listen to me: It may be that the Shawanese would not have been so foolish if it was not put into their heads by some bad people who live with them & are paid by the English to tell them lyes.

Brother: There is Alexd^r McKee & some others who do great harm to your Grand Children by the Lies they tell them, & now I desire you will send four or five of your strong men to take McKee & more if they can & bring them to me so that I may have a piece of meat.

Brother: I will pay sixty Bucks to your men that bring McKee & twenty Bucks for any of the Girty^{s1}

Brother: This is the way to strengthen our friendship. Captⁿ Montour struck the Mingoes now let us both be strong

---

¹ The three Girty brothers were Simon, James, and George. A sketch of James is given in *Frontier Defense*, 234, note 98. George, the youngest, was born in 1745. He was captured in 1756 and lived for three years among the Delaware Indians. After his release, he became an interpreter and trader, and in 1778 was a lieutenant on Capt. James Willing's Mississippi expedition. Returning with Capt. Robert George to the Illinois, George Girty deserted in May, 1779 from Kaskaskia and brought a party of like-minded soldiers to Detroit. There Girty was at once employed in the Indian department, and accompanied Bird's expedition to Kentucky. George Girty was with the Shawnee in 1780 when Clark raided their towns. Later he lived with Captain Pipe's band of Delawares, and spent all the rest of his life with the Indians, among whom he married. He is thought to have died shortly before the War of 1812 at his brother James' post on the Maumee.

MORAVIAN AID ASKED

[Col. Daniel Brodhead to Rev. David Zeisberger. 3H14–15. Transcript of Letter Book.]

FORT PITT, Dec' 2nd, 1780.

DEAR SIR:

Being desirous of laying in a larger supply of salt provisions than from the present appearances will be laid in by the commissaries for the supply of my troops, I take the liberty to propose to you the sending fifteen or twenty of your best hunters to the best & nearest place of hunting buffalo, bear & elk near the Ohio River, & salting the same in canoes made for that purpose. If you approve of this proposal, please send two or three of your people with some horses to take out the salt that may be necessary to preserve such quantity as they may lay in: And upon their delivering the meat to a party of men I shall send to receive it, they shall be paid the full value on my order at this place.—M' Irwin will write the process of curing the meat, but if M' Bull[1] would go with the party I suppose he will stand in no need of instructions.

Should your people exert themselves in laying in a large quantity of meat, they will particularly recommend themselves to the esteem of their countrymen. I shall be happy to have an immediate answer, & am &c.

D. B.

REV. D. ZEISBERGER.

[1] John Bull, called by the Moravian Indians Schebosch or Shabosh, was a white man who lived among the Mission Indians, having married one of their number. He was favorable to the American cause, and aided Heckewelder in keeping the Delaware chiefs loyal. In the autumn of 1781 Bull was taken prisoner by a scouting party, commanded by Capt. John Biggs. At Fort Pitt the commandant released him, and he proceeded to Bethlehem, thus escaping the massacre in 1782 at the Moravian towns, wherein his son Joseph was killed. Bull rejoined the missionaries in July, 1783, bringing to their settlement near Detroit news of the Peace of Paris. Thenceforward he remained with the western missionaries, and died Sept. 5, 1788 at their settlement of New Salem, in Erie County, Ohio.

CONDITIONS ON PITTSBURGH FRONTIER

[Col. Daniel Brodhead to Richard Peters. 3H17–22. Transcript of Letter Book.]

FORT PITT, Decr 7th 1780.

SIR:

I am honored with your favor of the 21st Oct^r & 3^d ult—I am thankful for the contents, & happy in the hope of receiving supplies.

For a long time past I have had two parties commanded by field officers in the country to impress cattle, but their success has been so small that the troops have frequently been without meat for several days together; & as those commands are very expensive, I have now ordered them in. Indeed I am so well convinced that the inhabitants on this side the mountains cannot furnish half enough of meat to supply the troops, that I have risked the sending a party of hunters to kill buffalo at Little Kenhawa, & to lay in the meat until I can detach a party to bring it in, which cannot be done before Spring.

I am exceedingly distressed on account of the want of blankets, shirts, and many other articles of clothing, being very sensible that the soldiers must suffer much for want of them, & apprehensive that many will follow the example of those who have already deserted to a warm climate on that account. I shall not again send an officer for clothing, & I hope the Clothier General will not forget to send them when they come to hand.

The Delaware Council of Coochocking have declared war against the Senecas, & Capt. John Montour was in consequence of this declaration immediately sent with two Delawares & one whiteman to bring a prisoner from their towns; at French Creek (Venango) he fell in with a party of eight Senecas, who a few days before had taken a woman & two children from Westmoreland County. He shot one of the Indians on a raft in the Creek, & the rest ran away. But after a few minutes one of them returned, under cover of some timber, and asked Montour who he was? He answered, he & his men were Delawares, that they were sent by their chiefs, & that he might thank God the waters prevented his getting at them; when the Seneca expressed some mark of contempt, & followed his own party. This relation may be depended on. Capt. Montour is now in pursuit of another party of Indians; his party is composed of Delawares, & the party pursued are supposed to be either Tory Delawares or Muncies; they were discovered by a Delaware runner on their way towards these settlements.

I learn more and more of the disaffection of many the inhabitants on this side the mountain. The King of Britain's health is often drunk in companies; & I believe those wish to see the Regular Troops removed from this department, & a favorable opportunity to submit to British Government.

The Delaware Chiefs are very desirous to pay a visit to Congress in the spring. I wish I knew the sentiments entertained by that Honb[le] body respecting them. I have endeavored to preserve inviolate the articles of Treaty entered into by the Commissioners, & make them useful, which I conceive could be brought about if aught was furnished to clothe them. Some of the Nation, particularly the Coochocking Council, is very much attached to our interest, & I am persuaded try all they can to prevent others coming against our inhabitants, & are desirous to go with our troops when they are in force, but the want of goods is a great impediment. I have never been particularly instructed with respect to Indians in amity with us, & as there appears to be a jealousy among the ignorant inhabitants & an attempt has been made to murder some who [were under] our immediate protection I should be happy to receive full instructions for my future government.

I am much obliged by the honorable notice taken of my recommendation of M[r] Ferrol; I am sensible he will acquit himself with the greatest integrity.

In one of your former letters you did me honor to inform me that his Excell[y] the Commander-in-Chief, had demanded of our State 7000 galls. of rum, & now the Commissioner of Western lands informs me that he has verbal instructions from the Executive of our State to purchase that quantity of whiskey on this side the mountain. I hope we shall be furnished with a few hundred gall[s] of liquor fit to be drank.

I have the honor to be, with sentiments of the utmost respect & esteem, Sir, Your most obedient h[ble] servant,

D. B.

P. S. I take the liberty to enclose the copy of a letter I lately rec[d] from Gov[r] Jefferson relative to supplies.

Honb[le] Rich[d] Peters.

HENRY BAUBEE'S DRAWING OF FORT LERNOULT AT DETROIT

FRONTIER RETREAT 303

[Summary of a letter of Col. Daniel Brodhead, Fort Pitt, Dec. 7, 1780, to Gen. George Washington. 3H22–26. Printed in Sparks, *Corr. Amer Rev.*, III, 162–65.][1]

Courts-martial and their proceedings. Two impressing parties; party sent to kill buffalo around Little Kanawha. Delawares have begun war on Seneca. Partisan strokes encouraged. Inhabitant's attempt to murder friendly Indians frustrated. Disaffection west of mountains. A half-Indian named Baubee brought a draft of works at Detroit; sketch enclosed. Baubee confined as a probable spy.

REDUCTION OF ARMY

[Col. Daniel Brodhead to Gen. Anthony Wayne. 3H29–30. Transcript of Letter Book.]

FORT PITT, Decr 7th 1780.

DEAR GEN^L:

I am honored with your favor of the 2^d ult, & the enclosure. Enclosed is the return of the officers of my reg^t The Genl return made in pursuance of his Excellency's orders will be herewith transmitted to the Orderly office. My reg^t is very small indeed, but expiring enlistments have, I presume, thinned others nearly as much.

The honorable provision made for officers who choose to retire is indeed a great inducement, & I have no doubt many will accept it. I am sensible it would be greatly to my advantage to retire, but I love the cause in which we are engaged, & wish to entertain the pleasing reflection that I did not quit the field until I had seen the Freedom of my country fully established, and have entered the list for the war.

My situation is at present very remote which deprives me of an opportunity to solicit a particular reg^t, but I expect from you the most ample justice, according as my rank may entitle me. I have only this favor to ask, which is, that the officers and men who have so long been under my command, & are well acquainted with

[1] See a letter from Col. Daniel Brodhead to Pres. Joseph Reed, dated Fort Pitt, Dec. 8, 1780, in *Pa. Archives*, VIII, 640–41.

my disposition, may be continued in the reg^t which you may be pleased to assign me.

Please present my compliments to my adopted son Fishburne, and believe me to be, &c,

D. B.

BRIG. GEN^L WAYNE.

CONDITIONS IN KENTUCKY

[Col. John Floyd to Col. William Preston. 17CC133–34. Transcript.]

BEARGRASS December 8th. 1780.

DEAR SIR:

Capt. Lees[1] return to the settlement gives me an opport^y of writing tho' I have little or no news. Our Spies returned a few days ago from the Miamia but made no discovery of a number of Indians who it was said were on their march to attack the Fort at the Falls; so that it is probable we may be safe till spring. I think this is the first week since March that we have been without an alarm.

What can be gone with Crockett and his reg^t? do you expect we shall have any reinforcements early in the spring? if not I shall dread the consequences, if the French don't do something this Winter in Canady. I think provision will be laid up here to support a great many men on duty next summer but if we have no better regulations than has heretofore been I fear we shall fall a prey to the Enemy.

I have never had a line from you since your letter of the 23^d of June. I let young Jouett[2] have my fine mare last summer

[1] Henry Lee was born in Virginia in 1758, and came to Kentucky as a surveyor in 1779; was a representative in the Virginia legislature and in the convention which ratified the Federal Constitution in 1788. Lee was likewise a member of the convention that planned statehood for Kentucky. In 1785 he settled in Mason County where he served for many years as judge of the circuit court. He died in 1846 at his home near Maysville.

[2] John Jouett, a native of Albemarle County, Va., was an early surveyor in Kentucky. In 1780 and 1781 he was in Virginia, where in the latter year he warned the legislature in time to prevent Tarleton's attempted capture of that body; for this service he was given a fine sword together with other marks of public commendation. In 1782 Jouett married Sallie Robards, and the same year emigrated to Kentucky, where he was a member of the legislature, and a

purely to get some Goods, and he was to send them to your care: if you have an opport^y (which perhaps you may by Mr. Madison) pray remember him of it. My Brother Charles is come out and has had such bad fortune in getting us a few necessaries that I am next Wednesday to set out for Illinoise to endeavour to [blank in Ms.] a little Trade—I expected to have been able to do a little Surveying this Winter, but the Divisions of the County will I suppose prevent it till the Indians set to work in the Spring, & so we jog on—I want your opinion much about a certain affair but I am afraid you will have no safe conveyance. It is this. Whether you think patents could be obtained for Lands Entered & Surveyed below the Tenisee on the Waters of the Ohio? Is it contrary to Law or no? This [is] a matter which I have long wished to consult you about, but as I believe no one else in the country has thought of it, I cou'd wish to have the first chance if it is practicable. If you write me about it, let it be by some one who will deliver the Letter as I scarce ever received any but what are broke open—If you think the plan will do I shall want all the warrants you intend for your own use as soon as you can send them out. I want another cut in an untouched country—

May the Heavens preserve & bless you my Dear Friend

JNO FLOYD

COL. WILLIAM PRESTON.

P.S. don't mention the above affair to any person unless to some one who is interested & then in confidence.

FRENCH AGENT AMONG INDIANS

[Col. Daniel Brodhead to Maj. Daniel Maurice Godefroy de Linctot. 1NN70. Summary and transcript.]

Dec. 10, 1780.

Maj. G. Linctot requested to proceed to St. Vincent the Illinois &c to visit such other places as he may have influence with the savages, to induce them to wage war against our British & Indian enemies: As his commission is from V^a, he is to consult Col. Clark; if practicable to return to Fort Pitt by the 15th February.

publicist of importance. He died Mar. 1, 1822 in Bath County. See interview with his son in Draper Mss., 25S243.

SCARCITY OF PROVISIONS AT FORT PITT

[Col. Daniel Brodhead to Col. Ephraim Blaine. 3H30–31. Transcript of Letter Book.]

FORT PITT, Dec' 10th 1780.

DEAR SIR:

The troops have not tasted meat at this post for six days past, & I hear of none that we can purchase or procure by our compulsory means; indeed there is very little meat to be had on this side the mountains at any rate. I hope some means are devised for supplying this Department, if not I shall be under the disagreeable necessity of risking my men in most dangerous situations to kill wild meat, or march them to the interior part of the country, for it will scarcely be expected that they will be content to live on bread and water only.

I am impatient to hear from you, & am &c

D. B.

COL° E. BLAINE.

[Col. Daniel Brodhead to Dr. William Shippen.[1] 3H31–32. Transcript of Letter Book.]

FORT PITT, Dec' 10th 1780.

DEAR SIR:

Doctor Martin[2] has my permission to proceed to Philadelphia & lay before you the deficiencies of hospital stores, instruments &

[1] The medical department of the Continental army was organized July 25, 1775, according to the precedent of the British service. On April 1, 1777 William Shippen Jr., who in 1776 had been chief physician of the Flying Camp, was appointed director-general and chief physician of the army, a position he held until Jan. 3, 1781. Dr. William Shippen was a native of Philadelphia, son of one of its earliest physicians, Dr. William Shippen the elder. The younger man was born in 1735. He graduated from Princeton in 1754 and studied with his father until 1758, when he went to London and Edinburgh, graduating from the College of Medicine at the latter place in 1761. After a year in Paris he returned to Philadelphia and established a private medical course. It became the nucleus of the first medical school in the colonies, in which he held for many years the chair of anatomy. Among his pupils at this school was Dr. Benjamin Rush. After the expiration of his service in the army Dr. Shippen returned to private practice, which he maintained until his retirement in 1798. He died July 11, 1808 at his home in Germantown.

[2] Hugh Martin was a Virginia physician who in 1778 was appointed surgeon's mate of the Twelfth Virginia Regiment. In August of the same year he was

medicine. I have no doubt you will have this remote Department well supplied, & appoint a hospital surgeon, or make one of the regimental surgeons accountable for the stores.

Dr Martin has been very attentive hitherto, & I believe has given general satisfaction.

I have the honor to be, &c.

D. B.

DR Shippen.

REDUCTION OF ARMY

[Col. Daniel Brodhead to Gen. William Irvine.¹ 3H16–17. Transcript of Letter Book.]

Fort Pitt, Decr 14th 1780.

Dear Sir:

I am honored with your favor of the 19th ult. & am much obliged with the contents.

transferred to the Eighth Virginia, and on Mar. 7, 1780 became surgeon of the Eighth Pennsylvania. He retired from the army Jan. 1, 1781.

¹ Gen. William Irvine was born of Scotch ancestry Nov. 3, 1741 in County Fermanagh, Ireland. Irvine studied medicine at Trinity College, Dublin, after which he was appointed surgeon in the British navy, wherein he served throughout the Seven Years' War. At its close he emigrated to America and settled at Carlisle, Pa., where he married Anne, daughter of the Indian trader, Robert Callendar. In 1774 Dr. Irvine was elected a member of the first Provincial Convention of Pennsylvania, and on Jan. 9, 1776 was commissioned colonel of the Sixth Pennsylvania Battalion which was sent to reënforce the Continental army in Canada. He arrived in time to participate in the defeat of the American army, and, after wandering in the marshes near Three Rivers for many hours, he surrendered to the British authorities, who treated him with distinguished courtesy. At Quebec Irvine was released upon parole and soon thereafter returned to Pennsylvania. He was very impatient at his enforced inaction, which kept him from the army until he was exchanged, April 21, 1778. Meanwhile he had been commissioned colonel of the Seventh Pennsylvania, and on May 12, 1778 Congress appointed him brigadier-general. He served under Washington at the battle of Monmouth and in the campaigns of 1779 and 1780. In the latter year he was with General Wayne in an attack on Blockhouse Point, which served as the occasion for Maj. John André's satirical poem "The Cow Chase." In 1781 Washington detailed Irvine to the command at Fort Pitt, where he arrived in November, and where he remained until the close of the war. During the years 1783–85 General Irvine was a member of the Pennsylvania Council of Censors; later he represented Carlisle in the Continental and the Third Federal congresses. In 1785 he was surveyor for northwest Pennsylvania and in 1794 adjusted the agreement that made the triangle of Erie a

The new arrangement I had anticipated, but did not expect so great a reduction would take place; however, the number of regt⁸ may yet be sufficient, provided they be recruited to their full complement.

When Captn Finley arrived with the dispatches, the officers of my reg^t were chiefly on command, some upon hunting, & others on foraging parties. I immediately ordered them in, & expect they will be collected in a day or two—& so soon as I receive the arrangement of the reg^t it shall be forwarded to the War Office at Philadelphia, unless you wish to receive it at Carlisle.—I hear the Council & Assembly of our State have in contemplation the sending Militia or other raw troops to garrison these posts; if this is true I wish it may answer their expectations, but I confess my apprehensions of an immediate breach of faith with the friendly Indians, which must be productive of a general war with the Savages; an event which I have been instructed & by every address in my power have endeavored to prevent, & my exertions have been the greater on account of the disaffection of a very considerable number of the inhabitants on this side the mountain, who I am well persuaded are more anxious for a favorable opportunity to submit to a British Government, than to repel the hellhounds of the forest.

I have the honor to be, &c,

Gen^L Irvine.

D. B.

HUNTING FOR RATIONS

[Col. Daniel Brodhead to Capt. Samuel Brady. 3H32–33. Transcript of Letter Book.]

Head Qr^s, Fort Pitt, Decr 16th 1780.

Dear Sir:

I have your favor of this date & had signed the order you sent for liquor, but upon being informed that altho' the hunting party

part of the state's territory. Irvine commanded the Pennsylvania forces in the Whisky Rebellion, was presidential elector in 1797, and on Mar. 13, 1800 was appointed superintendent of military stores. In order to fulfill the duties of the latter office he removed to Philadelphia, where he died July 29, 1804. The town of Irvine is named in his honor. He was an upright and competent officer, and a personal friend of Washington. He served one term as president of the Order of Cincinnati. Many of his papers are in the Draper Mss., and will appear in the succeeding volume of this series.

now out was intended to provide meat for the garrison, yet out of the large quantity sent us only 400^{lbs} weight reached the public store. This being a subversion of my intentions, has determined me to recall both the officers and soldiers. You will, therefore, upon the return of the canoe & party get in as much venison as you may have ready, & the whole of the officers & men now on the hunting party are to proceed to this place without loss of time.[1]

I have the honor to be, &c.

D. B.

CAPT^N S. BRADY.

COMMANDANT FOR FORT McINTOSH

[Col. Daniel Brodhead to Capt. John Clark. 1NN70. Summary and transcript.]

Dec. 16, 1780.

Capt. John Clark ordered to go to Fort McIntosh, & relieve Lt. Tannehill, & take com^d there, wh. place to be garrisoned by the M^d corps. Lt. Thomas[2] to take the officers & men to F^t Henry, of the 9th Va. Reg^t

---

[1] Note on original manuscript: "It w^d seem that Brady had command of this hunting party—& within one day's reach of Pittsburg, sent for whiskey—& Brodhead ordered the whole party to return with what venison they had ready, upon the return to them of the boats sent for liquor: It does not appear that Brady was to blame—he 'sent' the 'large quantity' of meat, but how it happened that only 400 ^{lbs} reached the public store, does not appear. Perhaps the hungry soldiery seized it *nolens volens*—but if so, why recall the hunters? L. C. D."

[2] Lewis Thomas was commissioned, Dec. 19, 1776, second lieutenant of the Thirteenth Virginia, which became successively the Ninth and the Seventh Virginia regiments. Thomas attained the rank of captain-lieutenant, and was retired Jan. 1, 1783.

RECRUITS FOR VIRGINIA REGIMENT

[Summary of a letter of Col. John Gibson, Fort Pitt, Dec. 17, 1780, to Col. George Rogers Clark. 50J64. Printed in *Ill. Hist. Colls.*, VIII, 474.]

Letter received from Governor Jefferson to deliver surplus clothing to Captain Moore[1] for use of Clark's troops; those at Fort Pitt to be supplied from Continental stores. No prospect of getting a single stitch from the latter source; men of his regiment quite naked, and over one hundred drafts now on their way to join the regiment. Gibson going to Richmond, will endeavor to secure clothing for Clark. Refers to Captain Moore for news of this place.

HUNTING FOR RATIONS

[Col. Daniel Brodhead to Capt. John Clark. 3H33–34. Transcript of Letter Book.]

HEAD QR^s, FORT PITT, Decr 26th 1780.

DEAR SIR:

I am sorry to inform you that it is out of my power to supply your garrison with meat until further means are afforded.

---

[1] James Francis Moore was born Aug. 12, 1751 in Maryland, where in 1773 he married Ann Standiford, and the same year removed to Turkey Foot in Bedford County, Pa. There he was commissioned Mar. 19, 1776, lieutenant in Miles's Rifle Battalion, which the next August took part in the battle of Long Island. Soon thereafter Moore was appointed captain in the Twelfth Pennsylvania, whence he was transferred, July 1, 1778, to the Eighth Regiment, and in 1779 was honorably discharged. He then went to Kentucky and in April, 1780 was deputy commissary-general for Clark at the Falls of Ohio. Having visited Virginia in the fall of 1780 Captain Moore at the time of this letter was returning to Kentucky, where he arrived early in 1781. In April of that year he was tried and acquitted of charges of neglect of duty. *Ill. Hist. Colls.*, VIII, 519, 524. Moore became in later life a salt manufacturer, and a surveyor of Jefferson County. In 1789 he was appointed a trustee of Harrodsburg and Louisville. He also served on the commission to allot the land granted to the soldiers and officers of Clark. He was a Federalist member of the Kentucky legislature, and in the political duel fought in January, 1809 between Henry Clay and Humphrey Marshall, he served as the latter's second. Moore was in attendance at the legislature at Frankfort when he suddenly died Dec. 9, 1809. The site of his grave is not known. For many of the facts of this sketch obligation is acknowledged to Colonel Moore's descendant, T. W. Chamberlin of St. Louis.

Under these circumstances I must recommend the employing two or three faithful Indians to hunt near the fort, & paying them for their venison, &c, at a reasonable rate with flour, whiskey, or salt.

As soon as a quantity of meat can be procured, a large proportion shall be sent you, but not more then half rations of that article can be issued, at least for some time; & the deficiency shall be made up in Indian meal or flour.

With the compliments of the season, I am, dear Sir, Your most obed^t Servt—

        Dan^L Brodhead, Col^o Comm^g W. D.

Capt. John Clark.

VIRGINIA PLANS DETROIT EXPEDITION

[Gen. George Washington to Col. Daniel Brodhead. Washington Papers. Draft, partly autograph.][1]

     Head Quarters New Windsor 29th Decem^r 1780

Dear Sir:

The State of Virginia have determined to undertake an expedition, which I have ever had in view, and which I wished to carry into execution by a Continental force—but you are sufficiently acquainted with the situation of our affairs, both as to men and supplies, to know that it has been impossible to attempt it. It is the reduction of the Post of Detroit. His Excellency Governor Jefferson informs me that he thinks they shall be able, with the Aid of some Artillery and Stores already at Fort Pitt, to accomplish this most desirable object, and that should they even fail of carrying their point, much good will result from creating a diversion and giving the enemy employ in their own Country. The Artillery and Stores required by Governor Jefferson are

 4 field peices
 1600 Balls suited to them.
 1 Howitzer. 8 Inch
 300 shells suited to it

[1] This letter is printed also in Jared Sparks (ed.), *Life and Writings of George Washington* (Boston, 1855), VII, 343–45. The transcript presented here is taken from the original draft in the Library of Congress. The last paragraph of the letter is in Washington's handwriting.

2 Royals.
Grape Shot
necessary implements and furniture for the above
500 Spades
200 pick Axes
1 travelling forge
some Boats, should the State not have enough prepared in time
some ship Carpenters tools

Col° Clarke who is to command the expedition will probably be the Bearer of this himself,[1] and you will deliver to him or his order at such time as he shall require them, all, or as many of the foregoing Articles as you have it in your power to furnish. You will likewise direct the Officers with Company of Artillery to be ready to move when Col° Clark shall call for them, and as it is my wish to give the enterprize every aid which our small force can afford, you will be pleased to form such a detachment as you can safely spare from your own and Gibson's Regiment and put it under the command of Col° Clark also. I should suppose that this detachment cannot be made more than a command for a Capt or Major at most. You know the necessity of confining it to a Continental Officer of inferior Rank to Col° Clark.

Your good sense will, I am convinced, make you view this matter in its true light. The inability of the Continent to undertake the reduction of Detroit, which, while it continues in possession of the enemy, will be a constant source of trouble to the whole Western frontier, has of necessity imposed the task upon the State of Virginia, and of consequence makes it expedient to confer the command upon an Officer of the State. This being the case, I do not think the charge of the enterprise could have been committed to better hands than Col° Clarks. I have not the pleasure of knowing the Gentleman, but, independant of the proofs which he has given of his activity and address, the unbounded confidence which I am told the Western people repose in him, is a matter of vast importance, as I imagine a considerable part of his force will consist of Volunteers and Militia, who are not to be governed by military laws, but must be held by the ties of confidence and affection to their leader.

I shall conclude with recommending to you, in general, to give every countenance and assistance to this enterprise, should no

[1] This letter was enclosed in one from Washington to Jefferson, dated Dec. 28, 1780 (*ibid.*, 341–43), and was to be given to Clark at Richmond and to be carried by him to Fort Pitt.

circumstances intervene to prevent its execution. One thing you may rest assured of, & that is, that while offensive operations are going forward against Detroit & the Indians in alliance with the British in that quarter that your Posts with small Garrisons in them and proper vigilance, will be perfectly secure.—for this reason & the expedition's depending upon the supplies here rec^d I shall expect a punctual compliance with this order and am with great esteem & regard Dr Sir Y^r most ob^t Servt

G W

Col^o Brodhead.

OFFICERS FOR OHIO POSTS

[Col. Daniel Brodhead to Maj. William Taylor. 1NN71. Summary and transcript.]

Jan. 2^d 1781.

Orders Maj. William Taylor to march immediately the 9th V^a Reg^t to Fort Henry—leaving an officer (Ens^n Springer) serg^t, corporal & 12 rank & file to garrison Holliday's Cove—& detach a subaltern officer, with a Serg^t, corporal & ten rank & file to Col. Shepherd's Mill[1] for the protection of the same & the adjacent settlements.

[Col. Daniel Brodhead to Capt. John Clark. 3H34–35. Transcript of Letter Book.]

Head Qr^s, Fort Pitt, Jany 10th 1781.

Dear Sir:

I have rec^d your favor dated Pittsburg, Jany 7th 1780. [sic]

I see by the contents that you have taken upon yourself to give leave of absence to Ensign (whom you call Lieut.) Connor[2]

---

[1] Col. David Shepherd in 1775 built a single-geared mill on his land at the forks of Wheeling Creek, about six miles above Wheeling, near the present village of Elm Grove. After the siege of Wheeling in 1777 Colonel Shepherd removed his family to the settlement near Washington, Pa., when the Indians burned the abandoned blockhouse and other buildings, but did no injury to the mill. Occasionally in passing they would set it running. See Draper Mss., 2S182.

[2] In January, 1777 William Connor entered the army as sergeant of the Thirteenth Virginia Regiment, which on Sept. 14, 1778 was designated as the Ninth. On April 6, 1779 Connor received an ensign's commission, which he held until his resignation from the service, Jan. 4, 1782.

to go home for [?] weeks. because there is no doctor at your post.
This is a liberty I much disapprove, because it is unmilitary &
improper, and therefore shall not send another officer to supply
his place. If you will attend to the articles of war, you may read
in plain language that you have no authority to give leave of
absence to any officer without consulting me. You are upon no
pretence to give furloughs to non-commissioned officers or soldiers. Should any of the officers or men be so ill as to stand in
need of a doctor's attendance, you will give me the earliest notice
of it, & not send them to places where Doctors are not to be
found. I will immediately send a Doctor to visit Mr Connor &
report his complaint.—
I have the honor to be, &c.

D. B.

Capt^N Jno Clarke.

DELAWARES NEED HELP

[Gen. George Washington to Col. Daniel Brodhead. Washington Papers. Draft.]

Head Quarters New Windsor 10th January 1781.
Dear Sir:
I have rec^d your favors of the 17th of October and 7th of Decem^r.
It is to be wished that we had means of retaining the affections of
those Indians who appear friendly or of engaging those to take
part with us who are otherwise, but as that is not the case, it will
be a most desirable object to foment differences among themselves,
and as the Delawares have declared against the Senecas who
have been most troublesome to us they are certainly entitled to
our support and protection.

Major Genl Baron Steuben is at Richmond in Virginia assisting in compleating the new arrangement of the Virginia line.
He will write to you on the subject of Col^o Gibson's Reg^t and you
will be pleased to comply with his directions respecting throwing
the men into two Companies and calling down the surplus officers.

You will be pleased to attach the men of Rawlin's Corps and
the independent Companies to the Pennsylvania and Virginia
Regiments as they may respectively belong, should there be
any Marylanders for the War or for any considerable time to

come, you will send them down to Richmond under the care of an officers that they may join their line. The officers of those Corps retire upon half pay agreeable to the Regulations of the 3^d and 21st October You will transmit me a Return of the Names and Ranks.
COL° BRODHEAD.

[Delaware chiefs to Col. Daniel Brodhead. 1H151. In handwriting of Heckewelder.]

SALEM Jan^{ry} ye 13th 1781

William Penn and the Councellors of Cooshockung to Colonell Brodhead as follows—
BROTHER MAGHINGWE GEESHUCH:
Listen to me. You spoke to me twice already, and desired that we all who were Your Friends should live in one place together. I told You that I would do so, & promised to move to Cushcushkee.[1] I told You that what I said I also would do, and therefore You might depend on my Word

Now *Brother:* When I look upon my circumstances I find this matter almost impossible for me to perform, You know Yourself that I am poor and not able to undertake such a great Work without assistance, My Chilldren would suffer greatly, for it is Winter now, & when I consider Spring being so near, I cannot comprehend how I should do all this Work in such a short time, for I must always consider planting time as not to be neglected. As this is now a matter of consequence, I am coming to You to speak further about it.

Now *Brother:* All the Councellors have earnesly consulted one another concerning what You told me two Years ago, namely: That You would build a Fort at Cooshockung. A Year ago I told You to come and build me strong Houses, but it was not done on account of some of the Councellors being against it.˙ Brother Now We are all of one Mind, we have considered the Matter well, and therefore desire You to get ready and build a Fort at Cooshockung, and we furthur desire You to send 300 Men along to Live in that Fort.

Now *Brother:* If you will do this for me, I will send a good many of my Men to You to Guard You out, Then You will be at Coo-

[1] For this locality see *Frontier Defense,* 178, note 45.

shockung, and have an Opportunity of knowing every one. You have often told me, that there lives some with me who are not good. All these I suppose will withdraw themselves on Your appearance, and if any one should abide there, You will soon know such a one.

Brother: If any thing should happen unto You, while You are on the Way to Us. I mean if any of the Enemy should do harm, My Men that I send with You shall pursue them untill they get them.

Now *Brother:* You have heard me what I had to say to You, I am ready. But Brother, You told me last Year when the Wyondot Man was at Pittsburg, that I had no courage to speak to him, but that I hung my Head and was afraid of him, who was but one Man.

Brother: I assure You, that I am not afraid of any body, and I tell You now, that I am resolved to get up and Fight. I have considered this matter from my Heart. I am able to Fight any one of my Colour. I am no coward that You know Yourself, and You will find it so for the future.

My dear Brother: Now I and all the Councellors remember our Love to You.

Col° Brodhead.

Will^м Penn.

[Captain Killbuck to Col. Daniel Brodhead. 1H153. In handwriting of Heckewelder.]

Salem, Jan^{ry} ye 15th 1781.
Col° Henry to Col° Brodhead as follows.
Brother listen to me:

You will see the conclusion of Willm Penn and the Councellors of Cooshockung. When I left You I told You that in 30 or at most 40 Days You should hear me. I told You that in that time You should know in what place the Dellawares would assemble together. When I came as far as the Brethren Settlements then I was overtaken by those who deserted from You. Soon After Your Wampum was handed to me, both white & black with Your Words, namely: that I should do as I always had told You and keep my Promise. It is true what You say Brother, I know what I told You & that I said if that Man would desert, You should take me in his stead and put chains on me. I am sorry that I cannot do as I fain would. If it was in my Power I certainly would bring him back to You again. My heart is full of trouble on this account, but I tell You that You now can do as You please with me. I shall not desert You, but am ready for punishment as soon as You call me.

Brother: I do not blame any body but myself for what comes over me. I blame myself and some foolish People for it. Because I have broke myself now, I must desire You to chuse a better Man than I am out of the Turtle Tribe in my stead

Brother Maghingwe Geeshuch: You are a Turtle Yourself, & there are many Men in our Tribe, therefore You will not be at a loss to find one good one, who will speak the truth. You know that I told You last Fall, that I was weary of bearing the load of Lies laid upon me. You know that I told You, I never would be at ease untill I went & lived with the Brethren

I love You Brother and I know You also loved me untill this misfortune came upon me. I know of nothing at all that should hinder me from becoming a Christian, neither do I see You or the Councill of Cooshockung at any loss about me.

I am Your friend and Brother

COL° HENRY

COL° BRODHEAD.
[*Endorsed:*] Jn° Killbuck

SUPPLIES FOR CLARK'S TROOPS

[Col. Daniel Brodhead to Gov. Thomas Jefferson. 3H36–37. Transcript of Letter Book.]

FORT PITT, Jany 17th 1781.

SIR:
I am honored with your favor of the 12th Oct^r, & am thankful for the contents.

I have rec^d information from Detroit that the Indians are in a grand Council there, & it is expected that they are meditating with the British to attack these frontier parts as soon as the season will permit.

Your Excell^{ys} instructions to Mr Jas. F. Moore to make so large a purchase on this side the mountain as 200,000 rations, if actually made, will effectually distress the troops under my command, & probably greatly disappoint his Excell^y the Commander-in-Chief if he has not been consulted respecting the measure. It is with great sincerity that I profess to entertain the greatest respect towards your Excell^y; but circumstanced as I am, it appears to me that I can by no means be justified in suffering the provisions which are designed for the troops under my command, to be transported down the river,[1] unless I am so instructed to do by the Commander-in-Chief.

Col. Gibson takes down the arrangement and return of his reg^t & will have the honor of waiting on your Excell^y with this letter; he can inform you particularly of the circumstances of this District, wherefore I beg leave to refer to him.

I have the honor to be, &c.

D. B.

His Excell^y Gov. Jefferson

DRAFTS FOR VIRGINIA REGIMENT

[Col. Daniel Brodhead to Baron Steuben. 3H37–38. Transcript of Letter Book.]

Fort Pitt, Jany 17th, 1781.

Sir:

Your favor of the 24th of Novr I had not the honor to receive until yesterday.

Col. Gibson being desirous to transact some business at Richmond, will proceed thither without loss of time, & he has a return of his reg^t, also a list of the names and rank of his officers.

Col° Campbell informs me that the officers who were sent from hence to collect the drafts for the 9th Virg^a Reg^t are by his Excellency's orders immediately under my command; unless he is pleased to order otherwise I hope to see them join the reg^t early next spring.

I sincerely wish you great success, & have the honor to be, &c

D. B.

The Honb^le Baron De Steuben.

---

[1] Note on original Mss.: "I presume these supplies were designed for Gen. G. R. Clark's intended exp^dn ag^st Detroit, L. C. D."

CONDITIONS IN KENTUCKY AND ILLINOIS

[Summary of a letter of Col. Levin Powell,[1] Harrodsburgh, Jan. 21, 1781, to Col. Daniel Brodhead. 1NN51-53. Printed in *Pa. Archives*, VIII, 767-68.]

Since middle of December, when one man was killed at the Falls, no mischief done by Indians until lately when seven with a white prisoner came to steal horses. White man escaped to a station,[2] says Shawnee are fifteen miles from Pickawee town preparing for a vigorous attack. News from the Illinois of La Balme's defeat. Cannon on Maumee en route for Kentucky. Clark at Richmond, much expected of him. Accusations against commissaries. Montgomery and Dodge[3] in Illinois speculating with public funds.

[1] Levin Powell was born in 1738 in Loudoun County, Va., where in 1774 he signed the remonstrance of that county against British exactions. See *William and Mary College Quarterly*, XII, 234-36. In 1775 Powell was on the Committee of Correspondence; on Jan. 11, 1777 he was commissioned lieutenant-colonel of the Sixteenth Virginia Regiment, and served on the Trenton campaign after the winter at Valley Forge. On Nov. 15, 1778 Colonel Powell resigned and visited Kentucky where he was a trustee of the town of Boonesborough. He did not remain permanently in Kentucky, but returned to Virginia where he married Sarah, daughter of Burr Harrison. Powell was in the Virginia convention of 1778 which ratified the Federal Constitution, and served as Federalist member of the Sixth Congress. He died at Bedford, Pa., Aug. 3, 1810.

[2] This escaped prisoner was Martin Wetzel. See Draper Mss., 2S265, 11S36. Martin, the eldest son of Capt. John Wetzel, was born in December, 1757 in Rockingham County, Va. In 1769 he came West with his father's family, and in 1774 served in Dunmore's War. In 1777 Martin Wetzel was at the siege of Wheeling, and aided in burying the dead after Foreman's defeat. He was captured in April, 1779 and adopted into Cornstalk's Shawnee family. He escaped from a band of Indians by pretending a desire to go to Kentucky to steal horses. Sometime in 1781 Martin Wetzel returned over the Wilderness Road to his home near Wheeling. There he married Mary Coffle. During the remainder of his life he was much employed in scouting and claimed to have been in twenty-two skirmishes without receiving a wound. See Dr. Draper's interviews with Wetzel's sons, *ibid.*, 2E8-10, 2S307.

[3] For a sketch of Col. John Montgomery see *Dunmore's War*, 225, note 55; for John Dodge, see *Rev. Upper Ohio*, 143, note 48.

THE MORAVIAN MISSIONARIES

[Col. Daniel Brodhead to Rev. David Zeisberger. 3H39–41. Transcript of Letter Book.]

FORT PITT, Jany 21st 1781.

DEAR SIR:

I have your favor of the [blank in Ms.] '80, & am sorry to find that the proposal I made to obtain a quantity of wild meat was not accepted. It is probable that I said the Christian Indians declined assisting in the war, but I expected as a testimony of their attachment to American liberty they would not be averse to serving their country in affording supplies for the troops by every means in their power. But the reason you have assigned against the measure proposed must suffice. As to the mockery of the savages, it is common with them against persons living in a religious way.—I have just rec^d a letter from the Rev^d M Grube informing me that your packet which I sent by a son of the late Revd Mr Bruce,[1] was lost by them upon the road— which accident I am very sorry for, & if I can hear of it will immediately forward it by another hand.

Mr Connor[2] informed me that you & your worthy colleagues are without salt, wherefore I have ordered a half a bushel to be sent you a present, & shall be glad to furnish you with a further quantity or any other article in my power.

Our privateers have lately taken a few prizes near New York, in which they took 19,000 Bls of beef, 6000 bbls of pork, 600 bbls of raisins, 600 bbls of peas, & 500 firkins of butter, besides a considerable quantity of other stores & merchandize.

---

[1] Rev. David Bruce came to America from Scotland in 1741 with the Moravian missionary, Count Zinzendorf, and settled as pastor over an English mission in Bucks County, Pa. There in 1742 Bruce married Judith, sister of the philanthropist, Anthony Benezet. In 1744 Bruce was sent on a mission to the Iroquois; and in 1749 to the Mahican tribe, among whom a station was formed at Wechquadnach, in Dutchess County, N. Y., and there July 9, 1749 he died. One hundred years after his death a monument was erected to all the Moravian missionaries who had labored at Wechquadnach, on the border of the lake they called Gnadensee, now known as Indian Pond.

[2] For a sketch of Richard Conner see *Wis. Hist. Colls.*, XXIII, 246, note 1.

I send you a number of newspapers in which you will see how improbable it is, that the British can hold out much longer.
I have the honor to be &c.

D. B.

Postcript to Mr Zeisberger's letter—I am informed that your Indians have a great number of cattle & swine to spare. I must request you will not suffer them to be sent to the enemy. I have wrote for goods or specie to enable my Comm^y to purchase & pay for them.

D. B.

REV^D D. ZEISBERGER.

[Col. Daniel Brodhead to Rev. John Heckewelder. 3H42–43. Transcript of Letter Book.]

FORT PITT, Jany 21st 1781.

DEAR SIR:

I am honored with your kind favor of the 4th instant, and am particularly thankful for the acceptable presents from your good lady.

Killbuck appears to have acted with duplicity in regard to Bawbee; but I believe he has generally shewed as much attachment as any of the Coochocking Council, & it is probable as he is unsupported & much envied, that he conceived it too great a risk to interfere; however, his future conduct may determine how far he is culpable. I conceive that much confidence ought never to be placed in any of the colour, for I believe it is much easier for the most civilized Indian to turn Savage than for any Indian to be civilized. I am obliged to your people for the pains they took to get the whiteman from Bawbee—I do not despair of getting both him and Bawbee before long, for they will scarcely leave the continent; as to the villain whole [who] stole the skiff he with them will be remembered.

Bawbee being a notorious liar I do not believe what he has said as to the disaffected of the soldiers.

I shall be happy to hear from you by every safe conveyance, & hope you will be able to collect some interesting intelligence. I have directed my house-keeper to put up a small quantity of tea & coffee for your lady, & beg she will please to accept it as a mark of my particular esteem for you both.

I have, &c, &c.

D. B.

P. S.—For a putall of clear bear's oil, & a peck of tossimonany, I would cheerfully barter salt with any of your people who have it to spare.

D. B.

Rev[D] Jn[o] Hackenwelder.

SUPPLIES FOR FORT PITT

[Col. Daniel Brodhead to Maj. William Taylor. 3H38–39. Transcript of Letter Book.]

Head Qr[s] Fort Pitt, Jan[y] 22[d] 1781.

Sir:

I am favored with yours of the 15th instant, and am glad to find that no damage has happened to Capt. Biggs and his party. I conceive that if he is fortunate he will be able to furnish meat for your garrison, & the dependent posts at Holliday's Cove & Shepherd's Mill will probably be furnished by the inhabitants, until it may be in my power to send them a small supply from hence.

Our store of salt is nearly exhausted, & it will be necessary to retain what we have on hand to salt the beef which M[r] W[m] Wilson[1] is about to purchase.

M[r] Duncan will send some bags to Cap[n] Mitchel for which he is to account, & I expect you will have a considerable quantity of flour & meal laid in.

The Enemy at Niagara & Detroit are meditating on a descent on our posts early in the spring. I wish we may be able to give them a proper reception.

I am [&c]

D. B.

Major W[m] Taylor.

This is probably the person noted in *Rev. Upper Ohio*, 202, note 41.

[Col. Daniel Brodhead to Col. Abraham Hite.[1] 3H44. Transcript of Letter Book.]

FORT PITT, January 22^d 1781.

SIR:

The bearer Mr Wilson informs me that his brother has purchased some cattle for the use of the suffering troops in this District, & he is apprehensive a prohibitory law of Virginia will prevent his driving them hither. I have enquired into characters & have thought proper to address myself to you upon this occasion not doubting but your influence will be used in favor of troops who have already repeatedly suffered great want.

This frontier covering the settlements below the mountains will I conceive, interest every person concerned in the support of them. But was nothing said on this subject, I am satisfied your own good sense would point out the necessity of their being amply supplied.

I have the honor to be, &c,

D. B.

COL° A. HYTE.

[Col. Daniel Brodhead to Col. Ephraim Blaine. 3H54–55. Transcript of Letter Book.]

FORT PITT, Jany 22^d 1781.

DEAR SIR:

The hostile intentions of the enemy against the posts under my care & command, the present sufferings of my officers & men, & the disappointment Mr Wilson has met with, has determined me to send Mr Duncan to Philad^a to apply for money to purchase provisions. He can inform you particularly as to circumstances, wherefore I must refer you to him.

I am informed that the Moravian Indians have a great number of cattle & swine to dispose of, but these cannot be purchased for anything except goods & specie, & if that is not furnished they will be sold to the enemy.

I am very sensible that nothing in your power will be lacking to relieve us from further want.

[1] For Col. Abraham Hite, a prominent resident of the lower Shenandoah Valley, see *Dunmore's War*, 31, note 53.

I hope you are instructed to purchase some good spirit and brandy for this District, & that no time will be lost in forwarding it; at present we are destitute of every liquor, except vile whiskey warm from the dirty stills.

Please to write me a letter of comfort, & believe me to be &c

D. B.

Col° E. Blaine.

[Col. Daniel Brodhead to Richard Peters. 3H55–58. Transcript of Letter Book.][1]

Fort Pitt, Jany 22^d 1781.

Sir:

Mr Wm Wilson a few days ago wrote me that he had undertaken to furnish my troops with one hundred head of cattle upon private contract & with private money. This account, as there was no other prospect of obtaining meat, & the troops were suffering for want of it, whilst we were scarcely supplied with flour, was flattering & cheered the drooping spirits of both officers & men. But as meat could not be purchased on account of the great scarcity on this side the mountains, Mr Wilson immediately proceeded to the South Branch of Potowmack to perform the contract, & now I have the mortification to be informed by his brother who is just arrived from Old Town, that a prohibitory law of the State of Virg^a will prevent his getting the cattle he may have purchased for consumption here.

I sincerely wish there was no cause to trouble you with a further tale of misfortunes; but as it is the interest of the United States to retain in this district all the grain that has, under the protection of their troops, been raised in it; it might appear criminal in me was I to remain silent respecting certain instructions lately sent by Govr Jefferson for the purchase of 200,000 rations on this side the mountains for the use of the troops under Col° Clark, for which purpose he has already advanced 300000 pounds, & promise to furnish upon the first notice any further sum that may be necessary to complete the payment of that purchase: because this contract together with the consumption of multitudes of emigrants arrived & expected in this district, (chiefly to avoid militia duty & taxes) will scarcely leave a pound of flour for the regular or other troops which it may be necessary to employ

[1] On the same date Brodhead wrote a letter, which contains similar information, to Pres. Joseph Reed. See *Pa. Archives*, VIII, 706–10.

offensively or defensively against the enemy for the defence of this part of the frontier settlements.

A grand Council of British & other Indians is now holding at Detroit, & I am informed they are premeditating a descent on this post, & as I cannot rely on a private contract which may or may not be made as shall best suit the contractors, & it is at most insufficient; This & the other circumstances I have mentioned have induced me to send Mr Duncan (Col^o Blaine's Deputy) to apply for money to purchase & lay in provision for the troops that are or may be under my command, if possible before spring, so that if I should be unfortunate enough not to be sufficiently reinforced to enable me to pursue some hostile measure against the enemy, I may not be under the disagreeable necessity of shamefully abandoning posts of the first consequence committed to my care, & suffering the already much distressed inhabitants to be slaughtered by the merciless savages and their abettors.

I am unwilling to trouble you on the score of clothing or goods &c. for the Indians; I have hertofore wrote much on the subject.

The Moravian Indians have a considerable number of cattle & swine which might be purchased cheap for goods or specie, but without these they will be drove to market at Detroit.

I have wrote Govr Jefferson that I am not at liberty to permit the transportation of provisions out of this district until I receive instructions for that purpose.

I have the honor to be, &c.

D. B.

RICH^D PETERS, Esqr

[Col. Daniel Brodhead to Gen. George Washington. 3H58–61. Transcript of Letter Book.]

FORT PITT, Jany 23^d, 1781.

DEAR GEN^L:

(Here follows the explanation, substantially as the preceeding letter, about Wilson's failure to get cattle in Virginia, on account of the prohibitory law—& the instructions of Gov. Jefferson to raise supplies west of the mountains for Col^o Clark's troops—& that he (Brodhead) has written to Gov. Jefferson, &c)[1]

[1] The summary in the preceding paragraph is that of the transcriber, not that of the present editor. For the letter to Jefferson, written Jan. 17, 1781, see *ante*, 317.

A grand Council of British & other savages is now holding at Detroit, & I am informed they are premeditating an attack on this post early in the spring; without doubt the Indians will be more hostile next spring than they have yet been.

As I have not been honored with a line from your Excell[y] since the new arrangement of the army was ordered, I am at a loss what to do with the 9th Virg^a Reg^t, late Rawlin's corps & Capt. Heth's company, & shall continue them here until I know your pleasure.

The whole of my present force very little exceeds 300 men, & many of these are unfit for such active service as is necessary here; I hope you Excell[y] will be pleased to enable me to take Detroit the ensuing campaign, for until that & Niagara fall into our hands, there will be no rest for the innocent inhabitants whatever sums may be expended on a defensive plan.

My soldiers will be naked by the first of March, & yet I can obtain no clothing for them. If it is agreeable to your Excellency to permit me to wait upon you & make personal applications at Philadelphia for such articles as are necessary for the troops &c before the opening of the ensuing campaign, it would oblige me much, not account of any business of my own, but if possible to promote the public good.

The Moravian Indians have a considerable number of cattle & swine which we might purchase cheap for goods or specie, but without these we cannot obtain them, & they will probably be drove to market at Detroit.

I have never been furnished with any article of goods for the Indians, nor a shilling of money to enable me to transact business with them, neither has any person been employed to take the trouble of them off my hands. I take great pleasure in serving my country, nor will I count it a troublesome service, but I am sensible it will be agreed that it is necessary I should be supported, or our interest with the western Indians must be lost.

It appears to me that two complete regt^s with the volunteers that may be collected will be equal to any enterprise that may be undertaken in this part of the country—especially if goods could be furnished to pay some of the friendly Indians to act as spies, guides &c to prevent a surprise; & that number will be as great as can be well supplied without an immense expense of transportation.

I have the honor to be, &c.

D. B.

His Excell[y] Gen[l] Washington.

ALARM OF THE FRONTIER

[Col. Daniel Brodhead to Samuel Irwin. 3H61–65. Transcript of Letter Book.]

FORT PITT, Feby 2^d 1781.

SIR:

I have rec^d your kind favor of this date, & am much obliged by the contents. It is to be lamented that there should be such a seeming lapse of the administration of justice in the civil courts; for my own part, I could wish to see every court exercising the power of preserving the peace, enforcing the militia law, & punishing with rigor all persons guilty of treason, &c. But as to actions touching real estates, as that must in the prosecution involve a question as to the title, I conceive the Courts will act prudently by discouraging them until the boundary between the two states is finally determined, which I expect will be done as soon as the weather admits.

I am exceedingly distressed on account of the poor frontier inhabitants; they are doubtless under great apprehensions of danger, & I fear there is reason to apprehend it; wherefore I use every possible address with the savages, & have renewed my representations & requisitions to his Excell^y the Commander-in-chief, both for men & resources to enable me to afford the settlements ample protection at home, & if possible to avoid the inhabitants being called from that industry which is so essential to future operations, & their own happiness. As the Commanding officer of this Department, I conceive it to be my right to be consulted on every military plan which can be conceived, & that my assent is necessary to the execution. You entertain proper ideas of these matters, & I wish the inhabitants were made sensible of the impropriety of arming a body of men in the manner you have been informed without a proper concurrance; but their conduct should be construed unfavorably by those they ought to revere.

Had these gentlemen been so forward last summer or fall in affording supplies for the troops intended for an expedition against the enemy, they would probably have had less apprehension of danger, & I presume they might with greater propriety have furnished it on public credit then, than they can at their own expense hereafter, & that to answer a much less effectual protection to themselves and families. As I have rec^d no late letters from the Honb^le Congress, Board of War, or his Excell^y the Commander-in-chief, I cannot yet decide with precision how far it will be in my power to protect the inhabitants you mention; but I make no doubt there are several upon the communication to this place which will inform me fully.

In the present unsettled state of the bounday line, I conceive the inhabitants, waiving all prejudice, would act wisely by preferring a joint & respectful petition to the Honb^le Congress of the United States, setting forth their dangers & difficulties, & praying a reinforcement of Regular troops for their protection. This mode of application would doubtless procure men with certainty, & enable them to remain at home in safety & raise supplies for future operation, unless some unexpected event should intervene.

Give me leave to assure you that I have ever had the most sincere inclination to serve this young & much distressed part of the country, & that I only want the means to do it effectually.

I have the honor, &c.

D. B.

Sam^L Irwin, Esqr

DELAWARES EXHORTED

[Col. Daniel Brodhead to the Delaware chiefs. 2H78–82. Letter Book.]

Fort Pitt Feby 4th 1781

Mahingweegeesuch to Wm Penn & the Council at Coochocking

BROTHERS:

My Great Friend (Saml Evans) has delivered me your letter, also one from Caylelemend which is likewise answered by me

Brothers listen to me: I told you my reasons for desiring you to live at Cuscusky & you still remember them. but I do not wish you to do any thing that should prove injurious either to yourselves or Children. You know your own Circumstances & that I am desirous of doing the best service I can for your nation

Brothers: When I offered to build a fort for the protection of your women & Children I was ready to do it & nothing should have prevented me from building strong houses for you a year ago if you had been willing to have it done But I have told the Head warrior of the American Army that you were coming to live at Cuscusky & he thinks it will be so wherefore I cannot now comply with your request in building a Fort at Coochocking until I have sent your speech to him & to the Great Council of this Island & received directions from them & then you shall hear me, & if you see me on the Road or any Officer I may send come & take us by the Hand as you do at Fort Pitt for we are your true Friends

Brothers: I thank you for all your good words & I will not forget them because I believe they come from your hearts as mine do

Brothers: It is true I did observe that you did not speak so bold to the Wyandott Chief as I thought Delaware Chiefs ought to do. You must remember you have made me a great Chief of your nation & as such I cannot bear to see our nation who are the first Indian warriors spoken to by a Chief of another nation as if we were less than themselves, besides by our Confederation we are to be above all other nations

Brothers: I know you are good warriors & you know I am not the least amongst my Colour. I have promised to assist you against the Enemy & now I am much rejoiced to find that you are resolved to get up & fight. Be strong my Brothers & acquit yourselves like men & you shall see me with a great many men strike where you strike the Enemy

Brothers: As soon as I hear from the Great Council & the Chief Warrior I will let you hear what they answer to your Speech & in the meantime if any nation offer to strike you I can soon bring fifteen hundred or 2,000 good warriors to help you, & for this reason you may speak freely & with great Confidence to any nation who dare to threaten or offer to strike you

I am my Dear Brothers your Friend

[Col. Daniel Brodhead to Captain Killbuck. 2H74-78. Letter Book.]

FORT PITT Feby 4th 1781

Mahingwee Geesuch to Caylaylamend viz

BROTHER listen to me:

I have rec^d your letter of the 15th Ult. informing me that you rec^d my speech with some white & Black wampum, now when you see this you must know that I sent no speech to you about the Deserters, but I hear that Captn Thompson[1] who had likewise put himself in the place of Bawbee did send the Speech you rec^d by Springer.

Brother: I am sorry to hear you are in trouble, but why did you deceive yourself & me   I spoke plain to you & desired you not to trust Bawbee, but what you say is true you brought this trouble on yourself & you must get out of it as well as you can—

Brother: I have not forgot that you promised to leave Bawbees sister as a pledge for his good behaviour   you know I told you that I could not hurt the little Girl that was not my practice. But you forgot that you had a son in my power that you loved.   so that I must now tell you that it is best always to act honestly & in doing so we shall act wisely—

Brother: It is true that I am a Turtle & shall be glad to serve my tribe by Chusing a very good man to represent them in Council or by any other thing I can do to to make them a happy people so long as they listen to good Council & act wisely.   But until I can see the Chiefs & know who is best entitled to it I must be silent

Brother: I remember you talked to me of a desire you entertained to join the Brethren but your desire seemed to arise from Disappointment more than from a mere inclination to be a Christian, however if you know no reason that prevent you I have nothing to object, except that you have not told the truth in regard to Bawbee & have left your friends Thompson & Anderson in the Lurch

Brother: listen to me: It is true that I loved you & this proceeded from an opinion of your honesty—but you have said it is otherwise & what can I say to remove a suspicion of falsehood which you have proved by your own Confession

Brother: You see I have made a long talk but I have a few words to whisper in your ear.   First then I tell you when I am a friend to any man I do not easily cast him off without first giving him an oppertunity to retrieve his good name & I am just going to propose a method for you.   You & Anderson are bound for Bawbee & Charles helped him to run away; now Brother could you & Anderson Bawbee & Charles take two or three English men prisoners & bring them to your friends all might be well &

---

[1] John Thompson's Indian name was Coolpeeconain.   He was one of the delegates who visited Congress in 1779.   See *Wis. Hist. Colls.*, XXIII, 321, 353.

you might all be taken by the hand. Now if you are wise you will join with a proposal that comes from your Friend & Brother

MAHINGWEE GEESUCH

GIBSON'S REGIMENT TO JOIN CLARK

[Gov. Thomas Jefferson to Col. John Gibson. 10S43-44. Transcript.]

RICHMOND, Feb^{ry} 13th 1781.

SIR: Having obtained leave from Maj^r Genl Baron Steuben that you should concur in an expedition across the Ohio under the command of Genl Clark, I am to desire that you will in the first place take Baltimore in your way, at which place I have reason to believe four tons of powder[1] have been furnished us by the Continental Board of War which we mean for this expedition. The obtaining this powder was to be negotiated by the Speaker Harrison who has been desired to lodge a letter at Mr Goddard's, the printer in Baltimore, enabling you to take it under your care, yet it is possible it may have been furnished at Philadelphia instead of Baltimore, and that you may be obliged to take that in your route. In any event you will please to find it out, and see it safely conveyed to Fort Pitt, and delivered to Genl Clark, as the event of the expedition depends on his receiving this supply.

I send by you a letter to Col. Brodhead, desiring that your regiment may be joined in this expedition to Genl Clark's force, in which I hope to be gratified. You will take that or any other command which Genl Clark shall assign you. In the event of Genl Clark's death or captivity, your rank & our confidence in you, substitute you as his successor in the command; in which case you will prosecute the expedition under the instructions given to Genl Clark.[2]

COL.° J° GIBSON.

[1] As early as Jan. 29, 1781 Governor Jefferson gave orders that four tons of powder should be sent to Fort Pitt by the first of March. Draper Mss., 10S43.

[2] See letters of Feb. 13 and 19, 1781, from Gov. Thomas Jefferson to Gen. George Rogers Clark, printed in *Ill. Hist. Colls.*, VIII, 505, 507-8.

[Summary of a letter of Gov. Thomas Jefferson, Richmond, Feb. 13, 1781, to Col. Daniel Brodhead. Printed in *Pa. Archives*, VIII, 768.]

Has received his favor by Colonel Gibson. Sorry for his distress for provisions; this must arise rather from lack of money than from Virginia regulations. General Washington's letter sent to Brodhead by Gen. George Rogers Clark; his earnest espousal of the project for Clark's expedition to Detroit; reliance on Brodhead's cordial execution of commander in chief's requests. Colonel Gibson and his regiment ordered on the same service.

NEEDS OF FORT PITT

[Col. Daniel Brodhead to Gen. George Washington. 3H65–67. Transcript of Letter Book.]

FORT PITT, Feb[y] 18th 1781.

DEAR GEN[L]:

Since my last the half Indian Bawbee by concurrance of a serjeant belonging to late Cap[t] Heath's company, made his escape, & persuaded a fifer[1] of the 9th Virg[a] Reg[t] to desert to the enemy. The Delaware chiefs at Coochocking siezed the deserter & sent him back, & he is confined in irons, but cannot be tried until your Excell[y] is pleased to order a Gen[l] Court Martial.

I have heard nothing of M[r] Wilson since my last, indeed I am apprehensive he has not made the contract for cattle upon account of the opposition given him by the Commissioners. At present we have a considerable supply of flour, but not an ounce of meat, & unless M[r] Wilson has purchased a supply which he may forward, we must endeavor to live without it.

A report prevails amongst the inhabitants that the regular troops are to be recalled from hence, & as I could not positively say they were to continue, they are under the most dreadful apprehensions.

Should your Excell[y] be pleased to grant me an order to draw on the fixed magazines for such arms & amunition as may be necessary for the troops in this District it will prevent my troubling you with future applications on that score, & I will make a present use of it.

[1] For the trial of this deserter, whose name was John Hinds, see *post*, 490.

SAMUEL HUNTINGTON
From an Engraving in the State Historical Library

I take the liberty to enclose a copy of a letter lately received from the Delaware Council. I have told them that their request could not be complied with until your Excellency's pleasure was known, & I beg you will be pleased to instruct me respecting their message.

I have also taken the liberty to enclose an Indent of Ordinance Stores, signed by the commanding officer of Artillery. Should an expedition be carried against Detroit or Niagara from hence, I conceive the contents will be necessary.

Col. Presly Neville[1] will do himself the honor to hand you this letter, & will be able to inform your Excell^y of many circumstances which I may have omitted.

I have the honor, &c.

D. B.

His Excell^y Genl Washington.

[Col. Daniel Brodhead to Samuel Huntington.[2] 3H67–69. Transcript of Letter Book.]

Fort Pitt, Feby 18th 1781

Sir:

It is about two years since I was honored with the command of this District, & altho' I have taken upon myself to transact business of great consequence with the natives, I have never been properly authorized or instructed for that purpose, nor have I been supplied with any goods or money to defray the expense of rewards or negotiations; wherefore I have been compelled [to use] a considerable sum of money out of my private fortune & to

---

[1] Presley, son of Col. John Neville (for whom see *Rev. Upper Ohio*, 22, note 46), was born in 1756 in Virginia and educated at the College of Philadelphia. On Nov. 9, 1776 he volunteered and was commissoned ensign in his father's company of the Twelfth Virginia Regiment. In May, 1779 the younger Neville became captain, later rising to the rank of major, then to that of lieutenant-colonel, and serving for a time as aid-de-camp for Lafayette. Colonel Neville was captured May 12, 1780 upon the surrender of Charleston, S. C., and while upon parole visited his home on Chartier's Creek near Pittsburgh. Thither he retired after the war and here he brought his bride, Anne, daughter of Col. George Morgan. During the Whisky Rebellion of 1794 Col. Presley Neville assisted his father, who as revenue collector was the especial object of the insurgents' hatred. The death of the younger Neville occurred Dec. 1, 1818.

[2] Samuel Huntington, Connecticut signer of the Declaration of Independence, was president of the Continental Congress from Sept. 28, 1779 to July 6, 1781.

borrow from others, which I am unable to re-place at present: I therefore request the Honb^{le} Congress will be pleased either to appoint an agent to transact public affairs with the Indians, or give me such instructions as will be agreeable for the government of my future conduct respecting them, and order such goods and money as may be necessary to engage the savages in hostilities against each other, & to defray the expenses already accrued.

I take the liberty to enclose the copy of a letter lately rec^d from the Delaware Council, & shall be happy to know your pleasure respecting their request. I believe them to be sincere in their present professions of friendship, but I am not in force, nor have I any supplies to enable me to afford them any part of the protection they solicit. I presume a small quantity of goods, paint & trinkets might effect a great division of the savage interest, & direct the war from our frontiers.

I beg the favor of an answer, & have the honor, &c.
His Excell^y Saml Huntington, Esq.   D. B.

ALARM OF THE FRONTIER

[Col. Daniel Brodhead to Yohogania County officers. 1NN71. Summary and transcript.]

Feb. 20th 1781.

It having been represented to Col. Brodhead, by Col. Vallandigham, Col. Cannon & Capt. Swearingen,[1] that the inhabitants of Youghagania county are under great & immediate apprehensions of danger from the savages, & that they are about to forsake their habitations & retire to a more interior place for safety —Col. B. recommends them to collect by subscription or otherwise a sufficiency of salt or other meat to subsist four officers & 54 men two months— wh. provisions shall be p^d for out of the public funds: Likewise to provide a suitable quantity of flour or meal to be delivered on public account—& he will send the detachment.

[1] For Col. John Canon see *ibid.*, 221, note 63; for Capt. Van Swearingen see *Wis. Hist. Colls.*, XXIII, 360, note 1.

REDUCTION OF ARMY

[Col. Daniel Brodhead to Maj. William Taylor. 3H69–71. Transcript of Letter Book.]

HEAD Q^{rs}, FORT PITT, Feby 24th 1781.

SIR:

The Commander-in-Chief has been pleased to direct that the 9th Virg^a Reg^t be reduced to two companies, each consisting of one Captain, two subs, three serjeants, two drum^s & fifers, & one half the rank & file, which two companies are to be under your command until further orders—all the surplus officers are to repair to Richmond, Virg^a

The Maryland corps is likewise to march thither under the command of an officer; wherefore you are, immediately after arranging the companies, to detach a captain, two subs, & three serjeants, & 50 rank & file with a proportion of salt meat & craft to Fort McIntosh to relieve the garrison there. I wish to retain Capts. Biggs & Springer, Lieut^s John Harrison[1] & Thomas, & Ensigns Coleman & Winlock;[2] the Doctor and mate remain of course. If you have more than six serjeants regularly appointed, the surplus of them must march with the officers that are to proceed, & I would recommend it to the whole of them to march with

---

[1] John Harrison, son of Lawrence, and brother or cousin of Col. Benjamin, and Col. William Harrison, was born in 1754 in Westmoreland County, Va. He removed in early life to the Youghiogheny River, and was in Dunmore's division during the War of 1774. On the outbreak of the Revolution he left his plow standing in the furrow, took his father's gun, and joined Capt. John Stephenson's Rifle Regiment. On Dec. 16, 1776 Harrison was commissioned ensign of the Thirteenth Virginia, becoming second lieutenant Jan. 1, 1777, and first lieutenant Oct. 1, 1778. He served in the battles of Brandywine, Germantown, and Monmouth before being ordered West. He was promoted to a captain-lieutenancy Jan. 1, 1781 and was at Fort McIntosh at the time of the Crawford expedition in 1782. In 1785 Harrison, then brevetted major, removed to Kentucky and settled at Louisville, where he married·Mary Ann Johnston. He was present at Wayne's Treaty of 1795, and conversed with the Delawares in their own language. He was a great hunter and many stories are told of his prowess. See Draper Mss., 3S53–55. Maj. John Harrison was a prominent citizen of early Louisville, and died there about 1821. Dr. Draper interviewed two of his sons. *Ibid.*, 25S188–212.

[2] Joseph Winlock began army life Jan. 25, 1777 as corporal in the Ninth Virginia; he was promoted to an ensigncy Aug. 6, 1779 and commissioned second lieutenant May 26, 1781. He served until the close of the war. In 1812 Winlock was brigadier-general of Virginia militia; his death occurred in 1831.

the Maryland corps, as no soldier can be dispensed with to act as a waiter from this Department. Should your officers choose to go another rout, Mr Beck will be ordered to take charge of the Marylanders.

I am, &c.

D. B.

P. S.—Please present my complements to the gentlemen of your post—The surgeon or mate must go M°Intosh.

MAJOR W^M TAYLOR.

[Col. Daniel Brodhead to Capt. John Clark. 3H71–72. Transcript of Letter Book.]

HEAD QR^s FORT PITT, Feby 25th, 1781.

DEAR SIR:

His Excell^y the Commander-in-Chief has been pleased to order the Maryland corps from this Department. In consequence of which order, I have instructed Major Taylor to detach a part of the 9th Virg^a regt. to relieve your garrison, & to take with them a proportion of salt meat from Fort Henry, wherefore your present supply from hence will be small.

When you are relieved, you will take copies of the instructions you have rec^d from me, & deliver the original to the relieving officer, taking his receipt, & inserting the date or dates.

You will bring under escort of your garrison such quantities of amunition as the Dep^y Field Comm^y may require & your craft can safely carry, & without loss of time proceed to this post.

I am, &c.

D. B.

CAPT^N JNO. CLARKE.

BRODHEAD DISAPPOINTED

[Summary of a letter of Col. Daniel Brodhead, Fort Pitt, Feb. 25, 1781, to Gen. George Washington. 3H72–73. Printed in Sparks, *Corr. Amer. Rev.*, III, 243–44.]

Has received his letters of December 29 and January 10. Will execute every instruction to the utmost of his capacity. Captain

Heath's rank. Indians have killed one man on Ten Mile Creek; inhabitants are in consternation; frontier settlements will be deserted as he has no troops to protect them. Hopes Clark's proposed expedition will answer expectations; will assist his operations.[1] Requests leave of absence as force so much reduced. Continuance of garison at Fort McIntosh.

[Summary of a letter of Col. Daniel Brodhead, Fort Pitt, Feb. 25, 1781, to Pres. Joseph Reed. 3H74-76. Printed in *Pa. Archives*, VIII, 743-44.]

Instructions received to detach artillery and part of his small force for Clark's expedition, "who I am told is to drive all before him, by a supposed unbounded influence he has amongst the Inhabitants of the Western country." Informs Reed in confidence that he can afford little protection with such a dimished force. Artillery will never return. Depredations of Indians have already begun. Pennsylvania raising men for frontier, asks if they are to be under his command. The boundary line should be settled. Requests leave of absence.

DELAWARES BREAK ALLIANCE

[Rev. John Heckewelder to Col. Daniel Brodhead. 51J29. A. L. S.][2]

SALEM February 26th 1781

DEAR SIR:

I have received your kind favor of January 4th by which I saw the small present from my Wife was accepted of. I have likewise received the Almanack, & we all are greatly indebted to you for your kindness but my Wife in particular returns you thanks for what you sent to her,

In Killbucks letter you will find the true state of the People of Coochockung, I could never learn what they were properly about, for they kept theer matters very Secret—Now it is almost pub-

[1] See Col. Daniel Brodhead's letter to Gen. George Rogers Clark, dated Feb. 24, 1781, printed in *Ill. Hist. Colls.*, VIII, 509.
[2] This letter and the following one are printed in *Pa. Archives*, VIII, 769-70. The present printing is from the originals in the Draper Mss.

lickly known, that they are about no good business, & have been very busy in trying to decieve you this long time they have, as I am informed, also told lies of Us brethren, I must wonder at their stupidity but let me see, I think Killbuck, acquaints you of almost the same matter they Acuse'd Us as a chief arrant they themselves are on, therefore I apprehend they will find themselves in the trap at last

I indeed believe that the greatest part of them will be upon you in a few days, they have already been stop'd once or twice, but I daily hear they will go soon, they have ranged themselves into three partys, & if I am right one party is gone of already but I hope they will recieve what they deserve

As I understand the Councellors are to be here in a day or two, to have some letters read, brought by Saml Evans, I am determined to Unmask their faces and declare Unto them never to write a single Syllable for them any more—

Since my last letter to you I found that it was an impossibility for Killbuck to lay hold of bawbee in this part of the Country, for had he offere'd to have touched him he probably would have lost his life

Killbuck & Monture are those whom bawbee threatens to kill on account of his being imprisoned. Almost every body that comes here from Coochockung says that he utters the most horrid threats against these two persons, & it is apprehended, that if he cannot find an Opportunity to commit his design on the former, some of his Friends will have to pay for it

The Councel of Coochockung, have also been very busy, as it appears, to blacken the Character of Killbuck this proceeds from different reasons, of which I believe one to be that Killbuck is a Friend to the States, which they themselves are not, as it really now appears by their own Actions

Jno Monture has been no further than this place where he has had an opportunity of hearing what is passing, he will be able to give you a full account of all what is mentioned in Killbucks letter and more besides, I cannot think otherwise of either of those two, than that they are true to states—

As I understand, that you intend to go soon [down] the Country I have wrote a letter to the Rev^d [Mr.] Mathews at Litiz, directed to Mr Wm Henry Esqr Lan[caster] which I beg the favor of you to take to your Care Should it be concluded, on that a body of Men Shall march to Coochockung to punish these wicked People

I trust that your honor will do all that lies in your power to prevent mislesting any body belonging to our Towns, and you may depend Sir, that in case any of your Men should have occasion to come by any of our Towns, that they would meet with much kindness from our People.
I am with great respect Dear Sir, Your most Obed^t hu^l Servt
JN° HACKENWELDER
P. S. My best Compliments to all officers & Friends—

[Captain Killbuck to Col. Daniel Brodhead. 51J28. In handwriting of Heckewelder.]

SALEM February 26, 1781
Col. Henry to Mahingwo Geeshuch as follows
BROTHER MAGHINGWO GEESHUCH listen to me:
I have received yours of the 4th Instant, by which I see that some misunderstandings have rose between Us, which is partly derived from a speech brought to me Under your name which I now find to be a speech from Capt Thomson
Brother: I am not willing that our Friendship should be broke or disturbed in the least neither do I think, that if Friendship is settled on a good foundation it is to be easily overthrown, therefore have patience a few days longer, and I will be with you, when We will settle all these matters again.—
Now *Brother:* I have some other matters to acquaint You of, which I think needs your attention, more than the above mentioned, You know I told you when I cam away, that I should go no further than the Brethren Towns, I have been here all this time, The Council of Coochocking, have entirely stop'd my ears so that I know nothing—But Brother, a bird has whispered something in my Ear, & this I will acquaint you of, Viz, some days ago a Mingoe came to Coochocking, & received a speech from the Council there which made him go home laughing, The speech was to this purpose. Viz. I am your Friends and on your Side, and only wait to see what you are about, and then shall join you. There is none of Us here who think of being Friends to the Virginians, there is one Man who is a Friend to them, namely Calaylemont further Tatepawkshe and Mawquot are gone with a speech to the Wyondotts, to make up that matter which happene'd

last spring, namely when one of our Men, went with several of yours, & took two of their Weomen, at Saandusky Prisoners. Again every body here now knows, that the Coochockung Men are getting ready to go to fight you, & a party of five are gone off already, the Course they took was towards Wheeling, Three of these Warriors are Wm Penns near relations & one a Friend to White Eyes Cousin, & the Capt of the party is Jn° Lewis's Brother—Again a party of 5 of which Mouse Knife was Capt are come from War, and have brought with them the Scalp of one old Man and one Child, Again I heard some days ago that a pretty large party of Wyondotts was gone of towards fort—pitt, Again I hear 3 partys of Wingemunds Men are gone to War, likewise other small partys from the Shawnese Town but all Warriors are ordered in, in a very short time, for immediately at the Change of this Moon (that is the appearance of the next Moon) all Warriors are to be in one body, with all the English that are at Detroit, These are first to destroy all the Delawares that are Friends to the states, & then to proceed further to Beaver, & Fort Pitt the latter Account I communicate to you as I heard it, the former accounts you may depend on to be true—

Now *Brother:* This letter I send you, by Monture as soon as I see those Men here from Coochochung, which I have sent for, I will set of with them for Pittsburgh—

I am your Friend & Brother

COL. HENRY

COLL BRODHEAD COMMANDANT—

CLARK'S EXPEDITION ENDORSED

[Gen. George Washington to Col. Daniel Brodhead. Washington Papers. Draft.]

HEAD QUARTERS NEW WINDSOR 28th Feby 1781

DEAR SIR:

Your favor of the 23^d ult° reached me the 23^d instant. I cannot but regret that the irregular supply of provision still continues in your quarter, and I am sorry that the prohibitory laws of particular States should add to the difficulties; but it is not for me to interfere in cases of that kind.

FRONTIER RETREAT   341

The provision purchasing for Col° Clarke is for a very essential purpose—you have, I imagine been before this time informed of the object, by the receipt of a letter from me of the 29th Decem^r sent under cover to the Governor of Virginia to be delivered to you by Col° Clarke himself, or some person deputed by him. I make no doubt but you complied as fully as was in your power with the requisitions contained in that letter, as the least hesitation may have frustrated an enteprize of the highest importance to the peace and safety of the whole Western Frontier. I should have been glad, had it been in my power to have furnished you with a continental force sufficient to have carried on the expedition which Col° Clarke has in contemplation, with any tolerable probability of success, but the southern War is such a drain for our troops, that we shall with the greatest difficulty be enabled to spare bare Garrisons for our Frontier posts. If the English at Detroit were planning an attack upon Fort Pitt—Col° Clarke's expedition should be favoured and forwarded as much as possible, as the most likely method of counteracting them and obliging them to turn their view to the defensive.

I have no objection to your coming down the Country to represent the state of affairs to the Westward and to look after your private affairs, provided you leave a good Officer in command. Should my letter of the 29th Decem^r not have reached you, when you come away, you will leave the most pointed orders with the officer in command to comply strictly with the terms of it.

I am &c
COL° BRODHEAD.

MESSAGE OF CONGRESS TO DELAWARES

[Col. Daniel Brodhead to Delaware chiefs. 2H83–84. Letter Book.]

FORT PITT March 1. 1781

Mahingweegeesuch to Wm Penn & others the Delaware Council at Coochocking—
BROTHERS listen to me:
Sometime ago I wrote to the great Council of America & told them that some of their Delaware Friends wanted to see them & now you will hear what they say to the whole world about you,

the Small paper you find enclosed in this letter contains what they say[1]

Brothers: I likewise told them that our Friends were poor & I had nothing to give them; now it is enough the Honbl[e] Congress say that all those who join heartily against the Enemy shall not want. this shews how much they love you, & how much you should do for them as well 'as for yourselves

Brothers: Not only your American Brethren have heard that you have declared war against the Senecas but also your fathers the French & Spaniards likewise know it. Now Brothers be strong & dont disappoint them nor dishonor your nation

Brothers: I desire you will let me know how soon you will be ready & how many of you want to go down to Philad[a] you have seen what pains hath been taken with your boys that are at school & how well they are instructed. Now Brothers I recommend to you to take two or three other Boys that belong to some of you & have them likewise educated, this will make your nation wise & happy

I am your Friend & Brother

PUNISHMENT FOR DELAWARES

[Col. Daniel Brodhead to Col. David Shepherd. 2SS1. L. S.][2]

HEAD QUARTERS, FORT PITT March 8, 1781

DEAR SIR:

I have just received letters, by Cap[t] Monture, which inform me, that the Delawares of Coochockung, very few excepte'd,

[1] On Jan. 8, 1781, the following resolutions were passed: "*Resolved,* That Colonel Broadhead be informed, that it will be agreeable to Congress to receive the visit proposed to be made to them by some of the friendly Delaware Indians in the spring, as mentioned in his letter of the 7th of last month to the Board of War:

That Colonel Broadhead be also informed, that Congress will support, as far as their abilities will permit, such of the Indians of the Delaware tribe, as shall voluntarily engage in the service of the United States against the common enemy." *Jour. of Cont. Cong.,* XIX. 33. This resolution was later revoked. See *post,* 347–48.

[2] There is a similar letter to Col. Joseph Beeler, dated Mar. 4, 1781, in Brodhead's Letter Book. Draper Mss., 3H76–79.

have declare'd in favor of the British, and that some of them are already come against our Settlements.

I believe this intelligence to be Authentic, and that we shall now experience, what I have long strove to avoid, a general war with the Savages—

If We have any Friends amongst them besides the Moravian Indians, I expect they will be with us in a few days, & that they will be useful.

My force being much reduce'd, I cannot extend the protection I could wish to every part of the Frontier, but so far as I am enable'd, I am as Usual determine'd to give every Countenance to the Inhabitants—

Although it is to be wished that our endeavours to raise Supplies within this department, might not be interrupte'd, yet at this Crisis, it is highly expedient, that those Inhabitants who live in places of security should step forward, & lend immediate aid to the Frontier—

I have in contemplation an enterprize, against the deceitful Delawares, at and near Coochockung, but am much at a loss for supplies, therefore have thought it advisable that the County Lieutenants, & such commanding Officers of Battallions, as may be desirous of giving their attendance, do assemble at my Quarters on the 15th Instant at ten OClock in the forenoon, in order to deliberate upon ways and means to obtain supplies for an expedition, and to form some Suitable plan or plans, for the security of the Inhabitants[1]—

In the mean time encourage the Frontier Inhabitants to make a stand by collecting, into Forts or strong Houses, & by ranging in sufficient parties with great Vigilen[ce] & industry, & let all the Militia in your County be in readiness to repel an invasion—

Capt Monture was chased by Eight Indian Warriors & with difficulty, escaped to Fort McIntosh

I have the honor to be with great respect Dear Sir your most Obed^t Servt

DANIEL BRODHEAD Col^o command^g W. D.

COLO DAVID SHEPHERD Circular

[1] A letter from Col. Daniel Brodhead, Mar. [5], 1781, to Gen. George Rogers Clark, requesting the latter's presence at the officers' council on March 15 is printed in *Ill. Hist. Colls.*, VIII, 510.

[George McColloch, receipt to Capt. Benjamin Biggs. 5NN8. A. D. S.]

FORT HENRY, 8th March 1781.
Rec'ed of Benjamin Biggs (Capt) of the 9th Virginia Regiment four Bushels and four Quarts of Salt which was lodged in the Publick Store

GEORGE M^{c}COLLOCH, D: C: P.

CONDITIONS AT FORT PITT

[Col. Daniel Brodhead to Gen. George Washington. 3H81–83. Transcript of Letter Book.]

FORT PITT, March 10th 1781.

DEAR GENERAL:

I beg your Excell$^{y's}$ pardon for not returning the rank of the Maryland officers in my last—I have this moment got Captn Heth's, & shall enclose them together.

By letters lately rec^d from the Moravian Indian towns, it appears that we have lost the interest of the Coochocking Indians, & by what I have heard from Brig^r Clark it is more than probable we shall have a general war with the savages. I take the liberty to enclose copies of the letters above mentioned.

Mr Wilson has delivered 28 head of cattle at this post, which he informs me is all he can procure.

The troops under my command have been at half allowance of meat ever since the 26th of Dec^r, & frequently both before & since without any for several days together. Should the enemy be as active as is expected these out-posts cannot be maintained without sufficient magazines of salt provisions. I therefore entreat your Exll^y to order an immediate supply of that article to be forwarded from the interior country, as it cannot be procured on this side the mountains.

Brig^r Clark was kind enough to make me a visit, & I am sorry to inform your Excell^y that he is doubtful of receiving timely support for his enterprize. He understands your instructions to me in an unlimited sense, & has demanded considerable quanties of Q. M. stores, which I have ordered to be delivered; but as I conceive the same instructions to be limited to the articles therein mentioned I shall be happy to know whether it is your intention to permit a compliance with any order he may think proper to draw on the store-keeper.

I am informed that sometime last fall Col° de La Balme undertook an enterprize against one of the Miami Towns, aided by some of the inhabitants from the Illinois; that he surprized the town & took one hundred horse loads of plunder, but was soon pursued by the savages, & himself & thirty odd of his party were killed, & all his horses & plunder re-taken.

I have the honor to be, &c,

D. B.

HIS EXCELL^Y GEN^L WASHINGTON.

[Col. Daniel Brodhead to Samuel Huntington. 3H83–85. Transcript of Letter Book.]

FORT PITT, March 10th 1781.

SIR:

On the 20th ult I had the honor to receive your favor of the 12th of Jany enclosing an act of the Honb^{le} Congress respecting the the friendly Delaware Indians.

I took the earliest opportunity to communicate their pleasure to the Delaware Council as a means of securing their neutrality if not their interest, but by letters I have just rec^d by Captn Montour I am apprehensive it is too late, & we may now expect a general Indian war. I take the liberty to enclose copies of the letters rec^d by Captn Montour, and a copy of my letter to the Council.

I think it probable that a few of the Delawares may yet remain in our interest, provided they are well supplied; & if a few of the Oneida or Stockbridge Indians[1] could be sent to this place, the

[1] The one branch of the Iroquois or Six Nations which during the Revolution maintained an alliance with the Americans was the Oneida tribe. This was due in large measure to the influence of their missionary, Rev. Samuel Kirkland. Surrounded by British Indians, the situation of the Oneida grew so dangerous that they were removed to the neighborhood of Schenectady, where throughout the war they furnished spies and scouts for the border service. After the Revolution they returned to their early home in central New York whence in the third decade of the nineteenth century the entire tribe removed to Wisconsin where its members now live. The Stockbridges emigrated to this State about the same time. They are the remnant of a Mahican band, whose early home was in the Berkshire Hills of western Massachusetts. They, like the Oneida, aided the Americans during the Revolution.

address would make a material change in the councils of the western tribes; but they ought to come in good clothing.

The Indian Captains complain for want of clothing, & as they may be influenced by their tribe to join against us, it would be good policy to make it their interest to remain with [us] by affording them genteel clothing.

If it is possible to procure about one hundred match coats, some stroud for breech-clouts & leggins, & some paint, I should be happy to have them, as those articles would enable me to encourage partizan strokes, which with my present force is all that can prudently be attempted.

I have the honor, &c.

D. B.

His Excell^y S. Huntinton, Esqr.

[Col. Daniel Brodhead to Richard Peters. 3H80–81. Transcript of Letter Book.]

Fort Pitt, March 10th 1781.

Dear Sir:

I have done myself the honor to address a few lines to his Excell^y the President of Congress, & have inclosed to him copies of two letters lately rec^d from the Moravian Indian towns, the contents of which will doubtless be communicated to you, & you will thereby learn that the present temper of the Coochocking Indians is very unfavorable towards us; indeed I have other reasons to apprehend that we must now prepare for a gen^l Indian War.

My force is greatly reduced by detachments ordered to the Southward, & under the command of Brigad^r Clark to the westward so that [not much] can be expected from me, until I receive a re-inforcement from below; for in the present unsettled state of jurisdiction the militia cannot be called to aid me, nor could they be subsisted until we are better supplied.

I wish to annoy the enemy by encouraging partizan strokes, but I have nothing to offer as a reward, nor have I a match-coat, breech clout, leggin, or grain of paint, to equip the parties—& without these they can not pass into the Indian country.

I have the honor, &c.

D. B.

Honb^{le} Richd Peters, Esqr.

[Summary of a letter of Col. Daniel Brodhead, Fort Pitt, Mar. 10, 1781, to Pres. Joseph Reed. 3H85–88. Printed in *Pa. Archives*, VIII, 766–67.]

Letters from Moravians convince him of the imminence of a general Indian war. Has instructions to send Maryland corps to Richmond, and to detach artillery and troops for General Clark. Reenforcements necessary. Westmoreland remiss in furnishing militia; requests authority over them if called out. Alarming apprehensions in Kentucky. La Balme's party defeated. A few Oneida or Stockbridge Indians might effect a change in councils of Western Indians, if their message could be accompanied by some match-coats, paint, and strouding. Clark and his plans; shall not be surprised to see them fail. "It is clear to me that wise men at a great distance view things in the Western country very differently from those who are more intimately acquainted with circumstances and situation." Leave of absence requested.

[Summary of Board of War's report to Congress, Mar. 15, 1781. Printed in *Jour. of Cont. Cong.*, XIX, 279–82.]

Brodhead's letter of February 18 referred by Congress to Board or War "to report a state of the Western Department." Supplies extremely deficient, garrison of Fort Pitt and dependencies subsisted precariously for twelve months; distress so great there is danger of posts being abandoned. Colonel Blaine's responsibility. Brodhead has taken every measure to gain supplies, has been reduced to the expedient of sending a party to kill buffaloes; evidence of distress, rather than a hope of material aid. Offensive operations prevented by scarcity of provisions. Garrison consists of parts of two regiments, a detachment of artillery and some independent companies; recommends that an entire regiment be stationed at Fort Pitt, and these two disjointed commands be ordered down. Ruinous condition of Fort Pitt; Fort McIntosh well constructed, could not resist an attack for lack of supplies. Enemy Indians to the westward at first not more than 300, Delawares and Shawnee being much divided; have now an accession of strength from northern tribes, and unless some measures are taken to supply the neutrals, necessity will cause all to join British. Commandant should act as Indian agent. In present state of finances, imprudent to make large promises. Coshocton Delawares always friendly; visit of chiefs to Congress in 1778 [1779]; children now at Princeton. They proposed a new visit to which Congress agreed; will be expensive and dangerous to Indians because of frontier enmity. Strong escort needed on former visit; best to send presents to Fort Pitt, and obviate need of Indians coming to Philadelphia. Fort and garrison at Coshocton impracticable. Resolutions proposed: executive of Pennsylvania requested to place at Fort Pitt supplies for six months for a complete regiment of 612 properly officered; commandant to be directed to repair fortifications of Fort Pitt; commandant to act as Indian agent; money to be appropriated for Indian goods; expediency of visit of Coshocton Indians to be referred to Board of War, notwithstanding resolution of January 4 [8], 1781; commander in chief to draw the Western corps together as much as possible; Colonel Brodhead to be informed it is inexpedient to comply with the request of Indians in letter of January 13, 1781.

PREPARATIONS FOR EXPEDITION AGAINST DELAWARES

[Col. Daniel Brodhead to Col. David Shepherd. 2SS3. L. S.][1]

HEAD QUARTERS FORT PITT March 16th 1781
DEAR SIR:

You are requested to procure sixty—men including Officers from the Militia, to go upon an Expedition, both Officers & men must be furnished with at least Twenty Days provisions, each a Good Horse, Saddle & Bridle, & they are to be well armed & accoutred & to rendezvous at Fort Henry (Wheeling) on the fifth Day of next month—

Thirty Horses, Saddles & Bridles will likewise be necessary from your County to enable me to take out a part of the Regular Troops. The provisions & any unavoidable loss of Horses & Furniture will be paid by the publick—

You will be pleased to let me know by the first of next Month whether this requisition can be complied with. I hope there cannot be any Difficulty respecting it but our Force must be ascertained

---

[1] Similar letters were sent to the other county lieutenants of the vicinity naming different quotas of militia. That to Col. Archibald Lochry requests a levy of a hundred men from Westmoreland County. Draper Mss., 3H88–89.

FRONTIER RETREAT

to prevent the Expedition falling thro' to the Discouragement of the Inhabitants.

I am with great respect & esteem Dear Sir your most obed^t Servt

DANIEL BRODHEAD Col^o command^g W. D.

COL^o D. SHEPHERD.

[Col. Daniel Brodhead to Col. David Shepherd. 2SS5. A. L. S.]

HEAD QU^{RS} FORT PITT March 16th 1781.

SIR:

You are hereby requested to procure by subscription or otherwise three thousand weight of Beef pork or bacon for the use of the Regular Troops intended to be employed on an Expedition.

I am yours &c

DANIEL BRODHEAD COL^o command^g W. D.

COL^o D. SHEPHERD

WESTMORELAND TROOPS

[Summary of a letter of Pres. Joseph Reed, Mar. 17, 1781, to David Duncan. Printed in *Pa. Archives*, IX, 17.]

Has appointed him commissioner of purchases for Westmoreland. Limitation of amounts. Directs him to apply to late commissary, Perry, for effects.

[Summary of a letter of Pres. Joseph Reed, Mar. 17, 1781, to Col. Archibald Lochry. Printed in *ibid.*, 18.]

Authorizes him to raise a corps of fifty volunteers for four months; hopes ranging company already voted will be raised in early summer. Lochry is to dispose these troops to best advantage; new commissary will supply them. Accounts of expenditures; troops must be kept in active service.

TROOPS FOR CLARK

[Gen. George Rogers Clark to Col. David Shepherd. 2SS7. A. L. S.][1]

Sir:
         Crossings March 18th 1781[2]

I have been in hopes of Seeing you before this and am apprehensive my last letters never Reached you it now begins to be true that we should prepare our men for the Campaign, as I Could wish to set out as soon as possible at least to know our Strength Amediately the Shawonees Delawares and Sandusky Towns is our object

I expect one fourth of your Militia its left to yourself as to the mode of Raising them Either by Draft or Volunteers. Send me a return of the whole in as Short a time as possible the men are to serve during the Camp^n and no longer to Receive the same pay as other Troops the advantages of plunder & the fair prospect of Routing the Savages must be so pleasing to Every person that I have no doubt of a number of Volunteers Ingaging the defitiency must be made up by Draft I dont propose the men should Imbody untill we are Ready to set out except you want some of them to defend your frontier They draw pay from the time of their Ingagements be pleased to keep up a Constant Correspondence with me Mr Chaplin [Abraham Chapline] is in my imploy and will assist you

   I am D^r Co^l y^r Hl Servt
        G R Clark B G Co W. D. Virginia
Col. David Sheppard

OUTPOSTS WARNED

[Col. Daniel Brodhead to Capt. Uriah Springer. 3H91. Transcript of Letter Book.]

         Fort Pitt, March 19th, 1781.
Dear Sir:

I have rec^d your favor, & you are at liberty to come to this post after leaving proper instructions to Lieut. Thomas.

[1] See other letters of General Clark, dated Mar. 18–21, 1781, printed in *Ill. Hist. Colls.*, VIII, 511–15.

[2] This letter was written at Stewart's Crossings on the Monongahela, the site of the residence of Col. William Crawford.

I have received intelligence that an attempt will be made on your post by some Indians who will come under pretence of friendship to deceive. For this reason none are to enter the fort until it appears that they have no arms secreted under match-coats, &c.—In coming consult your own safety, & believe me to be with regard, &c.

D. B.

CAPT^N U. SPRINGER.

[Col. Daniel Brodhead to Capt. Benjamin Biggs. 3H92. Transcript of Letter Book.]

HEAD QR^s, FORT PITT, March 20th 1781.

SIR:

I have heard that the Indians intend to make an attempt on your post, & I believe the report to be true. You will, therefore, have the fort put in the best posture of defence, keep out a couple of active spies near the river & have all your garrison ready for action.

Any of the inhabitants who live near the post, & are willing to move into it must be encouraged.—

I am &c

D. B.

CAPT^N BENJ^N BIGGS.

TROOPS FOR CLARK

[Summary of a letter of Gen. George Rogers Clark, Crossings, Mar. 23, 1781, to Capt. Isaac Craig. 27CC30. Printed in *Ill. Hist. Colls.*, VIII, 515–16.]

Approves of Craig's going East to secure additional stores; Washington will aid; additional artificers and artillerymen advisable. Brodhead's approval. Return by May 1.

[Summary of a letter of Gen. George Rogers Clark, Mar. 23, 1781, to Pres. Joseph Reed. Printed in *Pa. Archives*, IX, 23–24.]

Doubtless Reed knows of his enterprise; hopes to visit Shawnee, Delaware, and Sandusky towns. Many western Pennsylvanians would join his forces but fear the disapproval of state authorities. Requests permission to enlist 500 men.

COMMAND OF WESTMORELAND TROOPS.

[Summary of a letter of Pres. Joseph Reed, Mar. 26, 1781, to Col. Archibald Lochry. Printed in *ibid.*, 28.]

Troops raised for Westmoreland defense are to be placed under Lochry's direction. Must not permit them to stay about Hannastown. During offensive operations Brodhead is to have command, not at other times.

LOYALISTS AND INDIANS NEAR FORT PITT

[Col. Daniel Brodhead to Gen. George Washington. 3H92–95. Transcript of Letter Book.][1]

FORT PITT, March 27th 1781.

DEAR GENERAL:

I am honored with your favor of the 28th ult. & am thankful for the contents.

I have acknowledged the receipt of your letter of the 29th of December, & shall give every encouragement to Gen¹ Clarke's intended enterprize. I wish he may be in readiness before the waters fail, & the Kentucke settlements are destroyed by the enemy, but I am informed that little or nothing has been done as yet at his boat-yards, & that the militia that he expected from this side the mountain are availing themselves of the unsettled jurisdiction.

Since my last a small paper was brought to me by some faithful Indians who found it neatly rolled up in a powder horn which a disaffected person had lost near the waters of Sandusky. I take the liberty to enclose a copy of it.[2] I have discovered the writer & put him in irons, but as too probably some of the garrison are concerned he may escape before he meets the reward of his de-

---

[1] This letter is printed also in Sparks, *Corr. Amer. Rev.*, III, 273–74.
[2] See letter dated Pittsburgh, Jan. 21, 1781, signed "Thomas Girty," but sent by Myndert Fisher, *post*, 491.

merit. Indeed this place is infested with such a set of disaffected inhabitants that I have been under the necessity of ordering some away, and others must soon follow to prevent greater injury to the service.

A number of Delaware Indians from Coochocking have been here since my last, & appear to be as friendly as ever. I am persuaded that a few are well affected, but they are now put to the trial by being ordered to remove hither without loss of time, & remain under our protection where their daily transactions will be seen & known.

I have called upon the County Lieuts. for a few of the militia, & if I am not disappointed as usual intend to surprize the Indian towns about Coochocking. Two Delaware Indians who in their cups spoke contemptuously of our service, I have confined in irons; but I am at a loss what farther to do with them until I see what number joins us, & hear what their general conduct has been.

Immediately after the termination of the intended excursion I will avail myself of your indulgence to represent the state of things in the District.

I have the honor, &c

D. B.

P. S.—By the arrangement it appears that Captn Brady is arranged into the 3^d Pen^a Reg^t, but as he cannot be more useful than he is in this part of the country, I hope he will be permitted to remain until the campaign is closed.

HIS EXCELL^y GEN^L WASHINGTON.

[Col. Daniel Brodhead to Richard Peters. 3H95. Transcript of Letter Book.]

FORT PITT, March 27th 1781.

DEAR SIR:

I take the liberty to enclose an extract of a letter I have just done myself the honor. to address to his Excell^y the Commander-in-Chief; it contains all the intelligence I have worthy your notice that I recollect.

Captn Craig will have the honor, & he is capable of answering most questions that may be put respecting this Department;

wherefore I beg leave to refer you to him for any circumstances I may have omitted.

Hon. Rh^d Peters, Esq.

D. B.

GARRISONS FOR ALLEGHENY POSTS

[Summary of a letter of Col. Daniel Brodhead, Fort Pitt, Mar, 27, 1781, to Pres. Joseph Reed. 3H95–96. Printed in *Pa. Archives*, IX, 39.]

In present circumstances impossible to garrison Fort Armstrong and Fort Crawford, until commander in chief gives directions to evacuate Fort McIntosh. Captain Brady is out on a scout; expects he will fall in with some Indian parties.

GREENBRIER RAIDED

[Col. Andrew Donnally[1] to Gov. Thomas Jefferson. 10S214. Transcript.]

Greenbriar, 27th March, 1781.

Sir:

On the 3^d instant a party of Indians came to the house of William Meek, living at the mouth of Indian Creek, which empties into New River, in this county, & took him and his family prisoners, & burnt his house and corn. A party of men belonging to Capt. Wood's company happened to be rendezvoused in the neighborhood, in order to march to join the troops who are to serve under Gen. Clark; these with some of the neighbors pursued the Indians, & after a continued march of near fifty miles they came up with them, killed one Indian, & wounded several, recovered all the prisoners and the plunder. By the prisoners we learn that there were eight Indians & two Canadian French in that party; & they told them (the prisoners) that another party of twelve more was to join them at that place where our men providentially defeated them. Lieut. Woods who commanded

[1] For a sketch of Col. Andrew Donnally see *Rev. Upper Ohio*, 183, note 17. See also *Wis. Hist. Colls.*, XXIII, *passim*.

our party deserves all praise for his spirited behavior & activity on this occasion, & I cannot forbear remarking that had it not been that these men happened to be so critically embodied at that juncture, that in all probability those unhappy people would have been carried into captivity by those merciless savages.* * *

ANDREW DONNALLY.

[Reminiscences of Rev. James Haynes.[1] 30S158-59.]

Wm Meek lived on Indian Creek about 4 miles from its mouth—opposite to which was Culbertson's Bottom—with his wife & children & mother, all taken prisoners by a party of eight Indians, on the 3^d of March, 1781. (Mr Haynes recollects the date from an old song about it) Capt. John Wood raised a party of some 10 men—among them James Elliston,[2] David Frazier—in the settlement & went in pursuit. Two men were [to] meet the party at the mouth of Big Blue Stone, with a canoe with which for the party to cross. When the two men reached the mouth of Blue Stone, they espied the Indians about making a raft—the men, undiscovered, crept ashore & hid themselves—after a little the Indians happened to see the canoe, availed themselves of it & crossed the river—New River there—the two men thought it imprudent to fire upon the Indians & kept out of sight—soon Capt. Wood came up with his party—constructed a raft & crossed—followed on the trail, discovered over night that they were close upon them —next morning very foggy, came upon the Indian camp, could see the fires at a distance—fired upon the Indians, killed one—the others fled—one, however, turned & in the act of firing at Capt. Wood he dodged as the gun flashed & escaped. All the prisoners were thus rescued. Where this rescue occurred, was near the head of Paint Creek, in the now County of Fayette.

[1] Rev. James Haynes was born Feb. 4, 1760, probably in Virginia. In the autumn of 1779 he visited Kentucky, where he remained about one year, returning in time to join the Virginia forces under Lafayette. Haynes made his home in Greenbrier County until 1790 when he removed to Tennessee, where near Paris in Henry County, about the year, 1843, he gave these recollections to Dr. Draper. The accuracy of Haynes' memory is attested by the marked correspondence of the details he narrated with those given in the contemporary document.

[2] James Ellison was captured in the autumn of 1781 near Blue Stone River by a party of three Indians, but succeeded in escaping after a short captivity. Draper Mss., 30S160.

BRODHEAD ACCUSED

[Alexander Fowler to Pres. Joseph Reed. Washington Papers. Contemporary transcript.]

PITTSBURGH 29 March 1781

SIR:

As a public servant and a citizen of the United States whose greatest ambition is to see them prosper, I can no longer remain silent. Indeed I think I should be undeserving of the trust reposed in me were I not to be explicit. For the indolence of public servants and the enormity of public abuses becomes more and more obvious

We are here Sir reduced to a contemptible situation and I am afraid we shall soon appear in a disgraceful one. For discipline is not only relaxed but totally neglected and private interest shamefully predominates over public œconomy. The indians and quarter masters who are equally objects of the people's jealousy and aversion are equally indulged here from motives mean and unwarrantable. An indian trade is carried on in this department on principles hitherto unknown to even our enemies in their lost and corrupt state. Under the auspices of our Commandant his harlot purchases furs and peltries from the savages which are paid for with liquor, salt &c from the commissaries store and sold for cash: and though this trade must be allowed to be snug, safe and profitable yet it is degrading, is unworthy of imitation and ought to be reprobated.

At the head of the quartermaster's department we have a grovelling ignorant man; but as he is servile and knowing and an adept in taking advantages in jobbing & making bargains, he appears to be principal confidant. While *David* can catch an advantageous private bargain *Daniel* can smile at public calamity. And while the people are complaining and almost ready to revolt, both can fatten on their distresses. These gents Sir are largely concerned in the land jobbing way. Their views and connections extend far and near and however unbecoming such conduct may be particularly by men who have public money to account for nothing else seems attended to. Indians have not only been countenanced but public criminals screened through base and interested motives. Hence Congress have been misled. With all due respect to that honorable body while they were bestowing commissions on savages the state of Pensylvania judged right by offering a bounty for their scalps.

Colonel Broadhead has not only rendered himself universally obnoxious to the people but also to many of his officers, who have refused for these twelve months past to dine or associate with him on account of his conduct, and what was then deemed only a suspicion is now rendered a fact. Nay some of his officers have charged him with *sporting with public money* and tho' he has on the one hand treated them with indignity they have on the other applied for a court of enquiry but nothing is done The officers are eager for a hearing and the commandant seems to sit silent under the reproach.

To enumerate to your excellency all the abuses & grievances here would be an endless task, I shall however endeavour to point out a few of them and their causes

Respecting commanding officers their expences are at present unlimited. By the single dash of a pen a commandant can make all fly before him. Thus the public stores are made not only subservient to his will, but caterers to his passions. By which means the safety and happiness of a country depends on individuals. False and destructive policy. In the british serv. Sir, there are many abuses, yet nothing of this kind can arise. With respect to the quarter masters department, it is a ruinous & destructive one. For having neither check nor controul of any kind they are enabled to ship the public at pleasure and make just what sum of money they deem necessary. Our Assistant D Q Master Mr *Duncan* tho' he can scarce write his name can employ just as many teams, artificers, labourers and workmen of all kinds as he thinks fit not for the benefit of the public, but the benefit of *he* that employs them, for the benefit of the very scum of America who seem to be destitute of all kind of knowledge as well as principle but that of amassing wealth. The Assistant Q^r Master has his farms, his assistants have theirs and for aught I know some of his waggoners, where their horses are employed in the summer season; and in the winter when agriculture is at an end and teams can do little from the shortness of the days and the depth of the roads, they are whipped into the public service, and while they are fattened and made sleek at public expence the poor continental horses are left to gnaw their hoofs & die in ditches. Public waggons, public geers and public artificers are employed for the private emolument of these men. Here your excellency may behold a public carpenter employed in mending & repairing the quarter masters waggons, for the use of which waggons he charges the public a high price. And the public blacksmith shoeing his horses making and repairing his plough irons as well as all kind of husbandry utensils, while many of the soldiery are employed in clearing his lands. Not only his land is cleared but houses are repaired & built and he puts what price he pleases on his timber. Even an artificer (a destructive bee of the quarter master's hive) has built a dwelling house with other conveniencies in the face of the garrison while he and his wasps were receiving high pay from the public & I believe double rations. And such hirelings as these shall even have their hirelings put on pay and rations by an assistant to a D Q Master and employed on their farms for weeks I believe I may say months together. So that every species of abuse and low peculation is practised that the art of man can invent. And while such public nuisances as these can not only supply themselves but their creatures & connections with every necessary and convenience, many who are entitled to attention from those gentry by resolutions of Congress are totally neglected. The abusers of public confidence, may it please your Excellency, are linked together in a chain of iniquity. One delinquent makes many until they are encreased without end. And indeed, Sir, I have often observed in my Rubbs through life that mean abilities are often attended with craft and he that knows nothing else knows how to be cunning So that besides *An Auditor of Accounts an inspector of abuses is necessary in this department.*

Your excellency will readily ask how such barefaced abuses can possibly arise without the knowledge of the Commandant ? How can an assistant to a D Q Master and his assistants employ their own teams in the face of a resolution of Congress ? Is it not the duty of a commanding officer to be as careful of public property as his own ? For my own part, Sir, I have ever thought so and that there cannot be a greater mark of virtue in a public servant than public œconomy. But when a commanding officer & an assistant D Q M become conjoint & connected it answers all these questions. It explains the whole & leaves nothing a mystery. The interest of the one becomes the interest of the other, and the interest of the public seems never to come under the consideration of either. With such public servants a country cannot prosper unless they are bitted [an]d bridled like untamed colts.

To remove the abuses enumerated and prevent them in future I beg leave to offer to your excellency the following hints.

Relieve the commandant and discharge the quartermaster. Indeed we can only act defensively in this quarter. And if a proper defensive plan was adopted, which is the only plan that can be adopted, that can either afford security or protection to the people the whole hive of wasps might be discharged and the public stores delivered to the care of capt Ferrel deputy field commissary who is a gentleman and worthy of trust; and all artificers that may be found absolutely necessary for the public service to be employd by the said field commissary & to be under his directions, by which means much treasure will be saved to the public.

Officers who are entitled to horses to find their own horses as well as forage & to be paid for the latter. This is very practicable here & I make no doubt but the officers, those expected that are connected with the quartermaster, would be better satisfied than in the manner they are now supplied

The fire wood necessary for the department to be found by contract which I am convinced I could have done here at one fourth the present expense.

Public stores and public money to be held sacred and by all means to fix an allowance for commanding officers

The above remedies on trial would I am convinced be found specific ones. But if it may be thought necessary that an assistant to a D Q Master and a swarm of his leeches are to be continued here I would beg leave to recommend such for that employment as have no farms in the neighbourhood and that his accounts should be audited on the spot; and for the benefit of the public I will with pleasure if agreeable take that trouble upon myself & report to the respective auditors. I can assure your excellency that these gentry are so accustomed to low cunning that they are not at a loss in putting a gloss of Justice and authenticity on the face of their accounts by well arranged vouchers, solemn affidavits and I know not what else besides which must naturally be admitted below and can only be detected here. I have many things in my eye which I cannot communicate to your excellency and which cannot be discovered by the most discerning & circumspect without he is on the spot. As I conceive it to be the duty of every honest public servant to detect abuses as well as give information thereof to those who may have it in their power to correct & prevent them I have thought it mine to

trouble your excellency with this letter which exhibits an un-
exaggerated detail of the disorders in the west and in doing so I
hope I shall not be by the virtuous & patriotic deemed officious.
They are of a dangerous & infectious nature & I hope a specific
remedy will soon be employed

I beg leave to assure your excellency that the public good is all
that I have in view by the letter. I bear resentment nor malice
to no man. But I cannot see America in some measure conquer-
ing herself and strengthening the hands of our enemies by the
depravity of public servants, without indignation: and I should
ill deserve the opinion which I flatter myself your excellency
entertains of me were I either to be intimidated by power or restrained by any other motive from giving you this information.
For as a great author observes "The enjoyment of liberty and
even its support and preservation consists in every man being
allowed to speak his thoughts and lay open his sentiments"

Y^r Excellency's most obedient & most humble serv

A FOWLER

HIS EXCELLENCY JOSEPH REED Esqr President of the state of
Pensylv^a Philadelphia.

[Memorial of Pittsburgh inhabitants. Washington Papers. D. S.][1]

To His Excellency the President and Supreme executive Council
of the State of Pennsylvania:

The representation and Memorial of the Inhabitants of the
Town of Pittsburgh, humbly Sheweth—

That we are greatly alarmed with the Claim of Colo Brodhead
Commanding officer at the Garrison of Fort Pitt, assuming authority to Exercise military power over this Town, which he conceives he has a Right to do, within the round of his Patroles, In
many cases he has actually exercised this authority taking away
the property, confining the Persons of the Citizens, and ordering
them to be tryed by a Court Martial. We know well that the
laws and Constitutions of our Country have fixed a precise
boundary to the Military power. It is limited to those who are
enlisted for the Service and under the Articles of War; it Cannot

[1] This document and the following one are not dated. The context shows
that they were drawn up and forwarded sometime in April, 1781.

extend in the least degree to a Citizen. Whether he happens to be within the walls of a Garrison, within the Cover of the Cannon, Within the sound of the Patroles, or at a Thousand miles distance. The commanding Officer at this place derive no authority from Congress to extend Military Law over the Inhabitants, The Congress are circumscribed by the articles of the Confederation and cannot interfere with the Laws and Internal police of a State; it is not in their Power by any Resolve to take away from one Citizen the right of being protected in his life, liberty and property by the laws of his Country; The Congress not being Possessed of this power cannot communicate it, and therefore no officer acting under them can exercise it. The assembly of the State could not surrender the people of this Spot to the authority of Military law but by a manifest Violation of the Constitution and bill of rights which have established that *no Freeman shall lose his liberty, but by the law of the land and the Judgment of his peers* The commanding Officer therefore Could not derive any authority from the assembly, and we have not heard of any act by which he can pretend to derive any authority to Exercise Military law over the People of this County. It cannot be pleaded that by custom or usage where a Garrison is placed in a Town, the Inhabitants of that town fall under the Power of the Military, because no Such usage or custom is known to our law, and we will Venture to affirm, to no Municipal law of any Country in Europe. It cannot be warranted by any law or Custom of Nations, because the laws or Customs of Nations have nothing to do in the Case.

It cannot be intended, that because a British commanding Officer before the Year 1768 possessing in Behalf of the Crown, by a Cession from the Natives, an Exclusive Right to the Soil within cannon shot, Exerted Military law over his own troops and the Retainers in the Garrison, that therefore now when the Soil is within ye State of Pennsylvania, and civil authority is Established, Military law should extend itself, and take place over Citizens.

It cannot be said that because the Jurisdiction of the Spot is contended by the State of Pennsylvania and that of Virginia, that therefore Citizens shall be Subject to Military law. Writs from the Courts of Both Commonwealths Run into this Town and Every Individual is amenable to Two Jurisdictions to Answer in cases of Debt, Trespass &c. or Criminal Offences. It would be hard therefore, & at the same time absurd, that this should be a

Reason, Why they should be made liable to a law issuing from a third Source, the will of a Commanding Officer.

Some of us who make this Representation have been Inhabitants of the Town of Pittsburgh many Years, have enjoyed the liberties and immunities of Citizens, have suffered in our persons, and fortunes for the Jurisdiction of Pennsylvania and all of us have contended for the cause of America, and are Willing to lay down our lives in the field but not to have our Liberty, our property, our lives suspended on the will of a Commanding Officer and a Court Martial.

Some of us have left our habitations to avoid ye Scalping Knife, and Tomhack of the Merciless Savage, and have gaind a Temporary Residence in this Town; We feel it peculiarly hard that we should be Supposed to have lost our Rights to the laws of our Country, at the same Time With our Possessions, and in removing to a different part of the County of Westmoreland to hold our Lives at the discretion of Military Power.

Having Represented these things, it is our prayer that his Excellency the President, and the Honourable the Council will lay this matter Before Congress and induce them to direct his Excellency Genl Washington to Remove Colo Brodhead from this Command, and give such Orders to the Succeeding officer at this Post, Whoever he may be, as Will Restrain him from such invasion^s of the rights the Citizens. If it Should be said that this Will be unnecessary as the laws of the Country and the Courts of Justice will Support every Individual against the Encrochments of Military power. We beg leave to Observe that it is not easy, but gives infinite trouble, & is almost impossible to obtain Redress by law against a Commanding Officer who can confine in his Guardhouse, from which even the posse commitatus cannot set at liberty, and who if he pleases to avoid an arrest Can be secure within the Cannon of the Fort, and Surrounded by his Guards.

We are Gentlemen your most obedient and Very humble Servants

THO. SMALLMAN	JOHN TEWIND
DAVERAUX SMITH	JAMES ROBINSON
ROBERT CAMPBELL	JOHN HAMILTON
JOHN IRWIN	W^M BARR
A. FOWLER	JAMES FLEMING
ROBERT MCKINLEY	JOHN HANDLYN

Samuel Evalt	Tho. Nichols
Wm Christy	Peter Rositor
Jno Broadly	Wm Amberson
John Ferry	James McLelland
Geo. Walace	And^w Robertson
Wm Reddick	D. Moor
David Tait	Edwd Ward

[Petition of Pittsburgh inhabitants. Washington papers. D. S.]

To His Excellency Joseph Reed Esqr and the Honorable the Executive Council of the State of Pennsylvania.

The Remonstrance and Petition of the Principal Inhabitants of the County of Westmoreland and Town of Pittsburgh; Sheweth

That the uncommon Stretches of power uniformly pursued and now adopted, by Colonel Brodhead Commanding in this Department, added to a connection formed with Mr David Duncan the Assistant to the Deputy quarter master of this State; is so truly alarming, that we trust a bare recital of them will Justify your Petitioners and mark the purity of their motives for this address.

1st That the Constitution and Laws, by which all ought to be governed, seems to become inadequate to the governing of one.

2^d The rights of free Citizens are invaded and property thereby rendered uncertain and precarious

3^d That a monopoly in Trade is created

4th That a Jobbing quarter master is favoured and indulged; and we have great reason to suspect that publick money is not appropriated to the purposes intended

5th That publick delinquents have been sheltered from punishment; while Innocence and Industry have been oppressed and injured

6th That discipline is neglected and relaxed and no attention whatever paid to the accommodation of the Officers and Soldiers, nor to puting the Garrison into a State of defence; and tho a number of artificers have been long employed by the Assistant Deputy quarter master at high wages, and a large allowance of provisions, nothing appears to have been done; and the Fort still continues as well as the Barracks in a ruinous untenable, and unmilitary State

7th That a great number of the Soldiers have been employed in the Quarter masters Department and still more at Head Quarters, while the protection of the frontiers have been totally neglected. Hence, under the specious pretext of publick good private pursuits are accomplished, some of which we have been informed, your Excellency and the Honorable the Executive Council, are not altogether unacquainted with. Indeed so obvious have these transactions appeared here, not only to the Citizen but the Soldier, that the latter in Conformity to a Resolution formed and unanimously adopted, when a Committee in 1779 treated Colonel Brodhead's invitation to dine; with marks of Contempt, while the former was reprobating him in terms of reproach. Thus with arms in our hands, defending our natural rights, your Petitioners unhappily find themselves under a Tyranny far more unsupportable, than that which they have successfully resisted, as the annexed despotick mandates and authentick documents will fully verify. But while many of your Petitioners feel the effects of Colonel Brodheads oppressions, and more are alarmed at the terrors suspended over them, we all with concern anticipate the consequences; They excite emotions in our Breasts, which tho we cannot describe, it would ill become us to conceal. For corrupt and depraved as the country may be, from whence we and our ancestors emigrated, military Tyranny there; is not yet countenanced; and while such a line of conduct cannot but distress and alarm your Excellency and Council; We are convinced that it must be reprobated and meet with a hearty, and determined opposition from every virtuous Citizen of the United States, whose Custom it has been, and we hope will be; to make those tremble who dare to attempt to make them miserable. Feeling and thinking like Free men in the manner we do, silence would become a crime; For History as well as observation evinces the truth of this simple position, that to live by the will of *one* entails misery on *all.* Therefore by giving you this faithfull information we humbly apprehend we are doing barely our duty as good Citizens, by rendering your Excellency and the Honorable the Executive Council all the assistance in our power, to promote the great objects of your trust, the Tranquility of Government and the welfare of the Governed.

Little did your Petitioners ever imagine that in the course of a war undertaken in defence of their Common rights, the Charecter of the Citizen should so soon become sunk in that of the Soldier.

The language of Complaint is painfull to us. but as an Illustrious Author observes; "Military Men belong to a profession which may be usefull, but is often dangerous." The truth of this observation is evident. The annals of every nation in Europe afford melancholy examples.—Even the American Revolution—Glorious and beneficial to mankind as it is.—Has not terminated without being shamefully tarnished with such proofs that we cannot even mention without indignation and Horror. Therefore the real and disinterested Friends of Freedom cannot be too tenacious of their rights,—too watchfull of thier preveleges, or too Jealous of the Ambitious and Interested who attempt to invade them.

Your Petitioners humbly apprehend that thier happiness and the security of thier invaluable rights depends in a great measure on thier own exertions and Spirit to protect and defend them. For the Political liberty of the Subject says Montisquie, is a Tranquility of mind arrising from the opinion each person has of his safety. And it is with heart felt concern, that we find ourselves bound by the strongest of Obligations to inform your Excellency and the Honorable the Executive Council, that instead of that Tranquility of mind; That safety mentioned by this ornament of mankind, the author of the Spirit of Laws, There has been unfortunately implanted in our Breasts, doubts, fears, Suspicions and Jealoucies, the natural production of Tyranny and Dispotism. your Petitioners are well aware of the disadvantagous light in which they may appear to your Excellency and the Honorable the Executive Council, From the partial Clamour raised here against the Generals, Hand, and McIntosh, and in which Colonel Brodhead himself (respecting the latter) bore a principal share. But we cannot command success, and there is a vast difference between doing our best to serve our Country and doing all in our power to serve ourselves. And indeed it is Generally admitted, that these General Officers had the public Interest warmly at heart, while it is allowed by all that Colonel Brodhead is actuated by motives, selfish and interested, and that his views are totally confined to Land, Manors, and Millseats. Duty to our Country our Constitution and our Rulers and a regard for our rights Franchises and Immunities has Induced us to address your Excellency and Council in Language which cannot we hope be displeasing, to which we beg leave to implore your attention. and Humbly Pray. That Colonel Brodhead may be removed from the Command of this Department, and M^r

David Duncan from the employment of assistant Quarter master as well as every other employment wherein he may be intrusted with Publick money and that for the benefit of the Publick his accounts may be settled in this Department. That an Officer may be appointed to Command here, who is more active and less Arbitary, and whose ambition and Study would be to afford us protection, promote the Good of this Country, and act in Unison with its Inhabitants. and that a Quarter Master may be appointed—if one may be found absolutely necessary—that has more pride and more principal than to descend to the mean and unwarrantable Task of becoming a Tool in Depeculation by sacrefiseing his time to create private Jobbs and promote advantageous bargains. It is therefore with a pleasing Confidence that we anticipate a ready attention to the Prayer of this Petition, and we beg leave to declare that it is not the man, but his Conduct that we arraign. And that had we an opportunity, Compliment would be more agreeable to your Petitioners than Complaint. And while we thus expose and are determined to oppose the dispotick and designing, we are determined at the same time, to support the virtuous and disinterested by every means in our power.

Patriotism will here find Friends and publick Good may depend on being Supported with our lives and fortunes.

N. B. The Inclosed List Contains the Names of the Subscribers:

Names of the Petitioners

Edwd Ward	John Handlyn	Samuel Osburn
Tho. Smallman	David Kenneday	Hugh Mc Daid
Deverux Smith	William Evans	Samuel Robertson
Andrew Robertson	John Reed	John Hall
John Gibson	James Agnew	Wm Robertson
James McLelland	William Reed	John Baird
Wm Reddick	Jno H. Reddick	Wm Collins
John Ferry	T. Wiatt	Jno Brandon
James Fleming	Mathew McKennie	Patrick Callen
Geo. Wallace	William Mooney	Robert Hall
James Robinson	William Aulls	Wm Cooper
Wm Amberson	Barry Chea	Peter Boyes
Hugh Gardner	Andrew Crowly	Gerret Homer
David Tait	Alex. Mitchel	William Lyon
A. Fowler	Joseph Hall	William Howey
John Irwin	Richard Steel	Joshua Clark

Wm Christy
John Irwin Junr
Robert McKinly
D^d Moor
William Barr
John Hamilton
Robert Campbell
Isaac Justice
Hugh OHara
John Bradly
Francis Dill
James Drain
James Deenan
Jacob Twebough
Thomas Young
Thomas Person
George Fubecker
Daniel Mathews
Alex. Maxwell
Mathias Hoyle
Daniel Hamilton
Abraham Scot
Wm Johnston
Wm Rigdon
Wm Marshal
James Glenn
Josua Spiers
David Devose
Elisha Rizsly
James Kerr
Ezekiel Hickman
Jeremiah Meek
John Killen
Joshua Armstrong
Henry Mead
Wm Pope
Josua Jenking

James Kuykendall
Abra. Kykendall
James Loagan

John Sumral
David McKee
George Swan
John Beck
Thomas Harper
Philip Jones
James Clark
James Johnston
Joseph Hall
John McConnell
Charles Milon
Andrew Burnside
Edwd Branner
Peter Harshey
James Brooks
Joseph Ross
Joseph McCune
Wm Nellerfield
Joseph Hill
Stephen Hill
Vincent Calvin
John Reed
James Davis
George Bruce
Ignatious Jones
James Bruce
Joseph Hopkins
John Tannyhill
Meniard Sturges
James McCraken
John Anstrod
Benj. Raid
John Flick
Robert Spears
Wm Gillmore
John Connolly
Wm Karey

Jno Beckit
Mitch^l Vanbush
David Parkison

Robert Smith
Thomas Maxwell
Alex. Young
Robert Young
Michael Graham
Robert Hall Junr
Robert Watson
James Watterson
Robert Jamison
John Cungill
Daniel Brooks
John Reed
James Brekenridge
Philip Taber
Thomas Brown
Tho Carroll
Hans Hamilton
Wm Colvin
Jno Vervill
And^w Ree
Henry Talen
Samuel Evalt
Wm Miller
John McDonald
Ben. Sweet
James Wallace
Oliver Miller
Jno Fife
Oliver miller Junr
Richard Waterson
James Parks
Thomas Miller
Samuel Glasgow
Jno Miller
Abraham Beam
Jno Stephenson
Samuel Hannah
Jno Stephens
Elias Pigg
Joseph Tobin
Geo. Martain

Thomas Comus
Arch[d] Ricords
Philip Delay
Jn° Wall
W[m] Anderson
W[m] Taylor
Jn° Anderson
Nathan Delay
Andrew Nye
W[m] Taylor
Henry Magnor
Hugh Brody
Jacob Pgly
Alex. Stewart
Nathan Tannyhill
John Barn
James Tannyhill
W[m] Tannyhill
Jn° Baird
Nathan Casebard
W[m] M°Connell
Jn° Hutson
Luck Decker

James Kerr
Jn° Martain Jun[r]
Peter Triplet
Philip Walker
W[m] M°Cue
Pat. Kelly
Jn° Dilrumple

Sol. Combs
James Hughs
Felix Hughs
Matthew Cain
Philip Walsh
Jn° Cain
Jn° M°Cann
Jn° Daugherty
Edward Davis

George M°Nabb
Jn° Ervin
And[w] Roberson
Geo. Young
Joseph Rope
John Kinny
Jn° Dean
Samuel M°Kinly
Geo. Gillespy. (200)
Philip Hollyday
Abr. Hendrise
John Salcon
Ben. Goodwire
Philip Lewis
Charles Wicklife
Rob[t] Wicklife
Jo. Cox
Nicholass Blake
W[m] Owens
Thomas Clare
Ben Brook
Jn° Scott
Randolph Snyder
Andrew Lee
James Alison
W[m] Fry
Jacob Fry
Tobias Woods
Jn° Stenson
Geo. Sickman
Jn° Woods
Jn° Reed
Joseph [sic]
Jonathan [sic]
James Rutherford
Adam Curry
Adam Loagan
Jn° Frezer
Robert Henderson
Jacob Fifer
Philip Flin

John Lamme
W[m] Rorke
Thomas Ogle
Basil Cooper
John Curry
Jerves Thompson
Jacob Sprinkle
Jeremia Simpson
Daniel Colvin
Henry Oats
Thomas John
Lewis Calzor
John Ewing
Andrew Robertson
Garret Clawson
Levi Hand
George Teatrick
Joseph Stillwell
John Hughs
W[m] Bushby
John Armstrong
Daniel Martain
Jn° Robins
Isaac Teatrick
Jn° Martain
Arthur Burns
William Bruce
Jacob Bousman
W[m] Deal
James Cron
W[m] Bell

James Mitchel
John Menate
Robert M° Nab
Jn° M°Cune
Robert M°Farren
Jn° Jamison
mar. Jamison
Jn° Jamison
Jn° Robertson

Benjamin Collins
Abra. Tout
Joseph Harris
Corard Winbidle
William Lea
Jno° Rock
Geo. Lickenburgh
Alex. Still
Hugh Sterling
Jn° Douglass
Thomas Bond
Mich^l Teggart
John Evans
Robt Bell
James McCormack
Paul Matthews
Joseph Forrester
Joseph Ker
Willm Richardson
John Clark
Hugh Murray
Thomas Miles
James Stoops
John Connor
Corneilus Connor Jn^r
Thomas Ramsey
Jos: McDowell
John Johnston
James Whitecker
Thos Sprott
Richd Carson
Danl Kyser
Mich^l Kyser
John Dunbar
John McKee
John Cunningham
John Glazier
Wm Broomfield
Wm Beatty
James McKee
Thos Cottrill

James Colter
John Taylor

John Killan
Robert Boyd
James Watson
Wm Tidball
Joseph Dermont
Edward Sharp
Adam Sharp
Charles Morgan
John Layson
John King
Thos Patterson
David McKee
John Niel
Gasper Reel
Charles M^{c}kinear [?]
Isaac Lan
Thos Lapoley
Phil^p Whitsel
Phill^p Francis
Wm Richmond
Phill^p Ross
Peter Body
John Creal
Benjn Reno
Corneilus Connor S^r
Christ^n Lisnit
Francis Lisnit
Richd Boyce
James Young

Wm Ralston
Arch^d Ralston
Wm Murdock
John Fawcett
Wm Snodgrass Sen
George Sharp
Wm Snodgrass J^r
Ja^s McLauchlin

Patrick Ohara
James Hamilton
Boston Frederick
John Small
William Woods
Sebastian Frederick
John Wolf
Thos McBride
Willm Powell
Nehemiah Sharp
George Custard
Christ° Owen
Wm Donnally
St^n Ritchards
Mordecai Ritchards
Mark Jordan
Jossias Gamble
Jos: Brown
Saml Brown
Matthew Ritchie
Craig Ritchie
John Boyce
Abell Morgan
And^w Munro
Hugh Bell
Charles Queen
Thos Nicholas
Jonathan Martin
Robt Miller
Thos McQueen
John Alexander
John Hayes

Robt Hayes.
Danl McCleod
Danl Ross
And^w Gibson
James Hayes
Wm Hayes
John Mc Donald
James Little

Ja⁸ Stephenson	David Stephenson	John Robb
Wᵐ Robb	Ja⁸ Robb	John Andrew
David Andrew	Wᵐ Glendy	Arthur Campbel
	George Berry	

RENDEZVOUS POSTPONED

[Col. Daniel Brodhead, circular letter to county lieutenants. 3H96–97. Transcript of Letter Book.]

HEAD QR⁸, FORT PITT, April 1ˢᵗ 1781.

DEAR SIR:

As I am informed that the court of Westmoreland county will be held this week, & that many good men will on that account be prevented from going on an expedition, I have postponed the rendezvousing the troops until the 10ᵗʰ instant; I expect they will attend as required by my last.

I am with great esteem, &c,

DANᴸ BRODHEAD, Col° Commanding W. D.

COL° Jɴ° EVANS, Circular.

ARTILLERY FOR CLARK

[Gen. George Rogers Clark to Board of War. 15S24. Transcript.]

YOUGH, April 2ᵈ 1781.

GENTᴹ:

I make no doubt but that you are fully acquainted with the design of the enterprise I am ordered on to the North West, the success of which greatly depends on the stores ordered by his Excellency, Genˡ Washington, to be furnished at Pittsburg. On examination its found that many articles are wanting that cannot be done without, as per the indent of Capt. Craig, who commands the artillery on the campaign. As you must know the sentiments of the Commander-in-Chief respecting those furnitures, and confident from the nature of the enterprise you would wish to give it every aid, I flatter myself the Captain will meet with no difficulty in procuring such articles as he may want to complete him. The Captain's company at present is very weak. I would take the liberty to solicit a re-inforcement to it; also nine or ten artillery artificers, and a tin plate worker. These favors I shall endeavor to acknowledge by doing all the service in my power to my country, and beg leave to subscribe myself, Gent[n], Your most obed[t] Serv[t],

G. R. CLARK, B. G. C. C. W. D. Virginia

WESTMORELAND RAIDED

[Summary of a letter of Col. Archibald Lochry, Twelve Mile Run, April 2, 1781, to Col. Daniel Brodhead. Printed in *Pa. Archives*, IX, 51.]

Has received three letters from Brodhead since writer's return from Philadelphia; bodily indisposition has prevented personal call. Had the county officers meet, and requested Colonel Cook to send an express to Brodhead to let him know what he may expect. "I am just returned from burying a man killed & scalped by the Indians, at Col° Pomeroy's house,[1] one other man is missing & all Pomeroy's effects carried off." Has been attempting to get some militia to protect frontier until relief comes. If the Cumberland militia arrive in time for the expedition they shall go and Lochry will go with them.

DELAWARES BREAK ALLIANCE

[Col. Daniel Brodhead to Col. David Shepherd. 2SS13. A. L. S.][2]

FORT PITT April 3rd 1781.

SIR:
I have received your favor of the 28th ultimo by M[r] Robeson, am glad to hear of the spirited Conduct of the good Men of your County and of your success in collecting provisions for the Expedition

[1] This raid took place in the Derry settlement of northeastern Westmoreland County, not far from Fort Wallace. For a sketch of Col. John Pomeroy see *Wis. Hist. Colls.*, XXIII, 46, note 4.
[2] Both the original letter, and the letter-book transcript of this manuscript are in the Draper Mss., the latter in 3H97–98.

Mʳ Duncan is hourly expected with a sum of Money sufficient to discharge the ballances for Provisions purchased by my instructions and to procure some more, when the Inhabitants know this circumstance the difficulty of obtaining a further supply for the regular Troops will probably be in some degree removed

I have inclosed to Col⁰ Valendigham the Copy of a letter just received from one of the Moravian Ministers which I have desired the bearer, Lieutᵗ Peterson, to take forward to you as soon as Col⁰ Valendigham had read it.

You will therein see how hostile the Indians in general are, & how necessary it is for the Inhabitants to be upon their Guard against them.

Mʳ Peterson takes a party as you have requested, to assist in collecting the Horses & Provisions. And I have directed him not to suffer the quantity mentioned in your Letter to be used, or any part of it, untill we march upon the Expedition, but in the meantime I hope you will be able to obtain a larger supply

I am Dear Sir with respect & esteem your most obedᵗ Servᵗ

DANIEL BRODHEAD Col⁰ commandᵍ W D.

COL⁰ DAVID SHEPHERD.

WESTMORELAND BLAMED

[Summary of a letter of Col. Daniel Brodhead, Fort Pitt, April 3, 1871, to Pres. Joseph Reed. 3H98–99. Printed in *Pa. Archives*, IX, 57.]

Rev. David Zeisberger goes to Philadelphia at Brodhead's request; a faithful and reliable man.[1] Copies of letters enclosed from Colonel Lochry and Colonel Perry prove how little support the Westmoreland militia accord Brodhead's project, and how necessary it is that the laws be enforced and taxes collected

[1] At the time this letter was written Zeisberger was on his way to Bethlehem to attend a synod of the Moravian church. On his return he visited Philadelphia, where he received the thanks of the president and the executive council of Pennsylvania "for his services among the Indians, particularly for his Christian humanity in turning back so many war-parties that were on their way to rapine and massacre." (*Ibid.*, 5D98.) Zeisberger was married June 4, and immediately thereafter set out for his mission station on the Tuscarawas, where he arrived July 15, 1781.

ASSEMBLING FOR DELAWARE EXPEDITION

[Col. Daniel Brodhead to Capt. William Crawford.[1] 3H99–100. Transcript of Letter Book.]

FORT PITT, April 5th 1781.[2]

SIR:

I have at this moment (at 11 o'clock P. M.) rec^d a letter from Col^o Evans, informing me that the militia from Monongehela[3] had marched to Wheeling agreeable to former instructions.

Having rec^d information that the Westmoreland militia or volunteers, many of whom would be prevented from going upon the expedition, I wrote to the several Lieutenants by express, to put off the rendezvousing the troops until the 10th instant, which it seems came to hand after some had marched, or before he could give them notice that the day of general rendezvous was put off.

It will not now be in my power to collect the different [divisions] to the place assigned until the 10th, wherefore I hope & expect the troops under your command will wait with patience until then, & they shall not be disappointed.

I have &c.

D. B.

COMMANDING OFFICER OF MONONGEHELA MILITIA, Wheeling.[4]

---

[1] Capt. William Crawford was born about the year 1737 near Chambersburg, Pa. Orphaned in childhood, he was bound to Samuel Combs of Loudoun County, Va., with whom he served until of age. Crawford then enlisted in a militia company raised for the French and Indian War on the Great Cacapon River. In 1769 he visited the West, and made an improvement on the Monongahela River near Redstone. The next year he brought his family and settled west of the river in what is now Greene County, Pa., then thought to be a part of Virginia. Crawford went out with McIntosh in 1778, and with Brodhead in 1781. He also served in Hardin's division on Harmar's expedition of 1790. He lived upon his Greene County farm until his death, Aug. 3, 1826. See narrative of his son, and letters of his grandsons in ibid., 6NN62–102. Capt. William Crawford was not related to the colonel of the same name who was burned by the Indians in 1782.

[2] On April 5, 1781 a British council with the Delawares and Shawnee was held at Detroit. See *Mich. Pion. & Hist. Colls.*, X, 462–65; and De Peyster's letters in *id.*, XIX, 613–15.

[3] For the muster roll of this company see *post*, 469.

[4] Note on original manuscript: "From the date of the last letter, April 5th, there are no letters entered in the Letter Book till the ensuing 19th August, a period of over four months. Most likely *** Col. Broadhead, immediately after the

BRITISH HEARTEN INDIANS

[Col. Guy Johnson to Alexander McKee. Printed in De Peyster (ed.), *Miscellanies by an Officer*, app., p. xlvii.]

NIAGARA, 7th April, 1781.

SIR:

The late letters from Detroit and from yourself, which have been communicated to me, has induced me, with General Powell's[1] approbation to send a message to encourage and strengthen the Hearts of the Indians in your quarter and particularly the Shawanese, and those who are most exposed to an Invasion. The great distance from hence, and the Uncertainty of affairs at present render it difficult to say how far the Six Nations may be able to help them; but I am sure they'll do so, as far as time and circumstance will permit. In the present state of things, from the acco'ts we have of the Rebels, and of the success of our Troops in Virginia, &c., as well as from the great distance and difficulty of the Route to Detroit, it does not seem probable they can come there in force within a short time; but the Vigilance of your Scouts will enable us to Judge farther, by procuring intelligence of their last motions. The person whom I have sent with the Message is Capt. Brant of my department, who is accompanied by 17 Inds., and from his Vigilance I expect the Message committed to him and the object of his Journey will be faithfully executed; he will show you his Instructions, and meet with your Assistance, and it will doubtless be pleasing to the Shawanese to see him and those of the Six Nations with him. Kayashota left this long

expedition, went to Phil[a], & *possibly* made only a verbal report of that affair. And yet I cannot bring myself to think, that during all this period he wrote no letters. There are no pages wanting in the letter book, at this point. The following letters—commencing in August, &c., appear to have been copied by another & better hand: L. C. D—30th May, 1846."

[1] Henry Watson Powell (1733–1814) came to America with his regiment during the French and Indian War and after 1768 was stationed in Canada. In 1771 he was commissioned lieutenant-colonel of the Fifty-third Infantry; by 1777 he had attained the rank of brigadier-general. Powell commanded the rear-guard of Burgoyne's army on its invasion of New York, and after the defeat made good his retreat to St. John's, Can. In 1780 he was appointed to succeed at Niagara Col. Mason Bolton, who was drowned in Lake Ontario on his retirement from that post. Powell remained at Niagara until the close of the war, when he was ordered to England, where in 1801 he became general of the army.

since with belts from the Eastern Indians, the Six Nations, and myself, but got a hurt and lyes ill at Kadaragaras.[1] I am with regard, Sir, Your very humble Servant,

G. JOHNSON.

ALEXR. MCKEE, Esqr.

[Col. Arent S. De Peyster to Delawares. Printed in *ibid.*, pp. viii–ix.]

Major De Peyster, Commandant of Detroit and its dependencies, to the Indians of Cooshawking—12th April, 1781.

INDIANS OF COOSHAWKING. I have received your speech, sent me by the half king of Sandusky; it contains three strings, one of them white, and the other two checkered.

You may say that you want traders to be sent to your village, and that you are resolved no more to listen to the Virginians, who have deceived you.

It would give me pleasure to receive you again as brothers, both for your own good, and for the friendship I bear to the Indians in general, being allied to them. But is it possible I can trust my traders amongst you, whose ears are open to every little French officer or trader who will tell you they come upon a mission from the French king? They easily make lies, and you as easily believe them. One of these people the Miamies killed,[2] and they brought me his papers, which are the copies of letters he wrote to Philadelphia, wherein he says he found you, the Cooshawking Indians, in a council he held with some of you at Fort Pitt, such believing fools, that he amused you with words, whilst the other nations required great presents from the English. I do not want to amuse you with words, I wish for an opportunity to serve you; and it depends on yourselves to put it in my power to serve you.

Send me that little babbling Frenchman named Monsieur Linctot, he who poisons your ears, one of them who says he can amuse you with words only—send him to me, or be the means of my getting him, and I then will put confidence in you. I then will deal with you as with other Indians, whom I call my friends, my brothers, and my children, and to whom I request of you to give free passage, and kind entertainment. If you have not an

[1] Probably this place was at the mouth of Cattaraugus Creek, which forms the boundary between Chautauqua and Erie counties, N. Y.
[2] A reference to the defeat and death of Colonel La Balme.

opportunity to bring me the little Frenchman, you may bring me some Virginia prisoner,—I am pleased when I see what you call *live meat*, because I can speak to it, and get information. Scalps serve to show you have seen the enemy, but they are of no use to me, I cannot speak with them. I request of you to give free passage to such Virginians as have a mind to speak with me— that you will not offer to stop them, but make a straight and even road for them to come to Detroit.

A. S. DE PEYSTER

EXPEDITION AGAINST DELAWARES

[C. W. Butterfield's narrative of Brodhead's Coshocton expedition. 5D91–97. A. D.][1]

On the seventh of April, 1781, Brodhead left Fort Pitt with over one hundred and fifty regulars, dropping down the Ohio river to Wheeling, where Shepherd had collected one hundred and thirty-four of the militia including officers, into four companies.[2] On the tenth, the united force made its way across the Ohio, taking the nearest route for Coshocton. The savages had received no warning of the approach of an enemy. They evidently felt secure in their wilderness home. With Brodhead was a few friendly Indians who evinced a keen desire for the scalps of the hostile Delawares.[3] As the army neared the objective point of

---

[1] Butterfield used as his sources Brodhead's report to Reed, Heckewelder, *Narrative*, and Rev. Joseph Doddridge, *Notes on the Settlement and Indian Wars of the Western Parts of Virginia and Pennsylvania* (Wellsburgh, 1824), 291–93. Doddridge lived in Ohio County, and knew personally many militiamen who participated in the expedition.

[2] The militia force was chiefly from Ohio County, Va., with one small company from Monongalia. It was organized into four companies, commanded respectively by Capt. Joseph Ogle, Capt. William Crawford, Capt. Jacob Lefler, and Capt. Benjamin Royse. See pay and muster rolls, *post*, 462–69.

[3] There is a persistent tradition, unverified by documentary evidence, that one of the friendly Indians by the name of Killbuck was slain at Wheeling by a group of militia. See Draper Mss., 2S155,181,215,283, 6NN46. The victim was not Captain Killbuck, but he may have been one of the Killbuck family. According to report Thompson the Indian and young Killbuck were asleep in the guardhouse when a mob of men headed by Lewis Wetzel broke in and killed Killbuck, but spared the old guide, Thompson. The assassins were severely punished, but were permitted to go upon the expedition.

the expedition an Indian was captured from whom was obtained some valuable information. Soon afterward two others were discovered and fired upon. One was wounded but both succeeded in making their escape. Fearing lest these Indians should give the alarm, Brodhead, although in the midst of a heavy fall of rain, ordered a rapid march for the town, in hopes of surrounding it before any of the savages had news of his coming. The troops marched in three divisions. The right and left wings approached the river a little above and below Coshocton, while the center moved directly upon it. The Coshocton Indians were completely surprised and their town laid waste; also Lichtenau, now occupied by them, two and a half miles below, on the same side of the river. Fifteen warriors were killed and over twenty prisoners—old men, women and children—taken. Large quantities of peltry and other stores were destroyed and about forty head of cattle killed.

About four miles above Coshocton, on the march down, Brodhead had detached a party to cross the river and attack about forty warriors who had just before crossed over with some prisoners and scalps and were then drunk, as he learned by the Indian whom the advance guard had taken prisoner; but the excessive hard rain having swelled the river bank high, it was found impracticable. Brodhead then marched up the stream about seven miles with a view to send for some craft from the "Moravian" towns with which to cross the river, so that he could pursue the Indians; but when he proposed his plan to the militia, he found they conceived they had accomplished enough and were determined to return; whereupon he marched to NewComer's town,[1] the home of Captain Killbuck and his followers. This chief and another had no sooner heard that Brodhead was upon the river than they pursued the fleeing Delawares, "killed one of their greatest villains," and brought his scalp to the American commander.

At the request of Brodhead, the missionaries and some of their converts from the "Moravian" towns visited him before he left the river. He renewed to them his proposition that they should break up their establishments and move to the border—urging them to accompany him to Pittsburgh. But this well-meant overture they declined. They, together with Captain Killbuck's band, supplied the army with corn and meat enough to subsist both men and horses to the Ohio river.

[1] For the site of this town see *Rev. Upper Ohio*, 45, note 72.

The Moravian Indians had become objects of suspicion to many of the frontiersmen, some of whom were of the militia in Brodhead's army. Among the prisoners captured at Coshocton were five of those Indians who, of course, were immediately released by the American commander; as they were simply visitors at their former home. As they were going up the river in a canoe on their way to Salem, some of the militia, contrary to express orders, followed them and in such a menacing manner as to induce them to leave the stream and take to the hills. They were in fact fired upon by those in pursuit and one of their number wounded though they all succeeded in reaching their town. So, also, while Brodhead was receiving the visits of the Moravian missionaries and some of their converts, as just described, there was manifested a strong desire upon the part of some of the militia to march to their settlements for the purpose of destroying them; but the movement was quickly repressed by those in command.

A proposition made by Brodhead to Captain Killbuck and his band to put themselves under the protection of the Americans and march with the army upon its return to the border, was gladly accepted; so, with this accession, and a large amount of plunder captured from the "Coshocton" Indians, the troops returned to Wheeling where the spoils were disposed of, netting quite a considerable sum. Both regulars and militia, upon this expedition, behaved with much spirit; and though there was considerable firing between them and the Indians not one was killed or wounded. Brodhead with his troops, accompanied by the friendly Delawares, then made their way back to Fort Pitt; while the militia were disbanded and returned to their several places of abode.

A circumstance thought by some damaging to the reputation of the enterprise was that all the warriors killed had been captured in the assault upon the town. These were pointed out by Pekillon, a friendly Delaware, who was with the army of Brodhead. A council of war was called to determine their fate. The fact that they had raided upon the border, killing indiscriminately the old and young of either sex was clearly established; and this, too, at the very time when others of their clan were making protestations of friendship to the commander at Fort Pitt. Their crimes were thought sufficient to justify a decree of death, by the council; and, in ordering the carrying out of that decision, Brodhead, himself a humane and chivalric officer, only acted upon the idea of a complete justification according to the usages of war. The warriors were bound, taken a little distance below the town, and dispatched with tomahawks and spears, and then scalped.

Another transaction—one of those unfortunate ones that the moralist must condemn, and which is too often seen in border warfare—was the killing, by the militia, to whose care they had been committed, of the residue of the prisoners, the women and children excepted. It was done immediately after the return march had commenced and without the knowledge of Brodhead or his principal officers.[1] The women and children were taken to Fort Pitt. An incident occurred on the march to New Comer's town which brings out in strong light the deep-seated hatred lurking in the breast of some of the bordermen to the savages, at that period—a frenzy of revenge, which only their extreme and long-continued cruelties and ravages could have engendered. An Indian presented himself on the opposite bank of the river and asked for the "Big Captain." Brodhead responded with the question as to what he wanted. To which he replied in substance that his desire was for peace. "Send over some of your chiefs," said the American commander. "May be you will kill them," was the reponse. He was answered that they should not be killed. One came across, a fine looking man, and entered into conversation with Brodhead. But while thus engaged, Lewis Wetzel,[2] one of the militiamen, came up behind the chief

[1] For a more detailed account of this incident see Thomas H. Johnson, "The Indian Village of 'Cush-og-wenk,' " in *Ohio Arch. & Hist. Quarterly*, XXI, 432–35.

[2] Lewis Wetzel was born in August, 1763 on the south branch of the Potomac River. About the year 1769 the family removed to the Monongahela, and three years later settled on the upper waters of Wheeling Creek. In 1777 or 1778 Lewis and his younger brother, Jacob, were captured by a band of Wyandot, and taken about twenty miles beyond the Ohio, where in the night they succeeded in loosening the cords with which they were tied, and having eluded the subsequent pursuit reached the river and crossed it on pieces of driftwood. Lewis thereafter was bitterly hostile to all the Indian race. In 1782 his brother, George, was killed while hunting; the same summer Lewis saw his companion, Joseph Mills, waylaid and shot and himself escaped a like fate only by his fleetness, and his ability to load his rifle as he ran. That autumn he detected an Indian lurking near Fort Henry imitating a turkey's call, and killed him without warning. The next year Lewis Wetzel was with young John Madison when the latter was waylaid and slain by Indians. Wetzel's vindictiveness towards the red race increased with the years. In 1784 in a time of peace he killed an

with a tomahawk concealed in the bosom of his hunting-shirt and struck him on the back of his head with the weapon, causing instant death.

A few days after the return of Brodhead from Coshocton, eighty hostile Delawares came up the Tuscarawas in search of Captain Killbuck and his band, breathing destruction to all of them. It was not, by any means, that they wished only to take them prisoners, especially Captain Killbuck and other chiefs and counsellors that they could thus have them under their control and prevent them governing the nation while the war lasted; it was, that they thirsted for their blood. The scalps of Captain Killbuck and his clan who had continued the allies of the Americans would have been esteemed as delectable prizes as those of any of their white enemies; for had not that chief already taken up the hatchet against them? From that moment, he was proscribed—he and all his followers. Not knowing of their leaving the valley with Brodhead, they felt sure of finding them. They finally reached Gnadenhütten but, of course, the objects of their search were not there. They were told by the Moravian Indians that all had gone off with the Americans. The Delaware band then endeavored to convince the "converts" that their only safety was in seeking a refuge to the Westward farther away from the border. Precisely the same advice had been given them by Brodhead when upon the Coshocton expedition, only with this difference, that they should go with him to Pittsburgh. It was thus that the belligerants saw, that it needed no prophet to forsee, the danger there was in the missionaries and their flock remaining in the valley of the Tuscarawas—literally between two fires; for, although they were to all intents and purposes the allies of the Americans, they were too far away from the border for any advantages of protection by them.

Indian known as "Old Crossfire" and rescued a captive girl At the Treaty of Fort McIntosh in 1785 Wetzel wounded a peaceful Indian, and after a similar deed at Marietta in 1789 was arrested by the commandant, kept some time in irons, and finally released because conviction could not be obtained from a frontier jury for the murder of an Indian. Wetzel was credited with stalking and hunting Indians as he would wild animals. Towards the close of the eighteenth century he visited New Orleans and was arrested by the Spanish on a charge of counterfeiting. This was never proved and Wetzel was released and made a final visit to the neighborhood of Wheeling. Then he returned South, where he died in 1808 not far from Natchez. Lewis Wetzel was a border hero because of his courage, his feats of agility, and his superior woodcraft. His attitude towards Indians was that of many of the lower class upon the frontier. Dr. Draper collected much material for a biography of Wetzel, from which this sketch is derived.

FRONTIER RETREAT

The Delaware band was not entirely unsuccessful in their endeavors to pursuade the "Moravians" to remove; as more than a dozen of those living in Salem concluded to go with them, "renouncing the gospel and falling back into heathenism." It was thus that there was to be found among the hostile Delawares a considerable element of what may be called "Moravianism;" false, of course, but such as enabled these before-time "converts" to appear, at least, to captives taken afterward, as veritable Moravian Indians; the deception being helped on, frequently, by their calling themselves such, and by their ability, in some instances, to speak pretty good German.

The Delaware warriors, before leaving, made three several attempts to take the life of Heckewelder, rightfully considering him as a chief obstacle in the way of inducing the removal of the "Moravians." It is probable they would have had still further success in inducing the "converts" to have the valley had it not been that a report reached their ears of an American army being again on its way to the Tuscarawas. So the warriors departed, leaving the "Moravian" villages again in peace—but only for a short time as small parties of Delawares continued to prowl through the valley, stealing the horses of the "converts" and whatever else they could find. One of these bands lay in ambush near a field at Gnadenhütten into which came the missionary Edwards and Young and began to plant potatoes. "Instantly seven of the savages cocked their rifles, took aim, and were upon the point of shooting them down," when their captain, seized by a sudden impulse of mercy, made a sign for them to desist. "The band crept away, and the two missionaries continued working in the field, ignorant of the death which had threatened them."[1]

[Extract from reminiscences of William P. Brady.[2] 7NN56.]

Does Gen'l Brodhead mention anything in his letter book about his Expedition to Muskingum. Brady was on The advance

[1] For the British report of Brodhead's expedition see *Mich. Pion. & Hist. Colls.*, X, 476. His approach greatly alarmed the Indians gathered in council at Detroit. See report of Simon Girty, May 4, from Upper Sandusky, *ibid.*, 478–79. Other rumors of the "Virginians" at Coshocton are in *ibid.*, 482–83, and *id.*, XIX, 634–36.

[2] This younger brother of Capt. Samuel Brady was born Aug. 16, 1766 near Shippensburg, Pa. William was with the family when his father and his brother

when the[y] struck the Tuskoragus. at Newcomerstown about ten miles above Coshoton old town opisite the mouth of White Womans C^r he heard some shooting down the river and moved on the firing Every now and Then Continued untill he arived it Was an Indian shooting at a Squerell he wanted it for beat [bait] to fish with Brady Waited untill The Indians Gun Was Empty When the[y] sprung on him and took him prisoner but unfortunately There ware two other Indians under the bank fishing when the[y] heard the noise took to their heels one of them though[t] to cross the branch but when he got to The opisite shore he was shot The other made his Eskeap and Give notice to the town when the[y] all fled when the troops came up the Indians fired a cross the Muskingum & Kill^d one man The Genl Then returned to Pittsburgh

ARTILLERY FOR CLARK

[Capt. Isaac Craig to Gen. George Washington. Washington Papers. A. L. S.]

PHILADELPHIA 15th April 1781

May it Please Your Excellency:

On Compearing the Indent of Ordnance Stores &c Requiered for General Clarks Expedition, with the Articles on hand it was found a Considerable Part was Wanting, it Appeared also that My Company was Much too Weake for the Duty to be done by it, and that nine or ten Artillery Artificers were also Necessary, in Consequence of which I Rec^d Orders to Prosceed to this Place, and forward with all Possible Expedition the Military Stores & Men Wanted to Fort Pitt.[1] I have found no dificualty in Obtaining the Stores, and I hope Your Excellency will see it Neceessary to Order me A Reinforcement. I Presume your Excellency is well acquainted with the Number & Calibers of the Ordnance

---

John were killed in 1778, and many years later he spent a month with his brother Samuel on a hunting excursion, when the latter related many of the thrilling incidents of his career. These the younger brother wove into a series of sketches which in 1832 he sent to R. B. McCabe of Blairsville, Pa., who about fifteen years later gave the manuscripts to Dr. Draper. William Perry Brady died sometime before 1845 at his home on Mahoning Creek in western Pennsylvania.

[1] For a list of the artillery stores that were ordered see *Ill. Hist. Colls.*, VIII, 535–37.

to be made use of on this Enterprize, My Company Consists of only thirteen Men, One Capt & one Capt Lieu^t General Clarke Assured me your Excellency was disposed to give every assistence to the Expedition. Co^l Procters[1] Reg^t to which I belong is now within A few Miles of Philadelphia from which I wish to have my Company filled up, the Artificers Can be had at Carlisle— it is not necessary to observe that one full Company will still be insufficient to Work Eight Peices of Artillery, and that I must still have Recourse to Militi[a] for further assistance. I Expect the Boats will be all finished and at Fort Pitt the 10th of next month, I shall wait Here with Impatience for Your Excellencys Instructions Respecting the Men

I have the Honour to be with Due Esteem Your Excellencys Devoted Most Obe^{dt} Servt

I Craig Capt Artillery

His Excellency George Washington Esqr.

[Gen. George Washington to Col. Daniel Brodhead. Washington Papers. Draft.]

Head Quarters New Windsor 16th Ap^l 1781.

Dear Sir:
I have received your favors of the 18th and 25th Feby and 10th of March.

Inclosed you will find a power for holding a General Court Martial at Fort Pitt for the trial of all persons who shall be brought before them. The proceedings, if any capital, or any which affect Comm^d officers, to be sent to me for approbation.

I shall write to the Board of War and desire them to send up such of the Stores demanded by Capt Craig as we have it in our power to furnish.

[1] Col. Thomas Proctor was born in 1739 in Ireland, whence he emigrated at an early age to Pennsylvania, and at the time of the Revolution was a master carpenter at Philadelphia. He was a member of the city's Committee of Safety in 1775 and in October of the same year raised a company of artillery. This became, in August, 1776, a battalion, of which Proctor was major. Later as a full regiment, Proctor's artillery served at Brandywine and Germantown, and on most of the campaigns in the eastern states. Proctor resigned from the army April 18, 1781, retiring with the rank of colonel. After the war he served as sheriff and lieutenant of the city of Philadelphia, and as general of the Pennsylvania militia. He died in the city of his adoption, Mar. 16, 1806.

It was not my intention to give Col⁰ Clarke an unlimited order upon the Magasines at Fort Pitt, By referring to the latest Returns from thence I found we could furnish the quantity of the several Articles mentioned in my letter. If his wants should be greater, and what he further requests can, in the opinion of the Commandant, be spared, I wish he may be supplied, but not otherwise. In short, it is my desire that every assistance, consistent with the safety of the post may be given to that Expedition if it should be prosecuted.

The keeping up the post of Fort M°Intosh must entirely depend upon the utility of it, and the means you have of supporting it. Of this you, who are upon the spot, will be the best able to judge. It would have been utterly out of our power to have built and maintained a Fort at Cuskuskei for the Cooshocking Indians even had they remained in Friendship with us, but as you seem to think in your last we have lost their interest, the matter falls of course.

I have never failed of transmitting your representations on the score of provision to Congress. Immediately upon the recipt of your last I wrote to them and informed them that the post must be evacuated in case of an invasion, if supplies were not immediately thrown in. When I was called upon last Fall to fix upon the places of deposit for the specific supplies demanded from each State, I directed Pennsylvania to form an ample Magasine at Fort Pitt—Why it has not been done, the Executive of that State can only answer?

I am &c

Col⁰ Brodhead or Officer Commanding Fort Pitt.

[Enclosure in above.]

A General Court Martial whereof [blank in Ms.] is to be president, is to sit at Fort Pitt at such time as the Commandant shall direct for the trial of all such persons as shall be brought before them.

Given under my hand and seal at Head Quarters at New Windsor State of New York the 16ᵗʰ day April 1781.

[Joseph Carleton to President of Congress. 15S24. Transcript.]

WAR OFFICE, Ap^l 16th 1781.

SIR:
The Board have the honor to lay before Congress an estimate of military stores wanted for an expedition into the Indian country, under the command Brig^r General Clark.—
I have the honor, &c.
JOS. CARLETON, Sec^y

Estimate: For Eight Inch Howitzer: 202 eight inch shells; 220 eight inch fuzes filled—& other apparatus.
Also for six pounders; for three pounder; & for royal howitzer Also 6000 musket flints; 6000 rifle flints—with many shot, shells $^{&c}$

WESTMORELAND RAIDED

[Col. Archibald Lochry to Pres. Joseph Reed. 46J65. L. S.][1]

WESTMORELAND COUNTY April 17th 1781

May it please your Excellency:
I have the honor (by the opportunity of Col° Proctor)[2] to send my accounts of Lieutenant of this County to the 20th Ul° I have likewise transmitted the Accounts of Col° Hays and Col° Campbell;[3] I have called on Colonels Cook & Perry[4] for their Accounts which they have omitted to render.

[1] This letter is printed in *Pa. Archives*, IX, 79–80; we publish from the original letter, signed by Lochry.
[2] For Col. John Proctor see *Rev. Upper Ohio*, 200, note 37.
[3] Col. Charles Campbell, who was captured by Indians in 1777, had been exchanged and was now serving as sub-lieutenant of Westmoreland County. See sketch of his life in *Frontier Defense*, 70, note 34.
Christopher Hays of the Sewickly settlement was at this time a member of the Supreme Executive Council of the state. He was also judge and sub-lieutenant of the county. Hays remained in Westmoreland until 1787 when he was induced by Col. George Morgan to embark on his Louisiana enterprise. On Hubbell's Creek in the Ste. Geneviève District Hays obtained a large Spanish concession on which he settled many families from Pennsylvania, and where he himself spent the last years of his life.
[4] For a sketch of Col. Edward Cook see *ibid.*, 110, note 75.
Col. James Perry settled at an early day at the mouth of Turtle Creek on the Monongahela River. From there he was elected to the First Provincial

I am doubtfull my Accounts are not in as good order as they ought to be, but I am in hopes our unhappy and distressed situation will in some measure appologize for their Irregularity.

The Savages have begun their hostilities,— since I came from Philadelphia they have struck us in four different places,—have taken and killed thirteen persons with a Number of horses and other Effects of the Inhabitants;—two of the unhappy people were killed one mile from Hannastown.

Our Country is worse depopulated than ever it has been:—I have got a few Militia to support the Frontiers, but am doubtfull I cannot keep them long on duty for want of Provisions;—our situation at present seems very deplorable and if the Savages were acquainted with our Weakness, they may very easily drive the people over the Yohogania.

There is no amunition in the Country but what is public property;—when the Hostilities commenced the people came to me from all Quarters for amunition, and assured me that if I did not supply them out of the public Magazine, they would not attempt to stand.—Under these Circumstances I gave out a large Quantity; and would be glad to have your Excellencies Approbation, as I am certain this County would have been evacuated had I not have supplied them with that necessary Article.

I have built a Magazine for the State Stores (in the form of a Block house) that will be defended with a very few men:— I have never kept men to guard it as yet, and will be happy to have your Excellencys Orders to keep a Serjeants Guard at our small Magazine;—the Consequence of moving to the interior parts of the Country would discourage those people on the Frontiers who have so long supported it.

I rest these Matters to your Excellencys Consideration and Wisdom, and beg leave to subscribe myself Your Excellencys Most obedient and very humble servant

A. LOCHRY

HIS EXCELLENCY JOSEPH REED Esqr President &c &c
[*Addressed:*] To His Excellency Joseph Reed Esqr President &c &c &c of Pennsylvania On Public Service p^r fav^r Col^o Proctor.

Conference of Pennsylvania and its Constitutional Convention of July, 1776. On Mar. 21, 1777 Perry was appointed sub-lieutenant of his county and served as such to the close of the war. He then removed to Kentucky, where he was still living June 19, 1802. Port Perry in Allegheny County, Pa., takes its name from this officer.

BRODHEAD ACCUSED

[Pres. Joseph Reed to Pres. Samuel Huntington. Washington Papers. Contemporary transcript.]

IN COUNCIL PHILADELPHIA April 18, 1781

SIR:
In answer to your excellency's favour of this morning enclosing general Washington's letter respecting fort pitt, I beg leave to inform you that proper measures were taken last fall to have meat salted at fort pitt Cattle were purchased in the adjoining counties of Virginia and salt sent up to that post, but some obstruction arose to the cattle going out of Virginia which was not got over till this spring, when twenty eight head were sent, but in a different condition than they should have been. Col Broadhead made a representation to us about the same time and of the same nature as that to the general upon which every step in our power has been taken and we hope by this time Mr Duncan's exertions and the money with which we supplied him have relieved not only the wants but the apprehensions of the garrison. As to flour and spirits there never has been any want. In this respect Col Broadhead's representation is too unqualified I must also beg leave to remark to your excellency that until the last requisition of Congress, beef was not comprized in the articles required from this state. Our whole exertion therefore was made on the other articles and when we inform your excellency that in the course of a few months six thousand and fifty four pounds fourteen shillings and one penny state money, when the purchases could be made with it nearly at a par with gold & silver, was sent to furnish the supplies of the garrison, and one thousand pounds lately we presume it will appear that this important post has not been neglected.
Whether these supplies have been furnished or applied with due œconomy and care we cannot determine, but the council have thought it proper to send the enclosed letter on this subject for the information of Congress. The writer is an auditor of the public accounts and deemed a man of character and intelligence.[1] We are sorry to add that the information of the inhabitants of

[1] This refers to the charges of Alexander Fowler against Brodhead, for which see *ante*, 356-70.

that part of the country corresponds in some degree with several particulars in the letter.

I am with much respect Your excellency's most obedient and very humble Servt

Jos: REED President

HIS EXCELLENCY SAMUEL HUNTINGTON President of Congress.

[Summary of a letter of David Duncan, Pittsburgh, April 24, 1781, to Pres. Joseph Reed. Printed in *Pa. Archives*, IX, 97–98.]

Has reached home after a long, hard ride, during which he bought thirty beeves; difficult to pass the state money. Petition being sent against himself and Colonel Brodhead wherein they are charged with speculating with public money. He denies the charge; it arises from his lack of money to pay public debts. His character at stake; has resigned all his estate for two years for support of public; every man has his enemies. Requests the appointment of another commissary in his place. "Colo. Brodhead is out on a Campaign against the Delaware Indians. I am not Certain of the Number of Men he has with him, some say when started from Wheeling he had about four Hundred, but no Certainty. We have heard nothing of him since, but expect him here in the Course of six or eight days."

BRITISH THREATEN FORT PITT

[Gen. George Washington to Col. Daniel Brodhead. Washington Papers. Draft.]

HEAD QUARTERS NEW WINDSOR 25th April 1781.

DEAR SIR:

The information contained in yours of the 27th ult° corresponds with intelligence I rece'd a few days ago, by a good channel, from New York. It is that Col° Conolly (who you must very well know) is to collect as many refugees as he can at New York and proceed with them as soon as the season will permit to Quebec— that upon his arrival in Canada he is to join Sir John Johnson and that they are to proceed by the Route of Venango against

FRONTIER RETREAT 389

Fort Pitt and the Western Frontier. It is added that Conolly is to carry with him blank Commissions for persons already in the Country and that he expects to be joined by several hundred disaffected in the Neighbourhood of Fort Pitt.[1] Upon this information and what you may have discovered, I think you should without loss of time secure or remove every suspected character from about you and to such a distance that they can not readily join the Enemy should they come down. I have communicated this intelligence to Congress as an additional motive to their taking measures to have a competent supply of provision thrown into the Garrison.

If Capt Brady is materially useful to you, you may detain him for the Campaign, giving the Commanding Officer of his Reg^t notice of the cause of detention.

I am &c
Col^o Brodhead or Officer Commanding Fort Pitt

[Gen. George Washington to President of Congress. Washington Papers. Draft.]

Head Quarters New Windsor 25^h April 1781.

Sir:

Since my letter of the 14th to your Excellency on the subject of an immediate supply of provision for Fort Pitt, I have received the following intelligence, thro' a good Channel, which makes the measures I then recommended more indispensably necessary—
"Colonel Conolly with his Corps to proceed to Quebec as soon as possible, to be joined in Canada by Sir John Johnston with a number of Tories and Indians said to amount to three thousand.

[1] For a sketch of Col. John Connolly see *Dunmore's War*, 42, note 77; see also *Rev. Upper Ohio*, passim. For Connolly's own account see his pamphlet *A Narrative of the Transactions, Imprisonment and Sufferings of John Connolly an American Loyalist and a Lieut. Col. in His Majesty's Service* (London, 1783). This is republished in *Pennsylvania Magazine of History and Biography*, XII and XIII, and also in a pamphlet printed in New York in 1889. In it Connolly gives an outline of the plan Washington here mentions, but says that in October, 1780, when first proposed, it was too late in the year to carry it into effect. In April, 1781 Connolly was ill, and soon thereafter was ordered to Virginia. See a recent study of Connolly's career by C. M. Burton in American Antiquarian Society, *Proceedings*, October, 1909. Therein it is stated that he died at Montreal Jan. 30, 1813.

(The number must be exagerated).¹ His Route is to be by Buck Island,² Lake Ontario and Venango and his object is Fort Pitt and all the adjacent posts. Conolly takes with him a number of Commissions for persons now residing at Pittsburg and several hundred men at that place have agreed to join to make prisoners of Col⁰ Brodhead and all friends to America. His (Conolly's) great influence in that Country will, it is said, enable him to prevail upon the Indians and inhabitants to assist the British in any measure" The latter part of this intelligence agrees exactly with a discovery which Col⁰ Brodhead has lately made of a correspondence between persons at Fort Pitt and the Commandant of Detroit. Some of whom have been seized by him. I have immediately transmitted the above to Col⁰ Brodhead and have directed him to secure or remove every suspected person in the Vicinity of his post. The security of the Frontier of the State of Pennsylvania so immediately depends upon the support of Fort Pitt, that I think the Executive cannot fail, upon a representation being made to them, of taking measure to afford the proper succours, while the thing is practicable. Upon the first appearance of an enemy, the communication between that post and the settlements below will be intirely interrupted.

I have the honor to be &c
PRESIDENT OF CONGRESS.

ARTILLERY FOR CLARK

[Gen. George Washington to Capt. Isaac Craig. Washington Papers. Draft.]

HEAD QUARTERS NEW WINDSOR 25 April 1781
SIR:

I have rec^d your fav^r of the 15th. The present State of Col⁰ procters Reg^t does not admit of your Company's being made up to its full complement, but I have, by this conveyance desired Genl St Clair to let you have as many Men as will put you on a level with the others. This is all that can now be done. I have already desired the Board of War to send six Artificers to Fort Pitt,

---

¹ The sentence enclosed in parentheses is in a different hand from that of the rest of the letter.
² Buck Island was later known as Carleton, for which see *ante*, 54, note 4.

you may wait upon them with this letter and ask three on four more, if they can be spared.[1]

I would wish the enclosed for General Clarke and Col⁰ Brodhead to reach them as speedily as possible; you will be pleased to take charge of them yourself, if you do not meet with a good opportunity previous to the time you intend setting out.

I am &c

CAP^T CRAIG 4th Reg^t Artillery care of Board of War Phila^d

RAID IN SOUTHWEST VIRGINIA

[Col. Arthur Campbell to Gov. Thomas Jefferson. 10S190–92. Transcript.]

WASHINGTON, April 25th, 1781.

SIR:

I enclose for your Excellency's information a letter just received from Col. Martin[2] and another from Major [Aaron] Lewis, whom I had instructed to drive off the Indians from their haunts near Cumberland Gap. I have no hopes now that the Cherokees will sue for peace,[3] whilst Augusta, Georgia, is in the enemy's hands, and they can receive supplies from thence—several hundred of the Indian women and children being now subsisted in that State by the British.

Col. Elijah Clarke[4] has by meeting with Major Dunlop and his corps of partisans on this side the Savannah river,[5] failed giving the blow that was intended.

[1] For Washington's communication, April 20, 1781, to the Board of War, and the list of artillery stores needed see *Ill. Hist. Colls.*, VIII, 535–37. See also Craig's letter to Gen. George Rogers Clark, *ibid.*, 547.

[2] For a sketch of Col. Joseph Martin see *Dunmore's War*, 235, note 64.

[3] Col. Arthur Campbell had returned about three months before the date of this letter from a campaign against the Overhill Cherokee, wherein he had inflicted much damage upon that tribe. See description in Theodore Roosevelt, *Winning of the West* (New York, 1889), II, 298–305. Campbell's official report is in Draper's Mss., 9DD24.

[4] Elijah Clarke was born about the year 1742 in Virginia; he removed to North Carolina, and in 1774 to Georgia. Clarke was captain of militia in 1776; he later became colonel, and in 1782 brigadier-general. He was much employed against the Loyalists and the hostile Creek Indians. In 1794 Clarke embarked in Genet's abortive plan for the capture of Florida. Afterwards he lived in retirement until his death Dec. 15, 1799 at his home in Wilkes County, Ga.

[5] James Dunlap was a Loyalist, who on Nov. 27, 1776 was commissioned captain in the Queen's Rangers. During the first years of the war he was in

The Northward Indians have visited us three different times this season, with small parties, in all killing one person, capturing two, and wounding two or three. These different parties came up Sandy river, and the last time penetrated into the settlement on Holstein, making prisoner a son of Capt. Bledsoe's.[1]

These troubles at home, and the apparent continuance of them, induced a number of the officers of this county to apply to me, to request that the Executive would countermand the order of the 29th of March last for sending two hundred militia out of the county to join the Southern army; or, at least, that the number might be lessened. The men in general at present are unable to fit themselves for so distant a trip, having received no pay for their different exertions last year. The Executive, I trust, will direct some regular mode for supplying with stores the company that ranges in Powell's Valley.

As to Lieut. Col. Martin's proposition, I am satisfied of the good effects it would have, could it be put into execution; but I suppose that the pressing calls from other quarters will prevent it, a force of at least two hundred men being necessary, as a defeat in the enemy's country might be the cause of our being overwhelmed suddenly.

I am, with respect, Your Excellency's most obedient serv^t,

ARTHUR CAMPBELL.

To Gov. JEFFERSON.

PENNSYLVANIA TROOPS PAID

[Summary of a letter of Pres. Joseph Reed, May 2, 1781, to Alexander Fowler and William Amberson. Printed in *Pa. Archives*, IX, 114–15.]

Encloses their appointments as auditors to settle accounts of Eighth Pennsylvania Regiment; gratuities for men enlisted for war, bounties for new recruits. Certificates and acts of assembly the North, participating in the battles of Brandywine and Monmouth. In 1780 Dunlap carried on partisan warfare in South Carolina, and on Mar. 24, 1781, while on a foraging expedition, his troop was attacked near Little River, twenty-two miles from Ninety-six, and totally defeated by Clarke's Whig forces from Georgia. The engagement is known as that of Beattie's Mills. Dunlap surrendered to a Whig officer who in the heat of passion slew the defeated commander.

[1] For a sketch of Col. Anthony Bledsoe see *Dunmore's War*, 106, note 53.

relative to these matters sent by Hon. Christopher Hays. Captain Craig has secured funds to pay the Artillery, attention to that branch not to alarm other troops, who are equally deserving.

PROTECTION FOR WESTMORELAND

[Summary of a letter of Pres. Joseph Reed, Philadelphia, May 2, 1781, to Col. Archibald Lochry. Printed in *ibid.*, 115–16.]

Acknowledges receipt of Lochry's letter of April 17; regrets mournful accounts, other counties having like afflictions. Can devise no new means of protection. Recommends that Captain Stokeley's company be raised. Cumberland militia ordered to Westmoreland six weeks ago. Ammunition very scarce, not 1,000 pounds of lead in this city. Magazine for powder at Lochry's not approved; more exposed to danger from the enemy than if kept at sundry places. Money sent by Christopher Hays for emergencies and for pay of Stokeley's company. Boundary line to be run this spring.

BRODHEAD ACCUSED

[Gen. George Washington to Alexander Fowler. Washington Papers. Draft.]

HEAD QUARTERS NEW WINDSOR 5th May 1781.

SIR:

His Excellency the president of Congress has lately transmitted to me the Copy of a letter from you to the president of Pennsylvania, in which, are a number of charges against Colonel Brodhead and the Deputy Q^r Master General at Fort Pitt for mal conduct, and insinuations against others not named. Congress have thereupon directed me to take measures to have the matter investigated, and the delinquents brought to justice. You must be sensible that it is as difficult to support as to defend a general charge, and as yours are chiefly of the latter nature, I am under the necessity of calling upon you to specify those against the D^y Q^r Master General or any other persons in the Staff dipartment, and deliver them to the commanding officer who has my orders to bring them to treat by Court Martial.

There is a necessity of proceeding in another Manner against Col° Brodhead. It being impossible to hold a Court at Fort Pitt proper for the trial of an officer of his Rank, it must be done at the Army, and the proofs and defence must be supported principally by depositions taken upon the spot, in presence of the parties, as all the Witnesses cannot be brought down without infinite expence and much inconvenience. The Judge Advocate General sends a deputation to the person usually officiating as Judge Advocate at the post authorising him to take these depositions. You will therefore specify your Charges against Col° Brodhead, deliver him a Copy of them and be ready when called upon to make the requisite depositions. When the whole are finished, The Judge Advocate at the post will transmit them to the Judge Advocate General and Col° Brodhead will be ordered to attend for trial. If you yourself or any other Witnesses can make it convenient to attend it will be well, for depositions should not be made use of but upon necessity.

I am &c

ALEXANDER FOWLER Esq: Auditor Western Department Fort Pitt.

[Gen. George Washington to Commandant at Fort Pitt. Washington Papers. Draft.]

HEAD QUARTERS NEW WINDSOR 5th May 1781.

SIR:

Mr Fowler will put into your hands sundry Charges against Mr Duncan D^y Q^r M. General at Fort Pitt, on which you will have him arrested and brought to trial. The proceedings you will transmit to me. Should Mr Fowler bring Charges against any other person who may, from their Ranks or Stations, be properly tried by the Court which shall be convened, you will likewise arrest and bring them to trial. Inclosed you have a power for holding a Court.

Mr Fowler has charges also against Col° Brodhead, who, on account of his Rank, cannot be tried at Fort Pitt. You will therefore, after filling up the Blank for the name, deliver the inclosed deputation to the Gentleman who usually officiates as Judge Advocate, and he will take the depositions of the parties on the spot, which will enable a Court Martial with the Army to determine the matter.

I am Sir Y^r most ob^t Servt

Col.° Brodhead or Officer commanding Fort Pitt.

[Gen. George Washington to Col. Daniel Brodhead. Washington Papers. Draft.]

Head Quarters New Windsor 5th May 1781.

DR Sir:

Mr Fowler having in a late letter to the president of Pennsylvania made several charges against you for mal conduct in your command, The president of the state communicated it to Congress, who have been pleased, thereupon, to direct me to investigate the matter and bring you to treat upon the matters alledged against you. Mr Fowlers charges having been rather general, I have desired him to specify them, and to furnish you with a Copy of them. You must be sensible that no Court can be constituted at Fort Pitt for the trial of an Officer of your Rank. It must therefore be held at the Army; but as it will be impossible to bring down all the necessary Witnesses, the Judge Advocate General sends by this Conveyance a deputation to the Gentleman usually officiating in that capacity at the post, autherising him to take depositions in the presence of the parties. These, by a Resolve of Congress, are made admissible evidence in Court. When the necessary depositions are finished, you will repair to the Army and take your trial.

You will see the propriety of giving up the command to the Officer next in Rank while this business is transacting. It will take off every objection that can be made against the validity of the depositions, as having been taken under your influence as Commandant.¹

I am &c

Col.° Brodhead.

¹ On May 6, 1781 Brodhead turned over to Gibson the command of the Western Department, and the next day left for Philadelphia. Draper Mss., INN71. Gibson had been ordered to reënforce Clark, but his orders from Brodhead conflicted with this plan. See Gibson's letters in *Ill. Hist. Colls.*, VIII, 547, 559.

[Inhabitants of Pittsburgh to President of Congress. Washington Papers. A. L. S. of Fowler.]

PITTSBURGH 9th May 1781.

SIR:

Aware that Colonel Brodhead may attempt to injure our reputations, for thus doing our duty to ourselves and our Country, by detecting Publick Abuses, and Praying for a redress of Greivances by the removal of a Man from this Command, whom we cannot but consider as a Publick Nusance. We beg leave to declare to your Excellency, that our motives are pure and Disinterested, and that we have no View but one in this Remonstrance —The prosperity of this Country, and the Happiness of the Community. Therefore should Colonel Brodhead attempt to reflect on us for what we have done, or to throw any specious, or flimsey veil, over his Conduct, and Connections here, as represented in our remonstrance; we hope and wish an opportunity will be afforded us to confront him with such Evidence as will fully prove to your Excellency, to Congress, and to the World, that the Allegations we have set forth against him, are founded on the most stubborn Facts.

We have the honor to be with the greatest veneration and respect, Sir, Your Most Obed. Humble Servants

        A. FOWLER
        THO. SMALLMAN
        EDW. WARD
        ROBERT CAMPBELL
        DEVEREUX SMITH
        JOHN IRWIN

TO HIS EXCELLENCY THE PRET OF CONGRESS &c &c &c

The Original Depositions and other proofs which Accompanies the Remonstrance to the President & Council of the State of Penna we make no doubt will come before your Excellency & Congress. In the mean time we beg leave to trouble your Excellency with a Copy of one of them respecting the Conduct of our Assistant Quarter Master.

        A. FOWLER
        EDW. WARD
        ROBERT CAMPBELL
        DEVEREUX SMITH
        JOHN IRWIN
        THO: SMALLMAN

PENNSYLVANIA TROOPS FOR CLARK

[Summary of a letter of Col. Archibald Lochry, Twelve Mile Run, May 11, 1781, to Gen. George Rogers Clark. 51J48. Printed in *Ill. Hist. Colls.*, VIII, 549.]

Would gladly aid Clark in the intended expedition; entering the enemy's country is most effective means of retaliation. Frontier of Westmoreland is badly harassed; is raising companies of rangers. Thinks an order might be obtained from executive of the state for these troops. Volunteers will doubtless join.

[Summary of a letter of Pres. Joseph Reed, In Council, Philadelphia, May 15, 1781, to Gen. George Rogers Clark. 51J49. Printed in *ibid.*, 550.]

Has received Clark's letter of March 23; considers a Detroit expedition under Clark's care as important to Pennsylvania as to Virginia; has much confidence in Clark's ability and good conduct. Will be much gratified if inhabitants volunteer; authorizes the statement that Pennsylvania officials consider the service highly meritorious; but are not in condition to grant financial aid. Will correspond with Brodhead and Jefferson on the subject.

DISCHARGE FOR A VOLUNTEER

[Certificate for John McColloch.[1] 4NN96. A. D. S.]

This is to Certify that John M°Cullough served as a Soldier in my Company on the Expedition with Colonel Broadhead Nine-

[1] John McColloch Jr. was born in 1752 on the south branch of the Potomac in what is now Hardy County, W. Va. When twenty years of age he removed with his father's family to the waters of Short Creek, Ohio County, Va. There the McCollochs became famous hunters and during the Revolution and the Indian wars served as scouts and spies. John was out under Brodhead in 1781, and under Williamson in 1782. In July of the latter year he and his elder brother, Samuel, were scouting when they fell into an Indian ambush; the latter was killed, and John made a hairbreadth escape from capture at the hands of the enemy. In 1792 John McColloch was captain, and three years later major,

teen Days furnish^d his Own horse & Provision. Given under my hand This 14 Day May 1781

JOSEPH OGLE Capt

CLARK AT FORT PITT

[Summary of a letter of Gen. George Rogers Clark, Fort Pitt, May 20, 1781, to Gen. George Washington. 16S38. Printed in *Ill. Hist. Colls.*, VIII, 551–53.]

Lack of men for his expedition due to British invasion of Virginia. Baron Steuben gave orders that Clark's forces were to be enlarged by Col. John Gibson's regiment and Captain Heath's company. Colonel Brodhead thought he was not at liberty to order them on campaign. Appeals to Washington for permission to have them accompany him. Two hundred additional men might ensure success. Forts may be garrisoned with militia as no attacks will be made during his advance. Hopes to make peace at Detroit. Troops will be ready to march at an hour's notice.

[Summary of a letter of Gen. George Rogers Clark, Pittsburgh, May 21, 1781, to Gen. George Washington. Printed in *ibid.*, 553–54.]

Has just received Washington's letter of April 25, not alarmed at the intelligence, has heard similar rumors by way of the Illinois. Thinks the plan is not to advance by the Allegheny, but by a western route as a thousand Wabash Indians have again declared for Americans. Is well acquainted with Colonel Connelly and would be glad to meet him if he has no regulars with him. Has written to Pennsylvania for consent to enlist men from their frontier. Apprehends no danger by way of Venango.

of the county militia. In 1793 he commanded an important reconnoissance into the trans-Ohio region. After the war McColloch and his wife, née Mary Bukey, lived on the paternal estate at Short Creek until the former's death, April 6, 1821. See interview with one of his sons in Draper Mss., 2S273–75.

EXPEDITION AGAINST DELAWARES

[Summary of letter of Col. Daniel Brodhead, Philadelphia, May 22, 1781, to Pres. Joseph Reed. Printed in *Pa. Archives*, IX, 161-62.]

Has pleasure to report the expedition carried on against the revolted Delawares. With about 300 men, nearly half being volunteers he surprised the towns of Coschocton and Indaochaie,[1] killed fifteen warriors and took upwards of twenty odd men, women, and children prisoners. About four miles above the former town he detached a party against forty drunken warriors who had just crossed the river with prisoners and scalps; river so swollen by rains that crossing was impracticable. Destroyed the towns, took great quantities of peltry and other stores, and killed forty head of cattle. Then marched seven miles up river in order to send to Moravian towns for craft to cross and pursue the enemy's party. Volunteers refused to go farther; determined to return. Then marched to Newcomers town whither about thirty Indians faithful to alliance had withdrawn. Killbuck and La Luzerne pursued the party. Killed one of the greatest villains and brought in his scalp. Were treated with great kindness by these and by the Moravian Indians; provisions supplied. Plunder sold at Fort Henry for £80,000. Montour, Wilson, and three other faithful Indians accompanied expedition. Although considerable firing occurred, no man was killed or injured, and only one horse was lost.

CONDITIONS AT FORT PITT

[Extract of a letter from Col. John Gibson to Gov. Thomas Jefferson. 11S21. Transcript.][2]

FORT PITT, May 30th 1781.

General Clark will write your Excellency by this opportunity, & I make no doubt give you every information relative to the intended expedition. I am much afraid he will not be able to

---

[1] Indaochaie was the Indian name for the abandoned Moravian village of Lichtenau. See *ante*, 377.

[2] This letter is also printed in Sparks, *Corr. of Am. Rev.*, III, 323-25, where it is wrongly dated May 26, 1781.

get many of the militia from this quarter, as I have just heard that three hundred men from the counties of Monongehala & Ohio, have crossed the river at Wheeling & are gone to cut off the Moravian Indian towns; if so, they will hardly turn out on their return. Indeed, it appears to me, they have done this in order to evade going with Gen¹ Clark. The Moravians have always given us the most convincing proofs of their attachment to the cause of America, by always giving us intelligence of every party that came against the frontiers; & on the late expedition they furnished Col° Brodhead & his party with a large quantity of provisions when they were starving.

Speaks of his reg^t not having rec^d a shilling for services for the twenty months past; speaks of going, as ordered, from Richmond to Philadelphia, for powder for Gen¹ Clark, & the expenses getting it from Carlisle to Fort Pitt.

JOHN GIBSON

[Col. Daniel Brodhead to Samuel Huntington. 14S120–21. Transcript.]

PHILAD^A May 30th, 1781

The troops at Fort Pitt & the dependant posts have suffered uncommon hardships from a great scarcity of provisions & clothing, which misfortune they have hitherto borne with uncommon fortitude. But it cannot be expected, that under such sufferings a proper subordination can much longer be preserved.

The British force which, it is said, is to attack Fort Pitt, will proceed from Niagara down the Alleghany river; consequently Gen¹ Clark's expedition to the westward will by no means cover the principal settlements west of the Mountains; & the same force with which we are threatened from Niagara may pursue him down the Ohio River unless a sufficient force can be raised to prevent their success in the attempt. * * * The parties which I have hitherto employed against the Indians are destitute of paint, & cloth for leggings & breech clouts, & cannot act to advantage until they are furnished with those articles The non-commissioned officers & soldiers of the 8th P^a Reg^t, & the Maryland Independent corps, are entirely destitute of shirts & other clothing, & the shoes of all the troops are worn out.

BRODHEAD ACCUSED

[Pres. Samuel Huntington to Gen. George Washington. Washington Papers. L. S.]

PHILADELPHIA June 2, 1781

SIR:

By the enclosed Order of Congress of the 29th Ulto, I am directed to lay before your Excellency the Letter of the 9th Ulto signed A. Fowler &c with the other Papers referred to, which are herewith enclosed

Col. Broadhead is now in this City. The Complaints of the Inhabitants in the Vicinity of Pittsburgh respecting his Conduct are very great, and his with Respect to them are not small. It seems necessary that due Enquiry be speedily made respecting those Matters and in such Manner as that Justice may be done.

I have the Honor to be, with very great Regard Your Excellency's Most obedient & most humble Servant

SAM. HUNTINGTON President

HIS EXCELLENCY GENERAL WASHINGTON

PENNSYLVANIA EXPEDITION PROPOSED

[Summary of a letter of Gen. George Rogers Clark, Crossings, June 3, 1781, to Westmoreland County officers. Printed in *Pa. Archives*, IX, 189.]

Hearing that the officers of Westmoreland are determined to distress the savages during the summer Clark presents the following plan: His objective point is the Shawnee, Delaware, and Sandusky towns.[1] The Delawares formerly on Muskingum have removed west of the Scioto; those of the Allegheny to Sandusky. Proposes that an expedition of drafted men from Westmoreland attack the Sandusky towns and then form a junction with Clark's army. If supplies cannot be obtained for such a long expedition, it would be advisable to join Clark's army. If peace does not take place this fall, it will be due to the inhabitants.

[1] Clark did not publicly announce that Detroit was the object of his expedition lest volunteers should be discouraged thereby.

CONDITIONS IN SOUTHWEST VIRGINIA

[Col. Arthur Campbell to Gov. Thomas Jefferson. 10S192–94. Transcript.]

WASHINGTON, June 4th 1781.

SIR:

This day your orders of the 28th of May came to hand, and I am sorry our situation at present is such that I have but a small prospect of forwarding the aid required. The murmuring and distresses occasioned by the misconduct of Commissaries, and the want of pay for militia services performed last year, together with the dread a man commonly has to leave his family exposed to the danger of being destroyed by the Indians before his return, are objections not easily answered. If the militia were paid off, I believe I should succeed well in complying with your Excellency's orders of the 12th of April last; and to this I have hopes to add one troop of horse.

Our frontier is now threatened with an invasion from the Creek Indians, Cherokees, Tories, &c. By a letter from Col° Sevier to Col° Isaac Shelby, of which he favored me with the perusal, a certain Crawford just made his escape from the Cherokees, says that the British Agent, some Tories, and a large body of Indians were preparing to come in, in order to give a blow to confound the project of a treaty. The account is so far believed in Carolina, that part of their militia are embodied. To me, it is doubtful, on account of the want of provisions, and information I have from Georgia, that Govenor Galvez has succeeded against Pensacola, treated with the Creek Indians in behalf of America as well as the Spaniards, and that General Pickens at Ninety Six, and Colonel Clarke at Augusta, were in a fair way to reduce those posts. General Greene's Head Quarters at Orangeburg, Sumter at Monk's Corner, and Marion carrying off a picquet from the Quarter House.

I am, Sir, your most obedient humble servant,

ARTHUR CAMPBELL.

P. S.—We are in want of amunition; none of that ordered last fall are come to hand, neither has Col. Preston received it.

To HIS EXCELLENCY, THE GOVERNOR.

THE BOUNDARY DISPUTE

[Summary of a letter of Col. James Marshel,[1] Washington County, June 5, 1781, to Pres. Joseph Reed. Printed in *Pa. Archives*, IX, 193-94.]

Opposition to organization of Washington County[2] militia created by Pentecost[3] and the Virginia faction, who are resolved to remain under Virginia jurisdiction until the line is actually run. Pentecost is assumed on old commission as county lieutenant of Yohogania County. John Canon and Daniel Leet,[4] the sub-lieutenants, refuse to do anything. Indians have done no damage in this county so far because of Brodhead's recent, and Clark's prospective, campaign. Requests some ammunition.

WESTMORELAND RAIDED

[Recollections of James Chambers.[5] 3S100-101.]

A party of nine Indians under Capt. John Harris, captured Joseph McNulty on Youghyoughogany on the 6th of June, '81,

[1] For a sketch of Col. James Marshel see *Wis. Hist. Colls.*, XXIII, 258, note 1.

[2] On Mar. 28, 1781 the legislature of Pennsylvania erected a new county from the territory formerly in dispute between their state and Virginia. The projected county comprised all south of the Ohio and west of the Monongahela and was named for the commander in chief of the American army. On April 2, 1781 James Marshel was appointed county-lieutenant with John Canon and Daniel Leet as sub-lieutenants.

[3] For Dorsey Pentecost see *Dunmore's War*, 101, note 47.

[4] Daniel, son of Isaac Leet, was born Nov. 6, 1748, on the New Jersey side of the Delaware about thirty miles above Philadelphia. Having been educated for a surveyor Daniel Leet secured a commission from Virginia as deputy under Col. William Crawford to survey lands on the Kanawha River for Washington, and was thus occupied when the Revolution began. Leet enlisted in the Thirteenth Virginia and was appointed quartermaster and paymaster of the regiment, and in 1778 served as adjutant under General McIntosh. In 1782 he was brigade-major of Crawford's unfortunate expedition, and after his return settled on Chartier's Creek, three miles above the tract which his father had purchased in 1779. Afterwards the younger Leet was a justice of the peace and a member of the Pennsylvania legislature. He died June 18, 1830 at the home of a daughter. See interview with his brother, Jonathan, in Draper Mss., 2S4.

[5] For James Chambers see *Frontier Defense*, 41 note 82.

& plundered his house: Five of the party took McNulty & started with the prisoner for their towns; while Capt Harris & 3 others remained, & next day captured my informant, James Chambers, on Sewickley in Westmoreland, in the path near Capt. Thos Stokeley's—wh. the Indians had waylaid. This party stole 8 horses & started off; & when trying to force the horses over from the eastern to the western bank of the Allegheny, two or 3 miles below Puckety creek,[1] Ensign Morrison[2] with 20 men, passing down the opposite bank from Franklin to Pittsburgh, discovered the Indians & horses. The horses w^d swim in a little distance & return back. The Indians hastily fled, one giving one of the horses a tomahawk cut in the rump, from wh. he recovered: They took their prisoner with them, & the young Indian who had been wounded on Brodhead's campaign in '79 abused Chambers,[3] struck him &c; & Chambers appealed to Capt. Harris, who lived much with John Harris of Harris' Ferry, now Harrisburgh,[4] & could talk good English—a tall Indian 6 feet 2 or 3 inches—was kind to Chambers; he s^d the young Indian's sourness arose from the death of his brother & himself being wounded on Brodhead's campaign.

When ensign Morrison appeared, & the Indians decamped, they left behind them a bell, tea-kettle, tea-pot, pair of shears, saddle, bed quilt, &c., taken at McNulty's house, near Pendergrass'

[1] Pucketty Creek forms part of the boundary between Allegheny and Westmoreland counties.

[2] Dr. Draper thought that the officer here mentioned was probably the one who later became Col. James Morrison of Lexington, Ky. The latter was, however, of the Pennsylvania line, while this Lieutenant Morrison belonged to a Virginia regiment. He had been sent to the heads of the Allegheny to look for signs of Connolly's descent toward Fort Pitt. Morrison found no sign of a warlike invasion. For his report see *post*, 406.

[3] Gen. Robert Orr told Dr. Draper that his father married for his third wife a sister of James Chambers, and "from her he learned, that when Chambers was taken prisoner by the Indians, they compelled him to sit down upon a hornet's nest—& when they pinioned & fastened him for the night, they had the point of a knife so fastened & placed just behind him, that if he moved his head back in the least, it would come in contact with the point of the knifeblade." Draper Mss., 6NN150–51.

[4] Captain Harris the elder was a Delaware Indian of the Turtle tribe who lived before 1728 near Nazareth, Pa. He was the father of the celebrated chief, Teedyuscung, and had another son who inherited his name of Captain Harris. Probably this son or a grandson was the captor of Chambers.

John Harris Jr., who in 1785 laid out the town of Harrisburgh, was born there in 1726. He was the son of the elder John Harris, an early Indian trader. The father emigrated from Yorkshire and died at his ferry in 1748.

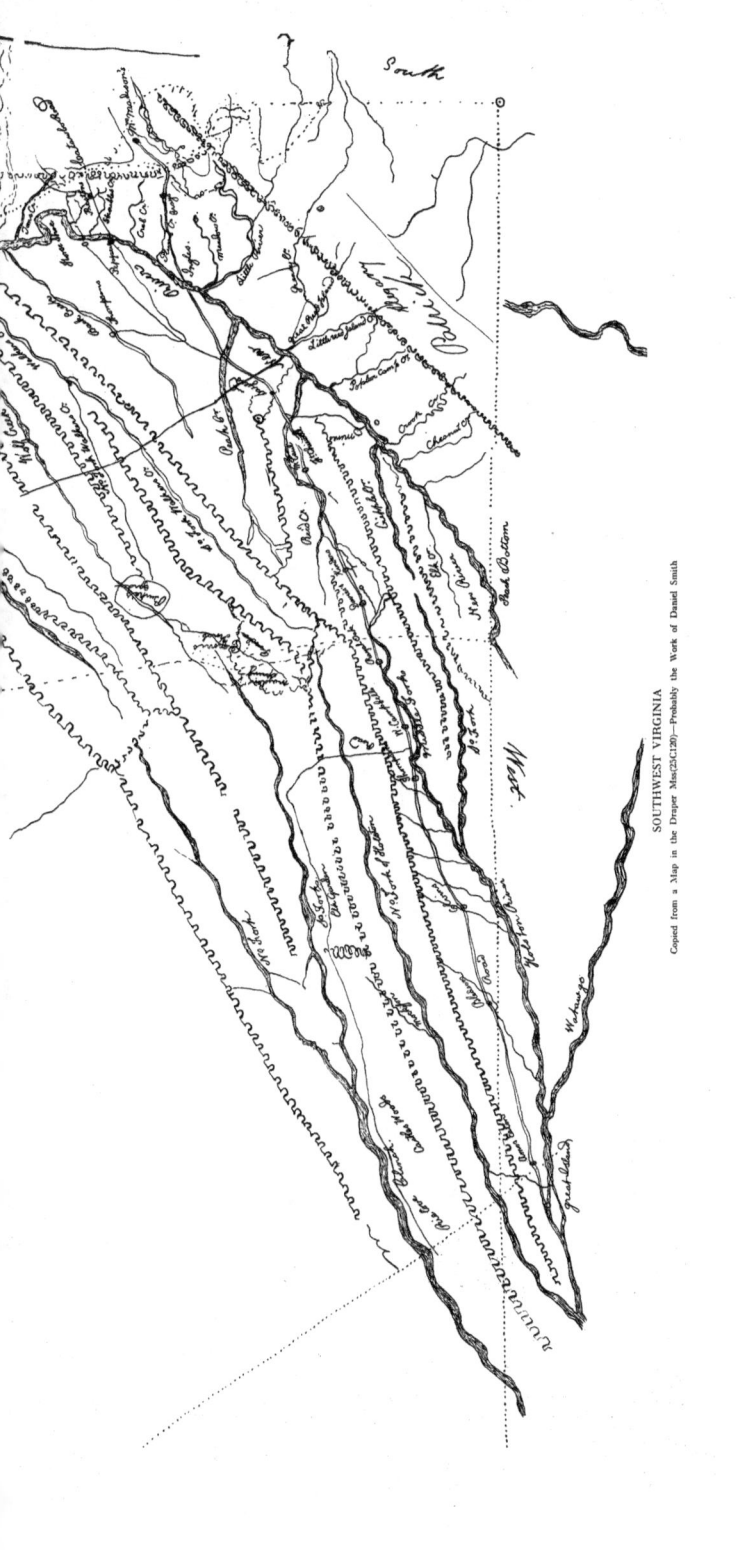

FRONTIER RETREAT   405

Station, at wh. station his family was when he was taken. Morrison took the horses & plunder to Pittsburgh for their owners; Capt. Brady was immediately despatched up Beaver to try & head the party & were in great haste, & one of the Indians followed to straighten up the grass, &c to prevent being trailed & finally got off. At Sandusky the two fragments of Capt. Harris' party met. There Chambers had to run the gauntlet.

BRODHEAD ACCUSED

[Gen. George Washington to Pres. Samuel Huntington. Washington Papers. Draft.]

HEAD QUARTERS NEW WINDSOR 7th June 1781.

SIR:
I have been honored with your Excellency's favors of the 2^d and 3^d Instants. I had, upon the former complaints exhibited against Col^o Brodhead and Mr Duncan the D^y Q^r M^r. Genl at Fort Pitt, directed the proper measures to be taken for calling them to an account, and as the Complainants in the present instance are principally the same as in the first they will have an opportunity of bringing and supporting their charges before the Courts which have been already ordered.

I have written to the Governors of Pennsylvania Maryland and Delaware and have desired them to send the Militia required by the Resolution of the 31st May to Virginia or Maryland as circumstances may require. I must trouble your Excellency to forward the inclosed to the Executives of those States.

Your Excellency's Circular Letter of the 1st instant cannot, I think, but have a happy effect, unless the States are determined, for want of proper energy at the moment when they ought most to exert themselves, to lose those advantages which they have it in their power to secure at the proposed Negociation. A Little success on our part will overballance any exorbitant terms or claims which the partizans of Great Britain may attempt to impose or demand.

The intelligence from the West Indies which your Excellency has been pleased to communicate is both interesting and agreeable. Could our generous Allies but once obtain a compleat

Naval superiority, the happiest consequences would undoubtedly insue.

I have the honor to be &^{c}

P. S. Inclosed is a Return of all the Recruits who have joined this Army from the 1st of January to the 1st of June amounting to 2574. A few have joined the York Regiments of Infantry and perhaps about 60 the Jersey. Your Excellency will be pleased for the information of Congress to call upon the Board of War for the monthly return of May in which the above are included. And by deducting from that return the detachment under the command of the Marquis de la Fayette, The two Regiments of New York and Hazens Reg^t now upon the Northern Frontier, you will be able to form a judgment of my efficient Strength at this place and in Jersey.

His Excellency Sam^L Huntington Esq.

CONDITIONS AT FORT PITT

[Summary of a letter of David Duncan, Pittsburgh, June 9, 1781, to Pres. Joseph Reed. Printed in *Pa. Archives*, IX, 200–1.]

Cannot make full returns since Perry has not delivered the stores. Hopes to save fully one third on prices that Perry paid. Hard to get people to take state money since exchange went to 175. Had men trying to purchase beef in the Glades, no one would sell except for hard money. Hopes to be continued in office. "Lt Morrison, of the 9th Virg^a Reg^t, have been up French Creek as far as the Carrying place, to see if they could make any Discoveries of the Indians & English that was said to be there & Coming against us; he and his men made no Discovery of any kind, nor no signs at the Carrying place; so from that we may hope the report we had of it was false, and no truth in it. I am very much of the opinion Genl Clark's Campaign will fall through, as it seems he wont get any men worth while on this side the Mountains; it's thought one Hundred is the most he will get."

BRODHEAD ACCUSED

[Gen. George Washington to Alexander Fowler. Washington Papers. Draft.]

HEAD QUARTERS 12th June 1781

SIR:
I wrote you under the 5th of May last respecting a Number of Charges & Accusations exhibited thro the President of Congress against Colo Broadhead—since which I have received thro' the same Channel which conveyed the former, a frish Number of Exhibits, Depositions & Complaints, on the same Head, in which your Name appears. As this matter seems to involve a Variety of Crimination—& in its present State appears very diffuse—in its Prosecution before a Court Martial must be attended with great Trouble & Expence—I have to request that you will make a particular Stating of all the matters of Charge & Accusation against the Col° brot into one clear Point of View, with the several Alligations & Supports properly arranged, that the whole may be attended to under one comprehensive Prospect. The particular mode for obtaining & forward^g the Evidences which are to be taken in the Case has been already pointed out in the abovementioned Letter of the 5th ulto. On Compliance with the above Order a Court Martial will be instituted, when I hope this troublesome Affair will have an Issue

I am &c

ALEXANDER FOWLER ESQ. Auditor W Dep^t Fort Pitt.

[Gen. George Washington to Pres. Samuel Huntington. Washington Papers. Draft.]

HEAD QUARTERS, NEW WINDSOR 16th June 1781

SIR:
I have the Honor of your Excellencys Fav^r of the 6th Instant inclosing sundry Petitions, Complaints &c against Col° Broadhead, having before this received a Number of other Papers respect^g Col° Broadheads Conduct—& observing that these Complaints have been exhibited in a very diffuse manner, & will involve a Variety of matter, I have written to Mr Fowler A[u]ditor of the Public Accounts at Fort Pitt, who appears to be a Principal in these Complaints to State them all in one general View,

exhibiting the several Charges in distinct Heads, with their several Supports & Evidences—when these are received a Court will be instituted & Col° Broadhead will have a Trial upon the Charges, And I hope the matter will be brot to a proper Issue.

Your Excellencys Fav^r of same Date with the above containing Intelligence from the Souward—& inclosing a Resolution of Congress of 2^d Instant respecting the Bills of Credit issuing in Pursuance of the Act of 18th Mar. 1780 is also duely received.

By Letters from Genl Greene of the 10th & 16th of May, our Affairs seen to wear a promising Aspect. I most since[re]ly congratulate your Excellency on this happy Event.

I have the honor to be with much Respect & Esteem Your Excellencys most Ob^t

HIS EXCELLENCY THE PRESD^T OF CONGRESS.

PENNSYLVANIA TROOPS FOR CLARK

[Summary of minutes of a meeting of Westmoreland County officers, June 18, 1781, at the house of Capt. John McClellan.[1] 51J60. Printed in *Ill. Hist. Colls.*, VIII, 566–67.]

Meeting called by legislative member, Christopher Hays. Adopted resolutions to furnish 300 men for Clark's expedition from the battalions of Col. John Pomeroy, Col. Benjamin Davis, and Col. George Beard.[2] Encouragement in money and grain for volunteers. Colonel Lochry entrusted with raising the men. A rendezvous appointed at home of Col. William Crawford.

[1] Capt. John McClellan lived on Big Sewickly Creek in that part of Westmoreland County which was afterwards included in Fayette County. McClellan served in 1778 as captain of militia and escort for provisions to Fort Hand. In 1782 he was chosen field-major on Crawford's expedition, was wounded during the retreat, taken prisoner, and tortured to death by Indians.

[2] Benjamin Davis was lieutenant-colonel of the second batallion of the county militia. His home was near the site of Greensburg, of which in 1785 he was a trustee. Davis was also a magistrate in his locality.

George Beard (or Baird) was lieutenant-colonel of the third battalion of Westmoreland militia.

[Summary of minutes of meeting of officers of several counties, at the Crossings, June 23, 1781. 51J62. Printed in *ibid.*, 569–70.]

Colonel Lochry, Colonel Shepherd, and officers of Pennsylvania and Virginia present. Resolved that the troops join General Clark at any time or place that he shall appoint; that one-fifth of the militia of what was West Augusta district will equal the 300 Westmoreland men, that therefore one-fifth of the militia of Monongalia, Yohogania, and Ohio counties be prepared for the expedition; that emigrants be enrolled as militia, and that in this time of emergency all factional disputes should be laid aside.

GARRISON AT FORT HENRY

[Col. John Gibson to Capt. Benjamin Biggs. 4JJ56. Transcript.]

HEAD QUARTERS, FORT PITT, June 23^d 1781

DEAR SIR:

I have at last been able to send Lt Neily[1] and a party of men to relieve you & the garrison of Fort Henry. You will please to deliver him all the orders you may have received from Col^o Brodhead or any other person respecting it.

You will repair with the officers & men under your command with all possible despatch to this post, bringing with you everything belonging to the reg^t, & as many boats as you can work.

As I hope to have the pleasure of seeing you soon, I shall defer saying any more than to assure I am, Dear Sir, Your most obed^t humble serv^t,

J^{NO} GIBSON, Col^o Comd^t F. Pitt.

To CAPT. BEN BIGGS, Com^{dt} Fort Henry. (Honored by Lt. Neily.)

---

[1] Benjamin Neilly (Neely or Neily) was commissioned ensign in the Eighth Pennsylvania Aug. 9, 1776; he was promoted to be second lieutenant July 13, 1777, and became first lieutenant Oct. 4 of the same year. On the reduction of the army Neilly was retired, Jan. 17, 1781.

NEW STATE PROJECT

[Summary of a letter of Col. James Marshel, Washington County, June 27, 1781, to Pres. Joseph Reed. Printed in *Pa. Archives*, IX, 233–34.]

Enemies of the Pennsylvania government are trying to prevent County organization. On June 5 the Yohogania County militia officers met and drafted one-fifth of the county militia for Clark's expedition; the people deny their authority and refuse duty under any government until the line is run. Fears involving the county in civil war with new government party. Agitation is kept up to drive people into the scheme for a new government.[1] Those formerly elected to Virginia assembly have gone down to promote this business and delay the running of the line. There are 2,500 effective men in this county; unless commissioners come soon, will be reduced by internal or external enemies. June 17, twenty Indians attacked a frontier settlement, wounded one man, and took a family prisoners; frontier being evacuated.

BRODHEAD ACCUSED

[Alexander Fowler to Gen. George Washington. Washington Papers. A. L. S.]

PITTSBURGH 28th June 1781.

SIR:

I was Honored with your Excellencys Letter of the 5th of May, and shall agreeable thereto specify my Charges against Mr David Duncan, the Assistant to the Deputy Quarter Master General, as soon as the Necessary Accounts and Vouchers are returned from Philadelphia, for which I have Wrote to the Quarter Master General as well as the Board of Treasurey. I wish may it please your Excellencey to bring home the proofs and Convict on such Grounds as may create unanimity and leave the Court without doubts.

---

[1] Concerning the agitation for a new state west of the mountains see Boyd Crumrine, *History of Washington County Pennsylvania*, 231–35; and F. J. Turner, "Western State-Making in the Revolutionary Era," in *American Historical Review*, I, 85–87.

As to Colonel Brodhead, he had left this place before the arrival of your Excellenceys Letter, therefore as Law, as well as Custom require Colonel Brodheads presence at the taking of the depositions—so that he may have an opportunity of interrogating, and Crossexaming the Deponents—nothing can be done respecting that Gentleman untill his return, when Specifick Charges shall be exhibited against him, and such Depositions taken and transmitted to the Judge Advocate General in support of them, as I make no doubt will be found tantamount to the Accusations, and satisfactory to the Court.

I have hitherto officiated as Deputy Judge Advocate in this Department, therefore the Deputation from the Judge Advocate General came properly directed to me. However the Commanding Officer here Colonel Gibson, thinks it improper that I should Act in the double capacity of Judge Advocate and Prosecutor. For my own part, may it please your Excellencey, I should imagine that—by officiating as Deputy Judge Advocate—I naturally become the Prosecutor of a Publick Delinquent: But I wish that Colonel Brodhead and Mr. Duncan may have every Indulgence, and therefore humbly submit this point to your Excellency, and the Judge Advocate General.

I have the Honor to be with the greatest Attachment & Respect, Sir, Your Most Obed^t Humble Serv

A. FOWLER. A. W. D.

HIS EXCELLENCY G. WASHINGTON Esqr Generel and Commander in Chief &c. &c. &c. North America.

[Col. John Gibson to Alexander Fowler. Washington Papers. Contemporary transcript.]

HEAD QUARTERS FORT PITT June 29 1781.

SIR:

A General Court Martial is now Sitting I would therefore request if you have any Charges to Exhibit against Mr David Duncan or any other person you would send them into me that I may have them Arrested and bro^t to Tryal and that I may Comply with the orders I have received from his Excellency the Commander in Chief

I have the Honour to be Y^r most Ob^t S^t

J^{no} GIBSON Colo. Command^g F. Pitt.

ALEX^R FOWLER Esqr Auditor

[Alexander Fowler to Col. John Gibson. Washington Papers. A. L. S.]

Sir: FORT PITT 30 June 1781

From his Excellency the Commander in Chiefs Letter of the 5th May it appears that the deputation from the Judge Advocate was directed to me, as hitherto officiating as Deputy Judge Advocate at this post: I expect therefore to prosecute Mr David Duncan, as Deputy Judge Advocate, But Sir, as you thought there was an Impropriety in my Officiating in that Capacity, as Prosecutor, I have Submitted that point to his Excellency and the Judge Advocate General. In the mean time as I already inform'd you the necessary paper that I want and must have to Support a principle charge which I propose Exhibiting against Mr Duncan are sent for, and must Arrive here before I shall Specify my Charge ag^t him and till then he ought not to be Arrested. At ye same time I beg leave to Acquaint you that I shall Exhibit a Charge ag^t Mr John Johnston (a Clerk) to Mr Duncan I have Transmitted you a Charge ag^t Lt Arch^d Read[1] Pay Master of the 8th P. Reg^t and when the Acc^t is Ready for the Tryal of that Gent^n Shall appear in Support of it.

I have the hon^r to be Y^r mo. Obt hl S^t

A FOWLER A. W. D.

ARTILLERY FOR CLARK

[Capt. Isaac Craig to Gen. George Rogers Clark. 51J64. A. L. S.]

FORT PITT,[2] 30th June, 1781
DEAR GENERAL:

By Serjant Blackwood of my Company I have Sent A Return of my whole Detachment in order to obtain the Corse linnen you

[1] Archibald Read, formerly a noncommissioned officer, was commissioned ensign in the Eighth Virginia Regiment June 2, 1778, and his appointment was published at Fort Pitt Nov. 2, 1778. On December 13 of the same year Read was promoted to a lieutenancy in the place of Joseph Brownlee, resigned. Read acted as paymaster of the regiment until the arrival of General Irvine. For the court-martial proceedings at which Read was acquitted, see *post*, 484-90. He died in 1823 in Allegheny County.

[2] Captain Craig returned from Philadelphia to Pittsburgh about June 25.

Promist for Frocks to them, I am told it will Require three Yards for Each, Consequently the whole will Amount to one Hundred and thirty Yards; the Quanty of thread Necessary Can be Extimated by one of the Taylors in Coll. Crockets Reg^t—It is Necessary that all the Articals Brought by me from Carlisle Except the powder and flints be Sent here, in Order to have all the Ammunition fixed and put in proper Order, the Quantity of Duck and Cordage Necessary for the Boats I have not yet been able to Estimate, but Wish A Parcell of it to be Sent Down of Which proper Care shall be taken if Capt Lt Martin[1] is left New Store[2] before this Reaches you, the Bearer is Capable of taken Care of the Stores to be Sent here and will Attend at Head Quarters for Orders Respecting them, I have the Honour Dear General to be With Much Esteem, Your obediant Hum^{bl} Servant,

I. CRAIG Capt Artillery

BRIG^R GENERAL CLARK.

WESTMORELAND RAIDED

[Summary of a letter of Isaac Mason,[3] July 1, 1781, to Pres. Joseph Reed. 46J63. Printed in *Pa. Archives*, IX, 238–39.][4]

All the settlement "between the Allegania and Youghagania Rivers as high up as Sweakley" laid waste; a prisoner taken on

[1] William Martin of Pennsylvania entered the Continental army April 1, 1777 as first lieutenant in the Fourth Artillery. On March 21 of the next year he was surprised and captured in the skirmish at Hancock's Bridge, N. J. On June 1, 1778 he was commissioned captain-lieutenant, and this was his rank when released from imprisonment on Dec. 4, 1780. Martin came West with Craig, and after this service was appointed (Jan. 1, 1782) captain in the artillery regiment, being honorably retired the first of the following year.

[2] New Store was located on the east side of the Monongahela at what is now the town of Elizabeth. At this place was the rendezvous for Clark's expedition.

[3] Isaac Mason (sometimes spelled Meason) was a Virginian who came as early as 1770 to the region of the Youghiogheny. He first bought land on Jacob's Creek and there built an iron furnace. He afterwards made great investments in lands, bought the estates of Christopher Gist and Colonel Crawford, and was credited in 1799 with owning 6,000 acres. In 1796 Mason laid out the town of New Haven in Fayette County. He died in 1819 on the Mount Braddock estate, formerly the home of Gist. His descendants still own part of his lands. His wife was Catherine, sister of Benjamin and William Harrison.

[4] See reply of Reed, July 23, 1781, in *Pa. Archives*, IX, 303–4.

Braddock's road; unless the Indian country is invaded, all the inhabitants beyond the mountains will be driven back. Had great hopes of Clark, but he has but 140 Virginia regulars; Virginia militia refuse to enlist. Colonel Hays summoned a council of Pennsylvanians which resolved to assist Clark by draft or volunteers. Object of Clark's expedition is the towns of the hostile Indians, especially Sandusky.

[Summary of a letter of James Perry, Westmoreland County, Sewickley, July 2, 1781, to Pres. Joseph Reed. Printed in *ibid.*, 240–41.]

Country in great confusion. James Chambers captured three weeks ago; last Friday two young women killed in Ligonier Valley; this morning a garrison of twenty or thirty at Philip Clinglesmith's, four miles from Hannastown, was destroyed, only three escaping.[1] A party sent out to bury dead not yet returned. Frontiers are in a deplorable condition; companies posted are not able to discover enemy on such an extensive territory; they come in small bodies. Only hope of deliverance is a campaign into the Indian country.

CLARK'S TROOPS RENDEZVOUS

[Gen. George Rogers Clark to Col. David Shepherd. 2SS17. A. L. S.]

2^d July 1781

D^R COL:

This is to inform you that I have appointed the 15th Ins^t for the Genl Rendevouse of all the troops we can raise in this Country (Except yours) we shall endeavour to have every thing ready to set out by that day let our numbers be many or few I have sent Instructions to the different Ct^y Lieu^{ts} desireing them without fail to have their Quotas of Militia ready by that time. as it's most convenient for yours to Rendevous at Weeling. I am

---

[1] Peter and Philip Klingelschmit located on Brush Creek in Penn township of Westmoreland County prior to 1774. Their fort is thought to have been a mile and a half northwest of the present Harrison City. After the raid here described Philip, his wife and their four children were buried in one grave.

in hopes that you will have the whole ready to meet at any hour that shall be affix'd which I shall advertise you of I suppose it will be a few days after ye 15th there is a Considerable Quantity of flour at Wells & Mr Roberts Mills[1] to be lodged at Coxes Fort[2] on the Ohio River it appears by report from the T. C. Genl that it will be out of his power to get it transported to the river without a Guard for the waggon that he has employd, I hope sir that you will immeadiately order a party of men for that purpose I should not have made this request of you but the forces we have already imbodied are so few that all hands are Constantly employd in their Quarters to have every thing Compleat by the day of Rendevoze & of course are much Fateagued—this is a matter of Consequence, & I hope will not be neglected I have not a sylable of news to inform you of worth notice

I am D^r. Col. yours with Esteem

G R Clark B G

[Addressed:] David Shepherd County Lt Ohio Pr Express On Publick Service

[Endorsed by Shepherd:] Came to Hand 3^d July

PENNSYLVANIA TROOPS FOR CLARK

[Summary of a letter of Col. Archibald Lochry, Twelve Mile Run, Westmoreland County, July 4, 1781, to Pres. Joseph Reed. Printed in *Pa. Archives*, IX, 246–47.]

Details concerning accounts. Four months' company raised; Capt. Thomas Stokeley's ranging company is thirty-men strong. "We have very distressing times Here this summer. The Enemy are almost constantly in our County Killing and Captivating

---

[1] Wells's Mills were owned by Alexander Wells, who came West from Baltimore about the year 1772 and bought a large tract of land on Cross Creek in what is now Washington County, Pa. In 1775 he built mills at the junction of the north and main branches of the creek in the present Cross Creek Township, and operated them until 1796. He died in 1813, aged eighty-six years, leaving a large family, for one of whom the town of Wellsburgh, W. Va., was named. The site of Roberts' mill has not been identified.

[2] Cox's Fort or Station was on the Ohio just above Wellsburgh. It was the residence of Capt. Reuben Cox, who emigrated from Maryland about the year 1772. His sons, Isaac, George, Gabriel, and Joseph, were prominent in early western history. This Station was garrisoned in 1777; see *Rev. Upper Ohio*, 251, note 97.

the Inhabitants. I see no way we can have of defending ourselves other than by offensive operations." Meeting summoned by Col. Christopher Hays concluded to aid Clark. After harvest a considerable force can be secured. The object is to reduce the Shawnee, Delaware, and Wyandot Indians.

OPPOSITION TO CLARK

[Gen. George Rogers Clark to Col. David Shepherd. 2SS19. A. L. S.]

D[R] S[R]:
YOHOGANIA COURT HOUSE 8th July 1781

I Recievd yours of 3[d] Ins[t] and am heartily sorry that any Opposition should be likely to take place in your county when we are at present flatterd from Every other Quarter, That all Divisions are Subsiding and a general Compliance to orders, But I hope those that you allude to will see their folly and Honour your orders without any forcible Measures being taken—I would send you an armd force Immediatly but wait a few days in hopes that your business will go on more smooth, If not it shall be done, Since I saw you last Red. a Letter from the Council of Pensylvania giving greater Encouragement for men to turn out than even the Government of Virg[a] and the party in opposition when you were at the Xings is now faling into the plan, I shall be able on the day of Rendezvous at this place to inform you of the time that your troops should meet at Weelin I Expect a few days after. we are geting all our stores to Pitt for fear of the water

I am S[r] with perfect Esteem your Obed[t] Serv[t]

G R Clark B G

[Addressed:] David Shepherd Esq[r] County L[t] of Ohio P[r] Express On publick Service

LOYALISTS NEAR FORT PITT

[Affidavit of William Johnson. 51J66. Unsigned.]

H. Q. July 10, 1781

The Information of William Johnson it apears That on the 9th Ins[t] he was at the House of Lawrence Crow where was a number of persons assembled at a Reaping—amongst whom were Wm Howe Lawrence Crow, John Crow and Phillip Magain whose Conversation and Conduct during his Continuance, sufficiently Convincd him of thier Inemical princepals in Every Instance— That he at length have declard himself afriend to America was orderd to Quit the house—which he did. Farther saith that John Jackman W^m [blank] son in Law of afor ment^d How and Alexand^r Andrews were present whom seemed to be well pleased at their behaviour These Circumstances happend accidently under the Inform [ms. torn] as pasing by was Envited to stay

CLARK'S EXPEDITION STARTS

[Gen. George Rogers Clark to Col. David Shepherd. 2SS21. A. L. S.]

H. Quarters Yohogania Court House[1] 18th July 1781

Sir:
The twentyith Ins^t July is the day affix'd on for our Embarkation from the new store, a few days will Enable us to load and make our arrival at weelin, where you will please to Rendezvous your troops on wednesday next without fail, and wait my Coming —providence has most apparently Interpos'd on our behalf at present therefore let us avail ourselves of the opportunity of the water as we have not the Smalist Reason to Expect a Similar advantage this Season

I have the Honour to be Dr Col^o with Esteem your Devoted Servt

G R Clark B G

N. B. In one of my former letters I directed you to send a guard for the flour should you for any Reasons not havè Comply'd therewith, will be pleasd to observe they are still wanting and the Sooner despatchd the better

[1] Yohogania County courthouse was on the farm of Andrew Heath, not far from the present West Elizabeth in Allegheny County, Pa. As Clark's headquarters it was convenient to New Store, his point of departure.
For the excitement in the Indian country over news of Clark's approach, and for the plans to repulse him see *Mich. Pion. & Hist. Colls.*, XIX, 647–48.

PENNSYLVANIA TROOPS FOR CLARK

[Summary of a letter of Pres. Joseph Reed, July 23, 1781, to Col. Archibald Lochry. Printed in *Pa. Archives*, IX, 307–8.][1]

Reply to Lochry's letter of July 4. Settlement of accounts. Council heard with much pleasure of the plans to coöperate with Clark. Brodhead's insinuations with respect to Clark's intention are disproved on high authority. Hopes Clark may receive such aid and support as are necessary for his purpose; his expedition will afford the only effective relief for the distress of the frontiers. County affairs appear to have been negligently managed; disputes and divisions weaken the county. Petitions in Lochry's favor will be considered.

ARTILLERY FOR CLARK

[Capt. John Craig to Gen. George Rogers Clark. 51J74. A. L. S.]

FORT PITT 25th July 1781

SIR:

As it is Necessary to open most of the Powder Casks in Order to distinguish & Marke the Different Kinds on the Casks that Containe it A Cooper will be Wanted for that Purpose I have therefor to Request One to be Ordered from Col Crockets' Regt or elsewhere as Soon as Possible—

I am Sir with much Esteem Your Hble Servt

I CRAIG

B GENERAL CLARKE

N. B. I have sent by the Boy ½ Dozen Knives & forks Please to accept of them.

---

[1] See letters of the same date and of the same tenor from Pres. Joseph Reed to Christopher Hays, Col. James Marshel, and David Duncan in *Pa. Archives*, IX, 300, 304–5. A copy of this letter from Reed to Lochry was captured at the latter's defeat and sent to the Canadian authorities. It is printed in *Mich. Pion. & Hist. Colls.*, XIX, 651–52.

OPPOSITION TO CLARK

[Summary of a letter of Col. Dorsey Pentecost, Washington County, July 27, 1781, to Pres. Joseph Reed. Printed in *Pa. Archives*, IX, 315–19.]

Writer is in Clark's camp three miles below Fort Pitt, about to go on the expedition. Has heard that his conduct has been misrepresented. Presents explanations as follows: The country west of the Monongahela has been administered by Virginia since 1774; is now included in Pennsylvania, but no line run; country in utmost confusion, Indians very troublesome; gentlemen met and chose a general committee for defense, planned to engage 100 men. James Marshel, a newcomer, went to Philadelphia, had Washington County erected and himself commissioned lieutenant, recorder, and register. While he was away General Clark came, preparing an expedition against the savages; every effort made to raise volunteers. The Yohogania County officers requested Pentecost to take command and save the country. Consulted with Clark, and he urged him to raise the militia which he has now encamped. His acts misconstrued. Marshel and friends represent him as opposing the authority of Pennsylvania. Pentecost offered to retire in favor of Marshel, who did all possible to perplex the people, advised them to refuse obedience to Clark's draft, after he had promised the latter he would do what he could to assist him. Animadversions against Marshel; it is not well for one man to hold three positions. As Pentecost is leaving the country offers his explanations and defends his motives, which arose from great anxiety for the welfare of the country.

ATTACK ON BOGGS'S FAMILY

[Recollections of Mrs. Lydia Cruger. 2S155–56.]

On the 30th of July, 1781, Capt. John Boggs, then living on Buffalo creek—Twelve Indians came & hid themselves among the shocks of grain in the field, Wm Boggs,[1] then in his 18th year

[1] "Wm Boggs, when taken in '81, was tied to stakes at night—rained on him; & when reaching the Indians he run the gauntlet—took the ague, 2 times a day, he was greatly afraid he would be recognized as aiding in killing Kill Buck

(who the spring before with Lewis Wetzel, at Wheeling tomahawked Kill Buck, chief—) went to the field to drive out the calves, & was taken by 5 Indians; while the other seven (a foggy morning) came towards the house, & Capt. Boggs siezed his gun & kept the Indians at bay, several times shot at by the Indians, until the family ran half a mile to James Newell's & then Capt. B. escaped. Then all the families in that region commenced forting at Wm Sparks[1] (father doubtless of Rh^d S. for Rh^d was in Capt. Ogle's company on Brodhead's campaign in spring of '81[2]—& Ogle lived on Short Creek) In this fight, the Mrs Cruger had previously been badly snake bitten & with difficulty could hobble around, ran to Newell's & was the first to reach there—never once thinking of her disabled limb!—

In August 1781, Capt. Boggs removed to Wheeling; & was there when the Indian party appeared there as already stated, in Sept.[3]

A few weeks after—the same party under Sam Gray, a half breed, who had taken young Boggs—appeared & killed Capt. Sam. Teter & another man on the head of Buffalo.

The party that took [William] Boggs, previous to reaching Capt. [John] Boggs, [on the] Dutch fork of Buffalo, met Danl Harris [sic] & a negro, both on horseback, fired at, Harrison w^d in the hip—both escaped—Harrison lay in a clump of willows all night—chased the negro &^{c}.

—He was finally, with young Presley Peek, & others sold to the British at Detroit, & finally exchanged, & got home after 18 months captivity." Draper Mss., 2S180–81.

[1] William Sparks was captain of militia on Hand's expedition of 1778.

[2] For Capt. Joseph Ogle see *Frontier Defense*, 36, note 69. The roll of his militia company is printed *post*, 464–66.

[3] Documents concerning the attack on Wheeling in September, 1781 will appear in the next volume of this series.

OPPOSITION TO CLARK

[Summary of a letter of Thomas Scott,[1] Washington County, July 31, 1781, to Pres. Joseph Reed.[2] Printed in *Pa. Archives*, IX, 324-25.]

Elections for justices have just occurred; commissions for several officers; Duncan's resignation requested; difficult to find a person of integrity to recommend in his place. Money totally fallen into disuse. Clark's preparations have been greatly injurious to Pennsylvania interests and abusive to individuals. Has used a commission to exercise an arbitrary jurisdiction over those formerly subjects of Virginia, no matter where they live. His proceedings have contributed to prevent the organization of Washington County militia and the regulation of that of Westmoreland. Instances of high treason against the state not less than forty.

[1] Thomas Scott was born about the year 1739 in Chester County, Pa., passed his early life in Lancaster County, and in 1770 removed to Dunlap Creek in Westmoreland County. As a partisan of Pennsylvania in the boundary dispute with Virginia Scott was arrested in 1774, tried before Lord Dunmore, and released on bail. In 1779 he protested against Virginia surveys in the disputed region, and upon the erection of Washington County was chosen its first prothonotary and clerk of court. Scott represented his county in the Continental Congress and in the First and Third Federal congresses. He died Mar. 2, 1796.

[2] For Reed's response see *Pa. Archives*, IX, 374.

Appendix

OHIO COUNTY COURTS-MARTIAL

[Court-martial Book for Ohio County, Virginia. 2SS39-49. D. S.]

At a Court Martial held at the House of Ezekiel Dewitt In And for Ohio County On Fryday the 8th day of October in the Year of Our lord one thousand Seven hundred & Seventy Nine
Present
Colonel David Shepherd President }
Col° Silas Hedges } Field Officers
Maj' Samuel M°Colloch }
Joseph Ogle }
Samuel Tetter }
Jacob Leffler } Captains
David English }
John Boggs }

Ordered that Derrick Hogland Shall Attend the Court as Provist Martial during the Time of Sitting

Andrew Robinson being Appointed and having Taken the Oath as Clark for the Court

Ordered that Henry Harvey of Cap^{tn} Ogles Comp shall pay a fine of Twelve pound for disobedience of Orders in not Going to Serve his Tour of Duty when Ordered

And the Sheriff is hereby ordered to Collect the Same

John Braddock Rezin Pumphrey Nicholas Pumphrey Richard Dickinson William Markland and Thomas Knox of Captain John Boggses Company each fined in the Sum of Twelve pounds— for disobedience of Orders when Ordred to the Station Except William Markland and Thomas Knox who Shall pay only the Sum of Two pounds Eight Shillings each and the Sherif ordred to Collect the same

Also Brice Virgin of the Said Company for disobedience of Orders fined Three pounds

The Court Having heard the Appeal of Brice Virgin Ezekiel Dewitt Abraham Rodgers John Baker Samuel Willson Richard Dickinson And William Leet Shall have their fines of the 13th of April 1779 Remited

Present Captain Davi^d Williamson A member of the Court

William Huston came into Court and Satisfied the Court that He was of the Age of fifty years and obtaind an exemption from Future Service according to law

James Richardson came into Court and was Exempted from future Service being Defective and lame in his Right Hand

James Armstrong exempt from future Service being lame in one of his Ancles

Abraham Enlow Discharged or exempted from Future Duty in This County being fifty Years of Age

Matthias Scarmahorn exempted from future Duty having made it appear that he is Liable to falling fitz.

Isaac Miles Exempted from Future Service through Visable Infirmities

Henry Moore exempted from future Service in this County he having Satisfied the Court that a number of infirmities Render him Unfit for Service

Robert Eagar Exempt from Duty having Satisfied the Court of a Defect in one of his Knee Joints and the frequent Dislocations thereof.

William Carrell and John M°Kneight each ordered to pay Fines for disobedience of Orders Viz^t William Carrell Six pounds And John M°Kneight Three Pounds and Sheriff Shall Collect the Same.

James Gillespee Esqr Jesse Martin Joseph Willson Isaac Cox Fined by the Court for Disobedience of Orders each in the Sum of Twelve pounds

Francis Reiley & Andrew Scott Also fined for Disobedience of orders Each fined Twelve pounds

Jacob Millar Junior Fined by the Court Six pounds for Disobedience of Orders and the Sherif ordred to Collect The Same

Absent Captain David English

Derrick Hogland is appointed a Recruiting Officer by the Field officers of this County agreeable to an Act of May Session 1779 For Recruiting Soldiers Sailors and Mariens

The Same Burser as formerly appointed Shall act Untill A future Court Disolve or Remove him

The Same Fees shall be paid to the Adjatant Provist Martial And Clark as Allowed by a former Court Martial For their Services.

DAVID SHEPHERD C^{oy} Lieu^t

ANDREW ROBINSON Clark

At Court Martial held at the court house of Ohio County November the 7th 1780

Present

Col° David Shepherd President
Coln Silas Hedges
Col° David M°Clure
Maj' Sam¹ M°Colloch

Captains

Cap John Mitchel
   Joseph Ogle
   Sam¹ Mason
   David Williamson
   David English

Resolved that Isaac Taylor be appointed Clk.

Whereas it appears to this Courtmartial that the Draugh alredy ordered to Fort Henery are not yet gone agreeable to Col Broadheads Order

It is hereby ordred that Each Captain upon Receipt hereof do forthwith Cause each draught from his Company to be Imadiatly sent to Fort Hennry under such a guard as he shall think necessary to be deliverd to Cap' Boggs And that Return be Imediatly made to the County Lieutenent how the[y] have Executed these Orders as there is a necessity for a suply of Provisions there Orderd that Cap Mitchel supply the statio[n] at Fort Henry Accordingly

DAVID SHEPHERD president

At a Courtmartial Held at the House of Ezekiel Dewitt on Tuesday the 20th of March 1781

Present

Col° David Shepherd President ⎫
Col° Silas Hedges   ⎬ Field Officers
Col° David M°Clure   ⎪
Maj' Samuel M°Colloch   ⎭

John Mitchell ⎫
Joseph Ogle   ⎬ Captains
John Boggs   ⎪
David Inglish ⎭

Andrew Robinson appointed Clark and Sworn Accordingly

Ordred that Three hundred Dollars Shall be Paid Captain Joseph Ogle for a Drum for the Use of his Company

Out of the fines of the Delinquents

Ordred that Jacob Leffler Strike John Best Juniors name of his Roll or the list of his Company of Militia till he Comes of the Age to do Duty as a Soldier

Whereas it appears to this Present Court Martial on the disposition of Stephen John Francis that Alexander Young a Militia Soldier in Capt[n] Joseph Ogles Company being ordred to Serve a tour of Duty at Fort Henry in October last he Contemptiously Refusing to Obey the said orders—Ordred therefor that he Shall be Delivered to a Continental Officer to Serve the Time Proscribed by Law

Whereas it appears to this Present Court Martial on the Confessions & depositions of Francis Reiley Serjant in Capt[n] Guillelands Company of Militia that said Francis Reily Joseph Scott David Randles & John Ferguson of the Same Company Soldiers Being Ordred to Serve a tour of duty At Fort Henry in October last they Contemptiously Refused to Obey the Said Orders—Ordered therefore that they shall be delivered to an Continental Officer belonging to this Commonwealth to serve the time Proscribed by law as a Soldier

Ordred that the Militia living on the West Side of the main Branch of Brush Run Shall Serve and do Duty under the Captain that Shall Command Capt[n] Ellises Company of Militia.

And all those living to the East of the Said Run in Cap[tn] David Williamsons Company

Whereas it appears to Court Martial on the Deposition of Capt[n] Isaac Phillips that William Huston & James Latimore Soldiers in his Company of Militia that they Being Ordred To Serve a Tour of Duty at Fort Henry in October last They Contemptiously Refusing to Obey the Said Orders Ordered therefore that they Shall be Delivered to a Continental officer belonging to this Commonwealth to Serve the Time Proscribed by law As Soldiers

Whereas it appears to the Court Martial that Capt[n] David Williamson Having Neglected to make a Return of his Company & Delinquencys Ordered therefore that he Shall pay a fine of fifty Pounds and the Sheriff ordred to Collect the Same

Ordred that the Delinquencys in Captain David Williamsons Capt[n] Inglishes & Capt[n] Mitchles Companys Shall Have notice given them by their Captains to appear on the first day of May

Court Martial to be held at the Courthouse to answer for their disobedience of orders

Whereas it appears to this Court Martial on the Deposition of Jacob Wolf that Henry Moore a Soldier in Captn Isaac Phillipses Company is fit for Duty

Ordred that he Shall be enrolled by Said Captn & do duty in his Tour as others

DAVID SHEPHERD President

ANDREW ROBINSON C. of the C. Martial

At a Court Martial held at the Courthouse of Ohio County on Monday the 7th day of May 1781

Present

Col^o David Shepherd President }
Col^o Silas Hedges   } Field Officers
Major Saml McColloch   }

John Mitchell   }
Samuel Mason   }
David Williamson   } Cap^{ts}
Jacob Lefler   }
David Inglish   }

David McClure appointed Clerk & Sworn Accordingly Alex^r Young being called according to Law he not Appearing therefore Ordered that his Former Judgment be Confirmed

Francis Ryley being Duly Called and appearing Ordered that his Former Judgment be put in Execution

Whereas it Appears to this Court Martial that Wm Huston & James Latimore having sent men on this Late Expedition therefore Ordered that the[y] be Acquited

Likewise Ordered that Robert Henry & Isaac Cox be acquited

Ordered that this Court Martial adjourn Untill tomorrow

DAVID SHEPHERD

the Court Martial Met According to Adjournment
                Present
Col° David Shepherd President
Col° Silas Hedges
Major Saml M°Colloch

John Mitchell   ⎫
Joseph Ogle   ⎪
David Williamson   ⎬ Cap^ts
Jacob Lefler   ⎪
David Inglish   ⎭
& David M°Clure Clerk

Whereas it appears to this present Court Martial that the Cap^ts of this County has not acted upon the Order of the Law therefore Ordered that the Severall Delinquents in this County be Cleared from any Condemnation as Regular Soldiers
Ordered that the Court Martial be adjourned
                                    DAVID SHEPHERD

*   *   *   *   *   *   *   *

At a Court Martiel Held For the County of Ohio on Thursday the 26th Day of July 1781
        Field officers   Cap^s
Present
        David Shepherd   John Mitchel
        Silas Hedges   Joseph Ogle
        Samuel M°Colloch   David English

Capt Jacob Lefler Being arrested for Resigning his Commition when ordred to Draft his Company is aqutted of the Same.
Present Capt Jacob Lefler

John M°donald a draft of Capt Ogles Company Complains is not able to Do proper Duty as a Soldier is acquitted of the present Campaign

Joseph Wells Sr Likewise acquited for the above Reason
Robert French to be Recommend to the General
William Milburn Being Subject to fits he is Excus[ed]
                                    DAVID SHEPHERD President

ORDERLY BOOK OF EIGHTH PENNSYLVANIA REGIMENT

[Official orderly book.[1] 2NN109-178. Transcript.]

HEAD QUARTERS, PITTSBURGH, Jan. 8th 1780.[2]

General Orders.

At a Court of Inquiry held at Pittsburgh Sept' 21st 1779, whereof Col. John Gibson was President—the court after hearing the allegations of Lts. Hardin & Crawford relative to their seniority of rank in the 8th Pa Regt, are of opinion that Lt. Crawford is entitled to the seniority.

They also are of opinion that in the dispute between Lieuts. Nielly & Peterson of the same regt relative to seniority of rank, that Lieut. Nielly is entitled to the seniority.

HEAD QUARTERS, PITTSBURGH, Jan. 13th 1780.

The Commandant having received information that the troops have had the presumption to pull down & carry away a part of the frames erected for drying hides, by which means a great number of them are exposed to ruin: He, therefore, positively forbids such practices in future on pain of the severest punishment: And he likewise offers twenty dollars reward to any person who shall discover one or more of the offenders.

At a general court martial, whereof Lt. Col. Campbell is President, William Freehold, a Horse Master in the service of the United States, was tried for neglect of duty pertaining to his men's wages, & on suspicion of selling a continental horse—& was found guilty of the charges exhibited against him, & sentenced him to make good all damages which the public has sustained by his neglect, to forfeit his pay & to be dismissed from the service, & rendered hereafter incapable of holding any place or employment whatever in the service of the Untied States.

Serjt Samuel Porter, of the 8th Pa Regt, was tried by the same court for disobedience of orders & neglect of duty & sentenced to receive one hundred lashes, to be reduced to the ranks & to ask pardon of Serjt Majr Wood at the head of the 8th Regt.

[1] For a description of this document see *Wis. Hist. Colls.*, XXIII, 423, note 1.
[2] The last preceding entry was dated July 29, 1779.

The Commandant approves of the proceedings of the Court, & directs that Wm Freehold remain a prisoner at this post until the judgment of the Court is fully complied with. The sentence aganist Saml Porter is to be executed to-morrow at 12 o'clock

PITTSBURGH, Jan. 14th 1780.

At a General Court Martial, whereof Lt. Col. Campbell is President, John McPherson, a private soldier in ye 8th P^a Reg^t, & Hyatt Lazier a private soldier in the 9th V^a Reg^t, were tried on suspicion of theft & acquitted.

The Commandant approves of the proceedings of the Court— & the said John McPherson & Hyatt Lazier are immediately to be released from their confinement.

HEAD QUARTERS, PITTSBURGH, Jan. 18th 1780.

At a general court martial, whereof Lt. Col. Campbell was President, Edwd Wilkins, a private soldier in ye 8th P^a Reg^t was tried for being absent from his quarters without leave, & for attempting to desert to the enemy—& was acquitted of the charge of attempting to desert to the enemy, but found guilty of being absent from his quarters without leave, in breach of the 2^d article of ye 18th section of the Articles of War, & sentenced to receive one hundred lashes.

Patrick McGuire, a private soldier in ye 9th V^a Reg^t, was tried by ye said Court Martial on suspicion of stealing a surtout coat out of the dwelling house of Jacob Bowsman, & by unanimous voice of the court was acquitted of the charge.

The Commandant approves the proceedings of the court: The sentence against Edwd Wilkins is to be executed to morrow morning at 12 o'clock—& Pat^k McGuire is to be immediately released.

PITTSBURGH, Jan. 24th 1780.

Upon the representation of Col° Gibson, that Capt. Beal of his reg^t, has declined to act as Paymaster—that his men are in great want of money—that Mr Josiah Tannehill is desirous of accepting an Ensigncy in his Reg^t & act in the duty of Paymaster in the same;—& that he has recommended him to the Govr & Council of the State of Virginia for their approbation—Wherefore, the Command^t directs that Mr Josiah Tannehill be considered as Ensign and Paymaster of the 7th V^a Reg^t by the approbation of the officers of that corps until the pleasure of the Governor & Council aforesaid & the Board of War is signified.

Each Colonel commanding a regiment is to be furnished with ten quarts of rum—each other field officer with eight quarts—each captain with six quarts, & each subaltern with four quarts—& the civil staff of the army in proportion to the other officers of the line.

HEAD QUARTERS, PITTSBURGH, Jan. 31—1780.

Whereas, some doubts have arisen whether Capt. Beal & Lt. Reid were released from their late arrests. The Commandant hereby declares that it was his intention (which he conceives to be implied by his remission of a sentence, & approbation of the sentence of the General Court Martial at their trial—& they are hereby released accordingly.

HEAD QUARTERS, PITTSBURGH, Feb. 4th 1780.

An additional sum of money having been issued from the Board of Treasury for the payment of the troops in this Department, the pay abstracts are to be made out immediately for pay & subsistence to the 30th of September last past, agreeably to the Muster Rolls.

Mr John Hollaway is appointed Dep't^y Must^r Master for this department, & is to be respected accordingly.

Muster Rolls are immediately to be made out to the last day of December last past

HEAD QUARTERS, PITTSBURGH, Feb. 9th 1780.

At a General Court Martial, whereof Lt. Col. Campbell is President, Lieut. Arthur Gordon, of the 9th V^a Reg^t, was tried—1st for behaving unbecoming the character of an officer & a gentleman by not returning two Continental horses & one pack-saddle which he got at this post—& for taking a horse & pack-saddle from the pack-horse men & not returning it, & keeping said horse tied up near 24 hours in this town—2^{nly} for ungentlemanly & unsoldierly conduct by framing lies & pawning his honor for the truth of them: 3dly—In an indirect & fraudulent manner obtaining Continental stores from Capt. Simeon Morgan which he had in charge, in the absence of the Regimental Clothier.

And, in the opinion of the court, both charges were duly supported—wherefore he falls under the 21st article of the 14th Section of the Articles of War, & the court sentence him to be discharged from the service as said article directs.

Lt. Gordon is to be continued under arrest until the pleasure of his Excellency the Commander-in-Chief is known.

At the same court Mr Matthew Vanleer, ass^t Q. M, was tried for insolence to the Commandant, & for repeated absence without leave; &, in the opinion of the court, the charge of insolence was not fully supported—wherefore he was acquitted of that charge: But he was found guilty of being absent without leave from the commandant, in violation of the 2^d article of the 13th Section of the Articles of War—& sentenced to be severely reprimanded in Genl Orders—& to ask the Commandant's pardon in the presence of the field officers of the Western Department.

The Commandant approves the proceedings of the Court. He is sorry to say that Mr Vanleer appears to be void of military knowledge, & a competent degree of decency: He considers his crime to be of the worst kind, & his defence to be a compound of ignorance & insolence. He hopes, however, that Mr Vanleer will learn a proper submission to his superiors, & be convinced that nothing but the lenity of the General Court Martial could have prevented him from the mortifying affliction of having been dismissed from the service with disgrace—& that he will, in future, conduct himself with great propriety in the execution of his duty.

The Commandant earnestly exhorts all his officers when they have leisure to employ a great part of their time in reading military treatises, as well as the law by which, as military men, they must be governed—which will instruct concerning the necessity of discipline & subordination, without which the best concerted plans, & the greatest force may be defeated,—besides the advantage that would accrue to the public whom they serve, they would reap the advantage of rendering their duty familiar & easy to them & their service more acceptable & honorable to their country—& of course avoid much trouble to themselves, as their would be little occasion for gentlemen properly instructed in their duty either to appear before, or, from a principle of necessity, be called to sit upon General Courtmartials, especially for the trial of officers.

The Commandant sincerely laments that Court Martials are so frequently called, but whatever his feelings may be upon such occasions, yet as the officer commanding in this Department, he is determined to support discipline against every attempt that may be made to destroy it—& he will always entertain a proper respect to such of his officers who, by a steady attention to the duties of their respective stations, assist him in supporting it.

The second part of the sentence against Mr Vanleer is to be put in execution at five o'clock this evening at Head Quarters, when all the field officers are requested to attend to be witness of his submission, agreeably to the intention of the General Court Martial.

Mr Vanleer will be released from his arrest when he has complied with the sentence of the court.

HEAD QUARTERS, PITTSBURG, Feb. 10—1780.

Mr Matthew Vanleer, As^t Q^r Mast^r having made his submission agreeably to the sentence of the General Court Martial, is therefore released from his arrest.

Returns of the names & rank of the officers in the different corps in this Department are to be immediately made out to the auditor to enable him to make returns to the Board of Treasury agreeably to a resolve of Congress.

The Commandant calls upon such commanding officers of corps as have not made out returns of arrearages of clothing due the troops for the year 1777, agreeably to the extracts of General Orders, to make out the same immediately & lodge them with the brigade-Major, in order that the same may be presented to the commissioners appointed to settle the same, agreeably to a Resolve of Congress of the 2^d of March, 1779.

To-morrow being his Excellency the Commander-in-Chief's birth day, thirteen cannon are to be fired from the fort upon the occasion.

Each soldier is to be furnished with half a pint of whiskey, & the same allowance of rum is to be issued to the officers of the line & staff, as was issued in pursuance of the last General Order of ye 31st Decr last past.

At a General Court-Martial, whereof Lt. Col. Campbell was President, John Young, a private soldier in Capt. Heth's company, was tried for leaving his post when centinel, & was sentenced to receive 100 lashes on the bear back with a cat-o-nine tails, by drummers of the Regiment. The Commandant approves the sentence of the Court, & directs that it be put in execution this evening at retreat beating.

HEAD QUARTERS, PITTSBURGH, Feb. 12—'80.

At a Genl Court Martial of the line, whereof Lt. Col. Campbell is President—Captn Thos Ferrol, Dep't^y Commiss^y Genl of Military Stores, was tried for beating & abusing a soldier of Capt. Heth's company, in a very unbecoming manner, and afterwards threatening to put him to death. And was found guilty of the charges, in violation of the fifth article of ye 18th section of the articles of war—& sentenced to be severely reprimanded in Genl orders, & to acknowledge his error to the soldier in the presence of his Captain; & the Court recommend it to Capt. Ferrol not to wear his sword in future while in the staff department.

The Commandant approves the proceedings of the Court.

The Commandant is sorry to see a gentleman who has seen so much service as Capt. Ferrol, & who has very reputable credentials of having signalized himself in former wars, through petulance or want of prudence, reduced to the necessity of making acknowledgments to a private soldier, of a crime committed against rules of discipline & good order, & that he at ye same time must have the mortification to feel the justice of the sentence, & the propriety of the injunction to lay by his sword until he can put it on for a better purpose than threatening the lives of men upon whose virtue & service the future happiness, & present safety of our country in a great measure depend: He hopes that upon a serious view of what has been said upon this occasion Capt. Ferrol will reflect upon the folly of too sudden passion & will avoid a consequence so big with danger to his reputation as well as injurious to his peace of mind, & the tranquility of those with whom he associates or transacts his business. Captn Ferrol will be released from his arrest immediately after he has fully complied with the sentence of the court.

Soldiers are exhorted not to discover the least contempt to their officers nor to persons in the staff. But, on the contrary, they are to expect the severest punishment where they disobey the orders of any gentleman who is regularly set over them. They ought always, without murmuring, to pay an implicit obedience to their orders; if they, conducting themselves with propriety, are aggrieved, they will be heard by their officers, & their wrongs will be redressed.

PITTSBURGH, Feb. 23^d 1780.

At a General Court Martial, whereof Lt. Col. Campbell was President, Joshua Still & Robt Broad, private soldiers in ye 9th V^a Reg^t, were tried for breaking open a store-house—from thence stealing flour, & selling it to the Indians, & were found guilty of the charge, in violation of the 5th art. of ye 8th Sec. of ye Articles of War—& sentenced to receive one hundred lashes each, on their bare backs, with a cat-o-nine tails by the drummers of the Reg^t

Charles Bodkin, of the same reg^t, was tried by the same court for desertion and mutiny, and was acquitted of the crime of desertion but found guilty of the charge of mutiny in violation of the 3^d art. of the 2^d Sec. of the Articles of War, & sentenced to receive one hundred lashes, on his bare back, with a cat-of-nine-tails by the drummers of the Regiment.

The Commandant approves the proceedings of the court, & directs that the sentence be put in execution to-morrow at 12 o'clock.

HEAD QUARTERS, PITTSBURGH, Feby 29th 1780.

At a general Court Martial, whereof Lt. Col. Campbell was President, Heath Murray, a private soldeir in ye 9th V^a Reg^t, was tried for refusing to join his regiment & obtaining his discharge unjustly, & found guilty of the crime laid to his charge in violation of the 5th article of the 8th Sec. of the articles of war. Wherefore he is sentenced to receive 100 lashes on his bare back with a cat-of-nine-tails by the drummers of the Regiment.

The Commandant approves of the proceedings of the court, & directs that the sentence be put in execution at 3 o'clock this afternoon. The court martial is dissolved.

Lt. Col. Campbell is requested to discharge such of the soldiers of ye 9th Virginia Reg^t, as appear to be entitled to their discharges by the opinion of the different courts of Enquiry, unless he can discover sufficient cause why any of them shall not be discharged.

PITTSBURGH, March 1st 1780.

Every officer in the line who lodges, or is quartered in the town of Pittsburgh, is immediately to remove into the fort—such only excepted who may obtain a special licence for the contrary. This order is not to effect any who are particularly stationed.

HEAD QUARTERS, Pittsburgh, March 4th 1780.

The Court of Enquiry, whereof Captⁿ Clark was President, ordered to examine into the loss of the public flour by the brigade under the direction of John Hamilton, horse-master, & to ascertain the reason of such deficiency, are of opinion that the deficiency of flour in Mr Hamilton's invoice arose from unavoidable accidents. Mr Hamilton is to return to his duty as usual.

HEAD QUARTERS, PITTSBURGH, March 10th '80.

A garrison Court-Martial, whereof Maj. Vernon is appointed President, is to sit to-morrow morning at 10 o'clock for the trial of such prisoners as are confined in the guard-house, to consist of the President & four members.

HEAD-QUARTERS, PITTSBURGH, March 14th '80.

At a garrison Court Martial, whereof Maj. Vernon was President the following prisoners were tried—John Darraugh, soldier 8th P^a Reg^t, & Wm Marlough, private of ye Maryland corps, charged with cutting up Continental tents. The Court are of opinion the prisoners are not guilty of the charge, & do acquit them.

Joseph Atchinson, soldier 8th P^a Reg^t, charged with stealing goods out of John Gibson's store. The Court after examining thoroughly into the matter are of opinion that the prisoner is not guilty of the charge, & do accordingly acquit him.

The Commandant approves the above sentences, & orders the prisoners to be immediately released.

HEAD QUARTERS, PITTSBURGH, March 16th '80.

Each field officer is to be supplied with 2 gallons of rum—each Captain with 6 quarts & each subaltern with 4 quarts: Each non-commissioned officer and soldier is to draw half a pint of whiskey to-morrow morning, & none are to be upon fatigue, except the standing fatigue for providing fuel. The civil staff are to draw an allowance of rum in proportion to the officers of the line.

HEAD QUARTERS, PITTSBURGH, March 23^d '80.

It having [been] represented to the Commandant that several officers have taken upon themselves to employ soldiers for their own emolument, as well as for others, without leave: He, therefore, directs that all such soldiers be immediately call^d into the garrison, likewise all soldiers upon furlough.

The Civil staff are immediately to make returns of all non-commissioned officers & privates employed in their departments respectively, specifying the corps they belong to, & the service they are now performing—to the Brigade Major, in order that the Commandant may determine whether they are properly employed or not.

The Commandant directs that no furloughs be granted, except upon the most pressing occasions, & not then without his consent. And he strictly enjoins all his officers not to presume to employ soldiers at their discretion in future without leave first obtained from him: Likewise that they attend to the orders issued heretofore against their strolling from the garrison, upon pain of arrest & trial before a Genl Court Martial. And as the garrison is deficient of men, he requests that his officers will endeavor to accommodate with one waiter to each two Capt^s & Sub^s whilst they remain in Quarters.

HEAD QUARTERS, PITTSBURGH, 29th March '80.

A general Court Martial, whereof Lt. Col. Campbell is appointed President, is to sit to-morrow morning at 9 o'clock at the President's Quarters, for the trial of such prisoners as shall be brought before the Court: All witnesses & parties concerned are to be punctual in attendance.

An orderly captain of the day is to be daily appointed to see that all the artificers & fatigue parties employed about this garrison, perform their duties respectively,—to confine all delinquents, & make reports to the Comm^{dt}

An orderly sub. is likewise is likewise to be daily appointed to visit the barracks & other quarters of the troops & see that they be kept clean; he is likewise to see that the soldiers make use of clean utensils & cook their provisions in the best manner possible, to preserve their health; he is likewise to see that the fort & its environs are kept clean—& make report of occurrances to the Commandant.

HEAD QUARTERS, PITTSBURGH, April 1st '80.

At a general Court Martial, whereof Col. Campbell was President, Nich^s Creduser, a private soldier of ye 9th Virginia Regiment, was tried for desertion—found guilty, & sentenced to receive 50 lashes on his bare back.

At the same court was tried Danl Murray, a private soldier in ye 9th V^a Reg^t, & John Gretsinger, of the Maryland corps, for theft, were found guilty—& Dan¹ Murray was sentenced to receive one hundred lashes on his bare back well laid on—& John Gretsinger to receive twenty five lashes.

The Commandant approves the above sentences & orders them to be put in execution to-morrow morning at troop-beating. The court is dissolved.

HEAD QUARTERS, PITTSBURGH, Ap^l 5th '80.

A Court of Enquiry, whereof Capt. Thos Beal is appointed President, is to sit to-morrow morning at nine o'clock to enquire into the terms of enlistment of Capt. Heth's Independent Company, & make report of ye names of such as are enlisted for during the war, & such as are enlisted for three years.

HEAD QUARTERS, PITTSBURGH, Ap^l 8—1780.

Whereas, it is essentially necessary that all the out-posts should be supplied with salt provisions, & it appearing from the returns that there is not a sufficient quantity in the magazines at the present ration, the Commandant finds himself under the disagreeable necessity of reducing the rations of meat one quarter of a pound—& he directs that one half pound of bread, flour, or Indian meal be issued in lieu thereof, until a supply of fresh provisions can be furnished, when the usual rations will again be issued to the troops.

HEAD QUARTERS, PITTSBURGH, Ap^l 13—'80

A General Court Martial whereof Col. Campbell was President, Christopher Wint, an artificer in the service of the United States, was tried for abusing the Commandant & threatening to kill him—for cursing & abusing all the officers in the Department, particularly the officer of the day—& for threatening to cut Capt. Tannehill's throat when reprimanding him for his conduct, & afterwards threatening to kill him, & several others when released from confinement—in violation of ye 3^d art. of the 2^d section of the articles of war—& sentenced to receive one hundred lashes on his bare back with a cat-of-nine tails by the drummers of the regiment.

James Kelly, W^m McDowell, Jos. Lane & Chas McCaffey, artificers in the service of the United States, were tried by the same court for disobedience of orders, & refusing to do their duty—& the Court upon a full consideration of facts did acquit W^m McDowell & Jos. Lane of the charge; but found Jas. Kelly &

Chs McCaffey guilty of a breach of ye 5 art. of ye 2^d section of the articles of war—& sentenced them to receive 30 lashes each, on their bare backs, with a cat-of-nine-tails, by the drummer's of the Regiment.

The Commandant approves the proceedings of the Court, & directs that the sentences be execut?d at 3 o'clock this afternoon. W^m McDowell & Jos. Lane are released, & the General Court Martial dissolved.

HEAD QUARTERS, PITTSBURGH, April 16th 1780.

The Court of Enquiry whereof Capt Thos Beal is President, is to sit to-morrow morning at 9 o'clock to hear & determine the claims of not only Capt. Heth's soldiers respecting discharges, but likewise of late Capt. O'Hara's company.—Each field officer is to be furnished with 2 gallons of Rum—each captain with 6 quarts—each sub. with one gallon—the officers of the civil staff in proportion.

PITTSBURGH, April 23^d 1780.

A garrison Court Martial, whereof Maj. Vernon is President, is to sit this morning at 10 o'clock for the trial of the prisoners in the Guard House—& the evidence & parties are to attend punctually.

PITTSBURGH, April 26th 1780.

At a Court of Enquiry, whereof Capt. Thos Beal was President, constituted to enquire into the enlistments of Capt. Heath's & late Capt. O'Hara's men & to make report—ye s^d court report as follows—viz:

That Andrew Glass, George Manes, Anth^y Glass, Richd Earls—Ja^s Ryan—Jac^b Whittaker—Thos Finn—James King—Jacob Bewling & Philip Conley, of Capt. Heath's company are entitled to be discharged—& that Serj^t George Such—Thos Shoughney, Alex^r Mc Adams—& John Evans are enlisted to serve during the war.

Likewise that John White—Wm Rankin—John M. Cushing & John Whiteman, are entitled to be discharged; & that Benjn Brooks, Laughlin M'Clean & George Whellps, of the same company are regularly enlisted to serve during the war.

And the Court do likewise report that Samuel Caswell, Cornelius Downey, & Alex^r Chambers of Capt. O'Hara's company are entitled to be discharged. And that Thos Wynn of the same company is enlisted during the war.

The Commandant approves of the opinion of the court, directs that such of the men as are entitled to discharges respectively, are to be discharged without loss of time.

HEAD QUARTERS, PITTSBURGH, Ap^l 29th 1780.

At a garrison Court Martial whereof Major Vernon was President, the following prisoners were tried—viz: John Callahan, private in ye 8th Penn^a Reg^t, charged with theft, found guilty, & sentenced to receive one hundred lashes.

Jos. Shaw, pack-horse driver of the United States, charged with buying a blanket from a soldier of ye 9th Virginia Reg^t, being public property, was found guilty of the charge, & sentenced to receive fifty lashes on his bare back, & to return a blanket of as good quality as the one he bought, to the officer of the company to which said soldier belongs.

Patrick Gwinn, soldier in the Maryland corps, was tried for stealing & selling public amunition—found guilty, & sentenced to recieve fifty lashes on his bare back.

Ferrol O'Neal & James Beers were tried for desertion & found guilty—& sentenced to receive each one hundred lashes on his bare back—& James Beers is to be imprisoned until he refunds to John Lane, soldier, the sum which he had advanced him to serve in his place.

Peter Griffin, soldier in the 9th Virginia Regiment, tried for drunkenness & neglect of duty—found guilty, & sentenced to receive fifty lashes.

William Moore, soldier in ye 8th Penn^a Reg^t, charged with selling or losing his accoutrements—the court acquit him of the charge, & he is to be released accordingly.

Bradwin Ashby, soldier of ye 9th Virginia Reg^t, charged with overstaying his furlough—the court find him guilty, & sentence him to receive fifteen lashes on the bare back.

The Commandant approves all the above sentences, except the last, & orders them to be put in execution to-morrow morning at troop beating. The Commandant is pleased to remit the punishment to be inflicted Gladwin Ashby, & he is to be enlarged.

The articles of war are to be read to the troops at retreat beating to-morrow evening on the grand parade, & regularly once a month afterwards.

HEAD QUARTERS, PITTSBURGH, Ap^l 30th 1780.

A garrison Court Martial, whereof Lt. Col. Campbell is appointed President, is to sit to-morrow morning at 10 o'clock for the trial of such prisoners as are confined in the guard house— & such as may be brought before them: The place of sitting to be appointed by the Pres^t.

Capt. Heath— 1
8th P^a Reg^t— 3 } Members.
9th V^a Reg^t 2

HEAD QUARTERS, PITTSBURGH, May 1st 1780.

Each non-commissioned officer & soldier is to be furnished with half a pint of whiskey for the celebration of the first of May.

PITTSBURGH, May 5th 1780.

Whereas sundry persons have taken the liberty of erecting houses & enclosing lands within the range of this garrison, without leave—the Commandant thinks it expedient to provide [prescribe] such practices in future—& to declare that he will punish every person who shall presume to erect a house, or enclose any part of the lands within cannon shot of this fort, until his permission is had in writing for that purpose.

HEAD QUARTERS, PITTSBURGH May 6th 1780.

As it appears from the returns of fatigue whiskey, that several draughts have been made for men who were ordered on trifling fatigues, only. The Commandant thinks it expedient that no fatigue whiskey be issued in future unless the returns are previously countersigned by Colonel Gibson or himself—& the Captain of the day is directed to make a return to him of the number of men on fatigue.

HEAD QUARTERS, May 8th 1780.

Every inhabitant in the vicinity of this garrison capable of bearing arms is to attend with his arms & accoutrements in the orchard to-morrow morning at 10 o'clock—where Lt. Col. Bayard will examine their condition & cause their names to be enrolled by their officers or such persons as they may elect to command them; & in future they are to parade every morning at troop beating on the green near Head Quarters, & have an alarm post assigned them. The Commandant has hitherto been disposed to avoid every trouble of this kind to the inhabitants; but as the

Enemy have lately increased their hostilities, he conceives it to be a duty that can no longer be dispensed with, until the garrison is reinforced, or the danger of an attack upon the town ceases.

HEAD QUARTERS, PITTSBURGH May 16th 1780.
Expiring enlistments & other casualties having rendered the garrison too weak to mount the necessary guards, & perform the other duties required, the indulgencies extended to the civil staff in allowing them waiters from the line, cannot be continued—& those gentlemen are requested immediately to send all soldiers employed in that way to join their respective companies.
Parole—Stottsberry—Countersign—Sutton.

HEAD QUARTERS, PITTSBURGH, May 17th 1780.
The Honble the Congress having been pleased to pass the following resolve, all persons concerned are requested to take due notice thereof:

In Congress, March 2d 1780.
Resolved—That the office of Commissrs of clothing Accts established by a resolve of Congress of ye 2d March, 1779, be discontinued after six months from the date hereof, & all persons having clothing accounts for the year 1777, & who do not exhibit them to the sd commissioners within that period shall not receive any compensation for any arrearages they may hereafter claim to be due to them.

HEAD QUARTERS, PITTSBURGH, May 19th 1780.
A Court of Enquiry is to sit to-morrow morning to enquire into the cause of the great deficiency of the stores brought to this place for the 9th Va Regt, & into the terms of enlistments of such non-commissioned officers & soldiers as claim their discharge. The court is to consist of a field officer & two captains, & their determination with respect to discharges is to be final & conclusive. All parties are to be punctual in their attendance.
Detail for the Court of Enquiry:
Major Taylor, of Virginia, Prest.
8th Pa Regt 1 captain.
9th Va Regt 1 captain.
Returns are to be immediately made out & signed by the commanding officers of regiments & corps, & delivered to the clothier for the number of shirts wanting to complete each serjeant with two, upon the receipt of which the clothier is directed to issue

the amount to the respective corps, except the Maryland corps, who are otherwise provided for.

HEAD QUARTERS, PITTSBURGH, May 22^d 1780.

A Court of Enquiry is to sit to-morrow morning at 9 o'clock to inquire into the nature of a dispute & some charge betwixt John Irwin, D. C. G. Issue, & Mr David Duncan, D. Q. Mr Genl, & make a report of its proceedings to the Commandant. Lieut. Col. Bayard is appointed President of this court, Lt. Col. Campbell & Maj. Vernon members.

The same court is to enquire into the nature of a charge against Lieut. Lewis, of the 9th V^a Reg^t, & report, &c.

Whereas it has been represented to the Commandant, that soldiers are frequently found among the inhabitants of Pittsburgh much disguised in liquor, even after tatoo beating; he therefore directs that the officers of the day do take with them at least two files of men from the fort guard, & at least twice a night patrol the streets & make prisoners of the soldiers found absent from their quarters after beating the tatoo—except where such soldiers have permission in writing from a field officer command^g a reg^t, to remain at their quarters in town & are not found in abuse of the indulgence.

The troops are to make use of the brush in the orchard for fuel as the teams cannot be spared to haul firewood until that is consumed.

The officers of the day are to seize all liquors in the possession of persons vending them to the troops or others, agreeably to form orders, & report their names in order that those tippling houses may be pulled down & destroyed.

PITTSBURGH, June 1st 1780.

At a Court of Inquiry whereof Maj^r Taylor was President, to examine into the claims of non-commissioned officers & soldiers of several regiments & corps demanding their discharges. The Court find that John Berry, John Finney, Baun^g Carter, Nich^s Carter, John Ross, Edwd Paul, John Guthrie, Wm Capes, John Kilgour, Thomas Johnes, Wm Smith, Michael Smith, & John McKinney of the 9th V^a Reg^t And James Clarke, Patrick Mooney, Martin Sheriden, John Cain, Arth^r Evans, Richd Hockley, & Danl Carr, of the 8th P^a Reg^t & David Miller, Nich^s Hagerty, Benjn Brooks, Jacob Adams, John Lapland & Christ^r Carpenter, of Capt. Heath's company—are properly enlisted during the war;

& that Tho⁸ Brownlee & Jeremiah Simpson of yᵉ 9ᵗʰ Vᵃ Regᵗ—Tho⁸ Flinn & Samˡ Blair are entitled to their discharges—& that Jeremiah MᶜCartney will be entitled to his discharge the 18ᵗʰ day of Jan. 1781.

The Court of Enquiry, whereof Lieut. Col. Bayard was President, appointed to enquire into the conduct of Lieut. Andʷ Lewis, of the 9ᵗʰ Vᵃ Regᵗ on a charge exhibited against him for being accessary to the death of Adam Dust, fifer, in the same regᵗ—are of opinion that Lieut. Lewis was not, by any means the occasion of the death of Adam Dust, but that he acted from liberal & generous motives.

The same court having examined into a dispute between Mʳ John Irwin. D. C. Issues & Mʳ David Duncan, A. D. Qʳ Mʳ Genˡ are of opinion that Mʳ John Irwine did not injure Mʳ Duncan in any manner whatever previous to their quarrel as was alledged, & that Mʳ Duncan has acted rashly & altogether unbecoming the character he ought to support.

A General Court Martial, whereof Col. John Gibson is appointed President, is to sit at Fort Pitt on Monday yᵉ 5ᵗʰ of June for the trial of such persons as shall be brought before them.

Given at Head Quarters, at Morristown, this 17ᵗʰ day of March, 1780.

    (signed)   Geo: Washington.

* * * * * * * *

Head Quarters, Pittsburgh, June 16ᵗʰ 1780.

At a General Court Martial, whereof Col. Gibson is President, James Bate, a serjᵗ in yᵉ 9ᵗʰ Vᵃ Regᵗ was tried for desertion & found guilty of yᵉ charge, in breach of yᵉ 1ˢᵗ article of yᵉ 6ᵗʰ section of yᵉ articles of war—& sentenced to receive one hundred lashes on his bare back, with a cat-o'-nine-tails by the drummers of the Regᵗ.

Edward Wilkie, a private in yᵉ 8ᵗʰ Pᵃ Regᵗ was tried by the same court—1ˢᵗ for leaving his guard & going up to town—2ᵈ for being drunk on his post when placed on sentry—3ᵈ for abusing & attempting to shoot Majʳ Taylor: 4ᵗʰ for abusing Capt. Heath: 5ᵗʰ for persisting in saying he would kill any field officer, and abusing Lt. Coleman—& found guilty of the five charges exhibited against him—in breach of yᵉ 5ᵗʰ article of yᵉ 2ᵈ section of yᵉ 5ᵗʰ article, of yᵉ 13ᵗʰ section of the articles of war—& sentenced to receive one hundred lashes for each crime, on his bare back, with a cat-o-nine-tails, by the drummers of the Regᵗ, & to be drummed out of the

8th Pa Regt as a vagabond unworthy of serving in the army of the United States.

The Commandant approves the proceedings of the court, & directs that the sentences be executed to-morrow morning at troop-beating.

Edward Wilkey is to be secured in irons until he has received his punishment—&, before he is drummed out, he is to receive a discharge, after which he is not to appear at any post in this Department upon pain of immediate death.

HEAD QUARTERS, PITTSBURGH, June 17th 1780.

At a general Court Martial whereof Col. Gibson is President, Gaverard Cavenaugh & John Marrick, private soldiers in ye 9th Va Regt, were tried for desertion, & found guilty of the charge in breach of ye 1st article of ye 6th section of the articles of war & sentenced to receive as follows—viz: Gavierd Cavaghnagh three hundred lashes, & John Merick one hundred lashes, with a cat-o-nine-tails by the drummers of the Regt.

Serjt Edward Petty was tried by the same court for neglect of duty by suffering some of his guard to go up into town, & found guilty of the charge—in breach of ye 5th arcticle of ye 18th section of the articles of war, & sentenced to be reduced to the ranks as a private sentinel.

John Burk, a private soldier in the Maryland corps, was tried by the same court for drowning a Continental horse, & was unanimously acquitted.

The Commandant approves the proceedings of the court & directs that the sentences be executed tomorrow morning at troop beating. But in consideration of the recommendation of the court the punishment of John Merick is remitted on account of his former good conduct, & he & John Burke are to be immediately released from their confinement.

HEAD QUARTERS, PITTSBURGH, June 22d 1780.

At a general Court Martial whereof Col. Gibson is President, John Jordan, a private soldier in the Maryland corps, was tried for desertion & found guilty of ye charge, in violation of ye 1st article of ye 6th section of the articles of war. & sentenced to receive one hundred lashes on his bare back, with a cat-o-nine-tails by the drummers of the regt.

At the same court Wm Batten, a serjt of the Maryland corps, was tried—1st for desertion—2dly for selling his arms—3dly for a breach of trust—& 4^{thly} for forgery—& is found guilty of the charges exhibited against him—in breach of ye 1st article of ye 6th section—ye 3^d art. of ye 13th section—& ye 5th art. of ye 18th section of ye articles of war—& sentenced to receive four hundred lashes, with a cat-of-nine-tails by the drummers of the regiment— to be reduced to the ranks as a private sentinel, & put under stoppages not exceeding half his pay until he makes good all damages sustained by Captn Tannehill & the public.

The Commandant approves the proceedings of the General Court Martial, & directs that the sentences be executed this evening at retreat beating.

The officers of this Department not having received regimental supplies regularly as in other parts of the army, & not having it in their power to purchase suitable liquors—the Commandant directs that each field officer command^g a Regiment be furnished out of the store-house with 3 gallons of rum each— other field officers with two gallons each—Capt^s—Regimental surgeons—Adj^{ts}—Qr. Mas^{trs} & Pay Masters with six quarts—& each subaltern with one gallon. Each Deputy in the civil staff Department with two gallons—each ass't. in service at this & the different posts, with one gallon—the Regimental surgeon's mates are to draw equal to subalterns.

Capt. Thos Beal having satisfied the Command^t that it was owing to some misconstruction of orders, & a dispute between Col. Campbell & himself that orders were not complied with, & that it was not owing to any intention in him—he is hereby released from arrest.

At the same gen^l Court Martial, whereof Col. Gibson is President, Benjn Brooks, a private soldier in Captn Heath's company, was tried for letting Indey, a prisoner, escape from the guard house, & was acquitted—he is to be immediately released from confinement.

PITTSBURGH, June 23^d 1780.

At a general Court Martial, whereof Col. Gibson is President, John Barnett, a serj^t of Capt. Heth's Independent company was tried for neglect of duty by letting Indey, a priosner, escape from the guard-house, in breach of ye 5th article of ye 18th section of the articles of war, & sentenced to be reduced to the ranks as a private centinel.

David Smith & Thomas Dunn, private soldiers in ye 9th V^a Reg^t, were tried by the same court for desertion, & were found guilty of the charge—in breach of ye 1st article of ye 6th section of the articles of war, & sentenced them to receive each 200 lashes with a cat-o-nine-tails on their bare backs by the drummers of the Regiment.

The Commandant approves the proceedings of the court, & directs that the sentences be executed this evening at beating the retreat.

HEAD QUARTERS, PITTSBURGH June 30th 1780.

Each soldier who has received only one shirt for this campaign is immediately to be furnished with another—& officers commanding corps are to sign returns for the same.

HEAD QUARTERS, PITTSBURGH, July 2^d 1780.

The fourth of this month being the anniversary of the glorious Independence of the freemen of America, & the beginning of the fifth year of our declared opposition to the tyrrany of the British King & his venal Parliament, in the support of the rights of mankind—all persons are to cease from fatigue, & each non-commissioned officer & soldier is to be furnished with half a pint of whiskey. The officers of the line & staff are requested to partake of a Dinner to be provided for them in the orchard at 3 o'clock, & Col. Bayard is requested to invite such of the inhabitants as he thinks proper. Thirteen cannon are to be fired with blank cartridges, & 13 rounds of blank cartridges or loose powder are to be fired by a party of fifty men to be paraded for that purpose by Adj^t Crawford.

The entertainment is to be conducted by Captn M°Intire, Dr Holmes, & Mr Gardner. The Com^dt hopes to see every part of the rejoicing conducted with the greatest decorum as usual, & the artillery & musketry will receive orders when to fire.

HEAD QUARTERS, PITTSBURGH, July 9th 1780.

At a general Court Martial whereof Col. Gibson is President, Thomas Kelly, a private soldier in ye 8th P^a Reg^t, was tried for desertion & found guilty of the charge, in breach of the 1st article of ye 6th section of the articles of war,—& sentenced to receive five hundred lashes on his bare back, with a cat-o-nine-tails, by the drummers of the regiment.

Nich^s Humler, a private soldier in the 8th P^a Reg^t, was tried by the same court for insolence to his superior, in breach of ye 1st article of ye 7th section of the Articles of War—& sentenced to ask pardon of Capt. M°Intire in presence of his commanding officer.

The Commandant approves the proceedings of the Court, & directs that the sentences be executed to-morrow morning troop beating, & that the regimental surgeon attend ye execution of the sentence on Kelly.

HEAD QUARTERS, PITTSBURGH, July 10th 1780.

Capt. M°Intire has permission to choose a party of men out of such of the corps as he thinks proper to be in readiness for command.

HEAD QUARTERS, FORT PITT, July 11 1780.

At a general Court Martial, whereof Col. Gibson is President, Hyatt Lazier, a private soldier in ye 9th Virginia Reg^t, was tried for stealing a canoe, the property of John Dousman—2dly for stealing a sheep, the property also of John Dousman: 3dly for quitting his command when sent express from Fort M°Intosh to this post—& was found guilty of the charges exhibited against him—in violation of ye 6th article of ye 18th section of ye articles of War—& sentenced to receive five hundred lashes, with a cat-o-nine-tails, by the drummers of the reg^t, on his bare back—& to pay to John [Dousman] the value of the sheep he stole from him, as also the value of the canoe, if not returned to said John Dousman in the same condition as when he, Lazier the prisoner, stole it.

The Commandant approves the proceedings of ye Genl Court Martial, & directs that the sentence be executed this eveing at beating the retreat.

HEAD QUARTERS, PITTSBURGH, July 29th 1780.

At a Genl Court Martial, whereof Col Gibson is President, Jos. Colman, a private soldier in y^e 8th P^a Reg^t, was tried for sleeping on his post, & was found guilty of y^e crime & sentenced to receive one hundred lashes, but in consequence of his general good behavior, the court recommend him to the mercy & clemency of the $command^t$. The $Command^t$ is pleased with the recommendation of the Court & does remit the sentence, in expectation that the offender will avoid giving any further trouble to court martials by a steady perseverance in his duty.

Hyatt Lazier a private in y^e 9th V^a Reg^t, having received part of the punishment awarded him, & undergone a tedious confinement, & as the Commandant hopes & believes he has experienced sufficient severity to excite him to better conduct in future, he is pleased to remit the remaining part of his sentence, & directs that be forthwith released from confinement.

The Commandant is sorry to find that (although repeated orders have been issued to prevent the wanton waste of amunition) a party cannot be had upon the most pressing occasion, until fresh quantities of amunition are drawn, he conceives that if the orders of his Excellency the Commander-in-Chief, issued at Middlebrook the 19th day of May, 1779, were attended to, & the arms, amunition, &c. of the respective regt^s & corps carefully inspected every morning at Roll Call, this abuse could not happen—& he strictly enjoins the officers to a punctual observance of that order.

The officers of the line & staff are to be furnished with a quantity of rum, equal to that ordered for, on ye 22^d of June last.

PITTSBURGH, July 29th 1780.

Regimental Orders.

The officers commanding companies are to examine every morning at Roll Calling the soldiers' arms & accoutrements & see that they are in good firing order & clean—& that the soldiers have not wasted their amunition.

A Regimental Court Martial to sit on Monday morning at 9 o'clock to try such prisoners as shall be brought before it.

S. BAYARD.

HEAD QUARTERS, PITTSBURGH, Aug. 2^d '80.

As beef & flour are equally plenty, the usual rations are to be issued, but not more than one pound of mutton is to be issued for a ration.

HEAD QUARTERS, PITTSBURGH, Aug. 3^d—1780.

At a general Court Martial, whereof Col. Gibson is President, Serj^t Maj^r Wood, of the 9th V^a Reg^t—Serj^t Dennison of the 8th P^a Reg^t, & Thos Shoughey, private in Captn Heth's Independent company, were tried for using unfair means to enlist a man, & defrauding him of his property. The court is of opinion that Serj^t Major Woods is not guilty of the charge exhibited against, & do therefore acquit him, & he is to be immediately released. Serj^t Dennison, in part for connivance, & Thos Shoughney fully were found guilty, & sentenced as follows—viz: Serj^t Dennison to be reduced to the ranks as a private centinel; & Thos Shoughney to receive five hundred lashes on his bare back by the drummers of the reg^t, & to refund to Conrad Ham the money he, Thos Shoughney, defrauded him of.

The Commandant approves the proceedings of the court, & directs that the sentence be put in execution to-morrow morning at troop beating.

HEAD QUARTERS, PITTSBURGH, Aug. 11th 1780.

At a general Court Martial whereof Col. Gibson is President, John Gosset, a private soldier in the 9th V^a Reg^t, was tried for cowardice & found guilty of the charge, in breach of ye 13th article of ye 13th section of the articles of war, & sentenced to receive five hundred lashes on his bare back by the drummers of the Reg^t.

The Command^t approves the proceedings of the court & directs that the sentence be executed to-morrow morning at troop beating. The surgeon of the reg^t to attend.

The sentences of David Gamble & Peter Davis will be published as soon as his Excellency's [wishes] the commander-in-chief, in regard to them, are known.

Serj^t Dennison, of the 8th P^a Reg^t, having generally supported a good character the Commandant is pleased to reinstate him in his former rank, & he is to be obeyed accordingly.

HEAD QUARTERS, PITTSBURGH, Aug. 16th 1780.

Returns are to be immediately made for shoes & blankets for the non-commissioned officers & soldiers who have not been lately supplied—& Lieut. Neilly will distribute a proportion of blankets to each corps. No non-commissioned officer or soldier is to be furnished with more than one pair of shoes in pursuance of this order.

PITTSBURGH, Augt 25th 1780.
Regimental Orders.

All officers, waiters, artificers, wood cutters, soldiers on standing fatigue, waggoners, &c. belonging to the 8th Penn^a Reg^t, are to attend Roll calls every Sunday, with their arms, accoutrements, amunition in good order. The officers of the Reg^t are requested to see these orders punctually obeyed.

S. BAYARD, Lt. Col.

HEAD QUARTERS, PITTSBURGH, Augt 26th 1780.

At a general court martial, whereof Col. Gibson is President, Lieut. Lewis Thomas, of the 9th V^a Reg^t, was tried for neglect of duty, & suffering David Gamble, a prisoner under sentence of a general court martial, to escape from the guard-house whilst he was officer of the guard—& by the unanimous opinion of the court was acquitted with honor—he is therefore released from his arrest.

As a part of the lands taken for public use, is now enclosed, no horses, cattle, sheep or swine (except such as are public property, or belonging to officers entitled to keep them at public expense) are to be suffered to remain within the enclosure, upon pain of having such trespassing horses, cattle, sheep, or swine impounded, & the trespass paid for in such manner & at such rates as shall be directed by the Command^t—Milch cows belonging to the garrison are to be turned out every morning at troop-beating, & drove in at beating the retreat.

The gates next the town are to be guarded by a sentinel from beating the Revilie until beating the retreat, when the officer of the day is to cause them to be locked—& they are not again to be opened, except for the purpose of going the rounds until break of day when the sentinel is to be posted.

HEAD QUARTERS, FORT PITT, Aug. 27th 1780.

All persons concerned who have not been made acquainted, or have been inattentive to the orders of the 14th of June last, are hereby enjoined to pay proper respect to them & govern themselves accordingly—the Commandant being determined to enforce a proper obedience to his orders.

HEAD QUARTERS, FORT PITT, Aug. 28th 1780.

At a general Court Martial, whereof Col. Gibson is President, John Gordon a private in the Maryland corps, was tried for neglect of duty, by suffering David Gamble, a prisoner under sentence of general court martial, to escape while he was placed over him as a sentry, & was acquitted—& is immediately to be released from his confinement.

At the same court John Moore, a private in the 8th P^a Reg^t, was tried for desertion & found guilty of the charge, in breach of ye 1st article of ye 6th section of ye articles of war—& sentenced to receive three hundred lashes on his bare back by the drummers of the Reg^t.

The Commandant approves the sentence of the court, & directs it to be put in execution this evening at beating the retreat.

HEAD QUARTERS, PITTSBURGH, Sept. 1st 1780.

At a general Court Martial, whereof Col. Gibson is President, Cha⁸ Parker & Conrod Ridnor, private soldiers in the 8th Pa Regt, were tried for having an intention to desert in company with John Maynard & some negroes: Ch⁸ Parker was found guilty, & sentenced to recieve one hundred lashes on his bare back. Conrod Ridnor & John Maynard were acquitted, & are to be immediately released.

The Commandt approves the sentence of the court on Ch⁸ Parker, & directs that it be executed to-morrow morning at beating the troop.

An allowance of Rum equal to that ordered on the 22d of June last, is to be issued to the officers of the line & staff.

HEAD QUARTERS, FORT PITT, Sept. 3d 1780.

Capt. Tannehill, of the Maryland corps, having represented that Captⁿ McIntire had beaten & injured one of his soldiers—& therefore requested that a court of Inquiry might be ordered to sit to enquire into the complaint & make report.

The Commandt has thought proper to direct that a court of Enquiry to consist of Capt. Craig, President & two members do sit to-morrow morning at the President's tent to enquire into the complaint & make report accordingly.

Capt. Brady, & [blank in Ms.], members.

HEAD QUARTERS, FORT PITT, Sept. 5th 1780.

At a court of Enquiry constituted to enquire into the nature of a complaint made by Capt. Tannehill against Capt. McIntire for having beaten & injured one of his soldiers: The court reports that the witnesses have been examined, & in their opinion, the conduct of Capt. McIntire ought not to subject him to a trial by a court martial.

At a general Court Martial, whereof Col. Gibson is President, James Burns, a matross in the 4th Regt of artillery, commanded by Col. Proctor, was tried for sleeping on his post when posted a sentry—& found guilty of the charge, in breach of the 6th article of ye 13th Section of the Articles of War—& sentenced to recieve two hundred lashes on his bare back, with a cat-o-nine-tails, by the drummers of the garrison.

The Command^t approves the proceedings of the court, & directs that the sentence be executed this evening at retreat beating.

A garrison Court Martial, to consist of Lt. Col. Bayard, Pres^t, & six members, is to sit to-morrow at such place as the President shall appoint for the trial of the prisoners in the guard-house. All witnesses & parties to be punctual in attendance. Lt. Ward for guard to-morrow.

HEAD QUARTERS, FORT PITT, Sept. 7th '80.

A court of Enquiry to consist of Captn Springer, Prest., Lt. Peterson, & Lt. Bradford, members, is to sit immediately to inquire into the enlistment of Ch^r Carpenter & such other soldiers as claim their discharges, & have not heretofore had the benefit of a Court of Inquiry. The said court to make report of their Inquiry to the Commandant.

At a garrison Court Martial, whereof Lt. Col. Bayard is President, Ch^s Crawford, a private soldier of ye 9th V^a Reg^t, was tried for drunkenness & neglect of duty, & by his own confession was found guilty of ye crime, in violation of ye 5th article of the 18th section of the articles of war, & sentenced to receive one hundred lashes—but his solemn promise having induced the court to recommend him for clemency—his punishment is remitted & he is to be immediately released.

At the same court Wm Cloyd & Wm Beaty, private soldiers, were tried for robbing the gardens of Thos Chambers & Jno Bradley—& found guilty of the charge—& sentenced to recieve each fifty lashes on their bare backs.

The Commandant approves the proceedings of the court, but in consideration of late Col. Rawlins' recommendation of Wm Beaty, his punishment is remitted, & as Wm Cloyd has (by the character given him by his Colonel) likewise supported a fair reputation, his punishment is likewise remitted—& both are to be immediately released.

The court is dissolved.

HEAD QUARTERS, PITTSBURGH, Sept. 9th 1780.

The Court of Inquiry, whereof Capt. Springer is President, report that Danl Lancy & Charles Bodkins, of the 9th V^a Reg^t, are entitled to a discharge, & that David Smith, of the same regt, & Chr' Carpenter & Sam¹ McCord, of Capt. Heth's company, are not entitled to be discharged.

Dan¹ Lancy & Ch⁸ Bodkin are, therefore upon application to be discharged from the service of the United States.

HEAD QUARTERS, Morristown, Ap¹ 30th 1780.

The Honble the Congress have been pleased to pass the following resolutions:

IN CONGRESS April 10th 1780.

Resolved,

That when Congress shall be furnished with proper documents to liquidate the depreciation of the Continental bills of credit, they will as soon thereafter as the state of the public finances will admit, make good to the line of the army & the Independent corps thereof, the deficiency of their original pay, occasioned by such depreciation and the articles heretofore paid or furnished, or hereafter to be paid or furnished by Congress, or the States, or any of them, as for pay, subsistence, or the compensate for deficiences, shall be deemed as advanced on accompt, until such liquidation as aforesaid shall be adjusted, it being the determination that all the troops serving in the continental army shall be placed on an equal footing (provided that no person shall have any benefit of this resolution, except such as were engaged during the war, or for three years, & are now in service, or shall hereafter engage during the war.

Resolved—That a committee of three be appointed to report a proper compensation to the staff of the army in consequence of the depreciation of the currency.

Extract from General Orders,

ALEX^R SCAMMELL, Adj^t General.

HEAD QUARTERS, FORT PITT, Septr 16th 1780.

Commanding officers of Reg^ts & corps are to make immediate returns of the state of their arms, & accoutrements to the commanding officer of artillery, agreeably to a form he has prepared for that purpose, in order for inspection, as directed in the late arrangement of the ordinance department, & where it appears that the arms in the hands of the men are not in the best firing order, & cannot immediately be repaired:—such arms are to be exchanged for good arms with the Commiss⁸ of military stores present, in order that all arms, &c. in this Department unfit for further service may be sent to the arsenal below the mountain & exchanged for new ones.

HEAD QUARTERS, F^T PITT, Sept. 23^d, 1780.

A subaltern officer & a fatigue are daily to be appointed to catch fish with the public Seine—the officer is to see that the fish caught by the party are weighed & delivered to the Commissary of Issues, who is to pass his receipt for the same, which receipts are to be lodged with the Brigade Major to be filed. Every Evening the seine is to be spread, & left in charge of the officer of the guard, who is not to deliver it to any person, except the officer warned to superintend the fishing fatigue.

As provisions are at present scarce, the Commandant expects that the officers appointed to the above service will exert themselves in having fish taken for the use of the troops.

HEAD QUARTERS, FORT PITT, Septr 29th 1780.

At a general Court Martial, whereof Col. Gibson is President, Alex^r M. Adams, a private soldier of Capt. Heth's Independent Company, was tried for neglect of duty by allowing Davis, a prisoner, to make his escape whilst he was placed over him as sentry—& was found guilty of the charge—in violation of ye 5th article of y^e. 18th section of the articles of war—& sentenced to receive fifty lashes on his bare back, with a cat-o-nine-tails by the drummers of the garrison.

Alex^r Chambers was tried by the same court for obtaining his discharge fraudulently, & by the unanimous opinion of the court was found guilty of the charge, & sentenced to be compelled to serve during the war.

John Phillips, Isaac Johnston & Stephen Winter, private soldiers in the 9th V^a Reg^t, were tried before the same court for breaking open the Commissary's stores at F^t McIntosh & stealing liquor therefrom; & John Phillips was found guilty of the charge, in violation of ye 5th article of ye 18th Section of the articles of war, & sentenced to receive one hundred lashes on his bare back with a cat-o-nine-tails by the drummers of the Reg^t And Johnston & Winter are found guilty of drinking part of the rum (knowing it to be stolen) & sentence the said Johnston (as corp^l) to do duty in the ranks as a private sentinel, & Winter to receive fifty lashes on his bare back by the drummers of the Reg^t.

John Darraugh & Saml Reed, private soldiers in the 8th Penn^a Reg^t were tried before the same court for desertion, & were found guilty of the charge, in violation of ye 1st article of ye 6th section of the articles of war—& sentenced to recieve each three hundred lashes on his bare back, with a cat-o-nine-tails, by the drummers of the Regiment.

The Command^t approves the proceedings of the court, but in consideration of the age & infirmities of Wm M. Adams, is pleased to remit his punishment—the rest of the sentences are to be put in execution to-morrow morning at troop-beating.

Parole—Rochester—Countersign—Rhine.

HEAD QUARTERS, FORT PITT, Octr 2^d '80.

At a General Court Martial, whereof Col. Gibson is President, Ens^n Thos Wyatt of the 8th P^a Reg^t, was tried for neglect of duty in suffering Davis, a prisoner under sentence of a general court martial for a capital crime, to make his escape out of the guard-house during his guard—& was acquitted.

The Command^t approves the proceedings of the court, & Ens. Thos Wyatt is released from his arrest.

At the same court Ens^n John Guthrie, of the same reg^t, was tried for disobedience of orders & behaving in a manner unbecoming an officer & a gentleman, & was found guilty of disobedience of orders, in violation of the 5th article of the 2^d section of the articles of war—& sentenced to be reprimanded in General Orders.

If Ensign Guthrie entertains proper ideas of the sacred character of an officer and a gentleman, his sentence will be a sufficient reprimand, & excite in him an attachment to that subordination which is the life & strength of an army, & without which no man is fit for an officer.

He is released from his arrest. The officers of the line & staff are to draw an allowance of liquor equal to the last general order for that purpose.

[Here ends the 1st vol., except the following entries on the closing fly-leaf:]

Capt. Clark	Guards	Court Martials Sept. 15 —	Commands.
" Dawson	....	....	....
" Swearingen	....	....	Aug. 8, '78.
" Carnahan	....	Sept. 15	....
" Jack	....	Sept. 15	....
" Cook	....	....	....

FRONTIER RETREAT

	Guards	Court Martials Sept. 15 —	Commands.
Capt. Stokely	....	....	....
" Jo^s Finley	....	....	....
" Prather	....	Sept. 15	....
" Moor	....	....	....
" Jn° Finley	....	Sept. 15.	....
Lt. Hughes	....	....	....
" Crawford	....	....	....
" Harden	....	....	....
" Peterson	....	Sept. 15, '78	....
" Niely	....	....	....
" Mickey	....	....	....
" Finley	....	....	....
" Amberson	....	....	....
" Graham	....	....	....
Capt. Clark	....	Peterson	Crawford
" Carnahan	....	Ward	Neilly
" Jos. Finley	....	Guthrie	Reed
" John Finley	....	Wyatt	Stotsberry.
C. Lt. Saml Brady.	....	Morrison	....
	....	Cooper	....

JOHN CLARK, Captain 8th P^a Regt.

THE VIRGINIA REGIMENT

[Officers of Ninth Virginia. 1SS195.]

Muster Roll of the field and Staff Officers belonging to ye 9. Virga Reg Taken for the Months of January, February and March, 1780

Names	Rank	Commisd or Appointd	Remarkes
Colonel Gibson		23 Octr 1777	
Lieut Colo Campbell	"		On Furlow
Major Taylor	"		On Furlough
Arthr Gordon	Adjutant	Apointd Feby 12th 1780	
Jacob Coleman	ditto	Octr ye 1st 1779	
Jossiah Tannihill	Pay Master	[word illegible] 3d March	
Geoe Berry	Qr Master	Apptd March 4th 1780	
Henry Dawson	Q Master	3 of May 1779	
David Holmes	Surgeon		On Furlough
John Knight	Surgn Mate		At Fort McIntosh
Thos Wood	Serjt Major		On Furlough
William Collis	Q M Serjt		
John Smith	Drum Major		
William Coxon	fife Major		Absent

ROLLS OF COSHOCTON EXPEDITION

[Ohio County officers. 4SS3–5. A. D.]

Pay Roll of the Field and Staff Officers of Militia belonging to the state of Virginia on ye Expedition to Coshockton in the service of the United States Commanded by Col^o David Shepherd Comm^g ye 10th April & Ending 28th Inclusive 1781 for 19 days

Names	Rank	No. days in service	Pay and subsistence per month		Whole amount of pay		Rec^d by us.
			Doll^s	90^{ths}	Doll^s	90^{ths}	
David Shepherd	Col^o	19	575	"	364	15	
Saml MColloch	Major	19	350	"	221	60	
Isaac Meeks	Adj^t	19	113	"	71	51	
W^m McIntire	Q. Master	19	113	"	71	51	
James Lemon	S. Major	19	20	"	12	60	
Jonothan Zane	Spy	19	"	"	19	"	
Total		"			760	57	

Pay Roll for hire of the Horses belonging to the field and Staff officers of the Virg⁎ Militia on the Expedition to Coshockton in the Service of the United States Commanded by Col° David Shepherd for 19 days Comm^g ye 10th Ap^l End^g 28th 1781.

Names	Rank	Horses in service	days in Service	pay per day		Amount of Pay		Rec^d by us
				Dollars	90^ths	doll^rs	90^ths	
David Shepherd	Col°	1	19					
Saml McColl°	Major	1	19					
Isaac Meeks	Adj^t	1	19					
W^m McIntire	Qu	1	19					
James Lemon	S. Major	1	19					
Jonothan Zane	Spy	1	19					
Total		6	19					

Pay Roll for Forrage due the field and Staff Officers of Militia to Coshocton for 19 days Ap^l 10, 1781

Names	Rank	N° horses in service	N° days in service	Corn		
				bush°	pecks	Qts.
David Shepherd	Col°	1	19	3	2	2
Saml M. Colloch	Major	1	19	3	2	2
Isaac Meeks	Adj^t	1	19	3	2	2
Willm M°Intire	Qu	1	19	3	2	2
James Lemon	S. Major	1	19	3	2	2
Jonothan Zane	Spy					
Total		6	19	21	1	4

[Officers and men. 4SS8–11, 22–23, 28, 32.]

Pay Roll of Cap.t Joseph Ogles Companie of Ohio Militia on the Expedition to Coshockton for 19 days Ap.l 10, 1781[1]

Men's Names	Rank	Time in service		pay per Month		Amount of Pay		Rec.d by us
		Mo.s	days	doll.s	90.ths	doll.s	90.ths	
Joseph Ogle	Cap.t	..	19	240	..	152	..	
Conrod Stroup	Lieu.t	..	19	126	..	79	72	
And.w Ramsey	Lieu.t	..	19	126	..	79	72	
Hugh M.cConnell	Ensign	..	19	120	..	76	..	
W.m Morrison	Serjeant	..	19	20	..	12	60	
Nathan Prater	ditto	..	19	20	..	12	60	
Garrat Applegate	ditto	..	19	20	..	12	60	
George Tate	ditto	..	19	20	..	12	60	
James Miller	Private	..	19	16	60	10	50	
W.m Harvey	d.o	..	19	16	60	10	50	
John Buskirk	d.o	..	19	..	..	10	50	
J.no M.cCormick	d.o	..	19	..	..	10	50	
Joseph Wells	d.o	..	19	..	..	10	50	
W.m Perrin	d.o	..	19	..	..	10	50	
Robert Moore	d.o	..	19	..	..	10	50	
J.no Scarmahorn	d.o	..	19	..	..	10	50	
W.m Scrichfield	d.o	..	19	..	..	10	50	
J.no Murphy	d.o	..	19	..	..	10	50	

[1] This roll is followed in the Draper Mss., by "A Roll of Horses belonging to Cap.t Ogles Companie April 10. 1781. for 19 days," sixty-six horses in all; "A Pay Roll for Retain'd Rations due Cap.t Ogles Companie," 1,163 rations; "Pay Roll for Forrage due Cap.t Ogles Companie for 19 days at 6 Quarts Corn per day," totaling 231 bushels, 3 pecks, and 4 quarts. As the names of the company's members are the same as those on this roll, we do not print the others.

FRONTIER RETREAT

Name	Rank							Note
Fras McGuire	do			19			10	50
Wm Gasten	do			19			10	50
Richd Applegate	do			19			10	50
James MGill	do			19			10	50
James Pierce	do			19			10	50
Richd Sparks	do			19			10	50
Wm Brazel	do			19			10	50
Robt Glass	do			19			10	50
Andw White	do			19			10	50
Geo: Ragor	do			19			10	50
Saml Wilson	do			19			10	50
Jacob Cox	do			19			10	50
M. Maitlind	do			19			10	50
Jno Sloughter	do			19			10	50
Jas Hughston	do			19			10	50
Anthony Linch	do			19			10	50
Jno Blane	do			19			10	50
Robt Henry	do			19			10	50	Joseph X Williams mark
Josh Williams	do			19			10	50
Thos Oar	do			19			10	50
James Clark	do			19			10	50
Hamilton Karr	do			19			10	50
Hairy Smith	do			19			10	50
Peter Nigswonger	do			19			10	50
Geo: Whitesale [Wetzel]	do			19			10	50
Lewis Whitesale	do			19			10	50
Jno Whitesale	do			19			10	50
Corns Gaiter	do			19			10	50
Wm Millburn	do			19			10	50
Isaac Pennington	do			19			10	50
Conrod White	do			19			10	50
Wm Boggs Senr	do			19			10	50
Wm Boggs Junr	do			19			10	50
Bartly McGie	Private	60	16	19			10	50	Barclay McGhee
David English	"	60	16	19			10	50
Isaac Phillips	"	60	16	19			10	50
Zac: Spriggs	"	60	16	19			10	50
Jas Mitchell				19			10	50
Jno MColloch				19			10	50

Mens Names	Rank	Time in service		Pay per month		Amount of Pay		Rec'd by us
		Moª	days	dollˢ	90ᵗʰˢ	dollars	90ᵗʰˢ	
Wᵐ Harris	"	"	19	"	"	10	50	
Thoˢ Mills	"	"	19	"	"	10	50	
Samˡ Worley	Private	"	19	"	"	10	50	
Jnº Green	"	"	19	"	"	10	50	
Benjⁿ Pyatt	"	"	19	"	"	10	50	
Jacob Paul	"	"	19	"	"	10	50	
Zechª Dewitt	"	"	19	"	"	10	50	
Jere: Clemens	"	"	19	"	"	10	50	
Alexʳ Stricklin	"	"	19	"	"	10	50	
Wᵐ Hawkins	"	"	19	"	"	10	50	
Eb: Zane	"	"	19	"	"	10	50	
Andʷ Scott	"	"	19	"	"	10	50	
Siloas Hedge	"	"	19	"	"	10	50	
David MClure	"	"	19	"	"	10	50	
John Biggs	"	"	19	"	"	10	50	
Total		"	"		"	1.112	74	Dollars

The above is a True Copy of Capᵗ Joseph Ogles Pay Roll, taken from yᵉ Original

Pay Roll of Capt Benjamin Royse's Companie for 19 days. April 10, 1781[1]

Mens Names	Rank	Time in Service Mo^s	Time in Service days	pay per month doll^s	pay per month 90^ths	Amount of pay doll^s	Amount of pay 90^ths	Rec^d by us.
Benjamin Royse	Capt	"	19	240	"	152	"	
John Miller	Lieu^t	"	19	126	"	79	72	
Wm Troup	Serj^t	"	19	20	"	12	60	
Alex^r Burns	d^o	"	19	20	"	12	60	
Corn^s Miller	Private	"	19	16	60	10	50	
John Goo[l]dwin	Private	"	19	"	"	10	50	
Joseph Jennins	d^o	"	19	"	"	10	50	
Nathan Bane	d^o	"	19	"	"	10	50	
Joseph Bane	d^o	"	19	"	"	10	50	
Zanes Linley	d^o	"	19	"	"	10	50	
Joseph Linley	d^o	"	19	"	"	10	50	
Edwd McVaw	d^o	"	19	"	"	10	50	
Isaac McVaw	d^o	"	19	"	"	10	50	
John Whiting	d^o	"	19	"	"	10	50	his John x Whiting mark
Eb: Osburn	d^o	"	19	"	"	10	50	
Jacob Husong	d^o	"	19	"	"	10	50	
Step^n Carter	d^o	"	19	"	"	10	50	
Caleb Linley	d^o	"	19	"	"	10	50	
Richd Bilby	d^o	"	19	"	"	10	50	
Benj^a Ross	d^o	"	19	"	"	10	50	
Wm Bennett	d^o	"	19	"	"	10	50	
Wm Morriss	d^o	"	19	"	"	10	50	
Danl Mcfarlin	d^o	"	19	"	"	10	50	
Saml Hardesty	d^o	"	19	"	"	10	50	
Nathan Evans	d^o	"	19	"	"	10	50	
Elias Kelly	d^o	"	19	"	"	10	50	
Jacob Rude	d^o	"	19	"	"	10	50	
Ab^m Hathaway	d^o	"	19	"	"	10	50	
Geo^a Dickeson	d^o	"	19	"	"	10	50	
James Guffey	d^o	"	19	"	"	10	50	
James Johnson	"	"	"	"	"			
Total						542	12	

[1] This roll is followed in *ibid.* by those for retained rations, pay rolls for horses and for forage for Captain Royse's company. The name of A. Burnett is found upon these rolls, in addition to those given on the roll here printed.

Pay Roll of Capt Jacob Leflers Comp^y for 19 days April 10, 1781[1]

Mens' Names	Rank	time in Service		pay per Month		Amount of Pay		Rec^d by us.
		Mo^s	days	doll^s	90^{ths}	doll^s	90^{ths}	
Jacob Lefler	Capt	"	19	240	"	152	"	
Francis Miller	Serj^t	"	19	20	"	12	"	
Ab^m Rice	Private	"	19	16	60	10	60	
Henry Ditts	d^o	"	19	"	"	10	50	
Jacob Miller	d^o	"	19	"	"	10	50	Jacob Miller
H. Fullinwider	d^o	"	19	"	"	10	50	
Danl Rice	d^o	"	19	"	"	10	50	
John Kenser	d^o	"	19	"	"	10	50	
John Huff	d^o	"	19	"	"	10	50	
Jno fulherborn [Geo. Plullerpurn]	d^o	"	19	"	"	10	50	
Peter fullinwider	d^o	"	19	"	"	10	50	
Total	"	"	"	"	"	260	20	

[1] This roll is followed in *ibid.* by those for retained rations, and pay rolls for horses and forage for Captain Lefler's company.

Pay Roll of Capt Wm Crawfords Company for 28 days April 2, 1781.[1]

Mens Names	Rank	Time in Service		Pay per Month		Amount of Pay		Rec^d by us.
		Mo^s	days	doll.	90^{ths}	doll.	90^{ths}	
William Crawford	Capt	"	28	240	"	224	"	
Wm Garritt [Jarratt]	Serj^t	"	28	20	"	18	60	
Jo^s [Jesse] Vanmetere	Private	"	28	16	60	15	50	
Richd Seaton	d^o	"	16	16	60	15	50	
John Cain	d^o	"	28	"	"	15	50	
John Bradford	d^o	"	28	"	"	15	50	
Thomas James	d^o	"	28	"	"	15	50	
Jere. Veatch	d^o	"	28	"	"	15	50	
Mich^l Catt	d^o	"	28	"	"	15	50	
George Catt	d^o	"	28	"	"	15	50	
Lewis Burnett	d^o	"	28	"	"	15	50	
Lewis Grinstaf	d^o	"	28	"	"	15	50	
Jacob Rifle (Rifle)	d^o	"	28	"	"	15	50	
Jacob Lawrence	d^o	"	28	"	"	15	50	
M. Baker	"	"	28	"	"	15	50	
Total						444	80	

[1] Capt. William Crawford's company came from the Monongahela River, hence the extra days for their time of service. This roll is followed in the *ibid.*, by those for retained rations, and by pay rolls for horses and forage for this company during the expedition.

WISCONSIN HISTORICAL COLLECTIONS

GENERAL COURTS-MARTIAL

[Trial of Lieut. John Ward, Maj. Frederick Vernon, president of court. Washington Papers. A. D. S.]

Proceedings of A General Court Martial held at Fort Pitt June the 29th 1781 In pursuance of A warrant from his Excellency the commander in chief, dated New Windsor the 16th April 1781, and by him transmited to the commandant at this Post.

Major Vernon President

Members:
Captain Craig
Cap: Springer
Capt. Brady
Lieu[t] Peterson
L[t] J. Harrison
L[t] L: Harrison

Capt: Clark
Capt[n] Biggs
L[t] Crawford
L[t] Springer
En[s] Dawson
En[s] Beck

Capt[n] John Finley D Judge ad:

The Court and Judge advocate being sworn Proceeded to the Trial John Ward L[t] 8th Pen[a] Reg[t]—

Lieu[t] John Ward came before the Court charged with Insolence, Disobedience of orders, and Taking part with the Enemies of the commanding officer of this District, and associating with those below the character of Gentlemen—

L[t] Ward pleads not Guilty—

Colo Stephen Bayard being sworn, saith a day or two previous to my arresting L[t] Ward or sending in the charges, I with a number of the officers of the 8th Pen[a] and 7th Virginia Regiments, were standing near M[r] Fausits, that we had not been standing long before we saw A Number of Men walking towards us, some of the Gentlemen said there comes the combind associators, let us not take any Notice of them nor shew them any Respect, nor even move our hats to them on hearing high words pass between Capt[n] Brady and L[t] Ward, I Desired L[t] Ward to hold his tongue (or words to that Effect) L[t] Ward Turned to me and said, he had a right to take their parts I told him he had no right to take their part there, or even to think about the Matter; he said he had as good a right to think or speak his sentiments there as I had; I told him to go about his business and Let me hear no more of it: he still kept Talking to me in that Insulting way; I desired him the second time to go away, his haughty imperious way provocked me, I told him I would put him Under an arrest. I asked him what Reg^t he belonged to, he said the 2nd Pen^a Reg^t. I told him he belonged to the 8th Pen^a Reg^t and must obey the orders of the commanding officer. after he was put under an arrest in walking to Mr Duncans, he walked along side of me and damn'd himself but he had as good a right to speak his sentiments as any man and would do it at any time. I told him I imputed it to his Ignorance of Military duty, and told him he was but a Boy in the service, or he would not have treated his commanding officer in that manner. I have observed Lt Ward Frequently associating with David Tait hooking arms together and riding out with each other—

Quest^n from Lt Ward to Colo Bayard—Did you not tell me previous to your arresting me, I was a boy, an Infant, and did not know my Duty—

Answer. I do not Recollect tho I might have said it

Quest^n from Lt Ward to Colo Bayard When you arested me, did I not tell you I would consider myself as such, and asked you for what, and did you not tell me it was for mutiny—

Answer. It implied that in part of the arrest.

Captn Saml Brady being sworn saith I was present with Colo Bayard when the Dispute hapned between him & Lieu^t Ward. I was the first that obseved the people coming up the Street, and I said there comes the combind Associators let us not treat them with Respect, for my part I dont know that I shall move my hatt to them. Lieu^t Ward Then Steped up and said he did not know that I had any Reason to treat some of them with Disrespect. I then took A second look at them and said there was an Individual there I would treat with common Respect. Col: Bayard then steped up and told Lt Ward he had no Right to take their parts. Lt Ward said he was not taking all their parts, but there was some he had a right to take their part. I then steped between Col: Bayard and Lt Ward and tryed to hush the matter as some of the Party had stoped near us to hear what was said Colo Bayard told Lieu^t Ward to hold his tongue (or words to that Effect) that he had not aright to think. Lieu^t Ward said he had a right to think. Colo: Bayard told him he was a boy and an Infant & did not know his duty, and desired him to go about his business. I cant Recollect the answer Lt Ward Returned. but that Colo. Bayard steped up and gave him A Slap on the breast and said I arest you for Mutiny. We then came to wards Mr Duncans &

I heard L⁺ Ward say he had A Right to think and speak his Sentiments as well as any other Gentleman Colo. Bayard told him he was A boy and he imputed his Conduct to his Ignorance of Military Disipline.

Captain John Finley being sworn saith on the 30th of May I with several other Gentlemen was present when a number of the Inhabitants of Pittsburgh was coming towards us. Captⁿ Brady said there comes the combind associators Let us not move our hatts to them or take any Notice of them for my part I will not move my Hatt or show them any Respect Lieuᵗ John Ward made answer and said he did not think Capt Brady had any Right to show them any disrespect. Captⁿ Brady said he had. Lᵗ Ward said it must be for some private Reasons. Captⁿ Brady said I have my Reasons. Lieut Ward said for his part he Looked on some of them to be be Gentlemen and would treat them as such. Colo Bayard then told Lᵗ Ward he was very wrong and acted out of the character of an Officer in taking the part of such Rascals or Villains, that no officer should be seen associating with or countenanceing such Damnd Scoundrals, that had been Mutinying against the commanding officer. Lᵗ Ward said there might be some such among them, but there was some of them Gentlemen, that was his Opinion and he thought he had a Right to enjoy it. Colo. Bayard said he had no Right to think any such thing. Lᵗ Ward said by god he had a Right to think and speak his thoughts & he would do it. Colo Bayard said he had not and it was his and Every other officers duty to suport the commanding officer and he had no Right to think. Lᵗ Ward said he had a Right to think and speak his thoughts if he pleased. Colo. Bayard said he was a boy an Infant and did not know his duty or he Would not Talk so, and told him to go away and Repeated the word Boy and Infant two or three times. Lᵗ Ward said he did not pretend to know a great deal of duty as he never had an opportunity of seeing much of it, but said he was an officer, and had don his duty as well as he knew how, and never Refused doing it; and would suport the commanding officer, in any thing he thought was Right. Colo. Bayard asked him if he was not an officer. he said he was. says the Col: in what Regᵗ. Lᵗ Ward said the 2ⁿᵈ Penᵃ Regt. Colo Bayard said he was not. Lᵗ Ward said that from the Arangment he thought he was, and said to Col. Bayard What Regᵗ do I belong to. Col. Bayard said the 8th and he Ought to be arested. Lᵗ Ward said if he had don anything that was out of the character of an officer he ought to be arested and Tryd. Colo. Bayard Said he would arest him for Mutiny, and desired him to consider himself under an arest Lt Ward said if it was his order he would. Col. Bayard said it was his orders.

Lieut. John Ward being put on his defence Saith— Gentlemen, I have been arested and araigned at your barr By Lt Colo. Bayard, for Insolence, Disobedience of Orders, and Taking part with the Enemies of the Command'g officer of this District, and associating with those below the Character of Gentlemen. To these Charges I have pleaded Not Guilty. In Support of the accusations, Colo Bayard who Exhibits them steps forth and deposeth That A day or two previous to his aresting Lt Ward, he with a number of officers were standing near Mr Fausits that they had not stood Long before they saw a number of men Walking Towards them. Some of the Gentlemen said there comes the associators Let us not Take any notice of them nor shew them any Respect It is needless to follow Colo. Bayard through his narative. However Towards the conclusion of it he says that he has seen me in company with Mr Tait. am I the only officer that has been seen in company with that Gentleman. I know nothing against Mr Taits Character. Nor do I keep company with any now but such whose company I formerly Frequented From the Evidence before the court it will I hope appear obvious that I was neither Insolent to Colo Bayar nor did I in any Respect Insult him or any other Gentleman. I admit that I told him that I had A Right to think, and speak my sentiments. This privilige is one of the greatest we hold and are contending for. and Notwithstanding the caprice of some and the Tyrany of Others I still hope we shall enjoy it. As an officer I have Ever obeyed with pleasure the Commands of my superiours, as a man I ever have and will enjoy my sentiments. Colo Bayard Imputes these Sentiments of mine to my Ignorance of military duty, and then deposeth that he told me I was but a boy in the Service But upon my asking him if he did not tell me previous to aresting me that I was a boy and did not know my duty He answers, He dos not Recollect that he told me tho he might have said it. How such Incoherancies and Contradictions can be Reconciled I leave to the Determination of the Court. Besides Gentlemen the Evidence of A prosecutor can have no Right did it ever opperate against me (tho Colo Bayard is of A different kind) For the mere Epsedixet of an accuser can never convict the accused. This is Repugnant to Law and Equity. Therefore the Evidence of Colo Bayard can only be considered as an Explanation, or Illustration of the Charge nor can it be taken up by the Court on any other ground whatever. I shall now proceed to the Evidence of Captn Brady This Gentleman Deposeth that he was the first that discovered The people coming up the Street, and said there comes the Combind Associators. Let us not treat them with Respect Lt Ward said he did not know that he had a Right to treat some of those Gentlemen with disrespect. That Colo Bayard Then told me I had no Right to take their part, Mr Ward then Replied he was not taking all their parts, but he had a Right to take part with some of them "that he Recollects that Colo Bayard told Lt Ward to hold his tongue" and that he had not A Right to think" and that Lt Ward answered he had A Right to think. That Colo Bayard told Lt Ward that he was A boy, and an Infant, and did not know his duty, And desired him to go about his business. that Lt Ward made some Reply which he dos not Recollect. When Colo Bayard steped up to him and gave him a slap on The Breast and told him he was arested for Mutiny. Captn Brady is called by the prosecutor Colo. Bayard and he proves The Substance of all I Could Either hope or wish. I am peremtorly Told to hold my Tongue and that I had no Right to think that I was A boy and an Infant &c and thereby Captn Brady clearly proves what Colo Bayard Endeavours to evade.

But I am particularly obligd to the Testimony of Captn John Finley who is also called in suport of the Prosecution this Gentleman is not only Candid but Explicit his memory is Retentive and he not Only Speaks the Truth but the whole truth and nothing but the Truth. I beg Gentlemen that you would advert to the Charge and Compare that with the Evidence of Captn Brady & Captn Finley. Hear I hope it will appear obvious that in place of being Insolent I was Treated with Insolence that I had Received ill Treatment and Unbecoming Language, but Returned None. It therefore depends on you Gentlemen to determine Whiether a commissioned officer bearing a Commission from Congress and carrying arms in Defence of Liberty and the Rights of mankind has the priviledge to think or not; and if the Articles of War doth not Prohibit us from enjoying this privilige. which it is impossible they can do I cannot be found Guilty of

Disobedience of Orders For Deposeth Captn Finley upon Colo Bayards saying it was his and Every other officers duty to suport the commanding officer & That Lt Ward had no Right to think, Lt Ward Replies he had a Right to think and speak his thoughts if he pleased. Can this be considered Disobedience of Orders I hope not I'm sure it cannot. such an Idea could only be Engendred by Violence Matured by Malevolence and pen'd by Indiscretion. and as to the latter part of the charge, Taking part with the Enemies of the commanding officer of this District, and associating with them below the character of Gentlemen. After being Repeatedly Insulted by telling me to be silent and that I was an Infant & a boy; and did not know my duty. What says Captn Finley. Lt Ward said he did not pretend to know a great deal of duty as he never had an opportunity of seeing much of it. but said he was an officer and had don his duty as well as he knew how and never Refused doing it, and would support the Commanding officer in any thing he thought was Right. Is there any thing like presumption or Insolence here, Is there any thing here like disrespect to my Commanding officer, or the Commanding officer of this district. Considering the Language I had Recieved from Colo Bayard and the manner he Treated me, are not my answers Mild Moderate and Respectfull. The Regard I have for the dignity of the Service and the Respect I bear for Commanding officers makes me desirous of throwing A Viel over part of the Evidence of Captn Finley. "Rascals, Villains, damn'd Scounderals" is a Language that never can do Honnour to any man. and I have an Effictionate Father* Gentlemen that merits no such appellation. He is A Citizen, and has associated with his Fellow Citizens, to obtain a Redress of Grievances which they have an Undoubted Right to do and which is fully Shewn by the Sixteenth art. of the Constitution and Declaration of the Rights of Inhabitants of the State of Pennsylvania which is as follows Viz—"That the people have a Right to assemble together to consult For their common good, to Instruct their Representatives And to apply to the Legislator for Redress of Grievances By Address, Petition or Remonstrances." Many of the associators as they are called are Gentlemen and all I believe are good Cittizens and Honnest men. To hear my Father Called a Scoundral without Rousing Resentment and Indignation would

*Col: Bayard observed Lt Wards Father was none of Number that was walking up the street, that he spoke of.

have argued that I was Destitute of Filiel affection, and that I had Neither the Feelings of a Son, nor the spirit of A man. Indeed to hear the cittizens of a free country, abused and Reprobated in such terms for Detecting Abuses, and applying for Redress of Grievances, was to me a Doctrine perfectly Novel. Congress, recommends attention and Respect to Cittizens, by The Following Resolves. Viz—

"That any Disrespectfull and Indecent Beheavour of any officer of any Rank under the appointment of Congress To the Civil authority of any State in the Union, will be discountenanced, and discouriged, and That a contrary beheavour will be considered as one of the Surest means to Recommend any officer to The Favour and notice of Congress."—and our Illustrious Commander in Chief sets daly Examples of This kind, even to the peaseant he is Respectfull as well as Just. Let us Follow his footsteps and Immitate his precepts. I shall conclude Gentlemen, with observing that the Constitution and Laws of my Country secures me from the Envenomd shafts of party and the Resentment of my Prosecutor. As an American while I stand a prisoner before my Countrymen my Peers, and my Brother officers and am conscious of my Innocence and Uprightness of having been attentive to my duty and Respectfull to my Supriours I have nothing to dread— While Candour dictates Honour will Justify. and what my Heart cannot Reprove, I hope my Brother officers cannot condemn, I mean my beheavour and conduct as an officer & A Gentleman on the thirtieth day of May last. My Honour, my Character, and my Reputation Gentlemen are now in Your possision. To A Soldier they are precious Gems, and to you I chearfully Intrust them. Convinced that You have too tender and nice a Regard for your own Reputation To Injure mine. and that as Gentlemen and men of honour You will act the part of Faithfull Guardians by Restoring That to me in its pristine State and Lusture.

The Court after Hearing the Evidences are of oppinion that Lt John Ward is not Guilty of the several charges Exhibited against him and therefore do acquit him.—and he is hereby acquitted.

       FRED^k VERNON Major & President—
       JOHN FINLEY D Judge ad^v pro tem

[*Endorsed:*] Proceedings of Court Martial Lt John Ward— (acquitted)

[Trial of George Wallace, commissary. Maj. Frederick Vernon, president of court. Washington Papers. A. D. S.]

July 1st

The Court met according to adjourment Lieutenant John Mills being sworn in Room of Lt Lawrence Harrison

George Wallace A. C of Issues came before the Court charged with neglect of Duty, and Insolence to Colo Bayard

Pleads not Guilty.

Colo. John Gibson being sworn, saith that Colo. Bayard came to him and told him that George Wallace A. C. of Issues had been Guilty of neglect of duty and behaved in an Insolent maner to him. that he (the deponent) desired Colo. Bayard to go to Adj^t Crawford and have Mr Wallace arested if he has behaved in such A maner

Colo: S: Bayard being sworn saith that previous to my aresting Mr Wallace I had immediate Occation for a Little salt. I made out an order for half a peck and told Henry Simmons (my Bowman) to go and try to get it. simmons went and got the order Signed by Samuel Sample A. D. Q. M. and waited to get it issued, after waiting some time he was told by Mr Sample that Mr Wallace had the key of the Store and Mr Sample sent him for it. Mr Wallace was with three or four Gentlemen. and said something to Simmons which will be releated to the Court in his Evidence. Simmons came and told me. I then had waited some time with impatience for his return when he came he said Mr Wallace sent word that he would wait his own time for it on which I sent Simmons Immediately to him and to tell Mr Wallace to let him have the salt without delay as the order had been signed, by his superior officer he had no right to say any thing in it. at the same time Desiring Simmons to bring Mr Wallace's answer to me. the answer I recieved was, go and tell Col: Bayard he would go when it suited him which provocked me as I expected to have Recieved civil answer from Mr Wallace. I then ordered Simmons to his duty. Some time after I was siting reading at my Window Mr Wallace, and Mr John Irwin pased by as they passed I called to Mr Wallace and repeated to him the Message he had sent me and asked him if he had sent it, he said he had— I then told him he did not know his duty or he would not send me such an impertinent mesage, he said he knew his duty as well as any man, he seemed much in wrath. I then told him he was A Rascal and an impertinent fellow for treating me in such a maner. Some short time after I came down to Col: Gibsons Quarters and told him in what maner I had been treated by Mr Wallace. Col: Gibson then ordered me to arest him—

Question by the prisoner Was that order drawn on me

Answer— it was not. but you was doing the duty of Mr Johnson, who was absent at that time—

Henry Simmons Soldier in the 8th Pen^a Reg^t being sworn, saith that I was sent by Col: Bayard with an order from him to Mr Duncan, D. Q. M. and he not being at home I went to Mr Sample one of his assistants Mr Sample after taking a Reciept told me that he had not the key of the Salt store and desired me to go to Mr Wallace for it. I went to Mr Wallace with Mr Sampels compliments to him to know if he had the key of the Salt store. Mr Wallace Replied I suppose I have. I then told him Mr Sample will be obliged to you for it as he is waiting. Mr Wallace said he could not go down then as he had not time; that he must wait his Leasure. I then went to Colo. Bayard and told him what Mr Wallace said, the Col: Desired me to go to Mr Wallace and Desire him to go Immediately. and told me to bring Mr Wallace's answer to him. I did so. and Mr Wallace Desired me to tell Colo. Bayard he would go when it suted him. I asked Mr Wallace if I would give that as his answer to Colo. Bayard, and he told me to give it—

Question by the Court Did you know what the order was for

Answer—It was for half peck of salt & one Quire of paper

Question by Mr Wallace When You presented Mr Sampels compliments to me did I not tell you I would be down immediately

An^s You said Mr Sample must wait your Leasure

Question by Mr Wallace did you tell me it was for to get salt that Colo. Bayard ordered me to the Fort

Answer I told you that the Col: wanted the key of the Salt store to get some salt—

John Irwin D. C. G. of Issues being sworn saith that he was at Mr Wallaces house with a design to call Mr Wallace to the provision store on some business. when Simons came that he heard the mesage Delivered, which was, that Mr Sample sent him for the key of the salt-store. Mr Wallace Replied he had not the key of the salt store there it was down in the Fort Locked up in the provision store where it was usually hung and that he was going immediately down to the Fort and would Either give or send the key to M[r] Sample, upon which the servant went away and Returned seemingly in great heast and informed M[r] Wallace that it was the Colo.s positive orders he should go Immediately down to the Fort. upon which M[r] Wallace with some degree of Surprise asked what Colo. it was that sent such A positive Order. the Servant answered it was Col: Bayard. then says Wallace if Colo Bayard takes upon him to send such positive orders to me I will go to the Fort when it sutes me for I know my duty. and instead of proceeding Directly to the Fort as he intended he then sat down in his house for some short time after some minuets had relapsed I then proposed to M[r] Wallace to go down to the Fort upon the busines's we intended upon which we proceeded together towards the Fort untill we came opposite Col: Bayards Quarters when Col: Bayard came to the door and called M[r] Wallace to him. I continued walking at a slow pace without halting for some time and did not distinctly hear what pased between them at First untill I halted at M[r] Smiths door and distincktly heard Colo. Bayard call M[r] Wallace an impertinent Rascal. upon which I turned round towards Colo. Bayard and told him that M[r] Wallace was not a Rascal that I knew him to be Qualified for all the duties of his publick station and that he Colo. Bayard was not capable of proving him a Rascal or of Treating him as such. upon which Col: Bayard again Repeated that my assistant was a Rascal

Question by the Court do you Recollect what M[r] Wallace said to Col. Bayard previous to his calling him A Rascal

Answer I did not hear what was said before Col: Bayard Called him a Rascal as I kept Walking. but when I was Talking with Colo. Bayard M[r] Wallace said some things which was prety warm but what they were I cant Recollect

Question by M[r] Wallace did you hear simmons telling me it was for salt that Colo Bayard was wanting me down

Answer I understood it was for the purpose of geting salt out for Col: Bayard that the key of the salt store was wanting

The court adjourns till tomorow morning. 9 OClook July 2nd

The court met according to adjournment

David Tait being sworn saith that I was present on the 13th Ult° in the House of George Wallace A. Com[y] of Issues when a Soldier Waiter to Colo. Bayard came with M[r] Samples compt. to M[r] Wallace for a key of the Salt store. M[r] Wallace told him it was in the provision store. and that he would be down in the Fort Immediately, and send, or Give it to Mr Sample. The Soldier asked Mr Wallace if he would not send the key of the provision Store to Mr Sample, to which Mr Wallace Answered that he did not trust any person with that key but himself. On this Conversation the Soldier went away but in A very short time returned and as he came to the door, he extended his arm toward Mr Wallace in an insulting and threatening maner and said, that it was the Colonels positive orders that he (Mr Wallace) should go to the Fort Immediately Mr Wallace asked him what Colo orders that was, the soldier said Col: Bayards. Mr Wallace asked him a second time if that was Colo. Bayards positive orders the soldier said it was. after a short silence Mr Wallace Told the soldier that he did not understand such orders and he kno his duty and he would go to the Fort when it it suted him— the soldier asked Mr Wallace if he would tell the Col: that—he said yes do—

Mr Wallace being put on his defense says as to the Charges of neglect of duty and Insolence Exhibited against me by Lt Colo Bayard I have Pleaded not Guilty— The first subject that calls for my Consideration is the proof which Colo Bayard hath produced in suport of these charges—he begins with his Own Evidence first and Consequently I must endeavour to trace him through that Labyrinth of nonsence in which he appears to Stray. he tells you that he made out an order for some salt and that his servant Went and got the Order Signed by Mr Sample A. Q. M.— This is strange indeed that A Lt. Colo Commanding a Regim^t should send his order to be countersignd by an A Q. M.— and it is still more strange that if the Issuing of this salt became the duty of an Issuing Comm^y Why an assistant, D. M. should have any thing to do in the matter, and send to me for the key of the salt Store as hath been made appear by Every Evidence adduced upon this Tryal—again he Informs you that he sent his Order "to go immediatly and let him have the salt" that the order was signed by my superior officer and I had no Right to say any thing in it—Most certain—I acknowledge that I had not the Least right to say a sylable upon the Occasion—and I think I can easily make it appear to the intire satisfaction of this Court that I had nothing Either to say or do in this Transaction—Colo Bayard has neglected to Inform the Court that the order he made out for the Salt was directed"To David Duncan

Esqr. D. Q. M. Genl W Dep^t but his servant (simmons) has clearly proven what he seems to have Evaded and swears that the Order was Directed to the said David Duncan. and he not being at home he went to Mr Sample his assistant" who took A Reciept thereon—and only told simmons to go to me for the lone of the key of the Salt Store— you see Gentlemen that this Transaction was intirely confined to David Duncan and his Ass^t whose duty it certainly was as both the disposing and Issuing of that parcel of Salt properly belongd to their Department of Business—Therefore if Colo Bayard met with any unexpected delays he ought to have confined his censures to those on whome he depended for this duty— Is it possible that any Rational creature could concieve that the Issuing of this salt became any part of my duty— or that I was bound to obey a positive indiscreet command, from a person who never had the least authority to give it.— Yet you see Gent^n that Col: Bayard is struck with this false Idea— and is presuming Enough to send a Peremptory command for me to go Immediately and let him have the Salt—and to compleat the nonsensical Farce. I am arrested in his own name for Neglect of duty, and Insolence—as I have already hinted at the Impropriety of Colo Bayard offering to command me upon this occasion it now becoms necessary to have a full and perfect Explanation of the subject.— I do asert that neither Colo. Bayard or any officer What Ever belonging to the line beneath the commander at this post *have any Right* to Command me; and that I am subject only to the command of my superiour officers in my own Departm^t of Business or the commanding officer of the Post or Detatchm^t to which I am assigned the Regulations for the Goverment of the Commiss^y Dep^t are particularly Explicit in every part of Our duty and Tenor of our Commission prepaired and calculated for the nature of Our service clearly and Expressivly fixes the Limits of our subordination.— If Staff Officers have neither Rank or Command in the line Consequently they Cannot be commanded by the Line as they stand arranged in a Department of Service Quite abstracted from the line of the Army.— Wherefore I insist that any command given by Lt Colo Bayard or any other officer not fully authorised for the purpose can only be dictated by Ignorance or ambition—I hope Gentlemen I have made clearly appear that the duty of the Issuing Comm^y at this post can be no ways concearned in Orders addressed to A D^y Q. M. Genl and that in the present Case Colo.

Bayard attempted an Illegal Stretch of authority in commanding me upon business not belonging to the duties of my Department— Wherefore I flatter myself that with Gentlemen of Candour, divested of Prejudice and disposed to do Justice I shall shortly Stand acquited of this Immaginary crime—neglect of Duty— With respect to the charge of Insolence it appears to be as ill grounded as the Other— Had he charg^d me with disobedience of Orders instead of Insolence he Would most Certainly have carried his point—because he gave a positive Command and I acknowledge that I as positively disobeyed it— If it can be deemd Insolence to disobey an Illegal, Unjust and peremtory Command then I acknowledge myself Guilty.— but it appears Very Evident to me that Colo Bayard must have been consious that I had no Right to Obey the Order he sent, Otherwise he would most Certainly have Exhibited the charge of Disobedience also then it follows that if there was no Right in giving the order, there can be no wrong in Refusing it Consequently I must Stand acquited of the Charge of Insolence— But Gentlemen, I beg your particular attention to the Evidence of Mr Irwin and Mr Tait, which fully proves my moderation and Ready attention when I was called upon for the key of the Salt Store my Reply was that I was going immediately down to the Fort and would Either send or give the key to Mr Sample Pray Gentl^n dos this savor the least of Insolence when Col: Bayard Stopd me in the publick Street and accosted me with the Epethit of "Rascal and impertinent fellow" you do not know your duty &. C. as already declared on his own oath What was my Reply to him ? why nothing more than telling him that I knew my duty that I was no Rascal and that he was not capable of Treating me as such. pray where was my Insolence upon this Occation— But I should Rather ask where was my Spirit and Resentment.— But he may be assured that a day will come and I believe it is not very distant when he must certainly attone for his conduct upon this occasion. Gent^n I have the Honour of being a Commissioned officer in the Civil Staff of the army and I am consious that I have for the space of four Years past most punctualy discharged all the duties of A Faithfull Servant to the public wherefore I will say without Vanity that I consider myself Justly Intitled to all the Respectfull Treatment that is due to those two Characters— Here Gent^n you see in place of my being Insolent I have been Treated with Insolence arrogance and disrespect.— You see how widely

Colo Bayard has Departed from the Character of A Gentleman and instead of observing that decensy and good Deportment that is customary among Gentlemen and due from one officer to another You see him decending to the lowest degree of Scurility and abuse— But Colo Bayard will find that there are articles of war provided to correct his Errors as well as mine,—and as I appear hear only in the Character of A defendant I shall desist from any further accusation and leave that for the business of a Future day

Gentlemen my Conduct in a public Capacity for several years past must be well known to the most of the Gent: of this Court— I therefore appeal to your own Experience Whether you ever Discovered in me a Spirit of Insolence or Neglect of Duty— I flatter myself that you will do me the Justice of Acknowledging that you have ever Experienced a very Diffirent Deportment in all the duties of my publick Station.— Gentlemen my Case is now submitted to your Consideration and with you I freely Intrust it— But Before you determine thereon would beg leave to try your feelings for a moment with an application of my case to yourselves.— Suppose Yourselves only for this moment in my situation and try how spirit and Resentment will Relish the Unmerited treatment I have Received for shewing only a becoming Resentment to an Illegal Unjust and arbitary command from a person not possesed of authority to give it I am not only Insulted and abused, but charged with neglect of duty and Insolince.— But Gentlemen it is Impartial Judgement that trys the Charge and I assure You I am Perfectly satisfy'd that your sentence Will be purely the dictates of Justice Honour and Truth—

The Court after hearing and maturely considering the Evidences for and against Mr Wallace are of Oppinion that he is not guilty of Neglect of duty and they do acquit him of that charge.—but the Court are of oppinion he is Guilty of Insolence to Colo Bayard it being A breach of the 5th Art: of the 18th Section of the Articles of War. and they do sentence him to be Reprimanded in Genl Orders—and he is hereby sentanced to be Reprimanded in G^l Orders—

       FRED^{r} VERNON Major & President
       JOHN Finley D. Judge ad. pro tem

[*Endorsed:*] Proceedings of Court Martial George Wallace C Issues reprimanded in Genl Orders

[Trial of Lieut. Archibald Read, Col. Stephen Bayard, president of the court. Washington Papers. D. S.]

July 9th.

The court Met according to adjournment

Lieu^t Colo: Stephen Bayard being sworn as presid^t in place of Maj^r Vernon, who was sick.

Members:
- Captn Craig
- Captn Biggs
- Captn Lt Martin
- Lieu^t Thomas
- Lieu^t Harrison
- En^s Morrison
- Captn Clark
- Captn Brady
- Captn Lt Lloyd
- Lieu^t Howel
- Lieu^t Ward
- En^s Dawson—

The court being sworn proceeded to the Tryal of Lieu^t Archibald Read Pay-Master to the 8th Pen^a Reg^t who came before the court charged (by Alex^r Fowler Esqr Auditor of Accompts W District) with Defrauding the Soldiers and Detaining From them their pay in a manner Unbecoming the character of an officer and a Gentleman.—

Pleads not Guilty to the charge.—

Alex^r Fowler Esqr Auditor of acc^{ts} W. D. produced to the court in support of the charge the Acc^{ts} of Money paid to the officers & Soldiers of the 8th Pen^a Regiment. With their Reciepts (for Moneys paid to them) in the Following Words. Viz. "We the Subscribers do Acknowledg to have Rec^d the Sums anexed to our names Respectively." And it appears that Serjeant William Lee & Serj^t George Armstrongs that is set to their Reciepts is not their Hand Writing, Mr Read acknowledges to have wrote their Names.—Mr Fowler produced to the court the Acc^t Stated at Settlement with Lieu^t Read, as Follows. Viz—

Dr The United States
    To Lieu^t Archibald Read paymaster

	Doll:	9ths
To the 8th Pennsylvania Reg^t		
To cash paid the officers and privates as p^r Receipts	22000	56
To do. Returned to the Dept^y pay master Genl Due dead Diserted and Absentees	1072	50
Ditto	C^r	
By cash Rec^d for pay and Subsistance of Said Reg^t on Warrant N° 71	23073	16

Mr Fowler likewise produced to the court the Oath taken by Lt Archibald Read at Settlement. Viz,

Lieu^t Archibald Read Maketh Oath that the above Acc^t at this time Exhibited to the auditor for Settlement contains A full Just & True State of all moneys Rec^d and paid by him as pay master to the 8th Pen^a Regiment, and that the Sum of One thousand and Seventy-two Dollars and Fifty ninetieth parts of A Dollar being the ballance stated in the same as due from him is the whole of money at this time in his hands belonging To the Said Regim^t or any Individual Therein the United States or any of them.—

ARCHIBALD READ pay master 8th Pen^a Reg^t

Sworn before me this 25th day of July—1780

ALEX^R FOWLER Aud^r W: Dep^t

Mr Fowler produced to the court Instructions for Regimental pay Master. Mr Read acknowledges to have Rec^d a coppy of them Viz "You are to make out a particular list wherein shall be contained the names of all prisoners Diserters and Dead men belonging to the Regim^t, the time of their Captivity, Disertion, or death, the Companies to which they Respectivly belong, and the Sums Remaining in your hands due each man particularly— and Likewise of all Absentees."—

The court adjourns till the 11th

July 11th

The court met according to adjournment—

William Lee Serjeant 8th Pen^a Reg^t being sworn in suport of the charge produced to the court a note (he Rec^d by Matthew McAffee Soldier in s^d Reg^t) from Arch^d Read pay-master to s^d Reg^t Viz. "I have sent you one Hundred and Forty five Doll: it being not Twelve months pay which is all that I have drawn."

sign^d

Arch^d Read.

Question by the court to Serjeant Lee.—did you ever call on Mr Read for the Remainder of your pay that was in his hands

Answer.— Yes, I call^d on him twice for the purpose of A Settlement.—

Question From the court to Serjeant Lee.—What answer did you Receive from Mr Read when you call^d on him for settlement

Ans^r— The First time I called on him he said I should wait on him another time.— The second time he told me to wait till Mr Boreman came up and he would settle with me.—

Question from the court to Serj^t Lee.— How long since you applied to Mr Read for A Settlement.—

Ans' Two or three months.—

Quest^n from the court to Serjeant Lee.— did you give M^d Afee (whom you sent by for your pay) Orders to sign your name to the Reciept

Ans' Yes if he Recd it.—

Question from the court to Serjeant Lee.— did you think M^r had an Intention of Defrauding you out of your pay

Ans' No.—

Question from Mr Fowler to Serjeant Lee— What was the Reason you did not apply sooner than three month ago to Mr Read for your pay.—

Answer. I applied in June or July 1780—

Question from Mr Fowler to Serjeant Lee.—Did you apply to Mr Read for a Settlement of your Due bills as well as your personal pay. in June or July 1780

Answer: I Expected a Settlement of the whole.—

Question from Mr Fowler to Serjeant Lee Did not Mr Read always tell you that you would be paid out of the money That Mr Boreman was to bring up now.—

Ans' he said he would pay me when Mr Boreman came up.—

Question from Mr Fowler to Serjeant Lee.—What is your oppinion now of Mr Read Since I told you he had drawn your pay and sign^d your name to the Reciept.—

Ans'— I thought he might have lent it and would Replace it again to me.—

Question—From Mr Read to Serjeant Lee.—When you calld on me first did not I tell you I was not at Leasure & for you to call on me another time.—

Answer.—you did and I said it would sute me as I was not in a want of money.—

Question from Mr Read to Serjeant Lee.—When you shewed me the due bills and orders, did not I tell you the men that gave you the orders were setled with, and that the money was not drawn to pay those orders.—

Answer.— Yes and I said I would wait till the money came up and they would be good at another payment.—

Question from Mr Read to Serjeant Lee.—Did not you say it would sute you to settle the due bills and orders at one time when Mr Boreman came up.—

Answer. Yes.—

Question from Mr Read to Serjeant Lee.—Did not Matthew McAfe tell you that I was going to Lay in my acc^{ts} and from the manner of keeping the Books it was necessary to have your Receipt, that I would Set your name down and for you to call on me when you would come down and I would pay you the Remainder of your pay.—

Answer.— When McAfee came up he gave me the money you sent me and the note, and said you would pay me the Remainder when I would go down.—

The court adjourns till the 17th.—

July 17th

The court met according to adjournment—

Lieu^t Archibald Read being put on his Defence Saith

Gentlemen I now stand arraigned before this most Worthy and Impartial Bench, Arested by Alexander Fowler. Esqr Auditor of acc^{ts} for the Western Dep^t, Charged with Defrauding the Soldiers and Detaining from them their pay in a maner unbecoming the Character of an officer and A Gentleman.— To Which charge I plead not Guilty.— In support of the charge Alex^r Fowler Esqr Adt^r of Acct, Produced to the court the accounts of monies paid to them in the Following words Viz. "We the Subscribers acknowledge having Rec^d the sums annexed to our names Respectivly" In which were Serjeants Lee. & Armstrongs names not in their hand writing, Which I acknowledg I myself wrote.— For so doing I give you my Reasons.— Near the time I was to lay in my Acc^{ts} Serjeant Lee was in the country, He sent in by one McAfee Soldier in the 8th Pen^a Reg^t to Recieve his pay. I gave s^d McAfee only part. the Whole change at that time I could not make out at The Same time mentioned to him I was to lay in my Acc^{ts} before the Auditor, that it was Necessary his Reciept should be there in the form the Books were kept, that it was Equally the same tho he had not the whole. I Disremember Whiether I asked McAfee to write his name, but I wrote it in his presence Which I thought was the same thing, and told him to acquaint Serj^t Lee when he came in I would settle the Remainder. When Serj^t Lee came in I Recollect his calling on me I hapned not Just to be at Leasure He said another time would answer, which agrees with Serj^t Lees Affadavit— That another time would sute him as he was not in a want of money.— A Long time afftter Serjeant Lee called on me and shewed me some Due bills and orders, I Examined them, and told him the men that gave the orders were setled with, that the money was not drawn to pay those orders as it was for the Year 1780—which money is now arived but at that time was daily Expected, which made Ser^t Lee Satisfied to wait and Settle the due bills and orders under me. this also agrees with his affidavit. Serj^t Lees Ans^r to Cap^n Fowlers Question is he applyd in June or July 1780 which you will observe was his first application. The Reason of no settlement is pointed out. The last application is near Twelve months after. the Reason of the time being so long I suppose is because Serj^t Lee had no occassion for Money or he would have called sooner, & when he applied his having the orders with the Due Bills, and the paymaster daily Expected he was fully satisfied to make but one settlement. It is plainly seen there was not the least Intention or design to defraud said person or I should Disputed his Right. but so far from that I did not Deny him a settlement Respecting Armstrong when I charged him as paid I was sensible I was doing wrong for long before it he had Rec^d more than the amount of his pay which I Borrowed for him before I Rec^d the pay of the Regiment, as he had a furlough to go down the country, and I told him I would charge him with it, When Setling with Mr Holaway an assistant to Mr Fowler I mentioned these things to him and asked him if I was not clear in doing it, he told me he thought I was.—after this one of the men came and setled for what, I answered Armstrong. had proper application been made the matter might been setled Armstrong himself cannot say I even meant or did Defraud him it was A misunderstanding —Gentlemen it is very evident in the manner their names were wrote it was not Intended for forgery or the least Intention of Fraud. had there been the least Imitation of their hand writing and they been denied their due it would appear Intentionally, Forgery is intended to decieve and blindfold, and your Judgement will determine Wheither there was any deception in the matter or not.—

I will now Inform you relative to the due bills, in august 1779 great part of the Regiment were discharged, all discharged I gave Due bills which was the same as pay, and for which bills I was answerable and accountable. numbers sold their Due bills Immediately for pay as the money was daily Expected tho it did not arive till the latter end of October During this interval those that had not sold their bills came sundery tim[es] Expecting the money was arived (which most of the Gentlemen officers are sensible of & I believe some here present) after the money came those that had purchased said Bills and laid them in Rec^d the amount & the name of the first Owner wrote in the Book. when I was setling my Acc^{ts} I was sensible there was bills that was not come in which stood against me, and it appeared clear to me I could not enter those bills in the Collum of absentees. I even mentioned these things to Mr Hollaway when Setling, I told him there was Due bills not come in for which I was accountable, that they were the same as pay, and could not be in the absentee collum.— Had I have thought otherwise I should have Returned the sum of the whole bills in the absentee collum.— Those who called on Captn Fowler was in my absence when sent to Fort McIntosh Had I been present they need not have called on him, and would been setled with— When I with Mr Hollaway went and laid in my acc^{ts} before the Auditor had not the matter appeared clear to me as well as to Mr Hollaway they would have been mentioned.— As to my Instructions I thought I was acting up to them. If I have not and have deviated from them I most candidly, & most solemnly Declare to you. it was far very Far from having the least Intention or Design of Injury, or doing the Unjustice to any person or persons Whatever. Gentlemen I know the nature of an Oath and when I gave my affadavit had I the most distant thought that I was not doing Right I could not have don it; it is imposible, my nature would forbid it

I have nothing more to offer but I appeal to you and Every Gentleman officer I am and Ever have been acquainted with, Relative to my character and prinseples, I appeal to the Diffirent parts of the world that are acquainted with me; I never did nor never wish to sound my Character, but I flater myself I can with safety say I ever bore a character that never brought the least blush upon me or any of my Relations Friends or acquaintances, & hope ever to bear the same, I will even appeal to the soldry whom I have long been with, wheither they ever had or now have the least thought of my having principles that would admit of so black a crime— I am happy in having it to say I never heard the Least murmuring or complaint with the Soldery Relative to my conduct, nor even do I at this present time, was it, the case it would be known.—

Gentlemen I now rest the matter entirely with you and Submit it to your most candid & impartial Judgement.—

The court after hearing the Evidence of Serjeant Lee are of oppinion that Lieu^t Archibald Read is not Guilty of the Charge

Exhibited against him, and do acquit him accordingly. and he is here by acquited.—

    S. BAYARD Col° 8th p. n President
      JOHN FINLEY Dep^y Judge ad.
[*Endorsed:*] Proceedings of Court Martial Lt Archibald Read P. M— (acquitted)—

[Trial of John Hinds. Col. Stephen Bayard, president of court. Washington Papers. D. S.]

July 25th

John Hinds Fifer in the 7th Virginia Reg^t was brought Before the court, Charged with Diserting, and asisting a Disaffected Indian to Make his Escape to the Enemy.

The prisoner pleads Guilty of Diserting But pleads not Guilty of asisting a Disaffected Indian to make his Escape to the Enemy— No Evidence appearing in support of the charges.

The prisoner being put on his Defence, says, that from the nature of my Enlistment, I thought I had a Right to my Discharge, and from the time the court of Enquiry gave Their oppinion I was to serve During the war I was Determined to Disert. and my Intention in going away with the Indians was to stay at one of the Indian towns till I could get going down the Ohio River—

From the prisoners maner of Diserting and in waiting in a boat with an Indian, till the one that was Confind in the Guardhouse for being Disaffected to the United States, came to them, and all going away together. (as was confessed by the prisoner) From these circumstances the court are of oppinion the prisoner (John Hinds) is Guilty of the Charges Exhibited against him, and the court do sentence him to be hanged by the neck till he is dead. and he is hereby sentenced to be hanged by the neck till he is dead.

    S. BAYARD Col° Comman^g 8th P. r. Presid^g
      JOHN FINLEY D Judge ad.

[*Endorsed:*] Jn° Hinds—for Desertion Sentenced to Death referred to Genl Irvine—

[Trial of Myndert Fisher. Col. Stephen Bayard, president of court. Washington Papers. D. S.]

July 26th.

Myndart Fisher A citizen Employd as a Guide, came before the court charged with holding A Traiterous correspondence with the Enemies of the United States.

the prisoner pleads not Guilty to the charge.

The Original Letter that the prisoner wrote to his Friends at Detroit was produced to the court, the prisoner confessed to have wrote it and sent it by one Graverod. it is as follows Viz

Pittsb^g Jan^y, 21st 178[1] Dr Gentlemen, If Mr Graverod would succeed with the help of You, the Errant he is going upon, would be of Infinite service both to Me your Brother, and himself, and friends here present, that is only waiting for his Return, and the Honorable Commanders answers from Detroit, which I suppose, there will be no less than one Hundred that will accompany him to said place, if the Commander will pleas to give him the least Encouragement possibly he ca[n] Thomas Girty—

The prisoner in his Defence says that Thomas Girty knew nothing of the letter being wrote, or of his name being sign^d to it, and says my Intention in writing that Letter, was to help Mr Graverod to get a Quantity of goods to bring to this place, that I had no ill meaning when I wrote the Letter.—and I submit my self to the mercy of the court—

The court is of oppinion that the prisoner Myndart Fisher, is Guilty of holding a Traiterous corrospondence with the Enemies of the United States it being a breach of the 19th art: of the 13th Section of the articles of war. they do sentence him to be hanged by the neck till he is Dead and he is hereby sentenced to be hang by the neck till he is Dead—

S. BAYARD Col^o Comman^g 8th P. R. Presid^g

JOHN FINLEY D Judge ad.

[*Endorsed:*] Myndert Fisher—sentenced to Death—Not approved —ordered to be released from Confinem^t

PARTICIPANTS[1]

Adams, Capt.—(11C41)
Alexander, Joseph (6ZZ66)
Amberson, James (3E60,3S60,4S7)
Amberson, William (2DD345,8NN99)
Anderson, George (5E32,19S238)
Anderson, Peter (6ZZ103)
Ashby, Capt.—(6ZZ48)
Askins, Serg. Thomas (2DD353)
Ballard, Bland (31J27)
Barr, Samuel (6ZZ69-70)
Barr, William (4S177,183,6ZZ129)
Basye, Capt. Thomas (30J89)
Beeler, Lieut. Joseph (7NN14)
Bendure, Thomas (3S163)
Biggs, Lieut. Joseph (6ZZ98)
Bonnet, Jacob (31J86)
Bonnet, Lewis (2S208, 31J85)
Bonnet, Peter (31J85,87)
Brown, James (2U67)
Brown, Ralph (5D208)
Buskirk, Capt. Lawrence Lewis (3E41)
Button, Joseph (29J109)
Byerly, Jacob (9E143)
Cackhill, Lieut. Isaac (2U54)
Caldwell, John (6ZZ61)
Caldwell, Samuel (6ZZ98)
Carrel, David (30J97)
Casber, Jonathan (6ZZ47)
Chaffin, Thomas (60J429)
Chambers, James (3S84)
Chapline, Moses (6ZZ98)
Chapman, Capt. John (29J109,30J76,31J81)
Coburn, Capt. Jonathan (31J85-87)

[1] The following list contains the names found in Draper Mss. either among pension statements, the recollections of pioneers, or original documents, of those who served on the Fort Pitt frontier during the years 1779-81. The notations in parentheses following the names are the pressmark references.

Coe, Lieut. Benjamin (31J41)
Day, Ezekiel (31J40)
Day, John (6ZZ49)
Dent, Lieut. John (6ZZ48)
Dickerson, Thomas (6ZZ170)
Downing, Timothy (6ZZ103)
Dunlevy, Francis (7NN14)
Duvall, Col. John P. (31J85–87)
Ellis, Jesse (2DD352)
Ellis, Capt. Nathan (2DD352,363,7NN14)
Farlan, Thomas (2U57)
Faukler, Jacob (2S194–95)
Field, Capt. Benjamin (31J92,104)
Fitzgibbon, David (4S180)
Fleming, Lieut. Lewis (2U54)
Fouts, Capt. Andrew (3E41,1SS145)
Gosset, John (5S34)
Hall, William (3S84)
Hardin,—(30J76)
Harrison, Lieut. John (3S53,5S2)
Harrison, Maj. John (25S191)
Hickerton, Michael (60J429)
Hoagland, Derrick (1SS145)
Hughes, Elias (31J1–21)
Hupp, Philip (2S307, 7J1,1SS179)
Jackson, Capt. George (31J81,87)
Jolly, Henry (6ZZ116)
Karr, Andrew (1SS145)
Leech, Capt. James (31J41)
Leet, Ensign William (1SS145)
Lockwood, Benjamin (6ZZ98)
Lowther [Louder], Maj. William (30J76,78,31J1–5,8)
McCarty, Capt. Edward (9S8)
McColloch, Abraham (6ZZ67)
McColloch, Capt. John (6ZZ98)
McColloch, Capt. Samuel (2DD353)
McDermott, Joseph (6ZZ47)
McGavock, Lieut.—(31J106)
McGuire, Capt. Francis (3E41,19S187)
McIntyre, Thomas (3S56)
McIntyre, Capt. William (2E79)

McMahon, Maj. William (3E41)
Marchand, Capt. David (2E79)
Mason, Capt. Samuel (6ZZ61,92)
Martin, William (6ZZ48)
Means, Francis (4S179)
Means, Capt. Isaac (9S8)
Metcalf, Allen (2S48)
Mills, John (6ZZ65)
Mills, Thomas (6ZZ1)
Mitchell, Lieut. Charles (6ZZ69–70)
Mitchell, Capt. Hugh (6ZZ69–70)
Mitchell, Nathaniel (6ZZ122)
Moon, Lieut.—(31J106)
Moore, Capt. Peter (18S103)
Morgan, Zackwell [Zachariah] (30J76,78)
Mounts, Thomas (2U54)
Murphy, Patrick (7NN45)
Owens, Capt. George (3S258)
Parchment, Peter (3S116)
Parsons, Capt. Baldwin (3E41,17S253,19S186)
Patton, Capt. Henry (2U57)
Paul, Lieut. James (30J76,78)
Perrin,—(2S194)
Pitts, Lieut.—(31J106)
Poe, Andrew (8S115)
Powers, William (31J4)
Pursley, David (3E41)
Richardson, George (11C41)
Riley, John (6ZZ59)
Ross, Capt. Philip (30J97)
Roush, George (3S187)
Ryan, Lazarus (7J1)
Schermerhorn, Lucas (2S194)
Scott, Capt. William (6ZZ103)
Shane, Timothy (4S161)
Shearer, Capt. John (31J41)
Sherlock, Edward (2S67,3S48)
Sills, Ensign Benjamin (31J85,87)
Skaggs, Archibald (2U57)
Skaggs, Henry (2U57)
Smith, Jacob (9E143,8NN84)

Spencer, Lieut. James (3E41)
Springer, Lieut. Jacob (6ZZ48,129)
Springer, Capt. Uriah (6ZZ48)
Sprott, John (19S265-66)
Stites, Capt. Benjamin (3S259)
Stokeley, Col. Jeremiah [Nehemiah] (6ZZ67-70)
Stokeley, Capt. Thomas (2DD353)
Stroup, Conrad (1SS145)
Thomas, Abraham (31J107)
Thompson, Thomas (31J41)
Tipton, Capt. Abraham (30J76,31J81)
Titus [Tilton], Samuel (6ZZ103)
Todd, Samuel (31J41)
Tomlinson, Lieut. Joseph (31J107)
Trigg, Capt.—(2U57)
Vallandigham, George (11E162,7NN14)
Waits, James (23J201)
Wallace, Capt. James (2U54)
Walls [Wales], Maj. George (30J76,185,31J81,106)
Ward, Lieut. John (5S17,7NN14)
Ward, Capt. Sylvester (31J87)
Watson, Ensign Thomas (2U54)
Weighley, Isaac (2E79)
Westfall, Capt. Jacob (31J81,87)
Whaley, Benjamin (30J76,78,89)
White, Capt. Jacob (3S324,2U56)
Whittaker, Daniel (3S218)
Winlock, Joseph (30J89)
Wise, Ensign Bealez M. (2DD353)
Wright, Alexander (4S161)
Yoho, Henry (30J47)
Young, Capt. Thomas (30J76,89,31J106)
Zane, Jonathan (7NN14)
Zane, Capt. Silas (6ZZ1)

INDIANS

Served with Americans
Montour, John (7NN14)
Thompson, John (5S15)
Wilson,—(5S17)

 # Index

Index

Abb's Valley, settlement, 156.
Abingdon (Va.), 196.
Aboite Creek, La Balme's defeat at, 200.
Adams, Capt. ——, 492.
Adams, Alexander M. See McAdams, Alexander.
Adams, Jacob, private, 445.
Adams, William M. See McAdams, Alexander.
Adams County (Pa.), 226.
Agnew, James, at Pittsburgh, 366.
Albany (N. Y.), 287.
Albemarle County (Va.), 131, 196, 304.
Alexander, John, at Pittsburgh, 369.
Alexander, Joseph, 492.
Alexandria (Va.), 58.
Allegheny County (Pa.), 110, 271, 386, 412.
Allegheny River, route via, 70, 275, 398, 400; Brodhead's expedition on, 14–15, 18, 39–44, 52–66, 76–77, 95–96, 100, 169; posts on, 19, 53–54, 117, 125, 164, 235, 272; scouting on, 100; site on, 270; Indian bands cross, 226, 404, 413; Indians remove from, 401.
Allison, James, at Pittsburgh, 368.
Almon, John, *Remembrancer*, 55, 76.
Amberson, James, 492.
Amberson, Lieut. William, commissary, 188, 235; at Fort Pitt, 459, 492; signs protest, 363, 366; auditor, 392–93; sketch, 188.
American Antiquarian Society *Proceedings*, 389.

American Historical Review, 167, 410.
American Pioneer, 82.
Amherst County (Va.), 267; troops from, 52.
Anderson, Delaware chief, 330.
Anderson, Indian chief, 41.
Anderson, George, 492.
Anderson, John, at Pittsburgh, 368.
Anderson, Peter, 492.
Anderson, William, at Pittsburgh, 368.
Anderson, William, family attacked, 41.
André, Maj. John, "The Cow Chase," 307.
Andrew, David, at Pittsburgh, 370.
Andrew, John, at Pittsburgh, 370.
Andrews, Alexander, Loyalist, 417.
Andrews, Rev. Robert, boundary commissioner, 107.
Anstrod, John, at Pittsburgh, 367.
Applegate, Garrett, sergeant, 464.
Applegate, Richard, private, 465.
Arkansas Post, Spanish fort, 81, 81; Rogers visits, 86, 89; sketch, 84.
Arkansas River, Rogers on, 84, 86, 89.
Armstrong, George, sergeant, 484, 487–88.
Armstrong, James, exemption for, 426.
Armstrong, John, at Pittsburgh, 368.
Armstrong, Joshua, at Pittsburgh, 367.
Armstrong, Col. Martin, suppresses Loyalists, 170, 252; sketch, 170.

499

INDEX

Armstrong County (Pa.), 55.
Arnold, Benedict, treachery, 286.
Artillery, for the West, 28, 30, 40, 102, 116, 120, 124, 136, 146–47, 173–76, 347, 382–85, 390–91; en route, 178, 180–81; arrives at Fort Pitt, 202; detailed for Clark's expedition, 32, 311–12, 337, 347, 351, 370–71, 412–13, 418; stores for, 333; pay for, 393; repairs arms, 456; at Fort McIntosh, 118; British, 118, 185, 192–93.
Ashby, Capt. ———, 492.
Ashby, Bradwin, court-martialed, 442.
Askins, Serg. Thomas, 492; wounded, 59.
Atchinson, Joseph, tried and acquitted, 438.
Auglaize River, portage to, 185.
Augusta (Ga.), held by British, 391; attacked, 402.
Augusta County (Va.), prison in, 144, 259, 263; residents, 167.
Aulls, William, at Pittsburgh, 366.
Austin, Capt. William, non-juror, 254.
Avon (N. Y.), location, 53, 65.

BABY, Jacques Duperon, at Detroit, 86.
Baby, Marie-Josephe, son, 86.
Bailey, William, capture and release, 226.
Baird, George. See Beard.
Baird, John, at Pittsburgh, 366, 368.
Baker, Evan, commissary, 193–94, 216.
Baker, Isaac, pioneer, 193.
Baker, John, fine remitted, 425.
Baker, M., private, 469.
Baker family, settlement, 193, 209.
Ballard, Bland, 492.
Ballston (N. Y.), 286.
Baltimore (Md.), port, 81; powder from, 331; emigrants from, 415.
Bane, Edward, enlists, 263.

Bane (Beane), James, Loyalist, 221–22, 247; trial, 263; gives bonds, 264.
Bane Jr., James, gives bonds, 228; enlists, 264.
Bane, Joseph, private, 467.
Bane, Nathan, private, 467.
Baptist Valley (Va.), Loyalists in, 254; sketch, 254.
Barbour, James, Virginia commissioner, 105.
Barn, John, at Pittsburgh, 368.
Barnett, James, house, 132; magistrate, 228; at Loyalists' trials, 258; sketch, 132.
Barnett, John, court-martialed, 448.
Barr, Samuel, 492.
Barr, William, at Pittsburgh, 362, 367, 492.
Basye, Capt. Thomas, 492.
Bate, James, deserter, 446.
Bates, Samuel P., *History of Greene County, Pennsylvania*, 274.
Bath County (Ky.), 305.
Baton Rouge (La.), captured by Galvez, 129–30.
Batten, William, court-martialed, 447–48.
Baubee (Bawbee), Wyandot chief, message from, 47.
Baubee, Henry, Wyandot spy, 295–97, 303; escape of, 316–17, 321, 330, 332; threatens Delawares, 338; sketch, 295.
Bavaria, envoy to, 201.
Bawbee, Wyandot chief. See Baubee.
Bayard, Col. Stephen, at Fort Pitt, 443, 445, 449; presides at court, 446, 455, 484, 490–91; order, 451; witness in Ward's trial, 470–71; accuser of Ward, 470–76; accuser of Wallace, 477–83.
Beall, Capt. Robert, commandant at Fort McIntosh, 49; impressing provisions, 289; message for, 294; declines to act as paymaster, 432; sketch, 49.
Beall, Capt. Thomas, orders for, 174, 178; court-martialed, 282;

INDEX

released, 433, 448; presides at court, 440–41; sketch, 174.
Beam, Abraham, at Pittsburgh, 367.
Beane, James. See Bane.
Bear, hunted for provisions, 300.
Beard (Baird), Col. George, militia officer, 408.
Beargrass Creek, in Kentucky, 186, 267, 304.
Beattie, Agnes, married, 196.
Beattie, Capt. David, opposes Loyalists, 196–97; sketch, 196.
Beattie, John, son, 196.
Beattie Jr., John, killed, 196.
Beattie, William, at King's Mountain, 196.
Beattie's Mills (S. C.), battle of, 392.
Beatty, William, at Pittsburgh, 369; court-martialed, 455.
Beaver, Abraham, enlists, 262; accusation of, 263.
Beaver County (Pa.), 151, 223.
Beaver Creek (Big Beaver River), trespassers on, 22; fort, 42, 76, 204, 340; proposal to remove Indians to, 134; Indian raids on, 159; Indian trail on, 191, 405; Brady rescues captives on, 203, 205–6, 224–25.
Beck, Ensign John, 367; letter to, 41–42; on escort duty, 336; member of court, 470; sketch, 41.
Beckit, John, at Pittsburgh, 367.
Bedford (Pa.), 319.
Bedford County (Pa.), 310.
Bedford County (Va.), Loyalists in, 27, 251; troops from, 51, 241, 252; native of, 93; prices in, 129; school in, 215.
Beeler, Col. Joseph, militia officer, 178, 234, 278, 281, 284; letters to, 182, 342; letter, 279; sketch, 234.
Beeler Jr., Lieut. Joseph, 492.
Beers, James, deserter, 442.
Bell, George, sheriff, 254.
Bell, Hugh, at Pittsburgh, 369.
Bell, Robert, at Pittsburgh, 369.
Bell, William, at Pittsburgh, 368.
Bender, P., *Old and New Canada*, 86.
Bendure, Thomas, 492.

Benezet, Anthony, philanthropist, 320.
Benezet, Judith, married, 320.
Benham, Robert, on Rogers' expedition, 83–84; dispatch bearer, 85, 87; wounded, 90–92; sketch, 83.
Bennett, William, private, 467.
Bentley, Thomas, in Illinois, 127, 165; sketch, 165.
Bergen County (N. J.), headquarters, 208.
Berkeley (Va.), transport from, 146.
Berkeley County (Va.), 126.
Berkshire Hills (Mass.), 345.
Berry, George, quartermaster, 460; at Pittsburgh, 370.
Berry, John, private, 445.
Best Jr., John, released from service, 428.
Bethlehem (Pa.), Moravians at, 119, 161, 189, 232, 300, 372.
Beverly Manor (Va.), 215.
Bewling, Jacob, discharged, 441.
Biddle, Capt. Nicholas, naval officer, 175.
Big Beaver River. See Beaver Creek.
Big Bone Lick (Ky.), 131, 159, 186.
Big Cat (M'hingwe Pushees), Delaware chief, 191; message from, 272–73.
Big Knife, Indian term, 173.
Big Sandy River, post for planned, 19, 51, 192; Indian trail on, 155, 392.
Biggs, Capt. Benjamin, at Fort McIntosh, 281, 289; at Fort Henry, 344, 350, 409; on hunting party, 332; retained in service, 335; member of court, 470, 484; letters to, 118, 121–22, 289, 351, 409; gives receipt, 168, 344; sketch, 118.
Biggs, Capt. John, scouting, 300; private on Coshocton expedition, 466.
Biggs, Lieut. Joseph, 492.
Bilboa (Spain), 81.
Bilby, Richard, private, 467.

INDEX

Billingsport, defense of, 175.
Bird, Capt. Henry, British officer, expedition, 19–20, 22, 26, 185, 220, 299; news of, 190–93, 269–70.
Blacklegs Creek, post at, 164.
Blacksnake, Seneca chief, recollections, 63–65; sketch, 63.
Blackwood, Serg. ——, of the Artillery, 412.
Blaine, Col. Ephraim, quartermaster, 285, 288, 292; letters to, 280, 291, 306, 323; deputy, 325; responsibility, 347; sketch, 280.
Blaine, James G., ancestor, 280.
Blair, Samuel, discharged, 446.
Blairsville (Pa.), 382.
Blake, Nicholas, at Pittsburgh, 368.
Blake, William, ranger, 113.
Bland County (Va.), 197.
Blane, John, private, 465.
Bledsoe, Col. Anthony, son captured, 392; sketch, 392.
Blevins, William, Loyalist officer, 247.
Blockhouse Point, attack on, 307.
Blount County (Tenn.), 197.
Blountville (Tenn.), 258.
Blue Licks (Ky.), salt makers captured at, 93, 185.
Blue Ridge Mountains, gap in, 236.
Blue Stone River (Va.), 355.
Boats, builders for, 77, 135–36, 312; built at Pittsburgh, 83–84, 88; escapes from Rogers' defeat, 91, 93–94; expense of building, 148; for Kanawha River, 243; for Clark's expedition, 312, 352, 383; at Fort Henry, 409.
Bodkin, Charles, court-martialed, 437; discharged, 455–56.
Body, Peter, at Pittsburgh, 369.
Boggs, Capt. John, defends family, 419–20; at courts-martial, 425–30; militia company, 425, 427.
Boggs, Lydia. See Cruger, Mrs. Lydia.
Boggs Sr., William, private, 465.
Boggs Jr., William, on Coshocton expedition, 465; captured by Indians, 419–20.

Bolton, Col. Mason, British officer, letters to, 52–54; letter, 47–48; drowned, 374; sketch, 47.
Bond, Thomas, at Pittsburgh, 369.
Bond County (Ill.), 267.
Boniface, William, witness, 199.
Bonnett, Jacob, 492.
Bonnett, Lewis, 492.
Bonnett, Peter, 492.
Boone, Col. Daniel, captured, 93, 185; in Dunmore's War, 156; explores Kentucky, 210.
Boonesborough (Ky.), relief for, 93; trustee of, 196, 319; Henderson visits, 141–42.
Boreman, John, agent, 485–86.
Botetourt (Va.), prices in, 129.
Botetourt County (Va.), sheriff, 241; protection for, 241; letters from, 50, 244; officers, 212, 242, 258; troops from, 51, 213, 251; delegate, 130; land commissioners in, 132; residents, 137, 230, 264, 266; prison in, 144; Loyalists in, 209; trials for, 257–64.
Bougainville, Louis Antoine, French naval officer, 296.
Bound Brook (N. J.), 100.
Bouquet, Col. Henry, expedition, 280.
Bourbon County (Ky.), 93.
Bousman, Jacob, at Pittsburgh, 368, 432.
Bowen, Charles, home, 197; sketch, 197.
Bowman, Col. John, letters, 184–86, 202; requests aid, 184, 192, 194, 248, 283; orders, 186; Shawnee expedition 1779, 104; sketch, 184.
Boyce, John, at Pittsburgh, 369.
Boyce, Richard, at Pittsburgh, 369.
Boyd, Robert, at Pittsburgh, 369.
Boyes, Peter, at Pittsburgh, 366.
Braddock, John, fined, 425.
Braddock's Defeat, 65.
Braddock's Road, raid on, 188, 414.
Bradford, Lieut. Charles, messenger, 293; member of court, 455.
Bradford, John, private, 469.

INDEX

Bradley, John, at Pittsburgh, 367, 455.
Brady, Gen. Hugh, reminiscences, 202-4; sketch, 203.
Brady, John, killed by Indians, 381-82.
Brady Jr., John, killed by Indians, 382.
Brady, Capt.-Lieut. Samuel, 459; on Brodhead's expeditions, 58, 60-61, 381-82; orders for, 150; reconnoitre to Sandusky, 30, 187-88, 219, 340; rescues Mrs. Stoops, 30, 202-8, 224-25; thanks for, 248, 280, 284; scouting, 39, 151, 354, 405; impressing provisions, 276, 280, 284, 288; enlisting, 114; leap a fiction, 204; hunting party, 308-9, 382; retained in service, 352; letters to, 276, 280, 308; dispute with Ward, 470-76; member of courts-martial, 454, 470, 484; scouts who served with, 202, 207; brothers, 203, 381; characterized, 225; sketch, 39.
Brady, William (Bill), scout, 178.
Brady, William P., reminiscences, 381-82; sketch, 381.
Brady's Lake, location, 204.
Branch Historical Papers. See *John P. Branch Historical Papers.*
Brandon, John, at Pittsburgh, 366.
Brandywine, battle of, 175, 335, 392.
Brannes, Edward, at Pittsburgh, 367.
Brant, Joseph, Mohawk chief, 53-54; raids, 248, 287; messenger, 374; sketch, 53.
Brauer, Lydia M., acknowledgments to, 10.
Brazel, William, private, 465.
Breckenridge, James, at Pittsburgh, 367.
Breckinridge, John, pioneer, 215.
Breckinridge Jr., John, letter, 198; sketch, 198.
Breckinridge, William, in Kentucky, 267; sketch, 267.
Brittain, Nathaniel, Loyalist, 212, 247, 254, 263; committed to prison, 263.

Broad, Robert, court-martialed, 437.
Broadley, John, at Pittsburgh, 363.
Brodhead, Col. Daniel, commandant at Fort Pitt, 18, 20, 23, 427; Allegheny expedition, 14-16, 48, 52-66, 95-96, 100, 404; Coshocton expedition, 33-34, 343, 348-49, 353, 370, 372-73, 376-82, 388, 397, 420; report of, 399; rolls for, 461-69; plans other expeditions, 28-32, 133-34, 154, 168, 172-75, 177, 214, 231, 234, 250, 265; postpones expeditions, 178-80, 234-35, 281, 284, 370, 373; abandons expeditions, 182, 188; Indian relations, 16, 44-47, 66-76, 97, 132-35, 139, 157-59, 166, 172-73, 182, 189-93, 217-20, 231-33, 250, 275, 295-99, 305, 328-29, 341-42; Indian policy, 333-34, 378-79; Indian title, 44; friction with officers, 98-99, 108, 120-21, 125-26, 136, 313, 352, 357, 364, 434-35, 440; relations with George Rogers Clark, 30, 32-33, 42, 77, 134, 150, 165, 182, 270-72, 276, 278-79, 331-32, 337, 343-44, 346-47, 352, 397-98, 418; disappointment, 327-28, 336-37; on furlough, 148, 337, 341, 347; rebuked, 136-37, 171; supported, 171, 176; declines to retire, 303; sends information, 285-87; charges against, 32-33, 118, 356-70, 387-88, 393-96, 405-12; summoned to Philadelphia, 395, 399-401, 411; replaced, 34-35; characterized, 31-32; Letter Books, described, 274, 283, 342, 373-74, 381.
Brody, Hugh, at Pittsburgh, 368.
Broken Straw Creek (Da-gah-sheno-de-a-go), Indian town on, 55, 63; island near, 62, 64, 66; camp on, 66.
Bronstetter, Andrew, Loyalist, 255.
Brooks Benjamin, at Pittsburgh, 368; private, 441, 445; tried and acquitted, 448.
Brooks, Daniel, at Pittsburgh, 367.
Brooks, James, at Pittsburgh, 367.

Broome County (N. Y.), 54.
Broomfield, William, at Pittsburgh, 369.
Brown, Basil, pioneer, 84, 88; on Rogers' expedition, 84.
Brown Jr., Basil, on Rogers' expedition, 84, 88–93; deposition, 88–91; recollections, 91–93; sketch, 84.
Brown, James, 492.
Brown, Joseph, at Pittsburgh, 369.
Brown, Ralph, 492.
Brown, Samuel, at Pittsburgh, 369.
Brown, Samuel, Loyalist, 239–40.
Brown, Thomas, at Pittsburgh, 367.
Brownlee, Lieut. John, plots against Indians, 290; sketch, 290.
Brownlee, Lieut. Joseph, resigns, 412.
Brownlee, Thomas, discharged, 446.
Brownsville (Pa.), 84.
Bruce, Rev. David, Moravian missionary, 320; sketch, 320.
Bruce, George, at Pittsburgh, 367.
Bruce, James, at Pittsburgh, 367.
Bruce, William, at Pittsburgh, 368.
Brunot, Dr. Felix, near Pittsburgh, 290.
Brunot's (Hamilton's, McKee's) Island, purchased, 290.
Brush Creek, raid on, 188, 414.
Brush Run, raid on, 179, 188; as a boundary, 428; sketch, 179.
Brushy Mountain (Va.), 254.
Bryan, George, boundary commissioner, 107.
Buchanan, Jane. See Floyd, Mrs. John.
Buchanan, Col. John, Virginia pioneer, 257.
Buchanan, Mary, married, 257.
Buck Island. See Carleton Island.
Buckaloons, Indian town, 55, 57; sketch, 55.
Buckingham County (Va.), troops from, 52.
Bucks County (Pa.), 320.
Buffalo, hunted for provisions, 300–1, 303, 347.
Buffalo (N. Y.), Historical Society, 49; *Publications*, 100.

Buffalo Creek (Va.), 419–20; Dutch fork of, 420.
Buffalo Township (Pa.), 110.
Bukey, Mary, married, 398.
Bull, John (Schebosch, Shabosh), a Moravian, 300.
Bull, Joseph, killed, 300.
Bull Town, Indian site, garrisoned, 117.
Bullock's Ford, on Clarion River, 56.
Burgoyne, Gen. John, surrender, 242, 374.
Burke, John, tried and acquitted, 447.
Burke County (N. C.), 211.
Burnett, A., private, 467.
Burnett, Lewis, private, 469.
Burns, Arthur, at Pittsburgh, 368.
Burns, John, mattross, court-martialed, 454–55.
Burnside, Andrew, at Pittsburgh, 367.
Burton, C. M. "John Connolly, Loyalist," 389.
Bushby, William, at Pittsburgh, 368.
Buskirk, John, private, 464.
Buskirk, Capt. Lawrence Lewis, 492.
Bustard, David, Loyalist, 255.
Butler, Col. John, Loyalist officer, 47, 129, 192, 194; letter, 53–54; raiding, 248; sketch, 53.
Butler, Mann, *History of Kentucky*, 81, 84–85, 87.
Butler, Maj. Walter, British officer, 47–48, 53; sketch, 47.
Butterfield, C. W., narrative of Brodhead's Coshocton expedition, 376–81; *History of the Girtys*, 17.
Button, Joseph, 492.
Byerly, Jacob, 492.
Byrn, Capt. ———, wounded, 266.
Byrn, James, letter to, 211–13; nonjurors in company of, 222; at Loyalists' trials, 258; brother, 266; sketch, 211.

CACKHILL, Lieut. Isaac, 492.
Caggley, George, Loyalist, 254.

INDEX

Cahokia (Ill.), 176; endangered, 20, 186; garrison, 195; letter from, 230; commandant, 231.
Cain, John, private, 445, 469; at Pittsburgh, 368.
Cain, Matthew, at Pittsburgh, 368.
Caldwell, Ezekiel, recollections, 62.
Caldwell, James, Ohio County magistrate, 110–11; sketch, 110.
Caldwell, John, on Brodhead's expedition, 62, 492; brother, 110; sketch, 62.
Caldwell, Samuel, 492.
Caleylemont, Delaware chief. See Killbuck.
Callahan, John, court-martialed, 442.
Callen, Patrick, at Pittsburgh, 366.
Callendar, Anne, married, 307.
Callendar, Robert, trader, 307.
Callensburg (Pa.), 56.
Calvin, Vincent, at Pittsburgh, 367.
Calzor, Lewis, at Pittsburgh, 368.
Camden (S. C.), battle at, 210, 282; retreat from, 210.
Campbell, Arthur, at Pittsburgh, 370.
Campbell, Col. Arthur, suppresses Loyalists, 26–27, 195–98, 210–11; letter to, 236–40; letters, 192–98, 210, 217, 244–45, 391–92, 402; sketch, 192.
Campbell, Col. Charles, sub-lieutenant of Westmoreland, 385.
Campbell, Capt. John, Virginia officer, 196, 237; sketch, 196.
Campbell, Col. John, American, captured, 18, 87, 93–94, 105–6, 123; letter, 94; sketch, 87.
Campbell, Col. John, British officer, 130; sketch, 130.
Campbell, Col. Richard, 448, 460; commands Fort Laurens, 39; orders for, 39, 44; illness, 121; at Fort Pitt, 122, 318, 445; letters, 149–50, 156–57; scouting, 180–81; presides at court-martial, 431–33, 435–37, 439–40, 443; sketch, 39.
Campbell, Robert, Pittsburgh inhabitant, 362, 367, 396.
Campbell, Capt. Thomas, 171; orders for, 79, 99, 109, 114, 118; commands rangers, 95, 120, 136; arrest ordered, 125–26; sketch, 79.
Campbell, Col. William, suppresses Loyalists, 24, 27, 208–9, 217, 222, 236–40; attempted revenge, 27, 267–68; at trial, 258; letters to, 217, 244–45; letters, 236, 240–41; handwriting, 240; sketch, 209.
Canada, attempt to recover, 29, 304; forces from, 248; education in, 86; Moravians in, 161; invasion of, 307.
Canadasega, Seneca town, 53.
Canawago. See Conewago.
Canawaugus, Indian town, 53.
Canborough Township (Ont.), 52.
Canon, Col. John, sub-lieutenant of Washington County, 403; warns of danger, 334; petition of, 82; sketch, 334.
Capes, William, private, 445.
Captina (Capteening) Creek, attack near, 168.
Carleton, Sir Guy. See Dorchester.
Carleton, Maj. Guy, leads expedition, 286.
Carleton, Joseph, secretary, 385.
Carleton (Buck, Deer) Island, British post on, 54, 390; sketch, 54.
Carlisle (Pa.), 81, 114, 280, 285, 307–8, 383, 400, 413.
Carmichael, James, 293.
Carmichael, John, impressing provisions, 293–94; sketch, 293.
Carmichael, Thomas, 293.
Carnahan, Capt. James, letters to, 117, 235; at Fort Pitt, 458–59; sketch, 117.
Carney, Martin, at Fort Jefferson, 230.
Carolina. See North Carolina and South Carolina.
Carpenter, Charles, claims discharge, 455; refused, 456.
Carpenter, Christopher, private, 445.
Carr, Daniel, private, 445.
Carrel, David, 492.
Carrell, William, fined, 426.
Carroll, Thomas, at Pittsburgh, 367.
Carroll County (Va.), 236, 251.

INDEX

Carr's Creek (Va.), 196.
Carson, Richard, at Pittsburgh, 369.
Carter, Bauning, private, 445.
Carter, Nicholas, private, 445.
Carter, Stephen, private, 467.
Casber, Jonathan, 492.
Casebard, Nathan, at Pittsburgh, 368.
Casgrain, P. B., *La Vie de Joseph-François Perrault*, 86.
Cashaquin, Indian letter from, 250.
Caswell, Samuel, discharged, 441.
Catherine's Town. See Sheoquaga.
Catt, George, private, 469.
Catt, Michael, private, 469.
Cattaraugus (N. Y.), letter from, 52.
Cattaraugus County (N. Y.), 63.
Cattaraugus Creek, Indian site, 375.
Cavenaugh, Gaverard, deserter, 447.
Cayashooto, Seneca chief. See Guyashusta.
Cayuga Indians, at Niagara, 50.
Chaffin, Thomas, 492.
Chamberlin, T. W., acknowledgments to, 310.
Chambers, Alexander, discharge for, 441; fraudulently obtained, 457.
Chambers, James, recollections, 403-5; captured, 404, 414, 492.
Chambers, Thomas, at Pittsburgh, 455.
Chambersburg (Pa.), 373.
Chapline, Lieut. Abraham, captured, 17-18, 87; escapes, 20, 185, 187, 192; accompanies Rogers, 87; son, 94; employed by Clark, 350; sketch, 87.
Chapline, Moses, 492.
Chapman, Capt. John, 492.
Charles, Delaware Indian, 330.
Charleston (Ind.), 180.
Charleston (S. C.), British at, 24, 129; refugees from, 27; captured by British, 145, 192, 201, 210, 226, 265; besieged, 202, 210; prisoners from, 268, 333.
Charlotte County (Va.), 137.
Charlottesville (Va.), 242.
Chartier's (Chertees) Creek (Pa.), 87, 180, 271, 333; captives from,
202, 204, 224; settlers on, 403; militia, 226.
Chautauqua County (N. Y.), 375.
Chea, Barry, at Pittsburgh, 366.
Cheat River, raids on, 94-95, 248-49.
Cherokee Indians, aid British, 24-25, 170; treaty with United States, 25, 40, 43; visit the Delawares, 45; intertribal relations, 51; expedition against, 210-11, 258; unite with Loyalists, 244-45, 402; mission to, 257; hostile, 391, 402.
Cherry Valley (N. Y.), raided, 48.
Chertees Creek. See Chartier's Creek.
Chester County (Ky.), 421.
Chew, James, clerk of land commission, 119.
Chicago (Ill.), fur-trade post, 164.
Chickamauga (Chuchamoga) Indians, location, 51; expedition against, 197, 258, 267; sketch, 51.
Chillicothe Indians, branch of Shawnee, 109; town of, 93.
Chippewa Indians, attitude toward Americans, 40, 43, 233; at Detroit council, 217-18; intertribal relations, 297.
Choconut (Chucknut, Chugnutt), Indian town, 54.
Choctaw Indians, aid Spanish, 130.
Chote (Chota), Cherokee town, 244.
Christian, Capt. Gilbert, at King's Mountain, 258.
Christian, Rosanna, married, 137.
Christian, Col. William, orders for, 50; on Cherokee campaign, 258; in Dunmore's War, 212; letters, 128-32, 267-68; removal to Kentucky, 131, 137; at trial of Loyalists, 257; sketch, 50.
Christian, Mrs. William, sister of Patrick Henry, 264.
Christy, William, at Pittsburgh, 363, 367.
Chubhicking, Indian name for Vincennes, 297.
Chucknut. See Choconut.
Chugnutt. See Choconut.
Cincinnati, Order of, president, 308.

INDEX

Cincinnati (Ohio), Indian battle near, 17–18, 83, 91–93.
Clare, Thomas, at Pittsburgh, 368.
Clarion County (Pa.), 56.
Clarion River (Pa.), 56.
Clark, Serg. ———, 178.
Clark, Benjamin, son, 230.
Clark, Gen. George Rogers, in the West, 18–19, 25–26, 186; Indian policy, 16, 29, 56, 104–5, 155, 305; influence of presence, 20, 34, 417; aid for David Rogers, 17, 83, 85, 87; supplies for, 86, 92, 324, 382–85, 400, 413; reënforcements, 179, 194, 209, 243, 354; Illinois expedition, 87, 127, 267; expedition of 1779, 72; expedition of 1780, 22, 30, 223, 230, 245–46, 249–50, 265–66, 271; expedition of 1782, 167; expedition of 1786, 83, 87; returns to Virginia, 180, 319; Detroit expedition planned, 32–34, 133–34, 165, 175, 312, 318, 331–32, 336–37, 341, 344, 346–47, 350–52, 370–71, 382–85, 397, 399–400, 406–9, 412–21; opposition to, 403, 415, 419, 421; rendezvous for, 413–15, 417, 419; a Virginia officer, 101; relations with Brodhead, 32–33, 42, 77, 106, 134, 150, 165, 173, 182, 337, 343–44, 418; officers with, 49, 180, 193, 195, 310; relatives, 126, 230; letters to, 42, 156–57, 182, 310, 337, 343, 391, 397; letters, 77, 93, 103–5, 350–51, 370–71, 398, 401, 414, 416–18; *Memoir*, 18.
Clark, James, 367; private, 465.
Clark, John, at Pittsburgh, 369.
Clark, Capt. John, of Eighth Pennsylvania, 59, 313–14, 458–59; orders for, 97, 103, 106–7, 125, 281, 309–11, 336; member of court, 438, 470, 484; sketch, 60.
Clark, Joshua, at Pittsburgh, 366.
Clark, Lieut. Richard, messenger, 231.
Clark, Lieut. William, letter to, 230–81; sketch, 230.

Clarke, Maj. Elijah, in Georgia, 391, 402; sketch, 391.
Clarke, James, private, 445.
Clarksville (Ind.), 230.
Clawson, Garret, at Pittsburgh, 368.
Clay, Henry, duelist, 310.
Clemens, Jeremiah, private, 466.
Cleveland, Col. Benjamin, suppresses Loyalists, 27, 210, 239–40; sketch, 210.
Clevings, William, Loyalist, 254.
Clinch River, as a frontier, 245; headwaters, 254; raids on, 155–56.
Cline, Mrs. ———, reminiscences, 151–52.
Clinglesmith. See Klingelschmit.
Clinton, Gov. George, of New York, 287.
Clinton, Sir Henry, at Charleston, 24, 129, 170, 268; letters to, 14, 50, 78, 122–23.
Cloyd, William, court-martialed, 455.
Coburn, Capt. Jonathan, 492.
Coe, Lieut. Benjamin, 493.
Coffle, Mary, married, 319.
Coho. See Cahokia.
Colchester (Ont.), 153.
Cold, Delaware chief, 45.
Cold Spring (N. Y.), site, 63–65.
Coleman, Coonrod, rescues captives, 200.
Coleman, Ensign Jacob, orders for, 40; witness, 200; retained in service, 335; abuse of, 446; adjutant, 460; sketch, 40.
Collins, Benjamin, at Pittsburgh, 369.
Collis, William, quartermaster's sergeant, 460; at Pittsburgh, 366.
Collyer, Isaac, on Rogers' expedition, 83, 90.
Colman, Joseph, court-martialed, 450.
Colter, James, at Pittsburgh, 369.
Colvin, Daniel, at Pittsburgh, 368.
Colvin, William, at Pittsburgh, 367.
Combs, Samuel, apprentice for, 373.
Combs, Sol., at Pittsburgh, 368.
Comus, Thomas, at Pittsburgh, 368.

Conesus, Seneca town, 62.
Conewago, Indian village, 44, 55; attack near, 52–54, 189; burned, 56; sketch, 44.
Congress, Continental, powers of, 101, 361; members, 421; issues commissions, 151, 183, 357; memorial to, 81; information for, 283, 384, 406; supplies for, 84; Indian visitors, 44, 47, 116, 181, 302, 330, 345, 348; Indian negotiations, 169, 341–42, 347–48; orders investigation, 393; resolutions of, 171, 174, 290, 342, 345, 395, 435, 444, 456, 476; president's letters to, 286–87, 333, 345–46, 389, 396; report to, 347–48, 385; *Journal*, 127, 171, 174, 290, 342, 347.
Conley, Philip, discharged, 441.
Connecticut, Indians of, 119.
Connecticut River, Indians from, 119.
Connellsville (Pa.), 278.
Connolly, John, at Pittsburgh, 367.
Connolly, Col. John, Loyalist, threatened invasion by, 388–90, 398, 404; sketch, 389.
Connor, Cornelius, at Pittsburgh, 369.
Connor Jr., Cornelius, at Pittsburgh, 369.
Connor, John, at Pittsburgh, 369.
Connor, Richard, among the Moravians, 320; sketch, 320.
Connor, Ensign William, leave of absence, 313–14; sketch, 313.
Conococheague (Pa.), transportation from, 291.
Continental army, reduced, 290, 303, 307–8, 335–37, 409; medical department, 306–7, 314; recruits for, 406.
Continental Congress. See Congress.
Continental currency, depreciation, 31, 128–29, 131, 227; disuse, 421; to be refunded to soldiers, 456.
Convention prisoners, in Virginia, 242.
Cook, Col. Edward, militia officer, 371, 385; sketch, 385.

Cook, Capt. Thomas T., at Fort Pitt, 458.
Coolpeeconain (John Thompson), Delaware chief, 330, 339, 495; life threatened, 376.
Cooper, Basil, at Pittsburgh, 368.
Cooper, Ensign William, at Fort Pitt, 459; signs protest, 366.
Copeley, Thomas, trial for Loyalism, 260.
Cornplanter, Seneca chief, 65–66; reservation for, 55, 59, 62–66; information from, 60; son, 62; sketch, 59.
Cornplanter (Pa.), site, 62.
Cornstalk, Shawnee chief, 319.
Cornwallis, Charles, earl, orders, 210; at Camden, 282; capture rumored, 296.
Coshocton (Coochocking, Coochoquin, Cooshawing, Cooshockung), Indian village, 161–62, 214, 274; council at, 97, 157–59, 168, 177, 189–90, 217–20, 233, 295–98, 301, 315–16, 321, 328, 332, 337–40, 342, 346, 348, 353, 375, 384; Indians from, 60, 172, 398–99; messages, 275; fort to be built at, 315, 329, 348; letters from, 44–46, 105, 157, 231, 273; letters to, 139, 177, 183; expedition against, 33, 343, 348–49, 353, 370, 372–73, 376–82, 388, 399; rolls of militia, 461–69; destruction of, 377; sketch, 44.
Cottrill, Thomas, at Pittsburgh, 369.
Courts-martial, proceedings, 94, 115, 135, 248, 303; method of procedure, 147, 283, 394–95; orders for, 148, 332; power to hold, 209, 383–84; at Pittsburgh, 116, 393–95, 411, 439–58, 470–91; approved, 282; for Brodhead, 394–95, 407–8; for Ohio County, 425–30.
Cowpens (S. C.), battle of, 211.
Cox, Gabriel, 415.
Cox, George, 415.
Cox, Isaac, Ohio County pioneer, 415; fined, 426; acquitted, 429.

Cox, Jacob, private, 465.
Cox, John, militia officer, 237, 239–40; son captured, 238–39; accused of Loyalism, 234; sketch, 237.
Cox, Joseph, 415; at Pittsburgh, 368.
Cox, Capt. Reuben, pioneer, 415.
Coxon, William, fife major, 460.
Cox's Station (Va.), 415.
Coyle, James, Loyalist, 239–40.
Crab Orchard (Va.), 197.
Craig, Capt. Isaac, artillery officer, 170, 393; men, 201, 383; at Fort Pitt, 202, 412; goes East, 353, 370–71; on courts-martial, 454, 470, 484; letters to, 181, 351, 390–91; letters, 382–83, 391, 412–13, 418; sketch, 175.
Craig, Neville B., editor, 283.
Crawford, ——, escapes from Cherokee, 402.
Crawford, Charles, court-martialed, 455.
Crawford, Lieut. John, of Eighth Pennsylvania Regiment, 431, 459; adjutant, 449, 477; member of court, 470.
Crawford, Sarah, married, 278.
Crawford, Capt. William, letter to, 373; on Coshocton expedition, 376, 469; sketch, 373.
Crawford, Col. William, surveyor, 403; at Fort Pitt, 81; expedition of 1782, 58–59, 335, 408; residence, 350, 408; death, 153, 373; daughter, 278; estate, 413.
Crawford County (Pa.), 61.
Creal, John, at Pittsburgh, 369.
Creduser, Nicholas, deserts, 439.
Creek Indians, hostile, 391, 402; treaty with Spaniards, 402.
Cresap, Michael, widow, 82.
Cresap Jr., Michael, interviewed, 82.
Cripple Creek (Va.), 236, 254; sketch, 254.
Crockett, Col. Hugh, suppresses Loyalists, 241, 268; sketch, 241.
Crockett, Col. Joseph, Western battalion of, 51, 131, 209, 266, 304, 413, 418; brother of, 241; letter to, 243–44; sketch, 51.
Crockett, Maj. Walter, brother, 241; suppresses Loyalists, 24, 198, 216, 237; letters, 170, 236; amnesty for, 239–40; sketch, 170.
Croghan, Col. George, dwelling, 270; sketch, 270.
Cron, James, at Pittsburgh, 368.
Crooked Run (Va.), 269.
Croom, John, Loyalist, 247.
Cross Creek Township (W. Va.), 415.
Crossings. See Stewart's Crossings.
Crow, Captain, Seneca chief. See Na-tah-go-ah.
Crow, John, Loyalist, 417.
Crow, Lawrence, Loyalist, 416–17.
Crowly, Andrew, at Pittsburgh, 366.
Crow's Island, in the Ohio, 223.
Cruger, Mrs. Lydia, interviewed, 82; recollections, 419–20.
Crumrine, Boyd, *History of Washington County, Pennsylvania*, 168, 410.
Cub Creek (Va.), church at, 137.
Cuba, Archives of, 130.
Culbertson's Bottom (Va.), 355.
Culpeper County (Va.), 126, 179.
Cumberland (Pa.), 207.
Cumberland (Tenn.), land in, 129, 131.
Cumberland County (Pa.), 160; militia office, 285; sheriff, 280; militia ordered West, 293, 393.
Cumberland Gap, war road in, 391.
Cumberland Mountains, Indian raids in, 187.
Cuming, Fortescue, "Tour," 290.
Cummings, Alexander, magistrate, 252.
Cungill, John, at Pittsburgh, 367.
Cunningham, John, at Pittsburgh, 369.
Curry, Adam, at Pittsburgh, 368.
Curry, John, at Pittsburgh, 368.
Cuscushing (Goschgoschuenk, Kushkushing), Munsee town, 56–57.
Cuscusky and Cushcushkee. See Kuskuskies.

510 INDEX

Cushing, John M., discharged, 441.
Custard, George, at Pittsburgh, 369.
Cuyahoga River, Moravians on, 161; scouting near, 175; leap across, 204.

DA-GAH-SHE-NO-DE-A-GO. See Broken Straw Creek.
Dah-gan-non-do, Seneca Indian. See Decker, Capt. John.
Darlington, Mary C., *Fort Pitt*, 179, 214.
Darraugh, John, court-martialed, 438; deserter, 457–58.
Darter, Nicholas, Loyalist, 254.
Daugherty, John, at Pittsburgh, 368.
Davereux, Nancy. See Devereaux.
Davis, ——, killed, 187.
Davis, Col. Benjamin, militia officer, 408; sketch, 408.
Davis, Edward, at Pittsburgh, 368.
Davis, James, at Pittsburgh, 367.
Davis, Col. John, quartermaster, 136; letter to, 285; sketch, 285.
Davis, Peter, court-martialed, 282, 452; escape of, 457–58.
Dawson, Ensign Henry, quartermaster, 460; member of court, 470, 484.
Dawson, Capt. Samuel, orders for, 43; at Fort Pitt, 458; sketch, 43.
Day, Ezekiel, 493.
Day, John, 493.
Day-oos-ta (It-is-light-to-be-lifted), Delaware Indian, 65.
Dayton (Ky.), site, 92.
Dayton (Ohio), 163.
Dead Man's Bend, on the Mississippi, 231.
Deal, William, at Pittsburgh, 368.
Dean, John, at Pittsburgh, 368.
Deaver brothers, killed, 150.
Decker, Capt. John (Dah-gan-non-do, "He who patches"), Seneca Indian, recollections, 65–66.
Decker, Luke, at Pittsburgh, 368.
Deenan, James, at Pittsburgh, 367.
Deer Island. See Carleton Island.

Deh-gus-way-gah-ent (Fallen Board), Seneca Indian, 65.
De la Balme. See La Balme.
Delaware, immigrants to, 119; militia ordered out, 405.
Delaware Indians, language, 335; towns, 53; intertribal relations, 46, 72–75, 219, 231, 233, 249, 295, 301, 303, 314, 339–40; Indian allies, 16, 66–76; American alliance of, 14, 23, 28, 56, 75–76, 112, 151, 172, 180, 183, 220, 376; visit Congress, 28, 302; children educated, 181, 342, 348; on Brodhead's expeditions, 41, 44, 48, 53, 60, 65, 376–82; French envoy among, 29–30, 176–77, 214, 249, 265, 273–75, 375–76; desire fort, 75–76, 315, 328, 384; urged to remove, 134, 136, 315, 353; information from, 41, 45–47, 116, 168–69, 250, 272–73, 276; messages, 157–59, 168, 172–73, 217–20, 275, 296–97, 315–17, 333; excuse trespassers, 97, 106–7; messages to, 28, 166, 177, 183, 295–96, 298–99, 328–29, 341–42; suspected, 150–51, 156, 180–81, 353; exonerated, 157, 159, 161–63, 165, 183, 191, 231–34, 274, 300, 334; on scouting parties, 181, 183, 188; return deserter, 332; refugees from, 50; western division of, 104, 119, 158; hostile bands of, 17–18, 65–66, 105, 191, 193, 224, 273, 275, 290, 297, 301, 340, 348, 350–51; lack of supplies for, 139, 274, 276, 284, 302, 314–17, 326; break alliance, 33, 337–40, 342–47, 372; at Detroit council, 373, 375–76; Brodhead's expedition against, 33–34, 343, 353, 372–73, 376–82, 388, 399, 416; remove westward, 401.
Delaware River, post on, 175; settlers, 403.
Delay, Nathan, at Pittsburgh, 368.
Delay, Philip, at Pittsburgh, 368.
Dennison, Serg. ——, tried and sentenced, 451; reinstated, 452.
Dent, Lieut. John, 493.

INDEX 511

De Peyster, Col. Arent Schuyler, commandant at Detroit, 16, 140, 220; at Indian council, 218–19, 373, 375–76; letter cited, 223, 373; desires prisoners, 376; *Miscellanies by an Officer*, 140, 374–75; sketch, 140.
De Peyster, J. Watts, editor, 140, 374.
De Peyster family papers, 140.
Dermont, Joseph, at Pittsburgh, 369.
Derry settlement, in Pennsylvania, 371.
Detrick, Charles, Loyalist, 254.
Detroit, commandants, 13, 16, 94, 140, 297, 390; garrison, 111, 115, 188; reënforced, 50, 135–36; scarcity at, 78; prisoners at, 86, 200, 206, 220, 297, 420; deserters, 299; Loyalists, 491; Moravians, 161, 300; importance of, 209, 329; message to, 230; Indians at, 14, 33, 46, 50, 122, 191, 193, 245; Indian councils at, 217–20, 317, 325–26, 373, 381; raids from, 18, 276, 322, 325–26, 341; plans to capture, 16–19, 40, 56, 70, 77, 94–95, 101, 111–15, 123–24, 136, 147, 165, 173, 176, 273, 282, 311–13, 318, 333, 374; information about, 117, 119–20, 162, 169, 254; spy from, 295; sketch of fort at, 303; Clark's expedition against, 32–34, 133–34, 165, 200, 331–32, 341, 397–98, 401–21.
Detroit River, island in, 16.
Devereaux, Charles, Loyalist, 252.
Devereaux, Nancy, letter, 252.
Devose, David, at Pittsburgh, 367.
Dewitt, Ezekiel, Ohio County pioneer, 425, 427; fine remitted, 425.
Dewitt, Zechariah, private, 466.
Dickerson, Thomas, 493.
Dickinson, Gideon, private, 467.
Dickinson, Richard, fined, 425.
Dickson, Col. Alexander, British officer, 129; sketch, 130.
Dill, Francis, at Pittsburgh, 367.
Dillon, Matthew, frontiersman, 41.
Dilrumple, John, at Pittsburgh, 368.

Ditts, Henry, private, 468.
Docksteder, John, Loyalist, 53–54; letter, 52–53; sketch, 52.
Doddridge, Rev. Joseph, manuscripts, 91; *Notes on the Settlement and Indian Wars of the Western Parts of Virginia and Pennsylvania*, 376.
Doddridge, Narcissa, sends manuscripts, 91.
Dodge, John, in Illinois, 127, 319; sketch, 319.
Dolly, ——, Virginia Loyalist, 170.
Donnally, Col. Andrew, letter, 354–55; sketch, 354.
Donnally, William, at Pittsburgh, 369.
Doonyontat, Wyandot chief. See Half King.
Dorchester, Guy Carleton, lord, 286.
"Doria," warship, 175.
Double-Door, Seneca Indian. See Gen-ne-hoon.
Douglas, George, Loyalist, 255.
Douglas (Duggless), James, Loyalist, confesses, 254–55.
Douglas, Thomas, Loyalist, 255; confession, 255–56.
Douglass, Ephraim, commissary, 99; sketch, 99–100.
Douglass, John, at Pittsburgh, 369.
Dousman, John, Pittsburgh resident, 450.
Dowler, ——, captured, 163.
Downard, Thomas, trial for Loyalism, 263.
Downey, Cornelius, discharged, 441.
Downing, Timothy, 493.
Doxtater family, in Wisconsin, 52. See also Docksteder.
Drain, James, at Pittsburgh, 367.
Drake, Benjamin, *Life of Tecumseh*, 119.
Draper, Lyman C., series named for, 9; prepares biography, 380; returns manuscripts, 240, 283; interviews, 59, 62, 65, 152–53, 160, 163–64, 202, 207, 319, 335, 355, 373, 398, 403; secures manuscripts, 58, 91, 125, 283, 382; conclusions,

Draper—Continued
61, 160, 186, 236, 404; narrative of Rogers' defeat, 79–88; correspondence, 109, 127; notes, 266, 309, 318, 373–74; *King's Mountain and its Heroes*, 196, 210.
Dry Fork, of Big Sandy, 155.
Dublin, college at, 307.
Dubois, Col. Lewis, regiment, 80.
Duncan, David, quartermaster, 223, 288, 294, 322, 387, 445–46, 478, 480–81; praises for, 291; house of, 471; goes to Philadelphia, 323, 325, 372; charges against, 356–60, 363–66, 388, 393–94, 405–6, 410–11; resignation asked for, 421; letters to, 349, 418; letters, 388, 406; sketch, 223.
Duggless. See Douglas.
Dunbar, John, at Pittsburgh, 369.
Dunlap, Maj. John, Loyalist in Georgia, 391; sketch, 391–92.
Dunlap Creek (Pa.), 421.
Dunlevy, Francis, 493.
Dunmore, John Murray, lord, conducts trial, 421.
Dunmore's War, outbreak, 9, 156; officers in, 58, 212, 230–31, 258, 278, 319, 335.
Dunn, Thomas, deserter, 448.
Duplantier, Capt. ——, French officer, among Indians, 231, 234, 249, 274; life threatened, 273; sketch, 249.
Dust, Adam, fifer, 446.
Dutchess County (N. Y.), 320.
Dutton, Philip, Loyalist, 255.
Duvall, Col. John P., 493; petition of, 82.
Dysart, Capt. James, opposes Loyalists, 196, 237; sketch, 196.

Eager, Robert, exemption for, 426.
Earls, Richard, discharge for, 441.
Eckenrode, H. J., *The Revolution in Virginia*, 237.
Edinburgh, medical college in, 306.

Edmiston, Capt. William, company, 197; opposes Loyalists, 196, 237; sketch, 196.
Edmiston, Maj. William, letters to, 193, 195, 198; sketch, 193.
Edwards, William, Moravian missionary, 161, 190; life threatened, 381; sketch, 161.
Eels, ——, Indian hunter, 112.
Eighteenth British Infantry, 224.
Eighth Canadian Infantry, 47.
Eighth Pennsylvania Regiment, at Fort Pitt, 103, 150; augmented, 94, 114, 125–26; term of service, 147; returns of, 290; officers, 99, 109, 224, 282, 310, 409, 412, 458–59, 470–76; paymaster, 484–89; surgeon, 307, 460; auditors, 392–93; privates, 438, 442, 445–46, 449–55, 457, 478; clothing for, 108, 142, 400; *Orderly Book*, 431–59.
Eighth Virginia Regiment, officers, 103, 230; surgeon, 307.
Elizabeth (Pa.), 413.
Elk, hunted for provisions, 300.
Elk Creek (Va.), 255.
Elkhorn Creek (Ky.), 137.
Elliott, Matthew, Loyalist, 185; sketch, 185.
Ellis, Capt. ——, militia officer, 428.
Ellis, Jesse, 493; *Recollections*, 58–59; sketch, 58.
Ellis, Capt. Nathan, 493.
Ellison, James, in rescuing party, 355; captured, 355.
Elm Grove (W. Va.), 313.
Emigration, to the West, 21–22, 41, 277; reasons for, 324; checked, 269–70, 293; militia from, 409.
English, David, Ohio County officer, 425–30; company, 428; private on Coshocton expedition, 465.
Enlow, Abraham, exemption for, 426.
Erfurt (Germany), 232.
Erie (Pa.), added to state, 307–8.
Erie County (N. Y.), 375.
Erie County (Ohio), 300.
Ervin, John, at Pittsburgh, 368.
Essex County (Ont.), 153.

INDEX 513

Estaing, Charles Henri Theodar, Count d', French admiral, 102.
Eutaw Springs, battle, 103.
Evalt, Samuel, at Pittsburgh, 363, 367.
Evans, Arthur, private, 445.
Evans, John, at Pittsburgh, 369; private, 441.
Evans, Col. John, letters to, 146, 168, 178, 182, 234, 370; information from, 174, 373; absence, 279; sketch, 146.
Evans, Nathan, private, 467.
Evans, Samuel, messenger, 328, 338.
Evans, William, at Pittsburgh, 366.
Ewing, John, boundary commissioner, 107.

FAIRFIELD (Can.), 161.
Fallen Board, Seneca Indian, See Deh-gus-way-gah-ent.
Falls of Ohio, 167, 277; Clark at, 16–19, 49, 77, 194, 310; Rogers' expedition, 17, 85, 87, 89; endangered, 20, 185–86, 192–94, 230, 304; powder transported around, 81; news of Rogers' defeat at, 94; unhealthy climate, 131; wounded at, 266, 319. See also Louisville.
Farlan, Thomas, 493.
Faukler, Jacob, 493.
Faulks. See Foulks.
Fawcett (Fausit), John, at Pittsburgh, 369, 470, 473.
Fayette County (Ky.), 137.
Fayette County (Pa.), 82, 84, 88, 408, 413; part of Virginia, 278; prothonotary, 100; mills in, 293.
Fayette County (Va.), 355.
Ferguson, John, court-martialed, 428.
Ferguson, Maj. Patrick, British officer, 145; killed, 258.
Ferroll, Capt. Thomas, commissary, 95; commended, 302, 359; court-martialed, 436; sketch, 95.
Ferry, John, at Pittsburgh, 363, 366.
Field, Capt. Benjamin, 493.
Fife, John, at Pittsburgh, 367.

Fifer, Jacob, at Pittsburgh, 368.
Fifth Virginia Regiment, officers, 195, 215.
Fifty-third British Infantry, 374.
Fifty-seventh British Infantry, 130.
Filson Club *Publications*, 137.
Fincastle County (Va.), sheriff, 212.
Fincastle Court House (Va.), 244.
Finley, Lieut. Andrew, at Fort Pitt, 459.
Finley, Capt. John, 459; assignments, 43, 109, 113; commended, 113; returns to Fort Pitt, 308; deputy judge advocate, 470, 476, 483, 490–91; testimony in Ward trial, 472, 474–75; sketch, 43.
Finley, Capt. Joseph, 459; recommended, 109; letters, 113, 116–18; sketch, 109.
Finn, Thomas, discharged, 441.
Finney, John, private, 445.
First United States Infantry, 269.
First Virginia Regiment, officer, 269.
Fish Creek, scouting to, 108.
Fishburne, Capt. Benjamin, message to, 304.
Fisher, Myndert, arrested, 352; trial, 491.
Fisher Branch (Va.), 236.
Fishing Creek, raid on, 160.
Fitzgibbon, David, 493.
Five Nations Indians. See Iroquois.
Fleming, James, at Pittsburgh, 362, 366.
Fleming, Lieut. Lewis, 493.
Fleming, Col. William, commissioner, 103; letters to, 103–4, 128–32, 137–38, 292; letter, 50–52; on Virginia council, 130; *Journal*, 160; sketch, 50.
Fleming, Mrs. William, sister, 137; care for, 138.
Flick, John, at Pittsburgh, 367.
Flin, Philip, at Pittsburgh, 368.
Flinn, Thomas, discharged, 446.
Florida, British in, 19, 24, 130; deserters seek, 77; Spanish secure, 131; attempted capture, 391. See also West Florida.

514   INDEX

Flower Gap, in the Blue Ridge, 236.
Floyd, Charles, message for, 267; emigrates, 305; sketch, 267.
Floyd Jr., Charles, with Lewis and Clark, 267.
Floyd, John, letters, 21, 141–42, 186–87, 265–67,. 304–5; killed, 267; sketch, 141.
Floyd, Mrs. John, in Kentucky, 187; message from, 267.
Floyd, William P., mentioned, 187, 267; sketch, 187.
Floyd County (Va.), 236.
Floyd's Station (Ky.), 266–67.
Forbes, Gen. John, expedition, 150.
Forbush, George, Loyalist, 254.
Foreman's Defeat, 319.
Forest County (Pa.), 56.
Forrester, Joseph, at Pittsburgh, 369.
Forster, Capt. Anthony, British officer, 129.
Forsyth, Robert, interviewed, 164.
Forsyth, Thomas, fur trader, 164; sketch, 164.
Forsyth, Mrs. Thomas. See Malott, Keziah.
Forsyth, William, sketch, 164.
Fort Anne, captured, 286.
Fort Armstrong, built, 40; location, 55; garrison, 79, 98–99, 107, 113, 180; evacuated, 117, 121, 136, 249, 354; regarrisoned, 164, 174, 272.
Fort Bute, captured, 129.
Fort Chartres, garrison, 224.
Fort Chiswell, at Virginia lead mines, 26–27, 198, 251, 268; garrison, 195, 212, 217; letters from, 208, 217, 236; sketch, 143.
Fort Clark, at Kaskaskia, 231.
Fort Crawford, garrison, 79; evacuated, 118, 121, 136, 235, 249, 354; regarrisoned, 164, 174, 272; Indians near, 178; sketch, 40.
Fort Cumberland, endangered, 230.
Fort Dillon (Dillars), attack near, 41.
Fort Duquesne, visit to, 65; captured, 150.
Fort George, captured, 286.

Fort Hand, garrison, 99; provisioned, 408; sketch, 79.
Fort Henry, at Wheeling, 19; garrison, 116, 118, 180,.281, 309, 409, 427; commandants, 118, 122, 309, 313, 409; letter from, 160; supplies for, 168, 322, 336, 344; a rendezvous, 169, 178; attack near, 271, 379; warning for, 350–51; booty sold at, 399; insubordination at, 428. See also Wheeling.
Fort Jefferson, planned, 19; Clark at, 20; relief for, 176; officers at, 230–31.
Fort Laurens, built, 184; evacuated, 18, 39–40, 43, 69, 71; soldiers killed at, 41; garrison, 41.
Fort McIntosh, 204, 206, 224–25, 343, 489; utility of, 42, 347, 354, 384; commandants, 49, 121, 281, 289, 309; garrison, 19, 23, 43, 103, 112, 116, 180, 335–37; attacked, 41; watched, 46, 231; Indians visit, 76, 132, 184, 220; trespassers near, 96–97, 107; Indian defeat near, 31, 223–26, 232, 245–46, 273; as a rendezvous, 214; supplies for, 310–11; express from 450; artillery at, 118; hospital, 122; surgeon, 460; court-martial for, 457; threatened, 275, 340, 350–51; treaty at, 41, 381.
Fort Nelson (Ky.), garrison, 87; built, 180.
Fort Ninety-six, attacked, 145, 402; battle near, 392.
Fort Pitt, in Pennsylvania, 280; importance of, 124, 287, 384, 390; inhabitants encroach on, 443; commandants, 14, 67, 81, 171, 307, 395; garrison, 19, 347; size of, 326; reënforcements for 113, 118, 126, 146–47, 208, 348; artillery for, 175–76, 202, 382, 390–91; supplies for, 88, 93, 109, 136, 174; scarcity at, 31–32, 202, 235, 248–50, 271, 273–78, 282–88, 291–95, 301, 306, 308–9, 322–26, 347, 387, 400; fishing for food, 457; hard winter at, 137; Indians

INDEX

visit, 56, 191; French officers, 29–30, 142, 161, 305, 375; Loyalists, 22–23, 277, 285, 302, 352–53, 389–90, 416–17, 491; expeditions from, 14–16, 33, 376; scouting parties, 79; watched, 46; raids near, 20–21, 150–54, 273, 340; endangered, 135, 176, 193, 230, 276, 286, 322–23, 340–41, 388–90, 400, 404; courts-martial at, 383, 431–58, 470–91; missionaries visit, 232, 400, 404; news of Rogers' defeat reaches, 18. See also Pittsburgh.
Fort Randolph, provisions for, 243–44; sketch, 52.
Fort Schuyler (Stanwix), garrisoned, 287.
Fort Stanwix. See Schuyler.
Fort Venango, captured, 65.
Fort Wallace, raid near, 371.
Fort Washington, captured, 79.
Fort Wayne (Ind.), site, 200.
Forty-seventh British Infantry, build post, 54.
Foulk, Andrew J., descendant of Brodhead, 283.
Foulks (Faulks), Elizabeth, captured, 150–54; attempt to rescue, 199; son, 152; sketch, 152.
Foulks, George, captured, 150–54; attempt to rescue, 199; sketch, 151.
Foulks, John, death, 151.
Foulks Jr., John, killed, 151–52.
Fourth Artillery Regiment, 391, 413, 454.
Fourth of July, celebration, 449.
Fourth United States sub-legion, 269.
Fourth Virginia Regiment, 126; officer, 230.
Fouts, Capt. Andrew, 493.
Fowler, Alexander, auditor, 392, 394, 407, 484–89; charges against Brodhead, 356–60, 393–95, 401, 407, 410–12; charges against Read, 484, 486–89; signs protests, 362, 366, 396; letters to, 392–94, 407, 411; letters, 224–27, 356–60, 396,

410–12; characterized, 387–88; sketch, 224.
France, alliance with, 14, 23, 122; envoy from, 28; financial aid, 80–81; army in America, 197, 209, 248, 264; naval aid, 210, 248, 264, 268, 282, 296, 405–6. See also French.
Francis, Capt. Henry, militia officer, 240.
Francis, Philip, at Pittsburgh, 369.
Francis, Stephen John, deposition, 428.
Francisco, Jacob, trial for Loyalism, 261; enlists, 262.
Frankfort (Ky.), 310.
Franklin (Pa.), site, 54, 61, 65, 404.
Franklin Mills (Ohio), 204.
Franklin Township (Pa.), 274.
Frazier, David, in rescuing party, 355.
Frederick, Boston, at Pittsburgh, 369.
Frederick, Sebastian, at Pittsburgh, 369.
Frederick County (Va.), 87.
Freehold, William, horse master, 431; sentenced, 431–32.
Fremont (Ohio), 152.
French, Robert, militiaman, 430.
French, as envoys to Indians, 29–30, 111, 124, 176, 188, 200–1, 214, 231, 249, 265, 273–75, 305; influence on Indians, 218–19, 234, 274, 375. See also France.
French and Indian War, 53, 65, 130, 210, 307, 373–74.
French Canadians, at Detroit, 13–14; attitude towards Americans, 29, 127, 218–19, 250, 273; follow La Balme, 200; with raiding parties, 354.
French (Le Bœuf) Creek, Brodhead's expedition on, 54–56, 60–61, 78; Montour's raid on, 301; Morrison's scout to, 406.
French Margaret, chieftess, 96.
Frezer, John, at Pittsburgh, 368.
Frontiersmen, attitude towards Indians, 29–30, 34, 60, 290, 302–3;

Frontiersmen—Continued
murder Indians, 376, 379–80; forting at approach of Indians, 420.
Fry, Jacob, at Pittsburgh, 368.
Fry, William, at Pittsburgh, 368.
Fubecker, George, at Pittsburgh, 367.
Fullerborn, John, private, 468.
Fullinwider, H., private, 468.
Fullinwider, Peter, private, 468.
Fur trade, in Louisiana, 86, 176; hunting for, 142; at St. Louis, 164.

GADDIS, Col. Thomas, letter for, 107–8.
Gaiter, Cornelius, private, 465.
Galalemend, Delaware chief. See Killbuck.
Galvez, Bernardo de, at New Orleans, 81, 83–85; conquests, 19, 129–30; captures Pensacola, 402; sketch, 129.
Gamble, David, court-martialed, 282, 452; escape of, 453.
Gamble, Josias, at Pittsburgh, 369.
Gap Store (Va.), 155.
Gardner, ——, at Fort Pitt, 449.
Gardner, ——, Kentucky pioneer, 267.
Gardner, Hugh, at Pittsburgh, 366.
Garlick, Gasper, Loyalist, 222; trial, 259.
Garritt. See Jarratt.
Gasten, William, private, 465.
Gates, Gen. Horatio, letters to, 168, 177; orders, 180; in battle of Camden, 210, 282; in South Carolina, 264.
Gehnhenshecan, Indian site, 158.
Geijashuta, Seneca chief. See Guyashusta.
Genesee River, Indians on, 64–65, 96.
Genet, Edmond Charles, French envoy, 391.
Geneva (N. Y.), site, 53.
Gen-ne-hoon (Double-Door), Seneca Indian, killed, 66.

George, Capt. Robert, 299; orders for, 42, 77, 165; letter, 77–78; message for, 231; sketch, 42.
Georgia, Loyalists in, 25, 143, 170, 253; British, 102, 391; information from, 402.
Gérard, Conrad Alexandre, relations with Indians, 44.
Gérard, Delaware chief. See Johnny, Captain.
Germantown (Pa.), 306; battle of, 335.
Gibson, Andrew, at Pittsburgh, 369.
Gibson, Capt. George, New Orleans expedition, 81.
Gibson, John, Pittsburgh merchant, 366, 438.
Gibson, Col. John, regiment, 120, 149, 314, 400; at Fort Pitt, 113, 122, 432, 443, 478; leave of absence, 114, 148–49, 173, 318, 460; returns, 177; relations with Brodhead, 58, 99, 395; ordered to join Clark, 33, 312, 331–32, 395, 398, 400; replaces Brodhead, 395, 411; as witness, 477; presides at courts, 431, 446–54, 457–58; letters to, 331, 412; letters, 289, 310, 395, 399–400, 409, 411–12.
Gibson, John B., interviewed, 81.
Gillehan, Thomas, Loyalist, 254.
Gillespee, James, fined, 426.
Gillespy, George, at Pittsburgh, 368.
Gillmore, William, at Pittsburgh, 367.
Girty, George, in Indian raid, 17; reward offered for capture, 299; sketch, 299.
Girty, James, reward for capture of, 299; sketch, 299.
Girty, Predeaux, sketch, 163.
Girty, Mrs. Predeaux, recollections, 163–64.
Girty, Simon, 60; captured when a boy, 59; marriage, 163–64; defeats Rogers' party, 17–18, 93; reward for capture of, 299; report, 381; sketch, 59.
Girty, Mrs. Simon. See Malott, Catherine.

INDEX

Girty, Thomas, near Pittsburgh, 352; letter forged in name of, 491.
Girty Jr., Thomas, interviewed, 163.
Gist, Christopher, explorations, 236; estate, 413.
Glade Road, route via, 150; advised, 181.
Glade Spring (Va.), 196.
Glades, of Holston River, 26, 198.
Glades, of Monongahela River, 294, 406.
Glasgow, Samuel, at Pittsburgh, 367.
Glass, Lieut. ———, orders for, 99–100.
Glass, Andrew, discharged, 441.
Glass, Anthony, discharged, 441.
Glass, Robert, private, 465.
Glaves, Lieut. William, militia officer, 215.
Glazier, John, at Pittsburgh, 369.
Glendy, William, at Pittsburgh, 370.
Glenn, James, at Pittsburgh, 367.
Gnadenhütten, Moravian village, 159, 162, 190, 380; missionary at, 161; ambush at, 381; massacre, 119, 232; sketch, 159.
Gnadensee. See Indian Pond.
Goddard, ———, Baltimore printer, 331.
Goodson (Va.), 194.
Goodwin, John, private, 467.
Goodwire, Ben, at Pittsburgh, 368.
Goodwood, Campbell's estate, 192, 194–95.
Gordon, Lieut. Arthur, adjutant, 460; court-martialed, 115, 135, 147–48, 433–34.
Gordon, Col. James, captured, 286.
Gordon, John, tried and acquitted, 453.
Goschgoschuenk. See Cuscushing.
Gosfield (Can.), 163.
Goshen (Ohio), Moravian mission village, 161.
Goss, Zechariah, Loyalist, 239; hung, 240.
Gosset, John, 493; court-martialed, 282, 452.

Graham, Lieut. Alexander, at Fort Pitt, 459.
Graham, Michael, at Pittsburgh, 367.
Grand River (Can.), land grant on, 52.
Granville (W. Va.), Indian raid at, 95.
Grant, William, enlists, 260–61.
Grave Creek (Va.), residents, 110; fort at, 160.
Graverod, Gerret, Loyalist, 491.
Gray, Sam, half-breed hostile, 420.
Grayson, John, trial for Loyalism, 259.
Grayson, Robert, Loyalist, 254; trial of, 258; sketch, 258.
Grayson, William, enlists, 262.
Grayson County (Va.), 237.
Greasy Creek (Va.), Loyalists on, 236.
Great Cacapon River (Va.), 373.
Great Kanawha River. See Kanawha River.
Great Miami River, mouth, 94; portage to, 185; Indians on, 51, 87; expedition on, 185, 192; post built on, 273; spies visit, 304.
Green, John, private, 466.
Green, Col. John, horses stolen, 236; sketch, 236.
Green Coat Rangers. See King's Royal Regiment.
Green River (Ky.), settlement on, 142.
Greenbrier County (Va.), protection for, 52; inhabitant, 355; land commissioners in, 131; raided, 354–55.
Greene, George W., *Life of General Nathaniel Greene*, 80.
Greene, Gen. Nathaniel, in South, 80, 156, 241, 402; victory of, 408; letters to, 42, 107, 136; *Life*, 80.
Greene County (Pa.), 274, 373; *History*, 274.
Greensburg (Pa.), trustee, 408.
Grenadier Squaw, accompanies La Balme, 201.
Gresham, ———, aids Loyalists, 247.

INDEX

Gretsinger, John, court-martialed, 439–40.
Grey, Capt. Joseph, issues warrant, 228; at Loyalists' trials, 258; sketch, 228.
Griffin, Cyrus, Virginia Congressman, 130.
Griffin, Peter, court-martialed, 442.
Griffith, John, Loyalist leader, 23–24, 144–45, 208, 252–56; report, 247.
Grimstaff, Lewis, private, 469.
Grube, Rev. Bernard Adam, visits Ohio missions, 232; return journey, 246; letter mentioned, 320; sketch, 232.
Guffey, James, private, 467.
Guilford Court House, battle, 156.
Guilleland, Capt. ——, militia officer, 428.
Guthrie, John, private, 445.
Guthrie, Ensign John, orders for, 178; at Fort Pitt, 459; court-martialed, 458; plots against Indians, 290; sketch, 178.
Guyandotte River, post for planned, 19, 51.
Guyashusta (Cayashooto, Geijashuta, Kayashuta, Kiasheeta), Seneca chief, 48, 226; visit to Wyandot, 189, 191, 193, 223; messages, 217; illness, 374–75; sketch, 48.
Gwinn, Patrick, court-martialed, 442.

HACKENWELDER, John. See Heckewelder.
Hagerty, Nicholas, private, 445.
Haldimand, Gen. Frederick, cited, 14; releases prisoner, 86; letter to, 47; letters, 50, 78, 122–23.
Hale, Thomas, Loyalist, 222.
Half King (Doonyontat, Pemowagen), Wyandot chief, 45, 153; kinspeople, 20, 45, 154, 218; negotiates with Americans, 66–72; hostilities of, 153, 158–59; relation to Delawares, 219, 233, 375; speech, 219; sketch, 45.
Hall, John, at Pittsburgh, 366.

Hall, Joseph, at Pittsburgh, 366, 367.
Hall, Robert, at Pittsburgh, 366.
Hall Jr., Robert, at Pittsburgh, 366.
Hall, William, 493.
Halsey, Francis W., *The Old New York Frontier*, 248.
Ham, Conrad, defrauded, 452.
Hamilton, Daniel, at Pittsburgh, 367.
Hamilton, Hans, at Pittsburgh, 367.
Hamilton, Henry, captured by Clark, 14, 30, 122; successor, 140.
Hamilton, James, at Pittsburgh, 369.
Hamilton, John, at Pittsburgh, 362, 367; horse master, 438.
Hamilton's Island. See Brunot's.
Hampshire County (Va.), 82.
Hancock's Bridge (N. J.), battle at, 413.
Hand, Gen. Edward, at Fort Pitt, 23, 83, 85, 204, 365; assistance, 207; letter to, 224.
Hand, Levi, at Pittsburgh, 368.
Handlyn, John, at Pittsburgh, 362, 366.
Hanging Rock, battle, 79.
Hannah, Samuel, at Pittsburgh, 367.
Hannastown (Pa.), expedition against, 65, 290; troops at, 98, 120–21, 125, 352; raids near, 171, 223, 414; public records at, 188; band to murder friendly Indians, 290.
Hannibal (Mo.), 152.
Hanover County (Va.), 267, 269.
Hanover Township (Pa.), 41.
Harbot, David. See Herbert.
Hardesty, Samuel, private, 467.
Hardin, Lieut. John, 459; on Brodhead's expedition, 55, 57–58; commended, 76; in Indian wars, 373; rank, 431; sketch, 55.
Hardin, John, 493; escapes from Indians, 163; attempt to rescue wife and children, 199–200.
Hardin, Mary, captured, 163; attempt to rescue, 199–200.

INDEX

Hardin, Thomas, escapes from Indians, 163.
Hardin, William, escapes from Indians, 163.
Hardy County (W. Va.), 397.
Harless, ——, Loyalist, 221.
Harmar, Gen. Josiah, in Indian wars, 83, 373.
Harper, Thomas, at Pittsburgh, 367.
Harris, Captain, Delaware Indian, 403–5.
Harris, John, Indian trader, 404.
Harris Jr., John, builds town, 404; sketch, 404.
Harris, Joseph, at Pittsburgh, 369.
Harris, William, private, 466.
Harrisburgh (Pa.), founder, 404.
Harris's Ferry (Pa.), 404.
Harrison, Benjamin, Virginia Speaker, 331.
Harrison, Capt. Benjamin, messenger, 40; joins Clark, 156–57; kinspeople, 335, 413; sketch, 40.
Harrison, Catherine, married, 413.
Harrison, Burr, daughter of, 319.
Harrison, Daniel, wounded by Indians, 420.
Harrison, John, trial for Loyalism, 260.
Harrison, Lieut. John, 493; retained in service, 335; on courts-martial, 470, 484; sketch, 335.
Harrison, Maj. John, 493.
Harrison, Lawrence, sons, 335.
Harrison Jr., Lieut. Lawrence, on courts-martial, 470; retires, 477.
Harrison, Sarah, married, 319.
Harrison, Capt. William, 278; kinsfolk, 335, 413.
Harrison City (Pa.), 414.
Harrod, Mrs. Amelia, letters for, 160, 187.
Harrod, James, Kentucky pioneer, 87.
Harrod, Capt. William, passport for, 49; letters, 160, 187; son, 160.
Harrod Jr., William, interviewed, 160.

Harrodsburg (Ky.), settled, 87, 266; commissioners at, 105; letters from, 141, 292, 319; trustee of, 310.
Harshey, Peter, at Pittsburgh, 367.
Hartford (Conn.), Washington at, 282.
Harvey, Henry, fined, 425.
Harvey, William, private, 464.
Hathaway, Abraham, private, 467.
Haven. See Heavin.
Hawkins, William, private, 466.
Hawtatscheek, Mingo warrior, 157.
Hayes, James, at Pittsburgh, 369.
Hayes, John, at Pittsburgh, 369.
Hayes, Robert, at Pittsburgh, 369.
Hayes, William, at Pittsburgh, 369.
Haynes, Rev. James, reminiscences, 355; sketch, 355.
Hays, Christopher, of Westmoreland County, 385, 393, 408; calls out militia, 414, 416; letter to, 418; sketch, 385.
Hazards' Pennsylvania Register, 226.
Hazen, Gen. Moses, regiment, 406.
Heath, Andrew, farm, 417.
Heath (Heth), Capt. Henry, at Fort Pitt, 67, 446; rank, 337, 344; company, 94, 115, 326, 332, 398, 435–36, 448, 457; terms of enlistment, 440–41, 445, 456; on courts-martial, 443; sketch, 67.
Heavin, Howard, Loyalist leader, 221, 260–61.
Heavin, James, takes oath, 261.
Heavin, John, Loyalist, 221; acquitted of charge, 261; letter, 227.
Heavin, Thomas, Loyalist, 246–47.
Heavin, William, enlists, 261.
Heckewelder (Hackenwelder), Rev. John, Moravian missionary, 161, 300; spelling of name, 246; marriage of, 232; information from, 45–46, 105–6, 159, 169, 173, 189–90, 273, 337–39; life threatened, 381; letters to, 169, 176, 232–33, 321; letters, 231–32, 245–46, 337–39; handwriting, 46, 105, 157, 172, 190, 217, 272, 315–16, 339;

Heckewelder—Continued
Narrative, 56, 119, 232, 376; sketch, 45.
Hedges, Silas, militia officer, 110–11, 425, 427, 429–30; private on Coshocton expedition, 466; sketch, 110.
Helm, Capt. Leonard, Clark's officer, 127.
Henderson, John, gives bond, 228–29; trial for Loyalism, 260.
Henderson, Col. Richard, in Kentucky, 141–42.
Henderson, Robert, at Pittsburgh, 368.
Henderson, Robert, trial for Loyalism, 263.
Henderson (Ky.), founded, 142.
Hendricks, George, escapes, 185; sketch, 185.
Hendrise, Abraham, at Pittsburgh, 368.
Hening, William W., *Statutes at Large of Virginia*, 28, 110.
Henry, Col. John, Delaware chief. See Killbuck.
Henry, Patrick, governor of Virginia, 81–84; estate, 264; letter to, 84–86; letters, 82–83, 264.
Henry, Robert, acquitted, 429; on Coshocton expedition, 465.
Henry, William, Pennsylvania merchant, 338.
Henry children, rescued, 203.
Henry County (Tenn.), 355.
Henry County (Va.), troops from, 51; Loyalists in, 264.
Herbert (Harbot), David, Loyalist, 251–53; confession, 253.
Herbert, Thomas, ferry, 236.
Herrod. See Harrod.
Hessians, prisoners, 242; reënforcements of, 286.
"He who Patches," Seneca Indian. See Decker, Capt. John.
Hickerton, Michael, 493.
Hickman, Ezekiel, at Pittsburgh, 367.
Higgins, Daniel, recollections, 59–64; sketch, 59.

Hill, ———, Loyalist, 222.
Hill, Joseph, at Pittsburgh, 367.
Hill, Stephen, at Pittsburgh, 367.
Hinds, John, fifer, deserts, 332; trial, 490.
Hite, Col. Abraham, letter to, 323; sketch, 323.
Hoagland, Derrick, 493; provost-marshal, 425; recruiting officer, 426.
Hobkirk's Hill, battle, 103.
Hockley, Richard, private, 445.
Hogland. See Hoagland.
Hollaway, John, deputy muster-master, 433; assistant auditor, 488–89.
Holliday's Cove (Va.), garrison at, 42, 116, 180, 281; commandant, 119, 313; supplies for, 322; sketch, 42.
Hollyday, Philip, at Pittsburgh, 368.
Holmes, Dr. David, at Fort Pitt, 449; on furlough, 460.
Holmes, Joseph, land commissioner, 118.
Holston River, Loyalists on, 23, 26, 198, 201, 254; removal to, 138; raid on, 392; settlers on, 194, 196–97; in Dunmore's War, 231; north fork, 244–45; south fork, 254.
Homer, Gerret, at Pittsburgh, 366.
Hook, John, Loyalist, 254.
Hopkins, Admiral Esek, naval expedition, 175.
Hopkins, Joseph, at Pittsburgh, 367.
Howe, William, Loyalist, 417.
Howey, William, at Pittsburgh, 366.
Howell, Lieut. Ezekiel, member of court at Fort Pitt, 484.
Hoyle, Mathias, at Pittsburgh, 367.
Hubbell's Creek (Mo.), 385.
Hudson, Thomas (Telenenut), Seneca chief, 95.
Hudson River, 79; highlands of, 30.
Huff, John, private, 468.
Huff, Leonard, Loyalist officer, 247, 254.
Hughes, Elias, 493.
Hughes, Lieut. John, at Fort Pitt, 459.

INDEX

Hughes, Felix, at Pittsburgh, 368.
Hughes, James, at Pittsburgh, 368.
Hughes, John, at Pittsburgh, 368.
Hughston, James, private, 465.
Humler, Nicholas, court-martialed, 449–50.
Humphrey family, in southwest Virginia, 137.
Huntington, Samuel, president of Congress, letters to, 333–34, 345–46, 387, 400, 405, 407; letter, 401; portrait, 383.
Hupp, Philip, 493.
Huron Indians. See Wyandot Indians.
Husk, ———, informer, 198.
Husong, Jacob, private, 467.
Huston, William, exemption for, 425; court-martialed, 428; acquitted, 429.
Hutchins, Thomas, map, 56.
Hutson, John, at Pittsburgh, 368.

ILLINOIS, in War of 1812, 164; troops withdrawn from, 19; endangered, 20, 186; La Balme in, 30, 200, 319, 345; officers in, 77, 224, 299; expedition against, 83, 87, 165, 180; news from, 104; reënforcements for, 126, 195; Clark in, 157; trade in, 305, 319; French agent sent to, 305.
Illinois Historical Collections, 17–19, 21, 25, 29–30, 34, 42, 77, 127, 155, 165, 176, 182, 192, 194, 199–200, 209, 220, 246, 310, 331, 337, 343, 350–51, 391, 395, 397–98, 408–9.
Illinois Historical Society *Transactions*, 165, 200.
Illinois Regiment, land grant for 230, 310.
Impressment of provisions, ordered, 31, 235, 276, 278, 284, 288–89, 293–95; necessity for, 277, 280; opposition to, 285; ill-success of, 301.
Indaochaie, Indian town. See Lichtenau.

Independence, of United States, recognized, 129.
Indey, prisoner, escapes, 448.
Indian Creek (Va.), raid on, 354–55.
Indian Pond (Gnadensee), mission site, 320.
Indiana, Clark's land grant in, 230, 310.
Indians, agriculture among, 15; horse-racing, 203; living conditions, 162; war trails, 108, 155; superstitions, 63; treatment of prisoners, 86; captives rescued, 199–200; attachment to French, 14, 28–30, 122, 176, 218–19; relations to British, 48, 50, 169, 186, 218, 345; councils at Detroit, 217–20, 340, 374–76; American negotiations with, 66–76, 334; in American army, 345; hunt for garrison, 112; trespassers on lands of, 22–23, 96–97, 103, 106–7, 112, 114–15, 168; maltreatment by frontiersmen, 29–30, 34, 60, 183, 290, 302–3, 376, 379–80; missionary influence on, 345; speak English, 404; illicit trade with, 356; superintendent of trade for, 120; British agents, 78, 140; American agents, 164, 347–48; untrustworthiness, 321. See also the several tribes.
Ingles, Col. Thomas, protected, 212; sketch, 212.
Ingles (Inglish), Col. William, Loyalist, 24, 129, 254; trial of, 257–58; sketch, 257.
Ingles Ferry (Va.), site, 236.
Inglish. See Ingles.
Ingram, James, enlists, 262.
Ingram, Jonathan, enlists, 262.
Ingram, Samuel, trial for Loyalism, 262.
Irish, at Pittsburgh, 59; in Pennsylvania, 81–82, 175, 207, 226; regiment, 204; in Virginia, 195–96.
Iroquois (Five Nations, Six Nations) Indians, favor British, 14, 123, 191, 233; Americans invade country,

Iroquois—Continued
14–16, 41, 78; alarmed, 47–48, 50, 52–54; apply for peace, 169; intertribal influence, 191, 374; divided between British and Americans, 218; missionaries among, 320. See also Cayuga, Mohawk, Oneida, Onondaga, and Seneca.
Irvine, Robert, pack-horse master, 194.
Irvine, Gen. William, letter to, 307–8; at Fort Pitt, 412, 490; sketch, 307.
Irvine (Pa.), site, 15; named, 308.
Irwin, John, Pittsburgh inhabitant, 362, 366, 396; commissary, 445–46, 477–82; witness, 478–79, 482.
Irwin Jr., John, at Pittsburgh, 367.
Irwin, Capt. Joseph, militia officer, 171, 300; orders for, 79, 99; commands ranging company, 95, 113, 120, 135; reprimanded, 98; arrest ordered, 125; letter to, 125; plots against Indians, 290; sketch, 79.
Irwin, Samuel, letter to, 327–28.
Isle aux Chevreuils. See Carleton Island.
Islor, Nathaniel, justice of peace, 91.
Israel, Delaware chief. See Johnny, Captain.
It-is-light-to-be-lifted, Delaware Indian. See Day-oos-ta.

JACK, Capt. Matthew, scouting, 39; recollections, 61; plots against Indians, 290; at Fort Pitt, 458; sketch, 39.
Jackman, John, Loyalist, 417.
Jackson, Capt. George, 493.
Jackson, Joseph, recollections, 93; sketch, 93.
Jackson's Fort (Pa.), raid on, 274.
Jacob's Creek (Pa.), iron works on, 413.
Jamaica, expedition against, 248.
James, Robert, grandson, 83.
James, Thomas, private, 469.

Jameson, Lieut. John, orders for, 107, 113, 117; sketch, 107.
Jamison, John, at Pittsburgh, 368.
Jamison II, John, at Pittsburgh, 368.
Jamison, Mar., at Pittsburgh, 368.
Jamison, Robert, at Pittsburgh, 367.
Jarratt (Garrett), William, sergeant, 469.
Jay, John, letters to, 95, 107.
Jefferson, Thomas, governor of Virginia, 25, 228, 302, 310–11, 325, 341, 397; purchases for Clark, 324, 331; letters to, 50–52, 143–44, 241–42, 277, 317–18, 354, 391–92, 399–400, 402; letters, 32, 113, 127–28, 133–34, 155, 209, 180, 331–32.
Jefferson County (Ky.), 180, 310.
Jefferson County (N. Y.), 54.
Jena (Germany), 232.
Jenking, Joshua, at Pittsburgh, 367.
Jenkins, John, Loyalist leader, 250, 253; confession, 252–53.
Jennings, Joseph, private, 467.
Jessamine County (Ky.), 167.
John, Thomas, at Pittsburgh, 368.
John P. Branch Historical Papers, 23–24, 26, 170, 192, 194, 198, 208, 210, 254, 267.
Johnes, Thomas, private, 445.
Johnny, Captain (Gérard, Israel). Delaware chief, messages, 44, 46–47, 157–59, 173; message by, 183; sketch, 44.
Johnson, Col. Guy, letters, 140–41, 374–75; sketch, 140.
Johnson, James, private, 467.
Johnson, Sir John, Loyalist, 78, 185; leads raids, 248, 287, 388–89; sketch, 78.
Johnson, Thomas H., "The Indian village of Cush-og-wenk," 379.
Johnson, William, affidavit, 416–17.
Johnson, Sir William, son, 78; example, 140.
Johnson family, papers, 140.
Johnston, H. Benjamin, information from, 170.
Johnston, Isaac, court-martialed, 457.

INDEX 523

Johnston, James, at Pittsburgh, 367.
Johnston, John, quartermaster's clerk, 412, 478; at Pittsburgh, 369.
Johnston, Mary Ann, married, 335.
Johnston, William, at Pittsburgh, 367.
Jolly, Henry, 493.
Jones, Ignatius, at Pittsburgh, 367.
Jones, Joseph, Virginia congressman, 130.
Jones, Joshua, Loyalist, 247, 254–55.
Jones, Philip, at Pittsburgh, 367.
Jordan, John, deserter, 447.
Jordan, Mark, at Pittsburgh, 369.
Joshua, Moravian Indian, 119, 161, 169–70; sketch, 119.
Jouett, John, Kentuckian, 304; sketch, 304–5.
Jouett Jr., John, interviewed, 305.
Justice, Isaac, at Pittsburgh, 367.

KADARAGARUS. See Cattaraugus.
Kalb, Baron Johann de, killed, 282.
Kanawha River, headwaters, 23; post for, 19, 42, 192, 243; route via, 90; Washington's lands on 403.
Karey, William, at Pittsburgh, 367.
Karr, Andrew, 493.
Karr, Hamilton, private, 465.
Kaskaskia (Ill.), 85, 87, 127, 231; merchant of, 165; commandant, 224; deserters from, 299.
Kayashuta, Seneca chief. See Guyashuta.
Kaylalemend, Delaware chief. See Killbuck.
Keenhanshicanink, Delaware hostile, 191; visit to, 273.
Keeshmattsee, Shawnee chief, 73.
Kelleleman, Delaware chief. See Killbuck.
Kelly, Elias, private, 467.
Kelly, James, court-martialed, 440.
Kelly, Pat., at Pittsburgh, 368.
Kelly, Thomas, deserter, 449.
Kelly's (Va.), post proposed at, 192, 243.
Kenjua Creek (Pa.), 66.

Kenjua Flats, Indian town on, 66.
Kennedy, David, at Pittsburgh, 366.
Kenser, John, private, 468.
Kentucky, explored, 196, 210, 266; surveyors in, 236, 305; early settlers, 142, 179; emigration to, 21–22, 41, 87, 128, 131, 138, 149, 163, 167–68, 176, 277, 283, 386; militia of, 22; protection for, 19–20, 26, 51, 180, 184–87, 192–95, 197, 265–67, 292–93, 319, 347, 352; troops for, 179, 182, 304; raids in, 17, 20, 28, 77, 94–95, 191, 220, 232, 234, 249, 270, 299; Loyalists in, 22; commissioners for, 103, 105, 137; new counties in, 131; college, 109; troops from, 49; hard winter in, 141–42; convention in, 196, 304.
Kentucky County, officer, 184.
Kentucky Resolutions of 1799, 137.
Kerr, James, at Pittsburgh, 367–68.
Kerr, James, sentenced for Loyalism, 263.
Kerr, Joseph, at Pittsburgh, 369.
Kiasheeta, Seneca chief. See Guyashusta.
Kilgour, John, private, 445.
Killbuck (Caleylemont, Col. John Henry, Galalemend, Gelelemend, Kaylalemend, Kelleleman), Delaware chief, 41, 97; several names, 46, 73, 157, 339–40; assists Brodhead, 339, 377–78, 399; speech, 73–75, 139; information from, 105–6, 190–92, 217–20, 250, 316–17, 339–40; messages to, 44, 46, 157–59, 172–73, 233, 328–30; intercedes for Baubee, 297; deceives Brodhead, 316, 321, 330; life threatened, 338, 380; village site, 377, 399; sketch, 41.
Killbuck, Moses, information from, 272.
Killbuck family, murder of member of, 376, 420.
Killan, John, at Pittsburgh, 369.
Killen, John, at Pittsburgh, 367.
Kinders, Peter, confesses Loyalism, 247, 254.

King, James, discharged, 441.
King, John, at Pittsburgh, 369.
King, Robert, confession of Loyalism, 256–57; trial and sentence, 262.
King's Mountain, battle, 28, 196–97, 210–11, 258; commander at, 245.
King's Royal Regiment (Green Coat Rangers, Royal Greens), sketch, 185.
Kingston (Ont.), fort at, 54.
Kinny, John, at Pittsburgh, 368.
Kinzie, John, fur trader, 164.
Kinzua (Pa.), site, 66.
Kirkland, Rev. Samuel, influence over Oneida, 345.
Kiskakoquille. See Mahusquechikoken.
Kishinotsey, Shawnee chief, 139.
Kiskiminitas Creek, scouting on, 79, 100, 174; garrison at mouth, 117.
Kittanning (Pa.), 56, 60, 283; post at, 19, 40.
Kittering, Lawrence, Loyalist officer, 247.
Klingelschmit (Clinglesmith), Peter, pioneer, 414.
Klingelschmit (Clinglesmith), Philip, killed by Indians, 414.
Knight, Dr. John, surgeon's mate, 460.
Knotts, John, on Rogers' expedition, 90.
Knox, Gen. Henry, orders for, 147; cited, 287.
Knox, Col. James, Virginia officer, 113, 131; sketch, 113.
Knox, Thomas, fined, 425.
Koonty, ——, armorer, 103.
Kushkushing. See Cuscushing.
Kuskuskies (Cuscusky), trail via, 184, 202; Delawares to remove to, 315, 328, 384.
Kuykendall, Abraham, at Pittsburgh, 367.
Kuykendall, James, at Pittsburgh, 367.
Kyser, Daniel, at Pittsburgh, 369.
Kyser, Michael, at Pittsburgh, 369.

LA BALME, Col. Augustin Mottin de, Western expedition, 29–30, 319, 345, 347; at Fort Pitt, 200–1; killed, 345, 375; cited, 34; papers captured, 375; sketch, 200.
Lafayette, Jean Paul Joseph Motier, marquis de, in the Revolution, 29; aide-de-camp, 333; defends Virginia, 355; troops, 406.
Lake Champlain, British on, 286.
Lake Erie, 30, 165.
Lake George, expeditions on, 286–87.
Lake Oneida (N. Y.), 287.
Lake Ontario, post on, 54; drowning in, 374; route via, 390.
Lake Superior, French posts on, 176.
La Luzerne, Delaware chief, message from, 275; faithful to Americans, 399; sketch, 275.
La Luzerne, Anne César, chevalier de, French minister, 200, 275; sketch, 200–1.
Lambert, Philip, Loyalist, 254; safe conduct for, 256.
Lamme, John, at Pittsburgh, 368.
Lan, Isaac, at Pittsburgh, 369.
Lancaster (Pa.), 189, 338.
Lancaster County (Pa.), 109, 421.
Lanctot, Major. See Linctot.
Lancy, Daniel, discharged, 455–56.
Lands, speculators in, 131.
Lane, John, private, 442.
Lane, Joseph, tried and acquitted, 440–41.
Lapandier, Lewis, Indian rescuer, 199–200.
Lapland, John, private, 445.
Lapoley, Thomas, at Pittsburgh, 369.
Laramie Creek (Ohio), 185.
Latimore, James, court-martialed, 428; acquitted, 429.
Laughlin, ——, mill burned, 188.
Lawer, Andrew, trial for Loyalism, 260.
Lawer, Henry, trial for Loyalism, 260.
Lawrence, Jacob, private, 469.
Laybrook. See Lybrook.
Layson, John, at Pittsburgh, 369.

INDEX

Lazier, Hyatt, court-martialed, 432, 450; part of sentence remitted, 450–51; acquitted, 432.
Lea, William, at Pittsburgh, 369.
Lead mines, in Virginia, 23–26, 143–45, 155, 197, 251; garrison at, 195, 212, 217, 236; danger for, 196, 209, 237, 241, 253; prisoners kept at, 211, 216, 252; trials at, 251–52.
Leatherwood, Henry's estate, 264.
Lebanon (Ohio), 83.
Le Bœuf River. See French Creek.
Lee, Andrew, at Pittsburgh, 368.
Lee, Henry, Kentucky settler, 304; sketch, 304.
Lee, William, sergeant, 484; testimony, 485–89.
Leech, Capt. James, 493.
Leesburgh (Va.), 151.
Leet, Daniel, sub-lieutenant of Washington, 403; sketch, 403.
Leet, Isaac, son, 403.
Leet, Jonathan, interviewed, 403.
Leet, William, 493; fine remitted, 425.
Lefler, Capt. Jacob, on Coshocton expedition, 376, 468; at courts-martial, 425–30; company, 428; roll of, 468; acquitted, 430.
Lemon, James, sergeant-major on Coshocton expedition, 461–63.
Lernoult, Capt. Richard B., commandant at Detroit, 94.
Letcher, ——, murdered by Loyalists, 236.
Lewis, an Indian. See Lapandier, Lewis.
Lewis, Capt. Aaron, opposes Loyalists, 196, 237; information from, 391; sketch, 196.
Lewis, Gen. Andrew, letters, 50, 243–44; sketch, 50.
Lewis, Lieut. Andrew, charges against, 445; acquitted, 446.
Lewis, Griffith, Loyalist, 254.
Lewis, John, Delaware chief, 340.
Lewis, Meriwether, explorer, 196.
Lewis, Miriam, married, 167.
Lewis, Philip, at Pittsburgh, 368.

Lewis, Thomas, boundary commissioner, 107–8.
Lewis and Clark expedition, 267.
Lexington (Ky.), danger at, 292–93; sketch, 292.
Library of Congress, material from, 9, 35, 311. See also Washington Papers.
Lichtenau, Moravian mission village, 161; Indian name for, 399; laid waste, 377, 399.
Lickenburgh, George, at Pittsburgh, 369.
Licking River (Ky.), 185; post for planned, 19, 51; Bird's expedition on, 20, 22, 249, 266; Rogers at, 88–89, 91; rendezvous at mouth, 246.
Ligonier (Pa.), 150; raided, 188.
Ligonier Valley (Pa.), raids in, 414.
Linch, Anthony, private, 465.
Lincoln, Abraham, opposition to, 58.
Lincoln, Gen. Benjamin, 100.
Lincoln County (Ky.), 137, 167, 268.
Lincolnton (N. C.), battle near, 210.
Linctot, the elder, death, 176.
Linctot, Daniel Maurice Godefroy de, French agent, 29–30, 176–77, 189, 200, 231; council at Fort Pitt, 201; negotiations, 190, 193, 218–19, 275; letter mentioned, 271, 275–76; life threatened, 273–74; British demand, 375; letters to, 214, 234, 265, 305; letter, 274–75; sketch, 176.
Linley, Caleb, private, 467.
Linley, Joseph, private, 467.
Linley, Zanes, private, 467.
Linn, Andrew, information from, 94.
Linn, Dr. Andrew Johnson, information from, 94.
Linn, Col. William, New Orleans expedition, 17, 81; at Rogers' defeat, 94; sketch, 94.
Lintot, Bernard, at Natchez, 176.
Lisnit, Christain, at Pittsburgh, 369.
Lisnit, Francis, at Pittsburgh, 369.
Lititz (Pa.), 338.

Little, James, at Pittsburgh, 369.
Little Beaver Creek, 151, 207, 219.
Little Holston River, 196.
Little Kanawha River, post planned for, 19, 82, 192; buffalo hunted near, 301, 303.
Little Miami River, fight at mouth, 17–18, 116.
Little Redstone (Pa.), 280.
Little River (S. C.), battle on, 392.
Little River (Va.), Loyalists on, 251.
Liveer, Adam, enlists, 261.
Livingston County (N. Y.), 53.
Lloyd, Capt.-Lieut. James, member of court at Fort Pitt, 484.
Lloyd's *London Evening Post*, 93.
Locke, Col. Francis, defeats Loyalists, 211.
Lockhart, Capt. Patrick, at Loyalists' trials, 257, 259, 262–63; letter, 244; sketch, 244.
Lochry, Col. Archibald, lieutenant of Westmoreland County, 235, 280, 372; relations with Brodhead, 95, 108, 125–26, 393, 418; plans to go with Clark, 408–9 416, 418; defeat, 418; letters to, 39, 98, 108, 121, 125–26, 164, 168, 174, 179, 182–83, 188, 214, 249, 270, 272, 348–49, 352, 393, 418; letters, 20–21, 121, 125–26, 170, 188, 265, 371, 385, 397, 415–16; sketch, 39.
Lochry, Capt. William, militia officer, 235.
Lockwood, Benjamin, 493.
Logan, ———, captured, 41.
Logan, Adam, at Pittsburgh, 368.
Logan, Capt. Benjamin, in Shawnee expedition, 266.
Logan, James, at Pittsburgh, 367.
Logan County (Ky.), 196.
Logstown, an Indian site, 180.
Lomax, Thomas, 264.
London, medical college in, 306.
Long Hunters, explorations of, 196.
Long Island (N. Y.), battle of, 310.
Lorimier, Louis, trader, 185.
Loskiel, G. H., *History of the Mission of the United Brethren*, 161.

Lossing, Benson, *Field Book of the Revolution*, 80.
Louder. See Lowther.
Loudoun County (Va.), 126, 319, 373.
Louisiana, Spanish in, 81, 83; governor of, 129–30; Morgan's colony in, 385.
Louisville (Ky.), 18, 87–88, 92–93, 163, 179, 193, 246; letter from, 103; troops at, 195; officers, 230; trustee of, 310; settlers, 335. See also Falls of Ohio.
Lowellville (Ohio), 205.
Loyal Land Company, grants, 237.
Loyalists (Tories), on the frontier, 22–23, 303; near Fort Pitt, 277, 285, 302, 352–54, 389–90, 416–17, 491; in Georgia, 391; New York, 47, 52–54, 78, 286–87, 388; North Carolina, 210–11; Southwest Virginia, 23–28, 143–45, 155, 170, 195–98, 208–13, 215–17, 220–22, 227–29, 236–42, 244–45, 402; regiment of, 185; encouraged, 192; pardon offered to, 246–47; punishment of, 242, 244, 268; trials, 250–64; give bonds, 228–29; letter of, 201–2; attempt revenge, 27, 267–68.
Lowther, Maj. William, 493.
Luzerne Township (Pa.), 84.
Lybrook (Laybrook), Henry, trial of, 261; enlists, 262.
Lynch, Col. Charles, suppresses Loyalists, 27, 241, 250–52; letter, 250–52; sketch, 241.
Lynch law, origin of term, 241.
Lynch's Ferry (Va.), 131.
Lyne, Edmund, Virginia commissioner, 105.
Lyon, William, at Pittsburgh, 366.

McAdams, Alexander (William), private, 441; court-martialed, 457; reprieved, 458.
McAfee, Matthew, of Eighth Pennsylvania, 485–87.
McAfee, William (Billy), wounded, 266; sketch, 266.

INDEX

McAfee Brothers, Kentucky pioneers, 266.
McBride, James, pioneer, 199.
McBride, Henry, contract for rescuing captives, 199.
McBride, Thomas, at Pittsburgh, 369.
McCabe, R. B., collector, 382.
McCaffey, Charles, court-martialed, 440–41.
McCandlass Township (Pa.), 270.
McCann, John, at Pittsburgh, 368.
McCartney, Jeremiah, discharged, 446.
McCarty, Capt. Edward, 493.
McCauley, Nancy, Brodhead's mistress, 118; accusations against, 356.
McCinney, John, ranger, 113.
McClean, Laughlin, private, 441.
McCleary, Col. William, militia officer, 278, 281, 284; letter, 279; sketch, 279.
McClellan, Capt. John, militia officer, 408; sketch, 408.
McCleod, Daniel, at Pittsburgh, 369.
McCloud, ——, soldier, 282.
McClure, David, militia officer, 110–11; at courts-martial, 427, 429–30; clerk, 429–30; on Coshocton expedition, 466; sketch, 110.
McColloch, Abraham, 493.
McColloch, David, interviewed, 399.
McColloch, George, Ohio County magistrate, 110–11; receipt, 344; sketch, 110.
McColloch Jr., John, 493; discharged, 397–98; private on Coshocton expedition, 465; sketch, 397–98.
McColloch, Maj. Samuel, 110, 493; on Brodhead's expedition, 58, 60, 461–63; petition, 82; at courts-martial, 425–30; killed by Indians, 397; sketch, 58.
McColloch family, residence, 110; fame as scouts, 397.
McConnell, Ensign Hugh, militia officer, 464.
McConnell, John, at Pittsburgh, 367.
McConnell, William, at Pittsburgh, 368.
McCord, Samuel, refused discharge, 456.
McCorkle, Capt. James, militia officer, 213, 251–52; accused of Loyalism, 254; sketch, 213.
McCormack, James, at Pittsburgh, 369.
McCormick, Alexander, sketch, 153.
McCormick, Mrs. Alexander. See Turner, Elizabeth.
McCormick, John, private, 464.
McCormick, John, recollections, 153–54.
McCracken, James, at Pittsburgh, 367.
McCue, William, at Pittsburgh, 368.
McCullough, ——, land dispute, 118.
McCune, John, at Pittsburgh, 368.
McCune, Joseph, at Pittsburgh, 367.
McDaid, Hugh, at Pittsburgh, 366.
McDermott, Joseph, 493.
McDonald, Edward, enlists, 258.
McDonald, John, at Pittsburgh, 367, 369.
McDonald, John, Loyalist, 222, 247; warrant for, 228; gives bond, 228; trial of, 259.
McDonald, John, Ohio County militiaman, exempt, 430.
McDonald, Joseph, tried for Loyalism, 258.
McDonald Jr., Joseph, enlists, 258.
McDowell, Joseph, at Pittsburgh, 369.
McDowell, Joseph (Quaker Jo), defeats Loyalists, 211; sketch, 211.
McDowell, William, tried and acquitted, 440–41.
McElroy, Patrick, on Rogers' expedition, 83, 90.
McFarlan, Joseph, Loyalist, 254.
McFarland, John, 205.
McFarlin, Daniel, private, 467.
McFarren, Robert, at Pittsburgh, 368.
McGary, Capt. Hugh, Kentucky officer, 246.

528 INDEX

McGavock, Lieut. ———, 493.
McGavock, James, letter, 208; house, 250; accused of Loyalism, 254; sketch, 208.
McGee, Bartley, private, 465.
McGee, James, gives bond, 228-29.
McGee, Robert, gives bond, 228-29; trial for Loyalism, 259; gives parole, 262.
McGill, James, private, 465.
McGuire, Capt. Francis, 493; private on Coshocton expedition, 465.
McGuire, Patrick, tried and acquitted, 432.
McIlwaine, Francis, orders for, 79, 99; relieved, 98.
Machingwe Keesuch (Great Moon), Brodhead's Indian title, 44, 46, 66-67, 71, 73, 75, 97, 105, 132, 135, 139, 166, 172, 183, 190, 192, 217, 220, 233, 272, 295, 315-17, 329, 331, 339, 341; signs for, 296, 298, 299, 329, 342.
McHingwe Pushees, Delaware chief. See Big Cat.
McIntire, Capt. Thomas. See McIntyre.
McIntire, William, 493; quartermaster on Coshocton expedition, 461-63.
McIntosh, Gen. Lachlan, at Fort Pitt, 42, 61, 365, 403; expedition, 184, 373.
McIntyre, Capt. Thomas, 493; on command, 181, 400; defeats Indians, 223-26, 275; thanks for, 248; company of, 76; on leave, 284; on entertainment committee, 449; reprimanded, 454; apology for, 450; messenger, 100, 108; letters to, 142, 151; sketch, 76.
McKee, Alexander, Loyalist, letters to, 140, 374-75; building post, 273; reward for capture, 299.
McKee, David, at Pittsburgh, 367, 369.
McKee, James, at Pittsburgh, 369.
McKee, John, at Pittsburgh, 369.
McKee's Island. See Brunot's.

McKeever, ———, mentioned, 154.
McKeever, Nancy, mentioned, 153.
McKennie, Mathew, at Pittsburgh, 366.
Mackinac (Michelemcanaugh), news from, 230; British post, 19, 104; commandant, 16, 440; expedition from, 19-20, 186.
McKinear, Charles, at Pittsburgh, 369.
McKinley, Robert, at Pittsburgh, 362, 367.
McKinley, Samuel, at Pittsburgh, 368.
McKinney, John, private, 445.
McKnight, John, fined, 426.
McLauchlin, James, at Pittsburgh, 369.
McLelland, James, at Pittsburgh, 363, 366.
McMahon, Maj. William, 494.
McNab, Robert, at Pittsburgh, 368.
McNabb, George, at Pittsburgh, 368.
McNulty, Joseph, captured, 403-5.
McPherson, John, tried and acquitted, 432.
McQueen, Thomas, at Pittsburgh, 369.
Macquichees Indians. See Mequochoke Indians.
McVaw, Edward, private, 467.
McVaw, Isaac, private, 467.
Madison, Gabriel, in Kentucky, 266; letter, 167; sketch, 167.
Madison, James, Virginia congressman, 130.
Madison, Rev. James, boundary commissioner, 107.
Madison, John, sons, 167.
Madison Jr., John, surveyor, 167; killed by Indians, 379; sketch, 167.
Madison, Richard, orders for, 167; sketch, 167.
Madison, Capt. Thomas, merchant, 305; letter to, 264; sketch, 264.
Madison, William, letter to, 167; sketch, 167.
Madison County (Ky.), 196.

INDEX

Madrid, aid from, 85.
Magain, Philip, Loyalist, 417.
Magazine of American History, 43, 55.
Magnor, Henry, at Pittsburgh, 368.
Mahanaim, Christian's estate, 128, 267.
Mahican Indians, converted, 119, 320; hostile, 157, 159.
Mahoning County (Ohio), 205.
Mahoning Creek, expedition on, 55–56; scouting on, 174; site on, 205–7; residents of, 382; sketch, 55.
Mahusquechikoken (Kiskakoquille), Indian village, 55; burned, 57, 61.
Maitland, M., private, 465.
Malott, Catherine, married, 163–64.
Malott, Joseph (Peter, Theodore), family captured, 163–64.
Malott, Keziah, married, 164.
Malott, Peter, captured, 163; settled in Canada, 164.
Malott, Theodore, captured, 163; later life, 164.
Malott family, attack on, 162–64.
Mamawókunund, Delaware chief, 44.
Manchac (La.), British post, 84–85; captured by Spanish, 129–30, 165.
Manes, George, discharged, 441.
Marchand, Capt. David, 494.
Marietta (Ohio), Indian killed at, 380.
Marion, Gen. Francis, in South Carolina, 402.
Markland, William, fined, 425.
Marlough, William, court-martialed, 438.
Marshall, Humphrey, duelist, 310.
Marshall, William, at Pittsburgh, 367.
Marshall County (W. Va.), 108.
Marshel, Col. James, magistrate, strictures against, 419; letter to, 418; letter, 403; sketch, 403.
Martain, George, at Pittsburgh, 367.
Martin, Daniel, at Pittsburgh, 368.
Martin, F. X., *History of Louisiana*, 81.

Martin, Dr. Hugh, at Pittsburgh, 306–7, 335; sketch, 306.
Martin, Jesse, fined, 426.
Martin, John, at Pittsburgh, 368.
Martin Jr., John, at Pittsburgh, 368.
Martin, Jonathan, at Pittsburgh, 369.
Martin, Gen. Joseph, cabin, 51, 192; information from, 391; proposal, 392; sketch, 391.
Martin, Capt. William, 494; artillery officer, 413; member of court-martial, 484; sketch, 413.
Martinsburgh (Va.), 126.
Martin's Fort (Va.), raided, 269.
Martin's Station (Ky.), captured, 20, 220, 266.
Maryland, pioneers from, 58, 193; residents, 163, 174; militia requisitioned, 405.
Maryland Journal, 56, 269.
Maryland Regiment, at Fort Pitt, 41, 116, 118–19, 174, 309, 314–15, 335–36, 344, 347, 400, 438–39, 442, 447, 453–54.
Mason, Col. David, case of, 287.
Mason, George, mentioned, 131.
Mason (Meason), Isaac, letter, 413; sketch, 413.
Mason, Capt. Samuel, 494; at courts-martial, 427, 429.
Mason and Dixon's line, authorized boundary, 280.
Mason County (Ky.), 304.
Massachusetts, Indians of, 345.
Mathews, Rev. ——, letter to, 338.
Mathews, Daniel, at Pittsburgh, 367.
Matthews, Paul, at Pittsburgh, 369.
Maumee Rapids, trading post at, 153.
Maumee (Omey) River, Indian name, 158; portage from, 185; expedition on, 185, 192, 319; trading post, 299.
Mawquot, Delaware envoy, 339.
Maxwell, Alexander, at Pittsburgh, 367.
Maxwell, Capt. James, killed, 155.

34

Maxwell, Thomas, at Pittsburgh, 367.
Maxwell (Va.), 155.
Maxwell's Gap (Va.), 155.
May, Capt. ——, militia officer, 244.
May, Capt. John, information from, 195; sketch, 195.
Maynard, John, tried and acquitted, 454.
Maysville (Ky.), 304.
Mead, Henry, at Pittsburgh, 367.
Meadville (Pa.), site, 61.
Means, Francis, 494.
Means, Capt. Isaac, 494.
Meason, Isaac. See Mason.
Mechmewocunund, Delaware Indian, 273.
Meek, Jeremiah, at Pittsburgh, 367.
Meek, William, captured by Indians, 354–55.
Meeks, ——, Loyalist, 236.
Meeks, Isaac, adjutant, on Coshocton expedition, 461–63.
Menate, John, at Pittsburgh, 368.
Mequochoke Indians, Shawnee branch, seek American alliance, 16, 56, 73–76; message, 139; sketch, 73.
Mercer County (Ky.), 87, 167.
Meriwether, George, land commissioner, 118–19.
Merrick, John, deserter, 447.
Metcalf, Allen, 494.
Miami Indians, village, 200; expedition against, 345; kill La Balme, 375.
Michelemcanaugh. See Mackinac.
Michigan Pioneer and Historical Collections, 16, 40, 94, 111, 185, 191, 220, 223, 271, 275, 373, 381, 417–18.
Mickey, Lieut. Daniel, at Fort Pitt, 459.
Michilimackinac. See Mackinac.
Middlebrook (N. J.), headquarters, 451.
Middleburg (N. Y.), attacked, 287.
Middleton Township (Pa.), 285.
Milburn, William, exempt, 430; on Coshocton expedition, 465.

Miles, Isaac, exemption for, 426.
Miles, Thomas, at Pittsburgh, 369.
Miles's Rifle Battalion, 310.
Mill (Pond) Creek, at Cincinnati, 93.
Miller, Cornelius, sergeant, 467.
Miller, David, private, 445.
Miller, Elizabeth, married, 83.
Miller, Francis, sergeant, 468.
Miller Jr., Jacob, fined, 426; private on Coshocton expedition, 468.
Miller, James, private, 464.
Miller, John, at Pittsburgh, 367.
Miller, John, ranger, 113.
Miller, Lieut. John, on Coshocton expedition, 467.
Miller, Oliver, at Pittsburgh, 367.
Miller Jr., Oliver, at Pittsburgh, 367.
Miller, Robert, at Pittsburgh, 369.
Miller, Thomas, at Pittsburgh, 367.
Miller, William, at Pittsburgh, 367.
Mills, John, 494.
Mills, Lieut. John, member of court, 477.
Mills, Joseph, killed by Indians, 379.
Mills, Thomas, private, 466, 494.
Milon, Charles, at Pittsburgh, 367.
Mingo Indians, territory invaded, 14–16, 40–44, 55–66, 94–95, 110; hostile raids, 17, 56, 65, 105, 109, 157, 162, 176, 179–81, 275–76; killed, 53, 74; towns, 55, 189, 275; influence, 67, 218, 339; intertribal relations, 189, 193, 218, 299, 301, 303, 314, 342; spurn message from Americans, 275. See also Seneca Indians.
Mingo Bottom (O.), 275.
Minor, Don Estevan, Spanish officer, 176.
Minor family, residence, 177.
Mississippi River, French posts on, 176; Spanish posts on, 15, 19–20, 123; British posts captured, 19, 129–30, 147; expeditions on, 17, 81, 83–86, 88–89, 195, 299; fur traders, 164, 176; boundary touches, 186.
Mississippi Valley Historical Association *Proceedings*, 130.

INDEX

Mitchell, ——, speculator, 129.
Mitchell, Alexander, at Pittsburgh, 366.
Mitchell, Lieut. Charles, 494.
Mitchell, Capt. Hugh, 494.
Mitchell, James, at Pittsburgh, 368; private on Coshocton expedition, 465.
Mitchell, Capt. John, at Fort Henry, 322, 427; member of court-martial, 427–30; company, 428.
Mitchell, Col. John, 102.
Mitchell, Nathaniel, 494.
Mobile (Ala.), captured by Spanish, 19, 130.
Mohawk Indians, at Niagara, 50.
Mohawk Valley (N. Y.), expeditions in, 47, 78, 248.
Mohican Indians. See Mahican Indians.
Monks Corner (S. C.), 402.
Monmouth (N. J.), battle of, 307, 335, 392.
Monongahela River, sites on, 84, 88, 350, 413; state of water, 249; settlers on, 119, 373, 379, 385; emigrant boats, 163; raid on, 269–70, 274; forks of, 270; militia from, 373, 469.
Monongalia County (Va.), officers, 178; militia from, 146, 168, 373, 376, 400; muster roll of, 373, 469; troops from for Clark, 409; raids in, 95, 107, 173, 270, 279; letter from, 167.
Monsy Indians. See Munsee Indians.
Montesquieu, Charles de Secondat, baron de la Brède et de, *Spirit of Laws*, cited, 365.
Montgomery, Capt. James, opposes Loyalists, 196; sketch, 196.
Montgomery, Capt. John, in Illinois, 127, 319; sketch, 319.
Montgomery County (Va.), residents, 217, 252; lead mines in, 23; troops from, 51, 194, 237, 240; troops commended, 241; Loyalists in, 24–27, 143–45, 170, 195–98, 202, 209, 212–13, 215–17, 220–22, 236–42; official trials for, 254–64; letter from, 241.
Montour, Andrew, kinswoman, 95.
Montour, Catherine, chieftess, 95–96.
Montour, John, Delaware chief, 54, 495; life threatened, 338, 343; on Brodhead's expeditions, 58, 399; messenger, 70, 340, 342, 345; kinspeople, 95, 219, 233; hostile to Mingo, 299, 301; sketch, 55.
Montour's Island, in the Ohio, 176.
Montour's Run (Pa.), 207.
Montreal, Loyalists at, 78, 389; merchants, 86; reported expedition from, 169, 286; garrison, 248.
Moon, Lieut. ——, 494.
Mooney, Patrick, private, 445.
Mooney, William, at Pittsburgh, 366.
Moore, ——, treasurer of Virginia, 130.
Moore, David, at Pittsburgh, 363, 367.
Moore, Henry, exemption for, 426; revoked, 429.
Moore, James, emigrant, 156.
Moore Jr., Capt. James, frontiersman, 156; militia officer, 216.
Moore, Capt. James Francis, commissary, 310, 317; at Fort Pitt, 459; sketch, 310.
Moore, John, deserter, 453.
Moore, Col. John, North Carolina Loyalist, 210.
Moore, Capt. Peter, 494.
Moore, Robert, private, 464.
Moore, William, tried and acquitted, 442.
Moorhead, Capt. Samuel, company, 94, 126; sketch, 94.
Moravian Indians, conditions among, 162; speak German, 381; protection of, 339, 378; information from, 380; assist Brodhead, 34, 119–20, 231–32, 343, 377, 399–400; hunt for provisions, 31, 300, 320; provisions for sale, 321, 323, 325–26; massacre of, 300; relapse into paganism, 381.

532 INDEX

Moravian missionaries, 117, 119, 161, 232, 320; information from, 18, 31, 33, 120, 133, 168–69, 344, 346–47, 372, 400; mission villages, 56, 161, 190, 275; invited to remove, 134, 169, 377, 380; removal, 159, 161–62; aid French agents, 274; converts among, 300, 316–17, 330; church synod, 372; threatened, 380–81.
Mores, James. See Moore Jr., James.
Morgan Jr., ——, Loyalist, 247.
Morgan, Abel, at Pittsburgh, 369.
Morgan, Abraham, Loyalist, 222; trial of, 259.
Morgan, Anne, married, 333.
Morgan, Charles, at Pittsburgh, 369.
Morgan, Gen. Daniel, brigade, 215.
Morgan, Col. George, commissary, 42, 135; Indian name, 47; son-in-law, 333; Louisiana enterprise, 385; letters to, 16, 22, 77; sketch, 42.
Morgan, Nathaniel, Loyalist, 347.
Morgan, Capt. Simon, commandant at Fort McIntosh, 103; storekeeper, 433; letter to, 142; sketch, 103.
Morgan, Zackwell, 494.
Morris, William, private, 467.
Morrison, Ensign James, on scouting expedition, 404, 406; member of court, 484; at Fort Pitt, 459.
Morrison, Col. James, of Kentucky, 404.
Morrison, William, sergeant, 464.
Morristown (N. J.), headquarters, 123, 147–48.
Mount Braddock (Pa.), 82, 413.
Mounts, Thomas, 494.
Mouse Knife, Delaware warrior, 340.
Muddy Creek (Pa.), residents, 49, 160; sketch, 49.
Muhlenberg, Gen. John Peter Gabriel, letter to, 268; sketch, 268.
Munro, Andrew, at Pittsburgh, 369.
Munsee (Monsey, Muncie) Indians, wolf tribe, 132; war parties, 44, 56, 60–61, 157, 159, 162–63, 272–

73, 275; Allegheny villages, 55–56, 59–61, 63; routed, 95, 100; peace overtures, 101; information from, 189; intertribal relations, 301; sketch, 44.
Murdock, William, at Pittsburgh, 369.
Murphy, John, private, 464.
Murphy, Patrick, 494.
Murphy, Samuel, recollections, 206.
Murray, Daniel, court-martialed, 439–40.
Murray, Heath, court-martialed, 437.
Murray, Hugh, at Pittsburgh, 369.
Muskingum River, 184; trespassers on, 22, 107; Indian towns, 33, 401; mission villages, 161; scout to, 181; expedition to, 381.

NAILOR, Ralph, captured, 163–64.
Nanowland (George Wilson), Delaware Indian, on Brodhead's expeditions, 60, 399, 495; commission for, 183; sketch, 60.
Naradago. See Yoghroonwago.
Na-tah-go-ah (Captain Crow), Seneca chief, 62–63.
Natchez, British post, 85, 89; plans to capture, 111–12, 121, 124, 147; captured by Spanish, 129–30, 147, 165; residents, 176, 231, 380.
Natchitoches (La.), route via, 85–86.
Nazareth (Pa.), 404.
Neal, Capt. William. See Neil, Capt. William.
Nechnawalend, Delaware messenger, 173.
Neeley, William, at Loyalists' trials, 258; sketch, 258.
Neely, Benjamin. See Neilly.
Neeshawsh, Mahican warrior, 157, 159.
Neil (Neal), Capt. William, opposes Loyalists, 196; sketch, 196.
Neilly (Neely), Lieut. Benjamin, 459; at Fort Henry, 409; seniority of service, 431; distributes clothing, 452; sketch, 409.

INDEX

Nellerfield, William, at Pittsburgh, 367.
Neville, Col. John, at Pittsburgh, 176; son, 333.
Neville, Presley, messenger, 333; sketch, 333.
New Gnadenhütten, Moravian mission village, 161.
New Haven (Pa.), founder, 413.
New Jersey, headquarters in, 208; residents, 210, 278, 403; recruits from, 406.
New Orleans, supplies from, 17, 81–87, 123; expedition from, 19, 88, 129–30; Wetzel at, 380.
New River (Va.), Loyalists on, 23, 27, 170, 196, 198, 210, 212–13, 215, 217, 236–42, 251, 254; Indian raid on, 354–55.
New Salem (Ohio), Moravian village, 300.
New Schönbrunn, Moravian mission village, 161.
New Store (Pa.), as a rendezvous, 413, 417; sketch, 413.
New Windsor (N. Y.), Washington's headquarters, 311, 314, 340, 383–84, 388–90, 393–95, 405, 407, 470.
New York (city), rumored capture, 202, 265; evacuated by British, 272, 286; prize port, 320; Loyalists at, 388.
New York (state), boundary, 15, 54, 59; movement from proposed, 140; Loyalists in, 47, 52–54, 78, 185; raids in, 248, 286–87; Indians migrate from, 52, 345; Burgoyne in, 374; recruits from, 406.
Newcomer's town, Delaware village, 377, 379, 382, 399.
Newell, James, pioneer, 420.
Newland, John, Loyalist, 255.
Newport (Ky.), 83.
Newtown, battle of, 48, 53.
Niagara, British post at, 15–16, 63, 116–17; garrison, 135; siege of, 65; commandant, 47, 374; importance of, 326; refugee Indians at, 50, 62, 65, 96, 100, 112–13,

141, 189; endangered, 78; plan to capture, 333; peace mission to, 100; invasion from, 135–36, 272, 322, 400; illness at, 189, 192; letters from, 140–41, 374–75.
Nicholas, ——, Loyalist, 236.
Nicholas, Thomas, at Pittsburgh, 369.
Nichols, Thomas, at Pittsburgh, 363.
Nicholson, Joseph, with Brodhead, 58–60; sketch, 58.
Nicholson, Thomas, sketch, 58.
Niel, John, at Pittsburgh, 369.
Nigswonger, Peter, private, 465.
Nimwha, Shawnee chief, 73; death, 139; sketch, 73.
Ninety-six (S. C.). See Fort Ninety-six.
Ningaracharie, Indian site, 54.
Ninth Virginia Regiment, at Fort Pitt, 277, 326; supersedes the Thirteenth, 40, 309, 313; commandant, 289; officers, 119, 157, 168, 282, 288, 335, 344, 406, 445, 455; list of, 460; privates, 437, 439, 442, 445–48, 450–53, 455, 457; terms of service, 120, 147, 149; additions to, 94, 120, 310; changes in, 314, 318, 326, 335; deserter from, 332; enlistments for, 122; supplies for, 142; garrisons posts, 103, 112, 313, 336.
Noble, Henry, pioneer, 58.
Nolan, Philip, wife, 177.
Nolichucky River, Loyalists on, 254–55.
Norris, Maj. James, journal, 49.
North Carolina, Loyalists in, 23, 25–27, 143, 170, 197–98, 210–11, 239–40, 251, 268; British conquer, 25, 27, 286; boundary, 236; surveyed, 142, 186, 245; forces in, 209; Moravians in, 232; Indians threaten, 245, 402; ratifying convention, 210.
North Strabane Township (Pa.), 170.
North Union Township (Pa.), 278.
Nova Scotia, 140.

INDEX

Nunns, Annie A., acknowledgements to, 10.
Nye, Andrew, at Pittsburgh, 368.

OANACKADAGO, Indian site, 53.
Oar, Thomas, private, 465.
Oats, Henry, at Pittsburgh, 368.
Oats, Roger, Loyalist leader, 250, 252–54.
O'Bail, Charles, recollections, 62–63.
Ogle, H., assassin, 222.
Ogle, Capt. Joseph, on Coschocton expedition, 376, 398, 420, 464; company, 425, 427–28, 430, 464–66; at courts-martial, 425–30; drum for, 427; sketch, 420.
Ogle, Thomas, at Pittsburgh, 368.
O'Hara, Hugh, at Pittsburgh, 367.
O'Hara, Capt. James, company, 94, 115, 120, 441; glassworks, 176; sketch, 94.
O'Hara, Patrick, at Pittsburgh, 369.
Ohio Archæological and Historical Publications, 161; *Quarterly*, 379.
Ohio County (Va.), officers, 82, 106, 425–30; county lieutenant, 113; militia called out, 98, 110–11, 169, 178, 182, 270, 275, 278, 281, 343, 348–49, 400, 427; troops for Clark, 350, 409, 414; raided, 173; militia commended, 371; residents, 397; courts-martial, 425–30;militia rolls, 461–68.
Ohio River, route via, 266, 270, 293; posts on, 280, 313, 415; as a boundary, 403; frontier line, 18–19, 22, 51, 97, 104, 131, 184, 195, 243, 331; hunting on, 300; lands on, 305; Indians cross, 152, 180, 219, 225–26; prisoners cross, 151; emigrants attacked on, 160, 162–64, 167–68, 175, 200; expeditions on, 81, 83–84, 87–89, 376–77, 400; Rogers' defeat on, 17–18, 90–93, 105, 185; Wyandot defeat on, 31, 223–26; scouting on, 180, 246.
Ohio Valley, British propose to conquer, 19, 230.

Old Crossfire, Indian, killed, 380.
Old Town (Md.), merchant, 82, 91; provisions from, 271, 324.
Old Town (Ohio), Indian village, 152.
Oldham County (Ky.), 288.
Omey River. See Maumee River.
O'Neal, Ferrol, deserter, 442.
Oneida Indians, accompany Sullivan, 49; aid Americans, 345, 347; remove to Wisconsin, 52, 345; sketch, 345.
Onondaga Indians, at Niagara, 50.
Ontario (Can.), Loyalists in, 52.
Opelousas (La.), route via, 85.
Orange (N. J.), Washington's headquarters, 248.
Orange County (N. Y.), 288.
Orangeburg (S. C.), 402.
O'Reilly, Alexandro, governor of Louisiana, 81.
Orr, Gen. Robert, recollections, 404.
Osborne, Capt. ——, militia officer, 237, 240.
Osburn, Edward, private, 467.
Osburn, Samuel, at Pittsburgh, 366.
Oswego (N. Y.), British post, 48, 140, 287.
Ottawa Indians, attitude toward Americans, 40, 43.
Ottawa River, Loyalists on, 185.
Ouitanon, fur-trade post, 176.
Overhill Cherokee, expedition against, 391.
Owen, Christopher, at Pittsburgh, 369.
Owens, Capt. George, 494.
Owens, William, at Pittsburgh, 368.
Oweny, Richard, Loyalist, 247, 254.
Ozark River. See Arkansas River.

PAINT Creek (Va.), 355.
Pakeeland, Delaware chief. See Pekelend.
Palfrey, Col. William, paymaster-general, 101.
Parchment, Peter, 494.
Paris (Tenn.), 355.
Parker, Charles, court-martialed, 454.
Parker, John, ranger, 113.

INDEX

Parkinson, David, at Pittsburgh, 367.
Parks, James, at Pittsburgh, 367.
Parsons, Capt. Baldwin, 494.
Passaic County (N. J.), 290.
Passaic Falls (N. J.), headquarters, 282, 286.
Paterson (N. J.), 290.
Patrick, Jeremiah, accused of Loyalism, 259; enlists, 263.
Patterson, Col. Robert, founder of Lexington (Ky.), 292.
Patterson, Thomas, at Pittsburgh, 369.
Patterson, William, horses stolen, 155.
Patton, Capt. Henry, 494; militia officer, 213; sketch, 213.
Paul, Edward, private, 445.
Paul, Jacob, private, 466.
Paul, Lieut. James, 494; statement, 82.
Peach Bottom, Cox's estate, 237.
Peak (Peek) Creek, Loyalists on, 212, 267; sketch, 212.
Pearl, Polly, married, 268.
Peek, Presley, captured, 420.
Peek Creek. See Peak Creek.
Pekelend (Pakeeland), Delaware chief, 132–35; robbed, 157; with Brodhead's Coshocton expedition, 378.
Pemberton, George, accused of Loyalism, 255.
Pemowagen, Wyandot chief. See Half King.
Pendergrass' Station (Pa.), 404–5.
Pendleton, Nathaniel, son, 126.
Pendleton, Philip, land commissioner, 118, 126; sketch, 126.
Penn, William, Delaware chief, 295–98; message to, 299, 328–29, 341; message from, 315–16; kinsmen, 340.
Penn Township (Pa.), 414.
Pennington, Isaac, private, 465.
Pennsylvania, boundary dispute, 22, 33, 107–8, 127–28, 167, 170, 235, 279–80, 284, 361, 403, 419, 421; boundary line, 393, 403, 410, 419; chief justice, 81; constitutional convention, 293, 386; officers, 174, 290, 307; executive council, 385; bill of rights, 361; defense of frontier, 21, 176, 180, 390; troops, 109, 314, 337; bounties for, 76, 95, 108, 392; militia, 61, 405; scalp bounties, 176, 183–84, 357; authorizes impressment, 31, 235, 276, 284; requisitions for, 287–88, 348, 384, 387; aids Clark's expedition, 32–34, 351–52, 397–98, 408–10, 414–16, 418; commends Zeisberger, 372.
Pennsylvania Archives, 16, 21–23, 34, 39–44, 55, 76, 78, 94–95, 98–99, 103, 106–9, 111–22, 125–26, 134–36, 142, 146, 150–51, 156, 164–65, 168–69, 171, 174–83, 188, 202, 214, 223, 234–35, 249, 265, 270–74, 276–81, 285, 290, 303, 319, 324, 332, 337, 347, 349, 351–52, 354, 370, 372, 385, 388, 392, 399, 401, 406, 413–15, 418–19, 421.
Pennsylvania Colonial Records, 58.
Pennsylvania Historical Society Bulletin, 157.
Pennsylvania Magazine of History and Biography, 389.
Pennsylvania road, route described, 150; dangerous, 181.
Pensacola (Fla.), British post, 19, 129–30; captured by Spanish, 402.
Pentecost, Dorsey, opposes Marshel, 403, 419; letter, 419; sketch, 403.
Peoria (Ill.), fur-trade post, 164; Linctot at, 176.
Pepper, Samuel, tried for Loyalism, 263.
Pepper family, in Virginia, 247.
Perrault, Joseph François, fur trader, 86–87; sketch, 86; memorial, 87.
Perrault, Louis François, son, 86.
Perrin, ———, 494.
Perrin, William, private, 464.
Perry, Isaac, killed, 160.
Perry, Col. James, militia officer, 385; letter, 414; sketch, 385–86.
Perry, Col. John, commissary, 293, 349, 406; letter to, 288; information from, 372.

Person, Thomas, at Pittsburgh, 367.
Peters, Richard, letters to, 136, 174, 181, 276–77, 301, 324, 346, 353; letter, 146; sketch, 136.
Peterson, Lieut. Gabriel, 459; scouting, 39; express, 372; seniority of service, 431; on court, 455, 470; sketch, 39.
Peteson, Jacob, Loyalist, letter of, 201–2.
Petty, Serg. Edward, reduced to ranks, 447.
Peyton, Francis, land commissioner, 118, 126; sketch, 126.
Peyton, Valentine, son, 126.
Pgly, Jacob, at Pittsburgh, 368.
Philadelphia, United States capital, 33, 81, 98, 101, 126, 128, 200, 308, 326, 371–72, 374–75, 395, 400, 419; residents, 175, 306; Indians visit, 28, 45, 172, 201, 342, 348; Indian council at, 76; Brodhead visits, 399–401; letters from, 136, 269, 382, 387, 393, 397, 400–1.
Phillerpurn, George. See Fullerhorn, John.
Phillips, Hezekiah, trial of, 261.
Phillips, Capt. Isaac, deposition, 428; company, 429; private on Coshocton expedition, 465.
Phillips, John, court-martialed, 457.
Pickawee, Indian town. See Piqua.
Pickens, Gen. Andrew, besieges post, 402.
Pickering, Timothy, letters to, 43, 76–77, 109, 112, 116, 181, 202, 223, 271.
Pierce, James, private, 465.
Pigg, Elias, at Pittsburgh, 367.
Pipe, Captain, Delaware chief, 47, 97, 105, 157, 273; message, 132–33; message to, 134–35; at Detroit council, 217–19; Loyalist with, 299; sketch 47.
Piqua (Pickawee), Indian town, 266, 319.
Piqua Indians, Shawnee branch, 109.
Pitts, Lieut, ——, 494.
Pittyslvania County (Va.), troops from, 51.

Plaquemine (La.), Rogers at, 85.
Pluggy's Town (Tankhonnetick), Indians from, 109.
Poe, Andrew, 494.
Point Pleasant, battle, 87, 212, 230.
Pollock, James, at Carlisle, 81.
Pollock, Oliver, agent at New Orleans, 81, 83–84; on Galvez' expedition, 130; letters to, 86; memorial, 81.
Polson, Swain, Loyalist, 244; trial of, 259.
Pomeroy, Col. John, militia officer, 408; home raided, 371; sketch, 371.
Pond Creek. See Mill Creek.
Pond's Settlement (Ky.), 267, 293.
Poopickhoover, Joseph, Loyalist, 221.
Poor Jr., ——, Loyalist, 247.
Poor, Peter, Loyalist, 247.
Pope, William, at Pittsburgh, 367.
Poppecaughfer, Joseph, tried for Loyalism, 259.
Port Perry (Pa.), 386.
Port Washington (Ohio), 190.
Porter, Serg. Samuel, court-martialed, 431–32.
Postlethwaite, Capt. Samuel, quartermaster, 285.
Potawatomi Indians, attitude toward Americans, 40, 43; at Detroit, 297.
Potomac River, 82, 91, 110; south branch, 324, 379, 397.
Pourée, Eugène, dit Beausoleil, merchant, 86; sketch, 86.
Powell, Gen. Henry Watson, commandant at Niagara, 374; sketch, 374.
Powell, Levin, letter, 319; sketch, 319.
Powell, William, at Pittsburgh, 369.
Powell's Valley (Va.), post for, 19, 51, 192; exposed, 245; rangers in, 392; sketch, 51.
Power, Capt. Thomas, British officer, 53; sketch, 53.
Powers, William, 494.
Prairie du Chien (Wis.), 176.
Prather, Capt. Basil, of Eighth Pennsylvania, 459.

INDEX

Prater, Nathan, sergeant, 464.
Presbyterians, in Kentucky, 138; at Pittsburgh, 204; in Virginia, 137.
Presqu'isle, route via, 70.
Preston, John, witness, 229.
Preston, Gen. John S., owns manuscript, 240.
Preston, Col. William, county lieutenant, 255, 257, 262, 402; witness, 229; suppresses Loyalists, 24-27, 143-45, 227-29, 237, 242, 257-64; message to Loyalists, 220-22, 246-47, 256; reward for assassinating offered, 208, 222; letters to, 141, 155, 170, 186, 192, 194-95, 198, 208-11, 227, 236, 240-41, 244, 250-52, 265, 267, 304-5; letters, 143-44, 211-13, 215-16, 220-21, 241-42, 268; sketch, 141.
Price, David, enlists, 262.
Price, Michael, Loyalist, 23-24, 221; messenger, 227; Loyalists' trials at house of, 252; letters to, 201-2, 220-22.
Prices, in Virginia, 128-29, 131, 138.
Prince William County (Va.), 126, 210.
Princeton College, students, 109, 137; graduates, 306; Indians at, 348.
Prisquille. See Presqu'isle.
Proctor, Col. John, sketch, 385.
Proctor, Col. Thomas, artillery officer, 175, 383, 390, 454.
Prophet, Shawnee chief, 119.
Pucketty Creek (Pa.), 404.
Pulaski, Count Casmir, in Revolution, 200.
Pulaski County (Va.), 236, 251.
Pumphrey, Nicholas, fined, 425.
Pumphrey, Rezin, fined, 425.
Pursley, David, 494.
Putnam, Gen. Israel, cited, 80.
Pyatt, Benjamin, private, 466.

QUAIFE, M. M., *Chicago and the Old Northwest*, 200.
Quaker Meadows (N. C.), 211.
Quarter House (S. C.), 402.

Quebec, British headquarters, 48; garrison, 248; prothonotary, 86; reported expedition from, 169, 388-89; rumor of capture, 296; prisoners at, 307.
Queen, Charles, at Pittsburgh, 369.
Queen's Rangers, Loyalist regiment, 391.
Quincy (Ill.), 164.
Quirk, Maj. Thomas, at lead mines, 26, 198; in Kentucky, 293; letter, 195; sketch, 195.

RACCOON Creek, raids on, 20, 41, 150-54, 156-57, 162-63, 199, 225-26.
Radcliff's Marsh (Va.), 237.
Ragor, George, private, 465.
Raid, Benjamin, at Pittsburgh, 367.
Ralston, Archibald, at Pittsburgh, 369.
Ralston, William, at Pittsburgh, 369.
Ramsey, Lieut. Andrew, militia officer, 464.
Ramsey, Thomas, at Pittsburgh, 369.
Ramsour's Mills, battle of, 26, 210-11, 254; sketch, 210.
Randles, David, court-martialed, 428.
Rankin, William, discharged, 441.
Raven, Cherokee chief, 25, 244; sketch, 244.
Rawlings, Col. Moses, letter to, 277; recommendation from, 455.
Rawlings' Regiment, at Fort Pitt, 40-41, 147, 174, 314; ordered East, 326, 335-36, 347.
Read, Lieut. Archibald, 459; charges against, 412; court-martial, 484-90; released, 433; sketch, 412.
Reburn, Joseph, surety, 262.
Red Bank Creek (Pa.), 56.
Reddick, John H., at Pittsburgh, 366.
Reddick, William, at Pittsburgh, 363, 366.
Red-Eye, Seneca Indian, 62-65.
Red Jacket, Seneca chief, sketch, 65.
Red River, route via, 85.

Red Stone, on the Monongahela, 83-84, 88, 91, 285, 288, 373; in Dunmore's War, 278.
Redstone Creek, mill on, 293.
Ree, Andrew, at Pittsburgh, 367.
Reed, John, at Pittsburgh, 366, 367.
Reed II, John, at Pittsburgh, 367, 368.
Reed, Joseph, president of Pennsylvania, memorials to, 360-70; report, 376; orders investigation, 395; letters to, 43, 76, 95, 109, 113, 121, 125, 135, 151, 170-71, 175, 180, 183, 188, 249, 265, 271, 274, 290, 304, 324, 337, 347, 351, 354, 403, 406, 413, 415, 421; letters, 108, 136-37, 175, 188, 235, 349, 352, 387, 392-93, 397, 413, 418, 421; sketch, 43.
Reed, Samuel, deserter, 457-58.
Reed, William, at Pittsburgh, 366.
Reed Creek (Va.), Loyalists on, 23, 197, 236, 254; sketch, 197.
Reed Island Creek (Va.), 236; Loyalists on, 251; sketch, 251.
Reel, Gasper, at Pittsburgh, 369.
Regulator movement, in North Carolina, 210.
Reid, Lieut. Archibald. See Read.
Reid, David, enlists, 263.
Reid, Gasper, tried for Loyalism, 259; sentence remitted, 263.
Remember, Reuben, Loyalist, 247.
Reno, Benjamin, at Pittsburgh, 369.
Reynolds family, captured, 163-64.
Rice, Abraham, private, 468.
Rice, Daniel, private, 468.
Richards (Ritchards), Mordecai, at Pittsburgh, 369.
Richards (Ritchards), Stephen, at Pittsburgh, 369.
Richardson, George, 494.
Richardson, James, exemption for, 426.
Richardson, William, at Pittsburgh, 369.
Richland County (Ohio), 152.
Richmond, William, at Pittsburgh, 369.

Richmond (Va.), 127, 129, 165; becomes capital of Virginia, 128; officers at, 310, 312, 314-15, 318-19, 335, 347, 400; letters from, 209, 243, 331.
Ricords, Archibald, at Pittsburgh, 368.
Ridnor, Conrad, tried and acquitted, 454.
Rifle (Riffle), Jacob, private, 469.
Rigdon, William, at Pittsburgh, 367.
Riley, Francis, fined, 426; court-martialed, 428-29.
Riley, John, 494.
Rittenhouse, David, boundary commissioner, 107.
Ritchie, Craig, at Pittsburgh, 369.
Ritchie, Matthew, at Pittsburgh, 369.
Rizsly, Elisha, at Pittsburgh, 367.
Roanoke River (Va.), 128.
Roark, James, family killed, 155.
Roark's Gap (Va.), 155.
Robards, Sallie, married, 304.
Robb, James, at Pittsburgh, 370.
Robb, John, at Pittsburgh, 370.
Robb, William, at Pittsburgh, 370.
Roberson, Andrew, at Pittsburgh, 368.
Roberts, ——, Loyalist officer, 210, 215.
Roberts, ——, mills, 415.
Robertson, Andrew, at Pittsburgh, 363, 366.
Robertson II, Andrew, at Pittsburgh, 368.
Robertson, Col. James, at Loyalists, trials, 258; sketch, 258.
Robertson, John, at Pittsburgh, 368.
Robertson, Samuel, at Pittsburgh, 366.
Robertson, William, at Pittsburgh, 366.
Robeson, ——, messenger, 371.
Robins, John, at Pittsburgh, 368.
Robinson, Andrew, clerk of Ohio County court, 425-26, 429; sworn in, 427.
Robinson, E. W., Ohio County magistrate, 110-11.

Robinson, George, Loyalist, 228.
Robinson, James, at Pittsburgh, 362, 366.
Robinson, Col. Joseph, Loyalist, 145.
Robinson, Samuel, gives bond, 228, 261.
Robinson, Capt. William, militia officer, 211–12; sketch, 212.
Robinson's Run (Pa.), 58, 110; raid on, 271–72; sketch, 271.
Robinson Township (Pa.), 226.
Rock, John, at Pittsburgh, 369.
Rock Island (Ill.), agency at, 164.
Rock River (Ill.), campaign, 127.
Rockbridge County (Va.), troops from, 51; settlers in, 156, 196.
Rockcastle County (Ky.), 196.
Rockingham County (Va.), 319.
Rodgers, Abraham, fine remitted, 425.
Roger, Michael, Loyalist officer, 247.
Rogers, Col. David, defeat, 17–18, 78–94, 104–6, 115, 123, 185, 192; letters, 84–86; death, 90, 123.
Rogers, Capt. John, Clark's officer, 126, 165, 230; letters to, 165; letter, 230–31; sketch, 126–27.
Rogers, Thomas, correspondence, 127.
Rome (N. Y.), 287.
Rome (Ohio), site, 152.
Romine, James, Loyalist, 255.
Roosevelt, Theodore, *Winning of the West*, 391.
Rope, Joseph, at Pittsburgh, 368.
Rorke, William, at Pittsburgh, 368.
Ross, ——, land speculator, 129.
Ross, Benjamin, private, 467.
Ross, Daniel, at Pittsburgh, 369.
Ross, David, Loyalist, 254.
Ross, John, private, 445.
Ross, Joseph, at Pittsburgh, 367.
Ross, Capt. Philip, 494; at Pittsburgh, 369.
Rossitor, Peter, at Pittsburgh, 363.
Roush, George, 494.
Rowe, Adam, attacked, 160; sketch, 160.
Royal Green. See King's Royal Regiment.

Royal Oak, Campbell's estate, 196, 237.
Royse, Capt. Benjamin, on Coshocton expedition, 376; company roll, 467.
Ruddell's Station (Ky.), captured, 20, 220, 266.
Rude, Jacob, private, 467.
Rush, Dr. Benjamin, physician, 306.
Russellville (Ky.), 196.
Rutherford, Gen. Griffith, defeats Loyalists, 210–11; sketch, 210.
Rutherford, James, at Pittsburgh, 368.
Rutledge, George, at Loyalists' trials, 258; sketch, 258.
Ryan, James, discharged, 441.
Ryan, Lazarus, 494.
Ryley, Francis. See Riley.

SADLER, Samuel, enlists, 263–64.
Saginaw Bay, fur trade on, 164.
St. Asaph, Kentucky station, 105.
St. Clair, Gen Arthur, defeat, 83; orders for, 390.
St. Clair County (Mich.), 161.
Ste. Geneviéve (Mo.), 385.
St. Johns (Can.), 374; garrison at, 248.
St. Joseph (Mich.), British post, 104.
St. Lawrence River, Loyalists on, 185.
St. Leger, Col. Barry, expedition, 47, 78, 185.
St. Louis (Mo.), British attack on, 19–20, 186; Spanish at, 84, 89; Rogers' expedition, 86–87; fur trade, 164; residents, 176.
St. Mary's River, portage from, 185.
St. Vincent. See Vincennes.
Salcon, John, at Pittsburgh, 368.
Salem (Ohio), Moravian village, 190, 378, 381; letters from, 217, 231, 245, 296, 315–16, 337, 339; sketch, 190.
Salem Township (Pa.), 56.
Salisbury (N. C.), 210.
Salt River (Ky.), lick on, 131.

540 INDEX

Sample, Samuel, innkeeper, 224; deputy quartermaster, 477–82.
Sanders, ——, in Southwest Virginia, 252–53.
Sandusky (Ohio), an Indian rendezvous, 17, 109, 112, 150–51, 185, 192, 219, 231, 298, 350–51, 375, 401, 405, 414; Moravians at, 161; Brady's scout to, 188, 202–4, 206–7, 340; Loyalists at, 352.
Sandusky River, Indians on, 30, 203; reservation, 152.
Sandy River. See Big Sandy River.
Saratoga County (N. Y.), 286.
Sauk and Fox Indians, agent for, 164.
Savannah (Ga.), attack on, 102.
Savannah River (Ga.), battle on, 253.
Sayers, Robert, pioneer, 215.
Sayers, Alexander, son, 215.
Sayers Jr., Capt. Robert, militia officer, 215; instructions for, 216; at Loyalists' trials, 258; sketch, 215.
Scalps, bounties for, 176; effect of, 183–84, 188; British object to, 376.
Scammel, Col. Alexander, adjutant-general, 112, 456.
Scarmahorn, John, private, 464.
Scarmahorn, Matthias, exemption for, 426.
Schebosch. See Bull, John.
Schenectady (N. Y.), 287; Indians near, 345.
Schermerhorn, Lucas, 494.
Schoharie (N. Y.), destroyed, 287.
Schönbrunn (Tupaking), Moravian mission village, 161, 190; letters from, 189–90, 193; sketch, 161.
Schuyler, Gen. Philip, gives Indian information, 146.
Scioto River, Indians on, 28, 401.
Scot, Abraham, at Pittsburgh, 367.
Scotch, emigrate to America, 320.
Scotch-Irish emigrants, 156, 210, 280, 307.
Scott, Andrew, fined, 426; on Coshocton expedition, 466.
Scott, David, daughters captured, 95.
Scott, Fanny, killed, 95.
Scott, John, at Pittsburgh, 368.

Scott, Joseph, court-martialed, 428.
Scott, Phebe, killed, 95.
Scott, Thomas, letter, 421; sketch, 421.
Scott, Capt. William, 494.
Scrichfield, William, private, 464.
Seaton, Richard, private, 469.
Second Pennsylvania Regiment, officer, 471–72.
Second Virginia Regiment, 288.
Seiler, Jacob, gives bond, 228.
Seneca Indians, captives among, 59; towns destroyed, 100; peace overtures, 101. See also Mingo Indians.
Seshahsee, Delaware Indian, 158.
Seven Year's War. See French and Indian War.
Seventh Pennsylvania Regiment, officer, 307.
Seventh Virginia Regiment, supersedes the Ninth, 309, 470; officers, 40, 103, 195, 215, 470; paymaster, 432; fifer, 490.
Sevier, John, Tennessee pioneer, 258; information from, 402.
Sewickly Creek, settlements on, 385, 408; capture on, 404; raids, 413; letter from, 414.
Shabosh. See Bull, John.
Shane, Timothy, 494.
Shannon's, site of, 212.
Sharon Center (N. Y.), battle near, 52.
Sharp, Adam, at Pittsburgh, 369.
Sharp, Edward, at Pittsburgh, 369.
Sharp, George, at Pittsburgh, 369.
Sharp, Nehemiah, at Pittsburgh, 369.
Shaw, Joseph, pack horse man, court-martialed, 442.
Shawnee Indians, branches of, 16, 73, 109; chieftess, 30, 201; towns, 94, 140, 152; characterized, 40, 43, 176, 294; refugees from, 50; intertribal relations, 104–5; prisoner among, 319; in British interest, 273–74, 374; at Detroit council, 373; hostile raids, 17–18, 21, 51, 71, 93, 105, 156, 159, 190, 193, 219–20, 319, 340; relations with Americans, 275, 347; immunity for, 69, 72, 75; ex-

INDEX 541

peditions against proposed, 28–29, 42, 83, 94, 104, 111, 135, 165, 173, 175, 350–51, 401, 416; Clark's expedition of 1780 against, 22, 180, 182, 223, 245–46, 249–50, 265–66, 271, 299; of 1786, 83. See also Mequochoke Indians.
Shearer, Capt. John, 494.
Shelby, Col. Evan, pioneer, 193.
Shelby, Col. Isaac, militia officer, 245, 258, 402.
Shenandoah Valley, 322.
Sheoquaga (Catherine's Town), Indian village, 95–96.
Shepherd, Col. David, lieutenant of Ohio County, 82, 110–11, 168; mill garrisoned, 313, 322; gathers militia, 376; information from, 106, 174; on Coshocton expedition, 461–63; furnishes troops for Clark, 409, 414–17; presides at courts-martial, 425–30; letters to, 96, 98, 127–28, 154, 168–69, 178–79, 182, 270, 275, 278, 281, 342–43, 348–49, 350, 371–72, 414–17; letter, 81.
Shepherd's Mill (Va.), garrison at, 313, 322.
Sheriden, Martin, private, 445.
Sherlock, Edward, 494.
Shippen, Dr. William, Philadelphia resident, 306.
Shippen Jr., Dr. William, letter to, 306–7; sketch, 306.
Shippensburg (Pa.), 381.
Short Creek (Va.), 110, 397–98, 420.
Shoughney, Thomas, private, 441; tried, 451–52.
Shull (Shell), Jacob, Loyalist, 202, 221, 227, 261.
Shull Jr., Jacob, tried for Loyalism, 259; enlists, 261.
Shull, John, enlists, 261.
Sickman, George, at Pittsburgh, 368.
Sidney, Andrew, Loyalist, 254.
Siebert, Wilbur H., "The Loyalists of West Florida and the Natchez district," 130.
Sills, Ensign Benjamin, 494.
Simmons, Henry, bowman, 477–82; witness, 478.

Simpson, Jeremiah, at Pittsburgh, 368; discharge for, 446.
Simpson, Cornet R., militia officer, 216.
Sinking Creek (Va.), Loyalists on, 145, 267.
Sixteenth British Infantry, 130.
Sixteenth Virginia Regiment, officer, 319.
Sixth Pennsylvania Battalion, 307.
Sixtieth British Infantry, 130.
Skaggs, Archibald, 494.
Skaggs, Henry, 494.
Slaughter, Maj. George, letter to, 179; en route to Kentucky, 180, 182; calls out militia, 186; regiment, 266; sketch, 179.
Slaughter, James, with Clark, 180.
Slaughter, John, on Coshocton expedition, 465.
Slaughter, John, with Clark, 180.
Slaughter, Joseph, with Clark, 180.
Slaughter, Lawrence, with Clark, 180.
Slaughter, Robert, sons, 179.
Slaughter, Thomas, in Kentucky, 179.
Slimp, Frederick, Loyalist, 255.
Small, John, at Pittsburgh, 369.
Smallman, Thomas, Pittsburgh inhabitant, 116, 175, 362, 366, 396; purchase from Indians, 290; sketch, 116.
Smith, Dr. ——, aids Fleming, 138.
Smith, Ballard, Continental officer, 269; sketch, 269.
Smith, David, deserter, 448; retained in service, 455–56.
Smith, Devereux, Pittsburgh inhabitant, 362, 366, 396; house, 479.
Smith, Francis, children of, 269.
Smith, Frederick, trial for Loyalism, 262.
Smith, Hairy, private, 465.
Smith, Jacob, 494.
Smith, John, drum major, 460.
Smith, Michael, private, 445.
Smith, Robert, at Pittsburgh, 367.
Smith, Susannah, married, 269.
Smith, William, private, 445.

542 INDEX

Smith, Capt. William Bailey, land warrant, 267.
Snido, Christian, officer, 261.
Snip, Captain, Shawnee chief, 152.
Snodgrass, William, at Pittsburgh, 369.
Snodgrass Jr., William, at Pittsburgh, 369.
Snyder, Randolph, at Pittsburgh, 368.
South Carolina, during Revolution, 210, 264, 296, 392; British conquer, 24–25, 27, 102, 143; reënforced, 123; Loyalists in, 145.
Spain, declares war on Great Britain, 19, 129–30; acquisitions in America, 131; fleet aids United States, 210, 248.
Spanish, influence on Indians, 14, 123, 201; furnish supplies to Americans, 17, 80, 83–86, 88–89, 93; conquest in Southwest, 19, 129–30, 147, 165, 402; post attacked, 20; protect deserters, 78; at New Orleans, 380; intrigues of, 53.
Sparks, Jared, *Correspondence of the American Revolution*, 30, 111, 135, 150, 173, 180, 187, 202, 223, 248–49, 271, 273, 276, 303, 336, 352, 399; *Life and Writings of George Washington*, 80, 311.
Sparks, Richard, militiaman, 420, 465.
Sparks, William, pioneer, 420.
Spears, Robert, at Pittsburgh, 367.
Spencer, Lieut. James, 495.
Spiers, Joshua, at Pittsburgh, 367.
Spriggs, Zachariah, private, 465.
Springer, Ensign Jacob, 495; letter to, 119; witness, 200; orders for, 313; message from, 330; sketch, 119.
Springer, Capt. Uriah, 495; impressing provisions, 276, 280, 285, 288; retained in service, 335; president of court, 455; on court, 470; letters to, 276, 278, 285, 350–51; sketch, 278.
Springer family, 119, 278.
Sprinkle, Jacob, at Pittsburgh, 368.

Sprott, John, 495; interviewed, 207.
Sprott, Samuel, recollections, 207–8; sketch, 207.
Sprott, Thomas, at Pittsburgh, 369.
Stafford, Henry, acquitted of Loyalism, 259.
Standiford, Ann, married, 310.
Staunton (Va.), Loyalists confined at, 24; settlers near, 156.
Steel, Col. Archibald, quartermaster, 42, 271; characterized, 107, 136; letters to, 116, 171, 177; message from, 202; sketch, 42.
Steel, Richard, at Pittsburgh, 366.
Stenson, John, at Pittsburgh, 368.
Stephens, Amelia. See Harrod, Mrs. Amelia.
Stephens, John, at Pittsburgh, 367.
Stephenson, David, at Pittsburgh, 370.
Stephenson, James, at Pittsburgh, 370.
Stephenson, John, at Pittsburgh, 367.
Stephenson, Col. John, rifle corps, 174, 335.
Sterling, Hugh, at Pittsburgh, 369.
Steuben, Gen. Friedrich W. A. H. F. von, at Richmond, 314; letter to, 318; consents to Gibson's joining Clark, 331, 398.
Stewart, Alexander, at Pittsburgh, 368.
Stewart, Mary, married, 267.
Stewart, Walter, Loyalist, 244; gives bond, 228, 261.
Stewart's Crossings (Pa.), Clark at, 350–51, 401; officers' meetings, 408–9, 416; sketch, 350.
Stiles, Capt. Benjamin, 495.
Still, Alexander, at Pittsburgh, 369.
Still, Joshua, court-martialed, 437.
Stillwell, Joseph, at Pittsburgh, 368.
Stockbridge Indians, aid Americans, 345, 347; sketch, 345.
Stokeley, Col. Jeremiah (Nehemiah), 495.
Stokeley, Capt. Thomas, at Fort Pitt, 459, 495; home raided, 404; company of, 393, 415; sketch, 235.
Stone Arabia (N. Y.), battle of, 287.

INDEX

Stoner, ——, land sold, 129.
Stoops, James, family captured, 204, 224; signs protest, 369.
Stoops, Mrs, Jane, rescued, 30, 202–8, 224–25.
Stoops, Mrs. Nancy, recollections, 204–6; sketch, 204.
Stoops, Samuel, rescues captive, 207.
Stoops, William, captured, 204–6; later life, 204, 206–7.
Stotesbury, Lieut. John, of Eighth Pennsylvania, 459.
Stover, Jeremiah, trial for Loyalism, 259.
Stricklin, Alexander, private, 466.
Stroup, Lieut, Conrad, militia officer, 464, 495.
Sturges, Meniard, at Pittsburgh, 367.
Such, George, sergeant, 441.
Sugar Creek (Pa.), 60.
Sullivan, Capt. James, 122; sketch, 122.
Sullivan, Gen. John, Iroquois expedition, 14–15, 41, 48, 54, 59, 62, 65, 96, 100, 129, 140, 175; Brodhead's messages to, 43, 49, 95–96; defeats Indians and Loyalists, 53, 96, 129; county named for, 245.
Sullivan County (N. C.), troops from, 245; sheriff, 258; sketch, 245.
Sumner, George, *Boston Oration*, 81.
Sumner County (Tenn.), 210.
Sumral, John, at Pittsburgh, 367.
Sumter, Gen. Thomas, battle, 79; headquarters, 402.
Surry County (N. C.), 236; information from, 170.
Susquehanna River, expedition on, 14, 41; Indian town, 54; mission, 232.
Swan, George, at Pittsburgh, 367.
Swearingen, Capt. Van, warns of danger, 334; at Fort Pitt, 458; sketch, 334.
Sweden, emigrants from, 119.
Sweet, Ben., at Pittsburgh, 367.
Swift, Capt. ——, brings information, 198.

TABER, Philip, at Pittsburgh, 367.
Taimenend, Morgan's Indian title, 47.
Tait, David, at Pittsburgh, 363, 366, 471, 473; witness, 479–80, 482.
Talen, Henry, at Pittsburgh, 367.
Tankhonnetick. Indian town. See Pluggy's town.
Tannehill, Capt. Adamson, 440, 448; messenger, 174–75; report, 454; commandant at Fort McIntosh, 289; relieved, 309; sketch, 174.
Tannehill, James, at Pittsburgh, 368.
Tannehill, John, at Pittsburgh, 367.
Tannehill, Josiah, ensign and paymaster, 432, 460.
Tannehill, Nathan, at Pittsburgh, 368.
Tannehill, William, at Pittsburgh, 368.
Tarleton, Sir Banastre, raids Virginia, 304.
Tate, George, sergeant, 464.
Tatepawkshe, Delaware envoy, 339.
Taylor, Capt. Francis, 288.
Taylor, Capt. Issac, letter to, 215–16; at court-martial, 427; sketch, 215.
Taylor, John, at Pittsburgh, 369.
Taylor, Capt. John, at Loyalists' trials, 257; sketch, 257.
Taylor, Maj. John, letter, 155–56; sketch, 155.
Taylor, Maj. Richard, at Pittsburgh, 112; promoted, 288; on furlough, 460; cousin of, 288; letters to, 112, 114, 116, 118, 121–22; letter, 121; sketch, 112.
Taylor, Robert, Ohio County resident, 110.
Taylor, William, at Pittsburgh, 368.
Taylor II, William, at Pittsburgh, 368.
Taylor, Maj. William, Continental officer, 295; commandant at Fort Henry, 313, 366; presides at court, 444–45; insolence toward, 446; letters to, 288, 293–95, 313, 322, 335–36; sketch, 288.
Taylor's Creek (Ky.), 288.
Taylorstown (Pa.), 110.

Tazewell County (Va.), 155–56.
Teatrick, George, at Pittsburgh, 368.
Teatrick, Isaac, at Pittsburgh, 368.
Tecumseh, Shawnee chief, 119, 153.
Teeduscung, Delaware chief, 404.
Teggert, Michael, at Pittsburgh, 369.
Telencnut, Seneca chief. See Hudson, Thomas.
Ten Mile Creek (Pa.), 83, 187; raid on, 274, 337.
Tennessee, explored, 196; pioneers of, 194, 355; troops from, 245; Loyalists in, 254; constitutional convention, 258.
Tennessee River, as a boundary, 305.
Teter, Capt. Samuel, killed by Indians, 420; at courts-martial, 425–30.
Terre Bonne Parish (La.), 177.
Tewind, John, at Pittsburgh, 362.
Thames River (Can.), 161.
The Olden Time, 67, 73, 283.
Thibau, Pierre, artillerist, 201.
Third Pennsylvania Regiment, officer, 353.
Third United States Sublegion, 278.
Thirteenth Virginia Regiment, officers, 40–41, 103, 112, 278, 335, 403; changes of name, 309, 313.
Thomas, Abraham, 495.
Thomas, Lieut. Lewis, orders for, 309, 350; retained in service, 335; tried and acquitted, 453; member of court, 484; sketch, 309.
Thompson, Capt. James, at Loyalists' trials, 257; sketch, 257.
Thompson, Jerves, at Pittsburgh, 368.
Thompson, John, Delaware chief. See Coolpeeconain.
Thompson, Samuel, 128; home, 247; accused of Loyalism, 254–55.
Thompson, Thomas, 495.
Three Rivers (Can.), 307.
Thwaites, Reuben Gold, editor, 9, 95, 290.
Tidball, William, at Pittsburgh, 369.
Tiger Valley. See Tygart's Valley.
Tioga (N. Y.), Sullivan at, 47.
Tilton, Samuel. See Titus.

Tionesta (Pa.), site, 56.
Tipton, Capt. Abraham, 495.
Titus (Tilton), Samuel, 495.
Tobacco, price, 128; payment in, 194.
Tobin, Joseph, at Pittsburgh, 367.
Todd Jr., Col. John, letter, 292–93; residence, 293; sketch, 292.
Todd, Levi, residence, 293.
Todd, Samuel, 495.
Todd County (Ky.), 267.
Tomlinson, Lieut. Joseph, 495.
Tonawanda (N. Y.), Indians at, 62.
Tories. See Loyalists.
Totowa (N. J.), headquarters, 290.
Tout, Abraham, at Pittsburgh, 369.
Town Run (Pa.), 56.
Transylvania Company, services, 142.
Treaty of Pittsburgh (1779), 66–72, 115.
Treaty of Paris (1783), 300.
Treaty of Fort McIntosh (1785), 41, 380.
Treaty of Greenville (1795), 151, 153, 204, 335.
Treaty of 1817, 152.
Trenton (N. J.), during the Revolution, 319.
Trespassers, on Indian lands, 22–23, 96–97, 103, 106–7, 112, 114–15, 168.
Trigg, Capt. ——, 495.
Trigg, Capt. Daniel, militia officer, 212; at Loyalists' trials, 258; sketch, 212.
Trigg, Stephen, in Kentucky, 131, 138; brother, 212; sketch, 131.
Trinity College, Dublin, 307.
Triplet, Peter, at Pittsburgh, 368.
Troup, William, sergeant, 467.
Tryon County (N. Y.), 47.
Tucker, ——, married, 151.
Tucker, Lewis, captured, 150–54; attempt to rescue, 199; sketch, 151.
Tucker, Mary (Polly), captured, 150–54; attempt to rescue, 199; sketch, 153.
Tug Ridge (Va.), 155.
Tupaking, Moravian village. See Schönbrunn.

INDEX 545

Turkey Foot (Pa.), 310; road from, 150.
Turner, Elizabeth, captured, 150–54; attempt to rescue, 199; sketch, 153.
Turner, F. J., "Western State Making during the Revolutionary Era," 167, 410.
Turner, George, killed, 154.
Turner, James, captured, 150–54; attempt to rescue, 199.
Turner, Mary, married, 151.
Turner, William, children captured, 153.
Turner Jr., William, killed, 154.
Turtle, Delaware tribe, 317, 330, 404.
Turtle Creek (Pa.), settler on, 385.
Tuscarawas County (Ohio), 190.
Tuscarawas River, Indian villages on, 119, 161, 190; mission villages, 232, 372; war parties, 41, 153, 172, 193, 231, 380; negotiations at, 75; fort on abandoned, 69, 71; expedition to, 376–82.
Twebough, Jacob, at Pittsburgh, 367.
Twelfth Pennsylvania Regiment, officer, 310.
Twelfth Virginia Regiment, 179; surgeon of, 306; officers, 333.
Twelve Mile Run, Lochry's home on, 265, 370, 397, 415.
Tygart's (Tiger) Valley, raided, 173; purchases in, 288, 294.

ULLERY, Catherine, married, 151.
Unadilla (N. Y.), 287.
Unamy Sepu. See Maumee River.
Uniontown (Pa.), 82.
Unzaga, Luis de, governor of Louisiana, 81.
Upper Louisiana, traders, 86.
Upper Sandusky, Indian town, 203, 219; sketch, 203.

VALLANDIGHAM, Clement L., letter, 58.
Vallandigham, Col. George, on Brodhead's expedition, 58, 495; warns of danger, 334; letter to, 272, 372; sketch, 58.
Valley Forge, suffering at, 80, 82; officers, 319.
Vanbush, Mitchell, at Pittsburgh, 367.
Vance, Capt. Robert, orders for, 112, 114; sketch, 112.
Van Leer, Matthew, court-martialed, 434–35.
Vanmetre, Jesse, private, 469.
Van Rensselaer, Gen. Robert, defeats invaders, 287.
Vaudreuil, Louis Philippe, marquis de, in Virginia, 176.
Vault, Andrew, Loyalist, 254–55.
Vault, George, Loyalist, 255.
Veatch, Jeremiah, private, 469.
Veech, James, *Monongahela of Old*, 168.
Venango, Indian site, 48, 57, 78, 301; route via, 388, 390, 398; sketch, 48.
Venango Trail, described, 56, 60.
Vernon, Maj. Frederick, 445; on Brodhead's expedition, 60; charges against Brodhead, 118; presides at courts-martial, 438, 441–42, 470, 476–77, 483; illness, 484; letters to, 288–89, 292, 294; sketch, 60.
Vervill, John, at Pittsburgh, 367.
Vestal (N. Y.), site, 54.
Vincennes (Ind.), an American post, 16, 19, 133, 165, 176, 200; news from, 104–5, 297; captured by Clark, 127, 231; message from, 230; French agent sent to, 305.
Virgin, Brice, fined, 425.
Virginia, boundary line, 194, 236; jurisdiction, 109, 352, 361, 403, 419, 421; boundary surveyed, 142, 186; boundary dispute, 22, 33, 107–8, 127–28, 167, 170, 235, 279–80, 284, 361, 403, 410; constitutional convention, 126, 304, 319; committee of correspondence, 319; commissioners to adjust land titles, 103, 105, 118–19, 126–27, 131, 137; troops, 115, 129, 136, 314; volunteers, 94; militia, 61, 110–11, 194,

546 INDEX

Virginia—Continued
414; officers, 77, 82, 188, 249, 305; bounties, 76; Western defenses, 19, 50–52, 113, 192, 243; aid for Kentucky, 20, 26; convention prisoners in, 242; prohibits exports of provisions, 323–25, 332; drafts on, 86; supplies for, 17, 83–84; information for, 107; Indians visit, 176; Indians threaten, 245; Indian raids in, 155–56, 391–92, 401; British invasion of, 355, 374, 398; Tarleton's raid in, 304; Loyalists in, 23–28, 143–45, 155, 170, 195–98, 208–13, 215–17, 220–22, 227–29, 236–42, 244–47, 250–64, 267–69, 402; Detroit expedition planned by, 32–34, 131, 133–34, 282, 311–13, 397, 414; reënforcements for, 405; assembly, 128–29, 180, 304; *Journal of House of Delegates*, 24.
Virginia Archives, 81–84.
Virginia road. See Glade road.

WABASH River, Indians on, 16, 104, 158–59, 398; route via, 70; expedition on, 87, 230.
Waggoner Jr., ——, Loyalist, 247.
Waggoner, Jacob, Loyalist, 247.
Waits, James, 495.
Walawpachtschischen, Delaware chief, 157, 159, 172–73.
Waldeckers, at Baton Rouge, 130.
Wales. See Walls.
Walker, John, Virginia congressman, 130.
Walker, Philip, at Pittsburgh, 368.
Walker, Dr. Thomas, boundary commissioner, 186.
Walker's Creek (Va.), Loyalists on, 23, 208, 212, 222, 254; sketch, 212.
Wall, John, at Pittsburgh, 368.
Wall, John, Virginia Loyalist, 221–22.
Wallace, Rev. Caleb, letter, 137–38; sketch, 137.
Wallace, George, at Pittsburgh, 363, 366; trial of, 477–83; verdict, 483.
Wallace, Capt. James, 495; signs protest, 367.

Walls (Wales), Maj. George, 495.
Walsh, Philip, at Pittsburgh, 368.
Walter, George, trial for Loyalism, 260.
Wampum, used at Council, 217.
War of 1812, participants, 153, 164, 278, 335.
Ward, Edward, Pittsburgh inhabitant, 116, 175; signs protest, 363, 366, 396; officer's father, 475–76; sketch, 116.
Ward, Cornet John, in Montgomery County, 215.
Ward, Lieut. John, 495; on guard, 455; at Fort Pitt, 459; trial of, 470–76; acquitted, 476; member of court, 484.
Ward, Richard, Loyalist, 254–55.
Ward, Capt. Sylvester, 495.
Warren (Ohio), 59.
Warren (Pa.), site, 62, 65.
Warren County (Mo.), 268.
Warren County (Pa.), sites in, 54, 64, 66.
Washenaws, Munsee warrior, 157; attacks Malott family, 162–63.
Washington, Gen. George, commander-in-chief, 307, 318, 362, 370; camps, 80, 260; plans, 14, 28, 32, 340–41, 351; instructions, 18, 332, 387, 451, 470; Indians visit, 47; birthday celebrated, 435; visits the West, 270, 403; county named for, 403; letters to, 32, 40, 55, 94, 106, 111, 115, 120, 133, 135, 146, 149–50, 173, 180, 187, 202, 223, 245, 248–49, 271, 273, 276, 283, 303, 325, 332–33, 336, 344, 352, 382, 398, 401, 410, 412–13; letters, 100–2, 114–15, 123–24, 147, 208, 248, 282–83, 286, 311, 314, 340, 383, 388–90, 393–95, 405, 407; handwriting, 310; *Calendar of Correspondence*, 159, 249; *Papers*, in Library of Congress, 100–2, 114, 146, 149, 161, 189–90, 193, 231, 245, 250, 286, 311, 314, 340, 356, 360, 382–83, 387–90, 393–96, 401, 403, 405, 407, 410–12, 470, 477, 490–91.
Washington (Pa.), 313.

Washington County (Pa.), 271; erected, 403, 410, 421; emigration to, 21, 87; residents, 110, 151, 160; elections in, 421; raids in, 41, 274; letters from, 403, 410, 421; *History*, 168; sketch, 403.
Washington County (Va.), Loyalists in, 23–24, 143, 195–98, 209; aid from, 26, 193–94, 217; protection for, 51, 241, 402; settlers, 196; militia, 392; letters from, 391, 402; sketch, 51.
Watauga River, troops from, 245.
Watson, James, at Pittsburgh, 369.
Watson, Robert, at Pittsburgh, 367.
Watson, Ensign Thomas, 495.
Watterson, James, at Pittsburgh, 367.
Watterson, Richard, at Pittsburgh, 367.
Wayne, Gen. Anthony, in Indian wars, 83, 207; in the Revolution, 307; makes Indian treaty, 151, 153, 204, 335; letter to, 303; letter, 290.
Wayne Township (Pa.), 61.
Webb, George, treasurer of Virginia, 130.
Wechquadnach, Moravian mission, 320.
Weighley, Issac, 495.
Welawpachtschiechen, Delaware chief. See Walawpachtschischen.
Welch, Nicholas, North Carolina Loyalist, 210.
Wells, Alexander, mills of, 415; sketch, 415.
Wells Sr., Joseph, exemption for, 430; on Coshocton expedition, 464.
Wells, Moses, Loyalist, 255.
Wellsburgh (W. Va.), 415.
Welsh, as Loyalists, 24, 251–52.
West Augusta (Va.), officials, 82, 103; troops, 409.
West Elizabeth (Pa.), 417.
West Florida, captured by Spanish, 129–30. See also Florida.
West Indies, route via, 86; operations in, 248, 405.
West Liberty (W. Va.), 110.
West Point (N. Y.), headquarters, 100, 114.

West Union (Ohio), 109.
West Virginia, raids in, 95.
Western state movements, 167, 410.
Westfall, Capt. Jacob, 495.
Westmoreland County (Pa.), 290; surveyor, 109; lieutenant, 39, 352; emigration to, 21, 207; trespassers from, 168; militia, 98, 164, 168, 174, 179, 347–48, 373; battalions of, 408; ranging companies, 79, 95, 107–8, 113, 120–21, 125–26, 135, 137, 171, 188, 214, 265, 349, 397, 415; raids in, 14, 20–21, 39, 150–51, 170–71, 179–81, 187–88, 226, 301, 362, 371, 385–86, 397, 403–5, 413–14; protection for, 174–76, 178, 235, 249, 265, 272, 393; supplies, 271, 349; petition from, 267–70; reproached for inactivity, 372; meeting of court, 370; raises men for Clark, 408–9, 415–16; Clark's proposed side expedition from, 401.
Westmoreland County (Va.), 335.
Wetzel, George, on Coshocton expedition, 465; killed by Indians, 379.
Wetzel, Jacob, captured, 379.
Wetzel, Capt. John, pioneer, 319.
Wetzel Jr., John, private, 465.
Wetzel, Lewis, murders Indian, 376, 379–80, 420; on Coshocton expedition, 465; sketch, 379.
Wetzel, Martin, escapes from captivity, 319; sketch, 319.
Whaley, Benjamin, 495.
Wheeling (Va.), 110, 200, 376, 380, 420; post at, 19, 116, 118, 122; threatened, 31, 340; a rendezvous, 33–34, 348, 373, 376, 378, 388, 414, 416; powder at, 81; trespassers near, 97; scouting from, 108; besieged, 313, 319, 420. See also Fort Henry.
Wheeling Creek, raid on, 41; post on, 82, 313; settlers on, 379.
Whelps, George, private, 441.
Whinguakeshoo. See Machingwe Keesuch
Whisky Rebellion, 58; officer in, 308; revenue collector, 333.

Whitaker, George F., recollections, 152–53.
Whitaker, James, sketch, 152.
Whitaker, Mrs. James. See Foulks, Elizabeth.
White, Andrew, private, 465.
White, Conrad, private, 465.
White, Capt. Jacob, 495.
White, John, discharged, 441.
White Eyes, Delaware chief, 69; kinsmen, 340.
White Eyes, Nancy, present for, 250.
White River (Ind.), Indians on, 119.
White Woman's Creek (Ohio), 382.
Whitecker, James, at Pittsburgh, 369.
Whiteman, John, discharged, 441.
Whitesale. See Wetzel.
Whiting, John, private, 467.
Whitsel, Philip, at Pittsburgh, 369.
Whitsitt, William H., "Caleb Wallace," 137.
Whittaker, Daniel, 495.
Whittaker, Jacob, discharged, 441.
Whover, ——, Loyalist leader, 253.
Wiatt, T., at Pittsburgh, 366.
Wicklife, Charles, at Pittsburgh, 368.
Wicklife, Robert, at Pittsburgh, 368.
Wilderness Road (Ky.), protection for, 19; passage of, 319.
Wilkes County (Ga.), 391.
Wilkes County (N. C.), 210, 239.
Wilkie, Edward, court-martialed, 446–47.
Wilkins, Edward, court-martialed, 432.
Wilkinson, Gen. James, clothier general, 100, 120; letters to, 120, 142, 174.
Willett, Col. Marinus, victory, 52.
Willey, John, Loyalist officer, 247.
William and Mary College Quarterly, 319.
Williams, Maj. John, at Cahokia, 230; sketch, 230.
Williams, Joseph, private, 465.
Williamsburg (Va.), capital of Virginia, 127; French officer at, 29; letters from, 93, 127, 133, 155; surveyor's office, 167.

Williamson, Col David, expedition of 1782, 397; at courts-martial, 425, 427, 429–30; company, 428; fined, 428.
Willing, Capt. James, officers, 42, 77, 299.
Wilson, ——, information from, 323.
Wilson, George, Delaware chief. See Nanowland.
Wilson, Joseph, fined, 426.
Wilson, Samuel, fine remitted, 425; on Coshocton expedition, 465.
Wilson, William, commissary, 322–25, 332, 344.
Winbidle, Corard, at Pittsburgh, 369.
Winchester (Va.), 127, 211.
Wine, ——, married, 153.
Wine, Mary Tucker. See Tucker, Mary.
Wingenund (Wyngeenund), Delaware chief, 47, 97, 158; at Detroit council, 217–19; Brodhead's message to, 298; on war path, 340; sketch, 47.
Winlock, Ensign Joseph, 495; retained in service, 335; sketch, 335.
Wint, Christopher, court-martialed, 440.
Winter, Stephen, court-martialed, 457.
Wisconsin, New York Indians in, 52, 345.
Wise, Ensign Bealez M., 495.
Witchcraft delusion, among Indians, 119.
Withers, Alexander, *Chronicles of Border Warfare*, 95, 220, 269–70.
Wolf, Jacob, deposition, 429.
Wolf, John, at Pittsburgh, 369.
Wolf Creek (Va.), Loyalists on, 212, 254; sketch, 212.
Wolf tribe of Delawares. See Munsee Indians.
Wood, Capt. John, militia officer, 354–55.
Wood, Thomas, sergeant-major, 431; on furlough, 460; tried and acquitted, 451.
Woodford County (Ky.), 137.
Woods, John, at Pittsburgh, 368.

INDEX

Woods, Tobias, at Pittsburgh, 368.
Woods, William, at Pittsburgh, 369.
Worley, Samuel, private, 466.
Wright, Alexander, 495.
Wyandaughland, Delaware chief. See Wyondochella.
Wyandot County (Ohio), 203.
Wyandot (Huron) Indians, inter-tribal relations, 189, 191, 218–19, 249, 295–98, 316, 329, 339–40; at Detroit, 46; seek American alliance, 16, 40, 46–47, 56, 66–72, 76, 115, 296; deceive Americans, 43, 45, 106, 190, 193, 265; spy from, 295–97; hostile raids, 17, 20, 44–45, 105, 109, 150, 153–54, 158–59, 162–63, 219, 224, 234, 245–46, 249, 272, 340; prisoners among, 135, 162, 219, 297, 379; defeated, 30–31, 223–26, 273, 275; expeditions against planned, 30, 94, 223, 271, 284, 416; sketch, 66.
Wyatt, John, discovers Loyalist plot, 268–69; sketch, 268.
Wyatt, Ensign Thomas, court-martialed and acquitted, 458; at Fort Pitt, 459.
Wyngeenund, Delaware chief. See Wingenund.
Wynn, Thomas, private, 441.
Wyoming (Pa.), 63.
Wyondochella (Wyandaughland), Delaware hostile, 162, 191–92, 273; son, 273; sketch, 162.
Wythe County (Va.), 198, 236, 258.

Yadkin River (N. C.), 210.
Yahrungwago, Indian town. See Yoghroonwago.
Yellow Creek, Indian defeat near, 245.

Yoghroonwago (Naradago, Yahrungwago), Indian village, 54–55, 96; sketch, 55.
Yoho, Henry, 495.
Yohogania County (Va.), 88; militia officers, 58, 87, 94, 178, 419; letter to, 334; surveyor, 170; raided, 173, 271–72, 413; endangered, 334, 419; militia for Clark from, 409–10.
Yohogania Court House, letters from, 416–17; sketch, 417.
Youghiogheny River, as a frontier, 21, 171, 188; three forks of, 150, 289; settlers on, 335, 413; raid on, 403–5.
Young, ——, Moravian missionary, 381.
Young, Alexander, at Pittsburgh, 367; court-martialed, 428–29.
Young, George, at Pittsburgh, 368.
Young, James, at Pittsburgh, 369.
Young, John, court-martialed, 435.
Young, Robert, at Pittsburgh, 367.
Young, Capt. Thomas, 495; signs protest, 367.

Zane, Ebenezer, on Coshocton expedition, 466.
Zane, Jonathan, 495; scout on Coshocton expedition, 461–63.
Zane, Capt. Silas, 495.
Zeisberger, Rev. David, Moravian missionary, 190; visits East, 372; information from, 169, 189–90, 202, 231–32; services commended, 372; letters to, 117, 119, 134, 156, 169, 177, 300, 320–21; letters, 161, 189–90, 193; sketch, 117.
Zinzendorf, Nicholas Lewis, count, Moravian leader, 119, 320.

www.ingramcontent.com/pod-product-compliance
Lightning Source LLC
Chambersburg PA
CBHW052136300426
44115CB00011B/1400